Did Man Create God?

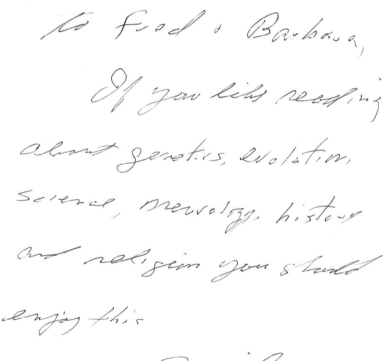

To Fred & Barbara,

If you like reading about genetics, evolution, science, neurology, history and religion you should enjoy this.

Sam

Cover illustration: Michelangelo's depiction of the creation of man in the chapter of Genesis on the ceiling of the Sistine Chapel 1508-1512.

Did Man Create God?

Is Your Spritual Brain at Peace with your Thinking Brain?

Including Intelligent Answers to Intelligent Design

by

David E. Comings, M.D.

Hope Press
Duarte CA

Hope Press
POB 188
Duarte, CA 91009

Other books by Dr. Comings
Tourette Syndrome and Human Behavior
Search for the Tourette Syndrome and Human Behavior Genes
The Gene Bomb

The drawings in Chapter 3. The Cambrian Explosion were from J. Gould's book *A Wonderful Life*, 1989. W.W. Norton & Co, Inc. The use of other copyrighted figures are credited in the chapter in which they appear.

Printed in China

Library of Congress Cataloging-in-Publication Data

Comings, David E.
  Did man create God? : is your thinking brain in conflict with your spiritual brain? : including intelligent answers to intelligent design / by David E. Comings.
      p. cm.
  Includes bibliographical references and index.
  ISBN-13: 978-1-878267-73-3 (hardback : alk. paper)
  ISBN-10: 1-878267-73-6 (hardback : alk. paper)
  ISBN-13: 978-1-878267-72-6 (pbk. : alk. paper)
  ISBN-10: 1-878267-72-8 (pbk. : alk. paper)
  1. Theological anthropology--Christianity. 2. Biology. 3. Evolution (Biology) 4. Spirituality. 5. Theology. I. Title.
  BT701.3.C66 2007
  210--dc22
                            2007011173

to

Sally — for being herself

Karen — whose wonderful spirituality gave me the idea
        to write this book

and

Jim — whose encouragement made it happen

Table of Contents

Preface—About Reading This Book

This book is intended for all inquisitive readers who are interested in why humans are such a spiritual species; whether Intelligent Design is a valid alternative to Darwinian evolution; whether our sacred books were written by man or by God; whether God created man or man created God; whether man made up the theory of God as our creator and protector; and whether our rational thinking brain can live in peace with our spiritual brain.

It is written for both those who are well acquainted with many aspects of science and those who are not. For the latter I have kept the scientific jargon to a minimum and defined or explained any terminology used. While a high school-level knowledge of biology would be helpful, the reader with no background in biology at any level can still read and understand this book. For those whose first reaction is, "Wow, over 650 pages!", I have sprinkled summaries of all of the important points in **red** text throughout the book. If a chapter repeats what you already know or bores or overwhelms you, just skip to the **red summary** and go on. *One could obtain the essence of the whole book in a very short time by just reading these summaries.* If you wish to understand the reasoning and evidence behind the red summaries, read the full chapter. Finally, if you would like to skip the chapters on evolution and cosmology and jump directly to the material about the rational and spiritual brain, go to Part IV.

Introduction

When I was in grade school I was very interested in all aspects of science. My father was a professor of chemical engineering at the University of Illinois and my mother was a bright independent thinker. They both encouraged my interests and attempted to answer each of my many questions. I collected rocks, minerals, and fossils, and stuffed every dead animal I could find. I found a set of *The Book of Knowledge* encyclopedias in our family library and read about all the geological epochs—Cambrian, Ordovician, Silurian, all the way to the Pleistocene. Each had a separate chapter, and as I progressed from one to the next I marveled at the unfolding evolution of life on earth. Darwin's theory of evolution by natural selection is a natural belief system that stayed with me my entire life. My parents, who were Presbyterian at the time, brought me to Sunday school and then to church whenever they were forceful enough to counter my pleas of "Do I have to?" Getting dressed up in a suit and tie on a beautiful Sunday morning when there were a thousand more interesting things to do seemed like a unique form of parentally induced torture. Even if we only went to church once or twice a month, it was taken for granted that the religious instruction I received was sinking in and that I believed in God. For a time, this was true. In Sunday school, although we discussed the book of Genesis, I lived in a university town where virtually everyone believed in Darwinism and most of us viewed the Genesis story as an interesting metaphor for the creative power of God. No one suggested we should take the seven days for creation literally.

By the time I was in fourth grade I had finished all the chapters on paleontology, read parts of Darwin's *The Origin of Species* and all the books I could find in the local library on astronomy, geology, archeology and other "-ologies." I remember to this day lying on my bed in my room, surrounded by shelves full of my collections of rocks and fossils, stuffed birds, and a reconstructed cat skeleton. As a mental exercise I slowly worked my way back down the evolutionary ladder from man to earlier and earlier forms of life. I eventually reached the long period of time when the earth was populated only by single cells without a nucleus—the bacteria. This flow of evolving life forms seemed so logical that there was no need for the hand of God to help the process over the rough spots. No need for a God of the gaps.

I also had read enough about astronomy to be able to take the process back further and further to the creation of the universe from clouds of gas. This was before modern cosmology and the Big Bang theory had been proposed, but the trend was the same—the whole complex universe and all life on earth evolved from more primitive precursors. By running the tape backwards one ended up with those simple precursors. It then occurred to me, lying there in the dark long after my bedtime, that the next question was, where did these simple precursors come from? There were two possibilities: they came from some form of matter or energy that was even simpler, or God made them. I had not yet heard of Occam's razor, the concept in science that the simplest explanation is usually the correct one. However, it seemed inherently reasonable that the simplest explanation was the best. To believe that God made the gases left a huge remaining question—Who Made God? God is the most complex concept or entity in all human thought, capable of incredible feats, pervasive, omnipresent, aware of our every thought and action, able to listen to, sort out and possibly act on the prayers of billions of people on a daily, hourly or even second-by -second basis. When considering primitive gases or God, based on the principle of Occam's razor, there was never an easier choice. Primitive gas was clearly the winner in the simplicity race. The question of "Who created God?" was then fairly simple—man created God. People in different parts of the world tailored God to conform to the unique aspects of their own culture and history, resulting in a wide range of different beliefs and religions.

Having come to this conclusion in the summer before fifth grade, my first thought was, "Now I am really in deep trouble." God is going to be very upset with me for doubting Him. Would He retaliate in some subtle way but cover His tracks so no one could really blame Him, like making me fall off my bicycle or get an F in my next math exam? "OK," I said to Him. "I will give you one week to do something about what I was thinking. If I don't hear back in a week, I will be forced to conclude that I was right. You don't really exist." Nothing happened. This issue was clearly not so simplistic that I would not believe in God just because I did not get an F in math the following week. But I was relieved to find that if He did exist, He must be a kind, understanding, and non-punitive God.

Since that evening many further developments in a range of scientific disciplines have strengthened my early conclusions and I have continued to believe that man created God. I have also continued to marvel at all the questions this answered that my theistic friends who believed in God were still struggling with. Foremost among these, if God was such a benevolent and loving being, how could He let such bad things happen to humans, such as the world war we were then in the midst of? If man created God, this was a non-issue. It made much more sense to believe we were in this universe alone and what we made of our lives, our country, and our world—was of our own doing. We should not screw it up, because no one was going to come to our rescue if we did.

My next hurdle was to tell my parents, especially my mother, of my conclusions about God. I waited several years before summoning the courage to do so. When I finally told her, the reaction was, "David, you don't really believe that." When I assured her that I did, I think she simply entered into a state of quiet denial and after that we never discussed it again. My father was nonplussed. Being well versed in science, I suspected that secretly he felt I had a valid point. By the time I was in medical school, if I went to church at all it was to meet girls. I went to the Unitarian church, where theists, agnostics, and atheists could all commune together in harmony. Long after I moved from home I was heartened to find that both my parents had joined the Unitarian church. I never subsequently discussed with them which of the above three categories they fit in, but I suspected it was the agnostic group.

When I was in high school, a good friend invited me to spend several weeks of a summer vacation with him and his parents in a cabin on the Gun Flint Trail in northern Minnesota. Being an amateur mammalogist, I immediately went to my *Field Guide of North American Mammals* to see what I might encounter. I was intrigued to find that the pigmy shrew *(Microtus agresti)*, both the smallest and the rarest of the North American mammals, had habitats in the area. Thus, I included in my suitcase a dozen mousetraps and a set of my mammal-skinning tools. A few days after arriving, I placed the traps near the water of a distant lake. I never dreamed that I would catch one, but the hunt for such a rare species was exciting. To my great astonishment, over the time I was there I caught five of these unique creatures. Since they were supposed to be rare, I felt five was enough. I skinned them and stuffed them with cotton to make what are called "study skins." I kept the skulls since the definitive identification of the species was based on specific characteristics of the teeth. Since they were so small, the muscles quickly dried, forming a mummified skull.

The best way to remove the muscle tissue from these skulls was to place them in a box with carrion beetles that feed on the flesh, leaving a pristinely clean skull. I did not have any carrion beatles, so several months after I returned home I went to visit the head of the department of mammalogy and curator of the Natural History Museum at the University of Illinois. I will refer to him as "George." I walked into his office and told him that I had five *Microtus agresti* skulls and proposed that if he would allow me to put them in his box of carrion beetles, I would let him keep a couple of the skulls and skins for the museum. I told him I was sure they were *Microtus agresti* because they had the characteristic tooth patterns of this species. He looked at me as though I was an alien who had just dropped down from a space ship. Here I was, a gangly teenager telling this head of the mammalogy department that I had not just one, but five skulls of the rarest and smallest mammal in the United States, while he had none. There was an unmistakable expression on his face that was a cross between total disbelief and a desire to show this young upstart that if I thought he was going to pass the skulls of a common house mouse off as *Microtus agresti* skulls he was going to quickly put me in my place and usher me out the door. He picked up a hand lens from his desk and began to examine the teeth. One of the greatest pleasures of my young life was to watch the smirk disappear, to be replaced by a jaw-dropping stare. He said, "These are *Microtus agresti;* where did you get them?" After I told him the story, he said he would be glad to clean the skulls up for me. To my utter astonishment, he next told me that he and two graduate students were planning a month-long expedition to New Mexico next summer. They could use some help and would I be interested in joining them. I agreed on the spot. By now you must be wondering, where is all of this going and what does this have to do with the issue of *Did Man Create God?* Be patient.

When next summer came, I did indeed join the group. They were interested in examining the sub-species of *Peromyscus* and other small mammals in the mountains of New Mexico. Being young and daring, I climbed down into a very steep gorge one day and placed about 160 mousetraps along the streambed. Unfortunately, I was far more successful than I planned and ended up collecting over 110 mice. When I got back to camp they were all excited about this success. I assumed we would make study skins of a representative sample and throw out the rest. That was not to be. George said we had to stuff all 110. At a rate of six mice per hour per person, that translated into five hours of work just for my mice. We would be working well into the night. We all sat at workbenches and talked while we worked. By midnight, the conversation turned from science to religion. Since I was with a group of fellow scientists I felt comfortable in telling them about my evening of revelation when I was in grade school, and how I felt that the only thing that made sense for me was that man created God, rather than the other way around. Instead of the "Amens" I expected from this scientifically sophisticated group, the mood instantly changed. My proud pronouncements went over like a child who had just yelled out a string of obscenities in church. To call this chill hostility was putting it mildly. Not a single one of the three scientists agreed with me, and each of them reacted with animosity and anger. We spent the rest of the evening silently finishing our job and went to bed. The next morning the silence continued through breakfast. We then went back into the field I was given the task of digging a hole, to what purpose I have long forgotten. In the process I got some dirt on George's shoe. He immediately smacked me hard in the face with the flat of his hand, sending me reeling backward to the ground. None of us said anything, but we all knew this was not because I got some dirt on his shoes. To top it all off, I never got any of my *Microtus* skulls back.

From that episode I learned that people take their religious views very seriously, to the point of physically assaulting those who threaten their beliefs. Being a scientist and being trained in the scientific method does not automatically prevent a person from having a belief system that is often in conflict with rational scientific thinking. This was the start of my beginning to think about what is going on in the brains of humans which allows them to be capable of the rational thinking that has become the basis of a remarkable scientific revolution and simultaneously be capable of a spirituality and faith system that may be in total conflict with rational thought. This episode also taught me to choose wisely with whom I discussed my thoughts about God.

The next time I summoned the courage to discuss my religious insight was in college. My parents had moved to Lafayette, Indiana, because my father had gotten a new job as head of the department of chemical and metallurgical engineering at Purdue University. My mother, in her great wisdom, realized it would be difficult for me to start a new school as a senior where the other students had known each other for years. At the time I was attending University High School in Champaign, Illinois. She investigated and found that I needed only a few more credits to graduate. Two summer school courses later I entered the University of Illinois at age 16. To help make ends meet, I found a job in a rooming house that provided room and board in exchange for my washing the breakfast and evening dishes. One evening after I had finished studying, I wandered into the room of a friend and a fellow dishwasher who was also the only other pre-medical student in the house. We sat talking for about an hour when the subject turned to religion. Since he was in pre-med and since we had become good friends, I thought he would be open to my views, and once again I opened my big mouth and began to relate my childhood revelation. After I completed the story his demeanor changed. He stared at me for a minute with hostile eyes, then flew across the room in a rage and started pounding on me. It took several others who happened to be in the hall to pull him off of me.

It always amazed me that I could sit and listen to others espouse their religious views for hours, respect them, and not get the slightest bit upset. By contrast, some would listen to my views for only a few minutes and fly into a rage. Why the difference? Perhaps others had never seriously questioned the beliefs they had been taught from childhood and were never exposed to anyone who presented a line of reasoning that potentially challenged those beliefs. If what I said was so outrageous that it made no sense, they would not feel challenged. However, if it did make some sense, suggesting their own life-long views might need some adjusting, it could indeed be threatening and engender anger and even rage.

After college I attended medical school at Northwestern University, then took my internship, internal medicine residency, and a fellowship in hematology at Cook County Hospital in Chicago. At the time I took hematology, Watson and Crick had just recently solved the structure of DNA; Vernon Ingram had just identified a single amino acid change in the hemoglobin molecule of children with sickle cell anemia, thus beginning the field of molecular medicine; and Marshall Nierenberg and Severo Ochoa were in the process of deciphering the genetic code. All of these extraordinarily exciting developments led me to take a second fellowship in human genetics with Arno Motulsky at the University of Washington in Seattle. I subsequently became the head of the department of medical genetics at the City of Hope National Medical Center in Southern California, where I stayed for 37 years.

I have enjoyed a wonderful career in human genetics. From 1968 until 1979 I was involved in both clinical genetics and basic research into human chromosome structure and DNA metabolism. In 1980 I undertook a major switch to become involved in the molecular and clinical genetics of human behavior especially relating to Tourette syndrome, attention deficit hyperactivity disorder (ADHD) and conduct disorder. Thus, my expertise is in genetics, human molecular genetics, neuroscience, and behavioral medicine. I was so involved in scientific writing that I never entertained thoughts of writing about religion and the subject of this book. However, several things happened in recent years compelling me toward this undertaking.

One reason I decided to write the book relates to the recent development of the Intelligent Design (ID) movement. After retiring from the City of Hope in 2002, I began to catch up on my reading in fields that were not directly related to medicine. One was James Hogan's book, *Kicking the Scared Cow,*[1] a compilation of chapters questioning some of the commonly accepted paradigms about a range of areas, one of which was examining various aspects of Darwin's theory of evolution. This introduced me to the difference between the creationists and the ID creationists. The creationists object to Darwinism because they literally accept the Book of Genesis and claim the world is less than 10,000 years old. The ID creationists tend to accept that the world is in fact 4.5 billion years old and that some form of evolution occurred, but they have concerns about certain more complex aspects of Darwinian evolution. These objections led them to conclude that ultimately only a supreme being could have created the universe, the world, and all life. While not necessarily saying the force is God, most Intelligent Design enthusiasts are self-avowed fundamentalist Christians. Their position is that if something cannot be easily explained by current evolution science or if it seems too irreducibly complex to have evolved by natural selection, it must have been created by a supreme power. Later I found that Hogan took many of his objections about evolution from Jonathan Wells's book, *Icons of Evolution Science or Myth?*[2] Wells' book carried the teaser line: *Why much of what we teach about evolution is wrong.*

The objections of the Intelligent Design group are often seemingly reasonable questions about the Darwinian theory of evolution. While some of their points are little more than pickiness, some do not have trivial answers and some have also been points of concern by mainstream scientific evolutionists, including Darwin himself. However, as pointed out by Forrest and Gross in their book, *Creationism's Trojan Horse: The Wedge of Intelligent Design,*[3] Intelligent Design is little more than neo-creationism. Phillip Johnson, the founder of the movement stated,

> …we should affirm the reality of God by challenging the domination of materialism and naturalism in the world of the mind. With the assistance of many friends I have developed a strategy for doing this….We call our strategy *The Wedge.*[4]

By their definition, naturalism was any form of science that provided answers that excluded God as part of the explanation.[5] Their preference was theistic realism that assumes that God[6] brought the universe and all of its creatures into existence. The originators of the Intelligent Design movement stated they were,

> …unhappy with the polarized debate between biblical literalism and scientific materialism. We think a critical re-evaluation of Darwinism is both necessary and possible without embracing young-earth creationism. [3p18]

Disturbingly, not only are they dedicated to a neo-creationist agenda, but also to toppling the scientific method from its pedestal in Western culture and to contaminating the teaching of scientific biology in our schools. *The Wedge* approach is asking us to abandon sound scientific methods and reintroduce divine entities and miraculous "explanations" into theories and theorizing. [7p197,284] This is, in essence, a return to the Middle Ages. They then insist we teach this in our schools.

This would be a tragedy for the economy of both our country and the world. Economists have attributed more than half of the gains in gross national product and up to 85 percent of the gains in per capita income over the past several decades to advances in science and and technology. [11]

Science works best in a culture that welcomes challenges to prevailing ideas and matures the potential of all of its people. Scientific ways of thinking and of re-evaluationg one's views in light of new evidence help strengthen a democracy. [12]

From the perspective of a molecular geneticist, I found that many of the Intelligent Design concerns and objections were based on a profound ignorance of aspects of evolutionary theory and molecular genetics having to do with mutation rates, gene duplication, repetitive DNA, molecular evolution, molecular genetics of embryonic development, developmental genes, gene regulation, and others. One of the themes of this book is that the theory of evolution provides a more-than-adequate explanation for how life was created and evolved than does Intelligent Design.

Another reason for deciding to write this book came from recent developments in the field of cosmology. In my childhood musings, the furthest back I could take my evolutionary logic was to some vague, ancient, nebulous gases. What, if anything, could possibly be simpler than that? The latter half of the twentieth century saw impressive gains in our understanding of the universe, with findings relating to quantum mechanics, relativity, black holes, the accelerated expansion of the universe and most recently string theory and M theory. String theory suggests that all the major forces (gravity, electromagnetic, strong, and weak) and all the subatomic particles are formed by different lengths and levels of vibration of extraordinarily small strings of energy. String theory dramatically pushes back the boundaries for simpler precursors.

The recent decision by Judge Jones against the efforts of the ID community to attempt to promote the teaching of ID in the Dover, Pennsylvania schools was a remarkable victory for keeping the teaching of religion and creationism out of the schools. In part, the decision read,

> Both defendants and many of the leading proponents of ID make a bedrock assumption, which is utterly false. Their presupposition is that evolutionary theory is antithetical to a belief in the existence of a supreme being and to religion in general. Repeatedly in this trial, Plaintiffs' scientific experts testified that the theory of evolution represents good science, is overwhelmingly accepted by the scientific community, and that it in no way conflicts with, nor does it deny, the existence of a divine creator. [8]

Judge Jones characterized the attempt by the Dover School Board to introduce ID in the classroom as "breathtaking inanity." However, this has only slightly dampened the enthusiasm of the attempts to introduce ID and to destroy the teaching of the scientific method in schools. This decision heightened the effort of creationists to advance their theories in other parts of the world. The best defense against the ID movement is to make available to parents, schools, and teachers information that allows them to intelligently counter many of the ID claims. This is covered in Part II of this book. Up to this point I thought of naming the book *Intelligent Answers to Intelligent Design.* However, this would only be part of the story.

The individuals who have formulated the ID movement, planned *The Wedge* strategy, and written the books, are bright people. As pointed out by Michael Shermer in his book, *How We Believe,*[9] most of the ID supporters themselves are well-educated, intelligent individuals. In addition, it has been estimated that over 95 percent of the world's population believe in a supreme power, a supernatural being. More specifically, in the United States a 1996 Gallup poll showed that 96 percent believed in God, 90 percent believed in heaven, 79 percent believed in miracles, 73 percent believed there was a hell, 72 percent believed in angels, and 65 percent believed the devil is real. Clearly communication or connection with God and a belief in the supernatural plays an important role in most people's lives.

This raises the question, "Are those of us who believe in the supremacy of rational thought and are atheists or agnostics, and would answer negatively to all of the above questions, missing something? Do non-believers know something that the others do not, or is it the other way around?" Humans have been endowed with a brain that contains two remarkable and unique abilities—the capability for complex, analytical reasoning and thought, and the capacity for spirituality or the need to feel connected to something larger and outside of oneself. I term these the rational brain and the spiritual brain. Are these two brains fundamentally in conflict with each other? The spiritual need is usually satisfied by believing in a superior force or being, most often called God, or an equivalent concept in different cultures, languages, and religions. As noted in the Gallup poll, this is often associated with a belief in a wide range of entities that our rational brain tells us cannot and do not exist. Thus, an equally important aspect of this story is to attempt to understand how and why *Homo sapiens,* a highly rational and uniquely intelligent species, also has a capability and apparent need to adopt systems of belief and faith that often place the spiritual brain in conflict with the rational brain. Both of these abilities must have been selected in the evolution of man, suggesting they both played a critical role in allowing humans to evolve and function in complex societies.

So why write this book? It may just make a lot of people mad like it did in the two experiences I related above. My purpose is not to make people angry or mad. It is to make them think and consider things they may have not previously considered. Since my professional background is firmly rooted in the science of basic and molecular genetics, neuroscience, and the biology and psychology of human behavior, and since I have written nearly 500 papers and abstracts and three books on these subjects, I felt I was as qualified as any to write about these issues.

Scores of philosophers, theologians and scientists over the centuries have agreed on one thing—it is impossible to prove the existence or non-existence of God. Thus, it is not my purpose to be so bold as to attempt that. However, a different question, *Did Man Create God?* is clearly amenable to scientific inquiry. By this I refer to whether man himself was responsible for formulating the entity of an anthropomorphic God that for most people looks like a human being but has supernatural powers and under different names is the God for most of the world's major religions. Since one of the battlefields that the creationists have chosen is to question whether the man-made theory of evolution is correct, the question, *Did Man Create God?* could also be framed in terms of whether God is actually the result of a man-made Theory of God?* The essence of this book is well depicted in Michelangelo's Sistine Chapel fresco depicting the creation of man by the touching of the hand of God to the hand of man.

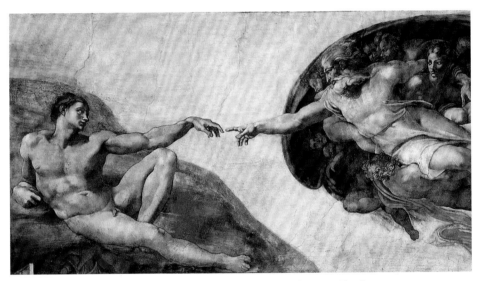

Figure 1. Michelangelo's Creation of Man in the Sistine Chapel.

The issue is, "Which way does the creativity flow? From God to man or from man to God?" The creation of God, embodied in the concept of the Theory of God, refers to a wide range of beliefs that include those about the creation of the universe, the earth, man and all other life on earth, the existence of a soul that lives on after we die, and the existence of an afterlife where we will be rewarded for leading a good and moral life.

Prior to the modern era, the Theory of God was the only viable explanation for many aspects of the natural world. An important added question is whether the sacred religious texts of the major religions, the Old Testament, the New Testament and the Qur'an (Koran), were also all essentially conceived and written by man rather than by God.

The questions "Did man create God?" and "Is the Theory of God a man-made

---

* A year-and-a-half after this introduction was written, Richard Dawkins also spoke of "The God Hypothesis" in his book, The God Delusion. [10] Two different sources for the same idea.

theory?" are fundamentally different from the question "Does God exist?" It is perfectly possible that the answer to the question, "Did man create God?" is "Yes," and yet a God still exists that does not bear the slightest resemblance to the anthropomorphic, personal God of the world's major religions and a God that played no role in conceiving or writing the sacred texts. Thus, readers who have a strong belief in God should not be put off thinking I am trying to destroy that belief. I am not. I am, however, suggesting that they consider many of the issues covered in this book. As a result, if they ever had any personal doubts about their faith, if their own rational brains have objected to some of the things they have been taught from childhood, they may be able to adjust their beliefs just enough to make peace with their rational brain and to develop a *rational spirituality.*

It is also my purpose to point out that spiritual values and a belief in God or some transcendent force can be very satisfying and religion can accomplish wonderful things, but if man created God, perhaps we should not take ourselves so seriously that we get into fights, wars, and terrorism over whose God is the best God, and whose sacred text is the best text—they are all equally valid and equally able to satisfy the spiritual side of human existence. I also explore the issue of whether it is possible to reconcile the rational and spiritual parts of our brain. Is it possible to develop a satisfying spirituality that rewards the spiritual part of our brain and at the same time does not insult the rational part of our brain? Again, I believe the answer to that is yes. If that is possible then perhaps many of the negative aspects of religious beliefs could be eradicated while retaining all of the positive aspects.

This book is divided into seven parts.

Part I. Evolution. In premodern times, the concept of God the creator was central to providing man with an answer to the questions, "Where did we come from? Where did all the creatures on earth come from?" After Darwin's momentous studies on *The Origin of Species,* these questions had a rational, scientific answer. Species evolved by evolution and natural selection. However, the validity of the central role of evolution in the creation of man and earth's creatures is contested by both the young world creationists and proponents of an old world but with Intelligent Design.

This section is about Darwin's theory of evolution and its more modern versions such as neo-Darwinism, post-neo-Darwinism and evolutionary developmental genetics. Darwin wrote his ground-breaking *The Origin of Species* in 1859 before DNA and genes were identified, before the development of the field of population genetics, and before all of human DNA as well as the DNA of many other organisms were completely sequenced. Because of this lack of knowledge of modern genetics, there were many issues that were left unexplained in Darwin's original theory and even in neo-Darwinism formulated in the 1940s. Many aspects of the fossil record were incomplete in the mid-nineteenth century and to some extent, still are.

Part II. Intelligent Answers to Intelligent Design reviews some of the ID objections to Darwinian evolution. Based on quite recent aspects of molecular biology and paleontology, I show that despite the ID objections the basic Darwinian theory of evolution is still strong and vibrant. I hope to explain some fairly complex science in a fashion that is easily understandable for the non-professional reader. This section has been presented in some detail because Intelligent Design arguments have been repeatedly used to validate the Theory of God. If readers are to come to their own conclusions about whether these arguments are valid or not, they need to know there are intelligent answers to all of the claims of the Intelligent Design creationists.

Part III. Cosmology. In premodern times, the concept of God the creator was also central to providing man with an answer to "Where did the earth come from? The sun? The stars? The universe?" If the reader thought that parts of Darwinian evolution were difficult to explain, some of the weirdness of quantum mechanics and string theory is even more so. Many of the new findings about astronomy and cosmology are highly relevant to issues of theology, religion, spirituality, and whether a God is necessary to create the universe. For example, does the Big Bang theory indicate that the universe was created from nothing? To many, the Big Bang proves the existence of God or at least the correctness of the Theory of God. Does it? Quantum theory shows that subatomic particles are instantaneously connected across the entire span of the universe. Some suggest this supports the concept of many Eastern religions that everything in the universe is interconnected. Does it? Does the combination of Darwinian evolution and cosmological evolution mean man is here by chance? Is he? If so does this affect our sense of purpose and the meaning of life? These and many additional spiritual implications of the new physics and modern cosmology are discussed.

Part IV. The Biology of the Rational and Spiritual Brain reviews the parts of the brain involved in consciousness, executive functions, rational and abstract thought, pleasure, social interactions, spirituality, meditation, self-healing, hope, happiness, and the biology of faith versus reason. Part IV shows that most of these traits and capabilities are hard-wired into the brain.

Part V. The Genetics of the Rational and Spiritual Brain reviews the role of genetic factors in bad behavior, altruism or good behavior, rational thought, and spirituality. When traits and capabilities are hard-wired into the brain this occurs because of the presence of a number of different genes interacting with each other and the environment.

Part VI. The Evolution of the Rational and Spiritual Brain. Complex, hard-wired, genetically regulated traits and capabilities do not just appear from nowhere. They are the result of evolution and natural selection over a period of thousands and millions of years. This section reviews the evidence relevant to the evolution of the rational brain (intelligence) and the spiritual brain (spirituality).

Part VII. Other Aspects of Spirituality and Religion. There are many additional aspects of human spirituality that are relevant to the question, "Did man create God?" This section reviews a number of these, including the origin of the major religions, mysticism, myth and ritual, and the role of psychedelics in spirituality and religion. In addition, the following questions are explored: Does God play favorites? Is one religion superior to another? Are there benefits to religion? Are there evils to religion? Is evil in the world incompatible with the existence of a kind and benevolent God? Are the sacred books literally true? and, Is God dead?

Part VIII. Summary. Parts I through VII have covered a wide range of complex subjects. Part VIII reviews these in relation to the subject of the book, *Did Man Create God?* Was man the author of the Theory of God? A range of issues are discussed concerning the meaning of life, whether morality or happiness is dependent on religion, and, most importantly, is it possible for you to develop a spiritual life that is not in conflict with your rational brain?

In recent decades there has been a dramatic increase in terrorism related to religious fundamentalism. This derives from the assumption that one religion is closer to being the true religion, one God is closer to being the true God, and one sacred religious book is better than another sacred religious book. All of these opinions are based on the assumption that God created man and that the sacred religious texts represent the spoken word of God. I challenge the reader to examine the validity of these assumptions.

While I personally do not believe in the existence of God, I am an unusual atheist in that I have the greatest respect for spirituality and many forms of religion. Some have referred to such individuals as "non-theists." Most Americans wrongly think that atheists are anti-theists, people who not only do not believe in God but also object to other's belief in God. A non-theist is simply "without a god-belief." In fact I argue that spirituality may have played such an important role in the evolution of man that without it we might not be here. Although I believe that a high level of spirituality does not automatically require that one also believe in God or be religious, I have respect for those whose level of spirituality has led them to believe in God and adopt religion as a means of expressing that belief. However, at the same time it is critical that people not hold the false beliefs that the universe, the earth, and all life could not have evolved without the helping hand of God, that one set of beliefs is superior to another, that one religion is better than another, or the false belief of fundamentalist religions that their sacred religious texts are the direct word of God and thus must be believed in their literal rather than in their metaphorical sense.

Knowledge of the biology of the spiritual brain helps us to understand why the majority of the human race believes in God. We owe it to ourselves and to the survival of the human race to understand where this need for spirituality comes from. We need to develop a *rational spirituality* that resists the adoption of rigid dogmatic religious systems and the belief in the superiority of one religion over another.

References

1. Hogan, J. P. *Kicking the Sacred Cow. Questioning the Unquestionable and Thinking the Impermissible.* Baen Publishing Enterprises, Riverdale, NY, 2004.

2. Wells, J. *Icons of Evolution Science or Myth? Why much of that we teach about evolution is wrong.* Regnery Publishing, Inc., Washington, DC, 2000.

3. Forrest, B. & Gross, P. R. Creationism's Trojan Horse. *The Wedge of Intelligent Design.* Oxford University Press, New York, 2004.

4. Johnson, P. E. *Defeating Darwinism by Opening Minds.* InterVarsity Press, Downers Grove, IL, 1997.

5. Johnson, P. E. *Wedge of Truth. Splitting the Foundations of Naturalism.* InterVarsity Press, Downers Grove, IL, 2000.

6.   Johnson, P. E. *Reason in the Balance: The Case Against Naturalism in Science, Law, and Education.* InterVarsity Press, Downers Grove, IL, 1995.

7.   Pennock, R. T. *Tower of Babel.* MIT Press, Cambridge, MA, 1999.

8.   Jones, J. T. Kitzmiller, et al. v. Dover Area School District, et al. United States District Court for the Middle District of Pennsylvania Case No 04cv2688. 1-139, 2005.

9.   Shermer, M. *How We Believe: Science, Skepticism, and the Search for God.* Second edition. A.W.H.Freeman Henry Holt and Company, New York, 2000.

10. Dawkins, R. *The God Delusion.* Houghton Mifflin Company, Boston, MA, 2006.

11. National Academies. *Raising Above the Gathering Storm: Energizing and Employing America for a Brighter Economic Future.* National Academies Press, Washington, DC, 2005.

12. Omen, G. S. Grand challenges and great opportunities in science, technology and public policy. *Science.* 314:1696-1704, 2006.

Is God the true creator of everything that exists, or is God a product of the human imagination, real only in the minds of those who believe?

Phillip Johnson
Reason in Balance [1p7]

Science is the only self-correcting human institution, but it is also a process that progresses only by showing itself to be wrong.

Astronomer Allan Sandage

Part I

Evolution

Since ancient times man has struggled to understand where he and the world around him came from. For many centuries the most common answer to this question was that we are here because a supernatural power put us here. While some may have found this explanation less than totally satisfactory, it was not until the publication of Darwin's *The Origin of Species* in 1859 that a viable alternative explanation existed. Thus, it was now possible to move from the statement,

"God created man and all living things"
to
"Evolution created man and all living things."

While it is not necessarily valid or logical to move to the next step—thus God does not exist—in the minds of many, this was at least a thought to consider. Because of this, Darwinism has been incorrectly considered by many to be one of the greatest potential threats to all religions that are based on the assumption of the existence of a supreme being that created heaven and earth. Because of the importance of the theory of evolution to the theme of this book, I have devoted Part I and II to the subject. Part I reviews Darwin's theory of evolution, using mostly his own words. Since the theory has grown to be more advanced and complex than it was in Darwin's time, I essentially review the evolution of the theory of evolution, i.e., Darwinism, neo-Darwinism, molecular genetics, and the molecular genetics of evolutionary development, so-called *Evo Devo*. Part II, Intelligent Answers to Intelligent Design will respond to the objections of the Intelligent Design creationists and show why none of those objections are valid and that Intelligent Design does not prove that a supernatural being or force was necessary to explain the creation of life in all of its wonderful diversity and forms.

References

1. Johnson, P. E. *Reason in the Balance: The Case Against Naturalism in Science, Law, and Education.* InterVarsity Press, Downers Grove, IL, 1995.

Chapter 1

Evolution of the Theory of Evolution

The theory of evolution itself has evolved from the initial concept of Darwin to the modern concepts of evolution based on the subsequent exponential expansion in our knowledge of biology, molecular genetics and development. I will start with Darwin.

Darwinian Evolution

In 1859 Charles Darwin (1809–1882) published his classic treatise *The Origin of Species by Means of Natural Selection or the Preservation of Favored Races in the Struggle for Life.*[1] Ernst Mayr[2] termed his theory of evolution,

> ...the greatest of all scientific revolutions. It represented not merely the replacement of one scientific theory ('immutable species') by a new one, but it demanded a complete rethinking of man's concept of the world and himself: more specifically, it demanded the rejection of some of the most-widely held and most-cherished beliefs of western man. In contrast to the revolutions in the physical sciences (Copernicus, Newton, Einstein, Heisenberg), the Darwinian revolution raised profound questions concerning man's ethics and deepest beliefs.

To give the reader a flavor of his book, I will frequently quote directly from Darwin, thus letting him explain his theory in his own words. In his introduction he stated:

> I can entertain no doubt, after the most deliberate study and dispassionate judgment of which I am capable, that the view which most naturalists until recently entertained, and which I formerly entertained—namely that each species has been independently created—is erroneous. I am fully convinced that species are not immutable; but that those belonging to what are called the same genera are lineal descendents of some other and generally extinct species in the same manner as the acknowledged varieties of any one species are descendents of that species. Furthermore, I am convinced that Natural Selection has been the most important, but not the exclusive, means of modification.

Ironically, although Darwin is known for his "theory of evolution," he only used that word once and that was the last word in the book.

> There is grandeur in this view of life, with its several powers, having been originally breathed by the Creator into a few forms or into one; and that, whilst this planet has gone cycling on according to the fixed laws of gravity, from so simple a beginning endless forms most beautiful and most wonderful have been and are being evolved.

> **The essence of Darwin's theory was that species evolved through a series of minor inherited variations and that by natural selection the variations that were the most favorable were retained. Over many generations this led to new species.**

The last sentence in his book indicates the thought that "the Creator" placed on earth a few or only one initial creature and all others evolved from that. In his section on Recapitulation and Conclusions he stated,

> I see no good reason why the views given in this volume should shock the religious feelings of anyone....A celebrated author and divine [clergyman] has written to me that 'he has gradually learnt to see that it is just as noble a conception of the Deity to believe that He created a few original forms capable of self-development into other and needful forms, as to believe that He required a fresh act of creation to supply the voids caused by the action of His laws.

Despite these caveats, all 1,200 original copies of the *The Origin of Species* sold out the same day it was released, and caused a storm of religious controversy.

Some of the data leading to Darwin's novel theory was collected when he was a naturalist on the H.M.S. Beagle that sailed the Pacific between 1831 and 1839. However, many years passed before the *The Origin of Species* was published. Darwin himself stated that an epiphany occurred when he read the book by Malthus called *Population* concerning the potential problems of human overpopulation. In his introduction, Darwin said,

> This doctrine of Malthus applies to the whole animal and vegetable kingdoms. As many more individuals of each species are born than can possibly survive; and as, consequently, there is a frequently occurring struggle for existence, it follows that any being, if it vary however slightly in any manner profitable to itself, under the complex and sometimes varying conditions of life, will have a better chance of surviving, and thus be naturally selected. From the strong principle of inheritance, any selected variety will tend to propagate its new and modified form.

One of the few diagrams in Darwin's book (Figure 1) illustrates his concept of the origin of new species.

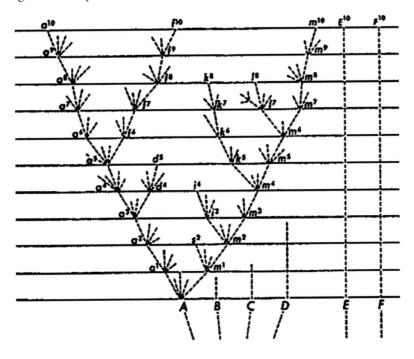

Figure 1. Diagram from Darwin's The Origin of Species. *See text.*

In referring to this figure Darwin said,

> As all the modified descendents from a common and widely-diffused species will tend to partake of the same advantages which made the parent successful in life, they will generally go on multiplying in number as well as diverging in character: this is represented in the diagram by the several divergent branches from (A). The modified offspring from the later and more-highly improved branches in the lines of descent will often take the place of, and so destroy, the earlier and less improved branches: this is represented in the diagram by some of the lower branches not reaching the upper horizontal lines. In some cases no doubt the process of modification will be confined to a single line of descent and the number of modified descendents will not be increased.
>
> After ten thousand generations, species (A) is supposed to have produced three forms, a^{10}, f^{10} and m^{10}, which having diverged in character during the successive generation, will have come to differ largely, but perhaps unequally, from each other and from their parent.

In this diagram Darwin laid out all of the important elements of his theory of evolution with minor changes slowly accumulating over thousands of generations to produce multiple branches and new species and old extinctions based on natural selection. Darwin even allowed for some species to progress through thousands of generations unchanged (E, F), but felt that this was fairly rare. This foreshadows the more-recent proposal of evolution by punctuated equilibrium, whereby rapid evolutionary change may be followed by long periods of no change.

Self-Criticism

Darwin was his own severest critic. He raised many of the concerns voiced by the Intelligent Design movement long before they did. His chapter VI was entitled, *Difficulties of the Theory.* He states:

> Long before the reader has arrived at this part of my work, a crowd of difficulties will have occurred to him. Some of them are so serious that to this day I can hardly reflect on them; but, to the best of my judgment, the greater number are only apparent, and those that are real are not, I think, fatal to the theory.

The following were some of his concerns:

1. Absence of intermediates. Darwin often viewed the fossil record as more of an embarrassment than as an aid to this theory. [3] Darwinian theory predicts the presence of many intermediate forms, if not in the present time, then at least in the fossil record. There was, however, an embarrassing dearth of such intermediate forms. He states:

> By this theory innumerable transitional forms must have existed; why do we not find them embedded in countless numbers in the crust of the earth?

His primary answer to this was that the fossil record was incomplete. The intermediate forms existed but they had not yet been discovered. There is some degree of truth to this. Paleontology has come a long way since Darwin's time, and in many cases, intermediate forms have been found, but in many cases they have not.

He also suggested that the intermediate forms existed for only a short period of time or in a very limited geographical area, thus greatly contributing to the difficulty of finding them in the vast excess of more developed forms. An additional reason he alluded to but did not explicitly state is that some forms, such as E and F in the figure, may have continued through thousands of generations essentially unchanged. Here the intermediate parental forms would be difficult to find in the vastness of unaltered forms.

2. Organs of extreme perfection and complication. In addition to few intermediate forms, the issue of complex structures is one of the most common objections to

Darwinian theory voiced by the Intelligent Design group. Darwin thought of it first. He stated,

> To suppose that the eye with all of its inimitable contrivances for adjusting the focus to different distances, for admitting different amounts of light, and for the correction of spherical and chromatic aberration, could have been formed by natural selection, seems, I freely confess, absurd in the highest degree.

He then stated he could find no other cases where the origin of a complex organ could not be explained by numerous, successive minor modifications. Other aspects of this subject so important to the Intelligent Design movement will be discussed later.

3. Organs of little apparent importance. A third area that Darwin found potentially troubling related to structures that seemed so unimportant that it was difficult to see how they could be formed by natural selection. His answer to this was that "organs now of trifling importance have probably been of high importance to an early progenitor."

4. The sudden appearance of groups of species. Darwin stated,

> The abrupt manner in which whole groups of species suddenly appear in certain formations, has been argued by several paleontologists as a fatal objection to the belief in the transmutations of species.
>
> I allude to the manner in which species belonging to several of the main divisions of the animal kingdom suddenly appear in the lowest known fossiliferous rocks.

It was known then that many new large groupings or phyla of animals seemed to have suddenly appeared in the Cambrian period. This was known as the Cambrian explosion. This interesting event is discussed in detail later. Darwin assumed there must have been a long period of animal evolution prior to the Cambrian explosion.

> Before the lowest Cambrian striatum was deposited, long periods elapsed, as long as, or probably longer than, the whole interval from the Cambrian age to the present day; and that during these vast periods the world swarmed with living creatures.
>
> To the question why we do not find rich fossliferous deposits belonging to these assumed earliest periods prior to the Cambrian system, I can give no satisfactory answer.

Again he blamed an incomplete fossil record and even suggested the missing fossils might be under the vastness of the Pacific Ocean. As we shall see later, his assumption of an incomplete fossil record does explain part of the story. The precursor life forms did not have the calcified exterior skeletons required to leave a good fossil record. Since Darwin's time some of the more subtle non-calcified records of life forms prior to the Cambrian period have been found. In addition, the field of molecular evolution, or the examination of the relationships between species based on the amino acid sequence of proteins and the nucleic acid sequence of DNA, has powerfully supported evolution but it was not even dreamed of in Darwin's time.

5. *Difference between Species and Varieties.*The first chapter of Darwin's *The Origin of Species* is entitled *Variation under Domestication.* We are all familiar with the wide variety in size, appearance, color, and other characteristics of different breeds of dogs and other domesticated species. Despite these differences, interbreeding produces fertile offspring. By contrast, interbreeding between species usually results in infertile or no offspring.

This puzzled Darwin, who stated,

> How can we account for species, when crossed, being sterile or producing sterile offspring, whereas, when varieties are crossed their fertility is unimpaired?

Each of these issues that bothered Darwin has been incorporated into the objections of the Intelligent Design group as evidence for the failure of Darwin's Theory of Evolution. Darwin thought of them first and, of course, did not view them as evidence against his theory. As outlined above he had an explanation for many of the anomalies. The solution of others would require waiting for further advances in biological knowledge.

> **Darwin was his own severest critic. He recognized that his theory was a work in progress and that some issues were troublesome, even to him. These included:**
> - **the frequent absence of intermediate forms**
> - **the existence of structures of great complexity**
> - **the presence of organs of little importance**
> - **the sudden appearance of large groups of species**
> - **the difficulty in defining a species versus a variety.**
>
> **These issues largely had to await the work of others to be fully resolved.**

Genetics and Neo-Darwinism

One of the major problems that Darwin faced was that the basic tenets of genetics had not yet been formulated. Thus, when he proposed that evolution was a result of the selection for advantageous inherited variations, the mechanism by which this could happen was a total mystery and would remain a mystery until 1900, 41 years after the publication of *The Origin of Species.*

Shortly after Darwin's work was published, Gregor Mendel, a monk in an Austrian monastery, was actually carrying out the experiments that led to an understanding of the basic concepts of genetic inheritance. He carefully recorded the results of crossing different varieties of peas. These results, published in a short monograph entitled *Experiments with Plant Hybrids,* showed that traits or mutations were inherited and transmitted as intact elements or units in successive generations. This work remained unappreciated until 1900, when three different scientists independently and almost simultaneously re-discovered Mendel's work.

This supplied an important missing link. In the first several decades of the twentieth century, remarkable advances were made in understanding the nature of these units called genes, the nature of dominant and recessive mutations, and how new mutations spread in populations. For example, H. Norton, a British mathematician, found that even *a small selective advantage of less than 10 percent led to drastic genetic changes in just a few generations.*

The combination of a rapidly increasing knowledge of genes and genetics, genes in populations (population genetics), and many related sciences led to the formulation of a new synthesis known as *neo-Darwinism.* Some of the most important publications for this new synthesis were Dobzhansky's 1937 book, *Genetics and the Origin of Species*[4] and Julian Huxley's 1940 books, *The New Systematics*[5] and *Evolution, The Modern Synthesis.*[6]

At a 1946 international symposium at Princeton, New Jersey, attended by all of the major workers in the field, there was unanimous endorsement of the gradualness of evolution, the importance of natural selection, the role of genes in populations, the role adaptation and diversification, the falsity of the inheritance of acquired characteristics, and the definition of a species as organisms that in nature mate to produce fertile offspring. [2]

This agreement was termed the *Modern Synthesis.* It was modern in that the new field of Mendelian genetics was now added. It was a synthesis in that it provided an agreement between two previously opposing groups. On the one hand there were the paleontologists who only saw the development of new species over long periods of geological time and referred to the process as macroevolution—the apparent sudden development of new species. On the other hand there were the population geneticists who saw evolution as a gradual change in the frequencies of variant genes due to selection or change in gene frequencies simply due to random genetic drift.

Remarkably they came to the agreement that the macroevolution of the paleontologists was the outcome of the continued and accumulative slow changes or the microevolution within a species observed by the population geneticists. Macroevolution in the sense of the sudden appearance of a new species, the "hopeful monsters" or "divine creation," did not exist. There was essentially no difference between microevolution and macroevolution. The difference was only a matter of degree. Of particular importance, studies of the mechanism of microevolution were relevant to macroevolution or speciation.

Molecular Genetics

The powerful addition of genetics to the theory of evolution occurred before Watson and Crick figured out the structure of DNA, thus setting off the revolutionary era of molecular genetics and molecular evolution.

In a one-page article published in *Nature* in 1953 James Watson and Francis Crick reported their work on deciphering the structure of deoxyribose nucleic acid or DNA.[7] In their opening paragraph they modestly state:

> "We wish to suggest a structure for the salt of dexoyribose nucleic acid (D.N.A.). The structure has novel features which are of considerable biological interest."

Their diagrammatic representation of DNA was as follows:

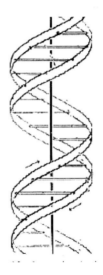

Figure 2. Diagram of the structure of DNA. From Watson and Crick.[7]

The legend for this figure read:

> The figure is purely diagrammatic. The two ribbons symbolize the two phosphate-sugar chains, and the horizontal rods the pairs of bases holding the chains together. The ventral line marks the fibre axis.

The phosphate-sugar and bases are arranged as follows:

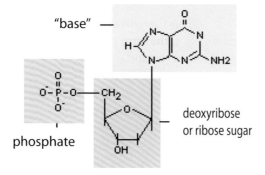

Figure 3. A deoxyribose nucleic acid

The key to the structure was the pairing by hydrogen bonds of the nucleic acids adenine (A) with thymine (T) and guanine (G) with cytosine (C) as follows:

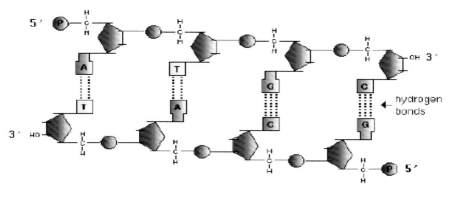

Figure 4. Base pairing of A:T, T:A, G:C and C:G. [8]

In this figure the sequence of base pairs is A-T, T-A, G-C, and C-G. If the top strand (5' to 3' strand) is read, the base sequence would be ATGC. If the bottom strand (3' to 5') is read, the complement sequence is TACG. The sequence of these base pairs is the key to understanding the entire field of genetics. In the sections of DNA that form the genes, this sequence is read into a second form of nucleic acid termed ribose nucleic acid or RNA, specifically messenger RNA. Based on the genetic code, where three bases code for each of the 20 amino acids, the messenger RNA is translated into specific proteins such as the globin of hemoglobin, or enzymes such as cytochrome oxidase.

Watson and Crick ended their article with the famous understatement:

> It has not escaped our notice that the specific pairing we have postulated immediately suggests a possible copying mechanism for the genetic material.

By this they referred to the fact that when the two phosphate-sugar chains separated, the specific A-T and G-C pairing allowed two new identical copies of DNA to be formed. This finally solved the problem of how one cell can divide to form two identical daughter cells with all the genetic information intact.

Over the next 15 years the genetic code was deciphered. The results are shown in Figure 5. This table shows the three-letter code for each of the amino acids. The letters in the left column show the first base, the letters on the top row show the second base, and letters for the third base are shown in each of the three letter codes. Thus, a sequence of CTT would code for the animo acid leucine *(leu or L)*. It can be seen that some amino acids such as leucine are produced by six different codes; some such as proline *(Pro or P)* are produced by four different codes, some such as cysteine *(Cys or C)* are produced by two codes, and some such as tryptophan *(Try or W)* are produced by only one code. *Ter* stands for termination. When this code is present, the synthesis of the protein stops.

	T	C	A	G
T	TTT Phe (F) TTC " TTA Leu (L) TTG "	TCT Ser (S) TCC " TCA " TCG "	TAT Tyr (Y) TAC TAA **Ter** TAG **Ter**	TGT Cys (C) TGC TGA **Ter** TGG Trp (W)
C	CTT Leu (L) CTC " CTA " CTG "	CCT Pro (P) CCC " CCA " CCG "	CAT His (H) CAC " CAA Gln (Q) CAG "	CGT Arg (R) CGC " CGA " CGG "
A	ATT Ile (I) ATC " ATA " ATG Met (M)	ACT Thr (T) ACC " ACA " ACG "	AAT Asn (N) AAC " AAA Lys (K) AAG "	AGT Ser (S) AGC " AGA Arg (R) AGG "
G	GTT Val (V) GTC " GTA " GTG "	GCT Ala (A) GCC " GCA " GCG "	GAT Asp (D) GAC " GAA Glu (E) GAG "	GGT Gly (G) GGC " GGA " GGG "

Figure 5. The genetic code.

When the sequence of amino acids in proteins in widely different species was determined it was found that they were similar. Since the differences were greater when the evolutionary distance between two species was greater, the study of protein sequences served as both a biological clock and a means of examining the branching in the tree of life such as that drawn by Darwin. As sequencing techniques improved, the sequence of bases in RNA and DNA were also determined. RNA differs from DNA in that uracil is used in the place of thymine, ribose is used in the place of deoxyribose, and RNA is usually single-stranded. The structural difference between deoxyribose and ribose is as follows:

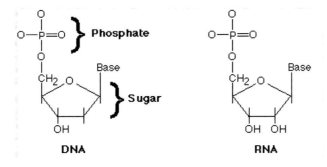

Figure 6. Deoxyribose versus ribose.

The difference is that ribose has two -OH groups while the deoxyribose of DNA has only one. The pathway by which genes in chromosomes code for proteins is diagrammed in Figure 7.

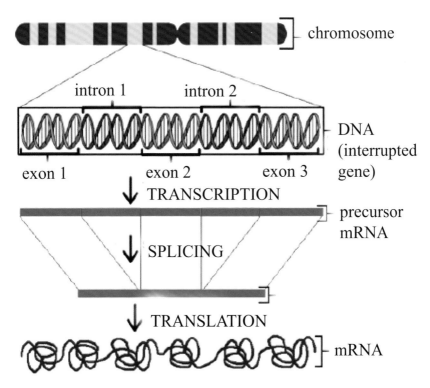

Figure 7. The chromosomes (top) contain a linear string of thousands of genes, one of which is shown. Genes are divided into exons whose sequence is utilized to determine the sequence of amino acids in proteins, and regions between the exons are called introns. The sequence of both the introns and the exons are translated into pre-messenger RNA, but the RNA corresponding to the introns is spliced out. This produces messenger RNA (mRNA) which directs the sequence of amino acids in the proteins. Most of the proteins are enzymes that catalyze specific chemical reactions in the body.[8]

From an evolutionary aspect, the important point is that organisms from bacteria to man possess many similar genes and proteins and the sequences of these genes and proteins show them to be genetically related. Half of the genes present in yeast are also present in humans. Actin is an important structural component of the cytoplasm of eukaryotes, analogous to the internal wooden framework of a house. The sequence of the actins of yeast and the actins of humans are 91 percent similar in their sequence. More than 99 percent of the genes of mice have homology to human genes. [9] As illustrated in subsequent parts of this book, the study of amino acid, RNA, and DNA sequences has provided an extraordinarily powerful verification of the inter-relatedness of the species and of their evolution from common ancestors.

> **Organisms from bacteria and yeast to mice and man possess many similar genes, and the sequences of these genes show them to be genetically related. This provides an extraordinarily powerful verification of the inter-relatedness of the species and of the evolution of modern species from common ancestors.**

Evolutionary Developmental Genetics

The final important development has been the marriage of molecular genetics with development termed *evolutionary developmental biology* and dubbed "Evo Devo." The most remarkable aspect of this part of the story is the identification of a constant set of genes involved in determining all the different body plans. This has been called the developmental "toolbox." These developments were described by Sean Carroll in *Endless Forms Most Beautiful: The New Science of Evo Devo.* [10]

> **Much of what we have learned has been so stunning and unexpected that it has profoundly reshaped our picture of how evolution works. Not a single biologist, for example, ever anticipated that the same genes that control the making of an insect's body and organs also control the making of our bodies.**

With these developments Darwin's original theory of evolution now had three powerful companions—genetics, molecular genetics, and molecular developmental genetics. In the following sections we will see how these help to provide effective responses to those who seek to attack the theory of evolution. I will first provide some general background information about the evolution of the earth and the Tree of Life.

References

1. Darwin, C. *On the Origin of Species by Means of Natural Selection or the Preservation of Favored Races in the Struggle for Life.* Murray, London, 1859.

2. Mayr, E. *The Growth of Biological Thought: Diversity, Evolution, and Inheritance.* The Belknap Press of Harvard University Press, Cambridge, MA, 1982.

3. Eldridge, N. & Gould, S. J. Punctuated equilibria: An alternative to phyletic gradualism. In: Schopf, T. J. M. & Thomas, J. M. *Models in Paleobiology.* Freeman, Cooper, San Francisco. 1972.

4.   Dobzhansky, T. *Genetics and the Origin of Species.* Columbia University Press, New York, 1937.

5.   Huxley, J. S. *The New Systematics.* Clarendon Press, Oxford, London, 1940.

6.   Huxley, J. S. Evolution, *The Modern Synthesis.* Allen & Unwin, London, 1942.

7.   Watson, J. D. & Crick, F. H. C. A structure for Deoxyribose nucleic acid. *Nature.* 171: 737, 1953.

8.   From arbl.cvmbs.colostate.edu/hbooks/genetics/biotech/basics/nastruct.html. By permission.

9.   Consortium, M. G. S. Initial sequencing and analysis of the mouse genome. *Science.* 420: 520-562, 2002.

10.   Carroll, S. B. *Endless Forms Most Beautiful: The New Science of Evo Devo.* W. W. Norton, New York, 2005.

Chapter 2

The Tree of Life

The purpose of this section is not to give a course in geology and paleontology but to introduce to the readers who may not be familiar with this material a brief, non-technical outline of some of the highlights of these fields of science. The unfolding of progressively more complex life forms over the long periods of geologic time has often been referred to as the Tree of Life. Geologic time is divided into progressively smaller units of time progressing from eons, eras, and periods to epochs. The time is given in *Ma,* or millions of years ago. These are summarized in Figure 2. The levels of atmospheric oxygen (O_2) are shown in blue on the left. The eons are very large blocks of time starting with the Hadeon, lasting one billion years from the birth of the earth 4.6 billion years ago to the very beginnings of primitive life. [1]

The **Archean** (ancient life) also lasted approximately a billion years and was the age of bacteria, especially the blue-green cyanobacteria (Figure 1).

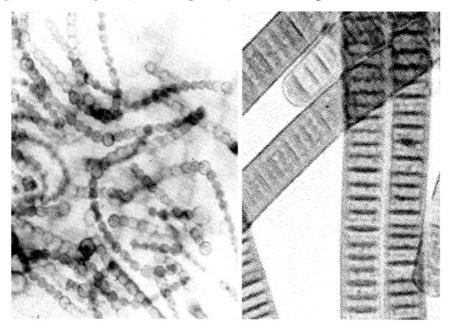

Figure 1. Blue-green Cyanobacteria [2]

Eon	Era	Period	Epoch	Age Ma	Tree of Life	O₂
Phanerozoic	**Cenozoic**	Quarternary	Holocene	.011	end of glaciers, rise of modern civilization	
			Pleistocene	1.8	fully modern humans, large mammals	
		Neogene	Pliocene	5.3	ice age, many mammals, recent mollusks	
			Miocene	23.0	moderate climate, mountain building, modern mammals and birds, first hominoids	
		Paleogene	Oligocene	33.9	warm climate, rapid evolution of mammals, modern angiosperms	
			Eocene	55.8	fully modern humans, large mammals	
			Paleocene	65.5	tropical climate, modern plants, large mammals	
	Mesozoic	Cretaceous	Late	99.6	Extinction of the dinosaurs / first placental mammals, flowering plants	
			Early	145.5	breakup of Gondwana, first birds	
		Jurassic	Late	161.2	gymnosperms especially conifers, ferns	
			Middle	175.6	many dinosaurs, small mammals, first birds and lizards	
			Early	199.6	breakup of Pangea into Gondwana and Laurasis	
		Triassic	Late	228.0	first dinosaurs, first mammals	
			Middle	245.0	many large amphibians	
			Early	252.6	modern corals, teleost fish	
		Permian		299.0	Permian extinction - 95% of life goes extinct / amphibians, gymnospermes, beetles and flies, Pangea	
		Carboni-ferous	Pennsyl-vanian	318.1	winged insects, amphibians common, first reptiles, coal formed, very high oxygen	
			Mississi-pian	359.2	large primitive trees, first land vertebrates, trilobites decline	
		Devonian		416.0	jawed fish common, aquatic amphibians	
		Silurian		443.7	first jawed fish, trilobites and molluscs	
		Ordovician		488.3	many invertebrates, first primitive vertebrates	
		Cambrian		542.0	Cambrian explosion of phyla, trilobites common, first vertebrates	
	Proterzoic	Ediacarian Vendian		630.0	first shelled organisms, soft bodied invertebrates, green algae	
				1,200	multicellular red algae	
				1,800	first eukaryotes	
				2,500		
	Archean			2,800	first bacterial stromatolites	
				3,200	first bacteria	
				3,600	origin of life, first microfossils	
	Hadean			4,600	formation of the earth	

Figure 2. See text

The cyanobacteria evolved early and subsequently changed little through to modern times. They were uniquely suited for life on a young planet where the atmosphere contained hydrogen, nitrogen, methane, carbon dioxide (CO_2) and little or no oxygen (O_2)—totally unsuitable for modern animals. Their blue-green color is due to the presence of chlorophyll. This allows for photosynthesis, the process of using the energy of sunlight to convert water (H_2O) and CO_2 to sugar and oxygen. Other bacteria perform respiration and reverse the process converting sugar and O_2 to water and CO_2. This is diagrammed as follows:

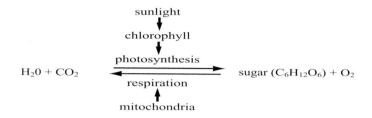

This process provided a major source of the oxygen that eventually accumulated in the atmosphere around 2.2 billion years ago. Cyanobacteria have been described as the most important organism to ever inhabit the earth. [3] This may come as a blow to those who think man is the most important organism. However the cyanobacteria have been present on earth for 3.6 billion years compared to man's one million years, 3,600 times longer. Bacteria have no nucleus and are thus termed prokaryotes (pro = before karyo = nucleus). This long period of time allowed prokaryotes to percolate for over 2.5 billion years before evolving to eukaryotes (eu = true) with a nucleus.

The other great contribution of the cyanobacteria is that they played a crucial role in the origin of plants. They possessed chlorophyll and thus in the presence of sunlight they had had the biochemical machinery to convert carbon dioxide and water into sugar and oxygen. Organisims that were precursors to plants ingested cyanobacteria and were able to convert the energy from the sun to oxygen.

The **Proterzoic** (before abundant life) ranged from 543 million to 2.5 billion years ago. During this period the bacteria continued to flourish, but a novel new group of organisms called archaeans appeared. The Proterzoic was also the period during which the cyanobacteria produced a build-up of oxygen in the atmosphere. This build up led to the extinction of many bacterial groups but also made possible the explosive evolution of the eukaryotes beginning 1.8 billion years ago. The oxygen levels increased to almost 30 percent during the Carboniferous and Permian periods, then dropped at the end of the Permian extinction. [4]

The **Vendian** is a period of time from 543 to 600 million years ago, in the late Proterzoic, during which the first multi-cellular organisms appeared. As noted above, Darwin was concerned about the apparent absence of life forms prior to the Cambrian explosion. He thought there was a long period of evolution of more primitive life forms prior to this but that the fossil record was still incomplete. He was correct. Since these earlier forms were soft-bodied they did not have calcified skeletons and thus were harder to find. The fossils of the Vendian period are important because they represent the first multicellular organisms. Figure 4 shows some of these fossils.

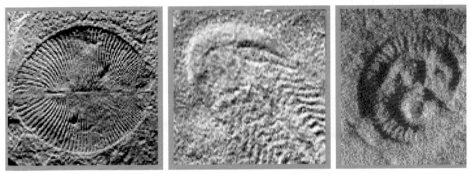

Figure 4. Vendian fossils. [5] Left. Dickinsonia possibly related to annelid worms or cnidarian polyps (jellyfish, corals, other stinging forms). Middle. Spriggia were initially thought to be an annelid (segmented worm) but later thought to be related to arthropods with external skeletons made of chitin. Right. Tribrachidium heraldicum, an unusual dish-shaped form with three-part symmetry. Possibly related to corals and anemones or sea urchins and seastars.

The **Ediacaran** period is concurrent with the Vendian and based on Ediacarian fossils found in Australia, Canada and China. Recent dating based on the decay of radioactive uranium to lead indicated this period was from 551 to 635 million years ago. [6] These fossils are similar to the other Vendian fossils. Since they have soft bodies that do not preserve well, the evidence for their existence often depended upon the trails they left in the mud.

Figure 5. Some pre-Cambrian fossils appear to be precursors of modern animals. Primitive worms made these simple burrow and trace fossils. These and other Ediacara forms survived the late Protozoic extinction and took part in the Cambrian explosion [7]

Most of the Vendian/Ediacaran organisms that populated the pre-Cambrian oceans became extinct as "failed experiments in evolution." Some, however, do appear to be precursors leading to the subsequent Cambrian explosion. Thus, as Darwin predicted,

> Before the lowest Cambrian striatum was deposited, long periods elapsed, as long as, or probably longer than, the whole interval from the Cambrian age to the present day; and that during these vast periods the world swarmed with living creatures.

He was absolutely correct.

Small shelly fauna. The first fauna with hard parts are called the *Tommotian* after a locality in Russia where they were first found. They were subsequently found worldwide. These have been termed *small shelly fauna.*

Figure 6. *Small Shelly Fauna from the Tommotian Age* From left to right, top to bottom: *Latouchella, a Helcionelloid mollusk; a Microdictyon-like form (the mineralized eye of a lobopod); Chancelloria—a spicule from a superficially sponge-like Procoelomate (Class Coeloscleritophora); a vermiform specimen and Tommotia, an angular shell from an animal of uncertain affinities, but presumably another Procoelomate—Class Tommotiida.* [8]

Like most of the Ediacara, the small shelly fauna were also a failed evolutionary experiment. The last great eon is the Phanerzoic (period of life). Its subdivisions are shown in Figure 2. The important points are the progressive increase in complexity of the different species and the periods of extinctions.

Extinctions. The red lines in Figure 2 represent periods of major and minor mass extinction of life forms. These extinctions were due to a range of factors including the impact of comets, dramatic shifts in temperature or in the composition of the atmosphere, and movements of the continents (plate tectonics). Mass extinctions of many species have played an important role in evolution. They clear out ecological niches and allow new species to fill in and evolve into the resulting empty spaces. Some of the most dramatic were the Great Permian Die-off at the end of the Permian period where more than 50 percent of families and more than 95 percent of species died off. The Cretaceous (K/T) mass extinction resulted in the extinction of all vertebrates that weighed more than 25 kg (55 pounds). Since these were the large dinosaurs, this is known as the dinosaur extinction. This extinction is believed to have been the result of a giant asteroid crashing into earth near the Yucatan Peninsula and producing a worldwide nuclear winter. The Pleistocene extinction resulted in the disappearance of large mammals and birds and coincided with the arrival of the first humans.

Many mass extinctions that occurred over geologic time periods cleared out old species from ecological spaces and played a major role in allowing the accelerated evolution of new species.

Tree of Life. One form of RNA is called *ribosomal RNA*. This is present in ribosomes, the structures that translate the specific sequence of nucleic acids in messenger RNA into a specific sequence of amino acids in proteins. This is a fundamental function that all organisms must perform in order to exist. The sequencing of ribosomal RNA by Dr. Carl Woese[9] provided the first evidence for the existence of a unique group of organisms, the archeans. These bacteria-like organisms lived at the high temperatures of volcanic hot springs and produced methane (CH_4). The sequence of their ribosomal RNA was distinctly different from that of either bacteria or eukaryotes. As a result of these studies Woese proposed three domains of life: eukaryotes, bacteria and archaea.

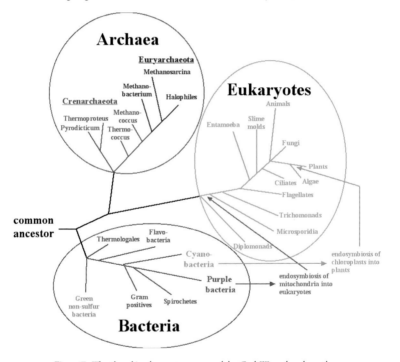

Figure 7. The three-kingdom system proposed by Carl Woese based on the sequence of ribosomal RNA. Most but not all of the sub-branches are shown. Modern eukaryotes contain mitochondria that were derived from purple bacteria by endosymbiosis (see purple arrows), and plants have chloroplasts derived from blue-green cyanobacteria by endosymbiosis (see blue-green arrows).

This diagram indicates that a very ancient ancestor was common to the three Kingdoms. The incorporation a whole organelles, such as chloroplasts, into a different organism is called endosymbiosis. This process was also responsible for the incorporation of mitochondria into the cells of eukaryotes. Mitochondria are membrane lined organelles with their own DNA. They are responsible for the respiration of oxygen. Figure 8 shows the membrane-rich mitochondria.

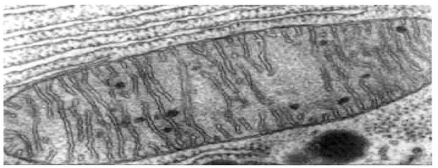

Figure 8. Electron micrograph of a mitochondria inside the cell. [10]

Plants are able to carry out photosynthesis because they contain chloroplasts with chlorophyll. Chloroplasts also have their own DNA and are also present as a result of endosymbiosis.

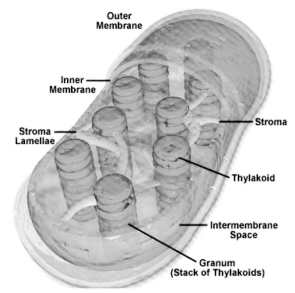

Figure 9. 3D reconstruction of a chloroplast. The thylakoids are the site of the initial conversion of sunlight energy into chemical energy ATP. [11]

Because these two organelles are surrounded by their own membranes and have their own DNA they are believed to have been free-living organisms at one time. They carried out vital functions related to the production of energy. Mitochondria were incorporated by endosymbiosis into purple bacteria, and chloroplasts were incorporated into cyanobacteria. These organelles contributed to the metabolism of these bacteria for several billion years. About 600 million years ago, further endosymbiosis provided eukaryotes with mitochondria and plants with chloroplasts.

Endosymbiosis indicates how innovative the process of evolution can be. Instead of repeatedly re-inventing structures, evolution simply incorporated "old parts" that functioned well in bacteria to make new, more-complex organisms.

Horizontal gene transfer. Evolution has carried the concept of "no need to re-invent the wheel" into two other areas—the horizontal transfer of whole genes and the re-use of parts of genes. While the tree shown in Figure 7 has a common ancestor, in reality the situation is not as clear-cut as it may seem. The complete sequencing of an archaea *Methanococcus janaschii* in 1996 showed that it shared only 11 to 17 percent of its genes with bacteria and that more than 50 percent of its genes were unknown to either bacteria or eukaryotes. This confirmed that archaea belonged to a distinct domain. While archaea were more closely related to eukaryotes than bacteria, assigning a clear root to this tree was difficult. All three domains shared the same genetic code indicative of a common origin. The bacteria and archaea carried their DNA in the form of a circle and had no nucleus. On the other hand, the archaea and eukaryotes share many features not seen in bacteria. Finally, the bacteria and eukaryotes have some characteristics of the chemical nature of their membranes not shared by archaea.

The solution to this confusion came when it was realized that horizontal gene transfer was taking place. This occurs when one organism takes up the DNA of another organism. The advantage of gene transfer is that if one species evolved a solution to a specific problem, another species could benefit by simply picking up the genes involved. This would accelerate the process of evolution. However, it would be a disadvantage if this process was too efficient since this would eventually retard evolution by widespread dissemination of "unique variations." How could an organism with an advantageous mutation maintain a selective advantage if its competitors quickly obtained the same mutation by horizontal gene transfer? The concept of patent protection had not yet been developed. The development of a nucleus around the DNA of multicellular organisms retarded horizontal gene transfer, resulting in a further acceleration of the pace of evolution.

The horizontal transfer of whole genes from one species to another was common early in evolution. While this could accelerate the adaptability of primitive organisms, the eventual restriction of this process was necessary for the evolution of more-complex organisms.

Transfer of parts of genes. A second change that occurred with the transition from prokaryotes to eukaryotes was a change in how genetic material was processed. The genes are separated into exons and introns. Exons code for different functions in a gene and this function (module) can be shared by different genes by a process called *exon transfer.* A reasonable analogy is a child's Tinkertoy® set. Tinkertoys® come with a range of different modules in the form of wheels, axels, struts, blades, motors, and many other parts used to construct anything the child's imagination desires. A basic set of modules can produce many thousands of different toys. Endosymbiosis, gene transfer, and exon transfer use the same modular or Tinkertoy® approach. Thus, once a working system, organelle, gene, or gene part has evolved, it can be used over and over to generate new life forms. We will see later how this modularity provides a solution for two of the Intelligent Design group's major concerns—the evolution of complex systems and the assumption that evolution would take too much time.

> **In addition to having a nuclear membrane, eukaryotes also divided their genes into multiple exons and introns. Each exon coded for a specific modular function in the resulting protein. Like biological Tinkertoys®, rearranging, shuffling and exchanging exons allowed for the rapid evolution of new genes and again prevented the need to re-invent a module.**

Preparation for the Cambrian explosion. A number of unique new aspects of the earth's atmosphere and the tree of life occurred in the late Proterozoic Era. These were:
- the accumulation of significant amounts of oxygen in the atmosphere
- partitioning DNA into chromosomes
- enclosing DNA in a membrane to form the nucleus and eukaryotes
- splitting the genes into exons and introns
- incorporation of mitochondria into eukaryotes
- evolution of the "developmental toolbox" (see Chapter 4)
- formation of multicellular organisms

The combination of all these novel features provided the major force for the sudden explosion of new life forms in the Cambrian Period.

> **For the first 2.5 billion years of life only single-cell bacteria existed. For the next 700 million years, single celled eukaryotes came on the scene. Immediately prior to the Cambrian Period there were two, largely failed evolutionary experiments, the Vendian/Ediacara fauna and the small shelly fauna. Following an accumulation of oxygen in the atmosphere and the development of multicellular organisms there came an explosion of new life forms—The Cambrian explosion.**

References

1. Carroll, S. B. Chance and necessity: the evolution of morphological complexity and diversity. *Nature.* 409: 1102-1109, 2001.
2. Figure from www.ucmp.berkeley.edu/bacteria/cyanointro.html. By permission.
3. Knoll, A. H. *Life on a Young Planet. The First Three Billion Years of Evolution on Earth.* Princeton University Press, Princeton, NJ, 2003.
4. Huey, R. B. & Ward, P. D. Hypoxia, global warming, and terrestrial late permian extinctions. *Science.* 308: 398-401, 2005.
5. Figure from www.ucmp.berkeley.edu/vendian/vendian.html. By permission.
6. Condon, D. et al. U-Pb ages form the neoproterozoic Doushantuo formation, China. *Science.* 308: 95-98, 2005.

7. Figure from geol.queensu.ca/museum/exhibits/ediac/ediac.html. By permission.
8. Figure from www.palaeos.com/Ecology/Biota/Tommotian.html. By permission.
9. Woese, C. R. and Fox, G. E. Phylogenetic structure of the prokaryotic domain: the primary kingdoms. *Proc Natl Acad Sci U S A.* 74:5088-5090, 1977.
10. Figure from Fawcett: *A Textbook of Histology.* Chapman and Hill, London, UK. 1994.
11. Figure from www.daviddarling.info/images/chloroplast.jp. By permission.

Chapter 3

The Cambrian Explosion

After all the necessary pieces were in place the stage was set for the age of the bacteria to come to an end and for multicellular eukaryotes to begin a rapid ascendancy. The most famous of the fossil deposits from the Cambrian Era were in the Burgess Shale in Yoho National Park in the Canadian Rockies. The sudden appearance of many different life forms was so dramatic that this is often referred to as the Cambrian explosion. The astounding aspect of the Cambrian explosion is that most of the modern animal phyla came into existence in this relatively short period of about 20 million years and no new animal phyla developed after that. Approximately 90 percent of the Burgess phyla became extinct.

The astounding aspect of the Cambrian explosion is that most of the modern animal phyla came into existence in this relatively short period of time and no new phyla developed after that.

This fossil bed was discovered by Charles Doolittle Walcott, who was both the director of the Smithsonian Institution and a paleontologist who worked in the field as well as sitting behind a desk. Walcott first discovered the Burgess Shale in 1909 late in the summer. Snowfall precluded extensive collecting but he recognized the value of his find and returned for a month each summer collecting fossils from 1910 through 1913. At the age of 67, he returned again in 1917. In all he brought back 80,000 specimens for storage in the Smithsonian Institution in Washington D.C. From 1911 to 1920 he wrote a series of reports on the Burgess fauna.

In his book *Wonderful Life,* Stephen Jay Gould[1] outlines in fascinating detail how Walcott "shoe-horned" all of the fauna of the Burgess Shale into a series of modern phyla. This fit perfectly with the classic Darwinian theory of slow progressive evolution from simpler to more complex forms of life, over time. These fossils then remained in storage for 50 years. Beginning in the 1970s three paleontologists—Harry Whittington and his two graduate students Simon Conway Morris and Derek Briggs, launched their own expedition. Instead of going to Canada they went to the dusty drawers in the back reaches of the Smithsonian Institution. They began a detailed re-examination of the Burgess Shale fossils and in the process launched a paradigm-changing re-assessment of the entire process of how evolution really works. A remarkable feature of the Burgess Shale fossils is that both hard and soft parts were preserved.

I would like to take the reader through a tour of this ancient Burgess Shale zoo to show the amazing diversity of this sudden explosion of multiple body forms, because the figures, taken from Gould's book, are a testament to the powerful creativity of evolution, and because the reconstructions by the artist Marianne Collins are things of beauty.

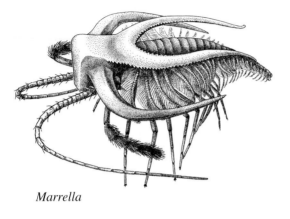

Marrella

The first organism to fall out of the Walcott shoehorn of modern phyla was *Marrella.* This remarkable creature possessed features that violated the key characters of every group of arthropods. Whittington struggled with how to classify it. He initially placed it in a group of trilobite-like organisms but quickly realized this was wrong. In reality it seemed to belong nowhere. Another organism called *Yohoia* with a large pair of grasping appendages also did not fit anywhere.

Whittington next examined *Opabinia,* an organism with a unique body plan consisting of five eyes in the head, a terminal claw, body sections with gills on the top and a tail piece in three segments. Two pairs of the eyes were on short stalks, a fifth was in the mid-line. While this unique phylum also went extinct, it is intriguing to

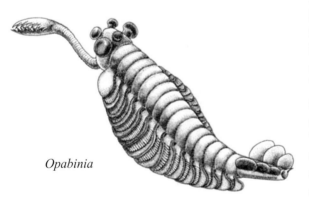

Opabinia

imagine what we might look like running around with five eyes if this organism had been at the bottom of the tree leading to humans. Whittington initially thought *Opabinia* was an arthropod, meaning "jointed foot." However, a careful dissection showed no such appendages. As unique as they were, with no modern counterparts, *Marrella* and *Yohoia* were at least arthropods. By contrast, Opabinia did not fit into any known phyla. Gould [1p136] stated:

> I believe that Whittington's reconstruction of Opabinia in 1975 will stand as one of the great documents in the history of human knowledge. How many other empirical studies have led directly on to a fundamentally revised view about the history of life? We are awestruck by *Tyrannosarus;*

we marvel at the feathers of *Archaeopteryx;* we revel in every scrap of fossil human bone from Africa. But none of these has taught us anywhere near so much about the nature of evolution as a little two-inch Cambrian odd-ball invertebrate named *Opabinia.*

While Whittington's approach to the treasure trove of Burgess fossils in the Smithsonian Institution was to first examine the most common organisms, Simon Conway Morris's approach was the opposite. He searched the many drawers for the rare oddball fossils. *Nectocaris* is the first oddball organism he described. This looked mostly like an arthropod in front and a chordate with a tail fin behind. It did not fit into any known phylum.

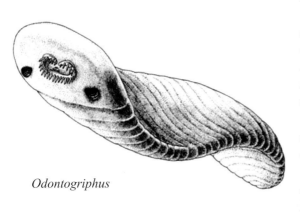

Odontogriphus was the second oddball organism described by Conway Morris. Its mouth was surrounded by tentacles and the pair of palps (probable sensory organs) are shown on the underside of the head.

There were no appendages or indication of hardened areas, suggesting it was gelatinous. This

Odontogriphus

further suggested the "Cambrian explosion" could simply be due to the absence of hard parts on the organisms allowing them to be visible as fossils. *Odontogriphus* also does not fit easily into any modern phyla.

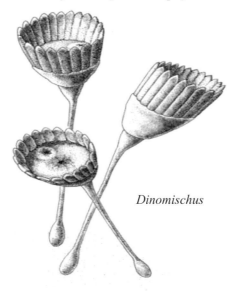

Dinomischus

Dinomischus was the third mystery animal described by Conway Morris. It represented another major functional design consisting of a creature with a radial symmetry, suited to receiving food from all directions. Both the mouth and the anus were located close together on the upper stalk. Be thankful this also did not become the model for us. This was also a "bizarre thing unto itself" and "has no obvious affinity with other metazoans and presumably belongs to an extinct phylum." [2]

A fourth organism described by Conway Morris was *Amiskwia*, a flattened, gelatinous, swimming animal with a pair of tentacles on the head, and side and tail fins. This creature also did not fit well with any known phylum.

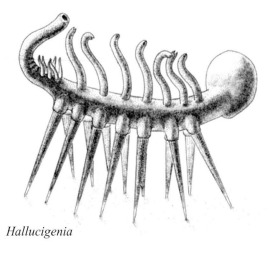

Hallucigenia

Hallucigenia, the fifth on Conway Morris's list, is the most stunningly bizarre of the lot. It is supported by seven pairs of unjointed struts allowing it to stand on the sea floor. There are seven tentacles with two pronged tips that extend upward from the large bulbous "head" to the opposite end "tail" Each tentacle may have been able to gather food and pass it to the communal gut. This organism was so difficult to classify that one consideration was that it was part of a larger, yet undiscovered creature, that would probably be even more bizarre. Some have suggested this figure is upside down with the tentacles on the bottom and the spikes on the top for protection. [3]

The third paleontologist of the trio, Derck Briggs, described a number of Burgess organisms, of which the first was *Branchiocaris*, considered by Walcott to be a Crustacea, which had five pairs of appendages in a specific arrangement. Careful examination showed it was not a Crusteacian and defied classification into any current group of arthropods.

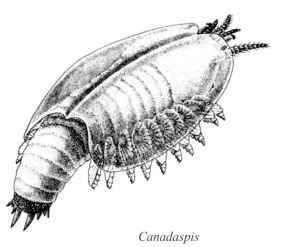

Canadaspis

Canadaspis, the second organism that Briggs studied, was also the second most common animal in the Burgess Shale. This was a true Crusteacea. This abundance was probably a sign of its potential for success. This is the first of all the Burgess animals described so far to be placed in a successful modern group of organisms.

Whittington examined a second Burgess Shale animal to survive past the mid-Cambrian era called *Naraoia*. This animal represented a twig on the branch of organisms that produced the trilobites. Trilobites survived to the end of the Paleozoic Era. A second Burgess Shale organism, *Tegopelte,* was also a trilobite.

Odaraia, a bivalved arthropod, had the largest eyes of any Burgess organism. The trunk contained forty-five limb-bearing segments, and a unique three-pronged tail more similar to that of sharks and whales than lobsters. This uniquely specialized organism was not similar to any other arthropod. A reconstruction of *Odaraia* in its natural habitat is from Conway Morris's book *The Crucible of Creation,* and is shown in Figure 1.

Figure 1. Odaraia (center) *with other Burgess Shale organisms including* Nectocaris *(middle right),* two Pikaia swimming in *upper* left, *an annelid worm Canadia (lower left), a Pirania sponge with spicules (lower right), a pair of Dinomischus (lower middle) and Ctenorhabdotus (upper right). From Conway Morris,* The Crucible of Creation, *Oxford University Press.* [4] *1998. By permission.*

Sidneyia

Another organism, *Sidneyia,* most closely resembled a group of arthropods called the merostomes, but it had a number of unique features indicating it was not a close relative of this group. Like other Burgess creatures it tended to be a grab bag of different features. For example, the first four of the nine body segments carried legs similar to those of merostomes, while the last five segments carried walking legs with gill branches. *Habelia* was yet another variant where for the 12 trunk segments, the first six had typical legs, while the last six bore only gill branches.

Sarotrocercus was one of the weirdest of the Burgess organisms. It had large bulbous eyes on stalks, nine body segments with gills but without leg branches, a tail with a tuft of spines at the end, and looked like a ride at Disneyland. *Sarotrocercus* was informally called *Santa Claws*

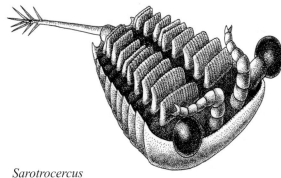

Sarotrocercus

to reflect the large and ferocious pair of front claws.

Wiwaxia is another weird Burgess wonder with no body segmentation and with no modern relatives. Other than the jaw that vaguely resembled a clam, there was nothing else about *Wiwaxia* that resembled other mollusks, living or dead.

Pikaia was the last Burgess organism that Gould described and is one of the most intriguing of the creatures described by Conway Morris. It appears to be the world's first known cordate. Chordates possess a notocord, the precursor of the spinal column which was required for the development of the nervous system.

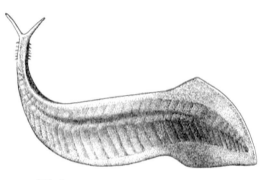

Pikaia

Figure 2. Anomalocaris has captured a trilobite. In the lower right *is the five-eyed* Opabinia. *In the* lower left *is* Wiwaxia, *and in the* lower middle *are three* Hallucigenia. *The two cup-like organisms at the bottom are Dinomischus. From Conway Morris* The Crucible of Creation, *Oxford University, New York. 1998.* [4] *By permission.*

This makes *Pikaia* a landmark in the history of the phylum to which all the vertebrates, including man, belong. Pikaia was a precursor to us. Gould [1p323] stated:

> ...if you wish to ask the question of the ages—why do humans exist?—a major part of the answer...must be because *Pikaia* survived the Burgess [extinction].

Gould [1p160] also stated that:

> Each one [of the Burgess arthropods] seemed to be built from a grab bag of characters—as though the Burgess architect owned a sack of all possible structures, and reached in at random to pick one variation upon each necessary part whenever he wanted to build a new creature....Where was order, where decorum?

47

In summary, most of the unique Burgess organisms are now extinct. The Burgess organisms that were precursors to later, but eventually extinct, organisms included the trilobites *Naraoia* and *Tegopelte*. The Burgess organisms that were precursors to modern organisms were *Canadaspis* (Crustacea) and *Pikaia* (Chordates)

Evolution is Not Directed

In reflecting on the wonders of the Burgess Shale fossils, Gould mused in *A Wonderful Life* [1p50] that if the tape of time were rewound and the period of the Burgess Shale replayed, the animals who survived and those who became extinct might be totally different and all subsequent life forms could have been different. The point and truth of this mental exercise is that as much as it may appear to have been goal directed toward a magnificent outcome (man), each step of the way was a crap-shoot of random events. The outcome of evolution is not predetermined.

The Burgess Shale fossil bed in Canada provided a treasure trove of fossils from the Cambrian Period. Over a time course of about 10 to 20 million years many modern and fossil animal phyla came into existence and no new phyla developed after that. Over 90 percent of the species became extinct, while others formed the beginnings of multiple modern phyla including chordates from which vertebrates including man evolved. The mechanisms by which the incredible burst of creation and diversity of body forms could have developed so quickly are discussed in the next chapter.

References

1. Gould, S. J. *A Wonderful Life: The Burgess Shale and the Nature of History.* W. W. Norton & Co Inc, New York, 1989.
2. Briggs, D. E. G. & Conway Morris, S. *Problematica from the Middle Cambrian Burgess Shale of British Columbia.* (eds. Hoffman, A. & Nitecki, M. H.) Oxford University Press, New York, 1986.
3. Ramsköld, L. & Hou, X. New Early Cambrian animal andonychophoran affinities of enigmatic metazoans. *Nature.* 351: 225-228, 1991.
4. Morris, S. C. *The Crucible of Creation: The Burgess Shale and the Rise of Animals.* Oxford University Press, New York, 1998.

The God of the gaps was actually a theological mistake. If God is the Creator, he is somehow connected with the whole show, not just the difficult or murky bits of what is going on.

John Polkinghorne
Quarks, Chaos and Christianity [1p22]

Part II

Intelligent Answers to Intelligent Design

There are two ways to respond to the threat to theism posed by the theory of evolution. One is to concede that the scientific evidence for evolution is so overwhelming that it is hopeless and irrational to believe otherwise. Accepting the validity of evolution does not prove that God does not exist. For many the next logical step is too great a leap. That step is that the theory of evolution is totally consistent with a belief in the existence of God if one adopts the view that God created the raw materials for the universe then went on to other more important things and left the creation of multiple life forms to evolution. The situation is illustrated by the joke related by Dembski. [2p38]

Scientists come to God and claim they can do everything God can do.
"Like what?" asks God.
"Like creating human beings," say the scientists.
"Show me," says God.
"Well we start with some dust and then"—God interrupts.
"Wait a second. Get your own dust."

I have included this because it is genuinely funny. However, it also illustrates why, in Part III, I discuss cosmology, since it is related to "getting our own dust."

Having once started things going, one must assume that out of curiosity God occasionally checked in to see what was happening. Of course the alternative that God does not exist is also quite possible. As pointed out in the Introduction, based on Occam's Razor, this seems the more logical of the two theories since it removes from the table the troubling and even more difficult next question, Who created God?

The second way to counter the threat of the theory of evolution is to claim that the scientific evidence for it is so deeply flawed in many of its aspects that we do not need to take it seriously, and yes, God really did create man and the universe. This has become a very popular approach. Five surveys in the United States over the past 20 years consistently show that 45 percent believe God created humans in their present form in the past 10,000 years, 37 percent believe God had a guiding hand in the development of humans, and only 12 percent believe God had no part in the process. Only a third believe Darwin's theory of evolution is well grounded in science. [3]

Respondents were also asked whether they believed more in creationism than in evolution. Of those who chose creationism, 28 percent still felt that humans have developed over millions of years from less advanced forms of life, but that God guided this process. Thus, not all self-avowed creationists reject the basic tenets of the theory of evolution.

There are two groups of detractors or anti-Darwinists—the creationists who believe in the total infallibility of the Bible and literally accept the account of creation as stated in the Book of Genesis, and those who propose the concept of Intelligent Design. The evidence against the young earth creationists' proposal that the earth is less than 6,000 years old is so overwhelming that I refer the reader interested in the evidence against this viewpoint to other books [4-15] and to the National Center for Science Education website www.ncseweb.org. It is not my purpose to respond to every single complaint of the old earth Intelligent Design Creationists. I have chosen only those given the highest visibility. The interested reader can refer to the National Center for Science Education website for responses to issues not covered.

Since young earth creationists believe the earth is young, and since a variety of radioisotope dating methods clearly show it is 4.5 billion years old, the young earth creationists spend a lot of effort attempting to disprove the validity of these dating methods. For those interested in a detailed account of why the creationists are wrong, and a description of the rubidium-strontium isochron dating with its self-calibrating and self-checking results, I refer the reader to Brent Dalrymple's book *The Age of the Earth*. [16] In contrast to these issues, I will answer some of the most relevant questions raised by the Intelligent Design group.

Darwinian Evolution "Just a Theory"

One of the most common objections to Darwin's theory of evolution is that it is "just a theory." In popular usage the concept of "a theory" often implies a rather weakly supported thought. However, in science, the term theory is a much stronger term. In science, theories are proposed, then tested and tentatively accepted or discarded. It is never possible to unequivocally prove that a scientific theory is correct. But theories can be disproved or, as scientists say, falsified. As Karl Popper stated, "We never prove a theory right; we merely fail to prove it wrong." [17] Science is a constantly moving collection of theories where no theory is sacred, but some are more sacred than others because numerous attempts at falsification have failed. Most good theories make a number of predictions. If those predictions turn out to be incorrect the theory is falsified and thus disproved. If the predictions turn out to be correct and if repeated attempts to falsify a theory fail, the theory is considered likely to be correct—but it is still called a theory.

The most famous example of attempting to falsify a theory occurred after Einstein published his famous theory of general relativity in 1915. The effect of gravity on the warping of space predicted that light would be bent as it traveled past the sun. The first attempt to falsify Einstein's remarkable theory was carried out by a group of scientists led by Sir Arthur Eddington. [18]

In 1919 these scientists went to Brazil and Africa to study a total eclipse of the sun. This allowed them to determine if the position of stars behind the sun was shifted because their light rays were bent by gravity when they passed by the sun. They were. Einstein predicted the light would be bent by 1.74 arcseconds. Eddington showed it was bent by 1.79 arcseconds. The minor difference was well within the range of measurement error. The general theory of relativity was not unequivocally proven, but a major attempt to falsify the theory failed. If enough attempts to falsify a theory fail, confidence that the theory is correct begins to build. While it has often been claimed that the theory of evolution is "just a theory," some of the most remarkable advancements and achievements of mankind are still referred to as theories, such as the Theory of Relativity or the Theory of Gravity or the Quantum Theory. One could say that the proposal that the sun will rise in the morning is "just a theory." It cannot be absolutely, unequivocally proven. However, since the sun has risen since the creation of the earth, all 4.5 billion x 365 or 1.64×10^{12} attempts to falsify this theory have failed, giving us confidence that the theory is correct. As discussed in this book, the massive evidence in favor of the Theory of Evolution has given scientists enormous confidence that it is true.

The Intelligent Design group continuously attempts to falsify the Theory of Evolution. In this book I am proposing that evolution is totally capable of explaining the origin of life in the universe and that Occam's razor is best satisfied by the proposal that man created God rather than God created man, since it best answers all related questions, including who created God? The purpose of this book, however, is not just to make this point. Its purpose is to examine the role of evolution in the formation of the two dueling parts of our brain—the part providing us with the capability for rational, analytical thought and the part thirsting for spirituality. Are they compatible? Can we have both? My story is cleaner and more robust if the theory of evolution is not falsified. Thus, I have devoted Part II to answering some of the attempts by Intelligent Design groups to falsify the theory of evolution. I cannot possibly answer all of their objections. Like a pile of cafeteria plates, when one is answered new ones are generated and pop up to take their place. All I hope to do is answer some of the most common objections. Each issue has its own chapter.

If you are already a staunch believer in evolution, you could skip to part III on Cosmology. However, reading the following chapters might allow you to better answer the Intelligent Design claims if you should be called upon to do so.

References

1. Polkinghorne, J. *Quarks, Chaos, and Christianity.* Crossroad, New York, 2000.
2. Dembski, W. A. *The Design Revolution.* InterVarsity Press, Downers Grove, IL, 2004.
3. Gallup. Substantial Numbers of Americans Continue to Doubt Evolution as Explanation for Origin of Humans. www.gallup.com/poll/content/login.aspx?ci=1942. 2001.
4. Ross, H. *A Matter of Days. Resolving a Creation Controversy.* NavPress, Colorado Springs, CO, 2004.
5. Eldridge, N. *The Triumph of Evolution and the Failure of Creationism.* W. H. Freedman, New York, 2000.
6. Pennock, R. T. *Tower of Babel.* MIT Press, Cambridge, MA, 1999.
7. Berra, T. M. *Evolution and the Myth of Creationism.* Stanford University Press, Palo Alto, CA, 1990.
8. Futuyma, D. J. *Science on Trial: The Case for Evolution.* Pantheon Books, New York, 1983.

9. Godfrey, D. J. *Scientists Confront Creationism.* W. W. Norton, New York, 1983.
10. Kitcher, P. *Abusing Science: The Case Against Creationism.* MIT Press, Cambridge, MA, 1982.
11. Montagu, A. *Science and Creationism.* Oxford University Press, New York, 1983.
12. Newell, N. D. *Creation and Evolution: Myth or Reality?* Columbia University Press, New York, 1982.
13. Ruse, M. *Darwinism Defended.* Addison-Wesley, Reading, MA, 1982.
14. Young, W. *Fallacies of Creationism.* Detrelig Entereprises, Calgary, Alberta, Canada, 1985.
15. Strahler, A. N. *Science and Earth History.* Prometheus Books, Buffalo, NY, 1987.
16. Dalrymple, G. B. *The Age of the Earth.* Stanford University Press, Palo Alto, CA, 1991.
17. Kopper, K. *The Logic of Scientific Discovery.* Routledge, London, 1972.
18. Aczel, A. D. *God's Equation. Einstein, Relativity, and the Expanding Universe.* Delta, New York, 1999.

Chapter 4

Does The Cambrian Explosion
Disprove Darwin's Theory?

Creationists and Intelligent Design proponents present the Cambrian explosion as a shining example of a phenomenon that evolution cannot explain. For them it is a prime example of the creative powers of a supernatural being. This became an exemplar of their cause by virtue of the fact that in Darwin's time (1859) and in Charles Doolittle Walcott's time (1900) knowledge about Precambrian life was non-existent. Not a single well-documented fossil had been found from any time before the Cambrian explosion, and the earliest evidence of multicellular life coincided with the earliest evidence of life. There could not be a better example of the creative touch of a supreme being.

The creationists and Intelligent Designers were not the first to see the hand of God in the Cambrian explosion. The apparent absence of life during most of the earth's history and its subsequent appearance at full complexity posed no problem for anti-evolutionists. Sir Roderick Imprey Murchison, the great geologist who first worked out the record of early life, viewed the Cambrian explosion as God's moment of creation, and read the complexity of the first animals as a sign that God had invested appropriate care in his initial models. [1] Writing five years before Darwin's *The Origin of Species,* he explicitly identified the Cambrian explosion as disproof of evolution ("Transmutation," in his terms), while he extolled the compound eye of the first trilobites as a marvel of exquisite design:

> The earliest signs of living things, announcing as they do a high complexity of organization, entirely exclude the hypothesis of a transmutation from lower to higher grades of being. The first fiat of Creation which went forth, doubtlessly ensured the perfect adaptation of animals to the surrounding media; and thus, whilst the geologist recognizes a beginning, he can see in the innumerable facets of the eye of the earliest crustacean, the same evidences of Omniscience as the completion of the vertebrate form. [2p459]

As reviewed previously, Darwin was forthright in exposing the difficulties of his theory and placed the Cambrian explosion at the pinnacle of his distress. He acknowledged the anti-evolutionary interpretation of many important geologists and recognized that this theory required an extensive Precambrian record of precursors for the first complex animals. Darwin has been vindicated by the subsequent findings of a rich Precambrian record, most discovered in the recent past. In his book, *Icons of Evolution,* Jonathan Wells [3] presents the following diagram purporting to represent Darwin's theory (top) and the reality of the Cambrian explosion (bottom).

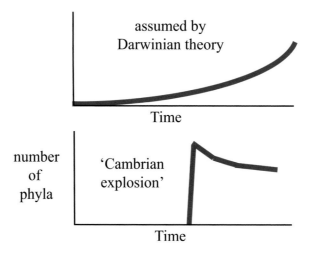

Figure 1. *Comparison of Darwin's evolutionary gradualism with the reality of the Cambrian explosion for phyla. From Wells.* [3] *By permission.*

The pattern for the number of phyla has been referred to as an upside-down tree of life and a failure of Darwin's prediction of progressive gradualism with many missing links. There are a number of caveats to this complaint.

First, to the casual reader this pattern gives the impression that all forms of life started with a single burst of creation in the Cambrian period. If this were really the case one might be justified in thinking this was surely proof that a supernatural being touched the surface of the earth and instantaneously brought forth this plentitude of life. However, the time scale for the Cambrian explosion was more like 10 to 20 million years, hardly a single touch. God would have had to linger quite awhile over this type of creation.

Second, note that pattern refers to animal phyla. Phyla are the major subdivisions of life based on body form. As reviewed in Chapter 2 several important groups of organisms such as the bacteria were present for several billion years before the Cambrian Period, again hardly a brief touch. Other forms such as red and green algae, other eukaryotes, soft-bodied invertebrates, "small shelly fossils," and the organisms of the Vendian and Ediacaran periods all proceeded the Cambrian explosion. All combined, based on the fossil record, there were many phyla in existence prior to the so-called Cambrian explosion. These included Proferia, Coelenterata, Nemertina, Echinodermata, Mollusca, and Anthropoda. [4] Thus, the widely held perception that all of the known phyla came into existence during the Cambrian Period is simply not correct.

Third, molecular clocks produce a tree of life based on the sequence of DNA, RNA and proteins. Such molecular results suggest that most of the major phyla originated long before the Cambrian explosion. Based on molecular clocks from different vertebrate species this diversification began more than one billion years ago. [5-7] Figure 2 is a diagram of the divergence times reported by Wray et al. [5] based on DNA sequencing of seven different genes.

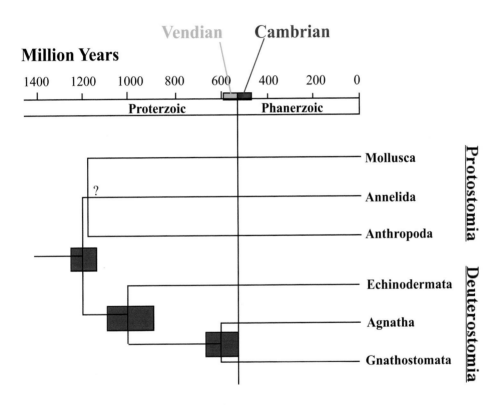

Figure 2. Divergence times for selected phyla. Standard errors are indicated by the red bars. The three estimated divergence times are in agreement with well-corroborated phylogenetic relationships. The chordate-echinoderm and chordate-protostome divergence times are significantly different from each other. From Wray et al. Molecular Evidence for Deep Precambrian Divergences Among Metazoan Phyla. Science. 274: 568-573, 1996. [5] By permission.

The molecular clock shown in Figure 2 agrees with the fossil record that diversification of major phyla began prior to the Cambrian explosion, but this clock also gives an earlier date than that proposed by the fossils record. As such this could represent what Darwin and others referred to as pre-Cambrian "hidden evolution." [8] It could be argued that when only a few genes are examined, the clock may not be accurate. The clock in Figure 2 is based on seven different genes. However, the molecular clock reported by Wang et al. [6] was based on 50 genes and gave a similar result.

Molecular clock studies based on invertebrates have given more recent times for the formation of bilateral body forms (bilaterians) shown as the first branch of the above tree. Peterson and colleagues estimated that the last common ancestor of the bilaterians arose between 573 and 656 million years ago. Microfossils of the Doushantuo formation in southern China have identified a primitive bilaterian called *Vernanimalcula* (small spring animal) (Figure 3) dating from 580 to 600 million years ago. [9]

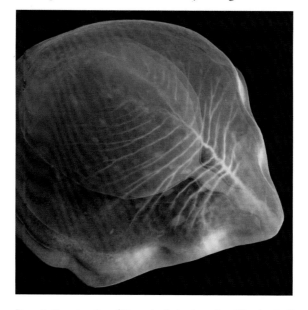

Figure 3. Reconstruction of Vernanimalcula, the earliest bilaterian fossil dating to 580 to 600 million years ago. From David Bottjer, "The Early Evolution of Animals," Scientific American. 293: 42-47, 2005. A. Bachar Illustration Design. By permission.

This time frame was 50 million years prior to the start of the Cambrian explosion. Thus, with a more complete fossil record and the results of studies of molecular evolution, the following more closely illustrates reality.

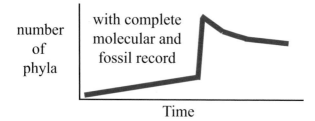

Figure 4. A more-realistic picture of the evolution of the Cambrian "explosion."

This is more like the end of a long slow crawl than a Big Bang or explosion. [10] Long after the Cambrian explosion many millions of species and hundreds of families (two divisions up from species and two down from phyla) continued to evolve. The following figure illustrates the number of new insect and four-legged animal (terrestrial tetrapod) families that evolved from the Devonian to the Tertiary periods.

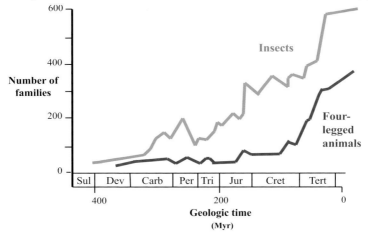

Figure 5. Rapid diversification of families of insects and four-legged animals since the Cambrian explosion. [11, 12]

Again, the pattern in Figure 5 hardly represents a single instant for the creation of all groups of species.

Despite these caveats, it is still necessary to explain how so many different phyla could come on the scene over a relatively short period of time. Gould made a distinction between disparity or the number of body forms and diversity—the number of different species. While diversity continued to increase, as shown in Figure 5, disparity peaked during the Cambrian explosion and then decreased, as shown in Figure 4. Before getting into the details of how the disparity increased so rapidly, it is necessary to present a few basic aspects of genetics relating to gene duplication and unequal crossing over.

Gene Duplication and Unequal Crossing-Over

The earliest single-cell organisms without a nucleus (prokaryotes) had only a small number of genes, numbering in the low hundreds. Mice, humans and other mammals have approximately 25,000 genes. How does the number of genes increase over time? This is accomplished by gene duplication through a process of unequal crossing over. Early animals started with a single copy of each gene, for example genes A and B.

Gene rearrangement. Most eukaryotes are diploid; that is, they possess one set of chromosomes from the mother and one set from the father. Random genetic changes in the sequence of DNA are very common. Sometimes they affect the function of the genes; more often they do not. As a result, the sequence of the maternal and paternal genes are often different. These sequence differences are shown by vertical yellow lines.

During *meiosis*, a special form of cell division associated with sexual reproduction, the chromosomes from the mother and father pair with each other. This allows crossing-over between the maternal and paternal chromosomes.

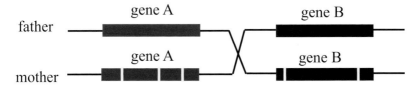

When the resultant products separate into individual eggs or sperm, the genes are rearranged.

This exchange and rearrangement of genetic information provides a powerful mechanism for increasing the genetic diversity and survivability of life forms.

Gene duplication. During meiosis, chromosomes may pair out of alignment to produce the following arrangement:

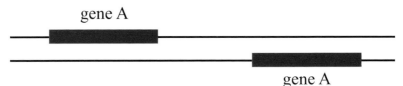

Now, crossing-over occurs between these two copies of gene A.

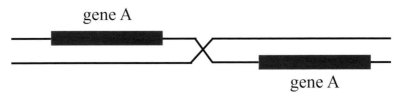

When the two chromosomes are segregated into an egg or a sperm, one has two copies of gene A

while the other chromosome has none.

If the germ cell missing the gene is involved in fertilization, the embryo will die and the chromosome with the gene deletion is usually lost. On the other hand, if the egg or sperm with the duplicated gene is involved in a fertilization, the resulting organism will now have two copies of the gene A, A and A' and more of the gene product will be produced. If this is of some advantage for the organism, it will be selected and soon the pair of duplicated genes will become fixed in the population. Since the organism still has a normally functioning gene A, gene A' is now free to have multiple random genetic changes that can alter the function of the gene to produce a new gene, B.

This is how the number of genes increases over evolutionary time. When the DNA of these genes is sequenced, because of the similarity of most of the sequence, the fact that gene A and B were originally one gene *can be deduced even millions of years after the duplication.*

Once a gene duplication of gene A, to A and A' has occurred, the rate of unequal crossing over can now occur much more rapidly. This is because the sequence of gene A and A' is so similar that A can easily but mistakenly pair with gene A'.

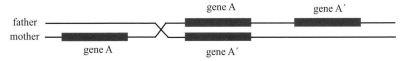

Now an unequal crossover between gene A and A,' will produce the following two chromosomes, one with three copies of the gene A,

and one with one copy.

This is the mechanism by which a whole series of genes with similar function can be distributed into a cluster or family on a given chromosome. Gene duplication is an exceptionally efficient mechanism for rapid evolutionary advance. [13,14] This now sets the scene for a review of the homeotic box, or *HOX*, genes.

The number of genes increased over evolutionary time by gene duplication. The presence of one or more duplicated genes adjacent to each other on a chromosome increases the probability of unequal crossing-over to produce even more gene duplication and gene clusters.

Homeotic Genes

In 1894, the British zoologist William Bateson published a book entitled *Material for the Study of Variations.* In it he had gathered together many examples of mutations that produced what he termed monsters. He was interested in these monsters because he thought that the sudden leaps into new body forms in a single generation might have relevance as a counterpoint to Darwin's slow and gradual changes. These monsters are now known not to be relevant to evolution. He divided the different monsters into those in which the number of repeated parts were altered and those in which one body part was transformed into the likeness of another. [15p46] He called the second group *homeotic* based on the Greek term *homeos,* meaning same or similar.

In 1915, the *Drosophila* geneticist Calvin Bridges discovered the first breeding homeotic mutant that caused the tiny hindwings of the fruit fly to develop into full-formed regular wings when under stress of heat, cold, or anesthesia. He termed this two-winged *mutant bithorax* (Figure 6).

Figure 6. The Drosophila melanogaster *bithorax mutant with two wings. Photo by Dr. Ed. Lewis.* [16]

HOX Genes

The bithorax mutation was studied extensively by the Drosophila geneticist Ed Lewis for which he received the Nobel Prize in 1995. These studies showed the presence of a cluster of duplicated genes that were called the *Bithorax Complex.* There were five genes that controlled the front half of the fly and three that controlled the back half. Remarkably, the order of the genes on the DNA strand was the same as the head-to-tail order of the parts they controlled. Since this formed a box-like set of genes they were termed *Homeo Box,* or *HOX,* genes. The arrangement of these genes and the parts of the body they regulate is shown in Figure 7.

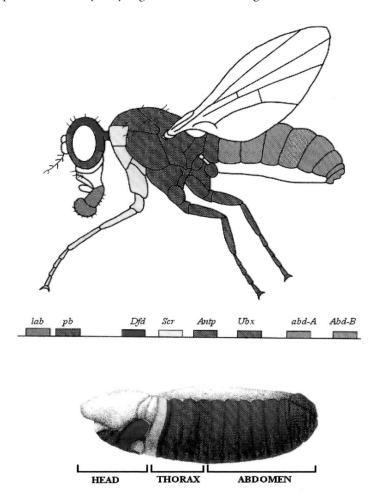

Figure 7. The eight HOX genes of Drosophila melanogaster. From Carroll et al. From DNA to Diversity, 2001. By permission from Blackwell Science, Malden, MA. [17]

A further striking aspect of the *HOX* genes was that the same set of genes, in the same order, was present in all animal species from insects to mice to humans. In mammals, multiple duplications of the entire cluster have produced four sets of *HOX* genes in the mouse. This is shown in Figure 8.

Drosophilia embryo

Head   Thorax   Abdomen

Drosophilia Hox C

Hypothetical common ancestor

Amphioxus Hox cluster
1 2 3 4 5 6 7 8 9 10

Mouse *Hoxa* a-1 a-2 a-3 a-4 a-5 a-6 a-7 a-9 a-10 a-11 a-13
Mouse *Hoxb* b-1 b-2 b-3 b-4 b-5 b-6 b-7 b-8 b-9
Mouse *Hoxc* c-4 c-5 c-6 c-8 c-9 b-10 b-11 b-12 b-13
Mouse *Hoxd* d-1 d-3 d-4 d-8 d-9 c-10 c-11 c-12 c-13

Mouse embryo

Figure 8. HOX genes in Drosophila and mice. The colors show that the linear arrangement of the HOX genes in both Drosophila (top) and mice (bottom) corresponds to the same head-to-tail effect of the genes on body form. The middle section shows that the linear arrangement of the HOX cluster of genes is the same in Drosophila as mice. In mice, the HOX cluster has been duplicated four times with retention of the gene order each time. From Carroll, S. B. By permission from MacMillan Publishers, Ltd., Nature. *376:479-485, 1995.* [19]

How Do the *HOX* Genes Work?

When the *HOX* genes were isolated and the 1000-plus bases sequenced it was found that each had a segment of 180 bases that were virtually identical across different species. The sequence of the *HOX* genes was stringently conserved because its function was to bind to a specific DNA sequence. The *HOX* genes are one of a huge group of genes called transcription factors. The specific DNA sequences recognized by transcription factors are in the promoter regions of genes. These regions are at the 5' end of genes as shown in the following diagram.

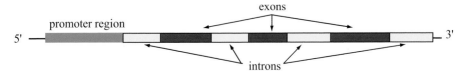

Promoter regions have a number of regions of specific DNA sequence called promoters. Different transcription factors bind to these different promoters and stimulate or suppress the function of the genes they are associated with. The HOX transcription factors bind to one of two, four base pair DNA sequences 5'-TTAT-3' or 5'-TAAT-3'. [18]

Since there are many genes that possess these promoter sequences, there are many proteins whose expression is controlled by the *HOX* clusters. These include other transcription factors, signaling proteins (associated with intracellular communication), and structural proteins. [19]

Switches and Evolution

In the promoter region shown above only a single promoter (TTAT or TAAT) sequence is shown. In reality genes have many different promoters. Some result in an increase in gene activity, some a decrease in gene activity. The level of activity of a gene in a given body organ depends upon the balance of the two. The effect of the homeotic genes on body structure can be altered by mutations that alter these switch regions. These mutations can be insertions or deletions that add or delete whole regions of DNA. *Simply altering the effect of genes that already exist rather than inventing new genes significantly enhances the rate of evolution.*

Other Homeotic Genes

Other homeotic genes are just as striking and informative as the *HOX* genes and like the *HOX* genes they were first described in *Drosophila* and then found to be present in all animals. Pax-6 is associated with eye development across all animals from the flatworms with primitive eyes to humans with very complex eyes. In humans this gene is called *aniridia* because its mutated form is associated with an absence of the iris. Another homeotic mutant is called *distalless* because its mutated form is associated with a loss of the outer or distal parts of fly limbs. This gene also controls limb structure across a wide range of animals from chicken legs, to fish fins, to legs of marine worms, to the siphons of sea squirts and tube feet of sea urchins. [15p69] A final additional homeotic gene is called *tinman* after the Tin Man in the *Wizard of Oz*, who had no heart. This gene controls aspects of the development of the heart in organisms ranging from insects to man.

Since the homeotic genes regulate many other genes that play a role in body form, any significant change in their sequence would not be tolerated since it would have a highly magnified deleterious effect. This accounts for the highly conserved sequence of homeotic genes over huge periods of time. The homeotic genes predate the evolution of bilaterally symmetrical organisms (bilateria) which occurred in the pre-Cambrian period. *This developmental toolbox was in place before the Cambrian explosion.*

Each body segment has the genetic ability to make a limb. The *HOX* genes do not actually make the limb; instead they either suppress limb development or modify it to create unique types of appendages. [19] The existence of a number of genes affecting body form provides many different targets for genetic variation.

Top-Down Versus Bottom-Up

Phyla are second only to Kingdom in being the broadest taxonomic classification of plants and animals. One of the additional complaints of the Intelligent Designers is that the Cambrian explosion, showing the rapid development of many new phyla, indicates a top-down form of evolution rather than the changes at the level of species or the bottom-up changes envisioned by Darwin. They propose that this falsifies Darwinian evolution. [20p20] In reality, this simply illustrates a lack of understanding of the "developmental toolbox." Evolution progresses by random changes in the sequence of DNA. If the changes happened to occur in *HOX* or *HOX*-like genes, the results will be major changes in body form. The taxonomic method of classification has been in place since the time of Linneaus [21] who placed such major changes at the level of phyla rather than at the level of species. Whether an evolutionary step appears to be top-down or bottom-up simply depends upon which genes are subjected to changes in DNA sequence.

Lysyloxidase

Ohno [4] has pointed out the importance of lysyloxidase in the development of more sturdy Cambrian organisms that make better fossils. One of the unique new aspects of the Cambrian Period is that atmospheric oxygen finally attained modern levels in the atmosphere. The function of lysyloxidase is shown in Figure 9.

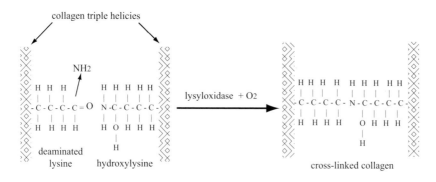

Figure 9. The cross-linking of collagen fibrils by lysyloxidase and oxygen.
After Ohno, S. PNAS 93:8475-8478, 1996. [4]

In the presence of oxygen, lysyloxidase was able to cross-link collagen fibrils, producing much stronger bodies, which made better fossils.

Hemoglobin

A second gene important in using the newly acquired atmospheric oxygen was hemoglobin, a combination of globin and heme. A single mutation allowed hemoglobin to pick up oxygen in the respiratory system and release it in the tissues, paving the way for the development of larger multicellular animals.

A Universal Cambrian Genome

The creationists and the Intelligent Designers foster the notion that the Cambrian explosion involved the rapid development of many organisms all with their own unique set of genes. If this was truly the case, they might have a point. In fact precursor animals all entered the Cambrian period with an almost identical set of genes, which Ohno called the *Cambrian pananimalia genome.* [4] *It was possible to form all of the different body forms by changing less than one percent of the genome*, and there were 10 to 20 millions years for this to occur—well within the capabilities of Darwinian evolution.

The Environment

The existence of a relatively empty environment to expand into is an additional important factor. Quantitative analysis of the morphological characteristics of the Cambrian arthropods showed no unusual degree of disparity, suggesting that the tempo of evolutionary change at that time was not unusually great. [22] Rather, the emergence of the different body plans seems related to an ecological breakthrough into rich, diverse, empty ecological niches. [23]

Evidence There was Plenty of Time for the Cambrian Explosion

We can now return to the central question of this chapter—did the phyla of the Cambrian explosion develop so rapidly that only a supernatural force could have been involved? There are many reasons to say no.

- The time period of 10 to 20 million years, while short in terms of the totality of geologic time, is still a substantial period. The entire evolution of a wide range of mammals occurred in a comparably short period of time after the extinction of the dinosaurs.

- While the strata suggest the organisms of the Burgess shale evolved over a period of 10 to 20 million years, a comparable collection of many different Cambrian fossils has been found among the Chengjiang fauna found in the Yunnan province of China. The Chengjiang fauna predate the Burgess by 15 million years, thus further extending the time available.

- All of the ten *HOX* genes and the other *homeotic* genes discussed above were in place prior to the Cambrian period. Thus, while the ten-fold duplication occurred by gene duplication, this process was completed and then locked in well over 550 million years ago, [15] prior to the Cambrian explosion.

- All of the animals of the Cambrian Period had virtually an identical genome (pananimalia) and changes in less than one percent of the genome were responsible for all the different body forms.

- It is clear now that the old concept that new genes must evolve to produce new body forms is incorrect. The secret is to teach old genes new tricks, rather than making new genes. [15] Flipping a switch to increase or decrease the expression of an already existing gene is much easier than making a new gene from scratch.

- The many variations in body form and the specialization of appendages for many different functions including feeding, walking, swimming, burrowing, breeding, sensing the environment, and defense were brought about by changing the expression of the different *HOX* genes in different body segments, not by the evolution of new genes.

- Molecular clocks show that while the fossils may have been difficult to find, the actual diversification of many of the phyla occurred as much as a billion years ago, some 500 million years before the Cambrian explosion.

- After several billion years of toil by the prokaryotic cyanobacteria and then the eukaryotic blue-green algae, the amount of oxygen in the atmosphere finally began to approach modern levels. This assisted in the triggering of the diversification of animal phyla in the Cambrian Period. [24] Minor modifications of only a few genes allowed Cambrian animals to utilize atmospheric oxygen. Mitochondria, the main energy producing organelle, had already been in place for over a billion years. [4]

- The few changes listed above allowed the newly evolving organisms to spread into a new virgin ecological space. This also fostered rapid diversification of phyla and species.

- Finally, the pressure of species diversification itself can accelerate further species diversification. [25] This is somewhat analogous to a fusion reaction in an atomic pile—the production of some neutrons promotes the production of more neutrons.

Multiple factors, including the formation of the "developmental toolbox" whereby the same small number of genes control changes in body form for all known animals; the availability of the core tools of this kit over a billion years ago long before the Cambrian Period; the ability of new body forms to be easily derived from old forms by minor modifications of the expression of toolbox genes rather than making new genes; the lack of modern levels of oxygen in the atmosphere until just before the Cambrian period; the availability of an empty ecological niche for the development of new species; and the accelerating effect that species diversification has on promoting further species diversification—all indicate that the Cambrian "explosion" was totally consistent with Darwinian evolution.

References

1. Gould, S. J. *Wonderful Life: The Burgess Shale and the Nature of History.* W. W. Norton & Co, Inc, New York, 1989.
2. Murchison, R. I. Siluria: *The history of the oldest known rocks containing organic remains.* John Murray, London, 1854.
3. Wells, J. *Icons of Evolution: Science or Myth? Why much of what we teach about evolution is wrong.* Regnery Publishing, Inc., Washington, DC, 2000.
4. Ohno, S. The notion of the Cambrian pananimalia genome. *Proc Natl Acad Sci USA.* 93: 8475-8478, 1996.
5. Wray, G. A., Levinton, J. S. & Shapiro, L. H. Molecular Evidence for Deep Precambrian Divergences Among Metazoan Phyla. *Science.* 274: 568-573, 1996.
6. Wang, D. Y., Kumar, S. & Hedges, S. B. Divergence time estimates for the early history of animal phyla and the origin of plants, animals and fungi. *Proc Biol Sci.* 266: 163-171, 1999.
7. Knoll, A. H. *Life on a Young Planet. The First Three Billion Years of Evolution on Earth.* Princeton University Press, Princeton, NJ, 2005.
8. Sterelny, K. *Dawkins vs Gould.* Icon Books, Ltd., Cambridge, UK, 2001.
9. Bottjer, D. J. The early evolution of animals. *Sci Am.* 293: (August) 42-47, 2005.
10. Lawrence, E. Pushing back the origins of animals. www.nature.com/news/1999/990204/pf/990204-4_pf.html. 1999.
11. Carroll, S. B. Chance and necessity: The evolution of morphological complexity and diversity. *Nature.* 409: 1102-1109, 2001.
12. Benton, M. J. Models for the diversification of life. *Trends Ecol Evol.* 12: 490-495, 1997.
13. Ohno, S. *Evolution by Gene Duplication.* Springer Verlag. New York, 1970.
14. McLachlan, A. D. Gene duplication and the origin of repetitive protein structures. *Cold Spring Harb Symp Quant Biol.* 52: 411-420, 1987.
15. Carroll, S. B. *Endless Forms Most Beautiful. The New Science of Evo Devo.* W. W. Norton, New York, 2005.
16. Photo by Dr. Ed Lewis, California Technology Institute.
17. Carroll, S. B., Grenier, J. K. & Weatherbee, S. D. *From DNA to Diversity. Molecular Genetics and the Evolution of Animal Design.* Blackwell Science, Malden, MA, 2001.
18. Ekker, S. C. et al. The degree of variation in DNA sequence recognition among four Drosophila homeotic proteins. *Embo J.* 13: 3551-3560, 1994.
19. Carroll, S. B. Homeotic genes and the evolution of arthropods and chordates. *Nature.* 376: 479-485, 1995.
20. Forrest, B. The wedge at work: How Intelligent Design creationism is wedging its way into the cultural and academic mainstream. In: Pennock, R. T. *Intelligent Design Creationism and Its Critics. Philosophical, Theological, and Scientific Perspectives.* The MIT Press. Cambridge, MA, 2001.
21. Linnaeus, C. *Systema naturae 10 edition.* Stockholm, Sweden, 1758.
22. Wills, M. A., Briggs, D. E. G. & Fortey, R. A. Disparity as an evolutionary index: A comparison of Cambrian and recent arthropods. *Paleobiology.* 20: 93-130, 1994.
23. Kirschner, M. & Gerhart, J. Evolvability. *Proc Natl Acad Sci USA.* 95: 8420-8427, 1998.
24. Ohno, S. The reason for as well as the consequence of the Cambrian explosion in animal evolution. *J Mol Evol.* 44 Suppl 1: S23-S27, 1997.
25. Emerson, B. C. & Kolm, N. Species diversity can drive speciation. *Nature.* 434: 1015-1017, 2005.

Chapter 5

No Intermediate Fossils Anywhere?

One of the most frequently stated objections to Darwin's theory of evolution by both the new earth creationists and the old earth Intelligent Designers is that the intermediate or transitional species predicted by Darwin do not exist. This is characterized as the "trade secret of paleontology." [1p62] As shown in Chapter 1, Darwin himself addressed this issue. The following is a typical example of the complaints by the creationist and the Intelligent Design group, as illustrated by a Jehovah's Witness pamphlet that stated:

> For evolution to be true, there had to be thousands, millions of transitional forms making an unbroken chain. In reality, such transitional forms are rare.

In answering this complaint, one of the first issues that needs to be addressed is whether intermediate or transitional forms are truly the usual expected outcome of the evolutionary process. It is clear that the classical Darwinian version of evolution, slow gradual transitions with many intermediate forms, so-called *phyletic* evolution, was the expected outcome. But is Darwin's version of speciation necessarily the correct one? Since Darwin's time, as more fossil evidence has became available, three accepted variations on Darwin's theory have developed: the punctuated equilibria of Niles Eldridge and Stephen J. Gould, the allopatric evolution of Ernst Mayr, and finding that the development of new species facilitates the development of additional new species. All three predict the rarity of intermediate or transitional forms.

Punctuated Equilibria Speciation

In 1972, in a book chapter entitled "Punctuated equilibria: An alternative to phyletic gradualism," Niles Eldridge and Steven J. Gould stated:

> The history of life is more adequately represented by a picture of "punctuated equilibria" than by the notion of phyletic gradualism. The history of evolution is not one of stately unfolding but a story of homeostatic equilibria, disturbed only "rarely" by rapid and episodic events of speciation. [2]

The following diagram illustrates the difference between punctuated equilibria and phyletic evolution:

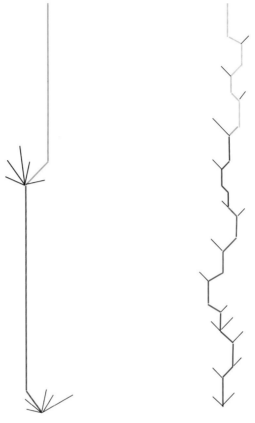

punctuated equilibrium   phyletic gradualism

Figure 1. See text.

In punctuated equilibria rapid diversification of species takes place in bursts (punctuation), and one of these species may be selected and remain unchanged for long periods of time (equilibria). By contrast, in phyletic graduated Darwinian-type evolution, a series of gradual changes takes place over time. As represented by the colors, transitional forms are expected to be present in the fossil record for phyletic graduated evolution. For the punctuated equilibria model of evolution they are much harder to find, since most of the time there are no morphological changes. Thus, the frequent apparent lack of intermediate links in an evolutionary line is easier to understand by the punctuated equilibria model where there are often no obvious intermediates. There is just selection of the best twigs of the bush, followed by long periods of equilibria with a species being at peace with its environment.

This subject was brought to the attention of a general scientific audience by a 1980 note in *Science* by Lewin[3] about a conference at the Field Museum in Chicago entitled *Evolutionary Theory Under Fire.* For Phillip Johnson, the originator of the Intelligent Design movement and of the Wedge philosophy, the apparent contradiction of Darwin's theory of gradualism provided just the fodder he needed to attempt to discredit the theory of evolution. In his book, *Darwin on Trial,*[4] Johnson suggested that Eldridge's and Gould's account of the seemingly instantaneous appearance of new species that then persisted relatively unchanged for long periods of time fit perfectly with how a divine creator would do things.

What Johnson failed to consider was that what Eldridge and Gould had really said was that there was an *apparent* instantaneous appearance of new species over geologic time.[2,5] Geologic time is a very long period, often millions of years. As shown in the following sections, a great deal of typical Darwinian gradualism can occur over such a stretch of time. As one example, 23 different species of elephants evolved over a period of only five million years.[6] When the gradual steps are left out because of an incomplete fossil record, it produces a pattern of punctuated equilibria.

As stated by Gould and Eldridge[5] even his own colleagues fell into this trap.

> …included the misunderstandings of colleagues who, for example, failed to grasp the key claim about geological scaling and misread geological abruptness as true suddenness, and then interpreted punctuated equilibrium as a saltational theory.[7]

By "saltational" they mean the instantaneous appearance of new species through some type of major change or rearrangement of the DNA sequence. In their 1993 review of the punctuated equilibria model, Gould and Eldridge[5] pointed out that most fossil records conform to the pattern of punctuated equilibria.

Speciation by Geographic Isolation

Allopatric speciation refers to the development of new species by geographical isolation in small founder groups at the margin of the geographic range of the parent species or on islands, usually triggered by some type of environmental stress. The famous Darwin finches of the Galapagos are a good example. This form of speciation was championed by Ernst Mayr.[7-10] A critical aspect of this theory is that small isolated founder populations are initially involved. In such small groups, individual new variants with a selective advantage can rapidly become the dominant species. This is somewhat analogous to the punctuated equilibrium model with the caveat that the diversity takes place in a small founder population. If one of these experiments is successful it can result in a new species that will not interbreed if exposed to the parent species. The resultant new species can spread outside the founder group such that new fossil species do not originate in the same place as where their ancestors lived. Allopatric speciation predicts that most variation will be found among samples drawn from different geographic areas rather than from different levels of the rock strata from the same place. Thus, as with the punctuated equilibria model, there would be few or no transitional forms in most fossil strata.

Gould and Eldridge[5] made this point themselves in a 1993 article in *Nature.*

> Mayr's peripatric theory of speciation in small populations peripherally isolated from a parental stock, would yield stasis and punctuation when properly scaled into vastness of geological time—for small populations speciating away from a central mass in tens or hundreds of thousands of years, will translate in almost every geological circumstance as a punctuation...

Allopatric speciation also carries with it an important definition of species as organisms that do not interbreed not because they can't, but because they are geographically isolated from each other. Thus, a species is a specific group of organisms that *in nature* do not interbreed. The *in nature* part is important because two different species can on occasion produce viable offspring, although they are often infertile.

Evolution by the phyletic gradualism of Darwin implies that new species can form even without geographic isolation. This has been termed *sympatric* speciation. Recent studies have suggested that it may in fact, be quite common. [11]

Acceleration of Speciation by Diversity

Studies of species diversity in islands have shown that the increased competition over limited resources due to species diversification promote both the extinction of some species and the development of more new species. [12] On balance, the diversification of species promotes the evolution of even more new species. When squeezed into a framework of geologic time, this important mechanism would contribute to the apparent explosion of new species during punctuations and to the diversification of new species in small founder populations.

All of these mechanisms: phyletic gradualism, sympatric speciation, punctuated equilibria, allopatric speciation, and the acceleration of speciation by diversity operate in different situations. Most would leave behind little or no evidence of transitional forms.

Major new models for the evolution of new species have been developed since Darwin's time. One is termed *punctuated equilibria* with bursts of new speciation (punctuations) followed by long periods of no change (equilibria). Another is allopatric speciation or speciation by geographic isolation. A third is the finding that when new species develop it may rapidly accelerate the development of even more new species. All play a role in speciation and would leave behind few if any transitional or intermediate forms. Thus, rather than falsifying the theory of evolution, when speciation takes place by these mechanisms, the absence of transitional forms is the expected outcome.

All of these models of speciation are likely to play a modifying role for different species, different geologic times, and different ecological niches. If the classical Darwinian model of gradualism plays a role in the development of some species, and is occurring within the geological periods of punctuation, there should be evidence for at least some transitional or intermediate forms. The following is part of a much larger list of examples where such intermediate forms do exist.

Horse Evolution

One of the more frequent examples of an apparent lack of intermediate forms cited by Intelligent Design creationists arises from the story about the evolution of horses. Hogan [13p27] complained that the apparent straight line of evolution from ancient to the modern horse with numerous transitional forms as presented in textbooks is a sham and the true situation, based on additional fossil evidence, is "more complicated and far from conclusive."

In 1876, Thomas Huxley, one of Darwin's most vocal early defenders, was on a speaking tour of the United States. One of his first stops was Yale, where he examined a large collection of horse fossils assembled by the paleontologist O.C. Harsh. Huxley found evidence for progressive stages of evolution, progressing from small 50-million-year-old Eocene "dawn" horses with four toes to the large single-toed horses of modern times. Henry Osborn, the director of the American Museum of Natural History, arranged the original display. It contained just four fossil horses. This displayed a progressive decrease from four toes to one, a change from leaf browsing to high-crowned grazing teeth, and an increase from the size of a fox to the size of a modern horse. Later, more specimens were added and the final result was displayed by the American Museum of Natural History and widely reproduced in textbooks [14] and other museums as a prime example of Darwinian evolution (see Figure 2).

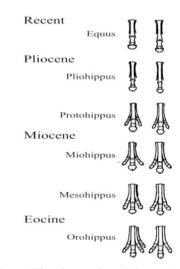

Figure 2. The early proposed smooth, linear path of evolution from small Eocene Orohippus with four toes to large modern Equus with one toe.

As more fossils were examined, it soon became clear that the pattern was more complicated. It was more like a bush with many branches than a linear tree with very few branches. The intermediate forms predicted by Darwin were not easy to find. Creationists [13] objected that the displays were wrong and artificially contrived to convey the original concept that Darwinian evolution progressed smoothly from early, presumably more-primitive forms, to later more-advanced forms. This example led many to conclude that evolution theory is flawed because the predicted intermediate forms were not obvious. A more-modern version of the evolution of horses is shown in Figure 3 [15] on the following page.

Modern Equus, shown at the top of that figure, evolved in the past 5 million years in North America. Studies of mitochondrial DNA from horse fossils indicate that in the late Pleistocene there were basically two species of the horse in North America, the true horses of the domestic type, and the "stiff-legged" horses. [16] Over the past 55 million years there was a diversity of extinct genera and species. [17] Rather than a linear increase in size, the horses from 20 to 50 million years ago were all small, ranging from 44 to 110 pounds. After that there was a wide range in size, with some early horses being as large as modern horses, some remaining in the 44- to 110-pound range, and some becoming even smaller over time. The shape of the teeth also varied widely for the past 50 million years, giving clues to whether they were mostly grazers, mixed feeders, or browsers. This variability is also shown in Figure 3.

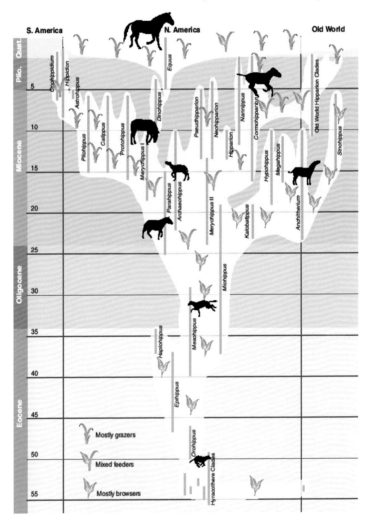

Figure 3. Evolution, geographic distribution, diet and body sizes of the horse family (Equidae) over the past 55 million years. From MacFadden, B.J. Fossil Horses—Evidence for Evolution. Science. 307:2005. [15] By permission.

Thus, in contrast with the linear progression proposed by the early proponents of Darwinism, the evolution of horses is characterized by a more bush-like pattern. The situation was summarized by Rudolf Raff: [18]

> The real record of horse evolution can be portrayed as a bush that at different times sprouted widely varying lineages between browsers and grazers. Most of those lineages became extinct and are not ancestral to the one surviving genus, Equus. The pull of the present as well as expectations of a linear pattern of evolution distorted the picture to make it seem that there had been a majestic 50-million-year evolutionary procession to the modern horse.

Thus, while the early depiction of the evolution of horses was overly simplistic, as knowledge advanced it has become clear that the evolution of horses progressed exactly as predicted by the modern theory of evolution, with much diversity in size, toe patterns, tooth shapes, feeding habits, and many extinct branches. Multiple genetic variations, selection, environmental changes, and geographical isolations resulted in many different species and multiple extinctions. One small twig of this large bush survived to become the modern horse. Thus, rather than being a faulty example of evolution, the story of horse evolution illustrates precisely how evolution works.

While the early depiction of the evolution of horses was overly simplistic, as knowledge advanced it has become clear that the evolution of horses progressed exactly as predicted by the modern theory of evolution, with much diversity in size, toe patterns, tooth shapes, feeding habits and many extinct branches. Multiple genetic variations, selection, environmental changes and geographical isolations resulted in many different species and multiple extinctions. One twig of this bush survived to become the modern horse.

After stating that evolution theory was flawed because there were no intermediate horse fossils, Hogan [13p28] then stated, "The known fossil record fails to document a single example of phyletic (gradual) evolution accomplishing a major morphologic transition and hence offers no evidence that the gradualistic school can be valid." In other words, not only were there no intermediate horse fossils, there were no intermediate fossils for any living or extinct organisms. This purported lack of transitional forms has been a common complaint of both the Creationist and the Intelligent Design community. As shown above, the complaint about the evolution of horses was without merit. Let us examine whether the statement that the known fossil record fails to document a single example of intermediate transitional forms is true. The following are some examples that falsify this statement.

The Burgess Shale

I left one organism out of the Cambrian explosion chapter so it could be discussed here. *Aysheaia* was a third Burgess organism to survive the Cambrian Period. It was one of the most widely discussed Burgess organisms representing the two P's: primitive and precursor.

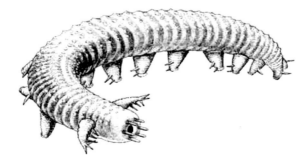

Figure 4. Aysheaia. *A Burgess shale species that may be a non-missing link between worms (annelids) and arthropods. From Gould.* [19]

Aysheaia was most closely related to a small group of modern invertebrates called the *Onychophora,* with characteristics of both annelids and arthropods. As a result it is often considered to be a rare connecting "non-missing link" between two phyla. Although it did not have the jaws typical of modern *Onychophora,* Gould [19] points out that the jaws may have simply evolved later, as occurred with other organisms, making it a true less-developed transitional form. While it is true that transitional forms are rare in the fossil record, *Aysheaia* is a reasonable candidate.

Diatoms

Diatoms are single-celled organisms that contribute to plankton in the sea. They often show remarkably beautiful bodies composed of silica as shown in Figure 5.

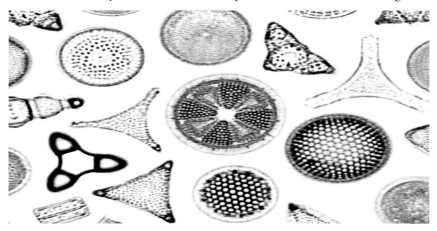

Figure 5. Diatoms [20]

Because of this mineral skeleton, they leave an excellent fossil record. Figure 6 shows such a fossil record for a diatom called *Rhizosolenia* between 1.6 and 3.4 million years ago. [21-22]

Approximately 3.1 million years ago a single ancestral species split into two species. One of the differences between the two species can be measured by a feature of the silicon skeleton, namely the height of a specific glassy (hyaline) area of the cell wall. This unusually complete fossil record shows the presence of transitional fossils of intermediate and decreasing height of the hyaline area between 3.1 and 2.7 million years ago, eventually forming a second species *Rhizosolenia bergonii* (solid dots). The height of the hyaline area of the parent species, *Rhizosolenia praebergonii* (open dots) remained constant.

This is a uniquely complete fossil record. Imagine if we only had fossils on the parent species from 3.3 million years ago and of the parent and derived species from 2.6 to 1.6 million years ago. This would mimic punctuated equilibria whereby new species arise by a split in paternal species seemingly almost instantaneously, in geologic time, and subsequently undergoing little change. With such an incomplete record it is also easy to imagine a creationist or Intelligent Designer complaining that since there were no intermediate species, Darwinism was falsified. This and some of the other examples in this chapter show that when the record is complete, transitional forms are indeed present.

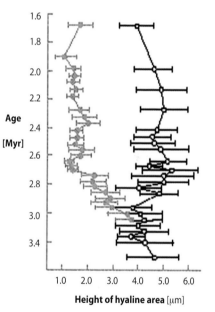

Mollusks and Species Extinctions

Jean Baptiste Lamarck (1744–1829) proposed the view that animals were able to pass on acquired characteristics. While this has subsequently been shown to be untrue, a number of Lamarck's ideas predated Darwinian evolutionary thought. [7] These ideas included the proposal that animals show a graded series of perfection or complexity, that these changes take place very slowly over enormous periods of time, and that this is not a problem because, for

Figure 6. The evolutionary split of the diatom Rhizosolenia praebergonii *into a second species* Rhizosolenia bergonii *from 3.1 to 2.7 million years ago. Cronin & Schneider. Trends in Evol Biol and Ecology. 5: 275-279, 1990.* [22, 23]

nature, time has no limits. Some of these conclusions were based on the fact that Lamarck took over the mollusk collection of the Paris museum after the death of the prior curator. The collection included both living and fossil mollusks. He found it was possible to arrange these specimens into a virtually unbroken phyletic series of species from the Tertiary period to modern living organisms. This led to the inescapable conclusion that many other animals had also undergone a slow and gradual change throughout time. [8] On the other hand, Williamson [23] described a well-documented series of mollusk faunas from the late Cenozoic. The evolutionary patterns in all lineages conform to the punctuated equilibrium model, and no gradualistic morphological trends occurred.

While Lamarck seamlessly integrated extinct and living species of mollusks into a phyletic series, for many eighteenth-century biologists the concept of extinct species was considered to be incompatible with the perfection and benevolence of God. If God's creations were all perfect they would not become extinct and through His benevolence He would not allow species to die out. Lamarck solved this problem by assuming that animals did not become extinct, they just gradually changed into other forms. Evolutionary change was then the solution to the problem of extinction. Lamarck recognized that the earth's environment was constantly changing. For a species to remain in harmony with its environment and thus avoid extinction, it had to constantly change. This is distinct from Darwinism where environmental changes led to extinctions and only natural selection of those individuals with advantageous mutations survived to form new species. For Lamarck and his contemporaries, and for church doctrine, extinction was impossible. For Darwin it was a necessary aspect of evolution.

Trilobites

Peter Sheldon, from the department of geology at Trinity College in Dublin, Ireland, reported his detailed studies of the fossil record of 15,000 trilobites from central Wales. As implied from the title of his *Nature* paper, [24] *Parallel gradualistic evolution of Ordovician trilobites,* he observed many intermediate trilobite forms occurring during this evolutionary period. Three of the eight trilobites reported are shown in Figure 7.

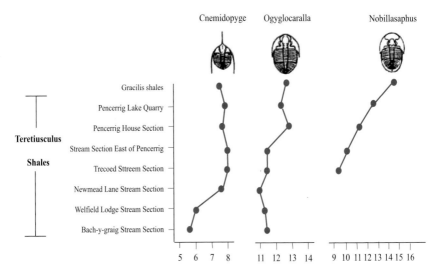

Figure 7. Three of the eight trilobite lineages reported by Sheldon showing parallel gradualistic evolution of Ordovician trilobites. Reprinted by permission from MacMillan Pubishers. Nature. 330:561-563, 1987. [24]

This clearly shows a slow progressive change over time with different rib counts for these three species, as well as the other five species not shown. Since Sheldon implied that many cases of apparent punctuated equilibria might show similar transitional forms if a detailed fossil record could be examined, his report resulted in a spirited debate with Eldridge and Gould. [25] However, as is often the case with scientific debate, all sides possess part of the truth. Some species evolve by a pattern of punctuated equilibria, some by allopatric speciation, and some by phyletic gradualism. If the precise fossil beds are discovered that present the full local details of the evolutionary experiment, it is likely that intermediate transitional forms will always be present.

Sea to Land

One of the greatest leaps in the evolution of vertebrates was the transition of animals that swam in the ocean to those that walked on land. This momentous event occurred in the Devonian period. The fossil *Acanthostega gunari* is a remarkable example of an intermediate form for this progression. It had internal gills, a fish-like skull and extremities, but was a land-based amphibian with lungs for breathing air. [26] An additional stage of this transition from sea to land was provided by the finding of a fossil fish *(ANSP 21350)* with fingers. [27,28] This fossil represented the intermediate condition between the primitive steering and braking functions of fins and a land-based walking gait. The relationship between *Acanthostega, ANSP 21350,* and other creatures in this progression are shown in Figure 8.

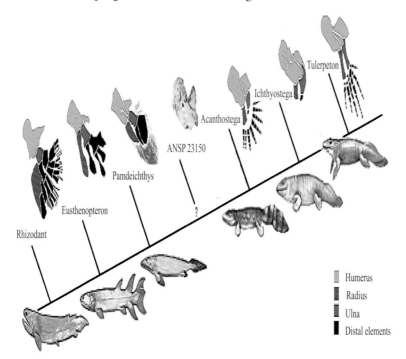

Figure 8. Progression of bone structure from fins to land based four-footed animals (tetrapods). Diagram from J. A. Clack. From Fins to Fingers. Science. 304:57-58, 2004. [29] By permission.

Subsequent reports identified entire skeletons of a transitonal species called *Tiktaalik roseae* with many characteristics of both fish and land-based amphibians. [30-31]

Land to Sea

One of the creationist's texts, *Of Pandas and People,* [32p100] states:

> The absence of unambiguous transitional fossils is strikingly illustrated by the fossil record of whales. By and large evolutionists believe that whales evolved from a land mammal. The problem is that there are no clear transitional fossils linking fossil land mammals to fossil whales.

In 1994, Behe [33] also challenged evolutionists to produce transitional forms for the Eocene period of migration of land animals into the sea to produce whales. In the same year, Gould [34] reported that three such species had already been discovered. One of these is the *Ambulocetus* whale. [35] Figure 9 shows *Ambulocetus* standing on land (A) and at the end of a power stroke during swimming (B).

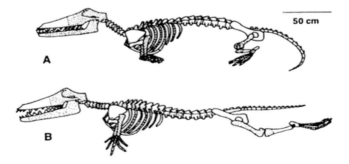

Figure 9. Reconstruction of Ambulocetus *whale standing on land (A) and at the end of the power stroke during swimming (B). Thewissen, et al.* [35] *By permission.*

This surely represents one of the shortest intervals between an anti-evolutionist claim that transitional forms do not exist and paleontologists finding the intermediates.

From Meat Eater to Leaf Eater

An intriguing interaction between a black market fossil dealer and a legitimate academic paleontologist [36] resulted in the discovery of a missing link between meat-eating (carnivorous) and leaf-eating (herbivorous) dinosaurs. [37] The new species *Falcarius utahensis* had five-inch claws consistent with carnivorous habits. However, instead of the serrated teeth of carnivores suited to slashing flesh, *Falcarius* had spoon-shaped teeth ideal for shredding plants (Figure 10). It was found in a massive fossil bed at Green River, Utah. The dinosaur's shift in diet may have been spurred by the advent of flowering plants. This illustrates again how changes in the environment result in evolutionary changes in animal structure. "It gives us amazing documentation of an evolutionary shift." [34]

Figure 10. Falcarius utahensis. *Illustration by Mike Skrepnick, University of Utah. Kirkland, J., et al. A primitive therizinosauroid dinosaur from the early Cretaceous of Utah. Reprinted by permission from MacMillan Publishers, Ltd.* Nature. *435: 84-87, 2005.*

And the list goes on and on. Intermediate fossil organisms transition between reptiles and birds, reptiles and mammals, and other taxonomic groups have also been described. Many of these intermediates have been found only recently. The finding of these intermediate fossils validate Darwin's assumption that in many cases "missing" intermediates would be found with time. They increasingly have been.

While intermediate or transitional forms are commonly missing, when the fossil record is very complete, the intermediate forms are often observed. When all of the above observations on the different mechanisms of speciation are considered it is clear that the apparent lack of some intermediate forms does not disprove the theory of evolution.

References
1. Johnson, P. E. Evolution as dogma: The establishment of naturalism. in: Pennock, R. T. *Intelligent Design Creationism and Its Critics.* The MIT Press. Cambridge, MA, 2001.
2. Eldridge, N. & Gould, S. J. Punctuated equilibria: an alternative to phyletic gradualism. in: Schopf, T. J. M. & Thomas, J. M. *Models in Paleobiology.* Freeman, Cooper. San Francisco, 1972.
3. Lewin, R. Evolutionary theory under fire. *Science.* 210: 883-887, 1980.
4. Johnson, P. *Darwin on Trial.* InterVarsity Press, Downers Grove, IL, 1991, 1993.
5. Gould, S. J. & Eldridge, N. Punctuated evolution comes of age. *Nature.* 366: 223-227, 1993.
6. Maglio, V. J. Origin and evolution of the Elephantidae. *Transactions of the American Philosophical Society.* 63: 1-149, 1973.

7. Mayr, E. *The Growth of Biological Thought. Diversity, Evolution, and Inheritance.* The Belknap Press of Harvard University Press. Cambridge, MA, 1982.

8. Mayr, E. *Systematics and the Origin of Species.* Columbia University Press, New York, 1942.

9. Mayr, E. *Animal Species and Evolution.* Cambridge University Press. Cambridge, MA.1963.

10. Mayr, E. *Populations, Species, and Evolution.* Cambridge University Press. Cambridge, MA, 1970.

11. Pennish, E. Speciation standing in place. *Science.* 311:1372-1374, 2006.

12. Emerson, B. C. & Kolm, N. Species diversity can drive speciation. *Nature.* 434: 1015-1017, 2005.

13. Hogan, J. P. *Kicking the Sacred Cow. Questioning the Unquestionable and Thinking the Impermissible.* Baen Publishing Enterprises. Riverdale, NY, 2004.

14. Simpson, G. G. *Major Features of Evolution.* Cambridge University Press, New York, 1953.

15. MacFadden, B. J. Fossil horses—evidence for evolution. *Science.* 307: 1728-1730, 2005.

16. Weinstock, J. et al. Evolution, Systematics, and Phylogeography of Pleistocene Horses in the New World: A Molecular Perspective. *PLoS Biol.* 3: e241, 2005.

17. MacFadden, B. J. *Fossil Horses, Systematics, Paleobiology, and Evolution of the Family Equidae.* Cambridge University Press, New York, 1992.

18. Raff, R. A. *The Shape of Life. Genes, Development, and the Evolution of Animal Form.* University of Chicago Press, Chicago, IL, 1996.

19. Gould, S. J. *Wonderful Life The Burgess Shale and the Nature of History.* W. W. Norton & Co, Inc, New York, 1989.

20. Figure from www.ucmp.berkeley.edu/chromista/diatoms/diatommm.html. By permission.

21. Cronin, T. M. & Schneider, C. E. Climatic influences on species: evidence from the fossil record. *Trends in Evolutionary Biology and Ecology.* 5: 275-279, 1990.

22. Cronin, T. M., Schneider, C.E. Climatic influences on species from the fossil record. *Trends in Evolutionary Biology and Ecology.* 5:275-279, 1990.

23. Williamson, P. G. Palaeontological documentation of speciation in Cenozoic molluscs from Turkana basin. *Nature.* 293: 437-443, 1981.

24. Sheldon, P. R. Parallel gradualistic evolution of Ordovician trilobites. *Nature.* 330: 561-563, 1987.

25. Gleick, J. in *New York Times.* New York, 1987.

26. Coates, M. I. & Clack, J. A. Fish-like gills and breathing in the earliest known tetrapod. *Nature.* 352: 234-236, 1991.

27. Daeschler, E. B. & Shubin, N. Fish with fingers? *Nature.* 391: 133, 1998.

28. Shubin, N. H., Daeschler, E. B. & Coates, M. I. The early evolution of the tetrapod humerus. *Science.* 304: 90-93, 2004.

29. Clack, J. A. From fins to fingers. *Science.* 304: 57-58, 2004.

30. Daeschler, E. B., Shubin, N., Jenkins, F. A. A Devonian tetrapod-like fish and the evolution of the tetrapod body plan. *Nature.* 757: 757-763, 2006

31. Shubin, N.H., Daeschler, E.B., Jenkins, F.A. The pectoral fin of *Tiktaalik roseae* and the origin of the tetrapod limb. *Nature.* 440:764-771, 2006.

32. Davis, P., Kenyon, D. H. & Thaxton, C. B. *Of Pandas and People. The Central Question of Biological Origins.* Haughton Publishing Company, Dallas, TX, 1989.

33. Behe, M. J. Experimental support for regarding functional classes of proteins to be highly isolated from each other. in: Buell, J. & Hearn, V. *Darwinism, Science or Philosophy?* The Foundation for Thought and Ethics. Houston, TX, 1994.

34. Gould, S. J. Hooking Leviathian by its past. In Gould, J. *Dinosaur in a Haystack.* Crown Paperbacks. New York, 1997.

35. Thewissen, J. G. M., Hussain, S. T. & Arif, M. Fossil evidence for the origin of aquatic locomotion in Achaeocete whales. *Science.* 263: 210-212, 1994.

36. Hotz, R. E. in *Los Angeles Times* A1, A20 Los Angeles, 2005.

37. Kirkland, J., Zanno, L. E., Sampson, S. D., Clark, J. M. & Beblieux, D. D. A primitive therizinosauroid dinosaur from the early Cretaceous of Utah. *Nature.* 435: 84-87, 2005.

Chapter 6

Not Enough Time?

A common complaint of creationists and the Intelligent Designers is that the mutation rate for advantageous mutations is so small that even the more than 3 billion years that life has been present on the earth is not enough to allow for Darwinian selection of advantageous mutations. The following is an example of this line of thought.

Based on the population frequency of a number of rare genetic disorders it has been estimated that the average deleterious mutation rate in humans is 10^{-4} or 1 in 10,000 to 10^{-6} or 1 in a million per generation. [1] Since this technique is based on the presence of disease, by definition all of these mutations are deleterious. As a specific example, Hogan [2] cites the case of the human cholesterol receptor gene located on chromosome 19. It consists of 45,000 nucleic acid base pairs and a coding sequence producing a protein of 772 amino acids. Over 350 mutations of this gene have been described. Again, since the case finding (ascertainment) was based on the presence of disease, none of them were beneficial.

This problem of biased ascertainment can be bypassed by performing epidemiological studies in which randomly selected members of the population are chosen for study, independent of disease. Such studies have been performed for many genes and many species. They show that the vast majority of mutations are neutral, that is, they are neither advantageous nor deleterious. Deleterious mutations are the next most common, and beneficial mutations are rare, but do occur.

If we take the average rate of all deleterious mutations as 10^{-4} or 1 in 10,000 generations per gene, the number of advantageous mutations per gene would be at least a thousand times less or 1 per 10,000,000 generations per gene. Humans and most other vertebrates have approximately 25,000 genes. If we assume that 1,000 of these could be the site of a beneficial mutation that would further the evolution of the species, this requires the passage of 10,000 generations before a beneficial mutation occurs. Since the average generation time for humans is approximately 20 years there would be one advantageous mutation per 200,000 years. Since many dozens of beneficial mutations would be required, it could be suggested, as the Creationists have, that the development of humans by Darwinian evolution is impossible.

One could argue that evolution by rare advantageous mutations is still possible for other organisms with a much shorter generation time. A twenty-fold decrease in generation time or one generation per year would help. A generation time of hours to days, as is typical of many prokaryotes, would be optimal. Some have argued that the ratio of beneficial to deleterious mutations is as high as 1/10,000 to 1/million per gene, [3p127] further exacerbating the problem for species, like humans, with a long generation time. Whether valid or not, it is claimed that advantageous mutations are too rare to allow for speciation by Darwinian selection. As a result Darwinian evolution is falsified and by default, a supreme being had to be responsible.

Well, not so fast (or I should say, not so slow). This line of reasoning ignores some of the most exciting recent advances in molecular genetics. There are two major types of genetic variation based on prevalence in the population—mutations and polymorphisms. Variations are called mutations when they are rare and occur in less than one percent of the population, usually in the 1-in-a-thousand to 1-in-a-million range. Variations are called *polymorphisms* when they occur in more than one percent of the population. Two major types of genetic variations are shown in Figure 1.

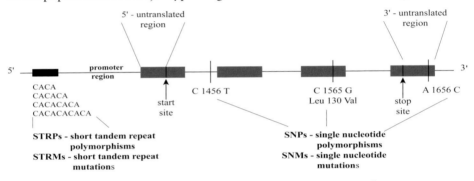

Figure 1. Two common types of polymorphisms. The exons containing the coding sequences are in red.

The first type of polymorphism involves single nucleotides. They are called single nucleotide polymorphisms (SNPs), if they are common and single nucleotide mutations (SNMs), if they are rare. The second type of polymorphism involves short repeated sequences. They are called short tandem repeat polymorphisms (STRPs), if they are common, and short tandem repeat mutations (STRMs), if they are rare. On average a SNP variant occurs every 200 base pairs along the entire DNA sequence of the genome. Since there are 3 billion base pairs in the human genome, this represents 15 million variants per genome. I will first discuss the SNPs and SNMs.

SNPs and SNMs. *Neutral* mutations or polymorphisms occur when a single base pair variation occurs in a relatively unimportant part of the gene such as an intron. A neutral variant is shown in Figure 1 as a change from a cytosine *(C)* to a thymine *(T)* at position 1456 in an intron of this gene. It is neutral becaue introns do not code for proteins. A neutral variation can also occur in the coding or exon regions of the gene if it does not result in a change in the amino acid sequence. This happens when the variation occurs in the third or redundant portion of the amino acid code. For example, refer to the genetic code in chapter 1. A T > C mutation or polymorphism resulting in a change from a CTT to a CTC would be neutral since both triplets code for leucine (L). Mutations that do produce a change in the amino acid sequence of the protein can also be neutral if that change has no effect on the organism (no phenotypic effect). Variations in the 5' [exclusive of the promoter] and 3' untranslated regions are also likely to be neutral since this is a non-coding region of the gene. SNMs can also be neutral.

Deleterious single nucleotide mutations occur when a SNM has an adverse effect on the function of the gene. This adverse effect can occur when the mutation changes the amino acid sequence of the protein and that change has a negative effect on the health of the organism. This is illustrated in Figure 1 by the C->G (guanosine) SNM at position 1565 resulting in an amino acid change from Leucine *(Leu)* to Valine *(Val)*. Deleterious mutations can also occur when an SNM is in the promoter region and alters the expression of the gene to the extent that it has a negative effect on the health of the organism. Since there is selection against deleterious mutations, they almost never become common enough to be polymorphisms.

Advantageous SNMs or SNPs can occur when the variant is in the promoter region and changes the expression of the gene in a positive fashion, or when the variant changes the amino acid sequence of the protein in a way that increases the viability of the organism. It is the advantageous SNMs that the Intelligent Design theorists refer to when they complain that the low rate of advantageous mutations falsifies Darwinian evolution.

STRPs and STRMs. STRPs are key to understanding many aspects of evolution and other aspects of genetics. What are they?

In the 1960s many experiments were performed in which DNA from a variety of organisms was split into its two strands (denatured) by heat. The strands were then allowed to come back together (renature) and the rate of this process was followed. Since there was so much DNA in the genome (3 billion nucleotides), it was anticipated that it would take a very long time for complementary strands to find each other and thus this should be a very slow process. Surprisingly, it was found that a large percent of the DNA renatured very quickly. The only explanation was that some sequences were repeated thousands of times. This, appropriately, was called *repetitious DNA.*

There are a number of different types of repetitious DNA also known as satellite DNA. Two of the types are called minisatellites and microsatellites. In minisatellites the length of the repeat sequence ranges from six to 65 base pairs. In microsatellites the length of the repeat sequence ranges from two to five base pairs. Since different individuals have different repeat lengths and since they are common, both minisatellites and microsatellites occur as short tandem repeat polymorphisms, or STRPs. These have also been called variable number tandem repeats or VNTRs. I will discuss the microsatellites.

Microsatellite DNA. The most common repeat sequence in microsatellites is CA/GT, as shown in Figure 1. Each different size is called an allele. The following are some of the important characteristics of the microsatellite STRPs.

- *Very polymorphic.* The number of different-sized alleles at a given STRP can vary from two to dozens. Thus, the different alleles of a CA two base pair repeat polymorphisms would be CA, CACA, CACACA, CACACACA, CACACACACA, etc. Since different individuals carry different common alleles this makes the STRPs the most polymorphic of the genetic variants. Thus, while the SNPs usually have only two variations or alleles in the population, STRPs have many alleles.

- *Very Common.* STRPs are very common with hundreds of thousands being present in the human genome. One to many are associated with each gene. They are usually clustered at the 5' end of the gene where most of the regulation of gene activity occurs.

- *Regulate gene function.* In our own laboratory we examined the possible association between STRPs at a number of genes and various human behaviors. One of the genes we examined was monamine oxidase A *(MAOA).* The *MAOA* enzyme plays a role in the breakdown of several brain neurotransmitters. The relationship between the different allele size groups of a STRP at the *MAOA* gene and a score for manic behavior is shown in Figure 2.

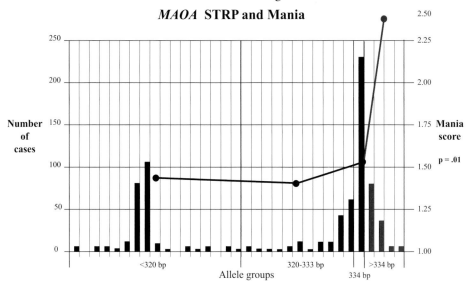

Figure 2. Relationship between the mania score and four different size groups of the MAOA STRP. From Comings et al. [4]

This shows that the mania score was fairly constant across several size groups of the MAOA STRP, except the group with the longest size repeats where the score was much higher. This and many other lines of evidence indicate that the STRPs play a role in regulating the rate of expression of the genes they are associated with. [4] The longer alleles may be associated with a greater (or lesser) degree of expression than the shorter alleles. Since each bar in Figure 2 represents a different allele, this also shows how polymorphic the STRPs can be.

- *Gene regulation occurs over long distances.* One of the most remarkable findings about STRPs is that not only do they regulate the expression of genes they are adjacent to, they can also regulate the expression of other genes "downstream." Because of the potential importance to understanding diabetes, one of the most intensively studied sets of STRPs are those associated with the *insulin* gene. Studies by Paquette and colleagues[5] showed that the effect of STRPs on gene function may extend across several genes. This is illustrated in Figure 3.

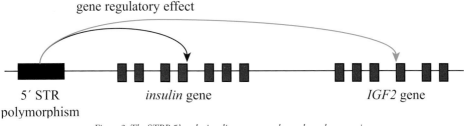

Figure 3. The STRP 5' to the insulin gene not only regulates the expression of the insulin gene, it also regulates the expression of the IGF2 gene 3' downstream. From Paquette et al.[5]

This shows that the 5' STRP not only regulates the expression of the *insulin* gene, but also regulates the expression of the insulin-like growth factor 2 (*IGF2*) gene, 3' downstream from the insulin gene. This indicates that not only are there many different levels of expression of a given gene and different levels of expression may also occur because of the effect of more distant STRPs. On the basis of these findings it is clear that the old idea that a gene occurs in two states, either "on" or "off," is wrong. Instead, most genes occuring in the population are set at many different levels of expression. This is illustrated in Figure 4.

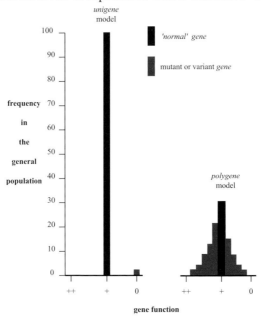

Figure 4. Unigene versus the polygene model. See text. From Comings.[6]

The diagram on the left illustrates the old concept that genes in the population are set at a specific "normal" level of expression, or if a deleterious mutation occurs, no expression. The association of genes with highly polymorphic STRPs, where different lengths of repeats are associated with different levels of gene expression, indicate that genes are actually present in the population at many different set levels of expression.

- *Very high mutation rate.* The mutation rate for single base pairs averages 10^{-9} or 1/billion per locus per generation.[7] By contrast, the mutation rate for microsatellite STRPs is much higher, in the range of 10^{-4} to 10^{-3} (1/thousand per locus per generation).[8-12] The mutation rate is related to the length of the repeat size, the longer the repeat the higher the mutation rate.[10-12] In some cases mutation rates in humans and other species have reached as high as 1/25 to 1/100/locus/generation.[11] *Thus, the mutation rate in STRPs is routinely a million to ten million times greater than for SNMs.*

    Mutations causing an increase in the number of dinucleotide repeats are more common than mutations causing a decrease in the number of dinucleotide repeats, up to a point. Mutations in very long repeats tend to decrease the number of repeats, thus preventing the progressive expansion of these polymorphisms.[12] The rate of mutation is also related to sex. In humans the mutation rate is five times faster in males than in females.[8,9] This sex difference is less striking in other species.[11]

- *STRP mutations are caused by replication slippage.* The very high mutation rate in STRMs compared to STMs is due to the fact that they have a unique mechanism of mutation—replication slippage.[12] This is due to the presence of loops in one of the DNA strands, due to the repeat structure of the STRPs. This in turn results in a deletion or insertion of one or more repeats during the DNA replication process. As a result, the mutation rate is related to the number of cell divisions that have occurred. In human males, production of sperm requires many more cell divisions. As a result, there is a higher mutation rate in males.

- *STRPs are present in many species.* STRP are present in humans, primates, dogs, turtles, lizzards, insects, and other species [11,12] indicating they have been present over long periods of evolutionary time.

Implications for evolution. By now the reader should appreciate the enormous significance the STRPs have for understanding the process of evolution and how the complaints of the Intelligent Designers that the beneficial mutation rate is too low to allow for evolution to occur are invalid. The mutation rate for STRMs is up to 10 million times faster that for SNMs. However, the story is still more elegant. I was so impressed with the implications of STRPs for evolution that in 1998 I stated the following:[4]

Evolution may not need to wait for mutations; they are always there. One of the tenets of evolution is a dependence upon the occurrence of just the right rare mutations that instead of being deleterious to the species, improve it, and allow selection to produce a new and better adapted species. This leaves open the question of how such rare events, i.e., mutations that affect the right gene, are advantageous instead of deleterious, happen at the right time, and have occurred often enough to provide for the rich diversity of species.

The concept of micro/minisatellite polymorphisms providing many alleleomorphic functional variants of each gene eliminates the need for this improbable sequence of events. Thus, new mutations or alleles do not have to occur, they are already present, and in great abundance and affecting most genes. It is not necessary for that rare advantageous mutation to just happen to occur at the right time and in the right gene, since all genes come in a rich array of functional variants. What is necessary to drive evolution is an environmental or ecological change to fuel the selection of a given set of genes better suited for the new environment. As an example, the evolution from primates to *Homo sapiens* required many different changes, including standing upright, thumb-finger opposition, the development of speech centers, the expansion of the frontal lobes, and many others. There is evidence that a number of different hominid species were simultaneously and independently undergoing these changes. [13] To accept that multiple advantageous new mutations of many different genes just happened to occur in the right temporal order, and in several different lineages, is difficult. However, if all the necessary mutations were already present, and environmental changes selected for the polygenic sets that were most advantageous, the parallel progression in multiple lineages is more readily understandable. This is not meant to imply that exon mutations in some critical genes do not also play a role in evolution, only that the presence of many functional alleles associated with micro/minisatellites may be a better explanation. [4]

The only addition I would now make is that because of the very high mutation rate of STRP loci, there could be selection for both new mutations and old variants when environment changes or other selective forces occur.

A number of unique characteristics of short tandem repeat polymorphisms (STRPs) make them uniquely suited to play a central role in evolution. These characteristics are:

- **Very variable (polymorphic) in different individuals in the population**
- **Very common, such that one to many STRPs are associated with each gene**
- **Occupy a preferential location at the 5' end of the gene, the usual site of gene regulation**

- Have a long-range of effect on gene regulation extending over more than one gene
- Can rapidly generate variation by replication slippage
- Have an extremely high mutation rate of one to 10 million times that of single base pair mutations
- Play an important role in the regulation of expression of the genes they are next to

As a result of these features there are a large number of pre-existing variations already present in the population. Potentially beneficial mutations and variants already exist waiting to be selected when changes in the environment call for them.

Even if an appropriately beneficial variant is not already present, the very high mutation rate can quickly produce it in the presence of environmental stress.

These features invalidate the complaints of Intelligent Designers that evolution cannot occur because mutation rates are to low and to rarely involve beneficial mutations to allow evolution to occur.

Proof of the role of STRPs in evolution. Given how enthusiastic I was about the explanatory role of STRPs for molecular evolution, I was especially excited by the subsequent studies of Fondon and Garner on the role of STRPs in evolution. [14] They took Darwin's lead that the variations in body form seen in domesticated animals over a short time span probably represents the same genetic process that occurs in evolution in nature, over much longer periods of time. Variants are incipient species. Since dogs are readily available, Fendon and Garner chose them to study the role of STRPs in the morphological variations seen in different breeds. They obtained DNA samples from 92 different breeds of dogs. Three-dimensional scans were made of the skulls of these dogs obtained from different museums. This allowed a total of 2.2 million individual measurements. They examined the STRPs associated with developmental genes, especially those known or suspected of being involved in the development of the face. These consisted of 21 *HOX* genes and 16 *HOX*-like genes. Their results indicated that selection for specific alleles of STRPs associated with genes involved in the bone structure of dogs played a significant role in the changes in body form involved in the selective breeding of dogs.

STRPs are especially associated with developmental and nervous system genes. Some STRPs consist of repeats of three bases (trinucleotide repeats) inside the coding regions of genes. Since the genetic code consists of three bases three trinucleotide repeats result in the presence of stretches of a specific amino acid in the protein gene product. These are called homopeptides (homo = same, peptides = small proteins). Two of the most common triplets are CTG and CAG, resulting in homopeptides consisting of leucine and glutamine respectively. These homopeptides may play a role in the regulation of the expression of genes. [15-17] These are all features that would also make this type of STRPs important in evolution. The following paragraphs show a specific example of the role of homopeptides in evolution.

The Face of a Dog and Homopeptides of the RUNX2 Gene. In addition to their remarkable findings about the important role of microsatellite STRPs in evolution, Fondon and Garner [14] also reported a role of STRPs due to a homopeptide polymorphism. *The RUNX2 gene codes for a master regulator of bone formation.* In addition the *RUNX2* gene contains two trinucleotide repeats for homopeptides, one consisting of alanine and the other of glutamine. The polyAlanine represses transcription of *RUNX2* while polyGlutamine stimulates it. In the dog gene there are 18 to 20 glutamines followed by 12 to 17 alanines. *Different ratios of the number of repeats in these two sections play a role in different levels of activity of the RUNX2 gene.* Fondon and Garner hypothesized that various aspects of the shape of a dog's head may be related to different polyGlutamine to polyAlanine ratios. They sequenced this region in 124 purebred dogs from 90 breeds, calculated these ratios, and correlated this with the slope of the snout. The results are shown in Figure 5.

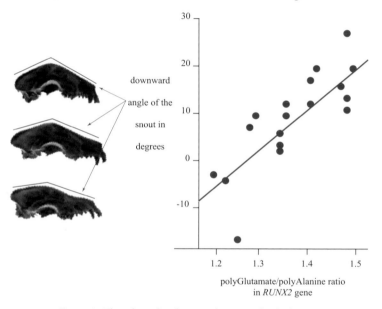

Figure 5. The relationship between the ratio of polyGlutamine to polyAlanine in RUNX2 and the angle of the snout in 90 different breeds of dog. Adapted from Fondon and Garner. PNAS. 101:18058-18063. [14] *By permission. National Academy of Sciences, USA. Copyright 2004.*

The greater the G/A ratio, the greater the angle of the snout. The correlation between the G/A and the angle of the snout was very high and significant (r^2 = .51, p = .0001, the r^2 value reflects the relative influence of the gene on the angle of the snout). 0 = no influence. 1 = 100 percent influence). There was also a high correlation with the midface length (r^2 = .63). This was another example of the important role of highly mutable, highly variable STRPs in the evolution of body form.

Darwin's Finches and Rapid Evolution

In Chapter 16, I describe the work of Peter and Rosemary Grant studying natural selection and evolution among the finches on the Galapagos Islands, made famous by Darwin. These studies showed that contrary to Darwin's thought that evolution proceeds very slowly over thousands of generations and millions of years, when major stresses such as droughts or floods occur, evolution proceeds very rapidly over one to a few generations and one to a few years. The reason it appeared to progress so slowly was that the changes produced by a drought and those produced by an excess of rain were in opposite directions. The end result was that over many years of alternating drought and flood seasons there was a false appearance of no change at all. However, if climatic or other environmental changes were to persist in a single direction, such as all drought or flood, evolution could occur very rapidly. It is likely that the genetic mechanism involves STRPs as described above.

The studies of Fondon and Garner have shown that the role of STRPs in evolution is more than theoretical. They showed that the inheritance of different STRPs in a range of homeotic genes were involved in the changes in body morphology brought about by the domestication and inbreeding of 90 different breeds of dog.

Studies of finches on the islands of the Galapagos have shown that natural selection and evolution can occur with great rapidity, over only a few years and generations. It is likely that changes of this degree of rapidity also take place by the selection of pre-existing STRP alleles.

The Role of Gene Splicing in Evolution

Eukaryote genes are divided into exons that actually code for proteins and introns that do not code for proteins. Both the exons and introns are transcribed into a large piece of RNA that remains in the nucleus and is called heterogeneous nuclear RNA (hnRNA). The RNA corresponding to the introns is spliced out of the hnRNA to produce messenger RNA (mRNA). The mRNA passes through the nuclear pores of the nuclear membrane, into the cytoplasm where it is read by the ribosomes to produce a specific sequence of amino acids resulting in a protein product.

Normal splicing is as follows:

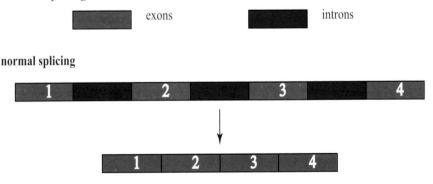

In humans the average gene is 28,000 nucleotides in length and contains an average of nine exons and eight introns. The exons average 120 nucleotides, while the introns can range from 100 to 100,000 nucleotides in length. Over 15 percent of gene mutations that cause disease act by causing alternative splicing. [18]

Exon skipping. One or more of the exons may be skipped during the splicing process.

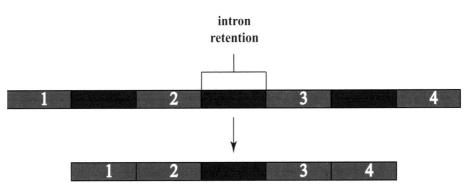

Exon skipping is the most common form of alternative splicing in mammals.

Intron retention. The splicing may fail to exclude an intron, resulting in intron retention.

This is probably the earliest type of alternative splicing to have evolved. [19]

Splicing seems like a lot of trouble. What possible advantage is it? It allows the shuffling of exons to easily make new genes without having to start from scratch. A second advantage is that in humans, for example, it allows 90,000 different proteins to be made from only 25,000 genes. In other words, by alternative splicing, each gene on average can make three or more different proteins. A third advantage is that it may allow evolution to evolve different species from the same basic set of genes. Thus, one quarter of the alternatively spliced exons in both species are specific to either humans or mice. [20]

Alu generation of new exons. One group of alternatively spliced exons is unique to primates and may have contributed to the divergence of primates from other species. The primate-specific exons are derived from a mobile genetic element called *alu*, which belongs to a larger class of elements known as retrotransposons. These are short sequences of DNA whose function seems to be to generate copies of themselves and then reinsert those copies back into the genome at random positions, rather like little genome parasites. Retrotransposons are found in almost all organisms and they have had a profound influence by contributing to the genomic expansion that accompanied the evolution of multicellular organisms. Almost half the human genome is made of transposable elements with *alu* sequences being the most abundant. [18]

The *alus* were long considered nothing more than genomic garbage, but they began to get a little respect as geneticists realized how *alu* insertion can expand a gene's protein-generating capacity. All it takes to convert some silent intronic *alu* elements into real exons is a single-letter change in their DNA sequence. [18] At present, the human genome contains approximately 500,000 *alu* elements located within introns, and 25,000 of these could become new exons by undergoing this single-point mutation. Thus, *alu* sequences have the potential to continue to greatly enrich the stock of meaningful genetic information available for producing new human proteins. Evolution works by presenting organisms with new options, then select and keep those that confer an advantage. Novel proteins created by the splicing in of new *alu*-derived exons probably helped to make humans the species they are today.

Alternative exon splicing adds a new capability to the evolutionary toolbox. In previous sections I discussed the great power of gene duplication to allow rapid evolutionary changes without having to make new genes from scratch. Exon splicing is in essence an alternative to gene duplication, but without the necessity of making a new gene. It allows the same gene to produce several different proteins, one of which retains the function of the original protein. Splicing may have become so prominent because of this powerful capability. It allows humans to have the diversity and capabilities of a 90,000 gene organism, while in reality having only 25,000 genes.

A role of STRPs in exon splicing. We saw in the first part of this chapter the powerful role that STRPs have in evolution. Lian and Garner [20] have now suggested that STRPs may also play an important role in alternative exon splicing. They found that while less than half of the proteins in the Human Alternative Splicing Database are known to be alternatively spliced, 84 percent of those that are alternatively spliced contain STRs. These complementary repeats could play a role in the regulation of alternative splicing. Since these sequences are known to have a high mutation rate this would contribute an additional method for rapid change during evolution.

During evolution alternative exon splicing provides a powerful mechanism for rapid changes in the way the genome expresses itself, yet requires few changes in the DNA sequence. For example, it allows humans to have the flexibility and diversity of 90,000 genes while possessing only 25,000 genes.

Other Mechanisms of Rapid Genetic Change

In addition to the above there are a number of other mechanisms by which the DNA sequence of the genome can change much more rapidly than by single base pair mutations. Some of these have already been discussed and are included here to make a complete list. All of these mechanisms utilize the principle of reusing previous solutions, previously developed modules, previously developed genes, or parts of genes. I have listed these in approximate order of the size of the reused module.

Endosymbosis. This has been discussed previously. It involves the reutilization of very large modules—chloroplasts and mitochondria—from bacteria. [21] This relieved newly evolved eukaryotes of the need of developing from scratch a mechanism for producing energy from light or sugar, a fundamental requirement for life.

Whole Genome Duplication. In 1970 Susumu Ohno suggested that during the course of vertebrate evolution, the entire genome was duplicated twice. [22,23] This doubling of the number of chromosomes is called *polyploidy*. It is especially common in plants and can rapidly lead to the evolution of new species. [24,25]

Gene duplication. Gene duplication is one of the most widely used mechanisms to make new genes by producing two copies of old genes, keeping one for the original function and allowing the other to diverge to take on new functions.

Hybridization. Hybridization occurs when two different but closely related species mate and produce fertile offspring. While the definition of a species usually implies two groups that do not mate in nature and would not produce fertile offspring if they did, the definition is not violated if the offspring are occasionally fertile. Certain environmental conditions may increase the probability of this occurring. The outcome is a wider range of alleles at the genes of each, and this may improve natural selection for more fit organisms and accelerate new speciation. [26,27]

Gene Displacement/Gene Opportunism/Cooption. Gene opportunism occurs when the protein product of a given gene has multiple functions. Each function is often in a specific place. Thus, one function may be inside the cell while the other function is outside on the cell surface. The difference can also be in different cell types. Proteins with these different functions have been referred to as moonlighting proteins. [28] This is a characteristic of many proteins. [29] The following are two striking examples.

First, one function of phosphoglucose isomerase is to catalyze the interconversion of glucose 6-phosphate and fructose 6-phosphate. However, other moonlighting functions include being a neuroleukin, which is both a nerve growth factor and an agent for maturing lymphocyte B cells; being an autocrine motility factor that stimulates cell migration; and being a factor that can cause the differentiation of human myeloid leukemia cells. A second example is the lens protein of the eye called *crystallin*. It also functions as heat shock protein, a stress response protein, and has seven different enzyme functions.

Gene displacement, or *opportunism,* or *polygeny* is a powerful mechanism in evolution. When speciation requires the development of a specific function, it is often possible to call upon the services of a protein whose gene is already present. Instead of inventing a new gene the only thing required could be a single mutation in a promoter or other gene region that *allows the gene to be expressed in a new organ or new place in the cell.* A related process is called *pleiotrophy.* This refers to the situation in which a single gene can be expressed as several different physical effects or traits or phenotypes.

This general phenomena has also been called *cooption*. Cooption is basically a shift in function in which a given system or gene product that had function A can subsequently be co-opted to have a different function B. This is especially easy to do if the gene was first duplicated so the original function A is not lost while the duplicated gene is coopted. Cooption was first proposed as a tool in evolution by Darwin.

Chromosome Rearrangement. Chromosomes contain hundreds to thousands of different genes. Many varieties and species, especially in plants, arise following various types of chromosome rearrangement. [30p603]

Horizontal Gene Transfer. As discussed previously horizontal gene transfer between species was so prevalent in prokaryotic organisms that it was not until the development of eukaryotes with a nuclear membrane that this process was slowed enough to allow for the evolution of more complex species. However, for prokaryotes, this process allows species to acquire new genes without the necessity of starting from scratch.

Jumping Genes. In 1948 Barbara McClintock began to report her studies in corn suggesting that genes could jump around in the genome. [31] These jumping units were called *transposons*. This was so bizarre to the scientific establishment that her work was ignored for years. However, over time the fact that her ideas were correct began to be accepted, and in 1983 she received the Nobel Prize for this innovative and groundbreaking work. Like the other mechanisms on this list, the presence of transposons allows the *rapid rearrangements of genetic material*. When beneficial the prevalence of the new arrangement in the population would be increased by natural selection.

Sexual Recombination. In asexual reproduction all of the genes of the parent, including new mutations, are passed to each offspring. Sexual reproduction involves the formation of an egg and a sperm, each of which have only half of the parent's genes. When a sperm fertilizes an egg, the full complement of genes is restored, half from the mother, half from the father. From the point of view of a strong parent wanting to pass his or her genes to their offspring, this is inefficient since only one half of the strong parent's genes are passed on. What advantage compensates for this inefficiency?

In addition to acquiring new genes, it is sometimes just as important in evolution to acquire specific combinations of genes. This is uniquely possible with sexual recombination. This form of reproduction started in the pre-Cambrian period and helped to accelerate evolution.

***Alu* sequences.** The important role of *alu* sequences was discussed above. However, there is part of this story that needs emphasis. *Alus* typically contain a poly A (adenine) sequence. Stretches of polyAdenine are added to the 3' end of messenger RNA after splicing. Thus, any sequence with polyAdenine is likely to have been derived from messenger RNA, the transcript that contains the essence of different genes. The ability to disperse such sequences throughout the genome to form new exons would provide a method of rapidly inserting sequences with proven functions into new genes.

Exon Shuffling and Domain Exchange. Proteins consist of multiple different domains each with a different function. Some proteins contain over a dozen such domains. These different domains are carried in different exons. As described previously, one of the major advantages of dividing genes into exons and introns is that exchanging exons, often called exon shuffling or domain exchange, allows the sharing of the same successful domains by many different genes. [32]

Repetitious peptides. The smallest modules that can be reused are short stretches of protein or peptides that have been used many times in many different genes in evolution. For example, albumin and alpha-fetoprotein contain tandem repeats of an 18-nucleotide-long primordial building block coding for a six-amino-acid peptide, and this contains smaller blocks of five and six nucleotides. [33] Many other proteins including collagen, β_2-microglobulin, different neurotransmitter receptors, and probably all genes, are also made up of similar repeats of short peptides. [34,35]

> Creationists and the Intelligent Designers repeatedly claim that the production of beneficial variants by single nucleotide mutations (STMs) is too rare and too slow to allow for evolution. This ignores the fact that much evolution is not the result of this type of rare genetic change. DNA composed of repetitious sequences in the form of short tandem repeats (STRs) mutate a million to 10 million times faster than STMs and play an important role in gene regulation and evolution. In addition to this mechanism, reusing or exchanging pieces of DNA that have already proven themselves in other situations accomplishes most evolution. The processes for rapid evolution include:
> - **Endosymbiosis**
> - **Whole genome duplication (polyploidy)**
> - **Chromosomal rearrangements**
> - **Gene duplication**
> - **Hybridization**
> - **Gene displacement**
> - **Horizontal gene transfer**
> - **Jumping genes**
> - **Sexual recombination**
> - **Retrotransposons (Alu sequences)**
> - **Exon shuffling and domain exchange**
> - **Repetitious DNA and repetitious peptides**
>
> These processes allow whole genomes, whole chromosomes, parts of chromosomes, whole organelles (chloroplasts and mitochondria), whole genes, specific combinations of genes, whole gene domains, and parts of gene domains to be put to new uses—over and over again. This reuse of what already works allows for the rapid acceleration of evolution and speciation and allows for a rapid response to environmental change and geographical isolation. As a result—there is plenty of time for evolution to occur.

References

1. Vogel, F. & Motulsky, A. G. *Human Genetics*. Springer-Verlag, New York, 1979.
2. Hogan, J. P. *Kicking the Sacred Cow. Questioning the Unquestionable and Thinking the Impermissible*. Baen Publishing Enterprises, New York, 2004.
3. Ross, H. *A Matter of Days. Resolving a Creation Controversy*. NavPress, Colorado Springs, CO, 2004.
4. Comings, D. E. Polygenic inheritance and micro/minisatellites. *Molecular Psychiatry*. 3: 21-31, 1998.
5. Paquette, J., Giannoukakis, N., Polychronakos, C., Vafiadis, P. & Deal, C. The INS 5' variable number of tandem repeats is associated with IGF2 expression in humans. *J Biol Chem*. 273: 14158-14164, 1998.
6. Comings, D. E. SNPs and polygenic disorders: A less gloomy view. *Molecular Psychiatry*. 4: 314-316, 1999.
7. Crow, J. F. How much do we know about spontaneous human mutation rates? *Mol Biol Evo*. 15: 1269-1274, 1993.
8. Weber, J. L. & Wong, C. Mutation of human short tandem repeats. *Hum Mol Genet*. 2: 1123-1128, 1993.
9. Brinkmann, B., Klintschar, M., Neuhuber, F., Huhne, J. & Rolf, B. Mutation rate in human microsatellites: influence of the structure and length of the tandem repeat. *Am J Hum Genet*. 62: 1408-1415, 1998.
10. Kayser, M. et al. Characteristics and frequency of germline mutations at microsatellite loci from the human Y chromosome, as revealed by direct observation in father/son pairs. *Am J Hum Genet*. 66: 1580-1588, 2000.
11. Ellegren, H. Microsatellite mutations in the germline: implications for evolutionary inference. *Trends Genet*. 16: 551-558, 2000.
12. Ellegren, H. Heterogeneous mutation processes in human microsatellite DNA sequences. *Nat Genet*. 24: 400-402, 2000.
13. Wills, C. *The Runaway Brain*. Basic Books, New York, NY, 1993.
14. Fondon, J. W., 3rd & Garner, H. R. Molecular origins of rapid and continuous morphological evolution. *Proc Natl Acad Sci USA*. 101: 18058-18063, 2004.
15. Karlin, S. & Burge, C. Trinucleotide repeats and long homopeptides in genes and proteins associated with nervous system disease and development. *Proc Natl Acad Sci USA*. 93: 1560-1565, 1996.
16. Gerber, H. P. et al. Transcriptional activation modulated by homopolymeric glutamine and proline stretches. *Science*. 263: 808-811, 1994.
17. Su, W., Jackson, S., Tjian, R. & Echols, H. DNA looping between sites for transcriptional activation: self-association of DNA-bound Sp1. *Genes Dev*. 5: 820-826, 1991.
18. Ast, G. The alternative genome. *Scientific American*. 292: 58-65, 2005.
19. Lee, C., Atanelov, L., Modrek, B. & Xing, Y. ASAP: the Alternative Splicing Annotation Project. *Nucleic Acids Res*. 31: 101-105, 2003.
20. Lian, Y. & Garner, H. R. Evidence for the regulation of alternative splicing via complementary DNA sequence repeats. *Bioinformatics*. 21: 1358-1364, 2005.
21. Margolis, L. *Acquiring Genomes*. Basic Books, 2003.
22. Ohno, S. *Evolution by Gene Duplication*. Springer Verlag, New York, 1970.
23. Ohno, S. Gene duplication and the uniqueness of vertebrate genomes circa 1970-1999. Semin Cell Dev Biol. 10: 517-522, 1999.
24. Stebbins, G. *Variation and Evolution in Plants*. University of North Carolina Press, New York.
25. Grant, V. *Plant Speciation*. Columbia University Press, New York, 1971.
26. Lewontin, R. C. & Birch, L. C. Hybridization as a source of variation for adaption to new environments. *Evolution*. 20: 315-336, 1966.
27. Grant, P. R. & Grant, R. Hybridization of bird species. *Science*. 256: 193-197, 1992.
28. Jeffery, C. J. Moonlighting Proteins. *Trends in Biochemical Sciences*. 24: 8-11, 1999.
29. Smalheiser, R. Proteins in unexpected locations. *Molecular Biology of the Cell*. 7: 1003-1014, 1996.
30. Mayr, E. *The Growth of Biological Thought. Diversity, Evolution, and Inheritance*. The Belknap Press of Harvard University Press, Cambridge, MA, 1982.
31. McClintock, B. Chromosome organization and genic expression. *Cold Spring Harb Symp Quant Biol*. 16: 13-47, 1951.
32. Gilbert, W. Why genes in pieces? *Nature*. 271: 501, 1978.
33. Ohno, S. Original domain for the serum albumin family arose from repeated sequences. *Proc Natl Acad Sci USA*. 78: 7657-7661, 1981.
34. Ohno, S. & Epplen, J. T. The primitive code and repeats of base oligomers as the primordial protein-encoding sequence. *Proc Natl Acad Sci USA*. 80: 3391-3395, 1983.
35. Ohno, S. Early genes that were oligomeric repeats generated a number of divergent domains on their own. *Proc Natl Acad Sci USA*. 84: 6486-6490, 1987.

Chapter 7

Complexity—Introduction

In 1691 John Ray published a book entitled *The Wisdom of God Manifested in the Works of the Creator.* In it he gave many examples where organisms or organs were so complex they must have been the work of a supernatural creator. In a similar vein, in 1802 William Paley [1] wrote that if it took a highly trained watchmaker to make a watch, then it must have taken a supernatural power to construct things as complex as those seen in the living world of biology. This famous statement led Richard Dawkins to entitle his book, *The Blind Watchmaker,* [2] explaining how evolution by random variation and natural selection could accomplish these biological wonders.

In his book, *Darwin's Black Box,* [3] Michael Behe claimed that not only have evolutionists not provided an explanation for some complex structures, he claimed they never would be able to provide such an explanation because some structures are "irreducibly complex."

> By irreducibly complex I mean a single system composed of several well-matched, interacting parts that contribute to the basic function, wherein the removal of any one of the parts causes the system to effectively cease functioning. [3p39]

To make sure he had made his point he further elaborated on this theme:

> An irreducibly complex system cannot be produced directly by numerous, successive, slight modifications of a precursor system, because any precursor to an irreducibly complex system that is missing a part is by definition nonfunctional. Since natural selection can only choose systems that are already working, then if a biological system cannot be produced gradually it would have to arise as an integrated unit, in one fell swoop, for natural selection to have anything to act on. [3]

Then in a modest, self-effacing evaluation of his own work he stated,

> The results of these cumulative efforts to investigate the cell—to investigate life at the molecular level—is a loud, clear, piercing cry of "design!" The result is so unambiguous and so significant that it must be

ranked as one of the greatest achievements in the history of science. The discovery rivals those of Newton and Einstein, Lavoisier and Schrödinger, Pasteur, and Darwin. [3p232]

At a minimum, his work helps us to understand why standard scientific findings presented in academic journals are subjected to impartial, independent review prior to publication. The evaluation of their worth cannot be left up to the authors themselves.

Many of the creationists' and Intelligent Designers' complaints against evolution involve what is termed *argument from ignorance.* This approach involves concluding that if the evidence for something is not currently available it never will be. We saw above that this failed when they claimed that since some of the important intermediate or transitional forms in evolution had not been found, they never would be found. In fact, they were quickly found. Behe uses the same faulty reasoning. If some mechanism about the evolution of a complex system is not known, it never will be known. In the following pages and chapters I examine and hopefully counter these claims. This introductory chapter presents some theoretical aspects of the complexity issue. In subsequent chapters I will directly address some of the Intelligent Designers' specific concerns.

Complexity and Cellular Automata

Stephen Wolfram, the author of the equation-solving computer program known as *Mathematica,* [4] published a book entitled *A New Kind of Science.* [5] His theme was that a wide range of very complex forms can be produced by a small number of initial rules. Because the program had a graphic format consisting of black or white cells, he used the term *cellular automata.* For example, we can take a piece of graph paper and blacken in one square.

One simple rule is that on the next row, any grid square that is either immediately below or below and adjacent to the original square is also blackened in.

When this process is continued many times, the following pattern develops.

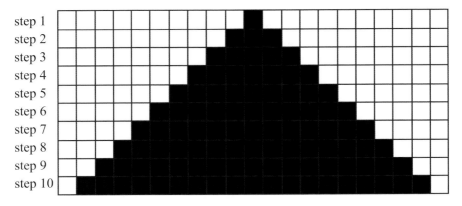

A set of eight simple sub-rules for this can be diagrammed as follows:

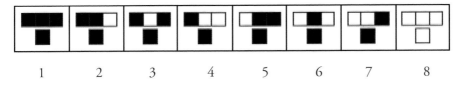

The top row shows the blackened squares already produced. The bottom row shows whether the square in the middle of the next row will be black or white. Boxes 1 to 8 show the rules when the eight different possible combinations of the top three cells are black or white. Since there are only two colors, black or white and eight possibilities, there are 28 or 256 possible sets of these rules. This was rule 254. Minor alterations in the rules can change the output from the above simple pattern to very complex patterns. For example, rule 90 is:

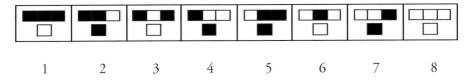

It differs from rule 254 in that for sub rules 1, 3, and 6 the bottom square is white instead of black. This now produces the following complex pattern:

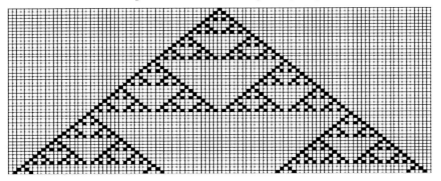

A further example is rule 30.

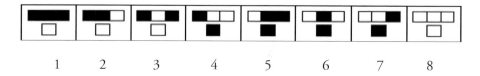

$$1 \quad\quad 2 \quad\quad 3 \quad\quad 4 \quad\quad 5 \quad\quad 6 \quad\quad 7 \quad\quad 8$$

This differs from rule 90 in that for sub-rule 2 the next square is white instead of black and for sub-rule 6 the next square is white instead of black. This produces the following pattern:

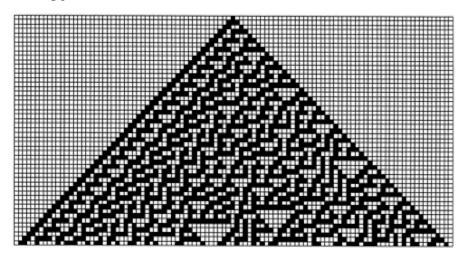

The important implication is that *very complex patterns can result from very simple starting rules*. While the reader may be skeptical about what relevance this has to the issue of whether Darwinian evolution and natural selection can produce very complex structures, I show in the following sections that it is remarkably relevant. The next section reviews studies of a computer program that was specifically designed to model evolution by genetic variation and natural selection. This simple program also produces very complex outcomes. Previously I reviewed the new field of evolutionary development dubbed "evo devo," which shows that a small set of body shape genes termed the developmental "toolbox" can account for the evolution of the enormous diversity of animal forms. Thus, some of the philosophical implications of cellular automata are relevant.

Theism and The Principle of Computational Equivalence. In addition to the above statement that very complex outcomes can result from simple starting rules, Wolfram examined the converse of this and found that if he attempted to produce even more complex patterns by using a set of even more complex rules, the result was a simpler rather than a more-complex outcome. The implications of this are quite profound, so much so that Wolfram elevated this observation to a grand concept he called the *Principle of Computational Equivalence.* He states, "In essence, the *Principal of*

Computational Equivalence introduces a new law of nature to the effect that no system can ever carry out explicit computations that are more sophisticated than those carried out by systems like cellular automata." [5p720] In other words, *no matter how complex the outcome, it is still likely to have been the result of a few simple rules.*

As discussed later, this concept certainly has validity for the string theory of the cosmos. Many religions, including Christianity, and the entire Intelligent Design movement, propose that the complexity of nature is so great that it can only be explained by the workings of a supernatural power. The *Principle of Computational Equivalence* suggests the opposite, that once a given level of complexity is attained, a level that is easily explained by a set of simple rules, a further increase in the level of complexity cannot be produced by evoking causative factors of still greater complexity. Since the concept of God is the most complex causative or creative factor ever proposed, the *Principle of Computational Equivalence* suggests evoking a God to explain complexity—is not necessary.

> **Very complex outcomes can result from simple starting rules.**
> **Artificially increasing the complexity of the starting rules leads to simpler rather than more-complex outcomes.**
> **This leads to the *Principle of Computational Equivalence,* which states that no system can ever carry out computations that are more sophisticated than those carried out by simple systems like cellular automata. This has the profound implication that it is not necessary to evoke the complex concept of God to explain the development of seemingly very complex organs or organisms.**

Computer Models of Evolution—Avida

Wolfram's cellular automata program demonstrated that great complexity can derive from a set of simple rules and that attempting to increase the complexity of the rules led to lower rather than greater levels of complexity. Natural selection of the results was not a part of the program. What happens when selection is a part of the program?

Christoph Adami and colleagues in the Digital Life Laboratory at California Institute of Technology in Pasadena and Richard Lenski and colleagues at Michigan State University in East Lansing developed a sophisticated program of this type called Avida. [6,7] Lenski had previously worked on evolution in bacteria but found the information provided by Avida to be so much more powerful that he switched to studying evolution in the digital world. Over a period of many years of work on bacteria, Lenski observed features that supported the concept of *punctuated equilibria.* Over 35,000 generations of bacteria evolved that were larger and grew faster. These changes were not smooth and linear but showed periods of rapid change alternating with periods of little change.

The advantage of computer-based evolution is that the time from one generation to the next is many thousands of times faster than for bacteria and many hundreds of thousands of times faster than for humans. In Avida all of the facets of Darwinian evolution are in place—replication, mutation, and natural selection. Instead of being restricted to examining evolution over 35,000 generations requiring years of experimentation, in the digital world evolution can be followed over millions of generations in minutes. The number of generations involved simulates the passage of geologic time.

Living animal organisms do things like respiration where they take in oxygen and put out carbon dioxide, and digestion where they consume food such as sugar and put out usable packets of energy in the form of ATP (adenosine triphosphate). What do digital organisms do? They work with food in the form of being fed numbers. One of the things that computer programs do is compare numbers. This is done by a fairly complex operation known as "equals" and involves a bit-by-bit comparison. The shortest program that can do the equals function requires 19 lines of computer code.

The chance that simple random events could produce this complex 19-step program is about 1 in a thousand trillion trillion. [7] What happens when random events are coupled with selection? In the digital world selection is represented by rewards for modest improvements on simple code and larger rewards for more complex code. Rewards take the form of supplying the program with more numbers (food).

As with living organisms, most of the mutations are either neutral with no effect, or deleterious and make things worse. Only a few mutations are beneficial. One experiment was set up so the organisms would replicate 16,000 times. This was repeated 50 times. Did selection improve the odds of producing a functioning equals program? Yes, dramatically, in that 23 of the 50 experiments produced a functional equals program, not the trillions of trials expected without selection. This illustrates the incredible power that can be obtained when random mutation is coupled with selection, even when beneficial mutations are rare.

When the rewards, i.e., selection, were taken away, none of the trials produced an equals program. Even more remarkable all 23 of the equals programs that were produced with rewards evolved in a different way. This is also consistent with a dictum of evolution—*the random process can come up with many different solutions for the same end product.*

These digital organisms also provide insight into another aspect of evolution. Ecologists have found that up to a certain point, the more energy or food provided by a given ecological niche, the more different types of organisms evolved. However, if too much energy (food) is supplied the number of organisms was more limited. The digital organisms showed the same phenomena. When plenty of energy (numbers) was supplied, only a single predominant program evolved. However, when the numbers were limited, multiple different programs evolved, each specialized for a different sub-function. Even more surprising, on a restricted diet of numbers the frequency of successful programs increased to 50 out of 50 trials and the equals programs evolved five times more rapidly. This represents the simple fact that the more stressful the environment (restricted diet) the more rapid the rate of evolution.

The Intelligent Designers have repeatedly pointed out that some complex multi-step or multi-component biological processes do not work if even one of the steps or components is left out. They argue that the probability of getting all steps working together by the process of random mutations and selection is so remote that Intelligent Design by a superior power must have been involved. As with these complex biological systems, the equals program also required multiple steps and if any one was left out the program did not work. Despite this, when exposed to a limited input of numbers, the equals programs evolved quickly and at a high probability (50 out of 50 times). This shows that *when random mutations and selection are combined irreducibly complex organisms can evolve rapidly and efficiently.*

Computer Models of Evolution—EV

Schneider[8] described another computer modeling of evolution. The programs were called *ev, ecd* and *lister.* A small population of 64 "organisms" was created; each genome consisted of 256 random bases, A, T, G or C. The organisms contained a target sequence of DNA to be recognized and the goal was to evolve a section of the genome that coded for a protein that recognized and bound to the target DNA sequence in a different part of the genome.

The organisms were subjected to rounds of selection and mutation. Mistakes were made in either failing to recognize the target DNA sequence or binding to a non-target DNA sequence. The number of mistakes made by each organism was determined. The "natural selection" component consisted of allowing only the half of the population with the fewest mistakes to reproduce by having them replace the other half that made more mistakes.

At every generation each organism was subjected to one random point mutation. At the start the organisms contained a random DNA sequence in which the information content of the binding sites was essentially zero. The results are shown in Figure 1.

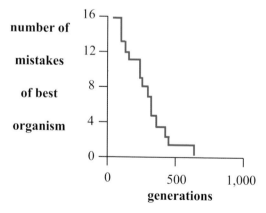

Figure 1. Number of mistakes for best organism in successive generations. From Schneider: Evolution of Biological Information, Nucleic Acids Research. *28:2794-2799, 2000. By permission.*

Remarkably, the cyclic mutation and selection process led to a mistake-free "organism" in only 704 generations. When "natural selection" was removed the information content of the recognition sequence rapidly decayed. This study showed how the information gain came about from mutation and selection, without the "outside influence" proposed by the creationists and Intelligent Designers.

The *ev* program also has relevance to the claims by Behe[3] of "irreducible complexity." The recognizer section and its binding site co-evolved in the *ev* program. They were interdependent upon each other, and destructive mutations in either immediately led to elimination of the organism. In this respect it was similar to the proposed irreducible complexity consisting of such interacting parts of a structure that the removal of one led to loss of function of the whole. However, *in ev, despite the interdependence of the two parts, the molecular evolution of the whole was straight-forward and rapid, in direct contradiction of Behe's thesis.*

In the *ev* program, the probability of finding 16 sites (recognition sites) averaging 4 bits each in random sequence was 5×10^{-20} (5 chances in one hundred billion billion). Despite this, the sites evolved from random sequences in less than 800 generations. This dramatic effect of combining natural selection with random mutation is similar to that observed in the Avida program.

> **Computer modeling of evolution using digital organisms shows that the combination of random mutations with natural selection is incredibly powerful and efficient. In one program the probability of a 19 component program evolving on the basis of random mutations alone was one in a thousand trillion trillion. When selection was added in combination with a "stressful environment," the probability increased to 1 in 1.**
>
> **In a second program the probability of finding a 16-site component was five in one hundred billion billion generations. When selection was added the component evolved in 704 generations, a thousand billion times faster.**
>
> **With this powerful combination of mutation and selection, irreducibly complex processes or organisms can evolve rapidly and efficiently.**

The Real Thing

While these computer models might be called simulations, they are not simulations but the real thing.[9] They do not simulate evolution; evolution is actually occurring. This is demonstrated by the fact that these studies have led to a new field of research called *evolutionary computation*. This involves using random changes in a computer program plus selection to design a wide range of practical things including airplane wings, manufacturing schedules, natural-gas transport pipeline networks, robots, and others.[9p105] In many cases the results are more creative and innovative than the efforts of very talented engineers and industrial designers. The power of this method is that a large number of random variations are tested. Those that work form the starting point for further changes. Those that fail are discarded. Evolutionary computational design is so effective that Boeing used the technique to design the geometry of the engine of the Boeing 777. [9p105]

Monkeys and Typewriters

One of the statements often made by those who advance the concept of Intelligent Design is to suggest that it is just as impossible for random mutations to result in the evolution of complex structures as it is for a series of monkeys randomly pounding on a typewriter to write poetry or literature. This complaint indicates a lack of understanding of how powerful the combination of random mutations, small steps, cumulative changes, and natural selection can be.

Let us suppose we had one thousand monkeys randomly typing on a typewriter and that they hit one key each second. Based on the keyboard I am currently using, there are approximately 28 letter or space keys. Thus, we will have the monkeys use a 28-key typewriter. Then let us take small steps in the form of groups of 10 letters or spaces. Natural selection will be in the form of a hypothetical English teacher who decides whether the words produced make sense and have the potential to tell a story (survival value). The following are some results that our form of natural selection might allow to "survive."

> There was…
> Once upon…
> Alice was…
> David was…

Without spending a lot of time trying to determine the exact number of selectable 10-letter outcomes, let us simply say there are 1,000 combinations of 10 letters and spaces that could be given the stamp of survival by our hypothetical English teacher. The chance that any one of these possibilities would occur after the monkeys were typing for one hundred years is $1/28^{10}$ x 1000 (possible outcomes) x 1,000 (number of monkeys) x 60 (seconds per minute) x 60 (minutes per hour) x 24 (hours per day) x 365 (days per year) x 100 (number of years) = 10. Thus, in only 100 years there would be 10 suitable outcomes that survived our form of natural selection. The final requirement is that once a suitable outcome had been selected, the process would start over to build on the 10 acceptable outcomes. Here the English teacher providing natural selection would have to select the new subsequent outcomes that were consistent with what had already evolved. It is reasonable that this requirement would cut in half the number of suitable outcomes, now requiring 200 instead of 100 years. Thus, if we take the first outcome listed above, the following are some possible second stage outcomes.

> There was…an old man

> There was…a nice boy
> There was…a bad girl

For subsequent rounds we could assume there would be even more restrictions on the number of suitable outcomes, as the form of the story began to take shape. However, the evolution of the final story can actually be rapidly accelerated by using previously completed modules, in this case words. As with evolution, it is not necessary to re-invent the wheel; once a word has evolved the whole word can be randomly used in subsequent "organisms." Eventually, a number of meaningful different stories would have evolved. This simple concept has a number of lessons and analogies relevant to real evolution.

1. Small steps. It is a common tactic of proponents of Intelligent Design to suggest that some things are too complex to be the result of random genetic change and natural selection. They invariably talk as though everything happened in one step. However, when taken in small cumulative steps, with natural selection at each step, quite complex organisms and structures, or in this case stories, can be produced.

2. Cumulative changes. The power of small steps is greatly multiplied by adding together the successive improvements, in this case, improvements in the unfolding story.

3. Non-directive. It has been repeatedly pointed out that Darwinian evolution is non-directive. That is, there is no predestined goal. It is truly blind. [2] The end result is simply what has survived the selection process. When we use *Homo sapiens* as an example of the outcome, our egos tend to lead some of us to believe we are the best possible outcome, and therefore a superior force directed the process. However, as in the many different stories in the above examples, biological evolution also has many different potential outcomes, as abundantly illustrated by the wide diversity of species on earth. Humans could have evolved to have four eyes instead of two, and three pairs of extremities instead of two, or even an average IQ of twice what it is currently. Had that been the outcome, we would probably view the thought of having only two eyes and two pairs of extremities as ugly, or inefficient, or both, and an average IQ of 100 as really stupid.

4. Multiple paths to the same goal. A similar but not identical concept is that an equally competent end result can be built from a number of different pathways. Here we may have had a similar outward appearance, but there may be more subtle differences in a number of metabolic pathways or internal organs producing multiple paths to a similar outcome. In the above analogy, the same story message could have been delivered using a wildly varying combination of words, sentences, and paragraphs, just as the concepts in these paragraphs could have been stated many different ways, and probably more elegantly, without losing the gist of the message.

5. Modularity. This refers to an interchangeability of parts. Thus, the above phrase, "There was an old man…" could be used as the beginning of many different stories without the need to evolve the phrase over and over. Internal to the story, the phrase, "He said," or "She said" could be used as a module over and over without needing to reinvent the phrase. Even single words would not have to be re-invented and could be reused. As described previously once a gene, an exon, or a domain has evolved and proven its survivability in natural selection, there is no need to reinvent it. By exon or domain shuffling, or in this case word or phrase shuffling, successful solutions are used and reused to accelerate the rate of evolution.

As with the digital model of evolution, a very simple model of 1,000 monkeys randomly hitting the keys of a typewriter, with every meaningful set of 10 letters being selected, shows the enormous power that small steps and natural selection play in the evolution of complex structures. Without small steps and selection, the Intelligent Design theorists and creationists would be correct—the probabilities of obtaining a meaningful outcome in a single step are remote in the extreme. However, the simple addition of multiple small steps with natural selection at each step allows the evolution of very complex structures and organisms.

Basic Argument from Improbability

One of the favorite ploys of the Intelligent Design group is to argue that the probability of something occurring in a single step is so remote that a supernatural being must have performed it. This whole area has been referred to as the *Basic Argument from Improbability (BAI)*. [10p126] The purpose is to "prove" that something cannot happen by displaying huge negative exponentials—then claiming that evolution or some aspect of biology is false because the mathematical probability of it occurring is so low that it is effectively impossible. For those uncomfortable with numbers and statistics, what does the term *huge negative exponentials* mean?

If 10 people are in a pool, betting on the outcome of a football game and only one person can win, the chance of winning is 1 in 10, or 1/10. Written in the decimal numbering system, this is 0.1. If there were a thousand people in the pool, the chance would be 1/1000 or .001. As the chances of winning get smaller, the number of zeros after the decimal point gets larger and soon it is difficult to keep track of them. Thus, the number can be written in its exponential form, in this case 10^{-3}. The $^{-3}$ indicates you have to count three positions in the minus direction (left) to find where to put the decimal point, i.e., .001. Thus, if we say the chance of X occurring is 10^{-10} this would represent .0000000001, or 1 in 10 billion, a very small chance.

As an example of BAI, in a book entitled *Scientific Creationism*, Morris [11] calculated that the chance of a given organism occurring in one step was 10^{-53} or one chance in a hundred million billion billion billion billion billion, or essentially no chance at all. The granddaddy of all BAIs is that of Hoyle and Wickramasinghe. [12] They estimated the chance that the amino acids would randomly line up to form the first hemoglobin molecule was 10^{-850}. This is a truly low probability since there are only 10^{80} atoms in the whole universe.

These statements make a number of fundamental mistakes. First, they assume the organism or structure in question was formed in a single step. The whole point of the theory of evolution is that many thousands if not millions of steps were required over several billion years to get to the point of discussion.

In the case of hemoglobin, it also ignores the fact that as long as the amino acid histidine was present to bind heme, there were thousands of different amino acid sequences that could do the oxygen-carrying work of hemoglobin. They also ignore the power of natural selection. As illustrated in the discussion above on digital evolution, a one-step probability of 1 in a thousand trillion trillion, or 10^{-26}, was reduced to 1 in 1, or 10^{-0}, when selection was added.

A final mistake is that BAI is often an exercise in absurdity. For example, using the above reasoning let's assume that I wish to determine the chance that I am really sitting at my desk. Given the size of the universe, there are at least 10^{+53} places I could be instead. Thus, there is only a 10^{-53} chance I will be where I am. Since this is such a small number, I must not exist! This is reminiscent of the story of the man who returns home early and hears a noise in the bedroom. He opens the door just in time to see the closet door close. When he opens the closet door he finds a naked man standing there and asks,

"What are you doing in my closet?"

To which the man replies, "Everybody has to be somewhere."

I too have to be somewhere. Adding up all the places I could be does not affect the probability that I am where I am.

> **Quoting ridiculously low probabilities that a gene or organ or organism could arise by chance in a single step ignores three fundamental features:**
> - **The evolution of these items took place in millions of small steps over billions of years, not in a single step.**
> - **Natural selection was also involved—an enormously powerful added factor.**
> - **By not taking these fundamental elements of evolution into consideration—random variation plus selection—it is easy to misrepresent the probability of events.**

Modularity

The power of reusing modules ranging from whole genomes to mitochondria, chloroplasts, whole genes, domains, exons, and sub-exons is of such importance that it will be emphasized and reemphasized. The examples of so called "irreducible complexity" given by Behe and other Intelligent Designers can all be answered by the power of modules. The following is a simple example of the power of the use of modules originally designed for one purpose, for a new purpose.

Evolution of a car. It could be claimed that a car is an example of irreducible complexity. Since many of its parts are critical to the function of the car, losing any one would result in a car that did not work. Therefore a car cannot be the result of evolution because the probability of simultaneously evolving all functioning parts is essentially zero.

The fallacy of this line of reasoning lies in two assumptions.

1. The car could not work when some of its parts are missing. For the purposes of this discussion and to keep it simple, I will assume that the chassis, motor, wheels and battery are the proposed irreducible components. The Intelligent Designers often state that a given example cannot function when one of its parts is removed. This is frequently not true. In the car example, a car without a motor or a battery is a cart—in use for centuries to carry goods. The motors only made it easier.

2. None of the parts had a function independent of the car. In my example, the chassis, wheels, motor, and battery also had other purposes before the car was invented. Figure 2 illustrates how a complex structure like the automobile is both reducible in that parts can be removed and still leave some functionality and modular in that the different component parts have other functions independent of the function they carried out in the automobile. This simple example illustrates three important points.

- The cases proposed by Behe and other Intelligent Designers are often reducible (not irreducible), since they can function at a more primitive level without needing every component.
- All the components do not have to evolve simultaneously—parts or modules often served other functions before they were incorporated into a more complex structure.
- A final important point is that the final structure may simply show what might be best called *pseudo-irreducibility*. The automobile serves as an example. If any of the four above components are removed the automobile does not work as an automobile. If we take out the engine, for example, it can no longer function as an automobile but it can function very well as a cart to transport things. In subsequent chapters I will further illustrate this concept.

Cases of so-called "irreducible complexity" are often not irreducible. In addition, the complex organ is often modular in that it is composed of modules that had a different use before being incorporated into the more complex function. This eliminates the necessity for all parts to evolve simultaneously.

In the following chapters I address some of the specific claims of irreducible complexity proposed by the Intelligent Designers and illustrate some of these points. For each claim I will ask two questions—It is really irreducible? Is it modular? The two questions are closely related; if the parts are modular, the system is reducible.

It is not my purpose to provide detailed answers to every complaint of the Intelligent Design creationists. My purpose is to show that when all the available information about these systems is examined, they are all both reducible and modular. For one of these systems, the immune system, I refer the interested reader to articles on the web by Inley [13] since it would have taken a very dedicated lay reader to ascend the learning curve necessary to follow the reasons why all the aspects of the immune system claimed by Behe [4] to be irreducibly complex are actually reducible and modular.

"Complexity" Evolution of the Automobile

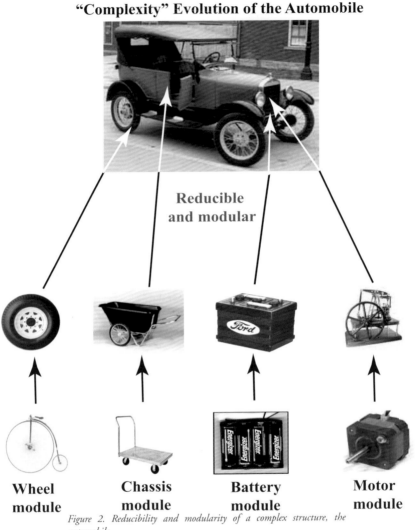

Figure 2. Reducibility and modularity of a complex structure, the automobile.

For several of the following chapters I thank the many other authors who have led the way in responding to Intelligent Design claims that some systems are irreducibly complex and can only be explained by Intelligent Design. [2,14-18] Two excellent web sites devoted to answering Intelligent Design are www.talkorigins.org and www.talkdesign.org.

References

1. Paley, W. *Natural Theology: Or, Evidences of the Existence of His Attributes of the Diety, Collected from the Appearances of Nature.* Fauldner, London, 1802.

2. Dawkins, R. *The Blind Watchmaker. Why the Evidence of Evolution Reveals a Universe Without Design.* W. W. Norton & Company, Inc., New York, 1996.

3.   Behe, M. J. *Darwin's Black Box.* The Free Press, New York, 1996.

4.   Wolfram, S. *Mathematica.* Wolfram Media, Inc., Champaign, IL, 1991.

5.   Wolfram, S. *A New Kind of Science.* Wolfram Media, Inc., Champaign, IL, 2002.

6.   Lenski, R. E., Ofria, C., Pennock, R. T. & Adami, C. The evolutionary origin of complex features. *Nature.* 423: 139-144, 2003.

7.   Zimmer, C. Testing Darwin. *Discovery.* 29-35, 2005.

8.   Schneider, T. D. Evolution of biological information. *Nucleic Acids Res.* 28: 2794-2799, 2000.

9.   Pennock, R. T. *Tower of Babel.* MIT Press, Cambridge, MA, 1999.

10. Forrest, B. & Gross, P. R. *Creationism's Trojan Horse. The Wedge of Intelligent Design.* Oxford University Press, New York, 2004.

11. Morris, H. *Scientific Creationism.* ed. Edition, P. S. Master Books, Green Forest, AR, 1974.

12. Hoyle, F. & Wickramasinghe, C. *Evolution from Space.* J. M. Dent & Sons, London, 1981.

13. Inlay, M. Evolving Immunity. A Response to Chapter 6 of Darwin's Black Box. www.talkdesign.org/faqs/Evolving_immunity.html

14. Shermer, M. *How We Believe. Science, Skepticism, and the Search for God.* A. W. H. Freeman, New York, 2000.

15. Pennock, R. T. *Intelligent Design: Creationism and Its Critics.* MIT Press, Cambridge, MA, 2001.

16. Young, M. & Edis, T. *Why Intelligent Design Fails.* Rutgers University Press, New Brunswick, NJ, 2004.

17. Perakh, M. *Unintelligent Design.* Prometheus Books, Amherst, NY, 2004.

18. Miller, K. *Finding Darwin's God.* Harper Perennial, New York, 1999.

Chapter 8

Complexity—Eyes

Being able to see where you are going, where your food is, and where your enemies are has such a powerful advantage for animal survival that it is little wonder that over 40 different independent solutions for serviceable image-forming eyes have evolved with at least nine different design principles. These include pinhole eyes (like ours), curved reflectors, and multiple types of compound eyes. [1] I have started these chapters on complexity with eyes because Darwin also discussed eyes as an example of how complex structures could have evolved. The following are some of the things Darwin said about the evolution of eyes:

> Numerous gradations from a simple and imperfect eye to one complex and perfect can be shown to exist, each grade being useful to its possessor.

Darwin viewed such evolution as occurring in multiple steps. One was connecting a nerve to light-sensitive areas of the skin.

> I may remark that some of the lowest organisms, in which nerves cannot be detected, are capable of perceiving light, it does not seem impossible that certain sensitive elements in their sarcode [protoplasm] should become aggregated and developed into nerves, endowed with this special sensitivity.

He quotes an M. Jourdain as finding

> …aggregates of pigment cells, apparently serving as organs of vision, without nerve cells and resting merely on protoplasm that serve only to distinguish light from dark. In certain star-fishes [sic], small depressions in the layer of pigment which surrounds the nerve are filled with transparent gelatinous matter, projecting with a convex surface, like the cornea of higher animals…this serves not to form an image, but only to concentrate the luminous rays and render their perception more easy [sic].

Darwin described numerous other intermediate forms of light and image perceiving organs. For example, bacteria are able to swim toward the light using nothing more than a nerveless, lensless patch of pigment containing light sensitive material. In essence he pointed out that the eye is not irreducibly complex because some organisms had primitive but functioning parts of the whole.

A Computer Model of the Evolution of Refractory Index

The eye is a unique organ for a computer-based analysis of evolution because specific numbers can easily represent the structures necessary for image formation. In this case the quantified variable is visual acuity or spatial resolution. It is the sole reason for the eye's optical design and is measured in terms of the ability for each photoreceptor to have a different field of view. [2] Nilsson and Pelzer [3] felt that the evolution of visual acuity of the vertebrate, pinhole-type of eye was especially amenable to examination by a computer simulation program.

They started with a simple patch of light-sensitive cells that was backed and surrounded by dark pigment.

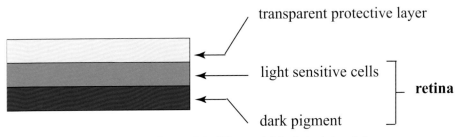

Figure 1. Initial stage of the Nilsson and Pelzer [3] simulation of the evolution of morphological aspects of the eye.

They then exposed this to selection for better and better visual acuity. There were two possible ways for this to occur: A) by forming a central depression in the light sensitive patch or B) by developing the pinhole. Both would reduce the angle through which the individual light-sensitive cells receive light. They found that initially deepening the pit was by far the most efficient. However, at a certain point, decreasing the aperture by forming the pinhole was more efficient. As the aperture decreased, the amount of light entering the eye also decreased. At a certain other point a further increase in visual acuity was only possible with the addition of a lens. Unlike man-made lenses, biological lenses do not have the same refractive index throughout. A smooth gradient of refractive index offers a superior design.

Nilsson and Pelzer made a conservative estimate that each evolutionary step based on genetic variation would make a one percent change in any quantitative character. The calculated number of one percent changes required between each stage was plotted against the number of resolvable image points within the eye's visual field. This showed that the spatial resolution improved almost linearly with morphological changes *indicating there were no particularly difficult steps in the process.* Figure 2 summarizes the different changes in the structure of the eye over time and the number of steps between each stage. The relative change in receptor diameter required to keep the light sensitivity constant throughout the sequence is represented by the letter *d.*

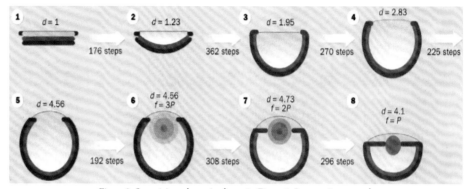

Figure 2. Stage 1 is as shown in shown in Figure 1. In successive stages the top protective layer deepens to form the vitreous body of the eye. The refractive index of the vitreous body is assumed to be 1.35, which is only slightly higher than water. In stages 4 and 5 the retina continues to grow (increasing d) but without changing the radius of the curvature. This causes a gradual shift from deepening the retinal pit to construction of the pinhole. In stages 6 to 8 a graded refractory index lens appears with a local increase in refractive index. The central refractive index increases from an initial 1.35 to 1.52. Simultaneously the lens changes shape from ellipsoid to spherical and moves to the center of the curvature of the retina. As the lens shrinks, a flat iris gradually forms by stretching of the original aperture. The focal length (f) of the lens gradually shortens, and in stage 8 it equals the distance to the retina (P), producing a sharply focused system. Figure from Nilsson and Pelzer. [3] By permission from Proc Biol Sci. 256: 53-58, 1994 as modified by Dawkins. [1]

Nilsson and Pelzer made a great effort to keep the model conservative. Thus, they allowed only a one percent change at each step and excluded parallel steps. Each step had to occur in series, a caveat that eliminated Behe's concerns that multiple simultaneous steps would be unlikely. Using additional conservative values for the selective advantages of each step, they estimated the entire process could be completed in fewer than 400,000 steps. In an article entitled "The eye in a twinkling," Dawkins [1] stated,

> ...the time needed for the evolution of the eye, far from stretching credulity with its vastness, turns out to be too short for geologists to measure. It is a geological blink.

Figure 3 shows a collection of different eyes from a simple eyespot to the complex eye, which has occurred independently at least a dozen times in natural history. This shows that the stages shown in Figure 2 are not purely theoretical but have some basis in real evolution.

The many different functioning eyes, from simple to complex, again illustrate that the eye is not irreducible. The fact that evolution produced so many different solutions to the need to see, and produced them many different times, indicates that eyes are not an impossibly complex problem for evolution.

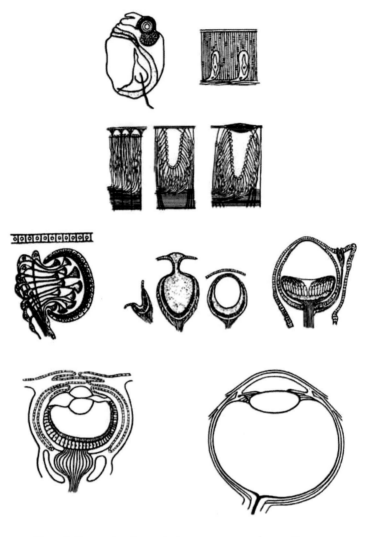

Figure 3. Eyes ranging from a single eyespot to a complex eye. From Michael Shermer, How We Believe. *2000. [4] By permission.*

In his section on "Organs of Extreme Perfection and Complication," Darwin himself recognized that while the eye was a challenge for his theory, there was plenty of evidence to suggest it evolved by many small steps, starting with a simple light-sensitive patch. Evolution has produced many different types of eyes, from simple to complex, many different times, indicating eyes are not irreducible and not an impossibly complex problem. Since many aspects of the eye can be easily reduced to numbers, Nilsson and Pelzer were able to perform a computer simulation of the evolution of the eye using tiny, non-overlapping steps. Despite using very conservative parameters, they found the modern eye could evolve in less than 400,000 generations—a blink of the eye in geological time.

References

1.   Dawkins, R. The eye in a twinkling. Nature. 368: 690-691, 1994.
2.   Snyder, A. W., Laughlin, S. B. & Stavenga, D. G. Information capacity of eyes. *Vision Research.* 17: 1163-1175, 1977.
3.   Nilsson, D. E. & Pelger, S. A pessimistic estimate of the time required for an eye to evolve. *Proc Biol Sci.* 256: 53-58, 1994.
4.   Shermer, M. *How We Believe.* A. W. H. Freeman, New York, 2000.

With maleus
Aforethought
Mammals
Got an earful of their ancestors
Jaw

John Burns
Biograffiti, 1975 [1]

Chapter 9

Complexity—Ears

Fish hear by sensing the vibrations in the water. These vibrations pass through sensory organs called lateral lines that run along the side of the body. Small neuromast structures sense this vibration and activate sensory nerves that pass these sensations to the inner ear located near the head. This system is very efficient because water is dense and the energy conveyed by vibrations is quite sufficient to activate the sensory nerves of the lateral lines and then the hearing apparatus of the inner ear.

Evolution then took a giant step and some animals evolved from fish to land based tetrapods. The inner ear, with its sensory hairs embedded in a liquid medium, remained fundamentally the same as for fish. But there was a problem. Air is much less dense, than water and it was now necessary to develop a method of amplifying the weak vibrations in air into vibrations that were strong enough to move the liquid in the inner ear.

Evolution of the Mammalian Jaw

The mechanism by which this took place is intimately wrapped up with the complaint by creationists that evolution from the jaw of the reptiles to the jaw of mammals was impossible since no intermediates had been found. The committed young earth creationist Duane Gish especially advanced this position in his 1978 book, *Evolution? The Fossils Say No:* [2p80]

> All mammals, living or fossil, have a single bone, the dentary, on each side of the lower jaw, and all mammals, living or fossil, have three auditory ossicles or ear bones, the malleus, incus and stapes…Every reptile, living or fossil, however, has at least four bones in the lower jaw and only one auditory ossicle, the stapes…There are no transitional fossil forms

showing, for instance, three or two jawbones, or two ear bones. No one has explained yet, for that matter, how the transitional form would have managed to chew while his jaw was being unhinged and rearticulated, or how he could hear while dragging two of his jaw bones into his ear.

With some modifications the same charges were repeated in his 1995 book *Evolution: The Fossils Still Say No.*[3] The following diagrams illustrate the issues. In the reptile *Pelycosaur*, the squamosal bone is just above and makes contact with the quadrate (Figure 1, in light blue).

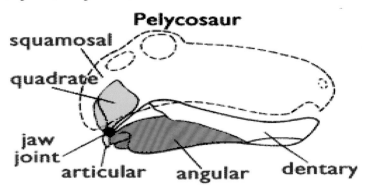

Figure 1. Reptile (Pelycosaur) jaw. From Kardong, Vertebrates. Comparative Anatomy, Function, Evolution. *McGraw Hill, 2002.*[4p275] *By permission.*

The jaw joint (black) consists of an articulation between four bones: the quadrate, articular, angular and dentary bones. By contrast the early mammalian jaw is shown in Figure 2.

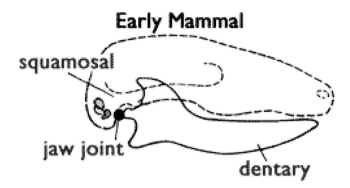

Figure 2. Early mammalian jaw. From Kardong, 2002.[4p275] *By permission.*

Here the jaw joint (black) consists of an articulation between two bones, the dentary and the squamosal. The quadrate has become the incus (blue), the articular has become the malleus (yellow), and the angular has become the stapes (pink). Thus, the issue raised by creationists was "how the transitional form would have managed to chew while his jaw was being unhinged and rearticulated, or how he could hear while dragging two of his jaw bones into his ear." Figure 3 shows the *Therapsid* transitional intermediate and provides the answer.

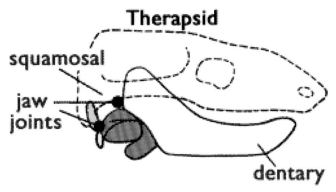

Figure 3. Therapsid jaw. From Kardong, 2002. [4p275] *By permission.*

This intermediate form has two jaw joints, retaining the reptile joint consisting of the articulation of only three bones, the quadrate (blue), the angular (pink) and now the articular (yellow). This freed up the dentary to form a second mammalian-like jaw joint with the squamosal bone. This, in turn, freed the quadrate to become the incus, the angular to become the stapes (pink) and the articular to become the malleus (yellow).

The positioning of these three early bones in the human ear is shown in Figure 4.

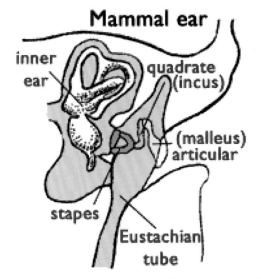

Figure 4. Human ear. Quadrate—incus (yellow), articular—malleus (yellow), and stapes (pink). From Theobald. [5] *By permission.*

Three little bones in the middle ear of mammals serve to amplify the weak vibrations in air so they can move the fluid in the inner ear and translate sound into nerve transmissions.

I have presented the evolution of the mammalian ear because it illustrates so well the dictum enunciated by Gould [6p101] that "Complex creatures exist by virtue of slop, multiple use, and redundancy." For example, the major purpose of the early stapes was as a structural support of the jaw. [7] It had a minor role in respiration and in hearing. When the jaw articulation was shifted to the squamosal-dentate of the mammalian version, the stapes was now redundant slop and free to shift to hearing as its major function. After the articulation of the squamosal and the dentary bones, a similar redundancy allowed the quadrate and the articular bones to shift from a primary function of support to a primary function of hearing. This point about multiple use and redundancy in evolution will be repeated in subsequent chapters.

The evolution of the ear well illustrates the dictum, "Complex structures exist by virtue of slop, multiple use, and redundancy." All three bones of the mammalian ear became slop and redundant when their prior function as part of the reptilian jaw was replaced by other bones. They could then be used for the critically important task of hearing.

References

1. Burns, J. M. *Biograffiti: A natural selection.* Demeter Press, New York, 1975.
2. Gish, D. T. *Evolution? The Fossils Say No.* Creation-Life Publishers, San Diego, 1978.
3. Gish, D. T. *Evolution: The Fossils Still Say No.* The Institute for Creation Research, El Cajon, 1995.
4. Kardong, R. V. *Vertebrates: Comparative Anatomy, Function, Evolution.* McGraw Hill, New York, 2002.
5. Theobald, D. *29+ Evidences for Macroevolution. Part I. The Unique Universal Phylogenetic Tree.* www.talk.origins.org. By permission.
6. Gould, S. J. *Eight Little Piggies.* W. W. Norton & Company, New York, 1993.
7. Clack, J. A. Discovery of the earliest known tetrapod stapes. *Nature.* 343: 425-427, 1989.

Chapter 10

Complexity—The Citric Acid Cycle

One of the most important things that a living cell needs is energy. In all forms of life this energy is supplied by a high-energy phosphate-phosphate chemical bond provided by a compound called ATP or adenosine tri-phosphate. This structure is shown in Figure 1.

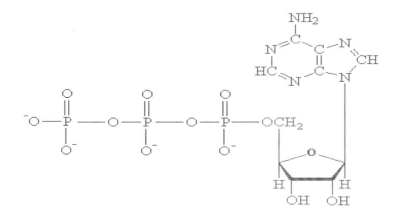

Figure 1. ATP. Adenine is in red, ribose in magenta, and the chain of three phosphate groups is shown in blue. [1]

The third phosphate group is the one that carries the high-energy bond and serves as the energy source of the cell. This chemical form of energy currency can be spent in many different chemical reactions in the organisms that need energy to work. The primary source of the energy is glucose (sugar). One sugar molecule is converted into as many as 38 ATP molecules. The first stage of this process is called glycolosis. This converts glucose into two pyruvate molecules and in the process produces 6 ATPs. An enzyme called pyruvate dehydrogenase converts pyruvate + coenzyme A (coA) to acetyl-coA, which is then converted by another enzyme into oxaloacetate. This is then passed through a series of eight chemical reactions using eight different enzymes, ending up again with oxaloacetate. The whole cycle is called the *citric acid cycle*. It is also called the *Krebs cycle,* after the biochemist Hans Krebs who first worked it out. It is shown in Figure 2.

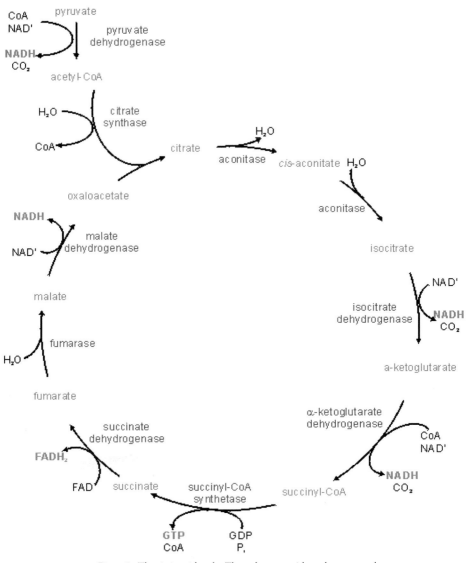

Figure 2. The citric acid cycle. The cycle starts with oxaloacetate and progresses through eight other chemical structures (blue) before ending up again with oxal-acetate. Names of the enzymes involved are in red. The various cofactors are in green. From www.pnf.org.

Talk about complex! The citric acid cycle is both one of the most important and most complex of the metabolic pathways. Surely if there was ever something with "irreducible complexity," this should be it. If this can be the product of Darwinian evolution, anything can. But how? Two research groups, Melendez-Hevia and colleagues[2] and Huynen and colleagues[3] have examined the evolution of the citric acid cycle. Melendez-Hevia and colleagues[2] pointed out that the citric acid cycle was the result of opportunism in molecular evolution.

Their introductory remarks are highly relevant to the issues raised by Intelligent Design and creationism.

> During the origin and evolution of metabolism, in the first cells, when a need arises for a new pathway, there are two different possible strategies available to achieve this purpose: (1) create new pathways utilizing new compounds not previously available or (2) adapt and make good use of the enzymes catalyzing reactions already existing in the cell. Clearly, the opportunism of the second strategy, when it is possible, has a number of selective advantages, because it allows a quick and economic solution of new problems. Thus, in the evolution of a new metabolic pathway, new mechanisms must be created only if "pieces" to the complete puzzle are missing. Creation of the full pathway by a *de novo* method is expensive in material, time-consuming, and cannot compete with the opportunistic strategy. [1]

It was found that only one "new" enzyme was needed to complete the citric acid cycle—succinyl-CoA synthase (see Figure 2). *All the other steps previously existed for a different purpose.*

In their study of the evolution of the citric acid cycle, Huynen and colleagues examined 19 different genomes that had been completely sequenced by 1999. These included four Archea, 14 Bacteria, and one Eukaryote. Many of these organisms still generated ATP despite missing one or more of the involved enzymes. In addition, for many of the organisms some reactions were catalyzed by more than one enzyme, a situation they called non-homologous gene replacement. This is equivalent to the evolutionary opportunism of Melendez-Hevia. Many of the enzymes involved had more than one function. Thus, the citric acid cycle was both reducible and modular.

Many of the mechanisms described in this chapter and Chapter 6, including horizontal gene transfer, gene duplication, domain, exon and sub-exon exchange, gene displacement, and evolutionary opportunism, were utilized in the evolution of the citric acid cycle. In summary, Melendez-Hevia and colleagues stated:

> The Krebs cycle was built through a process that Jacob[4] called "evolution by tinkering," stating that evolution does not produce novelties from scratch. It works on what already exists. The most novel result of our analysis is seeing how, with minimal raw material, evolution created the most important pathway of metabolism, achieving the best chemically possible design. In this case, a chemical engineer who was looking for the best design of the process could not have found a better design than the cycle which works in living cells. [2]

The citric acid cycle is an extremely complex metabolic pathway that is critical for energy production by living cells. Despite being complex it is highly reducible. Multiple different evolutionary mechanisms were involved in its evolution, including horizontal gene transfer, gene duplication, domain, exon and sub-exon exchange, gene displacement, and evolutionary opportunism. The citric acid cycle is an outstanding example of how complex pathways can be the product of a rich range of evolutionary tools.

References

1. Figure from www.bris.ac.uk/Depts/Chemistry/MOTM/atp/atp1.htm. By permission.
2. Melendez-Hevia, E., Waddell, T. G. & Cascante, M. The puzzle of the Krebs citric acid cycle: Assembling the pieces of chemically feasible reactions, and opportunism in the design of metabolic pathways during evolution. *J Mol Evol.* 43: 293-303, 1996.
3. Huynen, M. A., Dandekar, T. & Bork, P. Variation and evolution of the citric-acid cycle: A genomic perspective. *Trends Microbiol.* 7: 281-291, 1999.
4. Jacob, F. Evolution by tinkering. *Science.* 196: 1161-1166, 1977.

Chapter 11

Complexity—Blood Clotting

Like each of the systems discussed in previous chapters—vision, hearing, and energy production—the ability to keep from bleeding to death after an injury is also critical to survival. In vertebrates this has evolved into a complex, multi-step cascade that progressively and quickly amplifies the signal as the cascade progresses, finally providing for the development of a large fibrin blood clot to stem the potentially lethal flow of blood from a wound. This cascade can be set off by an extrinsic system responding to tissue damage, or an intrinsic system responding to vascular insults. The relationship of these two systems is shown in Figure 1 (next page).

The initial resting or inactive proteins are in red. These proteins are cut by an enzymatic reaction called *proteolysis*. The resultant products are in green or yellow. The enzymes doing the cutting are called *proteases*. Because they act at sites where the amino acid *serine* is present, they are called *serine proteases*.

If any one of the steps are left out, clotting does not occur or occurs too easily. Because of this, Behe [2] termed this a system of irreducible complexity and thus an example of Intelligent Design. As is true of most complex systems, he was not the first to wonder how they could have evolved. Russel Doolittle spent a lifetime researching the evolution of blood clotting. When he was a graduate student in the 1960s he asked himself, "How in the world did this complex and delicately balanced process ever evolve?" [3] In contrast to Behe, who simply threw up his hands and only heard the piercing cry of "design!", Doolittle set about attempting to answer the question in a more scientific manner.

Evidence that the cascade did not evolve all at once came from a careful examination of the molecular evolution of the clotting proteins see Table 1 (end of chapter) illustrates the fact that the first set of coagulation factors made their appearance 900 million years ago, while the last addition was only 200 million years ago.

The evolution of the clotting factors is a classic tale of gene duplication and exon and domain shuffling (Figure 2). As discussed previously, domains are segments of genes that have a proven function and can be exchanged between genes and used to facilitate the rapid evolution of new genes. Some of the domains involved in the clotting proteins are the GLA (**G**) domains that contain multiple γ-carboxy-glutamic acid residues whose synthesis depends upon vitamin K; EGF or epidermal growth

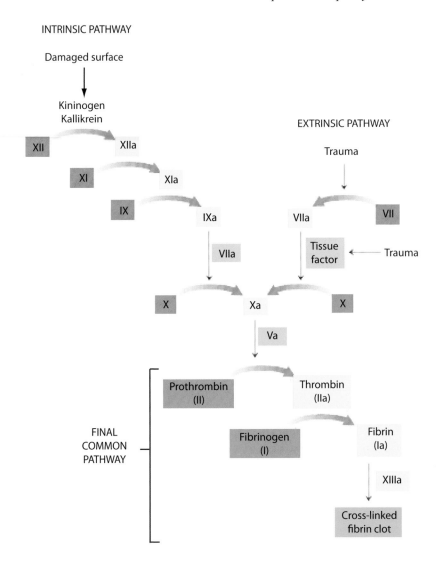

Figure 1. The blood clotting cascade. [4a] *See text.*

factor domains (**E**); kringles (**K**) which are modules involved in protein-protein binding [4]; PAN or proteasone-activating-nucleotidase domains involved in protein folding (**P**); fibronectin 1 (**F1**) and fibronectin 2 (**F2**) domains involved in cell adhesion; and serine protease (**SP**) domains. The details of what all these domains do are not as important as the concept that most of the coagulation proteins share many functions in common because they share many domains in common.

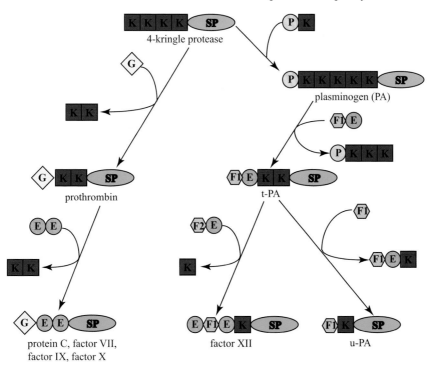

Figure 2. Evolution of coagulation factors. From Jiang and Doolittle, The evolution of vertebrate blood coagulation as viewed from a comparison of puffer fish and sea squirt genomes. PNAS. 100:7527-7532.[6] *By permission of the National Academy of Sciences, USA. Copyright 2003.*

Figure 2 shows how the different coagulation proteins can evolve from a common 4-kringle-serine protease precursor similar to that found in the sea squirt. As stated by Doolittle,[3] "This bespeaks of a wild frenzy of gene duplication and exon shuffling during a relatively brief episode just before the appearance of true vertebrates."

The mechanism of the evolution of the complex blood clotting cascade is understandable when it is observed that different components did not appear all at once but developed over a period of 400 million years and that most of the proteins involved are closely related serine proteases whose similarities are accounted for by gene duplication and whose differences are accounted for by the shuffling around of a small number of different functional domains.

How did the cascades evolve? In attempting to defend himself against the criticisms of his use of the blood clotting system as an example of irreducible complexity, Behe[2] criticized the invoking of gene duplication and exon shuffling as "so much hand waving." He claimed that gene duplication was irrelevant since it was not evidence *per se* for natural selection. This claim ignores the fact that gene duplication and natural selection are extremely interwoven concepts. As described previously, due to the power of gene duplication there are now two copies of a gene, one copy can continue to carry out its original function. Natural selection ensures that any mutations of the original gene would not be tolerated since they would likely reduce the fitness of the organism. At the same time, freedom from elimination by natural selection allows the duplicated gene to experiment with a number of random mutations. If, by chance, those changes provide a new function that is advantageous to the organism, natural selection now increases the fitness of the organism. Thus, *gene duplication has natural selection written all over it.*

Often when the environment changes there is a selective advantage to developing a new function. An Intelligent Design or supernatural solution would simply be a wave of God's hand and voilá—there would be a new gene. Since there are thousands of permutations of different amino acid sequences that could accomplish this task, the chance that the sequence of the new gene would resemble the sequence of any old gene would be remote. In fact, because of gene duplication, there is extensive similarity between the sequence or the old gene and the new gene. This alone falsifies the ID hypothesis and validates the process of evolution.

Behe's related complaint is that gene duplication and exon shuffling does not explain why nature found it necessary to build complicated multiple layers of actions into the blood clotting system and how it was done. Table 1 provides some clues and helps to answer Behe's complaint. The clotting system of 900 million years ago included only fibrinogen, prothrombin, tissue factor, and plasminogen. Figure 3 shows what such a system would look like back in the Precambrian or Proterzoic eon, when only the extrinsic pathway was in place. Clotting was adequate for the primitive, low-blood pressure organisms of that time. This illustrates what I mean by *pseudo-irreducible.*

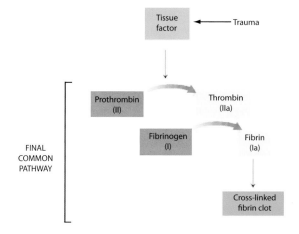

Figure 3. Figure 1, but with only the clotting proteins that existed in the Precambrian time.

If all the parts missing in Figure 3 were removed from a modern vertebrate, they would quickly bleed to death following injury. But the low "blood pressure"

Precambrian organisms obviously fared well—thus the term *pseudo-irreducible*. With this clotting system, trauma elicits the release of tissue factors. Factor X and Factor V are not yet present. These primitive organisms do not have an intrinsic clotting system because an elaborate vascular system did not exist. Clotting was a very simple system consisting of the conversion of fibrinogen to fibrin by the action of thrombin presumably produced by the direct action of tissue factor on prothrombin.

The modern clotting system is almost unique in requiring a finely tuned system of checks and balances. Too little clot and the organism bleeds to death. Too much clot and the organism dies of excessive thrombosis. Thus, as animal life evolved into more complex organisms with a better vascular system, there was also a need for an intrinsic activating system.

Five hundred million years ago Factors V, VII, X and XII were also present. Figure 4 (next page) summarizes this clotting pathway. The whole progress is now largely restricted to fine-tuning the extrinsic pathway. This makes sense because the Cambrian organisms still had a low-pressure primitive vascular system. The major dangers are still from external injury. Now, instead of acting directly on prothrombin, tissue factor acts by interacting with a series of serine protease factors VII, V, and X, all of which are easily produced by gene duplication. [3] Factor XII has come into existence as a primitive start of the intrinsic activating system. As a serine protease it can easily serve the function of Factor IX of later systems, also a serine protease.

Subsequent steps in evolution act to fine-tune this system. Thus, contrary to Behe's complaints, the slow addition of layers of the coagulation system over time—first to fine-tune the extrinsic system, then to initiate the intrinsic system, and finally to enhance sensitivity and provide for a more rapid response system when the increase in blood pressure makes a rapid response critical to survival—is both reducible and easy to understand.

The clotting system is not irreducible. In primitive Precambrian organisms, the presence of only fibrinogen, prothrombin, tissue factor, and plasminogen worked well for an extrinsic activation-only system in organisms with a primitive vascular system and low "blood pressure." Over the next 400 million years the major advance was to fine-tune the extrinsic activation system using two related serine proteases. Since that time, as the vascular system improved and blood pressure increased, there was a fine-tuning of the intrinsic activating system. These steps make the progressive addition by natural selection of multiple steps in the cascade easy to understand. This is hardly the picture of an irreducibly complex system that requires a divine creator to bring into existence all at once.

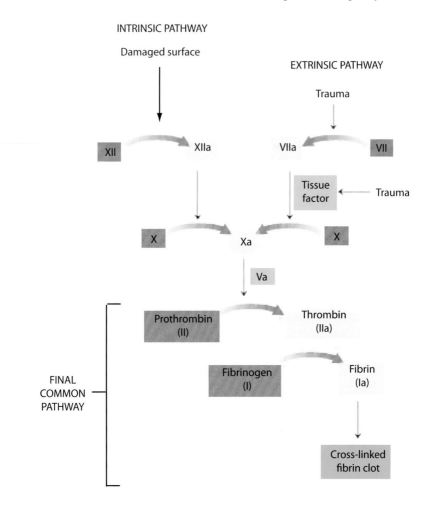

Figure 4. Clotting proteins as of 500 million years ago.

References

1. Figure from from wiki.cotch.net/index.php/Blood_clotting. By permission.
2. Behe, M. J. *Darwin's Black Box.* The Free Press, New York, 1996.
3. Doolittle, R. F. The evolution of vertebrate blood coagulation. A case of Yin and Yang. *Thrombosis and Hemostasis.* 70: 24-28, 1993.
4. Doolittle, R. F. & Feng, D. F. Reconstructing the evolution of vertebrate blood coagulation from a consideration of the amino acid sequences of clotting proteins. *Cold Spring Harb Symp Quant Biol.* 52: 869-874, 1987.
4a. From wiki.cotch.net/index.php/Blood_clotting. By permission.
5. Patthy, L., Trexler, M., Vali, Z., Banyai, L. & Varadi, A. Kringles: modules specialized for protein binding. Homology of the gelatin-binding region of fibronectin with the kringle structures of proteases. *FEBS Lett.* 171: 131-136, 1984.
6. Jiang, Y. & Doolittle, R. F. The evolution of vertebrate blood coagulation as viewed from a comparison of puffer fish and sea squirt genomes. *Proc Natl Acad Sci USA.* 100: 7527-7532, 2003.

Table 1. An Inferred Order of Appearance of Some Blood-Clotting and Fibrinolytic Proteins. *From Doolittle and Feng.* [4]

Factor	Million Years Ago
Fibrinogen	900
Prothrombin	
Tissue factor	
Plasminogen	
Factor V	500
Factor VII	
Factor X	
Factor XII	
Factor VII	450
Factor IX	
Factor XI	
Prokalikrein	200

Chapter 12

Complexity—Cilia

Cilia and flagella are high on the list of examples proposed by Intelligent Designers as showing irreducible complexity. Since cilia are a subpart of flagella, I will examine them first. Cilia are fine, hair-like structures that beat like a whip and are used to either aid in the locomotion of a cell like a sperm or to move objects around the outside of a cell. In the respiratory tract, cilia serve to move dust and other particles out of the lungs. A cross section of a typical cilium is shown in Figure 1.

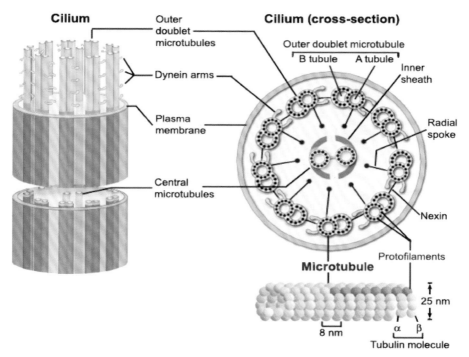

Figure 1. Structure of a lengthwise (left) and cross-section (right) of a cilium. [1]

The essence of a cilium is the presence of nine microtubule doublets in an outer circle and two single microtubules in the center. This is referred to as a 9 + 2 pattern. Cyanobacteria possess cilia that are of extremely primitive origin. The motion they provide give them a tremendous competitive advantage [2] by allowing the organism to pull food toward it and to escape from adversity. The other structures such as dynein and nexin attach to the microtubules and play a role in the mobility of the cilia. The doublets are formed by the fusion of two microtubules. Each microtubule is formed of 13 strands or protofilaments of the protein tubulin. Tubulin comes in two forms, alpha and beta, each with a slightly different amino acid sequence. The slightly different structure allows them to stack on top of each other, like a pile of saucers.

In addition to its role in cilia and flagella, tubulin is a module that also plays a critical role in cell division, where it forms the strands that the chromosomes are attached to during mitosis and plays a role in the transport of compounds inside the cell. Taxol, an important drug in the treatment of breast cancer, works by interfering with the function of tubulin, thus stopping cell division. This observation led to increased interest in the 3-D structure of tubulin. This was worked out by Nogales, Wolf and Downing[3] and is shown in Figure 2.

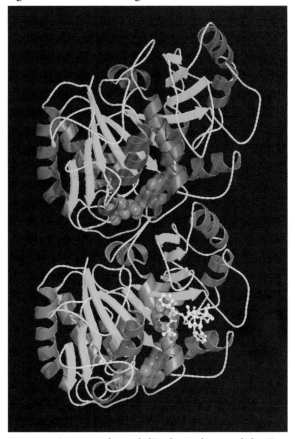

Figure 2. Structure of a tubulin dimer determined by X-ray crystallography at a resolution of 3.7 angstroms. Each monomer is formed by a core of two beta sheets (blue and green) surrounded by helices and each binds to a guanine nucleotide (pink). In addition to a nucleotide binding site, each monomer also has two other binding sites, one for protein and the other for taxol (yellow). From Nogales et al. Cell. 1999.[3] By permission.

Each monomer had three interlinked but different domains, one for binding to nucleotides (guanine in pink), one that binds to drugs like taxol (in yellow), and one that binds to other proteins.

Behe [4] reviewed biochemical studies of the mechanism by which cilia move. The energy for motion is supplied by ATP. When ATP is added to cilia that are stripped of their plasma membrane, they still move normally. However, when stripped of dynein they do not move. Dynein is considered the motor. When stripped of nexin the cilia get longer and longer, indicating the cross-linking by nexin is necessary to prevent this. Behe proposed that since cilia do not move without all three components—the microtubules, the motor and the linker—cilia were irreducibly complex.

Are cilia reducible? There are a number of reports of cilia that are different in structure than the usual form shown in Figure 1. The cilia of insect sperm are a particularly rich source of variation. [6] Many insect cilia show an additional single microtubule next to each doublet and thus have a 9 + 9 + 2 pattern. Some have a 9 + 9 + 1 pattern (Figure 3).

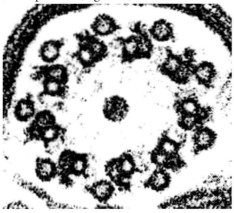

Figure 3. A 9 + 9 + 1 pattern of the sperm flagella of Culex. From Phillips, D. M. Exceptions to the prevailing pattern of tubules (9 + 9 + 2) in the sperm of flagella of certain insect species. The Journal of Cell Biology. *30: 28–43, 1969.* [5] *By permission.*

Some show an absence of the central tubules with a 9 + 9 + 0 pattern (Figure 4).

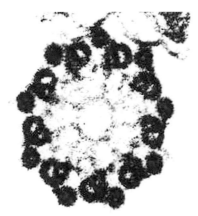

Figure 4. A 9 + 9 + 0 pattern of the sperm flagella of Tricorythodes. From Phillips, D.M. Exceptions to the prevailing pattern of tubules (9 + 9 + 2) in the sperm of flagella of certain insect species. The Journal of Cell Biology. *30: 28–43, 1969.* [5] *By permission.*

The absence of the central microtubules is not unique to insect flagella. The eel sperm shows a 9 + 0 pattern (Figure 5).

Figure 5. A 9 + 0 pattern of Anguilla anguilla eel sperm flagella. From Woolley, D. M. Studies on the eel sperm flagellum. J Cell Science. *110: 85-94, 1997.* [6]

In this species, in addition to the missing inner microtubules, the radial spokes and the outer dynein arms were also missing. In addition to a 6 + 0 pattern in Gregarine parasite, [6] a 3 + 0 pattern has been described in another parasite called Diplauxis (Figure 6).

Figure 6. A 3 + 0 pattern in Diplauxis hatti from Prensier et al.: Motile flagellum with a 3 + 0 ultrastructure. Science. *207:1493-1494, 1980.* [7] *By permission.*

The presence of dynein arms could not be excluded. This is the simplest of all cilia yet described. While these simpler forms of cilia are believed to represent loss and modification from an ancestral 9 + 2 pattern, they show that at least as far as the number of microtubules, the radial structures, and the outer dynein arms are concerned, cilia are reducible. Figure 7 shows that cilia are also modular. The dynein was coopted from prexisting brain, muscle and cytoplasmic dynein modules. The microtubule structure was derived from similar structures in mitotic and other cells. The nexin was derived from nestin modules in nerve, muscle and other cells.

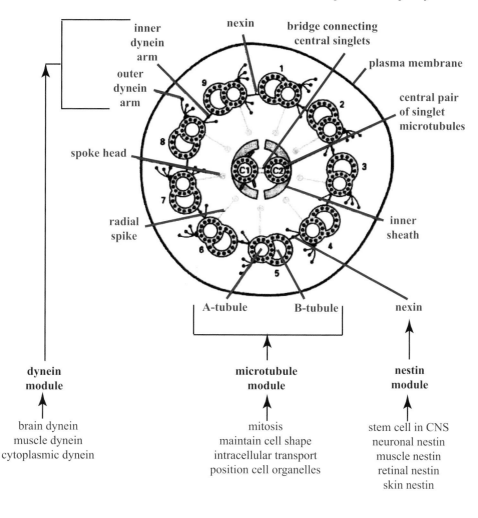

Figure 7. Modular nature of cilia. Each of the major component parts are used in a wide range of other structures and functions. Cilia diagram from Kenneth Miller's Finding Darwin's God. *8*

Thus each of the major component parts of cilia has an independent life elsewhere and thus cilia are highly modular. Even though some of these modules are used in structures that are more complex than bacteria, they illustrate the principle that each of these proteins can have functions that are independent of their function in cilia. Although the examples of simplified cilia such as 9 + 0 without radial arms or outer dynein arms show that the standard cilia are partially reducible, they do not include samples that were totally devoid of dynein and or nexin. Yet the essence of the irreducible complexity argument is that the probability of simultaneously evolving all three structures — microtubules, dynein and nexin — is remote. However, as we have seen in numerous prior examples, such as the citric acid cycle, when the individual components can exist as modules for other functions, cooption allows them to be assembled into complex structures with a new function. As a task for evolution and natural selection, putting the three cilia modules together would not be difficult.

Cilia are fine hair-like structures that wiggle and beat like a whip. This motion can either move the cell itself or move things outside the cell including food. There are three major component parts of cilia — dynein, nexin and microtubules made of tubulin. The microtubules are usually present as an outer circle of nine doublets and two central singlets. This is called a 9 + 9 + 2 pattern. Dynein and nexin play a critical role in the movement of cilia. Cilia are partially reducible in that they can exist in a much simpler form of 3 + 0, and missing some of the dynein, yet still function well. Cilia are highly modular in that the three major component parts have numerous other uses in other cells. As a task for evolution and natural selection, putting the three cilia modules together would not be difficult.

References

1. Figure from McGill Molson Medical Informatics Project. McGill University Faculty of Medicine. By permission.

2. Mitchell, D. R. Speculations on the evolution of 9 + 2 organelles and the role of central pair microtubules. *Biol Cell.* 96: 691-6, 2004.

3. Nogales, E., Whittaker, M., Milligan, R. A. & Downing, K. H. High-resolution model of the microtubule. *Cell.* 96: 79-88, 1999.

4. Behe, M. J. *Darwin's Black Box.* The Free Press, New York, 1996.

5. Phillips, D. M. Exceptions to the prevailing pattern of tubules (9 + 9 + 2) in the sperm flagella of certain insect species. *J Cell Biol.* 40: 28-43, 1969.

6. Woolley, D. M. Studies on the eel sperm flagellum. *J Cell Science.* 110: 85-94, 1997.

7. Prensier, G., Vivier, E., Goldstein, S., & Schrevel, J. Motile flagellum with "3+0" ultrastructure. *Science.* 207:1493-1494, 1980.

8. Miller, K. *Finding Darwin's God.* Harper Perennial, New York, 1999.

Complex creatures exist by virtue of slop, multiple use and redundancy.

Stephen J Gould
Eight Little Piggies[1p101]

Chapter 13

Complexity—Flagella

The bacterial flagellum represents the flagship of the Intelligent Design examples of apparent irreducible complexity[2] and with good reason. They are truly very complex structures. Even published experts in the field have made Behe-like statements. For example, in a 1978 review of bacterial flagella, Macnab[3] stated:

> As a final comment, one can only marvel at the intricacy, in a simple bacterium, of the total motor and sensory system which has been the subject of this review and remark that our concept of evolution by natural selective advantage must surely be an oversimplification. What advantage could derive, for example, from a "preflagellum" (meaning a subset of its components), and yet what is the probability of "simultaneous" development of the organelle at a level where it becomes advantageous?

The key, as usual, is "simultaneous" development. The flagellum of the bacteria *Escherichia coli,* the common bacteria of the human colon, is made up of approximately 20 major proteins and another 20 to 30 proteins that play a role in its construction.[4] Deletion experiments show that with few exceptions, when any of these proteins are removed, the flagellum either fails to function or to be assembled. While this meets the criteria of Behe[2] of being irreducible, it will be seen that this is really pseudo-irreducibility. Although the bacterial flagellum fails to function or assemble when parts are missing, the evolution of the flagellum was highly modular. The presence of many independently functioning modules removes the criteria of the individual parts needing to be "simultaneously" developed. It also eliminates the issue of irreducibility since the modules that were coopted during the process of evolution worked individually, before the other parts were added.

The following discussion relies heavily on the paper by Matzke *Evolution in (Brownian) space: A model for the origin of the bacterial flagellum.*[5] I have presented a fairly detailed description of the evolution of flagella because it plays such a major part in Behe's claims of irreducible complexity. I invite the reader to skip to the **red summary** at the end of the chapter if they are more interested in the conclusion than the gory details. Figure 1 shows a diagram of the bacterial flagellum with all of its component proteins and genes.

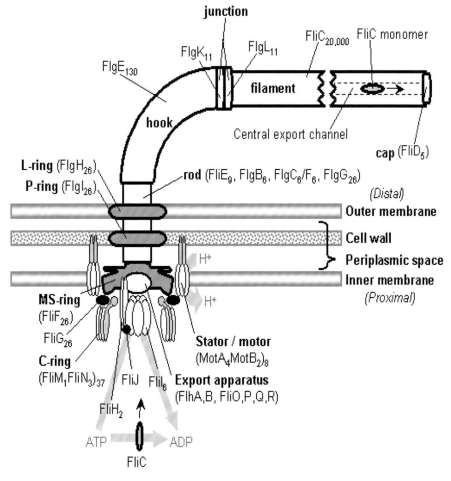

Figure 1. Diagram of a typical bacterial flagellum, shown in cross section. The names of substructures are given in bold, and the names of the constituent proteins are given in regular type. From Matzke.[5] By permission.

The cilia described in the previous chapter was a eukaryote flagella composed of tubulin. Bacterial flagella use a different protein called flagellin. The model proposed by Matzke makes extensive use of *cooption* or a shift in function for many of its components. This is a characteristic of a modular system in which a component serves a different prior function and is then coopted for use in the evolution of the flagellum. Figure 2 summarizes the Matzke model.

Stages 1 to 6 are presented in more detail below. Function of the core system refers to the functional state of the flagellum during evolution. Only at the last stage does it have full flagellar function. The analogs refer to the independent functions of the coopted modules before they became part of the flagellum.

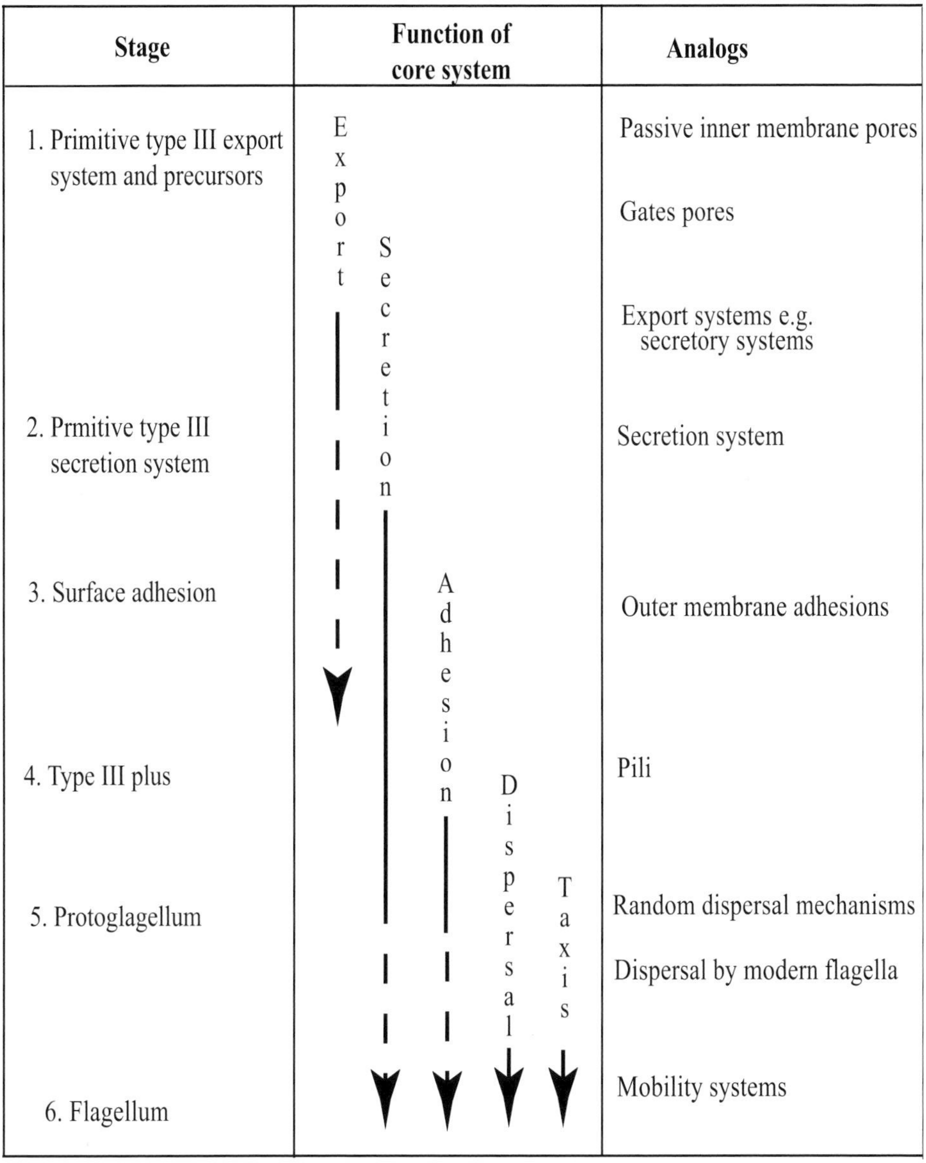

Stage	Function of core system	Analogs
1. Primitive type III export system and precursors	Export / Secretion / Adhesion / Dispersal / Taxis	Passive inner membrane pores
		Gates pores
		Export systems e.g. secretory systems
2. Prmitive type III secretion system		Secretion system
3. Surface adhesion		Outer membrane adhesions
4. Type III plus		Pili
5. Protoglagellum		Random dispersal mechanisms
		Dispersal by modern flagella
6. Flagellum		Mobility systems

Figure 2. Function and analogs at each stage of the Matzke model. [5]
By permission.

In the following discussion, the illustrations are all taken from Matzke. [5] Don't be put off by all the strange names. The names are not important; the concept of how this very complex flagellum was able to evolve by extensive use of co- opting other pre-existing modules is important. The structures in white have probable nonflagellar homologs that are coopted to flagellar function. The structures in grey have possible nonflagellar homologs also coopted for flagellar function. Export refers to the transport of proteins from the cytoplasm of the bacteria to the periplasmic space between the inner and outer cell membrane (see Figure 1). When the transport also crosses the outer cell membrane, it is called *secretion*.

The model begins with a primitive-type III export apparatus, with a passive, inner membrane pore (1a) composed of proto-FlhA and FlhB.

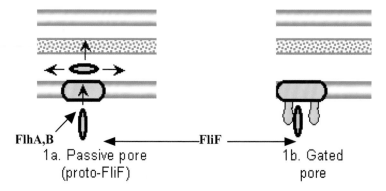

FlhA,B
1a. Passive pore
(proto-FliF)

FliF

1b. Gated
pore

The binding of FliF to this pore converts it to a more substrate-specific gated pore (1b) capable of transporting different components of flagellin protein.

As discussed in the section on the citric acid cycle, ATP is the primary currency for energy exchange in living cells. ATP synthase is a critical enzyme for the production of ATP and predated the development of flagella. DNA and protein sequencing studies have shown a 30 percent homology between FliI, a flagellar protein, and the F_1 subunit of F_1F_0-ATP synthase. ATP synthase has a built-in rotor, a perfect object for flagella to coopt for its own rotary purposes.

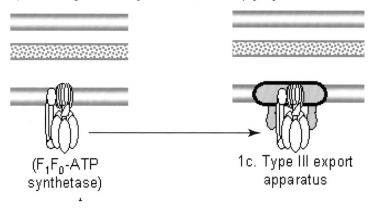

$(F_1F_0$-ATP
synthetase)

1c. Type III export
apparatus

The interaction of an F_1F_0-ATP synthetase with F_1hA/B produces an active transporter, a primitive type III export apparatus (1c).

The existence of a non-flagellar type III export apparatus shows that the argument that flagellar components are useless if they are not part of a fully functioning flagellum is not true. It answers McNab's and Behe's question, "What advantage could derive from a preflagellum?" the answer is that it is part of a preexisting module that served as an export system for the bacteria. This is also an example of what I refer to as a *pseudo-irreducible complex system.* Removing a part may inactivate the modern flagellum but many of its parts were able to function in the past as modules.

Another pre-existing module is the type III outer membrane secretion system. This is the ancient general *secretory (Sec)* pathway for protein secretion by cells. [6] Cooption of a type III secretion system which, with the outer cytoplasmic ring, converts the export apparatus into a secretion system passing through both membranes.

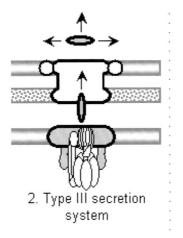

2. Type III secretion
system

A bacterium increases its chances of attaching to another structure by secreting adhesion proteins called *adhesins.* These are coopted for use by the flagellum and a mutation lets them bind to the outer side of the secretin (3a) and to then form a five-part surface adhesin ring (3b).

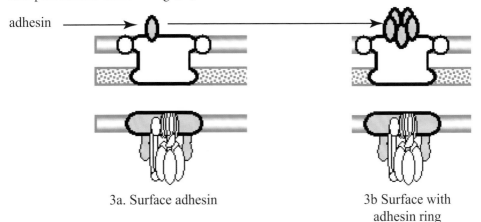

3a. Surface adhesin   3b Surface with
adhesin ring

The polymerization of this ring produces a tube, a primitive type III pilus (4a). All further axial proteins are descended from this common pilin ancestor by gene duplication. The binding together of multiple molecules of a pilin produces the cap that increases the speed and efficiency of assembly (4b). A duplicate pilin that loses its outer domains becomes the proto-rod protein, extending down through the secretin and strengthening pilus attachment by association with the base (4c).

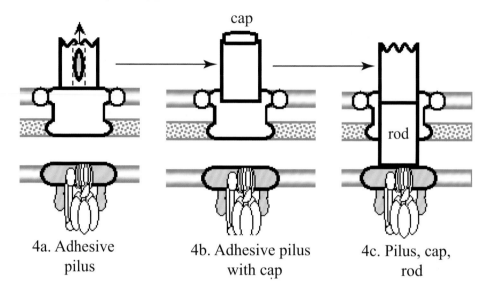

| 4a. Adhesive pilus | 4b. Adhesive pilus with cap | 4c. Pilus, cap, rod |

The flagellar motor is made up of two proteins, MotA and MotB. They were derived by cooption of the non-flagellar homologues, the Tol-Pal system,[7] members of the important chemical transport family of proteins that predate flagella. Rotation is aided by the interaction of MotA with FliG attached to the MS ring (FliF). (See Figure 1.)

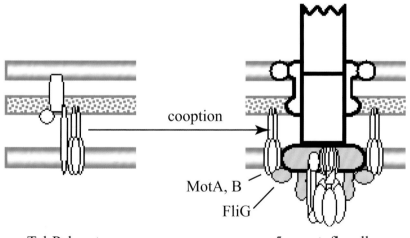

Tol-Pal system   5a. protoflagellum

In order to improve rotation, the secretin loses its binding sites to the axial filament, becoming the proto-P-ring, and the role of the outer membrane pore is taken over by the secretin's lipoprotein chaperone ring, which becomes the proto-L-ring (5b), and perfection of the L-ring results in 5c.

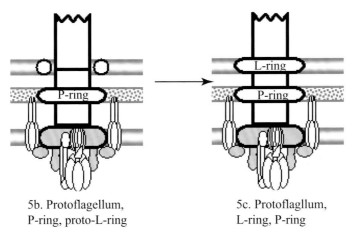

5b. Protoflagellum,
P-ring, proto-L-ring

5c. Protoflagllum,
L-ring, P-ring

Chemotaxis refers to an attraction or repulsion to chemicals in the environment. It is an ancient module found in bacteria, archaea, and eukaryotes. The proteins involved are termed *Che* (A, C, Y, Y-P and others). The final step in the process is the formation of the C-ring from the binding of a mutant proto-FliN, a CheC-like receptor, to FliG.

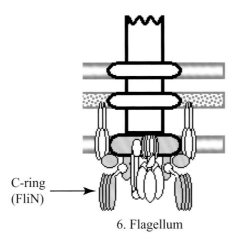

C-ring
(FliN)

6. Flagellum

This produces the final product—a chemotactic flagellum (6). I have spent a lot of time on the evolution of the bacterial flagellum because it is the centerpiece of the Intelligent Design argument that some structures are so irreducibly complex that a supernatural designer had to be involved. The essence of Behe's ID argument is the question, "How could flagella have evolved?" The Matzke model provides a reasonable explanation of how this could have occurred. *The bacterial flagellum is reducible and it is modular.* Darwin was right when he suggested that cooption would play an important role in the evolution of complex structures. *The widespread cooption of pre-existing modules is how the flagella evolved by natural selection.*

Despite the great complexity of the bacterial flagella, the Matzke model shows that it is both reducible and highly modular. Darwin was right when he suggested that cooption of previously existing structures and functions would play an important role in the evolution of complex structures. Widespread cooption is how the flagella evolved by natural selection.

References

1. Gould, S. J. *Eight Little Piggies.* W. W. Norton & Company, New York, 1993.
2. Behe, M. J. *Darwin's Black Box.* The Free Press, New York, 1996.
3. Macnab, R. M. Bacterial motility and chemotaxis: the molecular biology of a behavioral system. *CRC Crit Rev Biochem.* 5: 291-341, 1978.
4. Macnab, R. M. How bacteria assemble flagella. *Annu Rev Microbiology.* 57: 77-100, 2003.
5. Matzke, N. J. Evolution in (Brownian) space: A model for the origin of the bacterial flagellum. www.talkdesign.org/faqs/flagellum.html or www.talkorigins.org. 2003. By permission.
6. Cao, T. B. & Saier, M. H., Jr. The general protein secretory pathway: Phylogenetic analyses leading to evolutionary conclusions. *Biochim Biophys Acta.* 1609: 115-125, 2003.
7. Cascales, E., Lloubes, R. & Sturgis, J. N. The TolQ-TolR proteins energize TolA and share homologies with the flagellar motor proteins MotA-MotB. *Mol Microbiol.* 42: 795-807, 2001.

Chapter 14

Evolution Now: Introduction

A very common complaint of both creationists and Intelligent Designers is that man has not been able to observe evolution actually occurring. It is all something that happened in the past and thus is only hypothetical. The Creationists are all from Missouri—"show me evolution occurring 'now' or I don't believe it ever happened." By "now," I will assume this refers to the time that scientific records have been kept, or about the past 200 years. This could be referred to an "observable evolution," or "evolution in our time," or "recent evolution." In the following chapter titles I will refer to it as "Evolution Now."

Definition of a *darwin*

Because part of this issue concerns the rate of evolution, it raises the question of how to quantify the rate of evolution. In 1949 the geneticist J. B. S. Haldane[1] proposed a unit of evolution called the *darwin*. He sought to quantify the rate of changes in body form, such as size, over time. To allow the unit to be applied to animals of all sizes instead of referring to absolute size as in centimeters or feet, he used percent change and chose a change of one percent as his unit for size. Since geologic and evolutionary time periods are large, he chose one million years for time. Thus a *darwin* referred to a one percent change in some measurement over one million years. Haldane realized that the rate of change that animal breeders could produce was much higher than one *darwin*. However, Haldane meant this to be a measure of evolution as it occurs in nature. When evolution in nature is determined from fossil records, most organisms evolved at a rate of less than one *darwin*. In subsequent chapters, you will see that when examined carefully, some organisms evolve in nature several thousand times faster than that.

The first "Evolution Now" chapter recounts the story of one of the most famous examples of evolution now—Industrial Melanism and the Peppered Moth.

References

1.   Haldane, J. B. S. Suggestions as to quantitative measurement of rates of evolution. *Evolution*. 3: 51-56, 1949.

Chapter 15

Evolution Now: The Peppered Moth and Industrial Melanism

By the time of the mid-1800s the Industrial Revolution in England was in full bloom. In the days long before the Clean Air Acts, cities like Manchester, England became filled with dirty dust and soot.

> The sky resembled no sky on Earth so much as some Victorian vision of hell; dark even at noon, with roiling plumes of black smoke. So foul was the Manchester air in 1848, at the height of the Industrial Revolution, that mothers, it was said, could barely make out the outlines of their children across the street. [1p16]

As much as 50 tons of industrial fallout settled over each square mile of the city every year. The trees, houses, and every other surface around Manchester and the other dark mill towns were coated with black soot. The pollutants ran down the tree branches in rivulets, destroying the lichens that grew on the bark. Soon all the tree trunks were stripped of lichens. [1p17] The Peppered moth, *Biston betularia*, f. *typica*, sometimes called *Amphidasys betularia,* had a range that spread throughout England. The last part of its name, *typica,* refers to the variety or sub-species.

Figure 1. The Peppered moth, Biston betularia, F. typica. *From Coyne, J.:* Nature. *418:19, 2002.* [2] *By permission.*

In 1848, R. Edleston, an amateur moth collector living in Manchester, caught a rare dark, or melanic, form of the Peppered moth (Figure 2).

Figure 2. The Peppered moth, Biston betularia, F. carbonaria. From Coyne, J.: Nature 418:19, 2002 2 By permission.

He called it *Biston betularia,* F. *carbonaria.* In the latter half of the nineteenth century this black form spread rapidly throughout England. Edleston finally published his find in 1864. [3] By that time there were so many of the *carbonaria* that he wrote, "If this goes on for a few years the original type of *B. betularia* will be extinct in this locality." In fact, by 1895 the *carbonaria* form had reached a frequency of 98 percent in Manchester, and in many other places it had all but replaced the *typica* form. The Peppered moth produces only one generation a year. Thus, *to have virtually replaced the typica form in fewer than 50 years represents an astonishingly rapid change.*

The first person to suggest this rapid change was due to natural selection was J.W. Tutt. In 1896 [4] he proposed that the *typica* form was protected from predators by mimicking the lichens on tree trunks. He proposed that in industrial regions where the lichens had been destroyed by pollution and the tree trunks blackened by soot, the *typica* forms lost their protective mimicry and were rapidly eaten by birds. By contrast, the *carbonaria* forms flourished because now they were the ones that were hard to see against the black tree trunks. Since the melanism was due to a genetic mutation, the survivors passed this protection on to their offspring.

In some areas there was an intermediate form. These were called *insularia.* All three forms were due to multiple alleles at a single genetic locus. [5] The *carbonaria* form was dominant to the *insularia* and *typica* forms. This has been verified in studies of over 12 thousand progeny from 83 families. [6]

This was how the story of the Peppered moth and industrial melanism stood at the turn of the century and for the following 50 years. It was a beautiful, even fantastic, example of evolution in action. A dramatic change in the environment resulted in the selection of a rare new or preexisting genetic variant that was now better suited for survival and rapidly became more common in the population. Breeding studies showed it was an inherited genetic change, just as Darwin predicted.

One of the constant complaints of creationists was that the theory of evolution was flawed because one could not see it happening "in our time." They were not deterred when evolutionists explained that evolution occurred gradually and took a long time. The creationists kept saying, "If you can't show me, it does not exist." *Biston betularia*, F. *carbonaria* and industrial melanism allowed evolutionists to "show them" the striking rapidity with which natural selection could operate. *Evolution was real and was occurring both in real time and in our time.*

The brilliant Oxford geneticist John Burdon Sanderson Haldane further enhanced the melanism story. In 1924 he published a paper on the evolutionary genetics of the Peppered moth.[7] Based on the takeover of the *carbonaria* form in fewer than 50 years, Haldane calculated that for this to have occurred so rapidly it would require a selective advantage of 50 percent. Recall that prior to this Fisher had calculated that a selective advantage of only one percent was sufficient to fuel significant evolutionary change. Here was a selective advantage of 50 times that.

This raised a question that would take another 30 years to answer. What was the mechanism of this rapid selection? Was the lichen-centered mechanism the answer? Around the time that Haldane published his remarkable paper, Fisher had just met a fellow dedicated Darwinist, Edmund Brisco Ford. They both dreamed of a way of studying evolution not in the laboratory, but in nature, that was experimental, rigorous, and above all, quantitative. [1p53]

By 1937 E.B. Ford was a geneticist on the Oxford faculty. Bernard Kettlewell was a medical doctor working as a general practitioner in Cranleigh, Surrey, south of London. He was a passionate collector of butterflies and moths. On a collecting trip to the Black Wood of Rannock, in the Scottish Highlands, he met Ford who was there with a friend seeking a rare species of butterfly. [1p69] This chance meeting blossomed into a long, although somewhat tumultuous, friendship.

In 1951 E.B. Ford received a grant for studies in the field he had created, Ecological Genetics. He turned to his old friend Bernard Kettlewell to carry out the kind of studies he and Fisher had dreamed of years before. Kettlewell's objectives included direct observations of birds eating moths placed onto tree trunks and the marking of *typica* and *carbonaria* moths with a small spot of paint, releasing them and, after one to two days, recapturing them. They were then released onto trees in polluted and unpolluted woodlands.

The observation of birds preferentially eating moths depending upon their color and background was actually filmed in cooperation with Niko Tinbergen, a world-famous Oxford animal behavioralist. For example, in one filmed session involving nonpolluted trees, Tinbergen observed a spotted flycatcher eat 46 black moths and only eight typicals. The conclusion was that conspicuous insects were more vulnerable to predation than inconspicuous insects. Figure 3 shows the *typica* and *carbonaria* types on polluted and lichen covered trees.

The mark-release-recapture results were impressive. In the first such experiment, done in a polluted Birmingham woodland, of 447 melanics released, Kettlewell recaptured 123, or 27.5 percent. Of the 137 typicals released he recaptured only 18, or 13.0 percent, a 2-to-1 ratio of melanics to typicals. Two years later he performed the reciprocal experiment in an unpolluted woodland in Dorset. Of 496 typicals released he recaptured 62, or 12.5 percent, but of 473 melanics release he recaptured

Figure 3. Left. Carbonaria *(top) and* typica *(bottom) Peppered moths on polluted tree trunks.* Right. Typica *(top) and* **carbonaria** *(bottom) Peppered moths on nonpolluted lichen-covered tree trunks. The* carbonaria *form on the left and the* typica *form on the right were so hard to see they have been marked with a red arrow. These are posed pictures.*

only 30, or 6.3 percent, a 2-to-1 ratio of typicals to melanics in a reverse direction compared to the prior experiment. [8,9] He summarized his findings in a famous 1959 paper in *Scientific American* entitled "Darwin's Missing Evidence." [10]

The enactment of clean air acts in England and the United States further enhanced the Peppered moth story. In England these acts began to be implemented in 1956. By the 1980s three different surveys documented an extraordinarily rapid decline in the frequency of the *carbonaria* form, from over 90 percent to 40 percent. By 1994 in one survey it had decreased to 20 percent. [11] With comparable industrial polution there was a similar increase in the frequency of melanic forms of the Peppered moth in the United States. In an area near Detroit it had increased from zero to 90 percent. With the passage of clean air acts in 1963 the frequency of melanic forms in the same areas also dropped to 20 percent by 1995. [1p16]

Kettlewell's studies of industrial melanism rapidly became the poster boy for providing proof of Darwin's theory of evolution. The pictures in Figure 3 and others have been reproduced in countless textbooks of biology. The beauty of the Peppered moth story is that it is so easy to both see and to understand. One could not possibly dream up a better example and proof of the correctness of Darwinian evolution and natural selection. Or could they?

Attacks on the Peppered Moth Story

An attack on the Peppered moth story was launched largely with the help of Kettlewell's own scientific colleagues. While the creationists and Intelligent Designers have carried the banner, waved the anti-evolution flags and beat the drums, in fact, all they really had to do was sit back and pick up the pieces, with great glee. They pounced on this scientific debate with the same fervor that they pounced on "punctuated equilibria" when they overinterpreted the scientific debate and claimed that Eldridge and Gould had disproved Darwinism. The following are some of the slings and arrows that were unleashed. I will start with what Jonathan Wells said in his chapter on Peppered Moths in his anti-evolution book, *Icons of Evolution.* [12]

- *Imperfect correlation with pollution.* On both the upswing and the downswing, after the clean air acts there was not a precise match between the frequency of the *carbonaria* form and areas that were or were not polluted.
- *The exaggerated role of lichens.* The primary reason for suggesting that the *typica* form survived in nonpolluted areas was because they mimicked the presence of lichens on the trees. When the *typica* form increased in frequency after the Clean Air Acts were enacted, they did so before lichens returned to the trees. The same thing happened in the Unites States. The *typica* form increased without changes in lichen cover.
- *Peppered moths don't rest on trees.* Kettlewell placed all of his moths on tree trunks. However, Cyril Clarke, who was also an avid collector of Peppered moths, stated that in his many years of field work he had only seen the Peppered moth on a tree trunk once. The Peppered moth is nocturnal. During the day, they stay on the underside of leaves, not out in the open on tree trunks.
- *The Peppered moth pictures were staged.* Based on the positioning of the antennae and other aspects of the moths, it was clear that in some of the pictures the moths were dead and these photos were staged. In other pictures the moths were alive, but still staged.
- *Birds and UV vision.* While the studies of Kettlewell utilized evaluations based on human vision, birds use the ultraviolet spectrum in their vision. Thus, they may see past what looks like camouflage to human eyes.
- *Jerry Coyne's Santa Claus comment.* In the November 5, 1998 issue of Nature, [2] Jerry Coyne, a professor of ecology and evolution at the University of Chicago, reviewed a book by Michael E.N. Majerus entitled *Melanism: Evolution in Action.* [13] In the book, Majerus listed a range of criticisms of Kettlewell's studies. These included such things as A.) the moths do not usually rest on tree trunks, B.) bird vision is different than human vision, C.) the high densities of moth placement may have skewed the results, D.) problems with the timing of release, and others. Despite all his criticisms, Majerus still believed that Kettlewell's conclusions about the mechanism of natural selection were valid. Majerus stated, "My view of the rise and fall of the melanic Peppered moth is that differential bird predation in more or less polluted regions, together with migration, are primarily responsible, almost to the exclusion of other factors."

Jerry Coyne, however, was "horrified." [1p283] He had been teaching the standard version of the Peppered moth for years. He concluded, "we must discard *Biston* as a well-understood example of natural selection in action, although it is clearly a case of evolution." He capped off his comments with the statement, "My own reaction resembles the dismay attending my discovery, at the age of six, that it was my father and not Santa who brought the presents on Christmas eve." Talk about fodder for the creationist's anti-evolution diatribes. This was music to their ears. Here a member of the evolution establishment was trashing one of its own icons of evolution.

• *Hints of fraud.* To make matters worse, in her generally delightful book entitled, *Of Moths and Men,* Judith Hooper even implies that Kettlewell fudged his results. This was based in part on that fact that Kettlewell wrote to Ford about some initial disappointing recapture results. Hooper stated:

> We don't know exactly what state Bernard [Kettlewell] was in, but we can deduce something of it from a letter dated 1 July from Henry [Ford], who wrote, "It is disappointing that the recoveries are not better...However, I do not doubt that the results will be very well worth while." The message sounds benign enough, but knowing Henry, Bernard might have decided it to mean, "Now I do hope you will get hold of yourself and deliver up some decent numbers." He now felt that his fate as a scientist was hanging on this experiment. [1p114-115]

Hooper notes that the percent of recaptures immediately and dramatically increased after Kettlelwell got the note from Ford. Based on these problems, Wells gleefully termed the Peppered Moth study "the Peppered Myth."

Defense Against the Attacks

Are these criticisms fatal or are they simply the normal critical examination of studies by colleagues that takes place all the time and contributes to the power of science to find the truth? I will examine each issue.

The imperfect correlation with pollution. In general the correlation between the frequencies of the *carbonaria* form and the presence of pollution was quite high. However, it was not perfect. Unlike the pictures, the moths are not glued to the trees. They fly around and migrate from place to place.

The exaggerated role of lichens. In 1996 Sir Cyril Clarke, Grant and Owen wrote:

> The changes in allele frequencies in the moth populations we sampled occurred in the absence of perceptible changes in lichen floras. We suggest that the role of lichens has been inappropriately emphasized in chronicles about the evolution of melanism in peppered moths. [14]

However, they did not just leave the mechanism of selection hanging. They added that regional reductions in the soot component of atmospheric pollution meant that the surface reflectance from tree bark, even in the absence of lichens, would be lighter. [14,15] Grant and Howlett [16] also suggested that well-documented increases in the abundance of silver birch trees following the establishment of "smokeless zones" also changed the habitat.

In both Britain and the United States, the frequencies of the *carbonaria* form closely paralleled the increase and decrease in the levels of atmospheric sulfur dioxide. [14] It had been assumed that sulfur dioxide was killing the lichens and this affected the relative predation by birds. The observation by Clarke and colleagues that the increases and decreases in *carbonaria* frequency could occur in the absence of changes in lichens suggested the sulfur dioxide could work through a mechanism that was independent of bird predation. This work was covered in *The New York Times* with the statement, "While it is unclear exactly how natural selection is acting, it is very clear that selection is hard at work." [17]

Majerus [13] was not convinced and felt the Clarke report was not sufficiently detailed to make this sweeping generalization. In addition, a report by Cook [18] found that after the clean air act there was an increase in lichens in the most polluted areas, and this was reflected in an increase in the *typica* form.

As in most scientific quarrels, it is likely that both sides have a part of the truth. Lichens and bird predation were a factor, but not the only factor, leading to the changes in the frequency of the *carbonaria* form of the Peppered moth. However, both bird predation and the other factors acted through the mechanism of natural selection.

Peppered moths don't rest on trees. Peppered moths are nocturnal, and during the day they hide under the leaves, not on the tree trunks. Despite this, the above conclusion that bird predation and other factors cause differences in natural selection of the *carbonaria* and *typica* forms is still valid. In addition, recall the description of the level of pollution, at the beginning of this chapter. The soot and dirt were everywhere, providing plenty of places other than tree trunks for a *carbonaria* form to hide from birds.

Peppered moth pictures were staged. Given the difficulty of finding a *typica* and a *carbonaria* moth conveniently sitting next to each other on both a blackened tree trunk and a lichen-covered tree trunk, it is not surprising that Kettlewell placed living or dead moths on representative pieces of tree trunk simply to illustrate to the reader what he felt was the mechanism of the natural selection. As the above comments illustrate, the real story was not that straightforward. The staging of the tree trunk pictures does not change the real picture of a dramatic increase in the *carbonaria* form in polluted areas and the dramatic increase in the *typica* form when the pollution was eliminated, and of the replication of this pattern on two continents.

Birds and UV vision. Later research has shown that the moths are camouflaged in ultraviolet as well as in visible light. [19,20]

Jerry Coyne's Santa Claus comment. Despite his Santa Claus comments, in a review of Hooper's book, Coyne [2] strongly defends Kettlewell. Coyne refered to a colleague who described Kettlewell as "the best naturalist I have ever met, and almost the worst professional scientist I have ever known." As to Ford's letter he states, "This sounds familiar; many of us have offered similar consolation to students having a hard time in the field." As with Young and Musgrave (see next page) Coyne attributes the sudden increase in recapture rate on July 1 to a marked increase in the number of moths released, not to fraud. And yes, there were some problems with the study design, "but sloppiness is not fraud." Coyne suggests that Hooper unfairly smeared a brilliant naturalist.

Hints of fraud. Hooper[1] suggested that the sudden increase in moth recapture rate on July 1, the day Ford sent his letter "of encouragement," does not pass the fraud smell test. Young and Musgrave[20] presented a detailed response to this charge. They point out that from June 25 to 29 Kettlewell released an average of 31 moths per day and recovered (with a one-day delay) an average of 4.4 moths per day. On June 30 he released 102 moths, and on the morning of July 1, before he could have gotten Ford's letter, he released 114 moths. This resulted in an average recapture rate of 28.5 per day. On further analysis of the entire recapture experiment, Young and Musgrave showed there was a very high correlation (r = .80) between the number of moths released and the number recaptured. Thus, an increased release rate rather than fudging data in response to Ford's letter accounted for the jump in recapture rate. As further evidence of the validity of Kettlewell's findings, Majerus[12] reviewed five other subsequent studies, using modified experimental designs, that corroborated the fitness differences between carbonaria and typica in polluted and unpolluted regions.

In summary, no scientific study is perfect. As a scientist who has sat on many NIH study sections, reviewed hundreds of manuscripts, and had my own papers reviewed, I can say with confidence that virtually every study, every paper, and every grant receives its healthy share of criticism, with a special emphasis on methodology. A truism is, "If you don't like the conclusions, attack the methods." But that is the power of science. No scientist is immune from having their work very carefully examined. Sometimes the process is so contentious that good studies don't get published and many more don't get funded. When all of the difficulties of the type of study Kettlewell carried out are examined, it is questionable whether anyone could produce a study that could not be criticized. Despite all the criticisms the current state of the Peppered moth as an "icon of evolution" is well summarized by Grant.[21]

> The similarity of patterns between the British Isles and North America indicate parallel evolutionary changes that cannot be explained by anything other than selection acting independently on similar phenotypes in widely separated populations of the same species. On both continents, high frequencies of melanism and subsequent reductions correlate well to the same key factor: atmospheric pollution from regional industrial development and urbanization. No other evolutionary force can explain the direction, velocity, and the magnitude of the changes except natural selection. Certainly there are other examples of natural selection. Our field would be in mighty bad shape if there weren't. Industrial melanism in Peppered moths remains one of the best documented and easiest to understand.

Contrary to Jonathan Wells's characterization of the Peppered moth as "the Peppered Myth," with qualifications, the Peppered moth and industrial melanism still deserve to be in textbooks as classical examples of natural selection and of evolution in action and in our time.

The dramatic and rapid increase in the frequency of the black or melanic form of the Peppered moth in areas of England and the United States most severely affected by industrial pollution, and the equally dramatic decrease in the frequency of the blackened form after Clean Air Acts decreased the soot and sulfur dioxide in the atmosphere, is a classic example of natural selection. To attempt to determine the mechanism of selection, Bernard Kettlewell performed a series of experiments consisting of marking both forms of the moth, releasing, and later recapturing the survivors. He found that in polluted areas where the tree trunks and everything else were blackened, birds had difficulty seeing the black form and more of them survived. In nonpolluted areas, where the tree trunks were white due to lichens, birds had difficulty seeing the whiter form of the moth and more of them survived. This has been touted in textbooks as a classic example of natural selection.

Since these experiments, there have been many criticisms of Kettlewell's methods and of the basic hypothesis on which the study was based. As shown in the above discussion, it is clear that while some of these criticisms are valid, some are not. Despite this, industrial melanism as exemplified by the Peppered moth remains a powerful example of natural selection and of evolution in action and in our time.

References

1. Hooper, J. *Of Moths and Men. The untold story of science and the peppered moth.* W. W. Norton, New York, 2002.
2. Coyne, J. A. Evolution under pressure. Book review. *Nature.* 418: 19, 2002.
3. Edleston, R. S. *Amphydasis betularia. Entomologist.* 3: 150, 1864.
4. Tutt, J. W. *British Moths.* Routledge, London, 1896.
5. Lees, D. R. & Creed, E. R. The genetics of the insularia forms of the peppered moth *Biston betularia. Heredity.* 39: 67-73, 1977.
6. Creed, E. R., Lees, D. R. & Duckett, J. G. Pre-adult viability differences of melanic *Biston betularia* (L.) (Lepidoptera). *Biol J Linn Soc.* 13: 251-262, 1980.
7. Haldane, J. B. S. A mathematical theory of natural and artifical selection. *Trans Canmb Phil Soc.* 23: 19-41, 1924.
8. Kettlewell, H. B. D. Selection experiments on industrial melanism in Lepidoptera. *Heredity.* 9: 323-342, 1955.
9. Kettlewell, H. B. D. Further selection experiments on industrial melanism in the lepidoptera. *Heredity.* 10 (Part 3): 287-301, 1956.
10. Kettlewell, H. B. D. Darwin's missing evidence. *Sci Am.* 200: 48-53, 1959.
11. Clarke, C. A. B., Grant, A. B., Clarke, F. M. M. & Asami, T. A long-term assessment of *Biston betularia* (L.) in on U.K. locality (Caldy Common near West Kirby, Wirral) 1959-1993. *Linnean.* 10: 18-26, 1994.

12. Wells, J. *Icons of Evolution: Science or Myth? Why much of what we teach about evolution is wrong.* Regnery Publishing, Inc. Washington, DC, 2000.

13. Majerus, M. E. N. *Melanism: Evolution in Action.* Oxford University Press, Oxford, 1998.

14. Grant, B. S., Owen, D. F. & Clarke, C. A. Parallel rise and fall of melanic peppered moths in America and Britain. J. *Heredity.* 97: 351-357, 1996.

15. Clarke, C. A., Mani, G. S. & Wynne, G. Evolution in reverse: clean air and the peppered moth. *Biol J Linn Soc.* 26: 189-199, 1985.

16. Grant, B. and Howlett, R.J. Background selection by the peppered moth *(Biston betularia* Linn.): Individual differences. *Biol J Linn Soc.* 33:217-232, 1988.

17. Yoon, C. K. Parallel plots in classic evolution. *The New York Times.* C1, 1996.

18. Cook, L. M., Rigby, K. D. & Seward, M. R. D. Melanic moths and changes in epiphytic vegetation in north-west England and north Wales. *Biol J Linn Soc.* 39: 343-354, 1990.

19. Majerus, M. E. N., Brunton, C. E. A. & Stalker, J. A bird's-eye view of the peppered moth. *Journal of Evolutionary Biology.* 13: 155-159, 2000.

20. Young, M. & Musgrave, I. Moonshine. Why the Peppered moth remains an Icon of Evolution. *Skeptical Inquirer.* 29: 23-28, 2005.

21. Grant, B. S. Fine-tuning the Peppered moth paradigm. *Evolution.* 53: 980-984, 1999.

Chapter 16

Evolution Now: Darwin's Finches

It is a common misconception that Darwin first formulated his theory of evolution when the H. M. S. Beagle brought him to the Galapagos Islands where he noticed that the beaks of the finches were different on each island. He thought, as the myth goes, that a divine creator would have made a single species for all islands and that evolution involving natural selection would have fashioned each bird to match the type of seeds and the environment unique to each island.

Nothing could be further from the truth. In actuality, Darwin misclassified most the finches he collected as blackbirds, wrens and warblers and did not even bother to note which island they came from. [1,2] He thought they all represented species from the mainland of South America. He only noted the islands of origin for the mockingbirds he collected.

In his Pulitzer Prize-winning book, *The Beak of the Finch,* Weiner [3p27] notes that Darwin's earliest thoughts relevant to evolution came on the voyage home. In his notes he states that the mockingbirds on two of the islands seemed unique to those islands. He thought they were only varieties, but then wondered—"What if there were no limits to their divergence? What if they had diverged first into varieties, and then gone right on diverging into species, each marooned on his own island." As Weiner recounts,

> Darwin wrote, "the zoology of Archipelagoes—will be well worth examining, for these facts undermine the stability of Species." Then, in a scribble that foreshadowed two decades of agonized caution, Darwin inserted, "[this] would undermine the stability of Species."

On January 4, 1837, two months after the Beagle docked in Falmouth, England, Darwin gifted his bird collection to the Zoological Society of London. Immediately after examining these study skins, the ornithologist John Gould announced that they consisted of 14 new species that were unique to the Galapagos. [3p28] In addition, Gould also noted that the mockingbirds Darwin brought home were different depending upon the island from which they originated.

To determine if the finches also showed island-to-island variations, Darwin had to ask Fitzroy, the captain of the Beagle, if he could examine the birds Fitzroy and other shipmates had collected and labeled by the island of origin. While Darwin described the finches in his initial draft of *The Origin of Species,* he did not mention them in the final version, possibly because of the haphazard way he had handled the labeling of the specimens. Thus, mockingbirds, not finches, played the major role in the beginnings of Darwin's thinking about the origin of the species.

The following passage from his memoirs of *The Voyage of the Beagle,* written years later, probably contributed to the myth,

> In the thirteen species of ground-finches, a nearly perfect gradation may be traced, from a beak extraordinarily thick, to one so fine, that it may be compared to that of a warbler. I very much suspect, that certain members of the series are confined to different islands...

Despite this imperfect record, the finches of the Galapagos are now known as "Darwin's finches."

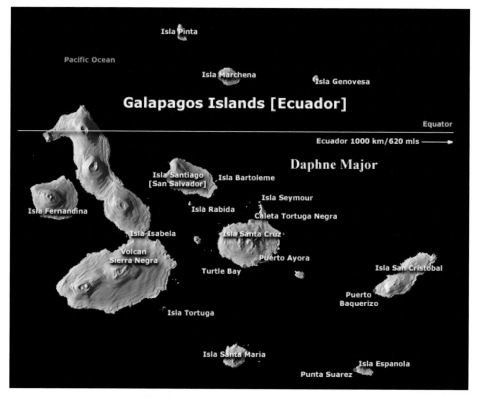

Figure 1. The Galapagos archipelago. The tiny island of Daphne Major is north of Santa Cruz island. [4] Courtesy of Mountain High Maps, Bugbog.com.

Studies by the Grants

Peter and Rosemary Grant studied Darwin's finches on Daphne Major, one of the smallest islands of the Galapagos archipelago (see Figure 1). Their studies lasted continuously from 1973 into the twenty-first century, the longest period of time ever recorded for such work. They have produced the most detailed record of evolution in action ever compiled. The results, eloquently related in Weiner's book, [3] have *enormous relevance to the understanding of many of the most fundamental aspects of evolution.*

The small size and remoteness of this uninhabitable island allowed the Grants to record a vast array of variables about the birds and their environment over the months they were on the island, without concern that things would be disturbed when they were not there. These variables included measures of the length, width, and depth of the birds' beaks; body weight, wing span; all of the species of plants; the size of all the seeds on the island; the amount of pressure required to break open the seeds; which birds ate which seeds; who mated with whom; who was left out of the mating game; how many progeny each bird had; who their parents, grandparents, and great-grandparents were; when each bird died; and many other important facts. Darwin's ground finches, from a drawing by the Grants' daughter Thalia, are shown in Figure 2.

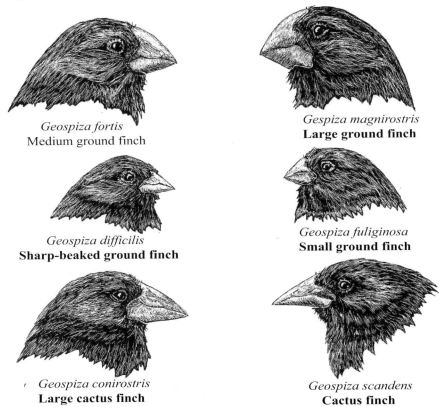

Geospiza fortis
Medium ground finch

Gespiza magnirostris
Large ground finch

Geospiza difficilis
Sharp-beaked ground finch

Geospiza fuliginosa
Small ground finch

Geospiza conirostris
Large cactus finch

Geospiza scandens
Cactus finch

Figure 2. Darwin's ground finches drawn by Thalia Grant. From Jonathan Weiner, The Beak of the Finch. [3]

A pair of male (dark) and female (brown) finches in color are shown in figure 3.

Figure 3. A pair of Darwin's finches from The Zoology of the Voyage of H.M.S. Beagle, Under the Command of Captain Fitzroy During the Years 1832 to 1836. [5]

The Drought

For the first several years of the Grant's data collection, not much happened. Then in 1977 there occurred one of the worst droughts ever recorded on the Galapagos. Figure 4 shows the changes this wrought on *Geospiza fortis*.

There was a dramatic decrease in the number of birds, with males dropping from 600 to 150 and females dropping from 600 to 25. The survivors were 6 percent larger than before the drought. The length of the bill increased from 10.68 to 11.07mm and the depth of the bill increased from 9.42 to 9.96 mm, when the birds before the drought were compared to the drought survivors. While an increase in the depth of the bill of only .54 mm may seem miniscule, it is a 5.7 percent change. As with the Peppered moth, this was one of the most intense episodes of natural selection ever recorded in nature.

These careful measurements showed that in the drought, when only the largest and most difficult seeds to break were available, the larger birds with the longest and thickest beaks were the ones to survive. This change, so small it is hard to appreciate by the naked eye, made the difference between life and death for the finches.

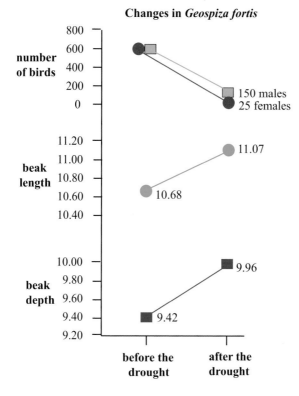

Figure 4. Changes in Geospiza fortis *following a severe drought on* Daphne.

As Peter Grant stated, natural selection takes place within a generation while evolution takes place across generations. Figure 1 shows the results of natural selection. Because data was also collected on mating, breeding, and offspring, it was also possible to study evolution. This also held some surprises. Because there were plenty of males but only a few females, each male had only a one in six chance of passing on its genes.

Remarkably, the females seemed to sense the crisis and only picked as partners birds that were the blackest, had the most mature plumage, were the largest, and had the largest beaks. Most of the males were left out of the mating game while every single female mated. Since the surviving females were also the largest, this, plus the choice by the females of the largest males, contributed to a 5 percent deeper bill in the next generation. This was evolution in action, resulting in larger, stronger birds with deeper bills—better equipped to open the largest seeds.

A statistical analysis showed selection was the strongest for body size and depth of beak. There was no selection for the length or width of the beak. Peter Grant wrote, "a narrow yet deep bill was the best instrument for performing the difficult task of tearing, twisting, and biting the mericarps [seed covering] of the *Tribulus* [plant] to expose the seeds."

This study proved Darwin correct when he proposed that evolution works by the natural selection of genetic variations that cause small changes but provide greater fitness and are passed on to subsequent generations. He undoubtedly would have been surprised by the incredible speed of the rate of these changes. More on this later.

The results of the Grants' study raised a number of intriguing questions. First, why didn't evolution just keep producing larger and larger birds who were better and better at uncovering the *Tribulus* seeds? It also raised the question of why evolution, as measured in the fossil record, progressed at less than 1 *darwin* per million years, while *G. fortis* posted a rate of 25,000 *darwins*? One could argue that this rate jumped because of extreme environmental stress, but surely there would be many comparable stresses over a period of a million years. These should be compounded to push the number of darwins to still higher levels. The answer came quickly.

The Flood

In 1982 the weather on Daphne went to the opposite extreme. December of that year saw rains that were greater than any since the founding of the Charles Darwin Research Station in 1960. The plant life was going from desert to jungle. One of the research team said, "The birds went crazy. The year before there had been no breeding at all. Now they bred like hell." [3p101] Females produced up to 40 eggs and up to 25 offspring per bird. One female went through four males, one after the other.

There were now ten times as many small seeds on the ground and big birds with big beaks had trouble feeding on the small seeds. An analysis of the data after the flood showed that now selection was reversed. Big birds with big beaks were dying while small birds with small beaks were surviving. Since they were larger they had to eat more seeds to stay alive. [3p105] In addition, males were dying at a faster rate than females. Thus, in flood conditions everything was the reverse of the selection that occurred in drought conditions.

The finding that drought pushed evolution in one direction while floods pushed it in the opposite direction provides us with great insight into several apparent problems in evolution. When examined over longer periods of time, organisms appear to evolve very slowly at a fraction of a *darwin*. However, the closer the observer examines life the more rapid the evolution, in some cases reaching over 60,000 *darwins*. The reason evolution appears to move so slowly over long periods of time is now clear—*the rapid oscillations cancel each other out.*

This could also explain both the punctuations and the equilibria of punctuated equilibria. The punctuations would occur when severe environmental stress accelerated variation and then speciation. Equilibria would occur when environmental stresses were balanced, thus resulting in balancing of the short-term but large evolutionary changes into long-term minor evolutionary changes.

Principle of Divergence

While competition among species is at the heart of Darwin's Theory of Evolution, he also proposed a *Principle of Divergence.* Here he predicted the general absence of competition. He proposed that in a large group of organisms all competing for the same food, variants might be different enough that they would occupy different habitats and thus significantly reduce competition. This would result in adaptive radiation (Figure 5).

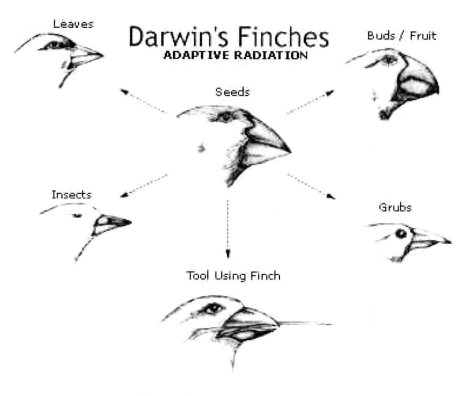

Figure 5. *The principle of adaptive radiation with the evolution of different beaks suited to different environmental conditions.*

In 1947 David Lack published a book entitled *Darwin's Finches.* [6] He found that in low-lying islands without mountains, either *G. fuliginosa* with small beaks or *G. difficilis* with sharp beaks were present, but never both. Here the competition was so great only one species survived. However, in islands with mountains, both species were present, but they occupied different ecological niches. The *G. fuliginosa* occupied the base of the mountain while the *G. difficilis* were near the top.

This supported Darwin's *Principle of Divergence,* or competitive exclusion. By adopting two different habitats, the two species could exist on the same island without competing with each other. Animals may evolve such that their physical characteristics are sufficiently different to allow them to occupy these different ecological niches, and thus escape from deadly competition. This is called *character displacement.*

Speciation by Hybridization

The Grants found that mating between species was rare, and under usual environmental circumstances the offspring of hybrids did not survive. However, following the flood, the competition for food was relaxed sufficiently for the offspring of those rare hybrids to survive. Hybridization between two related species has the advantage that it increases the range of genetic variation in an individual. Greater genetic variation increases the potential to survive dramatic changes in the environment. The Grants pointed out that while rare, this was another tool to facilitate speciation.

Death Knell to Anti-Evolutionists

These studies of the finches of the Galapagos rang a death knell to the many complaints of the Creationists. These studies showed that evolution is an ongoing process and that it occurs now and in our time. They explain why some species remain static over long periods of time while some rapidly diversify. Thus they explain both the punctuation and the equilibria of punctuated equilibria. They explain speciation by geographical separation (allopatric speciation) and evolution without geographic separation (sympatric speciation). They illustrate the intimate and often reciprocal interaction between animals and their environment. They validate Darwin's *Principle of Divergence*, competitive exclusion and character displacement by which species can actually escape from competition. They explain why the rate of evolution is often a fraction of a *darwin* when the fossil record is examined, but can be as high as 60,000 *darwins* when the interaction of a species with extreme environmental changes is examined over short periods of time. These studies falsify the claim that there is not enough time for evolution to occur.

The Creationists' Anti-Evolutionary Spin

In view of the above I was astonished to see Darwin's Finches and Weiner's book on the Grant's work mentioned in Jonathan Wells's anti-evolution book *Icons of Evolution*.[7] I would think that the last thing the creationists would want to do would be to call attention to this marvelous body of work. What possible spin could they come up with to claim this was evidence against evolution? The following is what Wells did.

First, rather than simply taking note of the interesting historical fact that Darwin was not that invested in the finches that were named after him, Wells treats this fact as some sort of conspiracy by evolutionists to mislead the public. In scientific studies, the record about who really discovered what gets corrected all the time without affecting the validity of the basic facts.

Second, Wells then attacks the beautiful studies of the Grants by saying that they did not actually observe speciation occurring and implied that the increase in beak size brought about by the drought would always be reversed by periods of flooding.

Finally, he attacked the Grants' studies on hybrids by claiming they prove that species fusion by hybridization is more common than species diversification. This ignored the statement by the Grants that cross-species hybridization is a rare event. The fact that over the lifetime of the earth over one billion species have evolved further indicates the absurdity of this claim.

The beauty of the finch studies is that they were field studies of actual evolution in action. They illustrated the mechanisms by which evolution occurs and illustrated the rapidity by which those changes can take place. The existence of many different ice ages; of continental shifts with the formation of mountains where sea bottoms once were and sea bottoms where mountains once were; the transformation of jungles into deserts and deserts into jungles; the occurrence of major climate change due to asteroids impacting the earth; and many other forces of nature have produced prolonged and lasting changes in both local and world-wide environments. The presence of these forces illustrated that in many cases the environmental changes continue in only one direction rather than undergoing short balancing cycles.

The Grants were observing the equilibrium part of punctuated equilibria. Punctuations resulting in new species are rarer. For a given trait, species tend to differ by 15 percent or more. If a single season of adverse climate were able to produce a 5.7 percent change, it would not require more than three or four successive seasons of the same type of adversity to result in a new species.

Now that we have observed the mechanism of evolution in action, it requires only a trivial amount of thinking to understand that when the environmental changes are unidirectional, new species and new punctuations can occur quite rapidly. Wells's slavish dedication to creationism seems to prevent him from this line of thinking. Strong support for the importance of climate in evolution is provided by detailed studies of 80,000 mammal fossils in three regions in Spain, covering a period of 22 million years. [9] Climate changes were assessed by geological and astronomical records. These studies showed that the evolution of new species was driven more by long-term climate changes than by competetion between species.

Studies of the finches of the Galapagos ring a knell to the complaints of the creationists. These studies show that evolution is an ongoing process and that it occurs in our lifetime. They explain why some species remain static over long periods of time while some rapidly diversify. They explain both the punctuation and the equilibria of punctuated equilibria, and speciation both with and without geographical separation. They illustrate the intimate and often reciprocal interaction between animals and their environment. They explain why the rate of evolution is often very slow when the fossil record is examined, but can be very rapid when the interaction of a species with extreme environmental changes is examined over short periods of time. They especially falsify the claim that there is not enough time for evolution to occur.

Other Examples. The stories of the Peppered moth and Darwin's Finches are so effective in illustrating the concept that evolution is an ongoing process and is occurring now that additional examples are not necessary. However, for the interested reader, John Endler, in his 1986 book, *Natural Selection in the Wild,*[8] listed examples of natural selection in over 110 species, often with multiple examples per species.

References

1. Sulloway, F. J. The Beagle collection of Darwin's finches (Geospizinae). *Bulletin of the British Museum of Natural History (Zoology).* 43: 49-94, 1982.
2. Sulloway, F. J. Darwin and his finches: The evolution of a legend. *Journal of the History of Biology.* 15: 1-53, 1982.
3. Weiner, J. *The Beak of the Finch. A Story of Evolution in Our Time.* Vintage Books A Division of Random House, Inc, New York, 1994.
4. Figure from www.bugbog.com/maps/south_america/ galapagos_islands_map.html
5. Darwin, C. *The Zoology of the Voyage of H.M.S. Beagle, Under the Command of Captain Fitzroy During the Years 1832 to 1836.* C. I. L. Ltd., Peterborough, UK, 1840 (1994).
6. Lack, D. *Darwin's Finches.* Cambridge University Press, Cambridge, UK, 1947.
7. Wells, J. *Icons of Evolution: Science or Myth? Why much of what we teach about evolution is wrong.* Regnery Publishing, Inc., Washington, DC, 2000.
8. Endler, J. A. *Natural Selection in the Wild.* Princeton University Press, Princeton, NJ, 1986.
9. Van Dam, J. A. et al. Long-term astronomical forcing of mammal turnover. *Nature.* 443:687-691, 2006.

Chapter 17

The Evolution of Man

While the theory of evolution and the origin of the species was a troubling concept for many, especially theologians, the idea that man evolved from the apes was especially difficult to accept. In his *Icons of Evolution,* Intelligent Design creationist Jonathan Wells simply resorts to denial by suggesting that the descent of man from lower primates is simply a myth, by pointing out that the Piltdown Man, once considered one of the supposed "missing links," was later found to be a fraud, and by pointing out that Neanderthals were not really direct ancestors of man. [1p208-228] The latter two points are well-known truths in evolution science and have no relevance to the overriding fact that 99 percent of the DNA sequence of humans and chimpanzees is identical, a clear indication they are closely related species.

Another common tactic has been to simply ridicule the notion that man is a primate rather than address the science. This common approach is illustrated by the religious controversy that met the release of Darwin's *The Origin of Species,* which culminated in a debate between Thomas H. Huxley, an avid proponent of Darwinian evolution, and Bishop Wilberforce, the Bishop of Oxford, England. The bishop attempted to put away his debating opponent by asking which side of his family did he claim was descended from the monkeys. Huxley's famous rejoinder won the day:

> I would rather have a miserable ape for a grandfather than a man highly endowed by nature and possessed of great means and influence, and yet who employs these facilities and influence for the mere purpose of introducing ridicule into a grave scientific discussion.

Nonetheless, the pain many felt about being just one more animal and one more twig on the evolutionary tree, rather than the unique image of God created by God, persisted and has been one of the issues most fought over by creationists.

Twelve years after the publication of *The Origin of Species,* Darwin published *Descent of Man and Selection in Relation to Sex.* [2] There was very little fossil evidence at that time relevant to the descent of man. Instead Darwin listed a wide range of human features that had a similar structure and function in animals, including primates. In the section on the mind of man he stated the following:

The differences in [the] mind between man and the higher animals, great as it is, certainly is one of degree and not of kind. We have seen that the senses and intuitions, the various emotions and faculties, such as love, memory, attention, curiosity, imitations, reason, etc., of which man boasts, may be found in an incipient, or even sometimes well-developed condition, in the lower animals.

Since Darwin's time a great deal more has been learned about the evolution of man. This remarkable journey is often considered to have entailed some of the following important steps: descent from the trees into the savannah or grasslands, walking upright, use of tools, development of speech and language, an increase in brain size, and the development of greater intelligence. The purpose of this chapter is to cover these aspects of human evolution. Since a main subject of this book is an examination of our analytical and spiritual brains, these aspects of human evolution will be examined in later chapters.

Lemurs — Our Earliest Ancestors

One of the earliest stages in the evolution of man involved the movement of the eyes from their usual position on either side of a large snout, as in the dog, to a more forward position. These early ancestors were the tree-living lemurs from the island of Madagascar and the tarsiers from Malaysia.

Figure 1. The lemur, a very early ancestor of man. [2a]

The advantage of forward-set eyes is that it provides improved three-dimensional vision, well suited for navigating without falling from the trees. The lemurs survived the K/T mass extinction that killed off the dinosaurs. We owe them a great debt for if they had not survived the devastation of the Yucatan comet, we would not be here. These small mammals with five strong fingers on each limb and a prehensile tail were the ancestors of other tree dwellers. To survive in the jungles of Africa, a larger and sturdier primate called *Proconsul africanus* (Figure 2) evolved. *Proconsul* thrived, spread throughout Africa and Asia and gave rise first to gibbons and orangutans, then to African gorillas and chimpanzees.

Descent to the Savannah and Bipedalism

About 6 million years ago a dramatic shift in climate occurred in Africa that lead to a decrease in the amount of land devoted to the jungles and forests and an increase in open savannahs. To survive the increasingly stringent struggle in the

Proconsul africanus

Trudge, C. *The Variety of Life,* 2000

Figure 2. Proconsul africanus an ancestor to hominoid apes. [2b]

forests, our ancestors came out of the trees to occupy this expanding habitat in the Great Rift Valley. This resulted in the environmental stimulus to push the evolution of many new features. One of the most important was the shift to an upright posture with locomotion by walking on two legs (bipedalism). Numerous benefits of this have been suggested, including better vision in the tall grass, better access to food, better regulation of body temperature by exposing less surface to the African sun, [3] and freeing up the use of the hands for carrying food and children and for making tools.

William Leonard of Northwestern University proposed that bipedalism evolved in part because it uses much less energy than walking on all fours. [3] Apes and monkeys living in the dense forest can obtain all the food they need within a one-mile radius. In the grasslands, food is harder to come by and may require traveling six to eight miles. The energy expended in acquiring food compared to the energy produced from the food, has important adaptive features for survival and reproduction. The increased efficiency of energy use brought about by bipedalism allows more energy for reproduction.

An additional effect of coming out of the trees was that now our ancestors roamed the savannahs in groups in search of food. Cooperation between individuals and groups of individuals made the task of finding and killing prey easier. These circumstances saw the earliest beginnings of human social structure.

The Human Tree

The ancestors to *Homo sapiens* separated from the chimpanzee about 5 to 6 million years ago *(myr).* [4] What then followed is the evolution of a complex mixture of different species with varying degrees of human traits. The names and times of appearance and disappearance of these species are shown in Figure 3.

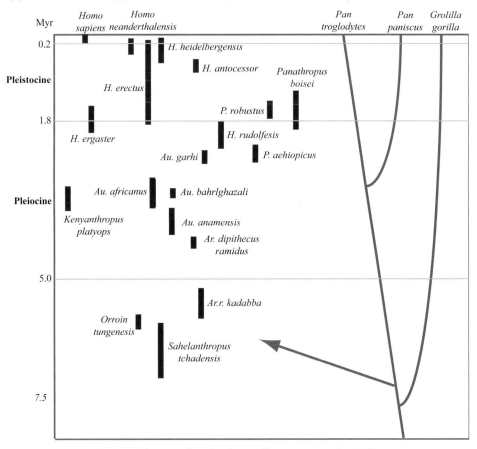

Figure 3. The time scale and evolution of human ancestors (hominids). Pan troglodytes (chimpanzee), Pan paniscus (bonobo), Gorilla gorilla (gorilla), and Pongo pygmasus (orangutan). After Carroll, S. B. Genetics and the making of Homo sapiens. Reprinted by permission. Macmillan Publishers, Ltd. Nature. 422:849-857, 2003. [5]

Since the exact ancestral relations between these species are not known they are presented as separate independent bars. Note that *Homo sapiens* had a very late appearance of approximately 200,000 years ago. *Pan troglodytes,* or the chimpanzees, are our closest relatives among living primates. The ancestors in the human line after divergence from the chimpanzee line are referred to as hominids.

African Mitochondrial Eve

I have previously described the analysis of DNA and ribosomal RNA sequences to determine evolutionary relationships between species. The cytoplasmic mitochondria have their own circular DNA, independent of the nuclear DNA. Since the rate of mutation is much greater than for nuclear DNA, it is ideal for determining evolutionary relationships between species and races that have diverged only recently.

Alan Wilson, Rebecca Cann and coworkers at the University of California, Berkeley, utilized the studies of mitochondrial DNA to examine the relationships between different racial groups.[6] They collected 147 samples from all over the world. In addition to its small size and higher mutation rate, mitochondrial DNA differs from nuclear DNA in that it is passed only from the mother to her offspring. This is because the mother's eggs contain mitochondria which are easily passed to the fertilized egg, while the small number of mitochondria in father's sperm do not pass easily to the egg. This makes analysis of genetic relationships easier.

The phylogenetic tree produced by the analysis of the mitochondrial DNA variation present in these samples indicated that its trunk began 200,000 years ago in Africa.[6] While the woman at the base of this tree was dubbed "mitochondrial Eve" it was only the peculiarities of the technique that made it appear the ancestor was a single person. It was more likely a small group of related individuals. An additional finding of the mitochondrial DNA studies was that there was no crossbreeding between *Homo sapiens* and Neanderthal man.

The human Y chromosome is present only in males and is passed only from fathers to their sons. In addition, there is litle crossing-over in the Y chromosome. Thus, except for random mutations, it tends to be stable over many generations. One of the most interesting uses of Y chromosome DNA studies has been to identify a long line of father to son Jewish rabbis dating back for thousands of years.[7]

Increase in Brain Size in Human Evolution

One of the most remarkable aspects of the evolution of man is the rapid increase in brain size over the past 3 million years. When only a few measures of a few species are included in the analysis, the results suggest there were leaps in brain size followed by plateaus, and then another leap, and that the process was complete after only a few leaps. This is illustrated in Figure 4.

This shows the apparent presence of several distinct brain size groups with rather large gaps in between. This pattern is reminiscent of the punctuated equilibria of Eldridge and Gould and of macroevolution. If true it would require some elaborate theories as to what the environmental factors were that could produce such leaps. However, such theorizing is obviated when a more extensive set of samples is examined.

Henneberg and Miguel[8] examined the cranial capacity and body weight of over 200 fossil homininae (humans, chimps, and gorillas) specimens. These were plotted in logarithmic format against dates in thousands of years before the present (ka BP) (Figure 5).

The regression coefficient for brain size = .95. When analyzed by both date and latitude, they concluded there were no discontinuities through time or geographic latitude. Thus, there were no punctuations and no giant leaps of macroevolution. Evolution of human brain size was occurring in typical Darwinian gradual steps.

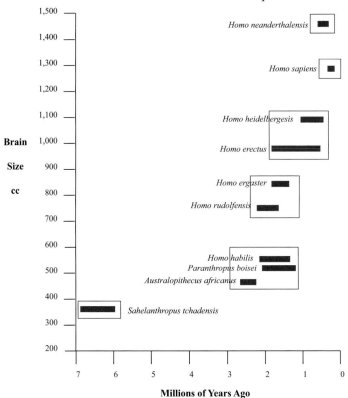

Figure 4. Apparent sudden leaps in brain size. Data from Carroll, S. B. Genetics and the making of Homo sapiens. *Reprinted by permission from Macmillan Publishers, Ltd. Nature. 422:849-857, 2003.* [7]

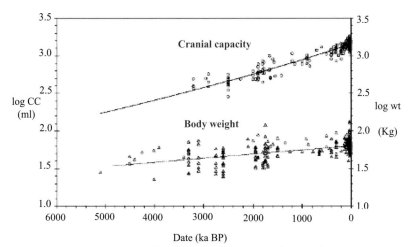

Figure 5. Regression of fossil hominin cranial capacity, log CC (ml) (top), body weight in log kg (bottom), and date in thousands of years before the present (ka BP). From Henneberg and de Miguel. Homo—Journal of Comparative Human Biology. *55:21-37, 2004.* [8] *By permission.*

The evolution of brain complexity. The complexity of the structure of the brain, especially the cortex, has also increased over evolutionary time. This is illustrated by the increase in the number of layers of the cortical plate as shown in Figure 6. Thus, some of the genetic changes between primates and humans produced an increase in the complexity as well as size of the brain.

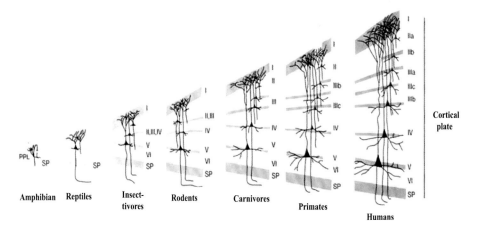

Figure 6. Evolution of the complexity of the cortical plate over time. Starting with layer I, layers are added progressively from deeper first (VI, V) to more superficial (III, II) last. In mammals with ever-larger brains, layers II/III/IV are progressively subdivided into II, III, IV, then IIa, IIb, and so on. From the Comparative Brain Atlas. [8a]

Microscopic changes. Since the 1990s scientists have identified a number of other microscopic features of the nervous system that are unique to humans and to a lesser extent, the higher apes. In 1999 Preuss and colleagues [49] found a layer of the visual cortex that was unique to humans, which may explain why we can detect objects against a background better than other animals. In the same year Hof and coworkers [50] found that a unique type of elongate slender cells called *von Economo neurons,* were unique to humans, the great apes, and whales. These cells may relay nerve impulses faster than other neurons. They are found in areas relating to cognition and advanced planning such as area 10 and the anterior cingulate cortex. [51] An additional microscopic feature, known as minicolumns, consist of 80 to 100 nerve cells bundled together vertically in the cerebral cortex. In Broca's area and area 10 these neurons are wider and more densely packed than in apes and chimps. [52,53]

Role of specific genes. *Microcephalin.* Genetic mutations that cause human disease can often provide clues to the identity of which genes are involved in specific traits such as brain size. A single gene mutation can cause microcephaly (small head) producing severe reduction in brain size without other gross abnormalities. [9-11] Individuals with this condition are mentally retarded and their brain size is comparable with that of early hominids. The gene involved is called *microcephalin (MCH1).* Studies of human populations have shown that *MCH1* contains different polymorphisms, many of which cause amino acid substitutions. The richness of these polymorphisms is likely to be due to a combination of population expansions and Darwinian selection. The analysis of the ratio of the polymorphisms that caused amino acid substitutions versus those that did not showed positive selection of *MCH1* during the origin of the last common ancestor to humans and the great apes, and corresponds to the drastic brain enlargement from the lesser apes to the great apes. [9,10] Much of the selection occurred on five polymorphisms that were associated with amino acid substitutions. An analysis that was extended back to 30 million years ago suggested that about 45 advantageous amino acid changes occurred over the evolution of our earliest primate ancestors. [11] A subsequent analysis indicated that one variant arose about 37,000 years ago. [10] This might have been relevant to the explosion of symbolic behavior occurring in Europe around that time. [12] These results clearly support the frequent occurrence of beneficial mutations in evolution.

ASPM (abnormal spindle-like microcephaly). ASPM is a second gene associated with microcephaly in humans. Similar analyses of the polymorphisms in *ASPM* also indicate that it experienced strong positive selection in the ape lineage leading to humans. [11,13-16] The evolutionary selection of specific segments of the *ASPM* gene was strongly related to brain size. One variant arose about 5,800 years ago and was quickly swept to high frequency. Direct studies in living humans show no association between *microcephalin* or *ASPM* variants with IQ. [10a]

SIGLEC11 (Saliac acid-binding receptor). This is a gene relevant to surface membranes and present in the microglia, the so-called "glue cells" of the brain. Since it is a human-specific gene [17] it may have played a role in the evolution of *Homo sapiens* and brain size. While other genes are likely to have been involved, these studies show that advantageous mutations in a small number of genes can be associated with a trait as complex as brain size.

Role of nutrition. Nutrition and energy metabolism played a unique role in the evolution of man. The brain in modern humans consumes an inordinate amount of energy, 16 times as much as a comparable weight of muscle. In the resting state the brain uses a whopping 24 percent of an adult human's energy needs [3] compared to 10 percent for nonhuman primates and five percent for other mammals. Leonard plotted the percent of resting energy allocated to the brain for our human ancestors against time in millions of years ago. This plot is shown in Figure 7.

In agreement with the data in Figure 5, this also shows a linear increase over time. A high degree of energy expenditure places a premium on the energy content of food. A meal of 3.5 ounces of animal meat provides up to 200 kilocalories, while a comparable amount of fruit supplies 50 to 100 kilocalories, and foliage supplies only 10 to 20 kilocalories. In addition, cooking food, especially starchy foods, significantly increases the available energy content by making complex carbohydrates more digestible. It has been estimated that the first hominid began using fire 1.8 million years ago. [3]

The spread of grasslands led to an increase in grazing animals. This source of food both provided more concentrated calories and led to hunting and gathering in cooperating foraging social groups. Freeing of the hands allowed the beginnings of the use of tools to aid in hunting and skinning the prey. The improved dietary quality alone cannot explain why hominid brains grew, but it appears to have played a critical role in allowing that change to take place. [18]

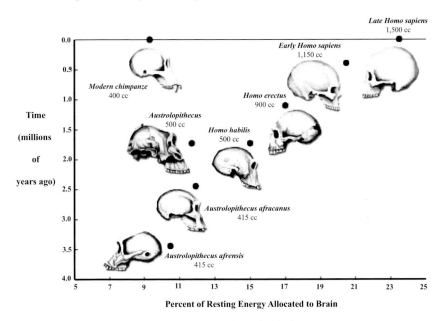

Figure 7. *Percent of resting energy allocated to the brain versus time in millions of years ago. From Leonard, W. R. Food for Thought.* Scientific American. *2002.* [3] *Drawing by Cornelia Blik.*

Origin of Speech

Larynx. Speech and language is one of the most unique of human traits. It plays a central and critical role in allowing the development of complex, interacting human societies. Phillip Lieberman, a linguist from Brown University, proposed that the critical change that paved the way for the development of speech was the migration of the larynx away from a close association with the jaw to further down in the neck. [19] He suggested that this lower location allowed for the production of a much-varied range of sounds, resulting in the ability to speak. The resulting increased power to communicate paved the way for the development of modern man and civilization.

Brain. As with other aspects of human evolution, new traits did not develop overnight. Even if a relocation of the larynx to the neck allowed speech to develop, the role of the brain in formulating speech also needed to develop. The two parts of the human brain most involved in speech are Broca's area and Wernicke's area. Their location in the human brain and comparable areas in the chimpanzee are shown in Figure 8.

Broca's area is part of the frontal lobe at the left inferior frontal gyrus. Individuals who suffer strokes or other damage to this area have expressive aphasia with impairment in the ability to produce language. Wernicke's area is part of the temporal lobe at the left superior temporal gyrus. Individuals who suffer strokes or other damage

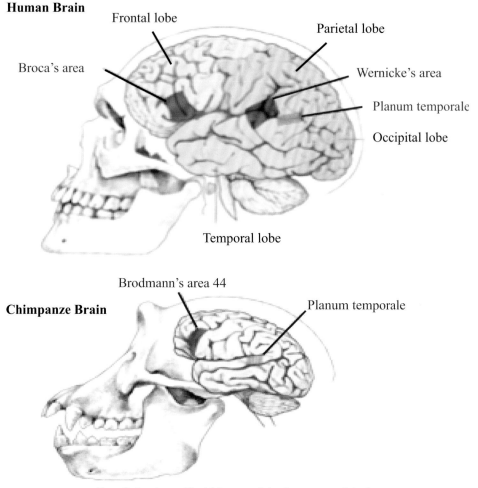

Human Brain

Frontal lobe

Parietal lobe

Broca's area

Wernicke's area

Planum temporale

Occipital lobe

Temporal lobe

Brodmann's area 44

Chimpanze Brain

Planum temporale

Figure 8. Broca's area, Wernicke's area, and the planum temporale in the human brain and comparable areas in the chimpanzee brain. After Carroll, S. B. Genetics and the making of Homo sapiens. *Reprinted by permission from Macmillan Publishers, Ltd.* Nature. *422:849-857, 2003.* [5]

to this area have receptive aphasia with impairment in the ability to understand language. While speech has a natural sounding rhythm it is jumbled and without recognizable meaning. The planum temporale is a key component of Wernicke's language area. In addition to speech it has been implicated in musical talent. These areas are present on the left side of the brain producing a right–left asymmetry in brain structure. Similar asymmetries have been noted for Brodmann area 44 and the planum temporale in the chimpanzee, suggesting the rudiments of expressive and receptive language in this species and that the lateralization of speech to the left size of the brain occurred prior to the divergence of the human and chimpanzee lines. [20,21] An area homologous to Broca's area has even been found in monkeys where it was involved in facial expressions, especially those involved in communication. It is likely that this area was coopted by human ancestors for control of expressive speech.

The *FOXP2* gene. In humans, severe impairment in expressive and receptive language is occasionally inherited in multiple family members as an autosomal dominant trait. When many individuals in one family are affected, linkage studies can identify the chromosomal region involved. In such a study of a family called KE by Lai et al. [22] the locus was mapped to the short arm of chromosome 7 (7p31) and given the name *SPCH1*. The same authors also found a separate individual with the same speech defect who had a chromosomal rearrangement (translocation) involving the *SPCH1* region. This allowed them to identify the specific gene involved. It was a transcription factor called *FOXP2*. Further studies showed that mutations at the *FOXP2* gene were actually a rare cause of speech and language impairment in children both with [23] and without autism. [24] Sites on several other chromosomes were involved in the most common forms of speech and language defects. [25]

Additional studies continued to support the important role of the *FOXP2* gene in speech. For example, functional MRI studies of individuals carrying the *FOXP2* mutation showed underactivity of Broca's area. [26] In a study in mice, when one of the *FOXP2* genes was experimentally inactivated there was a significant alteration in the ultrasonic vocalizations emitted by the pups when they were removed from their mothers. Finally, an analysis of the mutational changes in the *FOXP2* gene in humans, chimpanzees and mice showed that the human *FOXP2* gene experienced a greater than 60-fold increase in substitution rate compared to the animals without speech. There were two amino acid changes in a transcription domain that were unique to humans. [27,28] This clearly indicated that the *FOXP2* gene played an important role in the evolution of our ability to talk.

General Screen for Genes Involved in the Evolution of Man

It is known that the sequence of human DNA and that of his closest relative, the chimpanzee, is 99 percent identical, [29] attesting to the close relationship between man and this primate cousin. This still leaves room for many differences, and a number of researchers are searching for these differences. The *MCH1, ASPM,* and *FOXP2* genes studied above are what geneticists call *candidate genes.* Based on prior knowledge of their function they are examined because they seem like good candidates, in this case for brain size and speech respectively. However, there are approximately 21,000 human genes, many of which may be involved in human evolution but are not currently clear candidates for the job. To identify these, an alternative to examining specific candidate genes is used to perform mass screens of many genes. *The genetic variations present in different genes can be used to identify those that have been subjected to an unusual degree of natural selection.* The methods for doing this include the following: examining the differences in proteins themselves, the differences in the expression of messenger RNA in individual genes, the differences in DNA sequence, the differences in gene copy number, and the differences in regulatory RNA.

Examination of proteins. This is done by a technique called *two-dimensional gel electrophoresis.* The cellular proteins of a given organ are separated in one direction by size and the second direction by electrical charge. The 2-D gels of cell proteins of the human and chimpanzee frontal cortex from a study by Enard and colleagues[30] are shown in Figure 9.

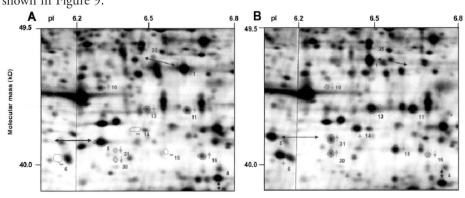

Figure 9. Two-dimensional gel electrophoresis of cell proteins from the frontal cortex (Brodman's area 9) of human (A) and chimpanzee (B). From Enard et al. Science. *296:340-343, 2002.[30] By permission.*

The advantage of examining proteins is that differences in mRNA levels do not necessarily translate into differences in protein levels, while examining the actual amount of a protein in the cell clearly does. If a mutation results in the substitution of an amino acid with no electrical charge, like proline, with an amino acid that has a negative charge, like glutamic acid, there will be a net -1 charge difference in the whole protein. These differences in charge due to mutations can be identified by 2-D gels. In the Enard study, brain, liver, and plasma were examined. The brain samples came from Brodmann's area 9, involved in cognition. A total of 538 spots were analyzed for the human-chimpanzee comparison. Of these 7.6 percent showed charge changes while 31.4 percent showed changes in the level of expression. The observed changes were more pronounced in the brain than the other tissues.

Examination of mRNA expression. The advantage of directly examining gene expression by examining the amount of messenger RNA produced is that many more genes can be tested. In addition, the function of most of the genes is known and specific organs or parts of organs can be compared. The technique for doing this involves the use of microarrays, produced by a technology similar to that used in producing tiny (micro) computer chips containing millions of transistors. In this case, instead of transistors, different nucleic acid sequences corresponding to different genes are attached to the microarrays. The basic aspects of this remarkable technique are illustrated in Figure 10. RNA is isolated from the two tissue samples to be examined, A and B. A DNA copy of these sequences is made by reverse transcriptase and in the process one is labeled with a red dye, the other with a green dye.

These sequences are then combined and hybridized to the array to which thousands of nucleic acid sequences corresponding to different genes are attached. The result is examined in a fluorescent microscope. If a given spot contains a sequence present in sample A, but less so in sample B, the spot will be red. If the sequence is present in sample B, but less so in sample A, the spot will be green. If the sequence is present in approximately equal amounts in A and B, the spot will be yellow. Variations in intensity and color allow the differences to be quantified.

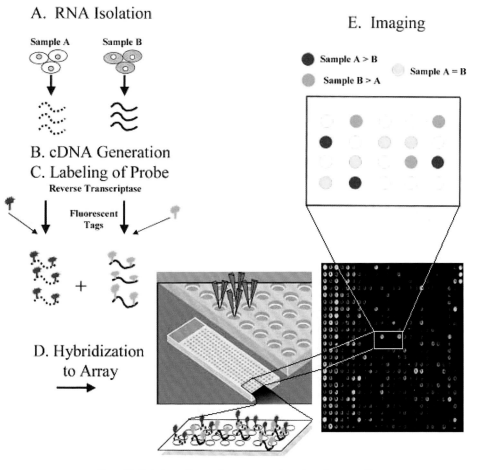

Figure 10. *Technique of comparing gene expression using microarrays.* [30a]
See text.

An advantage of this technique is that the expression of genes in a specific organ or organ part can be examined. Thus, we might be interested in the question, "What genes are involved in human cognition and reason?" Examining tissue from those parts of the brain that were involved in cognitive function could assess this. This is what Uddin and colleagues [31] did. They examined human, chimpanzee, gorilla and monkey tissue from the anterior cingulate cortex. Imaging studies show that blood flow is increased in this area when humans are involved in cognitive tasks such as making a decision between two interfering choices—otherwise known as judgment. Approximately 16,000 genes were examined. Based on our inherent sense of superiority it might be anticipated that the evolutionary changes were greatest in the human line. Surprisingly, the greatest changes in gene expression were seen in both the human and chimpanzee lines. This is consistent with the findings that chimpanzees engage in culture, [32] the use of tools, [33,34] and display rudimentary forms of language, [35] and is a further indication of how closely related these two species are. Up-regulation was noted in genes for energy metabolism and nerve function, consistent with the fact the human brain consumes a large percent of total energy resources.

An alternative method of examining gene expression data is to look at gene expression networks. This refers to how genes are co-expressed in different organs. For example, if gene A is active in the cortex gene B may also be active in humans but not in chimpanzees. Geschwind and coworkers found that in the cortex, 17.4 percent of co-expression networks were specific to humans. [35a]

Examination of DNA sequences. As with the gene expression studies, the advantage of examining DNA sequences is that many more genes can be examined and the precise function of most of these genes is known. However, these studies cannot examine for organ specific differences since the DNA sequence is the same in all organs.

Clark and colleagues [36] compared the sequence of 7,645 genes in humans, chimpanzees, and mice. They chose those genes that had similar sequences in the three animals (orthologs) and whose function was known. At the time this study was done the entire human and mouse sequence was known. This was not the case for the chimpanzee. They compensated for this by amplifying and sequencing the comparable exons from one male chimpanzee. Using a model that allowed the individual domains of the protein sequence to be tested, they identified 873 genes that showed evidence for a significant level of selection. Genes involved in smell showed the strongest selection. Genes involved in amino acid metabolism showed the second greatest level of selection. This is consistent with the prominent role of dietary changes in human evolution. Included in this set would be changes providing increased survival in times of famine. These could be the same genes that predispose to diabetes and obesity when food is plentiful. Other groups of selected genes include those involved in the skeletal development, brain development, embryonic development (homeotic genes) and hearing. This study only examined the coding part of these genes. Other studies are needed to examine the important regulatory sequences of genes.

Nielsen and colleagues [37] examined the sequence of 13,731 genes in humans and chimpanzees. Here the genes related to immune defenses appeared at the top of the natural selection list (Table 1).

Table I. Biological Categories of Genes Showing Positive Selection
From Nielsen et al. *PLOS Biology* 3:976-985, 2005. [37]

Biological Process	# genes	p-value
Immunity and defense	417	.0000
T-cell-mediated immunity	82	.0000
Chemosensory perception	45	.0000
Biological process unclassified	3,069	.0000
Olfaction (smell)	28	.0004
Gametogenesis	51	.0005
Natural killer-cell-mediated immunity	30	.0018

Spermatogenesis and motility	20	.0037
Inhibition of apoptosis (cell death)	40	.0047
Interferon-mediated immunity	23	.0080
Sensory perception	133	.0160
B-cell and antibody-mediated immunity	57	.0298

Genes involved in defense against viral infections and the important major histocompatibility complex were especially involved. As in the Clark study, there was selection for genes involved in smell and hearing. A large group of genes of unknown biological function was identified. The sequence of many of these suggested they coded for genes regulating transcription factors. They also found that genes involved in spermatogenesis and apoptosis (cell death) were strongly selected for. Table 1 lists all of the gene groups identified as experiencing strong selection.

Surprisingly, Nielsen and colleagues found that instead of showing evidence for strong selection, most brain genes were highly conserved. While this may seem to conflict with the results of Enard and colleagues, they may not. Most of the changes that the Enard study identified were in the level of expression rather than in amino acid substitutions. Nielsen did not test for levels of gene expression or changes in copy number. [37] Later studies, [38,39] including the report of the entire chimpanzee genome DNA sequence, [40] supported the findings of Nielsen and colleagues about the role of transcription and immune factors, but also found that *some of the most rapidly evolving genes were those involved in the function of the central nervous system.*

Changes in promoter regions. Promoter regions are located at the 5' end of the gene and carry the DNA sequences that interact with transcription factors to regulate the degree of expression of the genes. While the DNA sequences between humans and chimpanzees are 99 percent similar, a disproportionate number of these differences may occur in the promoter regions. This would drive the changes in gene expression described above. Some specific examples of this have been reported. For example, the prodynorphin gene *(PDYN)* produces the precursors to brain dynorphin and other morphine-like peptides. Variations at the *PDYN* gene have been reported to be associated with pain perception, social attachment, bonding, learning and memory. Sequencing studies have shown that the promoter region of the *PDYN* gene has accumulated six different nucleotide changes since the divergence of humans from the other primates. [41] This is illustrated in Figure 11.

These changes differ significantly (p < .0001) from those expected by chance and indicate that the *PDYN* gene plays an important role is some of the behavioral differences between humans and chimpanzees. They support the concept that many of the important DNA sequence differences between humans and other primates occur in the promoter regions of genes.

Changes in copy number. This refers to gene duplication, one of the major driving forces in evolution. Gene duplication results in an increase in copy number from one to two or higher. Fortna and colleagues [42] examined the copy number of 29,619 genes across five hominid species including humans. Copy number increases

position in 68 bp promoter

Primate	9	15	16	29	62	67
Human	G	G	G	G	C	A
Chimpanzee	A	C	A	A	T	T
Bonobo	A	C	A	A	T	T
Gorilla	A	C	A	A	T	T
Orangutan	A	C	A	A	T	T
Baboon	A	C	A	A	T	T
Pig-tailed macaque	A	C	A	A	T	T
Rhesus monkey	A	C	A	A	T	T

Figure 11. Nucleotide changes in the 68 bp PDYN gene promoter showing that all of these changes occurred after the divergence of humans from other primates. From Rockman, et al. PLOS Biology. 3:e387, 2005. [41]

were most pronounced in humans (134 sites). The genes involved included a number involved in the structure and function of the brain. A study of copy number by Demuth and coworkers showed that human and chimpanzee gene copy numbers differ by 6.4 percent. [42a]

Changes in non-coding RNA. It has been known for years that the expressed genes make up only about two percent of the total genome in mammals including humans. At one time the remainder was referred to as "junk" DNA, suggesting it had no real function. It was then found that the exons or parts of the genes that code for the sequence of amino acids in genes, is interrupted by many introns. These account for 30 percent of the genome. Introns are transcribed into RNA, but for years it was thought that this RNA was simply broken down and destroyed. It is now known that over 60 percent of the genome is transcribed into RNA, and this RNA comes in many different forms and sizes, including microRNA, siRNA (silencing RNA), and ncRNA (non-coding RNA). These originate from the introns, the DNA between the genes, and even the opposite DNA strand from that transcribed to produce mRNA. [43-45] Some of the noncoding RNA sequences are highly conserved while others show rapid changes in DNA sequence from species to species. All of these small RNAs play a major role in gene regulation.

Changes in human accelerated regions. Pollard and colleagues [46] identified 35,000 segments of DNA, averaging 140 bp in length, that showed virtually no change in sequence between mice and chimpanzees. They then searched among these segments and identified 49 that showed many base pair changes when compared to humans. These were termed *human accelerated regions (HARs)*. Remarkably, all but one of these *involved genes that coded for non-coding regulatory RNA rather than for proteins*. Of these 49, 24 percent were next to genes involved in brain development, indicating that *many of the HARs were brain-specific regulatory elements that had changed rapidly during human evolution*. The one that showed the most rapid evolution, with 18 base changes since diverging from the chimpanzee was termed *HAR1*. Further studies showed that this novel RNA gene was expressed in the human cortex between seven and 19 weeks after conception. *HAR1* was expressed in neurons that also repressed reelin, a protein involved in specifying the six-layer structure of the human cortex. Thus, this uniquely human structure of the human cortex, shown earlier in Figure 6, was in part directed by the rapid evolution of a single regulatory gene, *HAR1*.

Another study of the evolution of non-coding DNA was reported by Prabjalar and colleagues. [47] They examined human specific substitutions in 110,549 conserved non-coding sequences and identified 992 with a significant excess of human-specific substitutions. They then examined the genes that were adjacent to these sequences. The most impressive changes were next to genes for *neuronal cell adhesion* proteins that control the interactions between nerve cells. These studies support the concept that changes in regulatory non-coding DNA have played a major role in the evolution of man.

> **When all studies are combined, they indicate that the DNA sequence of brain genes show many changes in expression and copy number during the evolution of humans. Studies of non-coding DNA identified significant changes in a number of brain-specific genes during the evolution of man.**
>
> **Among the non-brain genes, the greatest selective forces have occurred in those for smell, hearing, immune defenses (especially against viruses), amino acid metabolism to allow for the greater energy requirements of the enlarging brain, and spermatogenesis.**
>
> **The fact that human and chimp genes are vastly more similar (99 percent) than they are different (one percent) provides overwhelming evidence that man evolved from the apes.**

Sex for all Seasons

While the development of speech led to improved socialization and bonding between humans, a second development also played an important role. Unlike other animals, man is unique in that both males and females are hormonally set up to mate throughout the year instead of only in certain seasons. This sex-on-call feature of humans further contributed to strong kin cohesion and pair bonding. The physiologist Jared Diamond considered this to be a key event in the evolutionary ascendancy of mankind. [48] Spirituality relates to the feeling of being connected with dimensions greater than oneself. Since pair bonding (marriage) and strong kin cohesion (extended family) are important parts of this greater dimension, it is likely that that capability for sex for all seasons played a role in the evolution of man's spirituality.

Other Distinguishing Features of *Homo sapiens*

Unlike finches, where a simple change in beak size can lead to a new species, the evolution of man was far more complex. It was not simply a matter of the development of a few new features but rather a whole symphony of new features. The following is a partial listing. [21]

> Advanced tool-making
> Body shape and thorax
> Brain structure (Broca's area, Wernicke's area, other areas)
> Cranial and facial features
> Decrease in protruding jaw
> Dimensions of the pelvis
> Increased brain size
> Long lifespan
> Opposing thumb and shortened fingers
> Presence of a chin
> Prolonged childhood
> Reduced hair cover
> Relative limb length (shorter)
> Skull balanced upright on vertebral column
> Small canine teeth
> S-shaped spine
> Speech and language
> Spirituality

Carroll [21] has pointed out that the large number of these changes is consistent with a gradual and progressive accumulation of many advantageous and adaptive polygenic mutational changes. The results of the gene sequence studies of Clark [36] and Nielsen [37] are consistent with the conclusion that man was made by microevolution, not by macroevolution or divine creation.

To some, the idea that humans evolved from the apes is even more disturbing than the idea that all other animal species are the product of evolution by mutation and natural selection. Some of the most dramatic aspects of human evolution include:

- **the descent from the trees to the grasslands**
- **standing upright and thus freeing the hands for multiple tasks, including holding food and babies, killing prey, and making tools**
- **the dramatic increase in brain size and complexity**
- **the development of speech and language**
- **the more rapid evolution of genes involved in smelling, hearing, immune defense, spermatogenesis, and brain**

development
- **changes in hormones to allow sex for all seasons**
- **spirituality**
- **and many others.**

The entire process of human evolution involved multiple steps and thousands of genes. Humans evolved by microevolution rather than macroevolution or divine creation.

References

1. Wells, J. *Icons of Evolution: Science or Myth? Why much of what we teach about evolution is wrong.* Regnery Publishing, Inc., Washington, DC, 2000.
2. Darwin, C. *The Descent of Man and Selection in Relation to Sex.* Murray, London, 1871.
2a. Figure from Nadersen, N. www.eyesondesign.net/2002gallery/lemur.jpg. By permission.
2b. Figure from Toug C. *The Variety of Life. A Survey and Celebration of All the Creatures That Have Ever Lived.* Oxford University Press, London, 2000.
3. Leonard, W. R. Food for thought. Dietary change was a driving force in human evolution. *Sci Am.* 287: (December) 106-115, 2002.
4. Wildman, D. E., Uddin, M., Liu, G., Grossman, L. I. & Goodman, M. Implications of natural selection in shaping 99.4% nonsynonymous DNA identity between humans and chimpanzees: enlarging genus *Homo. Proc Natl Acad Sci USA.* 100: 7181-718, 2003.
5. Carroll, S. B. Genetics and the making of *Homo sapiens. Nature.* 422: 849-857, 2003.
6. Cann, R. L., Stoneking, M. & Wilson, A. C. Mitochondrial DNA and human evolution. *Nature.* 325: 31-36, 1987.
7. Skorecki, K. et al. Y chromosomes of Jewish priests. *Nature.* 385: 32, 1997.
8. Henneberg, M. & de Miguel, C. Hominins are a single lineage: brain and body size variability does not reflect postulated taxonomic diversity of hominins. *Homo.* 55: 21-37, 2004.
8a. Figure from brainmuseum.org. The University of Wisconsin and Michigan State Comparative Mammalian Brain Collections and the National Museum of Health and Medicine. Funded by National Science Fundation and National Institutes of Health.
9. Wang, Y. Q. & Su, B. Molecular evolution of microcephalin, a gene determining human brain size. *Hum Mol Genet.* 13: 1131-1137, 2004.
10. Evans, P. D. et al. Microcephalin, a gene regulating brain size, continues to evolve adaptively in humans. *Science.* 309: 1717-1720, 2005.
10a. Balter, M. Links between brain genes, evolution, and cognition challenged. *Science.* 313:1872, 2006.
11. Evans, P. D., Anderson, J. R., Vallender, E. J., Choi, S. S. & Lahn, B. T. Reconstructing the evolutionary history of microcephalin, a gene controlling human brain size. *Hum Mol Genet.* 13: 1139-1145, 2004.
12. Balter, M. Evolution. Are human brains still evolving? Brain genes show signs of selection. *Science.* 309: 1662-1663, 2005.
13. Mekel-Bobrov, N. et al. Ongoing adaptive evolution of *ASPM,* a brain size determinant in Homo sapiens. *Science.* 309: 1720-1722, 2005.
14. Kouprina, N. et al. Accelerated evolution of the *ASPM* gene controlling brain size begins prior to human brain expansion. *PLoS Biol.* 2: E126, 2004.
15. Zhang, J. Evolution of the human *ASPM* gene, a major determinant of brain size. *Genetics.* 165: 2063-2070, 2003.
16. Bond, J. et al. *ASPM* is a major determinant of cerebral cortical size. *Nat Genet.* 32: 316-320, 2002.
17. Hayakawa, T. et al. A human-specific gene in microglia. *Science.* 309: 1693, 2005.
18. Leonard, W. R., Robertson, M. L., Snodgrass, J. J. & Kuzawa, C. W. Metabolic correlates of hominid brain evolution. *Comp Biochem Physiol A Mol Integr Physiol.* 136: 5-15, 2003.
19. Lieberman, P. *On the Origin of Language.* MacMillan, New York, 1975.
20. Gannon, P. J., Holloway, R. L., Broadfield, D. C. & Braun, A. R. Asymmetry of chimpanzee planum temporale: Humanlike pattern of Wernicke's brain language area homolog. *Science.* 279: 220-222, 1998.
21. Carroll, S. Cosmology: Filling in the background. *Nature.* 422: 26-27, 2003.
22. Lai, C. S., Fisher, S. E., Hurst, J. A., Vargha-Khadem, F. & Monaco, A. P. A forkhead-domain gene is mutated in a severe speech and language disorder. *Nature.* 413: 519-523, 2001.
23. Newbury, D. F. et al. *FOXP2* is not a major susceptibility gene for autism or specific language impairment. *Am J Hum Genet.* 70: 1318-1327, 2002.
24. Meaburn, E., Dale, P. S., Craig, I. W. & Plomin, R. Language-impaired children: No sign of the *FOXP2*

mutation. *Neuroreport.* 13: 1075-1077, 2002.

25. Fisher, S. E., Lai, C. S. & Monaco, A. P. Deciphering the genetic basis of speech and language disorders. *Annu Rev Neurosci.* 26: 57-80, 2003.

26. Corballis, M. C. *FOXP2* and the mirror system. *Trends Cogn Sci.* 8: 95-6, 2004.

27. Zhang, J., Webb, D. M. & Podlaha, O. Accelerated protein evolution and origins of human-specific features: *FOXP2* as an example. *Genetics.* 162: 1825-1835, 2002.

28. Enard, W. et al. Molecular evolution of *FOXP2,* a gene involved in speech and language. *Nature.* 418: 869-872, 2002.

29. King, M. C. & Wilson, A. C. Evolution at two levels in humans and chimpanzees. *Science.* 188: 107-116, 1975.

30. Enard, W. et al. Intra- and interspecific variation in primate gene expression patterns. *Science.* 296: 340-343, 2002.

30a. Figure from www.fao.org/documents. By permission.

31. Uddin, M. et al. Sister grouping of chimpanzees and humans as revealed by genome-wide phylogenetic analysis of brain gene expression profiles. *Proc Natl Acad Sci USA.* 101: 2957-2962, 2004.

32. Whiten, A. et al. Cultures in chimpanzees. *Nature.* 399: 682-685, 1999.

32a. Horvath, S and Geschwind, D.H. Conservation and evolution of gene expression networks in human and chimpanzee brains. *Proc. Nat. Acad. Sci. U.S.A.* 103:17973-17978, 2006.

33. Goodall, J. Behavior of free-ranging chimpanzees in the Gombe Stream Reserve. *Animal Behavior Monogr.* 1: 165-311, 1968.

34. Yamakoshi, G. & Myowa-Yamakoshi, M. New observations of ant-dipping techniques in wild chimpanzees at Bossou, Guinea. *Primates.* 45: 25-32, 2004.

35. Savage-Rumbaugh, E. S., Rumbaugh, D. M. & Boysen, S. Symbolic communication between two chimpanzees *(Pan troglodytes). Science.* 201: 641-644, 1978.

36. Clark, A. G. et al. Inferring nonneutral evolution from human-chimp-mouse orthologous gene trios. *Science.* 302: 1960-1963, 2003.

37. Nielsen, R. & al, e. A scan for positively selected genes in the genomes of humans and chimpanzees. *PLoS Biology.* DOI:10: 1371, 2005.

38. Dorus, S. et al. Accelerated evolution of nervous system genes in the origin of *Homo sapiens. Cell.* 119: 1027-1040, 2004.

39. Bustamante, C. D. et al. Natural selection on protein-coding genes in the human genome. *Nature.* 437: 1153-1157, 2005.

40. Consortium, T. C. S. a. a. Initial sequence of the chimpanzee genome and comparison with the human genome. *Nature.* 437: 69-87, 2005.

41. Rockman, M. V. et al. Ancient and Recent Positive Selection Transformed Opioid cis-Regulation in Humans. *PLoS Biol.* 3: e387, 2005.

42. Fortna, A. et al. Lineage-specific gene duplication and loss in human and great ape evolution. *PLoS Biol.* 2: E207, 2004.

42a. Demuth, J.P. et. al. The evolution of Mammalian gene families. *PLoS ONE* 1:e85, 2006.

43. Mattick, J. S. The functional genomics of noncoding RNA. *Science.* 309: 1527-1528, 2005.

44. Claverie, J.-M. Fewer genes, more noncoding RNA. *Science.* 309: 1529-1530, 2005.

45. Lu, C. et al. Elucidation of the small RNA component of the transcriptome. *Science.* 1567-1569, 2005.

46. Pollard et al. An RNA gene expressed during cortical development evolved rapidly in humans. *Nature.* epub, dol:10.1038/nature05113, 2006.

47. Prabjalar. S., Noonan, J. P., Paabo, S. and Rubin, E. M. Accelerated evolution of conserved noncoding sequences in humans. *Science.* 314:786, 2006.

48. Diamond, J. *The Third Chimpanzee.* Harper Perennial, New York, 1992.

49. Preuss, T. M., Qi, H. & Kaas, J. H. Distinctive compartmental organization of human primary visual cortex. *Proc Natl Acad Sci USA.* 96: 11601-6, 1999.

50. Nimchinsky, E. A. et al. A neuronal morphologic type unique to humans and great apes. *Proc Natl Acad Sci USA.* 96: 5268-73, 1999.

51. Allman, J. M., Hakeem, A., Erwin, J. M., Nimchinsky, E. & Hof, P. The anterior cingulate cortex. The evolution of an interface between emotion and cognition. *Ann N Y Acad Sci.* 935: 107-17, 2001.

52. Buxhoeveden, D. P., Switala, A. E., Roy, E., Litaker, M. & Casanova, M. F. Morphological differences between minicolumns in human and nonhuman primate cortex. *Am J Phys Anthropol.* 115: 361-71, 2001.

53. Balter, M. Brain Evolution Studies Go Micro. *Science.* 315: 1208-1210, 2007.

We cannot decide whether the origin of life on Earth was an extremely unlikely event or almost a certainty…

Francis Crick,

Life Itself[1]

Chapter 18

The Origin of Life

One of the most difficult problems in biology to understand is the creation of life on earth. In addition to Francis Crick's comment above, he also said that the origin of life appears at the moment to be "almost a miracle, so many are the conditions which would have had to be satisfied to get it going." [1] Coming from the Nobel Prize-winning scientist who co-discovered the structure of DNA, this comment was seized upon by creationists to validate their position that the origin of life had to be the result of divine creation. The purpose of this chapter is to show that there is clearly a viable alternative.

The Narrow Origin of Life Time Window

One thing has become clear—the time available for the creation of life was fairly short. The earth is 4.6 billion years old, and massive bombardment of the early earth by comets and meteorites apparently occurred until approximately 3.8 billion years ago. Since comets are large and composed predominantly of ice, they are believed to have been the source of the earth's oceans. [2] It was usually felt that the impact of these comets would have produced so much heat that it would have precluded the development of life during the first 500 million years of earth's existence. [3] However, recent observations on zircon microcrystals suggest *the earth may have cooled much more rapidly after its initial formation, perhaps in 100 million years.* [4]

Carbon dioxide (CO_2) in the atmosphere contains two isotopes of carbon, C^{12} in large amounts and C^{13} in small amounts. Since living organisms preferentially use $C^{12}O_2$ a high C^{12}/C^{13} ratio in fossils compared to the ratio in the atmosphere, is a marker for the presence of life forms. The combination of finding microfossils and of analyzing the C^{12}/C^{13} ratio in rocks suggests that life started as early as 3.5 to 3.8 billion years ago. [5,6] Based on initial estimates that it took about 500 million years for the earth to cool this would have left a very narrow time window for the evolution of first life of less than 200 million years and possibly as little as 10 million years. [7] If the earth cooled more rapidly, as the studies of the zircon crystals suggest, the window for the development of life on earth more likely ranged from 10 to 400 million years.

The Miller-Urey Experiment

One of the earliest scientific attempts to understand how life might have gotten started on earth was the 1953 experiment of Stanley Miller[8] at the University of Chicago. Miller was a graduate student of Harold Urey, a Nobel laureate in chemistry. Urey was interested in the primordial atmosphere of the earth and had just published a theory that it was poor in oxygen and rich in hydrogen.[9] Chemically speaking this would have been termed a *reducing atmosphere* as opposed to the modern oxygen-containing *oxidizing atmosphere.*

Many years prior to this, in 1924, a Soviet biochemist Alexander Oparin published an article entitled "The Origin of Life,"[10] and in 1936 wrote a book with the same title.[10] Both were later translated for English-speaking scientists to read. Based on the assumption that the atmosphere of primitive earth contained compounds such as ammonia (NH_3), Oparin proposed that these organic compounds formed a colloidal solution in the primordial ocean. These solutions then coagulated into so-called "coacervates." By absorbing sugars and amino acids, which could serve as catalysts in chemical reactions, a primitive form of metabolism could develop. Competition based on differences in adaptation to the environment brought about a form of evolution to more complex systems. This was in the days before the discovery of DNA and the understanding of its critical role in replication and information storage. As such, this was a "metabolism first" type of model.

In 1929 the British geneticist J. B. S. Haldane[11] wrote an article also entitled "The Origin of Life," and followed this up with a similar article in 1954.[12] Haldane also assumed a reducing atmosphere. Since oxygen (O_2) was absent, ozone (O_3), which protects the earth from ultraviolet rays, was also absent. Prior studies of Baly[13] showed that ultraviolet irradiation of carbon dioxide (CO_2) in water produced complex organic compounds. Based on these facts Haldane proposed that the UV light of the primitive earth resulted in a "hot soup" of organic compounds. As a geneticist, Haldane proposed a replicating "genes first" model in which a small primitive virus-like organism was able to replicate because the necessary precursors were present in this hot soup. This was likely to be an imperfect, error-ridden form of replication, and since replication with errors was the basis of evolution, primitive evolving life was able to get started.

In 1914, Leonard Troland, an American physicist, wrote a remarkably foresighted set of papers in which he proposed that "genetic enzymes" composed of nucleic acids suddenly appeared and were endowed with the ability to catalyze their own replication.[14] These papers were written years before it was recognized that nucleic acids contained the genetic information that was passed from generation to generation.

The reducing atmosphere models of Oparin and Haldane, utilizing methane, ammonia, hydrogen and water to form more complex precursors of life, were combined and called the *Oparin-Haldane hypothesis.* This hypothesis is illustrated in Figure 1.

In 1953, drawing from this hypothesis, Stanley Miller sought to determine experimentally if organic compounds really could be formed in these primitive earth conditions. Chemistry Nobel laureate Harold Urey, Miller's advisor at the University of Chicago, was so skeptical that he did not encourage his student to use this as a Ph.D. dissertation. Miller persisted and enclosed water vapor (H_2O), ammonia

(NH₃), methane (CH₄) and hydrogen (H₂) in a glass flask and used electrical discharges, simulating lightning, as a source of energy to facilitate chemical interactions.

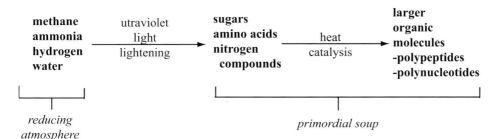

| methane ammonia hydrogen water | utraviolet light lightening | → | sugars amino acids nitrogen compounds | heat catalysis | → | larger organic molecules -polypeptides -polynucleotides |

reducing atmosphere   *primordial soup*

Figure 1. The Oparin-Haldane Hypothesis

Miller-Urey Experiment

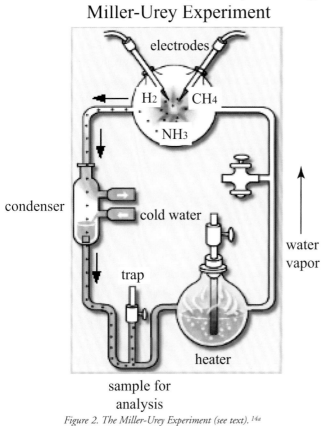

Figure 2. The Miller-Urey Experiment (see text). [14a]

Even Miller was astonished by the results. At the end of a week of allowing these reactions to occur, the water in the flask was deep red and turbid. About 10 percent of the available carbon was converted into organic compounds of which about two percent were amino acids, the building blocks of proteins. [8] These remarkable findings stimulated research around the world and started a new field of investigation in primitive earth or prebiotic chemistry. Importantly, some of these studies also showed the formation of short chains of amino acids known as *peptides*. [15p82]

In 1969 a meteorite fell in Murchison, Australia. Analysis of its chemical composition showed that it contained the same amino acids in the same relative amounts as the compounds produced in Miller's experiment. [16] These findings supported the Oparin-Haldane hypothesis about how organic precursors to primitive life could have been made. The Miller-Urey experiment was only a start toward understanding the possible origins of life on earth.

Creationists' Objections to the Miller-Urey Experiment

The conclusion that the earth's early atmosphere had a lot of hydrogen and was thus reducing, was based on studies of the atmosphere of the larger planets and the widespread presence of hydrogen in the universe. Although the smaller planets like the earth did not have the gravitational force to retain hydrogen in the atmosphere, the secondary atmosphere was still considered to be reducing.

Later evidence suggested that the primitive atmosphere of the earth was derived from volcanic action. Since modern volcanoes did not emit hydrogen, [17] the reducing nature of the early atmosphere was called into question. It was suggested that since water in the atmosphere could be broken down by UV light into oxygen, which would be retained in the atmosphere, and hydrogen would be lost because of its light weight, some oxygen was likely to be present.

A non-oxidizing or reducing atmosphere was necessary to preserve and protect the early organic compounds. The Oparin-Haldane scenario would be significantly weakened by the absence of a reducing atmosphere. The creationists, always searching for any conflicting opinions among scientists, have leapt on these developments to discredit the Miller-Urey experiment [18] and by implication, any non-divine origin of life. However, as often occurs in science, advances in knowledge bring improved clarity to complex issues. This improved clarity showed that there were only trace amounts of oxygen in the early atmosphere; there was a hydrogen-rich early earth atmosphere; comets and meteorites delivered huge amounts of organic compounds to the earth; and underwater hydrothermal vents provided the reducing conditions suitable for the origin of life.

There Was Virtually No Oxygen in the Early Earth's Atmosphere

The level of hydrogen and methane in the atmosphere of primitive earth is still debated. Some have suggested that methane was present and that the atmosphere really was predominantly reducing. [15p114] There is no debate about the fact that there was only a trivial amount of oxygen in the atmosphere prior to 2.1 billion years ago. [19,20] This was clearly not enough oxygen to produce an oxidizing atmosphere. The real issue has been, "Why did it take 1.5 billion years after life began before significant levels of oxygen accumulated in the atmosphere?" The critical point is that even when new Miller-type experiments were performed using various corrected atmospheric conditions the same wide range of organic compounds was produced. [21,22]

There Was a Hydrogen-Rich Early Earth Atmosphere

The escape of hydrogen from the early earth's atmosphere is likely to have occurred at a rate that is one hundred times slower than previously thought. [23] This suggests that the production of prebiotic organic compounds in such an atmosphere would have been more efficient than either of the following two mechanisms— delivery from space or hydrothermal vents.

Comets and Meteorites Provide Prebiotic Organic Compounds

One of the more incredible facets of our solar system is that comets, meteorites and interplanetary dust are loaded with a wide range of organic compounds, including amino acids, hydrogen cyanide, formaldehyde, adenine, and many others. [24] The amount of organic material currently deposited on the earth by meteorites and interplanetary dust is estimated to be about three hundred thousand kilograms, or 300 metric tones per year. During the early period of heavy bombardment this rate may have reached 50,000 tons per year. This rate would have produced the current total biomass in approximately ten million years. [15,25]

Comets are the richest source of organic compounds. [26p186,27] This organic material makes its way to earth in the form of micrometeorites, which are formed when the comets pass close to the sun. These micrometeorites are 50 to 500 um in size and currently reach the earth in huge amounts of 20,000 tons per year. [28] They contain tiny grains that contain clays, oxides, and sulfides of metals, which can act as catalysts in chemical reactions. As such they would function as chemical factories for the production of organic compounds.

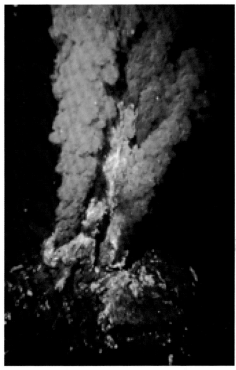

In addition to providing a rich source of organic compounds in prebiotic earth, it has also been proposed that cosmic debris bearing iron and carbon could contribute to a reducing atmosphere and lead to the production of hydrogen, methane, and ammonia in prebiotic earth, producing the conditions assumed in the Miller-Urey experiments. [26,29,30]

Hydrothermal Systems

The bottom of the ocean contains many volcanic, hydrothermal vents (Figure 3). These provide a remarkable ecologic niche. The gas from the vents

Figure 3. Undersea hot, volcanic, hydrothermal vents. [32a]

contains carbon dioxide and methane [31] and can serve as a hot reducing environment for the synthesis of prebiotic organic compounds. [32]

These vents have been proposed as sites for the evolution of life itself. [32,33] The high temperatures characteristic of these volcanic vents are especially suitable for the evolution of the heat-loving, or thermophilic, Archaea.

The complaints of Wells [18] and other creationists about the Miller-Urey experiments are without merit. All evidence indicates that

there was virtually no oxygen in the earth's atmosphere for 1.5 billion years after life, that it contained significant amounts of hydrogen and thus the primitive atmosphere really was predominantly a reducing environment. In addition, a huge amount of organic material was deposited on early earth by comets, cosmic dust, meteorites and micro-meteorites. Finally, Archaea, one of the very earliest forms of life, probably originated in the hot and reducing environment of undersea hydrothermal vents.

Theories of the Origin of Life

The Miller-Urey experiments related to the experimental examination of the Oparin-Haldane hypothesis for the synthesis of prebiotic organic compounds. This is a long way from the evolution of life itself. There have been many proposals for how such evolution may have occurred. The variables for the different models include the type of atmosphere (reducing or neutral); which system came first? (metabolism, cell membranes, protein synthesis, or nucleic acid-based replication); what was the source of energy? (feeding on organic food [heterotrophs] or light rays and chemicals [autotrophs]); which chemical world was involved (an RNA world versus a protein world); and which real world was involved (the earth versus an extraterrestrial origin of life).

It is not my purpose here to review the extensive literature on the origin of life in a short chapter. The excellent books of Iris Fry's *The Emergence of Life on Earth,* [15] and Christian de Duve's *Life Evolving* [34] and *Cosmic Dust,* [35] do this. It is my purpose to show that the creationist's complaint that the rapid evolution of life on primitive earth was so difficult that only a divine creator could do it, is false.

In the following paragraphs I have chosen one of the models that I find to be the most reasonable. This is the protometabolism-transfer RNA model of Nobel laureates Christian De Duve [34] and Manfred Eigen. [36-38] This model is summarized in Figure 4.

Protometabolism—A Chemical World

The first aspect of this model is *protometabolism.* One of the primary problems in modeling the chemistry of the origin of life relates to the issue of "Which came first, the chicken or the egg?" In the origin of life this translates to, "Which came first, proteins or nucleic acids?" It is clear that there are two critical parts of both current and primitive life. These are A) nucleic acids which code for the genes that produce the proteins and enzymes (replicases) that allow the nucleic acid to be made and replicated, and B) protein enzymes that carry out this synthesis and replication. Without the protein the nucleic acid cannot be synthesized and replicate. Without nucleic acids the protein enzymes cannot be made. This was a classic catch-22, a classic chicken or egg. *There is only one clear answer—they evolved together.*

It was also clear that the first nucleic acids had to be RNA, not DNA. RNA is single-stranded and much easier to make and replicate than DNA. Because it is single-stranded it can form complex secondary structures by virtue of some of the

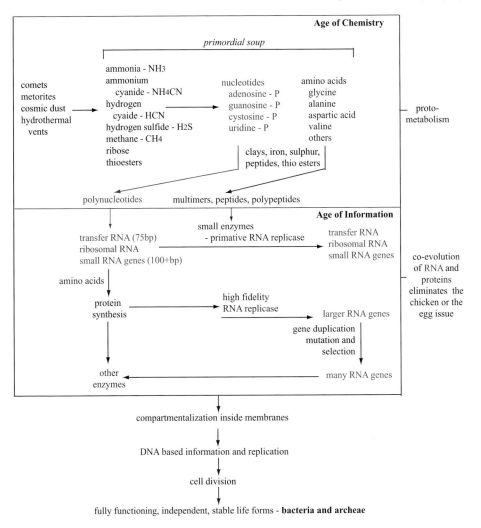

Figure 4. A protometabolism-transfer RNA model of the origin of life. The RNA parts are in red, the peptide and protein parts in blue. See text.

bases pairing with themselves (see transfer RNA in Figure 6 as an example).

It has actually been shown that these complex RNA structures can, in some circumstances, function as enzymes.[39] These are called *ribozymes*. It has been proposed that this would solve the "Which came first, RNA or enzymes?" problem, since RNA could be both a nucleic acid and an enzyme. This model was called *an RNA world*.[40] As elegant and exciting as this would be, De Duve[35] properly points out that this still did not answer the question of how such a complex piece of RNA got there in the first place. He felt that many more preparative steps had to be in place before this could happen. He termed these steps *protometabolism*, referring to chemical steps preceding the formation of complex structures such as RNA. This could be called a chemical world. The following are some aspects of this chemical world.

The primordial soup. The primordial soup that figures prominently in this protometabolism model does not refer to the oceans as a whole. That would represent a soup that was too dilute to feed anyone and certainly not feed the origin of life. The primordial soup concept refers to tidal flats or isolated lagoons where the evaporation of water can result in very concentrated solutions of prebiotic organic compounds.

Synthesis of adenine. One of the most critically important organic molecules involved in prebiotic soup was adenine. When combined with ribose sugar it formed adenosine, part of the energy-storage compound adenosine triphosphate or ATP. In 1961 Juan Oró[41] found that adenine could be formed in a single step from ammonium cyanide, a component of the prebiotic soup.

Non-enzyme catalysts by minerals. Catalysts are critical for any form of metabolism. They accelerate chemical reactions many thousand-fold by holding the chemical reactants close to each other. Enzymes are the catalysts of living organisms. The problem is they are composed of long stretches of different amino acids called proteins, and did not yet exist in prebiotic conditions. However, many organic compounds, especially those with negatively charged phosphorus or carboxyl groups (COO-), are attracted to positively charged inorganic compounds, especially those containing metals such as magnesium (Mg^{++}), copper (Cu^{++}), calcium (Ca^{++}), iron (Fe^{++}), zinc (Zn^{++}), cobalt (Co^{++}) molybdenum (Mo^{++}) and manganese (Mn^{++}). It is clearly no accident that many of the enzymes of modern life have these metals as part of their structure. De Duve called these similarities between prebiotic life and modern life *concordance*.

Some of the most frequently studied inorganic compounds that were considered as important as prebiotic catalysts were hydroxylapatite,[42,43] clay,[43] and iron-sulfur compounds (iron pyrite or fool's gold).[44,45]

Polymerization of amino acids. Polymerization (poly = multiple, mer = part) refers to the joining together of individual parts into a larger whole. It is similar to the phrase carried on the eagle of the U. S. Great Seal, *e pluribus unum,* meaning "out of many, one." One could say the original 13 colonies were polymerized into one nation. The non-enzymatic polymerization of prebiotic amino acids could provide for the formation of primitive enzymes. How could this take place? Four of the most

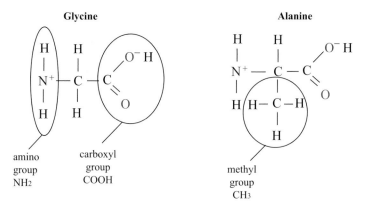

Glycine

amino
group
NH2

carboxyl
group
COOH

Alanine

methyl
group
CH3

Aspartic acid

Valine

$$N^+ - \overset{\overset{\displaystyle H}{|}}{C} - C\overset{O^-H}{\underset{O}{\diagup}}$$

common amino acids in the Miller-Urey type of experiments, in comets and meteorites, and in the prebiotic earth, were glycine, alanine, aspartic acid, and valine. The structure of these amino acids is as follows:

In order to polymerize amino acids it is necessary to form a peptide bond between the amino group of one amino acid with the carboxyl group of a second amino acid. This reaction is accomplished by removing an -OH group from the CO-OH carboxyl group and a hydrogen from the NH_2 amino group to form water and a peptide bond. This is shown in Figure 5.

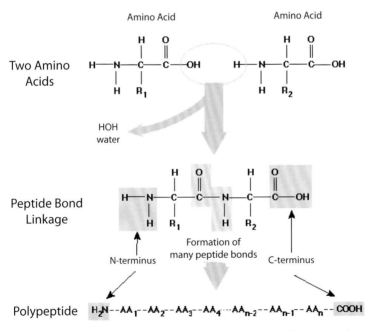

Figure 5. Diagram of the formation of a peptide bond during the polymerization of amino acids to form polypeptides. [45a]

In modern life this is accomplished by ribosomal RNA acting as a ribozyme. How could this important reaction have occurred in prebiotic times? One answer was provided in 1958 by Sidney Fox. [46] He found that simply heating a mixture of amino acids for three hours at 170°C produced a protein-like complex he called proteinoids that had some weak enzyme activities. A more satisfying possibility involves *thioesters.*

Thioesters. Esters are formed when an hydroxyl group (-OH) interacts with a carboxyl group (-COOH) with the removal of water as follows:

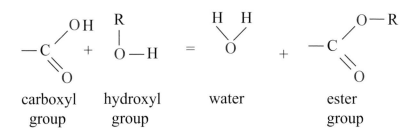

| carboxyl | hydroxyl | water | ester |
| group | group | | group |

Thioesters are esters with a sulfur molecule attached where the oxygen was.

The R refers to any chemical group. The thio group was derived from hydrogen sulfide (H_2S) that pervaded the prebiotic world and produced a putrid rotten egg smell. Theodor Wieland [47] found that when amino acid thioesters were mixed together in water, the amino acids polymerized to form peptides *even in the absence of any catalyst.* This ability to form primitive amino acid polymers that could serve as primitive enzymes provided an important step in the chemical world of protometabolism.

A thioester world. [35p43] As noted previously, adenosine triphosphate or ATP is an important energy source in modern organisms. De Duve felt that ATP was too complex a molecule to have been present in the protometabolism step. However, thioesters also contained high-energy bonds and were energetically equivalent to ATP. They could substitute for ATP and produce high energy inorganic P~P pyrophosphate bonds as a source of energy for polymerization of amino acids and the formation of nucleosides in the prebiotic soup. Thioesters provided the prebiotic world with two essential ingredients, energy and catalysis. [35p44] These above steps are summarized in Figure 4 in the top box called *protometabolism.*

The Co-Evolution of RNA and Proteins

The bottom box in Figure 4 is labeled "The co-evolution of RNA and proteins eliminates the chicken or egg issue." This stage represents the transition from the age of chemistry to the age of information. The following are a number of basic facts and issues involved in this aspect of the model.

Origin of the Four-Letter Code. As described previously, the secret of DNA replication and transcription is the pairing of guanine with cytosine by three hydrogen bonds and adenine with thymine (uracil in RNA) by two hydrogen bonds. Because the G-C pairing involves three hydrogen bonds, it is more stable than the U-T or A-T paring. Since it is likely that there were many other bases in the primordial soup, how were these specific ones chosen? The G-C and A-T based are typical of DNA, but DNA did not even exist yet. As shown in Figure 6, even though RNA is single-stranded it takes on a complex secondary structure by just this type of base pairing. Not only does this secondary structure provide RNA with much of its functional capacities, such as serving as ribozymes, it also protects itself from being destroyed. Single-stranded RNA is much more labile than double stranded RNA. Selecting the G, C, A and U bases would provide a very evolutionary force for ensuring that polymers would survive better than those that could not have a lot of secondary structure.

Transfer RNA. Transfer RNAs were likely to play a critical role in early evolving life. [36,37] This is because they are short (about 75 base pairs) and they provide a critical aspect of the genetic machinery. As shown in Figure 6 transfer RNAs serve as a bridge between the sequence of the bases in primitive genes and the amino acids assembled to form proteins. Just as the secondary structure of RNA was likely to have played an important role in selecting G, C, A and U bases, the attachment of amino acids to transfer RNA may have contributed to their stability and improved their ability to replicate. [35p62]

Transfer RNAs would play a critical role in evolving the early genetic code. Since GC-rich RNAs were more effective at base pairing than AT-rich RNAs, and since the middle position of the three-letter code can be any nucleic acid, the four initial codes were likely to be GGC, GCC, GAC, and GUC, coding respectively for glycine, alanine, aspartic acid, and valine. Sequencing studies indicate that these are, in fact, the most common amino acids in primitive proteins. [38] A genetic code based on the use of three nucleic acids would provide coding for 64 amino acids. However, because of redundancy in the code [p24] there are only 20 amino acids. Recent studies [48] suggest that the use of a two base code preceded the three base code. This would have considerably simplified the evolution of the genetic code. In addition, the temperature-sensitive amino acids glutamine and asparagine would have been left out. This would be consistent with a hot rather than a cold primordial soup.

Small is beautiful. In addition to the transfer RNAs, everything else also had to be small and short. Since the replication enzymes were primitive and not too accurate, the primitive genes had to be short, otherwise, the number of errors would be too great. Since the earliest protein enzymes were probably random chance combinations of amino acids and peptides, they would be short and their enzymatic functions would be crude and primitive. The fact that primitive enzymes were short negates one of the common arguments of creationists that the probability of the random formation of modern proteins that are hundreds of amino acids in length is so remote as to constitute a *Basic Argument for Improbability.* By contrast, there is a very high probability of forming short primitive enzymes in which a wide range of sequences could all work. Short primitive enzymes evolve into longer, more precise enzymes by mutation and natural selection.

Ribosomal RNA. Ribosomal RNA would also be one of the early primitive RNAs. In the absence of protein it can act as a ribozyme and catalyze the formation of peptide bonds. [49] This, in addition to the genetic RNA, was probably an important

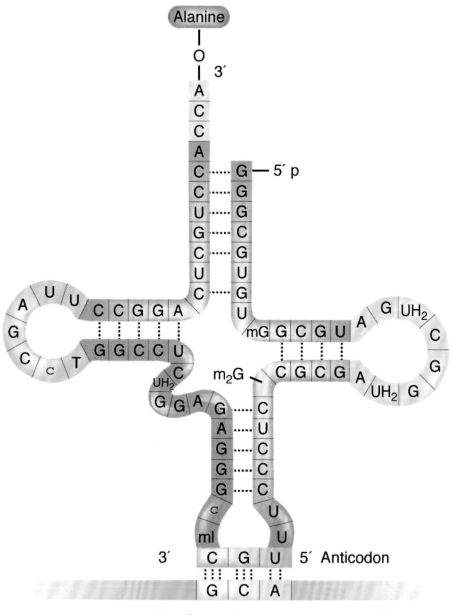

Figure 6. Alanine transfer RNA. The codon GCA in RNA is recognized by base pairing with the anticodon CGU, which in turn is attached to a short transfer RNA with a cloverleaf secondary structure and attached to the amino acid alanine. Thus, GCA (or GCC, GCU, GCG) coded for alanine in the resulting protein. [37a]

early biotic nucleic acid.

The linkage of energy and information. The utilization of ATP, CTP, GTP, and UTP as precursors in the synthesis of RNA is unusually efficient for primitive organisms since these are the same tri-phosphates that serve as important sources of energy in cell metabolism. The di-phosphates ADT, CDP, GDP, UDP and pyrophosphate P-P, are also energy sources. Thus, biological energy and information are intimately linked in nature. [34] These energy sources were likely to have played an important role in chemical reactions preparatory to the appearance of the first RNAs.

Co-evolution of RNA and protein. Since this is a truly irreducible system, all components would have to have evolved together. This was possible since many different short RNA and protein sequences were present in the primitive soup, and those components that worked were the ones utilized. These functioning mixtures of RNAs were called *quasispecies* by Eigen [38] and the complex dynamic interactions of multiple RNAs and protein was termed a *hypercycle.* This co-evolution eliminated the chicken or egg and the catch-22 problems.

Compartmentalization by membranes. Initially much of the assembly of primitive RNA and peptides took place in the primordial soup and was not sequestered behind cell membranes. This had the advantage that the solutions developed by multiple independent copies of primitive proteins or nuclei acids sequences could be shared. For example, the different transfer RNAs could be shared and the ones that worked the best would be used. The first genes would be short and the proteins they produced would be short. The minimum number of genes and enzymes required for independent cellular life is about 300. [50]

Evolution of a DNA-based genome. A double-stranded DNA genome is more stable than an RNA genome. The development of a DNA-based genome was most likely initiated by the development of a reverse transcriptase enzyme. This is well known in modern organisms and produces DNA from an RNA template.

Summary. All of these elements are present in the model shown in Figure 4. Since no one was there, it will be very difficult to prove the exact mechanism of the origin of life. However, the heavens, the earth, and present life forms have all left us with a wealth of clues. The above model cannot claim to be a proven mechanism for life's origins, but it is a reasonable model that is consistent with a wealth of clues. This model shows that the origin of life was not so intractable that only a divine creator could do it.

The question of "How did life first evolve on earth?" is one of the most intriguing questions in biology. The time window for this to occur may have been as narrow as ten million years. Examination of the wide range of modern organisms has provided a wealth of clues about some of the necessary chemicals and conditions required. While many models have been proposed, some are clearly better than others. One of the most likely is a protometabolism-transfer RNA model, consisting first of *The Age of Chemicals* providing the necessary organic compounds, followed by *The Age of Information* involving

the co-evolution of polymers of RNA and protein. **This model shows that the origin of life was not so intractable that only a divine creator could do it.**

Are We Alone?

One of the most impressive lessons learned is how rapidly life evolved, in as little as 10 million years, once the conditions on earth were suitable. This returns us to Crick's statement at the beginning of this chapter of "whether the origin of life on Earth was an extremely unlikely event or almost a certainty." The answer appears to be, it was almost a certainty. Given that there are trillions of planets in the universe that could support life it is virtually inevitable that life exists on many of these, forming what De Duve referred to as the universe's "vital dust." [35p292] Does this diminish us? Of course not. Will we ever communicate with these other forms of intelligent life? Given that most are over 100,000 light years away, probably not. However, one thing is certain, if God exists and is the personal God to all intelligent beings, he is not only going to be very busy but he also has a very difficult task. The speed of communication would have to vastly exceed the speed of light, yet nothing is supposed to exceed the speed of light. These required attributes severely stretch the credulity of our rational brain.

> **Given the rapidity and apparent ease of the origin of life on earth, it is likely that many of the other planets in the universe also have intelligent life. If God exists and is the personal God to this huge number of beings he has a very difficult task. The speed of communication would have to vastly exceed the speed of light. Since nothing is supposed to exceed the speed of light these required attributes severely stretch the credulity of our rational brain.**

References

1. Crick, F. *Life Itself.* Simon and Schuster, New York, 1981.
2. Owen, T. Comets, impacts and atmospheres. *Icarus.* 116: 215-226, 1995.
3. Sleep, N. H., Zahnle, K. J., Kasting, J. F. & Morowitz, H. J. Annihilation of ecosystems by large asteroid impacts on the early Earth. *Nature.* 342: 139-142, 1989.
4. Valle, J. W. A cool early earth? *Sci Am.* 293: 58-65, 2005.
5. Hayes, J. M. The earliest memories of life on earth. *Nature.* 384: 21-22, 1996.
6. Mojzsis, S. J. et al. Evidence for life on Earth before 3,800 million years ago. *Nature.* 384: 55-59, 1996.
7. Lazcano, A. & Miller, S. L. How long did it take for life to begin and evolve to cyanobacteria? *J Mol Evol.* 39: 546-554, 1994.
8. Miller, S. L. A production of amino acids under possible primitive Earth conditions. *Science.* 117: 528-529, 1953.
9. Urey, H. On the early chemical history of the earth and the origin of life. *Proc Nat Acad Sci USA.* 38: 351-363, 1952.
10. Oparin, A. I. The origin of life (Translation of 1924 article). in: Bernal, J. D. *The Origin of Life.* London. Weidenfeld and Nicolson. 1967.
11. Haldane, J. B. S. The origin of life (originally published in 1929). in: Bernal, J. D. *The Origin of Life.* London.

Weidenfeld and Nicolson. 1967.

12. Haldane, J. B. S. The origins of life. *New Biology.* 16: 21-26, 1954.

13. Baly, E. C. C., Davies, M. R., Johnson, M. R. & Shenassy, H. The photosynthesis of naturally occurring compounds. 1—The action of ultra-violet light on carbonic acid. *Proc R Soc Lond A.* 16: 197-202, 1927.

14. Troland, L. T. The chemical origin and regulation of life. *Monist.* 24: 92-133, 1914.

14a. Credit AccessExcellence.org.

15. Fry, I. *The Emergence of Life on Earth.* Rutgers University Press, New Brunswick, NJ, 2000.

16. Miller, S. L. Which organic compounds could have occurred in the prebiotic Earth? *Cold Spring Harb Symp Quant Biol.* 52: 17-27, 1987.

17. Levine, J. S. *The Photochemistry of the Atmosphere.* Academic Press, New York, 1985.

18. Wells, J. *Icons of Evolution: Science or Myth? Why much of what we teach about evolution is wrong.* Regnery Publishing, Inc. Washington, DC, 2000.

19. Copley, J. The story of O. *Nature.* 410: 862-864, 2001.

20. Rye, R. & Holland, H. D. Paleosols and the evolution of atmospheric oxygen: a critical review. *American Journal of Science.* 298: 621-672, 1998.

21. Rode, B. M. Peptides and the origin of life. *Peptides.* 20: 773-786, 1999.

22. Hanic, F., Morvova, M. & Morva, I. Thermochemical aspects of the conversion of the gaseous system CO_2—N_2—H_2O into solid mixture of amino acids. *Journal of Thermal Analysis and Calorimetry.* 60: 1111-1121, 2000.

23. Tian, F., Toon, O. B., Pavlov, A. A. & De Sterck, H. A hydrogen-rich early Earth atmosphere. *Science.* 308: 1014-1017, 2005.

24. Orgel, L. E. Origin of life on earth. *Sci Am.* 53-61, 1994.

25. Whittet, D. C. B. Is extraterrestrial organic matter relevant to the origin of life on Earth? *Origins Life Evol Biosphere.* 27: 249-262, 1997.

26. Gaffey, M. J. The early solar system. *Origins Life Evol Biosphere.* 27: 185-203, 1997.

27. Irvine, W. M. Extraterrestrial organic matter: A review. *Origins Life Evol Biosphere.* 28: 365-383, 1998.

28. Maurette, M. Carbonaceous micrometeorites and the origin of life. *Origins Life Evol Biosphere.* 28: 385-412, 1998.

29. Borowska, Z. K. & Mauzerall, D. C. Efficient near-ultraviolet-light-induced formation of hydrogen by ferrous hydrozide. *Origins Life Evol Biosphere.* 17: 251-259, 1987.

30. De Duve, C. *Blueprint for a Cell.* Neil Patterson Publishers, Burlington, NC, 1991.

31. Sakai, H. T. et al. Venting of carbon dioxide-rich fluid and hydrate formation in mid-Okinawa trough backarc basin. Science 248: 1093-1096, 1990.

32. Holm, N. G. Why are hydrothermal systems proposed as plausible environments for the origin of life? *Origins Life Evol Biosphere.* 22: 5-14, 1992.

32a. From en.wikipedia.org/w/index.php?title=Hydrothermal_vent&oldid=75032133

33. Baross, J. A. & Hoffman, S. E. Submarine hydrothermal vents and associated gradient environments as sites for the orgin and evolution of life. *Origins Life Evol Biosphere.* 15: 327-345, 1985.

34. De Duve, C. *Life Evolving.* Oxford University Press, New York, 2002.

35. De Duve, C. Vital Dust: *Life as a Cosmic Imperative.* Basic Books, NY, 1995.

36. Eigen, M. & Winkler-Oswatitsch, R. Transfer-RNA, an early gene? *Naturwissenschaften.* 68: 282-292, 1981.

37. Eigen, M. & Winkler-Oswatitsch, R. Transfer-RNA: the early adaptor. *Naturwissenschaften.* 68: 217-228, 1981.

37a. Figure from www.mun.ca/biology/scarr/MGA2-03-29.jpg. By permission.

38. Eigen, M., Gardiner, W., Schuster, P. & Winkler-Oswatitsch, R. The origin of genetic information. *Sci Am.* 244: 88-92, 96, et passim, 1981.

39. Kruger, K. et al. Self-splicing RNA: autoexcision and autocyclization of the ribosomal RNA intervening sequence of Tetrahymena. *Cell.* 31: 147-157, 1982.

40. Gilbert, W. The RNA world. *Nature.* 319: 618, 1986.

41. Oro, J. Mechanisms of synthesis of adenine from hydrogen cyanide under possible primitive earth conditions. *Nature.* 191: 1193-1194, 1961.

42. Gibbs, D., Lohrmann, R. & Orgel, L. E. Template-directed synthesis and selective adsorption of oligoadenylates on hydroxyapatite. *J Mol Evol.* 15: 347-354, 1980.

43. Winter, D. & Zubay, G. Binding of adenine and adenine-related compounds to the clay montmorillonite and the mineral hydroxylapatite. *Orig Life Evol Biosph.* 25: 61-81, 1995.

44. Wachtershauser, G. Groundworks for an evolutionary biochemistry: the iron-sulphur world. *Prog Biophys Mol Biol* 58: 85-201, 1992.

45. Wachtershauser, G. The origin of life and its methodological challenge. *J Theor Biol.* 187: 483-494, 1997.

45a. From www.science.siu.edu/microbiology/micr302/figure%207.07.jpg. By permission.

46. Fox, S. W. & Harada, K. Thermal copolymerization of amino acids to a product resembling protein. *Science.* 128: 1214, 1958.

47. Wieland, T. & Schäfer, W. Angew. *Chem.* 63: 146-147, 1951.

48. van den Elsen, J., Babgy, S. & Wu, H.-L. *Journal Molecular Evolution.* 2005.

49. Noller, H. F., Hoffarth, V. & Zimniak, L. Unusual resistance of peptidyl transferase to protein extraction procedures. *Science.* 256: 1416-1419, 1992.

50. Hutchison, C. A. I. et al. Global transposon mutagenesis and a minimal mycoplasma genome. *Science.* 286: 2165-2172, 1999.

Chapter 19

Evolution: Conclusions

The concept that a supreme being created us is an integral part of many religions. When we are born it was by the choice of "Our Creator." During our lifetime we are spiritually guided by "Our Creator," and when we die we go to meet "Our Creator." From the earliest times that humans acquired the ability to have such thoughts and when scientific alternatives were not available, the spiritual world and a belief in a supernatural force was evoked to explain our most critical questions such as, "Where did we come from?", "What is our purpose in life?" and "Who created life?" Other questions relating to our place in the world included "Did God put us at the center of the universe?" If this was true, then the sun must revolve around the earth.

When Galileo began to use the observational powers of science and actually peered into a telescope to view the solar system, he concluded that the earth revolved around the sun. The Catholic Church, which at the time represented the major Western form of organized religion, initially fought Galileo's conclusions. This concept, however, was not a major theological issue, and as the scientific evidence became overwhelming for a heliocentric solar system, religious resistance to the concept faded, culminating in a 1984 apology by Pope John Paul II for the manner in which Galileo was persecuted. [1]

However, when Darwin published *The Origin of Species,* many theologians found the concept that perhaps God was not "the Creator," and perhaps the world did not form in only seven days, and perhaps man was not created in the image of God but in the image of the lowly chimpanzee—way too much to accommodate. In the Middle Ages and even in modern times, many believed in the literal truth of the Bible. If God spoke every word, then every word had to be literally true. Under this view, the theory of evolution was the ultimate enemy. This view, however, was not universal. Many theologians assumed that men wrote the Bible and these men were simply trying to put into writing what they thought was the word of God. Since men are fallible, the Bible could be a metaphor for the truth rather than the absolute literal truth. Darwinism did not threaten theologians who held to this view, and many did hold it. [2]

There was, however, a very vocal minority who continued to believe in the literal truth of the Bible. These were the creationists. More precisely, they were the Young Earth Creationists. This movement was much stronger in the United States than in

Europe. In its effort to provide for freedom of religion for all citizens, the United States Constitution opted for the separation of church and state. A major challenge to this came in Tennessee in 1925 with the famous Scopes "monkey trial." Here, in the heart of the Bible belt, creationists attempted to prevent the teaching of the theory of evolution in the schools. This led to a classic battle of legal titans, Clarence Darrow versus William Jennings Bryan. Even though Darrow lost the case, the scientific position of the Young Earth Creationists was so weak that evolution continued to be taught in the schools.

One method to re-invigorate creationism would be to make it more scientifically palatable. The first item that had to go was the young earth part of creationism. The advent of radioisotope dating and advances in geology and cosmology made this view so untenable that no thinking person, and certainly no scientist, took it seriously. If the creationists were ever to have their views taught in our public schools that part of creationism had to go.

Enter Intelligent Design. Now it is agreed that the earth really is 4.6 billion years old as the radioisotope data clearly shows and yes, some aspects of Darwinism are correct. When pushed by environmental changes some natural selection and evolution can occur, but it is rarely able to actually account for the formation of new species. When some aspects of evolution are carefully examined, especially as related to certain structures and chemical pathways, they are claimed to be so complex and have so many critically interacting parts, that they could not possibly have evolved by the principals of Darwinian evolution. They had to have been the product of Intelligent Design. However, Intelligent Designers are very careful to never mention the word God—God forbid. This would make Intelligent Design sound too religious and this would keep it from being taught in schools as an alternative to the theory of evolution. Instead the Intelligent Design movement simply states that some force or power other than evolution was responsible. In addition, even though providing any testable hypotheses is vigorously avoided, and even though no papers on Intelligent Design have appeared in any of the peer-reviewed scientific literature, its proponents claimed that Intelligent Design is scientific and thus qualifies to be taught in the nation's schools. Finally, once that is accomplished, it is further proposed that any naturalistic scientific method that does not include the possibility of involvement of a divine force should be eliminated.

Our entire modern civilization exists as a result of naturalistic science and the application of the scientific method. This method consists of the generation of testable hypotheses and the dispassionate, unbiased testing of these hypotheses. Hypotheses that fail this process are discarded. Those that pass this process are accepted unless they are falsified by later studies. By contrast, Intelligent Design is not scientific because it does not use the scientific method. It is not dispassionate. It is not unbiased. It pre-judges the outcome and assumes that Intelligent Design is always the correct answer.

In its present incarnation, it appears that Intelligent Design's only enemy is the theory of evolution. However, the Wedge[3] philosophy is far broader than that. It proposes to dismantle all naturalistic science. This clearly would be catastrophic for modern civilization. The best way to counter Intelligent Design is to provide the truth.

The previous chapters illustrate the fact that none of the anti-evolution complaints of Phillip Johnson [4-6] and none of the examples of so-called "irreducible complexity," described by Behe [7] are valid. All of Behe's examples are either reducible or modular or both. A wise man once said "Science moves funereally. Scientists don't change their minds, they just die off." This is often true of non-scientists as well. We all have complex reasons for believing what we believe and those beliefs are difficult to change regardless of rational evidence that suggests they are incorrect. In this respect, this book is not intended to change the mind of any members of the Intelligent Design group. This is unlikely to ever happen regardless of the evidence. This book is instead aimed toward those who the Intelligent Design creationists are attempting to target—non-scientists who need to see all the evidence before they make up their minds. In this book, I am proposing that it is possible for humans to maximally use both their rational and their spiritual brains. To maximize the use of the rational brain, the role for evolution is critical for helping us answer important questions such as, "Where did we come from?" I hope to have made the point that the theory of evolution is incredibly powerful and capable of answering these questions.

It has often been said that the theory of evolution is unscientific because it poses no testable hypothesis. Not every hypothesis in science can be tested in the laboratory. Darwin's theory of evolution poses a wide range of testable predictions. For example, one prediction is that more primitive forms of life should be found in older strata and the more developed forms in later strata. This has been validated in thousands of field studies and evidence to the contrary has never been found. Another prediction was posted by Darwin himself when he stated that in many cases where there appear to be no intermediate forms in the evolutionary process, it is a result of an incomplete fossil record that would eventually be filled in. This prediction has been validated many times. Another prediction is that if all the species on earth are descended from a common ancestor, they should all use the same genetic code. There are 1.4×10^{70} informationally equivalent possible genetic codes. [8] Despite this, all of the thousands of species with sequence data show they use the same genetic code. [9] This is just a small sample of the thousands of testable predictions all of which are consistent with the theory of evolution.

By contrast, Intelligent Design creationism fails to provide testable predictions. Although the founders of Intelligent Design have desperately sought to obtain even the slightest degree of scientific recognition, they have never specified anything that their theory predicts. As pointed out by Kenneth Miller, [10p123] Johnson has assiduously avoided putting into the record what the implications of Intelligent Design would be for the sequential character of the fossil record. In fact, when asked to present any predictions he refused. Miller pointed out that Johnson is a lawyer, not a scientist. Just as a defense attorney's job is to instill reasonable doubt so their client will not be convicted, Johnson's goal is to instill doubt about the theory of evolution as an excuse to teach creationism in schools, not come up with a predictive theory of his own.

While the Intelligent Design creationists need to develop a testable theory of their own in order to have legitimate entry to the marketplace of science, they also need to explain some of the weirdness of their position that a designer was responsible for the creation of living organisms. Miller put it well:

> Intelligent design advocates have to account for patterns in the designer's work that clearly gives the appearance of evolution. Is the designer being deceptive? Is there a reason why he can't get it right the first time? Is the designer, despite all his powers, a slow learner? He must be clever enough to design an African elephant, but apparently not so clever that he can do it the first time. Therefore we find the fossils of a couple dozen extinct "almost" elephants over the last few million years. What are these failed experiments, and why does the master designer need to drive so many of his masterpieces to extinction?
>
> Intelligent Design does a terrible disservice to God by casting him as a magician who periodically creates and creates and then creates again throughout the geological ages. Those who believe that the sole purpose of the Creator was the production of the human species must answer a simple question—not because I asked it, but because it is demanded by natural history itself. Why did this magician, in order to produce the contemporary world, find it necessary to create and destroy creatures, habitats, and ecosystems millions of times over? [10p127-128]

Elsewhere he states:

> They hobble His genius by demanding that the material of His creation ought not to be capable of generating complexity. They demean the breadth of His vision by ridiculing the notion that the materials of His world could have evolved into beings with intelligence and self-awareness. And they compel Him to descend from heaven into the factory floor by conscripting His labor into the design of each detail of each organism that graces the surface of our living planet. [10p268]

Behe, another major Intelligent Design advocate, has been less reluctant to suggest a testable hypothesis. He suggested that the designer placed in the first cell, from which all subsequent organisms evolved, all of the genes required for complex structures but in an inactive state just waiting to be activated when they were needed, often many millions of years later. This prediction is extremely easy to falsify by examining the DNA sequence of prokaryotes versus eukaryotes. Not only do prokaryotes have less total DNA, they have far fewer genes than vertebrates and mammals. In addition, this hypothesis violates Behe's own statements that "natural selection can only chose systems that are already working." [7p228] If a gene is inactive for millions of years before being called upon to function, it will not undergo natural selection and will have accumulated so many deleterious mutations that it would cease to exist.

I have attempted to show in the prior chapters on evolution that none of the Intelligent Design arguments are valid. Since their focus is on complexity, I have focused on the most complex of the issues they have raised. Responses to any issues not covered in these chapters can be found on web sites such as the National Center for Science Education at www.ncseweb.org, evolution.berkeley.edu, www.talkorigins.org, and www.talkreason.org.

Is Darwinism Poison to Religion?

The source of much of the vitriol that both the Creationists and the Intelligent Design creationists displayed in trying to discredit evolution comes from the belief that it diminishes God and the teachings of Christianity. The literal Young Earth Creationists believe that if the account of creation in the Book of Genesis is falsified, then none of the teachings of the Bible can be believed. Apparently they have never heard of the use of metaphor as a powerful technique in literature. The Intelligent Design creationists have similar worries that if the job of creation is taken away from God, his role as Redeemer is somehow diminished. Both groups worry that if Darwinism is true then the whole moral fabric of humanity is somehow doomed. Do all Christians agree with these views? No. Robert Pennock put it well in his book, *Tower of Babel.*[11p39]

> Because almost all of the conflict that reaches the level of public debate involves creationists attacking evolution and scientists defending the same, most people have the erroneous, though understandable, view that this is just a battle between Fundamentalist Evangelicals and scientists, and do not recognize that many mainstream Christian theologians are equally involved in opposing creationism. They are appalled that creationists presume to limit the means by which God's creative power can operate and to claim that their anti-evolutionary view is the only true Christian viewpoint. Theologically they object to thinking of Genesis as giving a literal description of Creation as though it were a science textbook, and they caution us not to forget the notorious earlier "conflict" between the scientific and religious views about the movement of the earth and the heavens, and the aphorism that was the lesson of "the Galileo affair," namely that the Bible teaches how to go to heaven, not how heaven goes. Many mainline religions and Christian denominations have explicitly declared that they find no conflict with evolution.

A specific example is the statement of Pope John Paul II. In an October 22, 1996 message to the Pontifical Academy of Sciences, he explicitly endorsed the findings of evolutionary theory, stating that "fresh knowledge leads to recognition of the theory of evolution as more than just a hypothesis."

Judaism also has no issue with evolution. Rabbi Samson Raphael Hirsch (1808-1888), the great nineteenth-century Torah scholar, wrote that a totally naturalistic evolutionary explanation for life would show the "creative wisdom" of God in being able to design a set of simple rules that produces extraordinarily complex and rich results without any need for interference. Thus, neither mainstream Christian, Catholic, nor Jewish theologians believe that evolution is a threat to their religion.

The scientific method, what Johnson calls "scientific naturalism," is also no threat to religion. The scientific method cannot rule out a role for God as a causative agent in a given process; it simply does not start with the assumption that God is the cause. [11p202] The search for testable hypotheses comes first.

The point of the previous chapters is that the essence of science is to find truth by making and testing hypotheses. Hypotheses that fail this process are discarded. The hypotheses based on the theory of evolution have been validated over and over in thousands of studies. Intelligent Design creationists either provide no testable hypotheses or, for the one time they did, the hypothesis failed miserably. Intelligent Design is not a viable alternative to the theory of evolution. A belief in God and a belief in evolution are not mutually exclusive.

As pointed out in the introduction, the purpose of this book is to explore two fascinating capabilities of the human brain, the rational brain that seeks objective truth and the spiritual brain that seeks solace in spirituality and wants to be connected to something greater than itself. The past chapters were devoted to the conclusions that the rational brain would come to about the central question of "Where did we come from?" and "Who created us?"

Thus the purpose of Parts I and II was to provide information to counteract the assertions of the creationists that there are huge gaps in our knowledge about evolution and that these gaps can only be closed by divine intervention. While there will always be gaps in scientific knowledge, I hope to have shown that most of the gaps that matter have been filled in by modern science. The gaps are huge only if one chooses to avert one's eyes away from reality. If the listener is told only a biased viewpoint and does not have the background or expertise on which to base an informed decision, the decision will be a foregone conclusion—like a trial where only the prosecution gets to present its case. At a minimum, for those interested in listening, I hope I have provided the reader with a more balanced set of information on which to base a decision. Intelligent Design has not provided the correct answers. The theory of evolution, especially in its most modern versions, has.

Part III extends the discussion of "Where did we come from?" further back in time to the origins of the universe, to cosmology, to quantum theory, and quantum weirdness and its role in spirituality.

Part I of this book introduced some of the basic aspects of the theory of evolution. This has been attacked by the Intelligent Design neo-creationists as inadequate to answer some of the more difficult questions about complex systems and structures that have been claimed to have such irreducible complexity that a supreme being capable of Intelligent Design would have to have created them.

The chapters in Part II illustrate that none of the Intelligent Design creationist attempts to disprove the theory of evolution are valid. Good theories make testable predictions. For evolution, such predictions have been validated thousands of times. Most Intelligent Design creationists refuse to state testable predictions based on their theory. One testable theory proposed by Behe failed miserably. Intelligent Design is not a viable alternative to the theory of evolution.

As painful as it may be to some, life on earth and the development of all species of life on earth, can take place without divine intervention. Despite this, neither mainstream Christian, Catholic, nor Jewish theologians believe that evolution is a threat to their religion. Religions have no reason to fear evolution.

References

1. Golden, F. Rehabilitating Galileo's Image. *Time.* 1984.
2. Livingstone, D. N. *Darwin's Forgotten Defenders.* Regent College Publishing, Vancouver, BC, 1984
3. Forrest, B. & Gross, P. R. *Creationism's Trojan Horse. The Wedge of Intelligent Design.* Oxford University Press, New York, 2004.
4. Johnson, P. *Darwin on Trial.* InterVarsity Press, Downers Grove, IL, 1991, 1993.
5. Johnson, P. E. *Reason in the Balance: The Case Against Naturalism in Science, Law, and Education.* InterVarsity Press, Downers Grove, IL, 1995.
6. Johnson, P. E. *Defeating Darwinism by Opening Minds.* InterVarsity Press, Downers Grove, IL,1997.
7. Behe, M. J. *Darwin's Black Box.* The Free Press, New York, 1996.
8. Yockey, H. P. *Information Theory and Molecular Biology.* Cambridge University Press, New York, 1992.
9. Theobald, D. 29+ Evidences for Macroevolution Part I: The Unique Universal Phylogenetic Tree. www.talkorigins.org/faqs/comdewsc/section1.html. 2004.
10. Miller, K. *Finding Darwin's God.* Harper Perennial, New York, 1999.
11. Pennock, R. T. *Tower of Babel.* MIT Press, Cambridge, MA, 1999.

Truth is more of a stranger than fiction.

Mark Twain

Part III

Cosmology

Who are we? Why are we here? Was our universe created from nothing? If so is this proof that God exists? Did time start with the creation of the universe or was it always there. Has the universe been created from intense concentrations of energy? If so where did that energy come from? Could only God have put it there? Is the energy itself God? These and many other questions have relevance to the issues of theology and cosmology—the study of the origin, composition and fate of the universe. Cosmology is thus very relevant to a book about *Who Created God?* and a book about our rational versus our spiritual brain.

Two of the most common reasons cited by theists and Intelligent Design proponents as evidence that God exists come from different aspects of cosmology. These relate to the Big Bang and the Anthropic Principle.

- The Big Bang suggests that the universe was created from nothing—in one gigantic explosive inflation. Can only God create something from nothing or do the laws of physics allow this to happen? Does quantum theory allow this to happen? Would the existence of multiple universes allow this to happen?
- The Anthropic Principle states that the universe, life and man would not exist unless all of the cosmological constants were precisely what they are. Can only God bring about such an incredible feat of fine-tuning or are there other equally valid explanations that avoid the even more difficult question of — Who created God?

Who created us? Where did we come from? This question was addressed in relation to the origin and evolution of life on earth in Parts I and II of this book. These parts showed that life is the product of evolution and natural selection for variations that were brought about by different types of random changes in DNA. While evolution is not directed, it does tend toward the development of greater and greater complexity. This is the result of the simple fact that when significant environmental changes occur, more complex organisms often have a selective advantage over organisms that have remained unchanged. Because the earth formed 4.6 billion years ago, this story is limited to that time span. The study of cosmology allows us to explore our origins back to the beginning of the universe—13.7 billion years ago.

The past century has seen a series of remarkable new discoveries in relation to the theory of relativity, quantum theory and string theory. Some of the weird aspects of these theories have stretched the boundaries of our rational brain and have opened up new boundaries for our spiritual brain. Does the weirdness of quantum theory suggest there are things in the universe that are greater than the sum of its parts, or do we simply need to expand our belief in the rational laws of nature to accommodate this weirdness? Is there anything in cosmology and the weirdness of quantum mechanics that can provide the rational brain with a sense of peace, spirituality and connectedness to the universe? Can the rational brain find God in cosmology or is that kind of God too cold and too impersonal? There is still much about the universe that science cannot yet explain. Is this reason for theists to rejoice? Is this reason for believing in God? Or, as has occurred many times before in science, will the unknowns soon become known?

The following chapters are not meant to be a definitive study of all the remarkable cosmological findings and theories that have developed in the past and current centuries. That would require several books. Instead I have focused on those concepts that I feel are most relevant to the essence of this book, the conflict between our rational and spiritual brain, and whether the recent advances in cosmology prove that God exists. The first four chapters of Part III provide a basic review of the science of cosmology. The last chapter discusses the implication of these subjects for theology, religion, the conflict between our rational and spiritual brain, and the issue of *Who Created God?*

Einstein said that if quantum mechanics were correct then the world would be crazy. Einstein was right – the world is crazy.

David Greenberger

Chapter 20

The Weird World of Quantum Physics

Several of the aspects of physics and cosmology that are relevant to the issue of God and spirituality revolve around some of the weirder aspects of quantum physics. Some of the weirdest of these relate to interference, the uncertainty principle, and entanglement.

Interference

Christiaan Huygens, a famous seventeenth century scientist, argued that light was propagated by waves. Just as sound required air for its propagation, he proposed that light was propagated by what he called ether. He proposed that ether was composed of tiny elastic particles which when excited produced light waves. Another, even more famous seventeenth century genius, scientist and mathematician, Isaac Newton, thought Huygens was wrong and proposed instead that light consisted of tiny particles. By traveling at different speeds these particles produced different colors of light. This was the beginning of a long running feud over the question of whether light was a wave or a particle.

The issue appeared to have been solved with the experiments of a brilliant British physician and physicist, Thomas Young. His greatest contributions to physics came from his double-slit studies of light demonstrating interference. If a light beam was shone through a single slit it produced a single bright band of light (Figure 1).

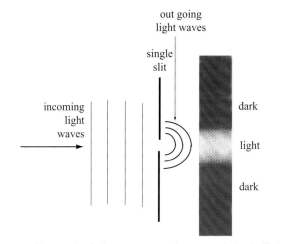

Figure 1. Single-slit experiment producing a single band of light on the detector.

In contrast, when light was shone through a double slit, an interference pattern of light and dark bands appeared on the detector (Figure 2).

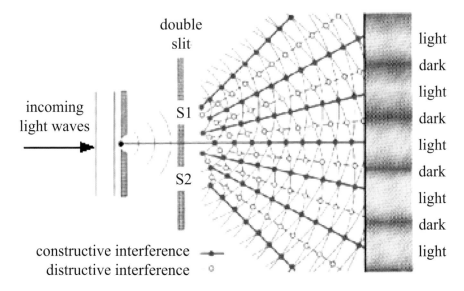

Figure 2. Double-slit experiment producing an interference pattern.

When the light passes through two slits the waves from each slit caused either constructive or destructive interference with the waves from the other slit. In constructive interference the amplitude peaks of the waves meet and the light signal is enhanced. In destructive interference, the troughs of the waves meet, the signal is canceled out and the light is diminished. This results in light and dark bands producing an interference pattern. Since such a pattern is explained by waves, Young proposed that his experiment proved that light is a wave. This theory held prominence for the next 100 years.

Planck's constant. Max Planck, a German physicist, initiated the field of quantum physics with his studies of energy. His doctoral dissertation was in the field of thermodynamics, or the study of the conservation of energy. He became interested in a phenomenon in physics known as *blackbody irradiation*. Thomas Wedgewood, the founder of the British Wedgewood porcelain, initiated the concept of blackbody irradiation. It had been known since ancient times that the hotter the object became, the more its color shifted from red to violet. During his work with porcelain kilns in 1792 Wedgewood discovered that the color of objects heated to a very high temperature depended only upon the temperature and not on other characteristics of the heated object.

A problem with blackbody irradiation was that at some temperatures the known physical laws relating to radiant energy broke down. He found that if he prevented one of the values in the equations from going all the way to zero, all of these problems disappeared. This minimum value was 6.626 x 10^{-34} Joule-seconds, a very, very tiny number. This was called Planck's constant, and the tiny packages of energy were called *quanta*. The equation for the quantum energy of a photon was E = hf, where E was the energy of a photon, h was Planck's constant and f was the frequency of the radiation. This was called Planck's law. In essence Planck's law states that *radiant energy exists in discrete quanta* that are proportional to the wave frequency. The concept that energy occurred in discrete packets provided the beginnings of quantum theory and transformed the field of physics.

Around the turn of the twentieth century physicists began to write about the photoelectric effect of light. This referred to the ability of certain metals to produce electricity when light was shone on them. The wave theory of light predicted that A) the more intense the light the more energy the electrons would have when they fly off the metal plate, B) if the light was very feeble it would be necessary to expose the plate for several seconds or minutes until enough waves struck it to knock electrons loose, and C) waves of any frequency should knock electrons free.

Experiments showed that none of these predictions were true. The energy of the electrons did not depend on the intensity of the light, the electrons always appeared as soon as the light reached the plate, and no electrons were produced if the frequency of the light waves were below a critical value.

In Einstein's 1905 miracle year, in which he produced four groundbreaking papers, one was entitled "On a Heuristic Viewpoint Concerning the Production and Transformation of Light." [1] In this paper he stated:

> In accordance with the assumption to be considered here, the energy of a light ray spreading out from a point source is not continuously distributed over an increasing space, but consists of a finite number of energy quanta which are localized at points in space, which move without dividing, and which can only be produced and absorbed as complete units.

He utilized Max Planck's finite energy concept and proposed that the energy of the electrons did not depend upon the intensity of the light because each electron absorbs only one packet at a time. If the absorbed energy is large enough to expel the electron from the metal, it leaves. If not, the electron dissipates its energy in collisions with nearby electrons and atoms before it can absorb another packet. As soon as a single packet containing sufficient energy strikes the source plate, it will knock an electron free. There is no need to wait for multiple waves to build up enough energy. Importantly, Einstein also predicted that no electrons are produced if the frequency of the light waves is below a critical value, and that the maximum energy of ejected electrons should increase with the frequency of the applied light. The photoelectric effect is diagrammed in Figure 3.

Einstein's work was consistent with both the particle and the wave theories of light. Subsequent experiments proved that Einstein's photoelectric theory was correct. The packets of light were later termed photons. Although the paper on the theory of relativity, for which Einstein is most famous, was published in the same issue as the

Photoelectric effect

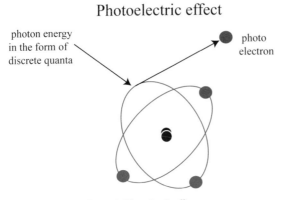

Figure 3. Photoelectric effect.

paper about the photoelectric effect, it was the photoelectric effect paper that won him the Nobel Prize. In 1924 the French physicist Louis de Broglie proposed that in addition to light packets, physical bodies such as electrons and other particles also had wave properties.

So where is the weirdness? So far, nothing is particularly weird about what has been described. The weirdness came when Young's experiments were repeated using light that was so weak that it emitted only one photon at a time. Now our rational brains would say that the interference pattern would no longer be produced because a single photon obviously cannot interfere with itself. If it did, the photon would have to pass through both slits at the same time. Since a particle cannot be in two places at the same time, this should be impossible and the interference should disappear. The remarkable thing was that the interference pattern did not disappear. It was still present, as shown in Figure 4.

In quantum physics, this phenomenon of appearing to be in two places at the same time is called the principle of the *superimposition of states.* I will refer to the strange parts of quantum theory and quantum weirdness.

Quantum weirdness #1: When interference experiments are performed with a light intensity so low that only one photon is emitted at a time, the interference pattern is still present. This is the principle of the superimposition of states. This indicates a particle can be in two places at the same time.

Some authors have brought different aspects of the weirdness of quantum physics into discussions of God and spirituality. However, to evaluate the spirituality issue it is important to determine the maximum size of the particles that are served by quantum laws. Studies of interference are

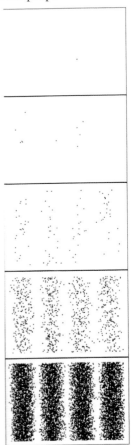

Figure 4. Results of sending one photon at a time through the double slit. The five panels show the results for 1, 10, 100, 1,000 and 10,000 photons. Each panel includes the results of the previous panel.[7]

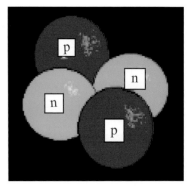

Figure 5. Alpha particle (helium nucleus) consisting of two protons and two neutrons.

Figure 6. A buckyball. [8]

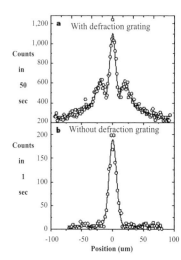

Figure 7. Demonstration of interference using a stream of buckyballs. A) With diffraction grating. B) Without diffraction grating. Arndt et al. Wave-particle duality of C60 molecules. Reprinted by permission from Macmillan Publishers, Ltd. Nature. 401: 680-681, 1999.

valuable in this regard. De Broglie predicted that—in addition to photons, electrons, neutrons—alpha particles and a wide range of other particles would also show a wave pattern. If so, they should also show interference, and they do. Figure 5 shows an alpha particle consisting of a helium nucleus with two protons with a positive charge, and two neutrons with no charge.

An alpha particle is much larger than a photon or an electron and it showed interference. What is the maximum-size particle that shows interference? This prize goes to buckyballs. A buckeyball is a molecule consisting of 60 carbon atoms arranged in a structure resembling a geodesic dome (Figure 6).

Buckyballs are named after Buckminster Fuller, who made such domes famous in architecture. In 1999 Arndt and colleagues [2] demonstrated wave-particle duality and interference with buckyballs consisting of 60 carbon atoms (Figure 7).

They showed that a stream of buckyballs passing through a diffraction grating produced an interference pattern that was not present when the diffraction grating was removed. The presence of the diffraction grating interactions at the wave troughs resulted in destructive interference-producing dips on both sides of the main peak.

The Uncertainty Principle

When light is shined through a prism, or through water droplets in a rainstorm, a beautiful spectrum of colors is produced. It had long been known that lines of different wavelengths appeared in the spectra produced when the source of light was a hot gas. Different elements produced different spectral lines as shown in Figure 8.

There are three types of spectra emitted by objects. The one we experience when we see a rainbow or pass light through a prism is a continuous spectrum. It does not contain spectral lines. With an emission spectrum, hot gases of various compositions produce the spectral lines as shown in Figure 8. An absorption spectrum is produced when a continuous spectrum passes

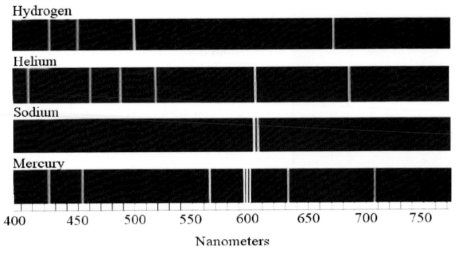

Figure 8. Spectral lines typical of different elements. [9]

through a cool gas. Here the spectral lines are removed, producing an inverse of the emission spectrum. These three types of spectra are illustrated in Figure 9.

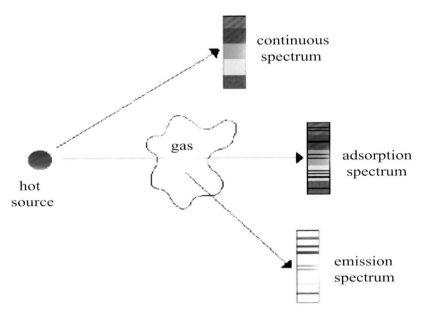

Figure 9. Three types of spectra.

The simplest atom is hydrogen, consisting of a nucleus with one proton orbited by one electron. A number of scientists described different frequencies at which the hydrogen atom produced different sets of spectra. These sets were named after the scientists who described them—Lyman for an ultraviolet series, Balmer for a visible light series, and Paschen for an infrared series. No one had an adequate explanation of what was producing these different, very specific spectra. No one, that is, until a Danish theoretical physicist, Niels Bohr addressed the problem.

Using Max Planck's theory as a basis, he quantized the energy of the atom and proposed that when the hydrogen atom drops from one energy level to a lower one, the energy that is released comes out as a single Einstein photon. This use of Planck's quantum theory to explain what happened in the interior of an atom was a major breakthrough for physics and further expanded quantum theory. It also finally explained spectral lines. *Every emitted frequency was due to an electron descending from one energy level to another.* The difference between the beginning and ending energies was emitted in the form of a quantum of energy. [3p43] This concept is illustrated in Figure 10.

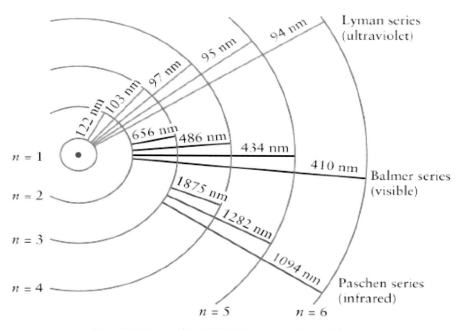

Figure 10. Diagram of how Niels Bohr's quantum theory of the atom explains the Lyman, Balmer and Paschen series of spectral lines. [10]

Each orbital drop produces a quantum packet of energy radiation resulting in lines with specific frequencies. In 1922 Niels Bohr received the Nobel Prize for his quantum theory of the atom. The story is told that following a discussion of Young's dual slit experiment and the principle of the superimposition of states, Bohr murmured, "To be…to be…what does it mean to be." [3p88]

Schrödinger's equation. Erwin Schrödinger was a professor of Theoretical Physics at the University of Zürich. He was anxious to make a major contribution to the field of physics. His colleagues such as Einstein and Bohr had made their groundbreaking discoveries in their early twenties, yet by age 37 Schrödinger had not produced anything outstanding. Although married, he was well known for keeping old girlfriends in his life. A few days before Christmas in 1925, he left for a vacation in a villa in the Alps. Although his wife did not join him, an unknown old girlfriend did. According to legend, the erotic tryst jarred his creative insights and he authored what is known as the *Schrödinger equation.* [3p62] It describes the statistical behavior of particles in the tiny world of quantum mechanics.

His equation had two important consequences. The first relates to statistical probabilities. In the macro world that we can see, if the initial location *(position)* and speed of a car *(momentum)* is known, it is possible to predict with great accuracy where the car will be at a given future time. By contrast, in the micro world of the atom, *it is only possible to describe a range of probabilities about where a particle will be.* The second consequence relates to entanglement and will be discussed later. In 1933 Schrödinger received the Nobel Prize for his famous equation.

Heisenberg's uncertainty principle. Werner Karl Heisenberg, using a form of mathematics called *matrix mechanics,* further expanded the issue of probabilities. The uncertainty principle states that in the subatomic quantum world, the position and momentum cannot both be accurately known. The more precisely the position is known, the more uncertain the momentum. The more precisely the momentum is known, the more uncertain the position. In other words, uncertainty cannot be removed from quantum systems. In 1932 Heisenberg received the Nobel Prize for his contributions to quantum theory. The uncertainty principle provides our second quantum weirdness.

> <u>Quantum weirdness #2:</u> **In the macro world that we can see, precise knowledge about position and momentum allows us to accurately calculate a new position. However, in the micro world of quantum mechanics, the more precisely position is known, the more imprecise our knowledge of momentum, or the more precisely momentum is known, the more imprecise our knowledge of position. This is known as *Heisenberg's uncertainty principle.***

Entanglement

While Einstein played a major role in the development of quantum theory, he was always uncomfortable with it as indicated by his famous statement, "God does not play dice." By this he meant chance should have no place within the laws of nature. While in the quantum world reality was always stated in probabilities or chance, he felt that a better or deeper theory would allow precise predictions rather than only probabilities. In this regard, he and two colleagues, Podolsky and Rosen, issued a challenge to the field of quantum physics, claiming it was incomplete. This was reflected in the title of their 1935 paper, "Can Quantum-Mechanical Description of Physical Reality be Considered Complete?" Based on the initials of its authors, Einstein, Podolsky, and Rosen, this is often referred to as the EPR paper.

They described what occurs when an atom gives off two photons in response to one of its electrons descending to a lower state of energy. While neither photon flies off in a definite direction, the pair will always be found on opposite sides of the atom.

That is, they leave the atom in opposite directions. These two photons are always intertwined. *The instant that one photon is changed, its twin—wherever it may be in the universe—will change instantaneously.* [3] This has been referred to as *entanglement,* a term coined by Schrödinger. In 2001, Amir Aczel published a delightful book on the subject. [3] He considered entanglement to be *the most bizarre of all the weird aspects of quantum theory.* Einstein termed this "spooky at a distance." The point that Einstein, Podolsky, and Rosen were trying to make with this thought experiment was that if quantum physics allowed such a bizarre phenomena to exist, then there must be something wrong with the theory.

Bell's Theorem. John Bell was a nuclear physicist whose day job was to design accelerators at European Center for Nuclear Research (CERN). He pondered the mysteries of quantum physics at night. He attacked the problem raised by the EPR paper. First a definition: *locality* refers to the concept that what happens in one place cannot instantaneously affect what happens at a distant location. That is, effects are local and do not occur at a distance. The issue of the EPR paper was that quantum theory and locality could not both be right. Einstein and John von Neumann felt that if particles appeared to be connected at a distance it was because there were *hidden variables* that conveyed how they should behave after they became separated, and the apparent non-locality was an illusion. If locality was truly correct, quantum theory was incorrect.

In its simplest form, Bell's theorem stated that if his equations, known as inequalities, could be violated by experimental results, this would provide evidence in favor of quantum mechanics and against the EPR complaints. In another paper, Bell proved that the hidden variables that Einstein and von Neumann assumed existed and would prove quantum mechanics was incomplete—did not exist. In summary, Bell's theorem was that *hidden variables* and *locality* had no place in quantum theory. Concerning Bell's Theorem, Aczel quotes a friend, Abner Shimony: [3p147]

> Bell was a unique individual. He was curious, tenacious, and courageous. He had a stronger character than all of them. He took on John von Neumann—one of the most famous mathematicians of the century—and with no hesitation showed that von Neumann's assumption was wrong. Then he took on Einstein.

Bell's theorem provided guidance to experimental physicists about how they could prove whether entanglement really existed. Many subsequent experiments proved entanglement and non-locality were real. [3] Instead of spelling a death knell to quantum theory, these experiments overwhelmingly supported it.

Quantum weirdness #3: When paired particles are emitted from an atomic source in opposite directions, their characteristics are entangled. When a property of one particle, such as spin, is changed, its twin will change instantaneously regardless of how far apart they are in the universe.

Entanglement and separation in space. Since distance has no meaning to entangled particles, entanglement would seem to break down our notion of spatial separation. However, if information cannot be transmitted, this connectedness across space and the universe has no meaning outside of the weird-world of quantum physics. Why can't entanglement transmit information? It all has to do with the role of the observer.

Role of the observer. In an extension of one of the experimental tests of entanglement, Yanhua Shih of the University of Maryland noted that when he could observe which of two paths were taken by a photon, no interference pattern was produced. In this "which-path" design, light acts as a particle. If he could not observe which of two paths was taken by a photon, it was a "both-paths" design. Now the photon was viewed as taking both paths simultaneously and an interference pattern was observed. This means that when not observed, the particle can take both paths at once, but as soon as the particle is observed or measured, "we force some quantum system to choose an actual value, thus leaping out of the quantum fuzz into a specific space." [3p251]

> <u>Quantum weirdness #4:</u> **Whether light acts as a wave or a particle depends on the observer. If the experiment allows one to determine which of two paths the photons take, light acts as a particle. If the experiment does not allow one to determine which of two paths are taken, the light takes both paths simultaneously and acts as a wave—and shows interference. The observer forces the quantum world to chose a specific value.**

The implication of this is that as soon as information is extracted from the system it collapses. Since the observer cannot choose what that state will be, only random information is obtained, unsuitable for transmission.

Entanglement and the speed of light. The phrase, "Its twin will change instantaneously regardless of how far apart they are in the universe," carries with it an apparent violation of Einstein's theory of relativity that states that nothing can travel faster than the speed of light. In an experiment designed to examine this issue, Anton Zeilinger performed an entanglement experiment in Switzerland using 16 miles of fiber optics. In this experiment, if there was a signal from one end informing the other end of its status, it would have had to travel ten million times the speed of light. [3p237] However, since entanglement does not allow us to send readable messages, it does not violate the speed of light limitation.

Despite the above caveats, some physicists still believe that "the spirit of relativity theory" has been violated since "something" travels infinitely fast between the two particles [3p252]. John Bell himself was of this opinion. One way out of this messy weirdness is to take the view that nothing is really transmitted between two parts because the parts are actually not separate entities. They are a single entity.

Do deeper principles underlie quantum uncertainty and nonlocality? The interpretation that once the path of a particle is observed, interference collapses, is called the *Copenhagen Interpretation* of quantum weirdness. The fact that this is still an issue is indicated by the fact that in its 125th anniversary issue, *Science* magazine asked scientists around the world what they thought were the major unanswered questions in science. One of the responses was, *Do deeper principles underlie quantum uncertainty and nonlocality?*[4] In addition to the Copenhagen Interpretation, one of the alternative explanations is the "many worlds" proposal. This suggests that interference, entanglements and other quantum phenomena are explained by posing that every possible quantum outcome really exists but in worlds parallel to our own. I personally am not convinced that this model is any less weird than the Copenhagen Interpretation.

Gravity and quantum weirdness—Do all objects occur in two places at once? Sir Roger Penrose at Oxford's Mathematical Institute has proposed a believable third interpretation. He is the author of *The Road to Reality: A Complete Guide to the Laws of the Universe.*[5] He pointed out that gravity is the only force physicists have been unable to explain in quantum terms. This is due in a large part to the fact that the force of gravity is by far the weakest of all the forces. It is so weak that theorists saw no problem with leaving it out of their equations. Penrose thinks this was a mistake. He points out that despite the tiny size of electrons, protons, and other particles that populate the quantum world, they also produce a warp in time and space, as Einstein proposed in his explanation of gravity.

If all objects can occur in two places at the same time, each would create its own distortions in space-time yielding two superimposed gravitational fields. It takes energy to sustain such a system, and the more energy required, the more unstable the system. Over time the unstable system settles back to its simplest, lowest energy state of one object in one place.[6] Tiny subatomic particles of the quantum world require so little energy they can persist in this unstable state forever. By contrast, bigger objects, like us, instantly settle into one state or the other. Penrose calculated that for a person, the time it takes to settle into one state is a trillionth of a trillionth of a second, too small to measure.

The beauty of this hypothesis is that it is testable. In addition, it removes some of the weirdness from the quantum world. There is nothing weird about the one force we all experience directly—gravity.

Is Quantum Weirdness Relevant to Human Spirituality?

One important question is, where does the boundary lie that separates the macro-world we see from the micro-world of quantum mechanics? If the boundary is too far into the micro-world, quantum weirdness would probably have no relevance to human behavior and experience. If the boundary encroaches on the macro-world, it may have relevance to human consciousness, thought, behavior, and a connectedness to something greater than us.

- Although Einstein complained about quantum weirdness by stating, "God does not play dice," Niels Bohr said, "Albert, stop telling God what he can do." Even more relevant to quantum weirdness, Stephen Hawking said, "God not only plays dice. He sometimes throws them where they cannot be seen."
- Does interference, and with it the idea that particles can be in two places at the

same time, have any relevance to Bohr's questions, "What does it mean to be?"?

- Should the uncertainty principle be viewed as one more reason, like evolution, to feel that we are just the probabilistic product of random events? Does that diminish us? Does that affect the question, "Do we have a purpose?" Does entanglement suggest that all humans are connected to each other and to nature, as the Eastern religions suggest, or is it just an interesting but irrelevant phenomenon since entanglement does not allow the transmission of information?
- Does the fact that certain aspects of quantum theory seem beyond human understanding allow our rational brain to more easily accept the concept of God—another concept beyond our understanding? Or should we behave as one scientist said to a colleague who didn't understand quantum weirdness, "Just shut up and do the calculations"?

One complaint of theologians and Intelligent Designers is that science does not include divine intervention as one of its primary hypotheses. Naturalistic science carries with it the implication of "That is all there is?" and "There is nothing here that is greater than the sum of its parts." Since supernatural beings are, by definition, greater than the sum of their parts, naturalistic science would seem to deny the existence of God. Many scientists agree with this, but not all. If there is any place in nature that God is hiding, or anywhere that the rational brain may feel comfortable with the thought that there may be something out there that is greater than the sum of its parts, the weirdness of quantum physics might be a reasonable place to go looking. However, if Penrose is right about the role of gravity, much of the weirdness disappears and with it many of these issues.

I have discussed the basic facts of quantum theory in some detail so the readers can have a firm background on what quantum mechanics is all about and can form their own opinions about whether quantum weirdness plays any role in their own spirituality. The above questions are just some brief teasers. Since many additional aspects of cosmology such as the Big Bang and string theory are relevant to religion, theology, and spirituality, a more complete discussion of the relevance of cosmology to these issues and to the potential conflict between our rational and spiritual brain is presented in Chapter 24.

A complete discussion of the relevance of quantum theory to spirituality is given in Chapter 24.

References

1. Einstein, A. Über einem die Erzeugung und Verwandlung des Lichtes betreffenden heuristisden Gesichtspunkt [On a Heuristic Viewpoint Concerning the Production and Transformation of Light]. *Ann Physik.* 17: 132-149, 1905.

2. Arndt, M., Nairz, O., Vos-Andreae, J., Keller, C., van der Zouw, G. and Zeilinger, A. Wave-particle duality of C60 molecules. *Nature.* 401: 680-682, 1999.

3. Aczel, A. D. Entanglement. *The Greatest Mystery in Science.* Four Walls Eight Windows, New York, 2001.

4. Anonymous. Do deeper principles underlie quantum uncertainty and nonlocality. *Science.* 309: 398, 2005.

5. Penrose, R. *The Road to Reality: A Complete Guide to the Laws of the Universe.* Alfred A. Knopf, New York, 2005.

6. Folger, T. If an electron can be in two places at once, why can't you? *Discover.* 26: 28-34, 2005.
7. From accad.osu.edu/~fkalal/vnv/final/light_spec_discrete.jpg
8. From www.godunov.com/Bucky/buckybal3.gif
9. From accad.osu.edu/~fkalal/vnv/final/light_spec_discrete.jpg
10. From Freedman and Kaufman (eds) *Universe: Stars and Galaxies,* p111. W. H. Freeman. By permission.

Chapter 21

The Big Bang

The Big Bang theory proposes that the universe suddenly arose from virtually nothing. It has been seized upon by theists as one of the "proofs" that God exists. This is based on their assumption that only God can make something out of nothing. Since such theological importance has been placed on the Big Bang, I will provide the reader with enough detail to allow them to understand what the Big Bang is, how the theory originated, and what was involved at the level of subatomic particles – so you can make your own judgments.

One of the four papers that Einstein wrote in his 1905 "miracle year" was entitled "On the Electrodynamics of Moving Bodies." This was his paper detailing the special theory of relativity. A second very short paper published later in the same year was entitled "Does the Inertia of a Body Depend on Its Energy Content?" These papers changed forever how physicists viewed time and space. In the latter paper Einstein wrote: [1p35]

> If a body gives off the energy E in the form of radiation, its mass diminishes by E/c²…The mass of a body is a measure of its energy content; if the energy changes by E, the mass changes in the same sense.

A simple rearrangement of this statement leads to the most famous equation in all of science: $E = mc^2$ where c^2 is the velocity of light squared. Since the velocity of light is very fast, 186,000 miles per second, when squared it produces a very large number. Thus, each unit of converted mass produces a huge amount of energy. We are most familiar with the implications this equation has for atomic energy where the conversion of tiny amounts of mass can produce enormous amounts of energy. However, the flip side of this equation provides great insights into the origin of the universe, since it shows that huge amounts of pure energy can be converted into mass. This is exactly what produced the universe—a quantum instability in huge amounts of energy started the development of the universe. This has been referred to as the *Big Bang*. This chapter is the story of that conversion of energy to mass. To better understand the story of where the universe came from, we must first review the building blocks of the current universe.

The Forces of the Universe
When Einstein wrote these papers only two types of physical forces were known:

gravitational force and electromagnetic force. We are all familiar with the force of gravity first proposed by Isaac Newton in 1867. It is what made the apple drop and what is responsible for the fact that our legs are always just long enough to reach the ground. We are also well aware of the electromagnetic force. This is responsible for electricity that runs our computers and telephones, for visible light that allows us to see, and for TV and radio waves that allow us to watch TV and listen to the radio. Figure 1 illustrates the different parts of the electromagnetic (EMF) spectrum.

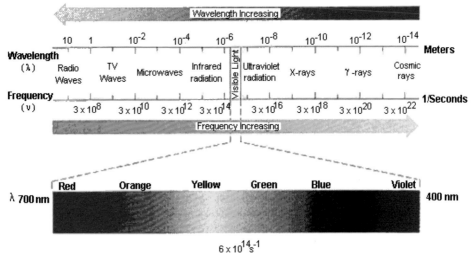

Figure 1. *The range of the electromagnetic spectrum.[4] Reprinted with permission of John Wiley & Sons, Inc.*

The visible light portion represents only a small part of the entire EMF spectrum. All of the different waves are composed of photons of different energy levels — the shorter the wavelength, the higher the frequency, and the greater the energy of the photons. The microwave portion of the spectrum is especially relevant to the story of the Big Bang. Although they are called microwaves, their wavelength is longer and they contain lower-energy photons than visible light. They are micro only in relation to radio and TV waves.

Einstein spent his remaining years attempting to develop a theory of everything that would unite the macro-world that his theory of relativity so well described and the micro-world of quantum mechanics, that he found so spooky and difficult to accept. However, he attempted to develop this theory without knowing about the two other forces of the universe, the strong force and the weak force. These were only discovered in the latter part of the twentieth century using powerful linear accelerators and are the nuclear forces of the subatomic world. The strong force is responsible for holding or gluing together the protons and neutrons of atomic nuclei. Without this force all matter would fly apart and we would not be here to discuss these forces. The weak force is responsible for the radioactive decay of elements such a uranium and cobalt.

Each of these forces is associated with a particle that represents the smallest possible unit of that force. These forces and their characteristics are listed as follows:

Force	Strength	Range (m)	Force Particle	Mass
strong	1	10^{-15}	gluon	0
electromagnetic	1/137	infinite	photon	0
weak	10^{-6}	10^{-16}	weak-gauge bosons	86, 97
gravity	6×10^{-39}	infinite	graviton	0

This shows how weak the gravitational force is compared to the other forces. The range of the strong force is equivalent to that of a medium-sized nucleus, while that of the weak force is that of a proton. All of these force particles have zero mass except the weak-gauge bosons that have a mass equivalent to 86 and 97 protons. All have been experimentally proven except the graviton, which is being vigorously pursued.

Particles of the Universe

In addition to forces, the second major components of the current universe are the fundamental particles. The term *atom* dates to the time of Democritus (460-370 B.C.) the ancient Greek philosopher. He used the term to define the smallest, uncuttable particle of nature. When nineteenth century scientists identified pure compounds such as oxygen, nitrogen and carbon, the smallest units were called atoms. The British physicist J. J. Thomson at the Cavendish Laboratory in England discovered the first subatomic particle in 1897. He was experimenting with cathode ray tubes. It was known for years that when a high voltage of electricity was passed through a vacuum tube, the tube glowed with beautiful colors. It was assumed that some type of ray was being produced, but the composition of the ray was unknown. Thomson made the bold prediction that these rays were composed of "corpuscles" that resided inside the atom and that all atoms were composed of these corpuscles. Further work showed the Thomson's corpuscles were tiny, negatively charged particles. They were called *electrons.*

After the discovery of the electron, it was realized that there must be a positive charge in the atom to balance the negative charge of the orbiting electrons. It was assumed that the electrons and positive particles were evenly distributed throughout the mass of the atom. Ernest Rutherford was a student of Thompson. He was researching the newly discovered phenomenon of radioactivity using uranium. In 1898 he confirmed an earlier observation of Henri Becquerel that the radioactive rays coming from uranium consisted of two parts that he termed *alpha* and *beta*. Alpha rays were easily adsorbed while beta rays were more penetrating. Rutherford used the same technique that Thompson had used in his discovery of the electron to measure the charge of alpha particles. He found that if the alpha particles were passed through a thin sheet of mica, the image on a photographic plate was blurred. This did not happen if the mica film was not present. He termed this effect *alpha scattering.*

In further studies of alpha scattering with two colleagues Hans Geiger and Ernest Marsden, Rutherford found that when a gold film was used instead of mica, the alpha particles scattered at a much greater angle and sometimes *bounced straight backward.*

He described this as the most incredible event in his life, "as if you fired a 15-inch shell at a piece of tissue paper and it came back and hit you." Such huge deflections were not consistent with Thompson's model of the atom. They could only be explained if all the positive charges of the gold atom were concentrated into a tiny mass capable of causing the alpha particles to bounce backward. In 1911 Rutherford proposed that the atom contained a massive nucleus that contained all of the positive charge, and that the lighter electrons were outside this nucleus. This nucleus had to have a radius that was 10,000 times smaller than the radius of the atom. As described in the previous chapter, in 1915 Niels Bohr further refined Rutherford's model by suggesting the electrons also existed as quanta and occurred in orbits at different distances from the nucleus. In 1919 Rutherford first termed the positively charged particle in the nucleus a *proton.*

It soon became clear that the story of the composition of the nucleus was still not complete. Things did not add up. The charge of atoms reflected the number of electrons and protons. However, except for hydrogen they did not add up to the total atomic mass. For example, helium has an atomic mass of four but a charge of only two. Rutherford suggested that one solution would be the presence of a nuclear particle with no charge. He termed this a *neutron* but it was only a hypothetical concept. Again using radioactivity, in 1932 James Chadwick identified the neutron and showed that its mass was approximately 0.1 percent greater than the mass of a proton. When Heisenberg showed that the neutron could not simply be a protein-electron pair, it was clear that the third subatomic particle had been

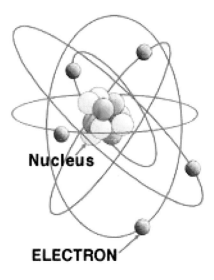

Figure 2. Structure of the atom. Yellow = neutrons. Red = protons. [5]

found. Figure 2 illustrates these three components of the atom.

The following table summarizes these three particles, their charge and mass in atomic mass units.

Particle	Symbol	Charge	Mass
electron	e-	-1	0.000548
proton	p+	+1	1.007276
neutron	no	0	1.008665

The fourth subatomic particle to be proposed and then discovered was the *neutrino.* In 1930 Wolfgang Pauli predicted the presence of the neutrino based on the need to explain aspects of beta radiation. The name *neutrino,* or *little neutron,* was proposed by Enrico Fermi to distinguish it from heavy neutrons. In the 1950s, using a nuclear reactor and a 400-liter tank of water and cadmium chloride, Frederick Reines and Clyde Cowan proved that neutrinos existed. The task was not easy because neutrinos can pass unaffected through a trillion tons of lead. Initially it was proposed to have no mass. Subsequently three types of neutrino were found each with a small but different mass (see Table below).

In the late 1930s *muons* were discovered in the course of studies of cosmic rays. They were the size of electrons but 200 times heavier. Brian Greene commented: [2p8]

> Because there was nothing in the cosmic order, no unsolved puzzle, no tailor-made niche, that necessitated the muon's existence, the Nobel Prize-winning particle physicist Isidor Isaac Rabi greeted the discovery of the muon with a less than enthusiastic, "Who ordered that?"

The theoretical physicist, Murray Gell-Mann, hypothesized that protons and neutrons were composed of three sub-sub particles. He termed these *quarks* after the whimsical name in James Joyce's *Finnegan's Wake.* In 1968 experiments at the Stanford Linear Accelerator showed that quarks were real. Each of the three types came in two varieties, *up* and *down.* Protons consisted of two up-quarks and a down-quark, while neutrons consisted of two down-quarks and one up-quark.

Further studies showed that all these particles were present in three families. Each family contained an electron or electron-like particle, one of three neutrinos, and two quarks—each of increasing mass. These are summarized in the following table where the mass is in multiples of the mass of a proton. [2p9]

Families of Fundamental Particles

Family 1		Family 2		Family 3	
Particle	**Mass**	**Particle**	**Mass**	**Particle**	**Mass**
Electron	.00054	Muon	11	Tau	1.9
Electron-neutrino	$<10^{-8}$	Muon-neutrino	<.0003	Tau-neutrino	<.033
Up-quark	.0047	Charm-quark	1.6	Top-quark	189
Down-quark	.0074	Strange-quark	.16	Bottom-quark	5.2

The final set of fundamental particles consists of antimatter particles for each of the above matter particles. These then are the players for understanding the components of the particle soup involved in the Big Bang. What about the theory of the Big Bang itself?

History of the Big Bang

In 1923, Edwin Powell Hubble discovered Cepheid variable stars in the Andromeda galaxy. Because of their properites they act as a "standard candle" and can provide accurate estimates of distance. This allowed Hubble to show for the first time that galaxies existed beyond our own galaxy, the Milky Way. In 1929 he announced, what has come to be called *Hubble's law,* that the galaxies are moving apart at a rate that increases with their distance. In other words, *the universe is expanding.* This observation was based on the fact that when galaxies are rapidly receding the light waves are longer and redder. This remarkable finding that the universe was expanding carried with it the implication that the *universe had a finite start.*

While Einstein had proposed that the size of the universe was constant, in 1922 a Russian mathematician, Alexander Friedman, argued that it was possible for the average density and radius of the universe to change over time, a theory that Hubble proved to be true. Einstein's equations were extremely difficult and complex. Friedman made a few simplifying assumptions that bypassed these equations. Now the solution to the equations depended on just three variables: H, the rate of expansion of the universe (Hubble's constant); *omega,* the average density of matter in the universe; and *lambda,* Einstein's cosmological constant.

In 1933, Belgian priest Georges Edouard Lamaître published a paper, "Discussion on the Evolution of the Universe." In it he suggested the expansion that Hubble described started by an initial explosion. He visualized a "primal atom" of incredible density containing all of the material for the universe in a sphere 30 times larger than the sun. This explosion sent matter off in all directions resulting in the expansion of the galaxies. In 1946 he expanded on this theory in his *Hypothesis of the Primal Atom.* In more poetic terms he wrote:

> The evolution of the world can be compared to a display of fireworks that has just ended: some few red wisps, ashes and smoke. Standing on a well-chilled cinder, we see the slow fading of the suns, and we try to recall the vanished brilliance of the origin of worlds. [3p51]

Background Micro-Radiation

In the 1940s George Gamow, a nuclear physicist, began to put the conditions for the early universe on a more formal and scientific footing. Like a paleontologist exploring ancient evolution by studying fossils, he sought out the "fossils" of the ancient universe. He proposed that Lamaître's primal atom was *an intense concentration of pure energy.* Einstein's famous equation allowed this energy to be the source of the matter in the universe. In 1948 his former student Ralph Alpher and a colleague, Robert Herman, published a famous paper entitled the "Origin of Chemical Elements." Using Einstein's equations they turned back the cosmic clock to the beginning of the universe. As the radius of the universe decreased, the temperature increased to the point that all of the particles and forces listed above were fused. From this starting point they calculated that the Cosmic Background Radiation (CBR) today should have a temperature of 5 degrees Kelvin. Kelvin degrees start at absolute zero, which is equivalent to -459°F.

At that time there was no way to measure CBR. This soon changed, almost by accident. Arno Penzias and Robert Wilson of the Bell Telephone Labs in New Jersey were interested in microwaves. These were very difficult to detect, but Bell Labs had a large horn-shaped antenna that could detect them. Bell Labs was interested in microwaves as a possible new mode of communication. Penzias and Wilson were attempting to determine the signal to noise ratio of microwaves. The noise part seemed to come from every direction above the horizon and did not change with time. They published their results in 1965 in the *Astrophysical Journal,* discussing it as a problem of "excess antenna temperature." It was quickly realized by others that this represented the CBR that Gamow, Alpher, and Herman had proposed. The background temperature was 2.7°K, remarkably close to what had been predicted. This was the first proof that what Fred Hoyle had called the Big Bang was true. It is perhaps worthy of note that purists point out the Big Bang was neither big nor a bang. The initial singularity was vanishingly small, and since there was no air there was no noise. However, any explosion that produces the entire universe certainly deserves the name "Big."

The first map of CBR was performed by NASA's **CO**smic **B**ackground **E**xplorer **D**ifferential **M**icrowave **R**adiometer (COBE DMR). The results made worldwide front-page news on April 24, 1992. The map showed the universe when it was 300,000 years old. The pattern showed an extremely uniform background radiation, but not totally uniform. The uncertainty principle states that the universe could not be perfectly smooth. Variations of one part in 100,000 were found. This was consistent with the predictions of quantum theory. The larger hot spots indicated where gravity would overcome expansion enough to allow the manufacture of galaxies. Had the variation been smaller the galaxies could not have formed. The larger cool spots evolved to become voids free of stars and galaxies. COBE had found the fossils Gamow was looking for.

George Smoot, the team leader from Lawrence Berkeley Laboratory, said, "It's like looking at God." Others have commented it is more like looking at a "baby picture" of the universe. [3p7] In his book, *Wrinkles in Time,* Smoot remarked, "There is no doubt that a parallel exists between the Big Bang as an event and the Christian notion of creation from nothing." Stephen Hawking described the findings as "the scientific discovery of the century, if not all time."

In recent years NASA's Wilkinson Microwave Anisotropy Probe (WMAP) launched in 2001, has provided a CBR map that was far more detailed than the COBE DMR map (Figure 3).

The hotter regions are in red, the slightly cooler regions in blue. These actually represent very tiny CBR variations with fluctuations on the order of a millionth of a decree K and represent variations in the density of the cosmos during the early years of the universe.

Current Version of the Big Bang

The current concept of the Big Bang in terms of how the various forces and particles outlined above, came into being, is summarized in Figure 4.

The following is a description of some of the aspects of the Big Bang that have the most relevance to religious and spiritual issues. For a much more detailed account

Figure 3. Map of the cosmic background radiation produced by the NASA Wilkinson Microwave Anisotropy Probe and the NASA and the WMAP Science Team. [6]

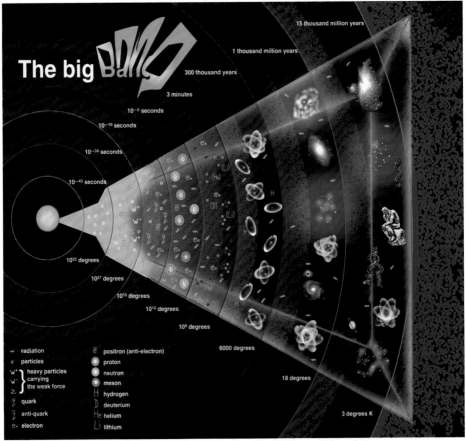

Figure 4. Diagrammatic representation of the Big Bang and the evolution of the universe. [7]

the reader is referred to the book *Origins,* by Neil de Grasse Tyson and Donald Goldsmith, [1] and *Parallel Worlds,* by Michio Kaku. [3]

One of the most critical questions is *what came before the Big Bang?* Did time start or has time always existed? The most popular version is that the universe began as a random fluctuation due to quantum instability in space that resulted in a single bubble that was the size of the Planck length, or 10^{-33} centimeters. This was hyperinflated 10^{50}-fold by space vacuum to fill the universe and started the universe on the path to the formation of matter based on Einstein's equation $E = mc^2$.

At the instant of the Big Bang, all four forces were unified into a single, coherent "superforce." All four forces had the same strength and were in perfect supersymmetry. Very quickly this symmetry began to break; the common force cracked and gave rise to the four currently known forces, with gravity being the first to split off.

The initial *inflation* stage of the Big Bang occupies such a short period of time and such a concentrated form of energy and particles, that it is difficult to conceive. Here Einstein's world of relativity and the micro-world of quantum mechanics are indistinguishable. The time of what is called the period of inflation was from 10^{-43} to 10^{-35} seconds, an extraordinarily short period of time. The energy for the inflation was produced in part by the splitting apart of the strong and weak force. The weight of the packed energy and matter was 100 trillion trillion trillion pounds. This degree of compactness is possible because the space filling atoms with orbiting electrons do not exist. During this period only energy and free particles existed. This universe was tiny (one inch in diameter) and extremely hot, 10^{32} °K.

The radiation was so energetic that the wavelength for the photon was in the cosmic ray range. The energy of the photons was sufficient for them to convert their energy into matter and anti-matter. This provides another place where everything could have gone wrong. When matter and anti-matter clashed, photons were re-formed. However, for every billion anti-matter particles formed, a billion and one matter particles were formed. Without this tiny difference all the matter of the universe, and eventually all life, would have never formed. [1p26]

Cosmic Weirdness #1: In the earliest stages of the universe, the energy of the photons was sufficient for them to convert their energy into matter and anti-matter. When that matter and anti-matter clashed, photons were re-formed. For every billion anti-matter particles formed a billion and one matter particles were formed. Without this tiny difference all the matter of the universe, and eventually all life, would have never formed.

The *first second* saw the formation of quarks, anti-quarks, leptons, electrons, protons, neutrons, and neutrinos. The temperature dropped to 10^9 °K.

The first three minutes saw the beginnings of the nuclei of the lightest and simplest elemental nuclei for hydrogen (one proton), deuterium (one proton, one neutron), and helium (two protons and two neutrons). If the universe had not cooled and expanded rapidly, all the hydrogen would have condensed into heavier nuclei. Then no water and no life would have been possible. These nuclei still had no electrons. At this time the universe was 330 trillion miles in diameter.

During the *first 300 thousand* years the universe continued to rapidly expand and cool, but it still was very hot. Electrons now orbited around the nuclei, forming the first common simple elements, hydrogen and helium. The capture of the electrons by atomic nuclei now allowed light to escape from the universe. The universe was 500 thousand trillion miles across.

After *100 million years,* with continued cooling and before the formation of stars, there was no light in the universe. Things were very dark. The universe was 10 million trillion miles across.

After *one billion years* stars had formed and their light, produced by thermonuclear fusion, brought light to the universe. They clustered to form galaxies and clusters of galaxies. The suns that were 10 times the mass of our sun had sufficient mass and pressure to fuse nuclei of lighter elements to form heavier elements. Some of the most important of these for life are carbon, oxygen, sodium, and calcium. When these stars died and exploded they dispersed these elements throughout the universe. The universe was now 60 million trillion miles across.

Now, *13.7 billion years later,* there are billions of galaxies each with billions of stars, many with planets. The current universe is 590 million trillion miles across. Our solar system formed about 8 billion years ago.

Inflation and the Speed of Light

In 1979 Alan Gurth at the Stanford Linear Accelerator Center in California proposed that in that time period from 10^{-43} to 10^{-35} seconds after the start of the Big Bang, the universe expanded at an incredible rate by a factor of 10^{50}. This super-rapid expansion was consistent with a flat universe model, since it flattened matter out like it was spread onto the surface of a huge balloon. Inserting this period of hyperinflation solved many thorny problems in cosmology. However, one problem it seemed to create was that this rate of expansion was considerably faster than the speed of light. How is that possible? Nothing is supposed to travel faster than the speed of light. Yet it can. The reason is as slippery as the famous comment, "It depends what your definition of is, is." Einstein's speed limit applies only to objects moving within space and not to the expansion of space itself.

> **Cosmic Weirdness #2: In the first fractions of a second of the Big Bang, the rate of expansion of the universe considerably exceeded the speed of light. Nothing is supposed to travel faster than the speed of light. However, this rule of Einstein's applies only to objects moving within space, not to space itself. Space itself can expand faster than the speed of light.**

The Rate of Expansion of the Universe is Accelerating

At the time that Einstein was producing his famous equations, there was no evidence from astronomers that the universe was either expanding or contracting. To ensure that his equations did not upset this cosmological stability, Einstein inserted a "cosmological constant." When Alexander Friedman proposed that the universe was unstable and Hubble proved it was expanding, Einstein pronounced his cosmological constant as his greatest blunder. Equations now had no need for a cosmological constant. No need, that is, until 1998. That is when two independent groups of astronomers published evidence that not only is the universe expanding, it is expanding at a constantly accelerating rate. Now a cosmological constant had to be re-inserted into the equations to ensure the universe continued to expand at an ever-increasing rate. Einstein was right after all.

<u>Cosmic Weirdness #3</u>: **The universe is expanding at an accelerating rate. It is not a balanced static universe. It is not even a balanced exploding universe. It is an exploding, exploding universe where the rate of expansion keeps accelerating.**

Dark Matter and Dark Energy

Of all of the incredible new knowledge of the cosmos one of the most incredible is two things we do not understand—dark matter and dark energy? As shown in Figure 5, the known normal matter consisting of the protons and neutrons of all the atoms of the universe makes up only 4 percent of the total universe.

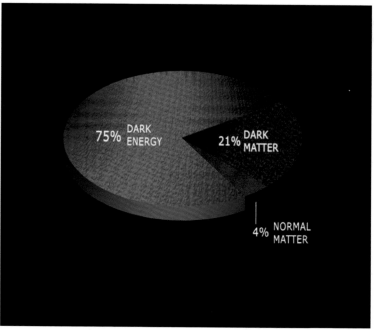

Figure 5. The proportion of dark energy and dark matter in the universe [8.]

Dark matter makes up 21 percent, and dark energy the remaining 75 percent. Since the make-up of these dark things is a mystery, the nature of a whopping 96 percent of the universe is unknown.

In 1933, in the process of measuring the velocities of galaxies whose gravity interacted with nearby galaxies, astronomers identified what was termed *missing matter*. Several years later Fritz Zwicky, an astrophysicist at the California Institute of Technology, was studying a cluster of galaxies known as the *Coma Berenices cluster*. He found that the velocity of some of the galaxies in this cluster was unexpectedly high. In fact the speeds were so high that the cluster of galaxies should have flown apart billions of years ago, but they did not. The cluster did not contain enough visible matter to prevent this from happening. Again, there had to be some missing matter. As shown in Figure 5, dark matter constitutes 21 percent of the mass of the universe. On average, across the universe it constitutes about six times the amount of visible matter. This has been called *dark matter* because the source of it is invisible. Dark matter and visible matter tend to occupy the same parts of the universe as though they had some type of interdependence. In the same issue of *Science* mentioned in the previous chapter in relation the quantum weirdness, the identity of dark matter was first on the list of important questions yet to be answered in science.

As with other aspects of the universe, the amount of dark matter was "just right." If there was too little dark matter, too much of the hydrogen would have been fused into helium. [1p72] If there was too much dark matter, the universe would be collapsing instead of expanding.

In the mid 1990s scientists realized that even after dark matter was included in the calculations, the total density of matter in the universe only came to one quarter of the critical density calculated by Einstein. After the 1998 studies, showing that the rate of expansion of the universe was accelerating, the question was raised, *What is causing this accelerated expansion?* The relevant equations constantly pointed to *dark energy*. Einstein showed that energy has mass and as shown in Figure 5, dark energy constitutes 71 percent of the total mass of the universe. Dark energy drives the expansion of the universe. As it expands more dark energy is generated and the rate of expansion increases still further. Dark energy arises from empty space, or to put it in the inverse, empty space contains huge amounts of dark energy.

> **Cosmic Weirdness #4: Only four percent of the universe is composed of visible matter, 21 percent is dark matter, 75 percent is dark energy. The exact nature of 96 percent of the universe is unknown to us.**

It has been proposed that empty space in fact buzzes with "virtual particles," which wink into and out of existence instantaneously. Quantum physicists refer to this as *quantum fluctuations in a vacuum*. When the amount of energy residing in a cubic centimeter of space is calculated, the result boggles the imagination; it's 10^{120}

times greater than the energy of supernovae explosions and the total CBR. It comes as no surprise that there is considerable controversy over the correctness of this conclusion. Tyson and Goldsmith said of this figure, "Some embrace it; some accept it only reluctantly; some dance around it; and some despise it." [1p99-102]

> **Cosmic Weirdness #5:** The amount of energy in a cubic centimeter of free empty space has been calculated to be 10^{120} times that of a supernova explosion and the total CBR.

Different values of the cosmological constant would produce many different amounts of dark matter over dark energy. Some would be consistent with life, but many would not. Some cosmologists have suggested our universe is part of a much larger "multiverse" in which many different universes with different cosmological constants exist. Since this concept is more relevant to Chapter 23, The Anthropic Principle, it will be discussed further there.

Black Holes

In 1915 Einstein published his theory of general relativity describing how space and matter interact. A short time later Karl Schwarzschild, a German physicist, showed that objects with sufficiently strong gravity would create a situation in which nothing, including light, could escape. This was called a *singularity.* In 1967 these objects were termed *black holes* by John Wheeler. The existence of black holes was soon proven. There is a black hole in the center of every quasar (quasistellar radio sources) and at the center of most giant galaxies. Astronomers estimate there are 300 million black holes in the universe.

Origin of the Solar System and the Earth

There have been many theories of the origin of the solar system, such as beginning as a rotating gaseous nebula that condensed in places to form the planets (nebular hypothesis); a collision of the sun with a passing star (catastrophe hypothesis); condensation of stellar dust; and others. Mathematical analyses have ruled out these models.

The currently favored model is a *solar nebula cold accretionary model,* with the formation of the earth 4.6 billion years ago. Harold Urey proposed that the terrestrial planets were formed at a relatively low temperature of 1,200°C. While this may seem hot to us, it is cold compared to the temperature of the sun. Turbulence and eddies in the solar nebula led to the formation of primitive planets. At this temperature the light elements such as hydrogen and helium were driven off, while the heavier elements were retained. The heaviest of these, such as iron and nickel, were retained and form the molten core of the earth. The less heavy elements, such as calcium, sodium, and potassium, formed the mantle and crust. The larger more distant planets such as Jupiter were composed of frozen methane, water and ammonia.

Is the Big Bang Relevant to Theology and Human Spirituality?

The Big Bang theory, positing the creation of the universe from nothing, has been a boon to theists. The relevance of the Big Bang and other cosmological weirdness to religious, theological and spiritual issues will be discussed in Chapter 24.

References

1. Tyson, N. D. & Goldsmith, D. *Origins*. W. W. Norton, New York, 2004.
2. Greene, B. *The Elegant Universe*. W. W. Norton Co, New York, 2003.
3. Kaku, M. *Parallel Worlds*. Double Day, New York, 2005.
4. From chemed.chem.purdue.edu/…/graphics/spectrum.gif
5. From extra.shu.ac.uk/cseCenterforScienceEducation, Sheffield Hallam University.
6. From map.gsfc.nasa.gov/m_mm.html
7. From eppog.web.cern.ch/eppog/
8. From chandra.harvard.edu/

Chapter 22

String Theory: A Cosmic Symphony

It is well known that for the last 30 years of his life Albert Einstein attempted to find a grand unified field theory that would unite the macro-world of relativity with the micro-world of quantum theory. He failed. As mentioned in the previous chapter, part of this failure was that he was not aware of two subatomic range forces in the universe—the strong and the weak forces. In addition, the subatomic particle soup was still only a half-cooked meal.

Every advance that has been made in the field of physics and atomic physics has come from identifying smaller and smaller units of energy and mass. For energy it was the discovery by Planck that energy comes in quanta, defined by multiplying Planck's constant, 6.626×10^{-34} Joule-seconds, by frequency. For mass, it was the identification of the subatomic particles: electrons, protons, neutrons, and neutrinos. This was followed by the identification of quarks as subparts of protons and neutrons. It should be no surprise then, that the next advance in cosmology has proposed something still smaller—strings.

Strings

Instead of a small particle, superstring theory, or more simply *string theory,* proposes an extraordinarily small vibrating loop like a tiny rubber band. The beauty of a loop instead of a still smaller particle is that variations in the length and rate of vibration of the loop can provide a basis for the formation of all of the forces and particles listed in the previous chapter. The amount of energy in a given string is reflected in its size and rate of oscillation. In our world the best analogy is a violin string. Differences in length produced by our fingers, and variation in oscillation produced by the bow, produce a rich range of sound. With string theory a single fundamental resonant pattern of vibration forms the basis of all the fundamental forces and particles. [1 p15] A diagrammatic representation of these strings is shown in Figure 1.

Since it is capable of uniting the world of relativity and the world of the quantum and since there is no need for a still deeper explanation, string theory and its latest incarnation, M theory, have been termed a *Theory of Everything,* or TOE. While the mathematics of these theories is incredibly complex, the concept itself and its cosmological implications are understandable to all. This understanding has been

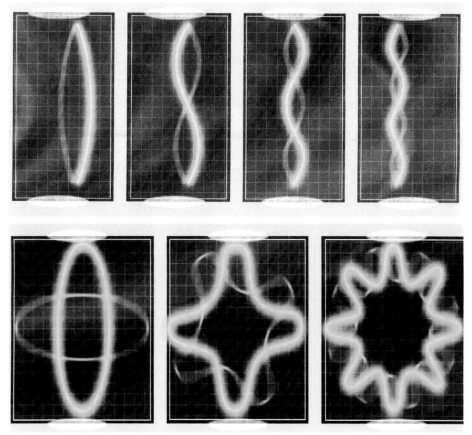

Figure 1. Diagram of different strings of string theory. From M. Kaku
Testing String Theory. Discover. 26:30-37, 2005. By permission.

made possible by the popular writing of some of the scientists involved. For readers who wish more details than the brief summary being presented here, I recommend Brian Greene's *The Elegant Universe*[1] and *Fabric of the Cosmos,*[2] and Michio Kaku's *Parallel Worlds.*[3]

String Theory

The problem with the standard model was that the force of gravity was not explained by the otherwise very precise quantum theories that unified the three other fundamental, non-gravity forces. At the submicroscopic scale of Planck's length (10^{-33}cm), the normally quiet and well-behaved space-time fabric became a chaotic sea of quantum jitters. A TOE. was needed that unified everything.

The first beginnings of string theory go back to 1968 when Gabriele Veneziano at CERN noted that an obscure mathematical formula proposed by Leonhard Euler, known as the *Euler beta-function,* seemed to explain many aspects of strongly interacting particles. In 1970 a group of three physicists, Yoichiro Nambu, Holger Nielsen, and Leonard Susskind, showed that if elementary particles were modeled as tiny vibrating strings their interactions were predicted by Euler's beta-function.

However, at that time this theory seemed to conflict with experimental high-energy physics relating to the strong force.

This apparent conflict appeared to be resolved in 1974 when John Schwarz and Joël Scherk showed that string theory could explain both the strong force and the force of gravity. Gravity represented the lowest vibration of the string with zero mass. Despite this, conflicts between string theory and quantum mechanics persisted until the 1984 landmark paper by Michael Green and John Schwarz showed that string theory could encompass all of the four forces, including gravity, and all of the fundamental particles. Thus, string theory is quantum theory plus gravity. This launched a period known as the *first superstring revolution*. Strings were the size of Planck's length—a millionth of a billionth of a billionth of a billionth of a centimeter. A persisting problem was that the mathematics was so complex that only approximations of the theory could be solved, and these failed to answer all of the questions involved.

An even greater problem was that over the years a number of different string theories had evolved based on adding new dimensions of space. There were now nine space dimensions and one time dimension. Thus, in addition to the three dimensions of space and the fourth dimension of time that we can directly experience, there were six additional dimensions curled up into such tiny structures that they were not available to our conscious perception. Five different versions of string theory evolved, each of which seemed to work. This plethora of suitable answers is not what scientists are used to. A much more satisfactory outcome is to fight over different possible answers, then eventually come to a single answer all could agree on. The existence of five suitable answers raised the disturbing possibility that perhaps none of them were correct. String theory seemed to be on the ropes, or more literally, on the strings.

M-Theory

The "second superstring revolution" was launched by a lecture by Edward Witten at a 1995 superstring conference. He had discovered a hidden unity that tied all five string theories together. Rather than being distinct, the five theories were actually five different ways of mathematically analyzing a single grand theory. [2p379] The unified theory had 11 dimensions, 10 for space and one for time. The new tenth space dimension was much smaller than the others but this allowed a unification of all five string theories. The new theory was called M-theory. Apparently, no one knows for sure what the M stands for: Membrane? Master? Majestic? Mother? Magic? Mystery? Matrix?—or all of the above.

The beauty of string theory is that the different properties of all 19 of the fundamental particles, their mass and force charges, are determined by the precise resonant pattern of vibration of different size strings. The greater the amplitude and the shorter the wavelength, the greater the energy of the string. Since Einstein showed the equivalence of energy and mass, the greater the energy, the greater the mass. Thus, heavy particles are composed of strings that vibrate more energetically. The different forces are determined by the manner in which the strings vibrate. All strings are the same and they represent the ultimate fundamental stuff of the universe. Current theory suggests everything is composed of vibrating strings and there is nothing below a string. The string truly provides us with a cosmic symphony. [1p146]

> **String theory and M-theory propose that the ultimate building blocks of the universe consist of tiny (10^{-33} centimeter) vibrating strings. Different lengths and vibration frequencies of these strings produce all four fundamental forces and all 19 fundamental particles. Since the force of gravity was now included in a unified theory, M-theory has been called the theory of everything, or T.O.E.**

Multiple Universes—Darwinian Selection of Universes

One of the thorny problems with the inflation part of the Big Bang was, "What put the brakes on the process?" "What stopped the inflation at just the right time?" This had to have occurred just when it did or the current universe could not have formed. The physicist Andrei Linde proposed a novel solution. He suggested that the brakes were applied randomly but that the quantum bubble in vacuum space that gave rise to our universe actually occurred millions of times, each with a different braking time. When omega was too large, the new universe immediately self-destructed. When omega was too small, the inflation went on indefinitely. By a form of *Darwinian selection of universes,* when everything was just right and the timing was perfect, it gave rise to the universe as we know it. In this model Big Bangs are happening all the time and new universes are budding or sprouting off to form a giant "multiverse." As shown in the next chapter, this concept of multiple universes also provides a possible answer to the anthropic principle.

Branes, Parallel Universes, and Cyclic Cosmology

Quantum theory states that there is a finite possibility that the seemingly impossible can happen. Thus, if one universe can be produced by a quantum instability in the vacuum of space, it is extremely probable that this will happen more than once, perhaps millions or billions of times, giving rise to many parallel universes. This concept has now been taken as a given by most cosmologists.

This concept is also consistent with M-theory which predicts multi-dimensional objects called *membranes,* or *branes* for short. This is such an integral part of M-theory that most physicists assume M-theory was so named for membranes it predicted. These branes can have three or more, but 10 or fewer spatial dimensions. This led to the possibility that our flat universe was a giant brane, and that the parallel universes are parallel three-dimensional branes.

As an extension of this, Paul Steinhardt and Neil Turok of Cambridge University proposed that we are living in the three-dimensional brane that collides every few trillion years with a parallel brane and that this collision is the cause of the Big Bang. This collision produces two new parallel branes that undergo accelerated expansion until they are largely depleted of matter. Then a new collision repeats the process resulting in a cyclic cosmology. [2] They referred to this as an *ekpyrotic model* of the cosmos. *Ekpyrosis* is Greek for conflagration.

A Universe from Nothing

The formation of our universe from so little and the notion of a multiverse with budding universes might seem to violate the laws of the conservation of matter and energy. However, as pointed out by Kaku, [3p94]

> The total matter/energy content of a universe may actually be very small. The matter content of the universe, including all the stars, planets, and galaxies, is huge and positive. However, the energy stored within gravity may be negative. If you add the positive energy due to matter to the negative energy due to gravity, the sum may be close to zero! In some sense, such universes are free. They can spring out of the vacuum almost effortlessly.
>
> In fact, to create a universe like ours may require a ridiculously small net amount of matter, perhaps as little as an ounce.

When the galaxies are compared, their total spin cancels out to zero and the positive and negative charges in the universe cancel out to 1 part in 10^{21}.[3p95] Thus, in addition to matter and energy, other aspects of our universe also tend to cancel each other out.

The total amount of matter + energy in the universe may be almost zero when the negative mass of the energy stored within gravity is summed with the positive mass of the universe. In this sense universes can spring out of the vacuum almost effortlessly.

Implications of String Theory for Theology and Spirituality

As with the Big Bang, there are some profound implications of string theory and multiple universes for theology and the existence of God. These theological implications will be discussed in the final chapter of Part III on cosmology.

The universe was formed from a tiny bubble randomly produced out of the quantum jitters of empty space. The space vacuum produced the hyperinflation initiating the Big Bang. If this could occur once, it could occur many times, suggesting there may be billions or trillions of parallel universes.

References

1. Greene, B. *The Elegant Universe*. W. W. Norton Co, New York, 2003.
2. Greene, B. *The Fabric of the Cosmos*. Vintage Books, New York, 2004.
3. Kaku, M. *Parallel Worlds*. Doubleday, New York, 2005.

Chapter 23

The Anthropic Principle

The *Anthropic Principle* states that the laws of nature are arranged so that life and consciousness are possible. Brandon Carter[1] first proposed this in 1973 during a symposium on *Confrontation of Cosmological Theories with Observational Data.* The symposium was celebrating the 500th birthday of Copernicus. The *Copernican Principle* claimed the opposite, that man does not occupy a privileged position in the universe. Carter's paper was entitled, "Large number of Coincidences and the Anthropic Principle in Cosmology." He stated that, "Although our situation is not necessarily central, it is inevitably privileged to some extent." The "large number of coincidences" refers to the extraordinary degree of fine-tuning of many of the constants of the universe so they are "just right" for the universe and life to develop — the so-called "Goldilocks" effect. This aspect of the Anthropic Principle has been widely used by Intelligent Designers and theologians in general to "prove that God exists."

In their extensive opus on the subject entitled *The Anthropic Cosmological Principle,* John Barrow and Frank Tipler[2] defined four flavors of the Anthropic Principle.

1. Weak Anthropic Principle (WAP).
The WAP is defined as: [2p16]

> The observed values of all physical and cosmological quantities are not equally probable but they take on values restricted by the requirement that there exist sites where carbon-based life can evolve and by the requirement that the Universe be old enough for it to have already done so.

A simpler, easier-to-understand, and more-modern version is:

> Among all possible multiple universes there is at least one that allows the evolution of intelligent life.

2. Strong Anthropic Principle (SAP)

The SAP is defined as: [2 p21]

> The universe must have those properties which allow life to develop within it at some stage in its history.

Or:

> The elementary particles and fundamental forces are uniquely those that allow the evolution of intelligent life.

The SAP is considered a strong version because it carries the implication that the constants and laws of nature *must* be such that life can exist. The SAP leads to a number of additional implications:

> **A.** There exists one possible universe "designed" with the goal of generating and sustaining "observers."

This is the teleological form of the Anthropic Principle and suggests "design" in its most unambiguous form. It is naturally favored by theologians but some astronomers such as Fred Hoyle ascribe to it as well. Hoyle stated: [3]

> I do not believe that any scientist who examined the evidence would fail to draw the inference that the laws of nuclear physics have been deliberately designed.

> **B.** An ensemble of other different universes is necessary for the existence of our Universe.

This B version receives support from the many-worlds interpretation of quantum mechanics. The third flavor of the Anthropic Principle was proposed by the physicist John Wheeler. [4,5]

3. Participatory Anthropic Principle (PAP)

The PAP states:

> Observers are necessary to bring the Universe into being.

PAP is a massive extension of one of the aspects of the Copenhagen Interpretation of quantum theory that an observer collapses the wave function of a particle or object and brings it into reality. This suggests a feedback loop between man, the observer, and the universe, and proposes the production of reality by observing works backward to the beginning of the universe.

4. Final Anthropic Principle.

This states that:

> Intelligent information processing must come into existence in the Universe, and, once it comes into existence, it will never die out.

What are the Constants that Must be Exactly as They are for Life to Exist?

There are many sources for the list of physical and cosmological constants that had to be just right for life to have occurred in our universe and in our solar system. I will start with those listed by Sir Martin Rees, the Astronomer Royal at Cambridge University in England. In his book *Just Six Numbers,* [6] he describes six numbers that seem especially significant.

N measures *the ratio of the strength of the electrical forces that hold atoms together, divided by the force of gravity between them.* Because the force of gravity is so small the number is huge—1,000,000,000,000,000,000,000,000,000,000,000,000, or 1×10^{36}. The very high value is a reflection of the weakness of the force of gravity. If the force of gravity was weaker, the stars would not have formed and the universe would be dark and lifeless. If gravity was stronger, the stars would heat up too fast and burn up too quickly for life to form.

ε (epsilon) is a measure of the *strong nuclear force* that defines how strongly atomic nuclei bind together. It has a value of .007. This means that hydrogen converts .007 of its mass into energy when it fuses into helium. Epsilon also controls the fusion of hydrogen atoms into heaver elements, including carbon and oxygen. If it were .006, protons and neutrons would not bind together. Our entire universe would have dissolved into hydrogen with no neutrons. If epsilon were .008, the fusion would have been so rapid that no hydrogen would have survived the Big Bang and the stars would burn their nuclear fuel too quickly for life to evolve.

Ω (omega) is the *cosmic density factor* and measures the amount of matter in the universe, including all the galaxies, diffuse gas, and dark matter. It is a *ratio of the importance of gravity pulling the universe together, and the expansion energy pushing the universe apart.* The current assessed value of omega is 0.3. For it to currently be anywhere between .1 and 10, the value of omega had to be accurate to an exact value of 1.00000000000000, one second after the Big Bang. If too small then the universe would have expanded and cooled too fast. If too large, the universe would have collapsed before life could start. Rees states,

> At one second after the big bang, omega cannot have differed from unity by more than one part in a million billion (10^{15}) in order that the universe should now, after 10 billion years, be still expanding and with a value of omega that has certainly not departed wildly from unity. [6]

Stephen Hawking weighed in as follows:

> If the rate of expansion one second after the big bang had been smaller by even one part in a hundred thousand million, [the universe] would have collapsed before it reached its present size....The odds against a universe like ours emerging out of something like the big bang are enormous. I think there are clearly religious implications. [17]

λ (lambda) is the *cosmological constant* which determines the rate of expansion of the universe. If much larger, antigravity forces would be created and blow the universe apart. If much smaller, the universe would have re-contracted into a singularity, giving too little time for life to develop. Alan Gurth [7] suggested that to prevent these problems λ had to be just right to one part in 10^{55} parts. This is probably an exaggeration. His paper was written in 1981 when the cosmological constant was thought to be zero, consistent with a universe that was expanding at a constant rate. Recent studies have shown that lambda is slightly greater than zero, yet here we are.

Q is the *ratio of two fundamental energies* and has a value of 1/100,000 or 10^{-5}. If it were smaller, the universe would be inert, smooth, and structureless, and the stars and galaxies would not have formed. If it were larger, the universe would be violent and dominated by black holes.

D is the *number of spatial dimensions in the world*. This refers to macro dimensions rather than the ultra tiny fourth to tenth spatial dimensions of string theory. Rees referred to these as the three dimensions of our visual experience. One or two dimensions would obviously not have worked. We would live in the world of *Flatland*. Four dimensions and the planetary and atomic orbits would be unstable.

Rees picked these constants because they are fundamentally independent in that one cannot be computed from any of the others. The following are two additional important examples from the literature.

Ratio of protons to anti-protons. This was mentioned previously but will be repeated here. Immediately after the Big Bang the energy of photons was converted to protons and anti-protons. When these interact they destroy each other with the release of energy. The current universe formed because the ratio of protons to anti-protons was 1,000,000,001/1,000,000,000. Without this tiny difference, all the matter of the universe would have never formed. [8p26]

α (alpha) or the *fine structure constant* = $e^2/2e_ohc$. It quantifies the relativistic (c) and quantum (h) qualities of electromagnetic (e) interactions involving charged particles in empty space (e_o). It is equal to 1/137.035599976, or approximately 1/137. This value accounts for why 137 has legendary status among physicists. There is some evidence that this value has changed slightly over the time of the universe, but if it had a significantly different value, matter and energy would interact in bizarre ways such that the distinction between the two could melt away. [9]

A More-Complete List of Anthropic Constants

Hugh Ross has published a longer list of anthropic constants [10p121] Those that are relevant for the whole universe are listed in Table 1 along with the consequences of higher or lower numbers. There is some overlap with the constants already discussed.

Table 1. Additional Anthropic Constants.

Constant	Consequence of larger#	Consequence of smaller#
Gravitational force	Stars burn too fast	No heavy elements
Strong nuclear force	No hydrogen	Only hydrogen
Weak nuclear force	Too many heavy elements	Too few heavy elements
Electromagnetic force	No sharing of electron orbits	Electrons fly off elements
Age of universe	No life possible	No earth-type suns
Expansion rate of universe	Universe would not form	Universe would collapse
Mass of universe	No galaxy formation	No heavy elements
Ratio electron/proton mass	Elements would not form	Elements would not form
Ratio EM force/gravity	Short life span of stars	No heavy elements
Ratio protons/anti-protons	No mass in the universe	No mass in the universe
Ratio protons/baryons	No galaxies would form	No stars would form
Ratio protons/electrons	No galaxy formation	No galaxy formation
Stability of the proton	Excess radiation lethal to life	Too little matter
Uniformity of universe	Too many black holes	No galaxies would form
Velocity of light	Stars too luminous	Stars too dim
^{4}He nuclear energy level	Too little oxygen and carbon	Too little oxygen and carbon
^{8}Be nuclear energy level	Excess nuclear fusion	No heavy elements
^{12}C nuclear energy level	Incompatible with C life	Incompatible with C life
^{16}O nuclear energy level	To little conversion of C to O	Excess conversion of C to O
Distance between stars	No heavy elements	Destabilize planet orbits
Rate of star luminosity	Excess greenhouse effect	Excess freezing of water
Distance between galaxies	Inadequate star formation	Disturb sun's orbit
Mass of neutrino	Stars would not form	Galaxies too close

Ross [10p129] also provided a list of constants that had to be just right for life in our solar system. These included:

The position of the solar system in our galaxy, the Milky Way. Our solar system is currently two-thirds of the way from the center of the galaxy, where a black hole lurks. If the solar system were too close to this black hole, the radiation it emits would be lethal to life. If the solar system were too far from the center, there would not be enough heavy elements, like iron, necessary for life.

The size of the earth. If it were smaller its gravity would have been so weak that the oxygen would not stay in the atmosphere. If it were larger many of the toxic primordial gases would have been retained. While it is likely that life could still have evolved, it would be dramatically different than life as we know it.

The size of Jupiter. The current size of Jupiter cleaned the solar system of asteroids that would have destroyed the earth. Jupiter is our asteroid protector. If Jupiter were much smaller it would not have been our protector.

Other figures include the age, color, and size of our sun; the distance of the earth from the sun; the size of the moon, and the tilt, rotation period, force of gravity, magnetic field, thickness of the crust, oxygen-to-nitrogen ratio, level of carbon dioxide, oxygen, and ozone level of the earth. Even these represent a partial list, but they clearly make the point that many constants of the universe, our galaxy, and our solar system had to be just right for life to occur. There are several interpretations of the Anthropic Principle.

- It is proof of the existence of God since only a divine presence could fine tune the universe with such accuracy.
- It is a tautological illusion.
- There are actually only a few true anthropic constants.
- It was a lucky accident.
- There are millions of universes and it was inevitable that in at least one the conditions would be suitable for life. If it were not, we would not be here to ask the question of "why?"

These are all discussed in the next chapter. For now, what do different scientists think of the Anthropic Principle?

Comments by Various Scientists

The Anthropic Principle elicits strong opinions from different people. Theists love it because it suggests intelligent design and thus "proves" that God exists. This position has been strongly voiced by Hugh Ross, a Christian astronomer who, while he believes in evolution and an old earth, [12] still believes in the literal truth of the Bible. He has written two books on the Anthropic Principle: *The Fingerprint of God* [10] and *The Creator and the Cosmos*. [11] The subtitles of these books, *Recent Scientific Discoveries Reveal the Unmistakable Identity of the Creator* and *How the Latest Scientific Discoveries Reveal God,* clearly indicate his view that the Anthropic Principle proves the existence of God.

In the book called *A Case Against Accident and Self-Organization,* Dean Overman, a lawyer and writer of a range of other books, proposes that the Anthropic Principle and other observations in nature argue against the proposition that the universe and the life in it could have developed from chance events. While he does not specifically mention God, this is an Intelligent Design-type of argument. It is clear that the Intelligent Design movement is meant to include cosmology as well as evolution. Other books that propose that the Anthropic Principle proves God exists include those by Nathan Aviezer, [13] Fred Heeren, [14] Patrick Glynn, [15] and others. John Polkinghorne, a particle physicist-turned-clergyman, can gave both a scientist's and a theist's opinion. He stated: [16]

The Weak Anthropic Principle amounts to little more than tautology.

"We're here and so things are the way that makes that possible." It fails adequately to encapsulate the remarkable degree of "fine-tuning" involved in spelling out the conditions that have permitted our evolution. Only a tiny fraction of conceivable universes could have been the homes of conscious beings.

He fundamentally believes that the world is fine-tuned because it is the creation of a Creator who wills that it be so.

Some physicists hate the Anthropic Principle because it suggests Intelligent Design and has been used to "prove" that God exists. Other physicists have suggested that we may have to accept the fact that the existence of life was built into the laws of physics from the beginning. Isaac Newton believed that the elegance of the laws he formulated pointed to the existence of God. Vera Kristiakowsky, an MIT physicist says, "The exquisite order displayed by our scientific understanding of the physical world calls for the divine." Physicist Freemon Dyson said "It's as if the universe knew we were coming." Stephen Hawking [17] said,

> It would be very difficult to explain why the universe should have begun in just this way, except as the act of a God who intended to create beings like us.

By contrast, Steven Weinberg was not convinced the anthropic principle meant anything. He stated:

> It is almost irresistible for humans to believe that we have some special relation to the universe, that human life is not just a more-or-less farcical outcome of a chain of accidents reaching back to the first three minutes, but that we were somehow built in from the beginning.

He concluded that the strong Anthropic Principle was "little more than mystical mumbo jumbo."

Strong Selective Effect

Whichever view is correct, it is clear that a strong *selection effect* is built into the Anthropic Principle. Thus, since humans represent "life and consciousness," the Anthropic Principle would not exist if the constants of the universe did not allow us to exist. Or, to put it differently, there is no Anthropic Principle in universes that have no life capable of thought and consciousness. If there were a trillion parallel universes it would be a virtual certainty that one of them would have the "just right" set of constants. The anthropic principle would be easily explained on that basis.

Is Life in the Universe Rare?

In their book, *Rare Planet*, Peter Ward and Donald Brownlee [18] expand even further the list of constants and conditions that had to be "just right" and in the Goldilocks zone for life to occur. On this basis they argue life is probably very rare in the universe. By contrast, as noted previously, based on the fact that life on earth evolved in such a short period of time and that there are probably billions of planets in the universe, De Duve came to the opposite conclusion and proposed that life has occurred in many worlds.

Religious and Spiritual Implications of the Anthropic Principle

Before it can be concluded that the Anthropic Principle has major implications concerning the existence of God and other spiritual matters, it is necessary to examine whether the whole concept is valid or simply a tautology. Only then can the religious and spiritual implications be discussed. Both of these issues are examined in the next chapter.

The Anthropic Principle states that the laws of nature are arranged so that life and consciousness are possible. This has been proposed because there are a number of cosmological constants that had to be "just right" for life to occur. Many individuals, including some scientists, have suggested that the Anthropic Principle proves that God exists, since only a divine presence could fine-tune the universe with such accuracy. Other interpretations that do not require a divine presence are discussed in the next chapter.

References

1. Carter, B. Large Number of Coincidences and the Anthropic Principle in Cosomology. In: Longair, M. S. *Confrontation of Cosmological Theories with Observations.* 2nd Copernicus Symposium. Boston, D. Reidel Pub. Co, 1974.
2. Barrow, J. D. & Tipler, F. J. *The Anthropic Cosmological Principle.* Oxford University Press, New York, 1986.
3. Hoyle, F. Religion and the Scientists. SCM, London, 1959.
4. Wheeler, J. A. in: Butts, R. E. & Hintikka, J. *Foundational Problems in the Special Sciences.* Dordrecht. Reidel. 1977.
5. Wheeler, J. A. The Universe as Home for Man. in: Gingerich, O. *The Nature of Scientific Discovery.* Washington, D. C. Smithsonian Press. 1975.
6. Rees, M. *Just Six Numbers. The Deep Forces that Shape the Universe.* Basic Books, New York, 1999.
7. Gurth, A. H. Inflationary universe: a possible solution to the horizon and flatness problems. *Physical Review.* 192: 440-441, 1981.
8. Tyson, N. D. & Goldsmith, D. *Origins.* W. W. Norton, New York, 2004.
9. Barrow, J. D. & Webb, J. K. Inconstant Constants. Do the inner workings of nature change with time? *Scientific American.* 57-63, 2005.
10. Ross, H. *The Fingerprint of God. Recent Scientific Discoveries Reveal the Unmistakable Identity of the Creator.* Promise Publishing Co., Orange, CA, 1991.
11. Ross, H. *The Creator and the Cosmos. How the Latest Scientific Discoveries of the Century Reveal God.* NavPress, Colorado Springs, CO, 2001.
12. Ross, H. *A Matter of Days. Resolving a Creation Controversy.* NavPress, Colorado Springs, CO, 2004.
13. Aviezer, N. *In the Beginning: Biblical Creation and Science.* Ktav Publishing, Inc., 1990.
14. Heeren, F. *Show Me God.* Day Star Publications, Wheeling, IL, 1998.
15. Glynn, P. *God: The Evidence: The Reconciliation of Faith and Reason in a Postsecular World.* Prima Lyfestyles, 1997.
16. Polkinghorne, J. *Beyond Science.* Cambridge University Press, Cambridge, UK, 1996.
17. Hawking, S. *A Brief History of Time.* Bantum Books, New York, 1996.
18. Ward, P. D. & Brownlee, D. *Rare Earth. Why Complex Life is Uncommon in the Universe.* Copernicus Books, New York, 2000.

Chapter 24

Cosmology, Theology, and Spirituality

There is enough material relevant to theological, religious, and spiritual issues in the previous four chapters to fill a library of books. In fact, just in recent years over 260 books have been written on the implications of modern cosmology and physics to theology, spirituality, and the existence of God. I will attempt to keep this chapter focused on the issue of whether some aspects of cosmology prove that God exists and whether our rational and spiritual brains can come to a mutually satisfying accommodation about these issues.

For many readers, the overriding approach to this material may be one of "Don't confuse me with facts; I have already made up my mind about God." Thus, based on their upbringing and other factors in their lives, most readers will approach these issues already knowing whether they are theists, deists, agnostics, or atheists — and interpret the material based on these beliefs. This is fine. This chapter is written to those who will approach this material with the view that they might be willing to change or expand their mind in one direction or the other. If some readers find a reason to reevaluate and broaden their prior spiritual views, that is fine also. If some readers chose not to change their spiritual views, that is also fine. They may at least enjoy the debate. I will discuss the issues in the order of the previous four chapters.

1. Quantum Physics

Does the Uncertainty Principle Mean We Have Free Will?

Following the publication of Newton's opus, *Philosophiae Naturalis Principia Mathematica [Mathematical Principles of Natural Philosophy]*, better known simply as *Principia,* it appeared as though the precise physical laws he described meant that everything in the universe was predictable and the the future was predetermined.

Pierre Simon Laplace, Napoleon's scientific advisor, claimed that using Newton's laws one could predict the future with the same precision that one knows the past. When he presented a copy of his masterwork, *Celestial Mechanics,* to Napoleon, the emperor was reputed to have said, "You have written this huge work on the heavens, without once mentioning God." Laplace replied, "Sire, I have no need of that hypothesis." [1p154]

Einstein, who did not believe in quantum mechanics and was also a determinist, stated:

I am a determinist, compelled to act as if free will existed, because if I wish to live in civilized society I must act responsible. I know philosophically a murderer is not responsible for his crimes, but I prefer not to take tea with him. [1]

His words might have been clearer if he had said, "Even though I am a determinist and thus believe there is no free will, I am compelled to act is if free will existed." He went on to say:

> ...each man explains in his own way the fact that the human will is not free....Everything is determined...by forces over which we have no control...for the insect as well as for the star. Human beings, vegetables, or cosmic dust, we all dance to a mysterious tune, intoned in the distance by an invisible player. [1]

The concept of determinism is common in most religions where predestination is linked with the idea of a powerful all-knowing God who knows what will happen to you in the future. The uncertainty principle of quantum theory has relevance to these philosophical and theological ideas. As stated before, during the probabilistic wave function, a subatomic particle such as an electron or a photon can exist in all possible states at the same time. It can be in two or more places at once. However, once an observation is made, the wave function "collapses" and the object goes into a definite state where its position is known. On a broader philosophical scale, for those who believe in quantum theory, like Niels Bohr, reality exists only after an observation is made. By contrast, Einstein, who was less than enthusiastic about quantum theory, believed in "objective reality," where objects can exist in definite states without human intervention. The Bohr approach reminds us of the old philosophical thought, "Does a tree falling in the forest where there is no one to hear it, really make a sound?"

I always thought this type of mental mischief was silly. Of course a falling tree makes noise whether a human, or other animal, is there to hear it or not. However, with the advent of quantum theory and the precise predictions it makes, this has been elevated to what could be called, "the observer problem." If an object's wave function only collapses when it is observed, perhaps the "falling tree" question is not as silly as it seems. In fact, some of the deepest thinkers in physics have struggled with this issue. [1p165] The Nobel laureate Eugene Wigner suggested that *human consciousness determines existence.* He stated:

> It was not possible to formulate the laws of quantum mechanics in a fully consistent way, without reference to the consciousness [of the observer]...the very study of the external world led to the conclusion that the content of the consciousness is the ultimate reality.

There was also the issue of "Wigner's friend." This alludes to the thought that if

I make an observation do I need someone else to observe me to collapse my wave function? Do I then need someone to observe that person, and on and on? This could be extended to an all-encompassing cosmic consciousness. There is more than one physicist who has voiced these views. Andrei Linde, one of the founders of the concept of the inflationary universe, states:

> For me as a human being, I do not know any sense in which I could claim that the universe is here in the absence of observers....A recording device cannot play the role of an observer, because who will read what is written on the recording device. In order for us to see that something happens, and say to one another that something happens, you need to have a recording device, and you need to have us....In the absence of observers, our universe is dead.

Others have taken a more circuitous route to resolve the philosophical questions generated by the role of the observer in the uncertainty principle. In 1970 the German physicist Dieter Zeh outlined an approach called *decoherance*. This was formulated in relation to the famous *Schrödinger's cat* problem that has often been used to explain the uncertainty and observer principle. Here a cat is placed in a box along with a radioactive uranium source. Since the decay of uranium is a quantum event, it is totally random and cannot be predicted ahead of time. There is a 50 percent chance the decay will occur and a 50 percent chance it will not occur. The box is set up so that if a decay occurs it sets off a Geiger counter, which sets off a hammer, which breaks a vial of cyanide, which kills the cat. Before the box is opened it is impossible to tell if the cat is alive or dead—in the quantum world the cat is both alive and dead. Once the box is opened, the cat's wave function collapses and it is observed to be either alive or dead.

Zeh pointed out that for the cat to be both alive and dead, the wave function of the alive cat and of the dead cat had to be vibrating in exact synchrony, a state called *coherence*. This, however, is almost impossible, since even the presence of a few randomly vibrating air molecules in the box would destroy the coherence and thus kill the cat without any observation taking place. By this approach, consciousness and human observers are not necessary. Decoherance occurs without them and thus *reality does not need an observer.*

The problem with the decoherance explanation is that is does not answer a question that disturbed Einstein. How does nature choose the final state of the cat? To show how much brain power has been expended on this issue, physicist Hugh Everett III suggested that the multiverse could come to the rescue. In this scenario, in one parallel universe the cat is alive and in another it is dead. An advantage of this is that the wave functions never collapse, they just keep splitting into more and more parallel universes. A disadvantage is that we have to put up with millions of parallel universes just to solve the cat problem.

We eventually get around to theology and religious issues because in a final suggested solution the observer is God. The universe exists because there is a deity to observe it. God decides whether the cat is alive or dead. God is responsible for collapsing the wave function of these objects that we see. Quentin Smith called this "the best scientific argument for God that is present in twentieth-century science. [2] Wheeler [3p583] quotes the following charming and relevant limerick:

> *There was a young man who said God*
> *Must find it exceedingly odd*
> *To think that this tree*
> *Would continue to be*
> *When there's no one about in the quad*
>
> *Dear Sir, your astonishment's odd*
> *I am always about in the quad*
> *And that's why this tree*
> *Continues to be*
> *Since observed by, yours faithfully, God*

My rational brain prefers a far simpler approach, that of Roger Penrose. As discussed previously, Penrose felt that the whole issue of the ability of subatomic particles to exist in several places at once was because the force of gravity was so weak, it could not collapse the wave function of tiny particles. By contrast the energy required to keep the larger objects in several places at once was so enormous, their wave functions immediately collapsed all by themselves. The beauty of this proposal is that the larger objects that are visible in our reality are collapsed not by an observer, man, decoherence, or God, but by gravity. Einstein was right in his belief in "objective reality" where objects can exist in definite states without human intervention. The subatomic particles that are beyond our visible observation can maintain their wave function forever until observed. In the larger reality of the real world, the wave function of objects is collapsed by gravity.

This discussion started with the issue of whether we have free will. Despite Einstein's concerns, quantum theory is correct. Determinism is not correct. The astrophysicist Kaku [1p346] put it well:

> The quantum revolution gave us an even more bizarre picture of the world. On one hand, the downfall of determinism meant that the puppets were allowed to cut their strings and read their own lines. Free will was restored, but at the price of having multiple and uncertain outcomes.

From a religious point of view, the Catholic biochemist Kenneth Miller [4] proposed that quantum indeterminacy formed the bridge between science and religion. He suggested that the element of uncertainty was deliberately introduced by God into the laws of his creation so that humans can be free to chose between good and evil and bear responsibility for their actions.

Despite this attempt to put a positive religious spin on quantum uncertainty, it clearly has negative implications for the common religious concept of pre-determinism. The uncertainty principle not only shows we have free will, it also shows we cannot predict the future and the future is not pre-ordained. Since God would not disobey his own laws, God also cannot predict or preordain the future. The preordaining aspect of the world's religions is relegated to our spiritual brains. Our rational brains realize it is not possible.

> **The advent of quantum theory and the Heisenberg Uncertainty Principle put an end to the philosophy of determinism. Free will was restored to humans but at the price of having multiple and uncertain outcomes. Because of this uncertainty we cannot predict our future. Since God would not disobey his own laws, God also cannot predict or preordain the future.**

Does Quantum Physics and Entanglement Support the Eastern Religious View of a Cosmic Consciousness Where All Parts of the Universe are Interconnected?

In his book, *The Tao of Physics,* Fritjof Capra [5] suggests there are parallels between quantum physics and Eastern mystic religions. Capra was trained in theoretical physics and became interested in Eastern mysticism. He confessed that overcoming the gap between his rational, analytical thinking and the meditative experience of mystical truth was very difficult. In a fashion somewhat similar to the theme of this book, Capra distinguishes between the rational brain and rational thought versus the mystical, spiritual, or intuitive brain and mystical thought.

> Rational knowledge is derived from the experience we have with objects and events in our everyday environment. It belongs to the realm of the intellect whose function it is to discriminate, divide, compare, measure, and categorize. In this way a world of intellectual distinctions is created. The realm of rational knowledge is, of course, the realm of science which measures and quantifies, classifies and analyzes.

This contrasts with what Buddhists call "absolute knowledge," a direct experience of reality which transcends not only intellectual thinking but also sensory perception. Eastern mystics insist that the ultimate reality can never be an object of reasoning or of demonstrable knowledge; it can never be adequately described by words, because it lies beyond the realm of the senses and of the intellect from which our words and concepts are derived. This is the basis of much of the meditative aspects of Eastern religions, where the basic aim is to silence the thinking mind and to shift the awareness from the rational to the intuitive mode of consciousness. When the rational mind is silenced, the intuitive mode produces an extraordinary awareness; the environment is experienced in a direct way without the filter of conceptual thinking.

This is the realm of the spiritual brain. Taoism is an ancient Chinese practice or tradition whose chief tenet is that there is a "Way" by which the universe flows, and that humans can learn to intuit this Way and live in accord with it or fight it.

So, what aspect of physics led Capra to conclude that it had a commonality with Eastern mystic religions? One aspect was that quantum theory and relativity theory, the two bases of modern physics, have made it clear that their reality transcends classical logic and we cannot talk about it in ordinary language. Capra states: [5p51]

> Probing inside the atom and investigating its structure, science transcended the limits or our sensory imagination. From this point on, it could no longer rely with absolute certainty on logic and common sense. Atomic physics provided scientists with the first glimpses of the essential nature of things. Like the mystics, physicists were now dealing with a nonsensory experience of reality and, like the mystics, they had to face the paradoxical aspects of this experience. From then on therefore, the models and images of modern physics became akin to those of Eastern philosophy.

Thus, Capra equates the weirdness of quantum theory and relativity with the mystic aspects of Eastern religions and as knowledge that is closer to the "absolute knowledge" of Buddhism than to the rational knowledge of Western thought. Even Einstein was shaken by this weirdness. He stated in his autobiography: [6]

> All my attempts to adapt the theoretical foundation of physics to this knowledge failed completely. It was as if the ground had been pulled out from under one, with no firm foundation to be seen anywhere, upon which one could have built.

There are a number of problems with Capra's concept of the unity of modern physics and Eastern mysticism. Capra leans heavily on Geoffrey Chew's 1970 "bootstrap" theory which attempted to do away with fundamental particles and replace them with the idea that every particle can be considered to be composed of other particles, with none more fundamental than any other. The success of the quark model, the Standard Theory, and M-theory all brought the bootstrap theory to a grinding halt. The demise of the bootstrap theory destroyed much of the apparent unity of modern physics with Eastern mysticism.

A second large part of the claim that modern physics and Eastern mysticism are similar is based on quantum entanglement. This assumes that if particles are instantly interconnected across the vastness of the universe, then all parts of the universe are connected to all other parts, just as proposed in Eastern religions. The problem with this is that information cannot be transmitted by quantum entanglement. All forms of communication, whether it is between societies, individuals, or within the nervous system of a single individual are based on a minimum of a one-way exchange of information and preferably a two-way exchange. If information cannot be transmitted, the so-called cosmic connectedness or cosmic consciousness is a meaningless fantasy.

While Nobel laureate Murray Gell-Mann once jokingly stated that "physics is very Zen" he also opined that most of the pop science books on the subject are "New Age pap." These attempts to transform modern physics into new age mysticism all play on the weirdness of quantum physics and modern cosmology. When carefully examined, their metaphysical claims do not hold up well to the reality that *quantum theory provides some of the most ultra-precise predictions available in all of science — a far cry from the claim of Eastern mysticism that "ultimate reality can never be an object of reasoning or of demonstrable knowledge" or "that there is no real valid physical model of the world."*

> **Quantum entanglement has often been used to support the philosophy of Eastern religions of a cosmic consciousness in which all parts of the universe are interconnected. However, since information cannot be passed by entanglement, and since communication is the key to any meaningful interconnection, basing cosmic consciousness on quantum theory is a fantasy.**

Quantum Physics and Metaphysics

In his *Discourse on the Method,*[7] the French philosopher Rene Descartes stated, "I think, therefore I am." This has arguably become the most famous thought in the history of philosophy. Descartes believed that thinking and the awareness of thinking (consciousness) was the real essence of being. He believed that the thinking mind was separate from the nonthinking body. This is the philosophy of dualism, or the separation of mind and body. Monism is the opposite of dualism and proposes that the brain part of the body is the seat of the mind. The failure of dualism and evidence for monism was eloquently described in Antonio Damasio's book, *Descartes' Error.*[8] The entire modern field of neuroscience and cognitive science repeatedly validates the role of the brain in cognition and thinking.

Despite this, many recent books[9-13] continue to suggest there is some dimension of the mind that is beyond neurochemistry and physics. This is the realm of metaphysics which is concerned with the ultimate nature of reality. A variant of this is vitalism or transcendentalism, the philosophy that living processes cannot be explained in terms of their physical and chemical composition and processes. These philosophies are related by the ideas that the "whole is greater than the sum of its parts." In *Quantum Questions: Mystical Writings of the World's Great Physicists,* Ken Wilber[14] noted:

> Plato announced that the whole of physics was nothing more than a "likely story," since it depended ultimately on nothing but the evidence of the fleeting and shadowy senses, whereas truth resides in the transcendental forms beyond physics (hence "metaphysics"). Democritus,

on the other hand, put his faith in the "atoms and the void," since nothing else, he felt, had any existence — a notion so obnoxious to Plato that he expressed the strongest desire that all the works of Democritus be burned on the spot.

This illustrates the truism that nothing under the sun changes. Now 2,000 years later, many still rail against the seeming inadequacy of science to explain "all there is." The weirder aspects of quantum theory provide a rich lode for mining by those who support this thought and they look to modern physics to validate their spiritual longings. As shown below, despite their own bents for mysticism, *none* of the major thinkers behind the modern physics revolution believed that relativity or quantum physics provided any support for these mystical and transcendental ideas.

2. The Big Bang

Do a Finite Universe and the Big Bang Prove God Exists?

Immanuel Kant (1724–1804) is considered to be the Father of Cosmology. Expanding on the work and ideas of Newton and other scientists of the time, he proposed a model of a mechanistic and infinite universe. He also swept away all earlier uses of cosmology to prove the existence of God. However, he was not an atheist. He was an agnostic and claimed that the question of God's existence was beyond the reach of man's knowledge. His views contributed greatly to materialism, determinism, and a number of other *isms,* including existentialism. [15p38] If the universe is infinite in time and space, with no starting time, no end, and no boundaries, as Kant proposed, then God was not the creator since the universe did not need to be created. [15p3] In his book, *A Brief History of Time,* Stephen Hawking states,

> If the universe is really completely self-contained, having no boundary or edge, it would have neither beginning nor end; it would simply be. What place then for a creator?

The famous astronomer, Fred Hoyle, also proposed a theory in which new matter was constantly being created, producing a universe with no beginning and no end — an infinite universe that just was.

By contrast to an infinite universe, if the universe is finite in time and space and if it was created out of nothing and has boundaries, this has been considered by many to provide proof that God exists, [15-18] since only God can create something from nothing. One or the other of these two concepts, a finite or an infinite universe, form the basis of most of the religions of the world. Western Christian, Jewish, and Muslim religions believe that God created the universe from nothing, while Eastern religions such as Buddhism and Hinduism propose a timeless universe with no beginning and no end. They also propose many levels of existence, with the highest being Nirvana. Nirvana is eternal and can only be attained by the purest of meditation.

Einstein's theory of relativity showed that Kant's model of an infinite universe was wrong. The Big Bang model, which is an extension of Einstein's theory, proposes that the universe originated from a singularity or a point of no size — nothing. Frederick Burnham, a science-historian, said of the Big Bang,

> These findings make the idea that God created the universe a more respectable hypothesis today than at any time in the last 100 years.

With a time scale that indicates the universe is 13.7 million years old, the Big Bang model is clearly not the view of the new earth creationists. With this exception, the Big Bang is a wonderful theory for theists since it is totally consistent with the view of God as the Creator. Eastern religions, by contrast, would agree with the new earth creationists but for opposite reasons, that the Big Bang is a seriously flawed bit of nonsense.

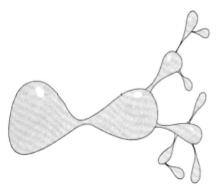

Figure 1. Budding multiverses. From Kaku. Parallel *Worlds. [1] By permission.*

In his book, *Parallel Worlds,* Michio Kaku, [1] whose parents were raised in the Buddhist tradition but who attended Sunday school and learned the parables of the Old Testament, proposed that there is theoretical evidence to support the existence of multiple universes or a multiverse in which entire universes continually sprout or "bud" off other universes.

If true, this would unify two of the great religious mythologies, Genesis of the Bible and Nirvana. Genesis would take place continually within the fabric of timeless Nirvana.

Our spiritual brain could choose to resolve this conflict between the philosophy of Eastern and Western religions either through multiverses or by suggesting that time and space are irrelevant to God. He is so powerful that He should be perfectly capable of creating either a finite or an infinite universe. By this view the Big Bang would not necessarily be proof that God exists and an endless universe would not be proof that God did not exist. Our rational brain could say that even this mental maneuvering is not really necessary.

While the scientific evidence for the Big Bang is overwhelming, the weirdness of quantum mechanics, or the collision of parallel universes, or the presence of multiverses, is sufficient to show how the inflation started and thus to explain the creation of the universe. No supernatural being is required.

Is God Required to Stabilize the Universe?

After the publication of his *Principia*, Newton received a letter from the Reverend Richard Bentley. He asked Newton why gravity, which is always attractive, did not result in the collapse of the universe into itself. If the universe was finite it should end up as one giant fiery superstar. On the other hand, if the universe was infinite, then the force on any object tugging it right or left would be infinite, and the stars would be ripped to shreds. This was known as the *Bentley Paradox.* [1]

Newton's response to Bentley was that the universe was infinite and uniform such that the gravitational forces were evenly balanced, producing a stable universe. However, Newton realized the inadequacy of this response in that even the tiniest jiggle of a star would start a chain reaction of instability. Thus, his ultimate answer came from his spiritual brain and suggested that *a divine force was needed to prevent its collapse.* Newton suggested that while God created the universe, which then obeyed Newton's laws of gravity, God needed to intermittently intervene to keep the universe stable.

Had Newton known about dark energy, his rational brain could have provided the answer without needing God's help. Dark energy keeps the universe expanding at an accelerating rate, preventing its collapse. Of course it is somewhat embarrassing that science does not yet know what dark energy is. Theologians might say dark energy is the hand of God, designed to stabilize the universe. We currently do not know what dark energy is, but in time we will.

Einstein, who also did not know about dark energy, was also confronted with Bentley's paradox. Instead of using his spiritual brain and evoking God as Newton had done, he used his rational brain and added an anti-gravity force to his equations in the form of a *cosmological constant.* He also regretted this and called it "his greatest blunder" when Hubble showed the universe was expanding and the cosmological constant was not needed. After his death, when astronomers found that the universe was expanding at an accelerated rate, the cosmological constant was needed again. Einstein was right after all. Whether it is a cosmological constant or dark energy our rational brain can once again say to God, "Thanks, but I really don't need your help."

3. String Theory

Does String Theory Eliminate the Theological Advantage of the Big Bang?

Prior to string theory the Big Bang assumed that when the equations were run backward to the singularity point, the universe would be infinitely small, a point so small that the universe appeared to have developed from nothing—perfect for the religious view that God created the universe from nothing and that only God could do this.

String theory prevents the universe from being created from nothing. This effect is similar to the manner in which string theory solved a paradox of Newton's theory of gravity. In his famous inverse square law, the force of gravity, G, increased as the square of the decreasing distance. Thus $G = 1/r^2$, where r is the distance between the bodies. The problem is that when this distance is zero, G is infinite. This problem was solved by string theory. Now r cannot be less than the size of a string, 10^{-33} centimeters and G is not infinite.

In the same vein, the universe did not arise from an infinitely small point it arose from something no smaller than a string. String theory places a limit on what was previously nothingness. While that limit is extremely small, 10^{-33} cm, it is not infinitely small. It is not nothing. Strings are not points; they have non-zero size. One could still ask, where did the strings come from? Did God create strings or have they always been there? The possibility that God and strings are the same is not very satisfactory, since ultra-minute strings do not provide for a very complex, warm, and fuzzy personal God. Strings are the simplest things in the universe. God is the most complex.

4. The Anthropic Principle

Does the Anthropic Principle Prove that God Exists?

Not everyone believes the Anthropic Principle is proof of design, or of Intelligent Design, or of the existence of God. There are a number of responses to the Anthropic Principle that do not require that type of interpretation.

The Anthropic Principle is just a tautology. A major criticism of the Anthropic Principle is that it is basically a *tautology,* or circular reasoning. Circular reasoning is a statement that is true by its own definition. In relation to the universe the tautology is that because we are here, we exist to ask the question. If we did not exist the question could not be asked. Or stated differently, if the features of the universe were incompatible with our existence, we would not be here to notice it.

The existence of many universes solves the Anthropic Principle. If we ignore the tautology and pursue the Anthropic Principle anyhow, the most common explanation is that the quantum fluctuations of space produce or attempt to produce billions of universes. Some have suggested up to 10^{500} [19] or untold trillions of universes. This has been referred to as a *megaverse*, a "huge landscape of possibilities—an enormously rich space of possible designs." [20] It is a mistake to think all of these other universes are as fully developed as ours. If a quantum instability began the birthing of a universe, but the constants were not right, it would never reach more than sub-microscopic proportions before it became extinct. Those latent universes that do not have the correct set of constants do not thrive. Those that do not have the right set of constants for life to exist do not have conscious beings capable of asking these questions. To Rees [21p247] the Anthropic Principle was one of the most compelling arguments for the multiverse. He commented,

> If the "constants" took different values in each universe, there would then be no need for surprise that some universes allowed creatures like us to exist. And we obviously find ourselves in one such subset. If you go to a clothes shop with a large stock of clothes, it isn't surprising to find a suit that fits you.

In their book *Origins,* Tyson and Goldsmith [22p99-104] argued that instead of providing evidence for God, the multi-universe proposal, which is an incredibly wasteful approach, clearly does not fit the concept of a perfect and efficient God.

Copernican Principle. The Copernican Principle is the opposite of the Anthropic Principle and states that humans do not occupy a privileged place in the universe. Successive astronomical discoveries seem to support this principle. In the Middle Ages it was assumed that God created man in his image, and as such, man and the earth were at the center of the universe. Copernicus and Galileo abolished the illusion that the earth was the center of the solar system and put the sun in its rightful heliocentric place. It was then found that the sun was not at the center of our galaxy, and Hubble showed that our own galaxy, the Milky Way, was not at the center of the universe. Finally, the multiverse concept suggests our universe may be just one of many constantly sprouting new universes, further diminishing the Anthropic Principle conclusion that the universe is here just for us. The Anthropic Principle emphasizes the rarity of life and consciousness while the Copernican Principle forces us to realize it was not all done just so we could exist.

There may be only a few or no true anthropic numbers. Carr and Rees [23] argued that although there appear to be a myriad number of so called anthropic coincidences or constants, only four are especially critical. These were *me* (mass of the electron), *mu* (mass of the up-quark), *md* (mass of the down-quark), and *g,* the Grand Unified coupling constant that determines the strength of the strong, electromagnetic, and weak forces. Taking this line of reasoning a step further, Kane and colleagues [24] proposed that:

> In string theories all of the parameters of the theory—in particular all quark and lepton masses, and all coupling strength—are calculable, so there are no parameters left to allow anthropic arguments...

Despite his sympathy for the concept of a God, Stephen Hawking's [25] latest studies also weigh in heavily against the Anthropic Principle. He proposed that our universe is much less "special" than the proponents of the Anthropic Principle claim it is. According to Hawking, *there is a 98 percent chance that a universe of a type as ours will come from the Big Bang.* Further, using the basic wave function of the universe as a basis, Hawking's equations indicate that such a universe can come into existence without relation to anything prior to it, meaning that it could come out of nothing.

The Anthropic Principle is a straw man, weakened by the fact that it is basically a tautology. It can be eliminated altogether by multiple universes, quantum mechanics and M-theory. The Anthropic Principle cannot be relied upon to prove that God exists.

The Participatory Anthropic Principle, Human Consciousness, and the Universe

In their opus on the Anthropic Principle, John Barrow and Frank Tipler [26] refer to Wheeler's feedback loop connection between mankind and the universe as *PAP,* or the *Participatory Anthropic Principle.* This has been taken to the extreme of assuming that the process of creating reality by human observation is retroactive to the beginning of the universe. John Wheeler stated: [27p18]

> The Universe starts small at the Big Bang, grows in size, gives rise to life and observers and observing equipment. The observing equipment, in turn, through the elementary quantum processes that terminate on it, takes part in giving tangible "reality" to events that occurred long before there was any life anywhere.

This proposes that the universe creates man, but man through his observations of the universe brings the universe into reality. Martin Gardner [28] seems to have placed the anthropic principle in some perspective:

> What should one make of this quartet of WAP, SAP, PAP and FAP? In my not so humble opinion I think the last principle is best called CRAP, the Completely Ridiculous Anthropic Principle.

Wheeler himself recognized how bizarre the concept of PAP was. In the discussion of his article entitled "The Universe as Home for Man," [3p261] he states: [3p580]

> At first even the words sound absolutely ridiculous. After all, we know that the scale of man's existence is extraordinarily short compared with the whole time scale of the universe. So it is preposterous to think that life and mind in these few hundreds of thousands of years of self-conscious existence will have any control or influence over the development of the universe in the ten billions of years past and in the several tens of billions of years to come.

And yet later, when the discussion turned to the concept of a Darwinian evolution of multiple universes, he stated:

> The universe allows mutation and Darwinian natural selection to proceed; this Darwinian evolution leads to consciousness, and consciousness of consciousness; mind at this level gives meaning to the universe, and without mind at this level and "participation"... embodied in the quantum principle, the universe...could not have come into being in the first place. [3]

In essence, Wheeler tends to vacillate between two concepts. Few could argue about one while the other fits his own description of "sounding absolutely ridiculous." The ridiculous concept is: "The universe just would not exist if it were not for consciousness to be aware of it." The similar, but drastically more acceptable concept, is: "The universe gives birth to consciousness; and consciousness gives meaning to the universe." The latter has an important kernel of wisdom—there is meaning to life that can be independently and naturally derived from human consciousness alone without requiring a divine power to provide that meaning.

> **There are two interpretations of the Participatory Anthropic Principle. One is ludicrous; the other is self-evident. One says, "The universe just would not exist if it were not for a human consciousness to be aware of it, and this effect is retroactive to the time of the Big Bang." This is the ludicrous one. The other says, "The universe gives birth to consciousness and consciousness gives meaning to the universe." This is the reasonable one and it has relevance to the issue of a meaning to life that can be independently and naturally derived from human consciousness alone, without requiring a divine power.**

Science and Mysticism

In *Quantum Questions,* Ken Wilbur [14] notes that modern physics has been used to both support and refute determinism, free-will, God, Spirit, immortality, causality, predestination, Buddhism, Hinduism, Christianity, and Taoism. To help us lesser beings understand these issues, Wilbur collected the relevant opinions and writings from the cream of the creative thinkers in modern physics: Heisenberg, Schrödinger, Einstein, De Broglie, Jeans, Planck, Pauli, and Eddington.

> The last thing these theorists would want you to surrender is your critical intellect, your hard-earned skepticism. For it was exactly through a sustained use — not of emotion, not of intuition, not of faith — but a sustained use of the critical intellect that these greatest of physicists felt absolutely compelled to go beyond [the old] physics altogether.

All of these great scientists had a mystical bent and "were mystics of one sort or another." And yet to a man they were unanimous in their agreement that *modern physics offers no positive support whatsoever for mysticism or transcendentalism of any variety.* Thus, none of these great geniuses would support the seemingly infinite varieties of new age "pap" that have sprung up based on the findings of the "new physics."

The New Physics and Reality. Despite this strong conclusion, we still need to ask why each of these scientists felt a kinship to some form of mysticism based on their creation of the new physics. Part of the answer was that these physicists felt they were looking at nothing but a set of highly abstract differential equations — not at reality itself. They were looking at shadow symbols of reality. Sir James Jeans put it this way: [29]

> We can never understand what events are, but must limit ourselves to

describing the patterns of events in mathematical terms; no other aim is possible. Physicists who are trying to understand nature may work in many different fields and by many different methods; one may dig, one may sow, one may reap. But the final harvest will always be a sheaf of mathematical formulae. These will never describe nature itself... our studies can never put us into contact with reality.

From this view science was at the opposite extreme of mysticism. Science deals with abstract symbols of reality, while mysticism deals with a direct, intuitive, faith based approach to reality itself. Thus, the claim that there are direct and central similarities between new physics and mysticism "represents a profound confusion of absolute and relative truth, of finite and infinite, of temporal and eternal." That is what repelled these physicists and led them to state that modern physics offers no support for mysticism.

This leads to the interesting question of what was the difference between the old physics and the new physics? The difference was profound. Both the old physics and the new physics dealt with shadow symbols, but the new physics *forced them to be aware that they were dealing with shadows and illusions, not reality.* With the new physics the shadowy character of the whole enterprise became much more obvious. It was this feeling that science was not yet in contact with reality that led the physicist to be sympathetic to mysticism in one form or another. It was the failure of the new physics to provide a total picture of reality, not similarities to mysticism, that led so many of the physicists to a mystical view of the world.

The alternate view of Murray Gell-Mann, who once characterized new age attempts to mysticize quantum physics as "flapdoodle," [30] stated that quantum theory provides some of the most ultra precise predictions available in all of science — a far cry from the claim of Eastern mysticism that ultimate reality can never be an object of reasoning or of demonstrable knowledge or that there is no real valid physical model of the world.

Gell-Mann was saying that simply because quantum mechanics is based on probabilities it does not make it less accurate. The new physics provides some of the most accurate predictions of reality ever conceived by man. If metaphysics is the search for the ultimate nature of reality, one could easily argue that based on the precision with which quantum theory predicts events in the micro-world and relativity theory predicts events in the macro-world—the ultimate reality has been found.

The philosophical and mystical views of the cream of the creative thinkers in modern physics show that most were unanimous in their agreement that modern physics offers no positive support for mysticism or transcendentalism of any variety. Despite this many had a mystical bent based on their feeling that the equations of physics may not represent the totality of reality. This illustrates the basic premise of this book — that humans with highly developed rational

brains can also have a well-developed sense of spirituality. However, other physicists disagree and correctly point out that the new physics provides an incredibly accurate prediction of reality, a picture that is far closer to the absolute truth than metaphysics could ever provide.

In conclusion, there is nothing in quantum mechanics, the theory of relativity, string theory, or the Anthropic Principle that provides proof of the existence of God, mysticism or transcendentalism. To the contrary, one could argue that quantum theory and string theory show us that the universe is capable of being created, if not from nothing, at least from almost nothing, without the need of divine intervention. These two theories certainly allow us to again use Occam's Razor to resolve the question: "Was the universe created as a consequence of features of quantum physics and M-theory, or was it created by God?" If the answer is that the universe was created by God, this again raises the infinitely more complex question of *Who Created God?* I suspect Occam would have chosen quantum physics as the creator of the universe.

There are, however, elements of the new physics that led many of the physics geniuses of the early twentieth century to feel that despite the incredible predictive power of quantum theory, they still only had a part of the total reality. Although some physicists disagree with this view, it is still clear that the spiritual brains of many scientists thirsted for more. This interaction between the rational versus the spiritual brain of these scientists is a reflection of the same conflict in everyone and is the core of the issues explored in the rest of this book.

References

1. Kaku, M. *Parallel Worlds. A Journey Through Creation, Higher Dimensions and the Future of the Cosmos.* Doubleday, New York, 2005. Figure 1 used by permission of Doubleday, a division of Random House, Inc.
2. Smith, Q. *Theism, Atheism, and Big Bang Cosmology,* 1995.
3. Wheeler, J. A. The Universe as Home for Man. In: Gingerich, O. *The Nature of Scientific Discovery.* Smithsonian Press. Washington, D.C. 1975.
4. Miller, K. *Finding Darwin's God.* Harper Perennial, New York, 1999.
5. Capra, F. *The Tao of Physics.* Shambhala, Boston, 1975, 2000.
6. Schilpp, P. A. ed. *Albert Einstein: Philosopher-Scientist.* Open Court Publishing Company, 1988.
7. Descartes, R. *The Philosophical Works of Descartes.* ed. (1970), Translated by Elizabeth S., Haldane and G. R. T. Ross. Cambridge University Press, New York, 1637.
8. Damasio, A. R. *Descartes' Error. Emotion, Reason, and the Human Brain.* A. Grosset/Putnam Books, New York, 1994.
9. Capra, F. *The Web of Life: A New Scientific Understanding of Living Systems.* Anchor Books, New York, 1997.
10. Capra, F. *The Hidden Connections.* Anchor Books, New York, 2002.
11. Myerson, J. Transcendentalism: A Reader. Oxford University Press, New York, 2000.
12. Talbot, M. *Mysticism and the New Physics.* Penguin, New York, 1993.
13. Talbot, M. *The Holographic Universe.* Harper Perennial, New York, 1992.
14. Wilbur, K. *Quantum Questions. Mystical Writings of the World's Great Physicists.* Shambala Press, Boston, 1985.
15. Ross, H. *The Fingerprint of God. Recent Scientific Discoveries Reveal the Unmistakable Identity of the Creator.* Promise Publishing Co., Orange, CA, 1991.
16. Ross, H. *The Creator and the Cosmos. How the Latest Scientific Discoveries of the Century Reveal God.* NavPress, Colorado Springs, CO, 2001.

17. Swinburne, R. *The Existence of God.* Second Edition. Clarendon Press, Oxford, 2004.

18. Strobel, L. *The Case for a Creator.* Zondervan, Grand Rapids, MI, 2004.

19. Brumfiel, G. Outrageous Fortune. *Nature.* 439: 10-12, 2005.

20. Suskind, L. *The Cosmic Landscape.* Little, Brown and Company, New York, 2005.

21. Rees, M. *Before the Beginning.* Perseus Books, Cambridge, MA, 1997.

22. Tyson, N. D. & Goldsmith, D. *Origins.* W. W. Norton, New York, 2004.

23. Carr, B. J. & Rees, M. J. The anthropic principle and the structure of the physical world. *Nature.* 278: 605, 1979.

24. Kane, G. L., Perry, M. J. & Zytkow, A. N. The Beginning of the End of the Anthropic Principle. arXiv:astro-ph/0001197 2: 1-13, 2005.

25. Hawking, S. en.wikipedia.org/wiki/Anthropic_principle. 2004.

26. Barrow, J. D. & Tipler, F. J. *The Anthropic Cosmological Principle.* Oxford University Press, New York, 1986.

27. Wheeler, J. A. Bohr, Einstein, and the Strange Lesson of the Quantum. In: Elver, R. Q. *Mind in Nature.* New York. Harper Row. 1981.

28. Gardner, M. WAP, SAP, PAP and FAP. *The New York Review of Books.* 23: 22-25, 1986.

29. Jeans, S. J. *Physics and Philosophy.* Cambridge University Press, New York, 1943.

30. Shermer, M. Starbucks in the Forbidden City. Eastern and Western science are put to political uses in both cultures. *Skeptic.* July, 2001.

Part IV

The Neurology of Reason and Spirituality

The prior three parts of this book were devoted to providing a review of some of the basic aspects of evolution and cosmology. While the wondrous complexity of life and of the universe might suggest design, the scientific knowledge that has accumulated in the past 150 years has provided us with an understanding of how life and the universe can be created without divine intervention. This is especially true since our very human desire is to know all there is to know and understand all there is to understand. If we assumed there was a creator we would still need to know and understand who created the creator. We now have the knowledge to avoid that added level of unsolved mystery.

Some would conclude that individuals who take this view would automatically be driven to shut down the spiritual part of their brain, would automatically be atheists or agnostics, would automatically be anti-religion, and would automatically assume that God is dead and probably never was alive in the first place. This ignores the simple fact that the vast majority of humans, including many scientists, revel in and are rewarded by spirituality of one type or another. Simply because our rational brain denies the need for a creator of life and a creator of the universe does not mean that our spiritual brain has to atrophy or die. Spirituality is such an integral part of being human that it is very likely to have been hardwired into our brain, and no amount of scientific knowledge will silence it. If this is the case, there would be three questions about this hardwiring to explore—What parts of the brain are involved? What genes are involved? And, in the evolution of man, what selective forces are involved? Part IV explores the first of these—what parts of the brain are involved in consciousness, planning, and other executive functions, pleasure, social interactions, rational thought, spirituality, meditation, happiness, self-healing, and how faith can bypass our thinking or rational brain. One of the fundamental principles of neuroscience is that all experiences are the result of brain activity. The scope of knowledge about this neural basis of behavior is immense and many aspects of it cannot be covered here. My focus will be on those behaviors that are relevant to the theme of this book. Since consciousness is a core trait, that is addressed first.

Consciousness is an awareness, a thinking, a knowing, a focusing of attention, a planning of action, an interpreting of present experience, a perceiving. These words are descriptive, but they hardly constitute a satisfactory description.

Penfield and Roberts
Speech and Brain Mechanisms [1]

Chapter 25

Consciousness, the Spirit, and the Soul

Consciousness, the spirit, and the soul are all related concepts. Consciousness is a scientific term, while the spirit and the soul are philosophical, theological and religious concepts. I will explore the scientific term first.

The essence of consciousness is being alive and being aware that we are alive. It is a sense of self-awareness. Consciousness is more than emotions and more than feelings. It is an awareness of our emotions and awareness that we are feeling our feelings. Consciousness resides at the nexus of the mind-body problem. A poetic description of consciousness was given by Julian Jaynes. [2]

O, What a world of unseen visions and heard silences, this insubstantial country of the mind! What ineffable essences, these touchless rememberings and unshowable reveries! And the privacy of it all! A secret theater of speechless monologues and prevenient counsel, an invisible mansion of all moods, musings, and mysteries, an infinite resort of disappointment and discoveries. A whole kingdom where each of us reigns reclusively alone, questioning what we will, commanding what we can. A hidden hermitage where we may study out the troubled book of what we have done and yet may do. An introcosm that is more myself than anything I can find in a mirror. This consciousness that is myself of selves, that is everything, and yet nothing at all—what is it? And where did it come from? And Why?

These are not easy questions. Here I address the first two: What is it? Where [in the brain] did it come from? For many years the subject of consciousness was primarily the purview of philosophers and psychologists. [3] It was considered so difficult for neuroscientists to study scientifically that many who attempted it commented that they risked doing so only after they had academic tenure, or better. Thus, two of the three scientists whose views I will discuss, and who have written extensively about consciousness, did so only after they had received the Nobel Prize for other work. These individuals were Gerald Edelman, who received the prize for his pioneering work in immunology, and Sir Francis Crick, the co-discoverer of the structure of DNA. Despite the impressive credentials of Edelman and Crick, I will start with the work of a third scientist, Antonio Damasio, M.D., since he is a neurologist and has gained extensive first-hand clinical experience with patients with impaired consciousness, and cover the studies of Edelman and Crick later.

Damasio and Consciousness

Based on his clinical studies, Damasio [4p16] proposed that there were two levels of consciousness: *core consciousness* and *extended consciousness.*

"*Core consciousness* provides the organism with a sense about one moment — now — and about one place — here. The scope of core consciousness is the here and now." It is like the knife blade of current existence, no past, no future, only now. It is constantly viewing, hearing, smelling, touching, feeling, and and being aware of the immediate environment, minute by minute, second by second. It is like remembering the present.

Extended consciousness. The more-complex *extended consciousness* provides the organism with an elaborate sense of self — an identity and a person, you or me, no less — and places that person at a point in individual historical time, richly aware of the lived past and of the anticipated future and keenly aware of the world beside it....Consciousness is the critical biological function that allows us to know sorrow or know joy, to know suffering or to know pleasure, to sense embarrassment or pride, to grieve for lost love or lost life. One of the realms of consciousness difficult to understand is how we get a "movie-in-the-brain," a metaphor for the many sensory tracts that provide us with an interface between the brain and sight, sounds, taste, smell and touch.

"Core consciousness is a simple biological phenomenon; it has one single level of organization; it is stable across the lifetime of the organisms; it is not exclusively human; and it is not dependent upon conventional memory, working memory, reasoning or language." By contrast, "extended consciousness is a complex biological phenomenon; it has several levels of organization; and it evolves across the lifetime of an organism." Damasio felt that extended consciousness was present at simple levels in some non-human organisms but it attained its highest level in humans. It depended on conventional memory and working memory and was enhanced by language. Human creativity is a level of knowing that is only allowed by the domain of extended consciousness. Neurological diseases that impair extended consciousness can leave core consciousness intact, but diseases that impair core consciousness destroy extended consciousness. Attention is necessary for some aspects of consciousness, but it is not sufficient for consciousness and is not the same as consciousness. Emotions and consciousness are also present or absent together.

For some, consciousness, mind, conscience, spirit, and soul are virtually indistinguishable. However, the mind has a broader scope than consciousness, per se. Conscience is a distinct concept with a flavor of morality and is discussed in a later chapter. The spirit and the soul are discussed at the end of this chapter.

Damasio also proposed the presence of three types of self: the *proto-self,* the *core self* and the *autobiographical self.* The *proto-self* is the unconscious self that monitors the internal awareness of the body. The *core self* is transient and is constantly re-created for each and every object with which the brain interacts. It monitors the external environment and produces a fleeting feeling of knowing that is reconstructed with each interaction. The *autobiographical self* is not transient. It is who we think we are. It is a collection of unique facts and ways of being that characterize us, as opposed to someone who is not us. These characteristics include our name, who our parents are, where we were born, the country, culture, and religion in which we were raised, our likes and dislikes, and many other features that identify us. The autobiographical self monitors our self-identify. These three types of self and the proposed parts of the brain responsible for them are shown in Figure 1.

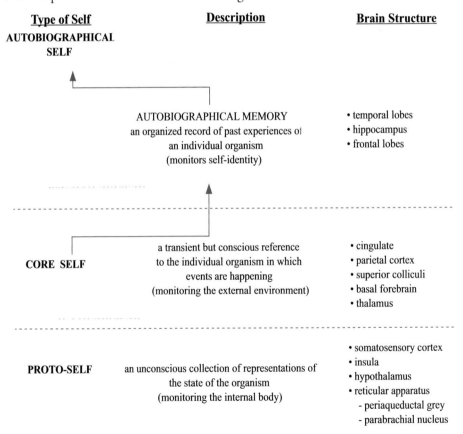

Type of Self	**Description**	**Brain Structure**
AUTOBIOGRAPHICAL SELF		
	AUTOBIOGRAPHICAL MEMORY an organized record of past experiences of an individual organism (monitors self-identity)	• temporal lobes • hippocampus • frontal lobes
CORE SELF	a transient but conscious reference to the individual organism in which events are happening (monitoring the external environment)	• cingulate • parietal cortex • superior colliculi • basal forebrain • thalamus

PROTO-SELF	an unconscious collection of representations of the state of the organism
	(monitoring the internal body)
		• somatosensory cortex
		• insula
		• hypothalamus
		• reticular apparatus
		  - periaqueductal grey
		  - parabrachial nucleus

Figure 1. Summary of Damasio's three types of self and two types of consciousness.

The Neuroanatomy of Consciousness

A number of clinical disorders have helped to understand the parts of the brain involved in the proto-self, core self and autobiographical self, and for the latter two the corresponding core and extended consciousness. The structures involved in core consciousness, and to some extent those involved in the proto-self are characterized by being in a central position in the brain, that is, near the mid-line. These are regions of old evolutionary vintage.

Proto-self. The unconscious proto-self monitors the feelings and status of the body itself. One of the structures involved is the insula (Figure 2). It is part of the cortex of the brain but is buried behind the temporal and parietal lobes which have to be pulled to one side to see it.

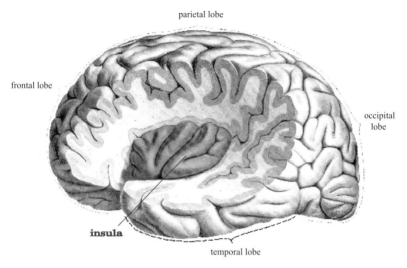

parietal lobe

frontal lobe

occipital lobe

insula

temporal lobe

Figure 2. Insula. Modified from Sobotta. [5]

The insula monitors feelings and sensations from the internal organs and thus plays a role in emotional sensitivity. [6] Functional MRI studies show that indices of negative emotional experience correlate with activity in the right insula. [7] The somatosensory cortex (Figure 3) of the partietal lobe also plays a role in monitoring the internal body.

The hypothalamus and basal forebrain are also involved in the proto-self. The reticular apparatus or the ascending activating system wakes up or arouses the brain. This especially involves two areas called the *periaqueductal grey* and the *parabrachial nucleus.* Thus, as shown in Figure 1, these are the structures involved in the proto-self.

The core self and core consciousness. Akinetic mutism is one of the neurological disorders that Damasio studied to provide information on the parts of the brain associated with core consciousness. Akinetic refers to lack of motion and mutism to lack of speech. He described a woman with akinetic mutism due to a stroke that affected her cingulate cortex (see Figure 4). Her body and face never expressed any emotion. She was awake but remained silent when spoken to. She was there but not there. One could attribute this state to either total muscle paralysis in the presence of an active and alert mind, like "locked in syndrome," or to a loss of core consciousness. When talking to her six months later, after she had emerged from this state, it was apparent that it was the latter. During this period she did not have a mind at all. She

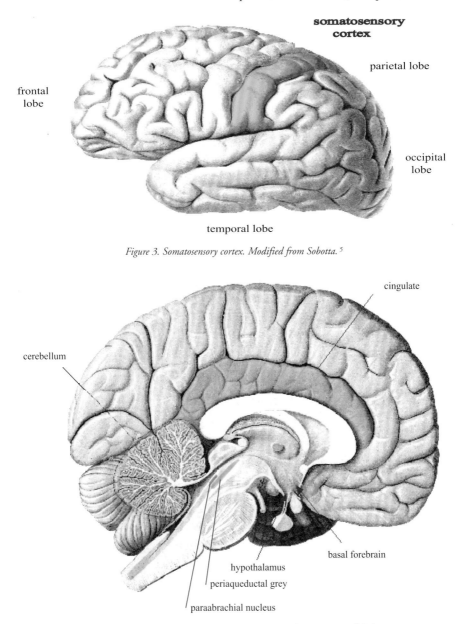

somatosensory cortex

parietal lobe

frontal lobe

occipital lobe

temporal lobe

Figure 3. Somatosensory cortex. Modified from Sobotta. [5]

cingulate

cerebellum

basal forebrain

hypothalamus

periaqueductal grey

paraabrachial nucleus

Figure 4. Hypothalamus, basal forebrain and cingulate cortex. Modified from Sobotta. [5]

had no recall of any experience. She felt no fear or anxiety and never wished to communicate.

The cingulate cortex is a large midline structure with many functions that involve both sensory and motor functions. It receives inputs from all of the somatosensory system and is thus involved in monitoring the internal body. It also monitors inputs from the musculo-skeletal system, which explains why it is involved in a large variety of complex movements. Not surprisingly, given its many internal sensory and motor connections, the cingulate is also involved in emotions. In this regard it is considered to be part of the emotional brain or limbic system. The cingulate may make a critical contribution to the "feeling of knowing," the special, high-order feeling that defines core consciousness. The superior colliculi also receive a multiplicity of sensory inputs from the retina, the visual and auditory cortex, thalamus, and somatosensory system. Because of the many interconnections Damasio suggested that these neural structures contributed to second-order patterns of consciousness.

The autobiographical self and extended consciousness. Since extended consciousness monitors the autobiographical self, it requires an intact working memory. This occurs in the hippocampus. These are structures with a unique snail-like shape that are part of the temporal lobe on both sides of the brain (see Figure 5). When they are destroyed by tumor or other pathology, all recent memory is lost.

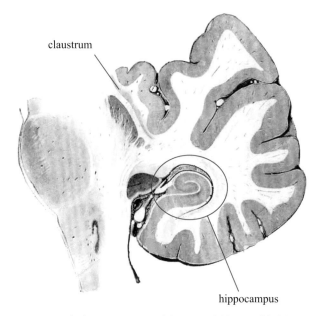

claustrum

hippocampus

Figure 5. The hippocampus part of the temporal lobes. Modified from Sobotta. [5]

Other structures, including the different sensory cortexes for sight, smell, hearing, and touch, are involved in extended consciousness, since this form of consciousness involves an integration of all of the senses.

In summary, based on a number of different disease states that comprise different types of consciousness, Damasio identified a number of brain structures that appear to play a role in core and extended consciousness. There is a tendency for core consciousness to involve the central midline structures that are evolutionarily old, and for extended consciousness to involve lateral structures that are evolutionarily more recent.

Edelman and Consciousness

The following is a description of the Edelman and Tononi[8] model of consciousness. For brevity I will refer to it as the Edelman model. For them, consciousness posed a special problem that was not encountered in other domains of science. Normal science involves connecting a physical entity such as an atom, with a law or principle such as quantum mechanics. By contrast, studies of consciousness involve connecting a physical entity such as the brain with a personal individual experience. Edelman adopted three working assumptions. First, there is no dualism. *Physical processes are all that are required to explain consciousness.*

Second, *consciousness evolved during natural selection in the animal kingdom.* This avoids attempting to characterize consciousness as a by-product of computational science or applying exotic scientific explanations like Penrose's notion of quantum gravity and consciousness while ignoring neurology.

The third relates to *qualia,* the private, subjective experience of sensations and perceptions. Examples include the subjective pleasure of seeing a beautiful face, hearing a bird sing, smelling the flowers, and the redness of a rose. No objective scientific description can adequately measure or quantify these sensations or take the place of the individual subjective experience of conscious qualia. This does not mean that the necessary and sufficient conditions for consciousness cannot be described, only that *describing them is not the same as experiencing them.* This strategy expands on William James's[9] prescient notion of consciousness as a process — one that is private, selective, and continuous yet continually changing. Edelman proposed an approach that differed somewhat from that of Damasio and of Crick. He stated: [8p19]

> As we shall see in a number of cases, it is likely that the workings of each structure may contribute to consciousness, but it is a mistake to expect that pinpointing particular locations in the brain or understanding intrinsic properties or particular neurons will, in itself, explain why their activity does or does not contribute to conscious experience. Such an expectation is a prime example of a category error, in the specific sense of ascribing to things properties they cannot have. We believe instead that what is practical is to concentrate on the processes, not just the brain areas, that support consciousness and, more specifically, to focus on those neural processes that can actually account for the most fundamental properties of consciousness.

Thus, their strategy was to focus on the properties of conscious experience that were the most general and are shared by every conscious state. They assumed that conscious experience would be associated with neural activity that was distributed simultaneously across neuronal groups in many different regions of the brain. Consciousness was neither a single thing nor a simple property. To support consciousness a large number of neurons must interact rapidly and reciprocally. They use the term *re-entry* for the reciprocal interaction between neurons. The more neuronal activity along certain pathways, the stronger those pathways become. "Neurons that fire together, wire together."

The two types of consciousness proposed by Edelman are similar to those of Damasio. They describe *primary consciousness,* which is comparable to *core consciousness,* and *higher-order consciousness,* which is comparable to *extended consciousness.* Primary consciousness is also present in animals and consists of constructing an immediate mental scene without using symbolism or language. It directs present or immediate behavior. It is the remembered present. It is the ongoing event-driven rush of consciousness. Higher-order consciousness is especially human and is accompanied by a sense of self (like autobiographical self) and the ability in the waking state to explicitly construct past and future scenes. It requires, at a minimum, a semantic capability and, in its most developed form, a linguistic capability. It is the state toward which mystics aim their devotions. Only organisms with higher-order consciousness are conscious of being conscious.

Edelman proposed that consciousness emerged in evolution when, through the appearance of new circuits mediating cross-talk or re-entry, the sensory cortex (sight, hearing, touch, taste, smell) occupying the back half of the brain became dynamically linked to the frontal cortex at the front part of the brain responsible for value-based memory. With this in place an animal would be able to build a remembered present — a scene that adaptively linked immediate or imagined contingencies to that of the animal's previous history of value-driven behavior. In Edelman's model consciousness is a result of the activation of the long nerve tracts connecting different parts of the cerebral cortex and thalamus.

The models of Damasio and of Edelman have much in common. The core consciousness and extended consciousness of Damasio is the primary and higher-order consciousness of Edelman. In both models the core or primary consciousness is for the present, while the extended or higher-order consciousness incorporates the past, present, future and knowledge of the self. Both recognize the need for cross-talk, integration or re-entry to allow communication between different neurons and regions of the brain. *This integration and interaction is the key to consciousness.*

The greatest difference between the Damasio and Edelman models is in the localization of the brain structures most involved in consciousness. While as stated above, Edelman cautioned against attempting to assign consciousness to a specific brain structure, he nevertheless suggested that the thalamo-cortical system (Figure 6) and other interconnections between different cortical regions played the major role.

The thalamus is reciprocally connected to the cerebral cortex. The six layers of the cortex each send and receive signals from specific sets of inputs and outputs. Edelman was confident that the activity of the cerebral cortex and thalamus was more important for primary or core consciousness than other brain regions. It formed a major part of a system of interacting neurons they referred to as the dynamical core. De Duve [11p222,] another Nobel Laureate, also proposed that the neural substrate of consciousness lay in the connections of the six layers of the cerebral cortex. These

During non-REM (NREM) sleep, the initial brain waves after TMS increased in magnitude (amplitude) and duration. Between 80 to 300 ms after TMS there was only a brief period of a significant response (in red) over background (in black). By contrast, in the wakeful state a significant response was seen throughout the 80 to 300 ms period. This indicates that during the loss of consciousness that occurs with NREM sleep there is a shutdown of the communication between the right and left hemispheres and a *shutdown of long-range connectivity.*

The master, or tertiary, association areas of the prefrontal lobes connect with virtually every other part of the brain. As described in the next chapter, they are also impressive candidates for a neurological location of consciousness. Combined, all of these studies are consistent with a *model of higher levels of consciousness that involves the long nerve tracts that connect and integrate disparate regions of the brain.* [24,25] This makes inherent sense when we realize that the concept of consciousness as that inner observing sense of self most likely comes from talk between the frontal lobes and all aspects of sensory input. To do this requires long and extensive lines of communication.

> **Consciousness is a self-awareness of feelings and awareness that we are feeling our feelings. It has only recently been considered a valid object of scientific inquiry. Two investigators who have independently written much about consciousness agree there are two types. The first is a core or primary consciousness representing an ongoing event-driven rush of consciousness operating in the here and now. The second is an extended or higher-order consciousness that provides the organism with an elaborate sense of self and provides us with the ability to explicitly construct past and future scenes. Studies of a range of diseases suggest core consciousness involves midline structures of the brain, while extended consciousness involves the cerebral cortex, the thalamus, and possibly the claustrum.**
>
> **A critical aspect of the neuronal structures involved in consciousness is a massive degree of information integration, interconnection and cross-talk between many different parts of the brain.**

The Spirit and the Soul

Consciousness, the spirit, and the soul are all interrelated concepts. The consciousness described above can exist independently of the soul. The concept of a soul as an entity that represents the essence of a person and that lives on after death, plays a prominent and central role in many religions. Plato is widely credited with the concept of a person as an immortal soul imprisoned in a mortal body. He also proposed that ideas have a real existence independent of the body and are eternal. Galen, the first-century Greek physician, divided the soul into several functions. He proposed that all of our motor and sensory abilities could be attributed to the soul along with rational functions such as imagination, reason and memory. These views were subsequently absorbed into the New Testament and form the basis of the classical Roman Catholic doctrine of a soul. [14] One of the catechisms of the Roman Catholic church poses the question, "What is the soul?" and suggests that, "The soul is a living being without a body, having reason and free will."

The French philosopher, Rene Descartes, proposed that the body was simply a machine composed of blood, bones, muscles, nerves, skin, and the other organs. The soul, by contrast, was present only in humans and was unique, ethereal, and immortal. It lived on after the death of the body. This theory was called *dualism.*

Julien de la Mettrie, a French doctor practicing and writing at the time of the Enlightenment, challenged this idea. In *L'Homme Machine (Man a Machine)* he proposed that humans are nothing more than complex machines. There was no need for souls or other mysteries to provide our vital spark. [26] In 1747 he wisely published the book anonymously. The implication that God was redundant was to much for the current French Establishment to tolerate, and when he was identified as the author he was banished and fled to Prussia. In Prussia he was treated as a *wunderkind,* received a pension, but died of a fever at age 43. In reality, the concept of man as just a machine was first espoused over 2,000 years ago by the ancient Greeks Leucippus, Democritus, and Epicurus.

In contrast to dualism, in the introduction to *The Astonishing Hypothesis,* [27p3] Crick states:

> The Astonishing Hypothesis is that "You," your joys and your sorrows, your memories and your ambitions, your sense of personal identity and free will, are in fact no more than the behavior of a vast assembly of nerve cells and their associated molecules. As Lewis Carroll's Alice might have phrased it: "You're nothing but a pack of neurons." This hypothesis is so alien to the ideas of most people alive today that it can truly be called astonishing.

If consciousness is a prerequisite for the soul, and consciousness is extinguished when brain damage causes the loss of core consciousness, it would also cause the loss of the soul. When the person dies, their consciousness, spirit, and soul also die. For those that criticize this as being a "reductionist approach" Crick responds: [27p8]

> There have been a number of attempts to show that reductionism cannot work. They usually take the form of a rather formal definition, followed by an argument that reductionism of this type cannot be true. What is ignored is that reductionism is not the rigid set of ideas at a lower level, but a dynamic, interactive process that modifies the concepts at both levels as knowledge develops. After all, "reductionism" is the main theoretical method that has driven the development of physics, chemistry, and molecular biology. It is largely responsible for the spectacular

developments of modern science. It is the only sensible way to proceed until and unless we are confronted with strong experimental evidence that demands we modify our attitude. General philosophical arguments against reductionism will not do.

Based on the above, our rational mind should be highly skeptical of the popular concept of a soul espoused by so many religions. Without a living, functioning brain there is no soul. If there is no soul, there is no afterlife, no hell, no purgatory, no reincarnation, no cosmic consciousness, and no reward in heaven for good behavior. The essence of many religions is lost without a soul. If there is no soul, is there also no obvious reason for moral behavior during life? Is the concept of a soul something simply conjured up by many religions to keep the flock in line by promising paradise after death? Is it just another aspect of the probability that man created God? Whether the existence of, or at least a belief in, the existence of a soul is an essential ingredient for morality is discussed in later chapters.

While the concept of a soul representing the essence of an individual and living on after death is central to many religions its existence is not supported by modern neuroscience which states that consciousness, the spirit and the soul are the product of neuronal activity and die when the person dies. This has major consequences for religion since without a soul there is no cosmic consciousness, no afterlife, no hell, no heaven and thus no reward in heaven for good behavior. In the same sense that some have said "evolution is real, accept it," we must also say that "the neuronal basis of the soul is real, accept it."

References

1. Penfield, W. & Roberts, L. *Speech and Brain Mechanisms.* Princeton University Press, Princeton, NJ, 1959.
2. Jaynes, J. *The Origin of Consciousness in the Breakdown of the Bicameral Mind.* Houghton Mifflin Company, Boston, 1976, 1990.
3. Block, N., Flanagan, O. & Güzeldere, G. *The Nature of Consciousness.* MIT Press, Cambridge, MA, 2002.
4. Damasio, A. *The Feeling of What Happened. Body and Emotion in the Making of Consciousness.* A Harvest Book, Harcourt, New York, 1999.
5. Sobotta, J. & McMurrich, J. P. *Atlas and Textbook of Human Anatomy.* W. B. Saunders Company, Philadelphia, 1914.
6. Craig, A. D. How do you feel? Interoception: the sense of the physiological condition of the body. *Nat Rev Neurosci.* 3: 655-666, 2002.
7. Critchley, H. D., Wiens, S., Rotshtein, P., Ohman, A. & Dolan, R. J. Neural systems supporting interoceptive awareness. Nat Neurosci 7: 189-195, 2004.
8. Edelman, G. M. & Tononi, G. *A Universe of Consciousness. How Matter Becomes Imagination.* Basic Books, New York, 2000.
9. James, W. *The Principles of Psychology.* Henry Holt, New York, 1890.
10. Crick, F. *The Astonishing Hypothesis The Scientific Search for the Soul.* A Touchstone Book, New York, 1994.
11. De Duve, C. *Vital Dust: Life as a Cosmic Imperative.* Basic Books, 1995.
12. Ribary, U. et al. Magnetic field tomography of coherent thalamocortical 40-Hz oscillations in humans. *Proc Natl Acad Sci USA.* 88: 11037-11041, 1991.

13. Skoyles, J. R. & Cagan, D. *Up From Dragons. The Evolution of Human Intelligence.* McGraw Hill, New York, 2002.
14. Koch, C. *The Quest for Consciousness.* Roberts and Company Publishers, Englewood, CO, 2004.
15. Dehaene, S. & Changeux, J.-P. Neural mechanisms for access to consciousness. In: Gazzaniga, M. *The Cognitive Neurosciences.* MIT Press, Cambridge, MA, 2004.
15a. Laureys, et al: Cortical processing of noxious somatosensory stimuli in the persistent vegetative state. *Neuroimage.* 17:32-41, 2002.
16. Dehaene, S., Sergent, C. & Changeux, J. P. A neuronal network model linking subjective reports and objective physiological data during conscious perception. *Proc Natl Acad Sci USA.* 100: 8520-8525, 2003.
17. Steinberg, D. Revelations from the Unconscious. *The Scientist.* 19: 17-19, 2005.
18. Laureys, S., Owen, A. M. & Schiff, N. D. Brain function in coma, vegetative state, and related disorders. *Lancet Neurol.* 3: 537-546, 2004.
19. Laureys, S. et al. Cerebral processing in the minimally conscious state. *Neurology.* 63: 916-918, 2004.
20. Tononi, G. An information integration theory of consciousness. *BMC Neurosci.* 5: 42, 2004.
21. Steriade, M., Timofeev, I. & Grenier, F. Natural waking and sleep states: a view from inside neocortical neurons. *J Neurophysiol.* 85: 1969-1985, 2001.
22. Ilmoniemi, R. J. et al. Neuronal responses to magnetic stimulation reveal cortical reactivity and connectivity. *Neuroreport.* 8: 3537-3540, 1997.
23. Massimini, M. et al. Breakdown of cortical effective connectivity during sleep. *Science.* 309: 2228-2232, 2005.
24. Schiff, N. D. et al. fMRI reveals large-scale network activation in minimally conscious patients. *Neurology.* 64: 514-523, 2005.
25. Tononi, G. & Edelman, G. M. Consciousness and complexity. *Science.* 282: 1846-1851, 1998.
26. Nunn, C. *De La Mettrie's Ghost. The Story of Decisions.* Macmillan, New York, 2005.
27. Crick, F. & Koch, C. Towards a neurobiological theory of consciousness. *Seminars in Neuroscience.* 2: 263-275, 1990.

Chapter 26

The Frontal Lobes

To understand the neurological basis of human behavior is to know the function of the prefrontal lobes. Where are the prefrontal lobes? The frontal lobes consist of three major parts, the motor cortex responsible for movement, the pre-motor cortex responsible for the regulation of movement, and the prefrontal lobes (Figure 1).

Frontal lobe

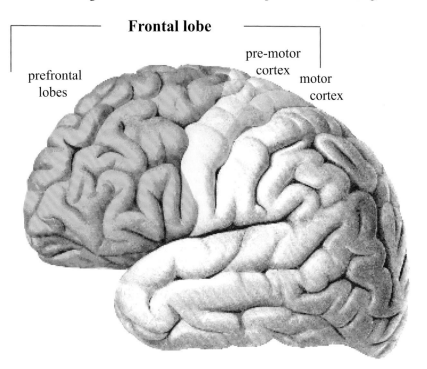

Figure 1. Frontal lobes consisting of the motor cortex (green) pre-motor association cortex (yellow) and the prefrontal lobes (pink).

Brodmann divided the surface of the brain into 52 areas that differ by structure and function. These are called the *Brodmann areas* (Figures 2 and 3).

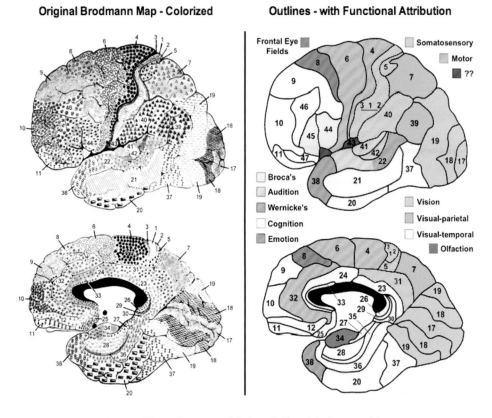

Figure 2. The Brodmann area of the brain (left) *and the functions of the different Brodmann areas* (right). [1a]

The prefrontal cortex consists of areas 8–13 and 44–47. These areas are characterized by the predominance of granular neural cells in cortical layer IV. The prefrontal cortex can also be defined by its neural connections. Thus, with regard to cortico-thalamic circuits, it receives projections from the dorsomedial thalamic nucleus, the highest station of neural integration in the thalamus. In terms of neurotransmitter circuits it receives projections from the dopamine system in the brain stem. The prefrontal cortex itself is divided into several areas including the *dorsolateral* and the *orbitofrontal*. The dorsolateral area consists of Brodmann areas 9 and 44–46. Area 10 is termed the frontal pole. It shares some functions with the dorsolateral prefrontal cortex. The orbitofrontal area consists of Brodmann areas 11 and 47.

Since the frontal lobes increased in size so rapidly during evolution they were once thought to be the site of intelligence but this proved not to be the case. Because their function was then unknown, they were often termed "the silent lobes." It turns out they were overwhelmingly important and anything but silent. Oliver Sacks [1] said of the frontal lobes:

Surface View

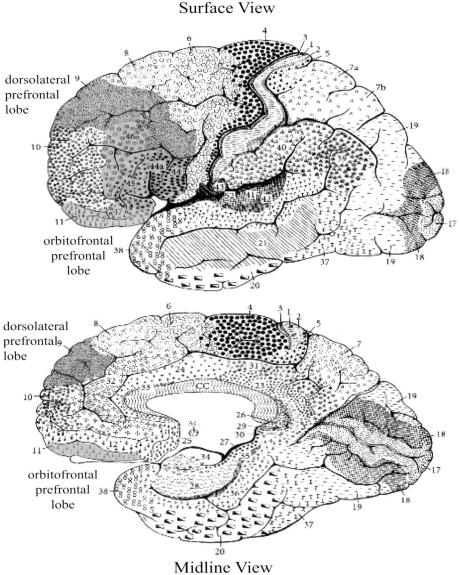

Midline View

Figure 3. Brodmann's map of the human cortex with the dorsolateral *and* orbitofrontal *prefrontal cortex in color.*

They are crucial for all higher-order purposeful behavior—identifying the objective, projecting the goal, forging the plans to reach it, organizing the means by which such plans can be carried out, monitoring and judging the consequences to see that all is accomplished as intended.

This is the central role of the frontal lobes, one which releases the organism from fixed repertoires and reactions and allows the mental representation of alternatives, imagination, freedom. Thus the metaphors…are of the frontal lobes as the brain's CEO, capable of taking "an aerial view" of all the other functions of the brain and coordinating them; the frontal lobes as the brain's conductor; the frontal lobes as the brain's leader, leading the individuals into the novelty, the innovations, the adventures of life. Without the great development of the frontal lobes in the human brain (coupled with the development of the language areas) civilization could never have arisen.

The intentionality of the individual is invested in the frontal lobes, and these are critical for higher consciousness, for judgment, for imagination, for empathy, for identity, for "soul."

How do we know this? We know this because of studies of individuals with various types of injury to the frontal lobes. The first thing that was clear from this work was that general intelligence was not affected and the frontal lobes were not directly the site of human intelligence. The real function was the executive control of the brain. In the days prior to MRIs and PET scans, what we knew about the function of the prefrontal lobes in humans came from brain injury cases. In 1868 J.M. Harlow[2] reported the most famous of them all. His patient was Phineas Gage. Harlow described what happened as follows:

> He was a shrewd and smart businessman, very energetic and persistent in executing all his plans of operation. One day while blasting a new roadway, an iron-tamping bar shot completely through the front part of his head.
>
> He gave a few convulsive motions of his extremities but spoke in a few minutes. He got out of the cart himself, with little assistance from his men…walked up a long flight of stairs and got into bed.…After a prolonged and stormy course he eventually recovered. Although all of his motor functions were intact his friends stated that he was no longer Gage. He was fitful, irreverent, indulging at times in the grossest profanity, (which was not previously his custom), manifesting but little deference for his fellows, impatient of restraint or advice when it conflicts with his desires, at times pertinaciously obstinate, yet capricious and vacillating, devising many plans for future operation, which are no sooner arranged than they are abandoned in turn for others appearing more feasible.

War Injuries. These findings were validated in studies of soldiers with war injuries affecting the prefrontal lobes.[3] These soldiers showed behavioral changes consisting of childish excitement, impatience, slowing and apathy, mood swings from euphoria to depression, short attention span, and some deterioration of intellectual capacity.

Surgical removal. Surgical removal of the prefrontal lobes for the treatment of tumors produced similar behavioral changes consisting of a loss of inhibitions, talkativeness, a tendency to joke, socially inappropriate behavior, loss of motivation, and concrete thinking with an impaired ability to make generalizations and to do abstract thinking. [4]

Lobotomy. Prefrontal lobotomy is a surgical procedure for the treatment of schizophrenia and other psychiatric diseases. With the advent of effective antipsychotic medication it has fallen out of favor. In addition to relieving psychotic symptoms surgically treated individuals showed a loss of motivation; socially inappropriate, rude and tactless behavior with a tendency to say the first thing that came into their mind; laziness; and carelessness. A prominent symptom was being "stimulus-bound" in the sense that they showed an overresponsiveness to immediate impressions and a decrease in the regulation of behavior that normally comes from learned past experience. The normal bond between immediate stimuli and the maturity of past experience seemed to have been broken. [5,6]

Luria and the Frontal Lobes

One of the richest sources of information on the function of the prefrontal lobes, especially for dorsolateral prefrontal lobes, comes from the famous Russian neuropsychologist Aleksandr Romanovich Luria. [7,8] The following are some of his observations. [9p348-350]

Consciousness, attention, and the initiation of programs. The prefrontal cortex serves as a tertiary association area of the brain. That is, it receives information from virtually every other area of the brain for final processing before a decision to elicit a motor response or act is made. Luria stated that the prefrontal lobes play "a decisive role in the formation of intentions and programs, and in the regulation of the most complex forms of human behavior." For a mental task to take place, a certain level of cortical tone is necessary and the prefrontal lobes regulate this activity. A critical task for this process is paying attention, and the prefrontal lobes are critical for sustained attention. He concluded that in man the frontal lobes participate directly in the state of increased activation which accompanies all forms of conscious activity. It is the prefrontal lobes that evoke this activation and enable the complex programming, control, and verification of human conscious activity.

Persevervation. Persevervation refers to the inability to change a course of action with the result that the same movement, behavior, or words are done over and over. Luria gave an example of a patient with frontal lobe damage who was asked to first draw a square and then a circle. The individual continued to draw squares. These patients are also able to recognize when others make mistakes but are *incapable of recognizing their own mistakes.*

Problems with complex programs. While lying in bed, one patient with frontal lobe damage was asked to raise her hand, which she did without problem. However, when the hand was placed under a blanket she could not carry out the more-complex program of removing the blanket first.

Memory. Normal subjects were able to memorize an average of six words. With practice this increased to ten words. Individuals with frontal lobe damage were only able to memorize an average of four words and this did not improve with practice. This damage also affected their ability to perform math problems other than simple addition and subtraction. When asked to perform more complex arithmetic that required holding a number in their head, they could not.

Animal Studies of the Frontal Lobes

Animal studies of the function of the frontal lobes have been particularly valuable since they allow an examination of the effect of the removal of specific brain regions and the direct measurement of electrical activity in specific brain areas. [9p352-355]

Lack of goal-directed behavior. Pavlov, the Russian physiologist famous for his studies of conditioned reflexes in dogs, also studied the function of the frontal lobes in dogs. [10] Dogs with their frontal lobes removed did not recognize their masters and responded to irrelevant stimuli in the environment. Since the animals' goal-directed behaviors were interrupted by senseless repetition of stereotyped behaviors, Pavlov concluded that the frontal lobes played an essential role in goal-directed behavior.

Inability to visualize information in working memory. In his early studies of the effects of the removal of the frontal lobes in primates, Jacobsen [11] noted that such animals could respond correctly to simple commands but could not synthesize and store information arriving from a variety of sensory inputs. This was tested using an approach called *delayed response.* Here the monkey was allowed to watch as food was placed under one of two or more cups on a table. An opaque screen was then lowered in front of the cups for one or two minutes. The screen was then raised and the monkey had to pick up the cup under which the food was placed. This part was easy, indicating memory was intact. However, when the food was placed under a different cup, the monkeys without frontal lobes perseverated, constantly looking under the cup where they had seen the food being placed. It was as though they could not *visualize in their minds* the possibility that the food might have been moved to the other cup.

Stimulus-bound and poor attention span. In related experiments [12-14], when different-shaped cups were used, the monkeys preferred the novel shapes over the familiar shapes, even if the novel-shaped cups never contained any food. As with Pavlov's dogs and humans with frontal lobe damage, these monkeys were stimulus-bound, reacting to novel aspects of the environment. As such, it was *very difficult for such animals to maintain focused attention* on a task.

Lack of awareness of the future. Karl Pribram carried out a range of studies with monkeys whose frontal lobes had been removed. [14,15] Such monkeys could not tolerate long pauses while awaiting certain experimental stimuli. They were also *unable to assess and correct their own errors.* From these and related studies Pribram concluded that the frontal lobes were necessary for orienting an animal not only in the present but *in the future.*

Hyperactivity. Monkeys without frontal lobes display driven motor hyperactivity as well as distractibility. [16] Dopamine has an inhibitory effect on the activity of the frontal lobes. When that inhibition is removed by the selective destruction of dopamine neurons, it results in motor hyperactivity. [17]

Orientation in space. The Morris water maze [18] is a clever way to test for spatial orientation in mice. This consists of a pan of water with a platform hidden somewhere under the surface. Once they have found the platform by random swimming, mice that have good spatial memory can quickly find the platform when placed in the water again. However, mice with their prefrontal lobes removed had much greater difficulty relocating the platform after each new trial.

In summary, these human and animal studies indicate that the frontal lobes represent the site for many of the actions of our rational brain, including abstract thought, orientation in space, judgment, focused attention, and planning complex actions for current and future goals.

The frontal lobes are critical for many of the most complex cognitive functions of humans, including paying attention, abstract thinking, spatial orientation, working memory, motivation, judgment, recognizing and correcting errors, the careful analysis of the information coming in from the senses before any action is taken, and planning complex behaviors for current and future goals.

The Prefrontal Lobes, Consciousness, and Civilization

In the previous chapter on consciousness, it was clear that the neural structures most likely to be involved in consciousness were those that had the greatest number of reciprocal connections with most or all of the other parts of the brain. The cingulate, the superior colliculi, the cortico-thalamic tracts, and the claustrum were all considered as reasonable candidates. However, while all of these may be involved, the most impressive candidate is the prefrontal cortex. As the final or tertiary association area of the brain, it receives the connections from all of the above and every other functional part of the brain. Of all the structures of the brain, only the prefrontal cortex is endowed with such a richly networked pattern of neural pathways. In 1928 the neurologist Tilney [19] suggested that the entire human evolution should be considered the "age of the frontal lobe." Luria called the frontal lobes "the organ of civilization." [20p2] Why? One the most important of human traits that allowed civilization to occur was the ability to move out of living only in the present and to both understand the concept of the future and to make and execute plans for the future. Goldberg [20p25] explains this as follows:

To conjure up an internal representation of the future, the brain must have an ability to take certain elements of prior experiences and reconfigure them in a way that in its totality does not correspond to any actual past experience. To accomplish this, the organism must go beyond the mere ability to form internal representations and models of the world outside. It must acquire the ability to manipulate and transform these models...It must go beyond the *ability to see the world through mental representations;* it must acquire the ability to work with mental representations. One of the fundamentally distinguishing features of human cognition, systematic tool making may be said to depend on this ability, since a tool does not exist in a ready-made form in the natural environment and has to be conjured in order to be made. To go even further, the development of the neural machinery capable of creating and holding images of the future, the frontal lobes, may be seen as a necessary prerequisite for tool making, and thus for the ascent of man and the launching of human civilization.

Of all the mental processes, goal formation is the most actor-centered activity. Goal formation is about "I need" and not about "it is." So the emergence of the ability to formulate goals must have been inexorably linked to the emergence of the mental representation of "self." It should come as no surprise that the emergence of self-consciousness is also intricately linked to the evolution of the frontal lobes.

Seen in this perspective, the advent of the use of tools may have both contributed to the rapid evolution of the human brain and to the development of consciousness. Consciousness was necessary to provide an image of the self that needs to do things for itself, both in the present and in the future. The enlarged prefrontal lobes in turn allow the further development of even more-complex use of tools, thinking, and rational thought. Consciousness, tool making, language, rational thought, and civilization are thus all intertwined.

Of all the structures of the brain, only the prefrontal cortex is endowed with such a richly networked pattern of neural pathways. This may be a critical prerequisite for the development of the "inner perception" characteristic of consciousness that was a necessary evolutionary advance to provide a sense of self around which plans could be made. This ability to plan for present and future events was an essential ingredient for the development of human civilization.

The Frontal Lobes and ADHD

The prefrontal lobes were the last part of the brain to evolve. In this regard it is of interest that they are involved in a wider range of behavioral disorders than any other part of the brain. It is as though the "last part to be added is the most likely to break." An analogy could be made to a computer program. A simple program with tight coding tends to run without making errors. If the code becomes very complex, despite its many new capabilities, it is more likely to break down. The disorders that involve malfunction of the prefrontal lobes include schizophrenia, autism, Pick's dementia, Alzheimer's disease, obsessive compulsive disorder, Tourette syndrome, conduct disorder, antisocial personality disorder, Attention Deficit Hyperactivity Disorder (ADHD), and others. Discussing most of these is outside the scope of this book. Antisocial personality disorder will be discussed in a later chapter. Since ADHD is especially relevant to the funcion of the frontal lobes, I will discuss it in more detail.

ADHD is a common, genetic disorder affecting approximately eight percent of school age boys and four percent of school-age girls. It is characterized by problems with impulsivity, inattention, and short attention span. The following is a list of symptoms common in ADHD children that are also common in individuals with prefrontal lobe lesions.

> concrete thinkers
> difficulty in carrying out complex tasks
> difficulty in changing plans
> difficulty in executing a sequence of complex behaviors
> difficulty in making plans for the future
> distractible
> do poorly on tests of frontal lobe function
> easily bored
> hyperactive
> impaired sequencing
> impatient
> impulsive
> learning disorders
> lie easily
> normal IQ
> poor abstract thinking
> poor judgment
> poor motivation
> poor planning
> poor spatial perception
> short attention span
> stimulus-bound
> unable to foresee the consequences of their behavior

Understanding the function of the prefrontal lobes provides us with great insight into the cause of ADHD. Understanding ADHD provides us with great insight about the importance of the evoluton of the prefrontal lobes to allow humans to develop an advanced civilization. Instead of being due to physical damage, ADHD is strongly genetic and caused by inheriting the wrong set of genes. The role of genes in human behavior will be discussed later.

The Dorsolateral Versus Orbitofrontal Areas

Separating the realms of the dorsolateral area and the orbitofrontal areas facilitates our understanding of the role of the prefrontal lobes in behavior. These differences are summarized and compared in Table 1.

Table 1. Behaviors Associated with Lesions of the Dorsolateral and Orbitofrontal Prefrontal Lobes.

Dorsolateral	Orbitofrontal
disinhibition	affective disorders
distractability	aggressive
impaired planning	poor self-control
impulsive	emotional outbursts
inattention	lack of guilt
no motivation	lack of remorse
poor abstract reasoning	lack of empathy
poor executive function	hypersexuality
poor organization	obsessive compulsive
	psychopathic

The dorsolateral cortex is especially involved in attention, motivation, organization, and rational thought, while the orbitofrontal area is more involved in empathy, antisocial, and amoral behavior.

The Dorsolateral Syndrome

One of the major characteristics of specific damage to the dorsolateral area is "pseudo-depression." Affected individuals appear to be depressed in that they tend to be apathetic, indifferent, sad, and uninterested in their environment. They find it hard to get out of bed and don't eat well or attend to other essential functions. However, the core feature is not depression in its usual sense but simply extreme inertia due to the inability to initiate behavior. That inertia is illustrated by Goldberg [20p119-122] who described the case of Vladimir, a patient with severe damage to the dorsolateral area.

> Vladimir spent most of his time in bed staring blankly into space. He ignored most attempts to engage him in any kind of activity...Asked to draw a cross, he would first ignore the instruction. I have to lift his hand with mine, place it on the page, and give it a little push, and only then would he start drawing. But having started, he could not stop and continued to draw little crosses until I took his hand in mine and lifted it off the page....When the task was to listen to a story and then recall it, Vladimir would start slowly and then carry on in a monotonous voice. He would go on and on and when asked to finish, he would say "Not yet." The never-ending monologue was an expression of "reverse inertia," an inability to terminate activity.

This example illustrates one of the ways in which the frontal lobes qualify as the "organ of civilization." Drive is a central requirement in a competitive, success-driven society. A normal functioning dorsolateral area is necessary for that trait. In the reverse sense, for a person to be successful, knowing what to not spend one's energies on is just as important as knowing what to spend it on. The dorsolateral area is as critical to stopping an activity as it is to initiating one. In a sense, it serves as both *the accelerator and the brake in daily activities.*

Imaging studies using PET or functional MRI have verified the role of the dorsolateral area in a range of functions including attention; [21-23,24] working, episodic and spatial memory; [25-30] the mental manipulation of information; [31,32] decision making; [33,34] motivation; planning; impulse control; [35] and initiation of action. [36] The symptoms of damage to the orbitofrontal area are relevant to morality and antisocial behavior. This and the role of both areas in decision-making are discussed in subsequent chapters.

Two important structures of the prefrontal cortex are the dorsolateral and the orbitofrontal areas. The dorsolateral area is especially important for the planning, starting and stopping of new motor programs, attention, decision-making, impulse control, motivation, organization, planning, working and spatial memory. The orbitofrontal area is especially important for socialization and moral behavior.

References

1.   Sacks, O. Forward. in: Goldberg, E. *The Executive Brain.* Oxford University Press, New York, 2001.
1a. From spot.colorado.edu/~dubin/talks/brodmann/brodmann.html
2.   Harlow, J. M. Recovery from the passage of an iron bar to the head. *Mass Med Soc Publ.* 2: 328-347, 1868.
3.   Black, F. W. Cognitive deficits in patients with unilateral war-related frontal lobe lesions. *J Clin Psychol.* 32: 366-372, 1976.
4.   Rylander, G. Personality changes after operations on the frontal lobes. *Acta Psychiat Neurol Scand.* Suppl 20: 3-327, 1939.
5.   Halstead, W. C. *Brain and Intelligence.* Chicago University Press, Chicago, 1949.
6.   Mettler, F. A. Physiologic effects of bilateral simultaneous frontal lesions in the frontal cortex. *J Comp Neurol.* 81: 105-136, 1944.
7.   Luria, A. R. *The Working Brain.* Basic Books, New York, 1973.
8.   Luria, A. R. *Higher Cortical Functions in Man.* Basic Books, New York, 1962.
9.   Comings, D. E. *Tourette Syndrome and Human Behavor.* Hope Press, Duarte,CA, 1990.
10. Pavlov, I. P. *Complete Collected Works.* Vol 1-6. Izd. Akad. Nauk., Moscow, 1949.
11. Jacobsen, C. F. Function of frontal association area in primates. *Arch Neurol Psychiatr.* 33: 558-569, 1935.
12. Malmo, R. B. Interference factors in delayed response in monkeys afer removal of the frontal lobe. *J Neurophysiol.* 5: 295-308, 1942.
13. Pribram, K. H. The intrinsic systems of the forebrain. In: Field, J. *Handbook of Physiology.* Vol II. (Section I). Washington, D.C. American Physiological Society. 1960.
14. Pribram, K. H. A review of the theory in physiological psychology. *Annu Rev Psychol.* 11: 1-40, 1960.
15. Pribram, K. H. A further analysis of the behavior deficit that follows injury to the primate frontal cortex. *J Exp Neurol.* 3: 432-466, 1961.
16. Kennard, M. A., Spencer, S. & Fountain, G. Hyperactivity in monkeys following lesions of the frontal lobes. *J Neurophysiol.* 4: 512-524, 1941.

17. Shaywitz, B. A., Yager, R. D. & Klopper, J. H. Selective brain dopamine depletion in developing rats: An experimental model of minimal brain dsyfunction. *Science.* 191: 305-307, 1976.
18. Morris, R. G. M. Spatial localization does not require the presence of local cues. *Learning and Motivation.* 12:239-260, 1981.
19. Tilney, F. *The Brain: From Ape to Man.* Hoeber, New York, 1928.
20. Goldberg, E. *The Executive Brain. Frontal Lobes and the Civilized Brain.* Oxford University Press, New York, 2001.
21. Seidman, L. J., Valera, E. M. & Makris, N. Structural brain imaging of attention-deficit/hyperactivity disorder. *Biol Psychiatry.* 57: 1263-72, 2005.
22. Kondo, H., Osaka, N. & Osaka, M. Cooperation of the anterior cingulate cortex and dorsolateral prefrontal cortex for attention shifting. *Neuroimage.* 23: 670-9, 2004.
23. Kane, M. J. & Engle, R. W. The role of prefrontal cortex in working-memory capacity, executive attention, and general fluid intelligence: an individual-differences perspective. *Psychol Bull Rev.* 9: 637-671, 2002.
24. Milham, M. P., Banich, M. T., Claus, E. D. & Cohen, N. J. Practice-related effects demonstrate complementary roles of anterior cingulate and prefrontal cortices in attentional control. *Neuroimage.* 18: 483-493, 2003.
25. Ranganath, C., Cohen, M. X. & Brozinsky, C. J. Working Memory Maintenance Contributes to Long-term Memory Formation: Neural and Behavioral Evidence. *J Cogn Neurosci.* 17: 994-1010, 2005.
26. Gilbert, A. M. & Fiez, J. A. Integrating rewards and cognition in the frontal cortex. *Cogn Affect Behav Neurosci.* 4: 540-552, 2004.
27. Gilboa, A. Autobiographical and episodic memory—one and the same? Evidence from prefrontal activation in neuroimaging studies. *Neuropsychologia.* 42: 1336-1349, 2004.
28. Numminen, J. et al. Cortical activation during a spatiotemporal tactile comparison task. *Neuroimage.* 22: 815-821, 2004.
29. Glahn, D. C. et al. Maintenance and manipulation in spatial working memory: dissociations in the prefrontal cortex. *Neuroimage.* 17: 201-213, 2002.
30. Petrides, M., Alivisatos, B., Meyer, E. & Evans, A. C. Functional activation of the human frontal cortex during the performance of verbal working memory tasks. *Proc Natl Acad Sci USA.* 90: 878-882, 1993.
31. Ptak, R. & Schnider, A. Disorganised memory after right dorsolateral prefrontal damage. *Neurocase.* 10: 52-59, 2004.
32. Windischberger, C., Lamm, C., Bauer, H. & Moser, E. Human motor cortex activity during mental rotation. *Neuroimage.* 20: 225-232, 2003.
33. Ernst, M. et al. Neural substrates of decision making in adults with attention deficit hyperactivity disorder. *Am J Psychiatry.* 160: 1061-1070, 2003.
34. Krawczyk, D. C. Contributions of the prefrontal cortex to the neural basis of human decision making. *Neurosci Biobehav Rev.* 26: 631-64, 2002.
35. Spinella, M. Self-rated executive function: development of the executive function index. *Int J Neurosci.* 115: 649-667, 2005.
36. Hunter, M. D., Green, R. D., Wilkinson, I. D. & Spence, S. A. Spatial and temporal dissociation in prefrontal cortex during action execution. *Neuroimage.* 23: 1186-1191, 2004.

Chapter 27

The Pleasure Brain

Understanding the capacity to experience pleasure is central to understanding the full dimensionality of the human brain. Why are humans so susceptible to becoming addicted to tobacco, alcohol, drugs, or gambling? The answer is simple. Nothing happens in a vacuum. If we want to keep from starving, we have to eat. To ensure we do, the brain possesses many mechanisms for allowing us to feel hunger, thus signaling when it is time to eat. To further ensure that we take in food, eating was made pleasurable. In addition, if we want our species to survive, we must reproduce. To ensure that happens, the process has also been made pleasurable. Eating, sex and love are called natural rewards and are critical to the survival of the species. Natural rewards stimulate the brain's reward pathways. These nerve pathways are rich in dopamine. The reason we become easily addicted to drugs, alcohol, gambling, and other activities is that these substances and activies also stimulate the same pleasure-producing dopamine reward pathways.

The Reward Pathways

How do we know that reward pathways exist? In 1953 Drs. James Olds and Peter Milner [1] placed wires into the brains of rats so they could stimulate different brain regions to study arousal mechanisms. They noticed that the animals kept returning to the part of the cage where they had received the stimulation. They seemed to "like" this area. This phenomenon became known as *place preference*. Animals liked a certain place because when they were there, something pleasurable happened.

Olds and Milner modified their apparatus so the animals could press a lever and stimulate themselves. This was so effective and so pleasurable that if left alone the animals would rather stimulate their own brains than eat, and they would soon starve to death. This study was a milestone in brain-behavior research. Using this technique they were able to map the pleasure pathways of the brain. These were subsequently shown to be dopamine-rich neurons. The reward pathways in the human brain are shown in Figure 1.

The two major dopamine pathways are shown in blue. The upper one starts in a part of the brain called the *substantia nigra,* and nerve fibers pass to the striatum or basal ganglia. The lower one starts in the *ventral tegmental* area, and fibers pass to the

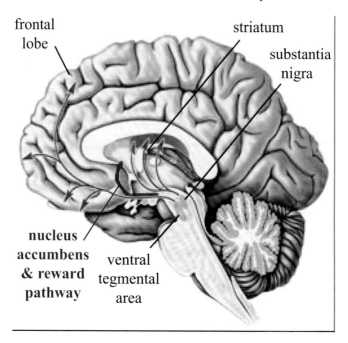

Figure 1. The dopamine pathways in the human brain (blue) and the reward pathways (red). [8]

frontal lobes. The red arrow points to the site of a large number of dopamine-rich nerve cells called the *nucleus accumbens,* and the red line represents other parts of the human reward pathway. The ventral tegmental area, or VTA, is the site of the cell bodies for the dopamine neurons that pass to the reward pathway and the frontal lobes.

In another classic study, DiChiara and Imperato [2] examined the effect of the administration of a number of drugs of abuse on dopamine levels in the nucleus

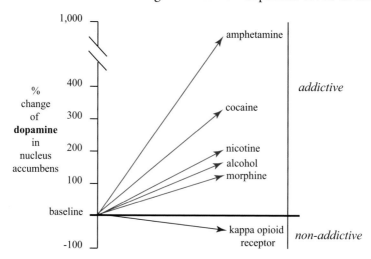

Figure 2. Effect of various drugs of abuse on dopamine in the nucleus accumbens of rats. Based on DiChiara and Imperato. Proc Nat Acad Sci USA. 85:5274-5278, 1988. [2]

accumbens of rats. These results are shown in Figure 2.

Amphetamine, or speed, resulted in the greatest release of dopamine in the nucleus accumbens. However, other common drugs of abuse such as cocaine, nicotine, alcohol and morphine also produced a significant release of dopamine in the same area. Morphine produced a release of dopamine by stimulating *mu* opioid receptors. As shown in the figure, the stimulation of a different opioid receptor *(kappa)* does not result in the release of dopamine, indicating the release is specific to dopamine and *mu* receptors. As a result of these and other studies, dopamine has become known as the "pleasure molecule." In addition to pleasure these pathways contribute to a general improvement in mood.

Pathological gambling. Pathological gambling is defined as gambling to such a degree as to interfere in a negative and major way with an individual's life. An addiction to gambling, or to sex, is a pure form of addiction in that no foreign substances are involved. As a result, brain imaging studies of gamblers are not complicated by the presence of drugs. In such a study, gambling was in the form of playing a video poker game. [3] PET scanning with ^{11}C-raclopride was used. The more dopamine released, the lower the RAC binding. The basal ganglia were examined

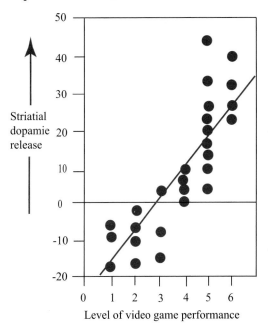

because they are large and particularly rich in dopamine, thus easy to image. The combined results for four different regions of the basal ganglia are shown in Figure 3.

There was a significant linear relationship between the level of video game performance and the release of dopamine in the basal ganglia. This provides a direct, objective demonstration of the role of dopamine release as an addicting reward in gambling.

Reward Deficiency Syndrome. While the fact that drugs of abuse such as alcohol, cocaine, speed, and tobacco stimulate the release of dopamine explains part of the question of why humans become addicted to these things, this does not explain why some people have serious problems with addictions, while others seem to be immune. While environmental factors play a role

Figure 3. The effect of video gambling on the release of dopamine in the basal ganglia. More negative values of ^{11}C RAC binding represent greater amounts of dopamine release. From Koepp et al.: Evidence for striatal dopamine release during a video game. Reprinted by permission of Macmillan Publishers, Ltd. Nature. 393:266-268, 1998. [3]

there is a significant variation in addictive potential among individuals exposed to the same environment. My colleagues and I proposed the existence of a reward deficiency syndrome (RDS). [4-6] This disorder is due to genetic defects in the dopamine reward pathways. As a result of such defects the natural rewards are no longer sufficient to improve mood and provide pleasure, and affected individuals turn to "unnatural rewards" such as alcohol, tobacco, drugs, gambling, and risk taking in the form of dangerous sports such as bungie and base jumping, sky diving, extreme skiing, race car driving, and others to stimulate their reward pathways.

One of the most innovative tests of this hypothesis was carried out by Nora Volkow and colleagues. [7] Dr. Volkow subsequently became the director of the National Institute of Drug Abuse (NIDA). They used two strains of mice. One strain liked drinking alcohol more than drinking water (alcohol-preferring), the other strain did not. If the preference for alcohol was due to a defect in the dopamine D_2 receptor, then increasing the level of the D_2 receptor in the reward pathways should eliminate the alcohol preference. This was done by injecting copies of the D_2 receptor gene directly into the nucleus accumbens. This resulted in a temporary overexpression of the D_2 receptor that lasted several days. The effect on the rats' drinking habits is shown in Figure 4.

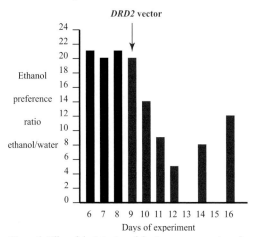

When DNA without the D_2 receptor gene was injected (dark blue) there was no decrease in alcohol preference. When DNA with the D_2 gene was injected (red), over the next four days there was a dramatic decrease in alcohol intake by 64 percent. As the D_2 gene began to decay, the preference for alcohol began to increase again. The authors concluded that over expression of the D_2 receptor gene reduces alcohol intake and that high levels of the D_2 receptor gene are protective against alcohol abuse.

Figure 4. Effect of the injection of the D_2 receptor gene into the nucleus accumbens of alcohol-preferring rats. From Thanos et al.: Overexpression of dopamine D^2 receptors reduces alcohol self-administration. J Neurochemistry. 78:1094-1103, 2001. [7] By permission.

The literature on the dopamine reward pathways is vast. The above discussion was just a small sampling to show that these pathways play a major role in survival by encouraging us to eat and reproduce, and when genetically defective they play a major role in susceptibility to addictive behaviors.

Dopamine-rich reward pathways are responsible for making eating, sex, and love pleasurable. These activities are essential for the survival of the species and are called *natural rewards*. Unfortunately a number of substances, including alcohol, amphetamine, cocaine, morphine, tobacco, other drugs, and a number of activities such as gambling and extreme sports stimulate the same pleasure pathways.

As a result, some people become addicted to these non-natural rewards. Individuals with a genetic defect in their dopamine reward pathways are particularly susceptible to these addictions.

References

1. Olds, J. & Milner, P. Positive reinforcement produced by electrical stimulation of septal area and other regions of the rat brain. *J Comp Physiol Psychol.* 47: 419-427, 1954.

2. DiChiara, G. & Imperato, A. Drugs abused by humans preferentially increase synaptic dopamine concentrations in the mesolimbic system of freely moving rats. *Proc Natl Acad Sci USA.* 85: 5274-5278, 1988.

3. Koepp, M. J. et al. Evidence for striatal dopamine release during a video game. Nature. 393: 266-268, 1998.

4. Blum, K., Cull, J. G., Braverman, E. R. & Comings, D. E. Reward Deficiency Syndrome. *American Scientist.* 84: 132-145, 1996.

5. Comings, D. E. & Blum, K. Reward deficiency syndrome: genetic aspects of behavioral disorders. In: Uylings, H. B. M., Van Eden, C. G., DeBruin, J. C. P., Feenstra, M. G. P. & Pennatz, C. M. A. *Progress in Brain Research.* Elsevier Science BV, Amsterdam. 2000.

6. Blum, K. et al. Reward deficiency syndrome (RDS): A biogenic model for the diagnosis and treatment of impulsive, addicitive and compulsive behaviors. *J Psychoactive Drugs.* 32 Supplement: 1-112, 2000.

7. Thanos, P. K. et al. Overexpression of dopamine D_2 receptors reduces alcohol self-administration. *J Neurochem.* 78: Sep 1094-1103., 2001.

8. From www.democrit.com/img/bio/drugs/dopamine_pathways.jpg

Chapter 28

The Social Brain

Appropriate social interactions between two or more people were critical for the development of human civilization. These include interactions between a mother and her child, a father and his child, between the mother and the father in a family setting, between individuals in daily work and play, between larger groups of individuals, and with society in general. These interactions include positive prosocial features such as caring, affection and love, bonding between a parent and a child or between parents, and a trust that allows personal interactions in the absence of fear. When these prosocial features are broken, antisocial behaviors such as aggression, rage, physical abuse, rape, robbing, stealing, and murder may occur.

To understand whether humans can have inherent morality without the threat of secular laws or divine damnation, it is necessary to understand why some people behave badly while others do not. Psychologists and geneticists have argued for years about whether such antisocial behavior is due to influences from a bad environment or bad genes, the classic question of nurture versus nature. In a word, the answer is clear—it is both. What is surprising to many is the degree to which genes play a role. This will be discussed in a later chapter.

Good social behavior is not just the absence of bad social behavior. Understanding the neurological defects that lead some people to behave badly is only one aspect of understanding why most people are well behaved and form loving, caring, bonding, and trusting relationships with spouses, children, friends, and larger social groups. Until recently it was largely a mystery why people spontaneously engaged in these prosocial behaviors. However, recent years have seen remarkable advances in this area, especially in relation to the prosocial effect of two hormones: oxytocin and vasopressin. The areas covered in this chapter will include the limbic system, the amygdala, the prosocial hormones oxytocin and vasopressin, the orbitofrontal cortex, the areas of the brain involved in "theory of mind" tasks, and the mirror neuron system. Together these structures account for much of our social brain. In terms of the goals of this book it is important to differentiate the realm of the social brain from the spiritual brain. While a well-functioning social brain is a necessary prerequisite for a healthy spirituality, as discussed in subsequent chapters, the spiritual brain is separate and distinct from the social brain.

The Limbic System

The limbic system can be considered the emotional brain. Since emotions are central to both prosocial and antisocial behavior, a brief description of the limbic system is in order. [1p321-332] In 1937 Papez published a paper entitled "A Proposed Mechanism of Emotion." [2] He had noticed that patients who died of rabies often experienced fits of extreme rage and terror in the hours before they died. When he examined the brains of these subjects he found that the virus preferentially affected specific areas of the brain that he called the "emotional brain." He suggested that, "Emotion can be considered as a way of acting and a way of feeling." The former was termed *emotional expression* and the latter *emotional experience.* Papez reasoned that the cerebral cortex had to participate in these activities in order for humans to experience emotional phenomena. He proposed that the cingulate cortex was the "emotional cortex" that could pass information to other parts of the cerebral cortex for "emotional coloring." The synthesis of the two parts of emotion required structures that could receive and integrate sensations and pass these onto higher conscious cortical functions—the psyche. He proposed what has come to be termed the *Papez circuit* (Figure 1).

Papez circuit

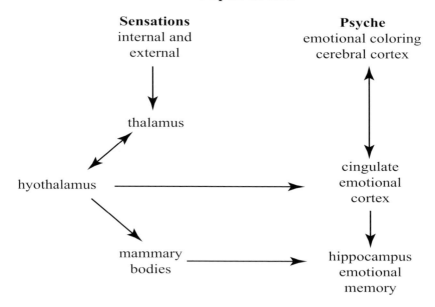

Figure 1. The Papez circuit.

The circuit involved a range of structures including the hippocampus, mammilary bodies, hypothalamus, thalamus, and cingulate and received inputs from various parts of the cerebral cortex. Papez's idea that there was a neurological structure as the basis of emotion was so radical for the time that it cost him his academic post.

Paul MacLean, director of the Laboratory of Evolution and Behavior at the

National Institute of Mental Health, named the structures of Papez's circuit the *limbic system.* [3] This name was derived from the fact that these structures surrounded the middle portions of the brain like an encircling limb. He pointed out that the microscopic structure of these areas was primitive compared to the other parts of the cortex. He also pointed out that there were strong connections to the smells or the olfactory apparatus. Because of this relationship the limbic system has sometimes been called the "smell brain." We all know that smells can elicit strong emotional memories. The structures that make up the limbic system are shown in Figure 2.

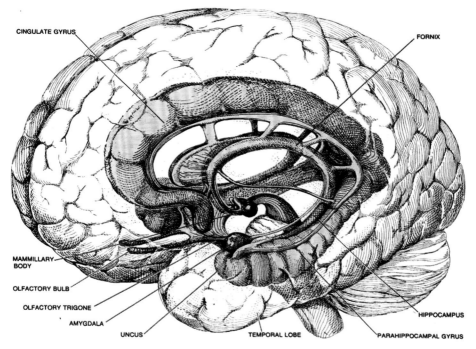

Figure 2. The human limbic system. From S. Snyder. Opiate Receptors and Internal Opiates. In Scientific American. *236:44-56, 1977.* [4]

MacLean also proposed the concept of a triune brain consisting of three evolutionarily distinct parts: the reptilian complex, the limbic system, and the neocortex. The reptilian complex was so named because in reptiles it constituted the major part of the brain. It is composed of the brain stem, midbrain, reticular activating system, and basal ganglia (caudate and putamen). These parts of the brain are involved in rigid, unthinking behaviors triggered by environmental cues. In reptiles, birds, and mammals, these portions are involved in basic survival behaviors such as mating, breeding rituals, imprinting, tracking prey, defense, and social hierarchies. Once triggered, these stereotyped behaviors are played out to completion like a mindless computer program. In his book, *The Dragons of Eden,* Carl Sagan [5] stated that "The reptilian mind is not characterized by powerful passions and wrenching contradictions but rather by a dutiful and stolid acquiescence to whatever behavior its genes and brain dictate."

The limbic system rescued animals from this robotic and reflexive pattern of behavior and allowed them to have an emotional involvement in life. Love, hate, anger, grief, jealousy, commitment and fear were now possible. The third and final layer of the triune brain—the neocortex—added extended consciousness, inhibitions, reflective and rational control over the raging emotions of the limbic system. One report of the electrical stimulation of the septum portion of the limbic system in a human subject produced feelings of euphoria. [6]

The Amygdala

The amygdala is included in the limbic system because it specifically adds the element of fear to the emotional repertoire. The amygdala is a tertiary association area located in the temporal lobe. It receives inputs from all the major senses: vision, hearing, touch, taste and smell (Figure 3)

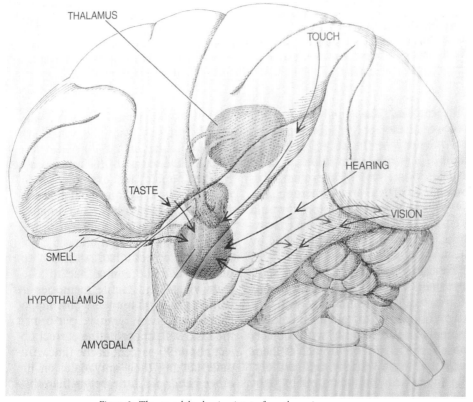

Figure 3. The amygdala showing inputs from the major sensory areas. From Mishkin and Appenzeller. The Anatomy of Memory. In Scientific American. 256:80-89, 1987. By permission.

Two years after Papez proposed his emotional circuit, Klüver and Bucy[7] described their studies of the effect of removing the temporal lobes, especially the amygdala, in monkeys. They developed what was referred to as *psychic blindness,* or *visual agnosia* (not knowing what was seen). The monkeys would approach all objects without hesitation even when they had previously been afraid of them. They would indiscriminately examine every object in sight by putting it in their mouths, rather than examining it by hand. They would also re-examine the same objects many times as if they had never seen it before. Their behavior seemed to be driven by uncontrolled irresistible impulses, but showed none of the usual fear and anger seen in normal monkeys. They were also hypersexual with excessive penile erection and manipulation. There was both homosexual and heterosexual behavior. A lesioned monkey might copulate continuously for 30 minutes, then leave the female, only to immediately mount her again.

The major symptom of humans with lesions of the amygdala is a lack of fear. Damasio [8p62-67] described a woman with bilateral calcification of both amygdala. She was normal in every respect except for her social history. She approached people and situations without fear and with a predominantly positive attitude. She was, in fact, excessively and inappropriately forthcoming and was eager to engage anyone in conversation. She did not shy away from friendly hugging and touching. As one might imagine, she made friends easily and formed romantic attachments without difficulty. "It was as if negative emotions such as fear and anger had been removed from her affective vocabulary, allowing the positive emotions to dominate her life." She was able to recognize facial expressions of all the emotions except fear. She had a gift for drawing but could not draw an angry face. This Pollyanna approach to the world can place such individuals at considerable risk for harmful social situations. Damage of the amygdala results in the loss of an individual's capacity to retrieve memories that contain emotional content. [9] A specific gene coding for a protein called *stathmin* has been found to play a major role in innate and learned fear. [10]

At the opposite extreme, children with severe shyness appear to have a hyperactive amygdala. These children showed increased brain activity in the region of the amygdala and were anxious about any face they could not decipher. [11]

The Prosocial Hormones Oxytocin and Vasopressin

The posterior pituitary gland secretes two hormones called *oxytocin* and *vasopressin*. They are made in the supraoptic and paraventricular nuclei of the hypothalamus and passed to the posterior pituitary [12] (green cells in Figure 4). Specific stimuli such as birth, breastfeeding, and certain types of stress cause them to be released into the blood stream.

Oxytocin has been implicated in many forms of social behavior, including parental care, grooming, nesting, sexual arousal, orgasm, breast-feeding, and birthing. Its important role in parental bonding was first shown in studies of two small mammals called voles. [13] One species, the prairie vole, *Microtus orcrogaster,* forms long-term monogamous relationships, and both sexes show a high level of parental care. In the laboratory they often sit side by side with a mate and attack unfamiliar adults. In early life the young show marked increases in ultrasonic calls and steroid secretion in response to social isolation. The other species, the montane vole, *Microtus*

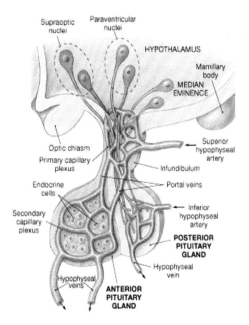

Supraoptic nuclei
Paraventricular nuclei
HYPOTHALAMUS
Mamillary body
MEDIAN EMINENCE
Optic chiasm
Superior hypophyseal artery
Primary capillary plexus
Infundibulum
Endocrine cells
Portal veins
Secondary capillary plexus
Inferior hypophyseal artery
POSTERIOR PITUITARY GLAND
Hypophyseal veins
Hypophyseal vein
ANTERIOR PITUITARY GLAND

Figure 4. Oxytocin and vasopressin are produced in the hypothalamus and passed to the posterior pituitary where they are released on demand. [13a]

montanus, lives in isolated burrows and shows no evidence of monogamy. In the laboratory they show minimal parental care and spend little time in close contact with each other. The pups show little if any behavioral or physiologic response to being removed from the nest. In a word, the prairie voles are social, while the montane voles are loners.

Because of the prior evidence that oxytocin might play a role in these behaviors, Insel and Shapiro, [13] from the National Institute of Mental Health, examined the distribution of the oxytocin receptor in the brains of these two voles. The prairie vole had much higher levels of oxytocin receptors in several parts of the limbic system, including the nucleus accumbens, ventral globus pallidus, the lateral part of the amygdala and the midline thalamic nuclei. The montane voles had higher levels in the cortical nucleus of the amygdala, the lateral septum, and other but different parts of the limbic system. In the female montane voles, the brain distribution of the oxytocin receptor changed within 24 hours after birth, coinciding with a brief burst of a postpartum period of bonding behavior.

The nucleus accumbens and ventral globus pallidus are parts of the dopamine reward pathway. The increased level of oxytocin receptors in these areas in monogamous voles suggests that one of the rewards for social attachment is the stimulation of the pleasure pathways. [14,15] This concept is strengthened by the observation that blocking the dopamine D_2 receptor, the primary receptor of the reward pathway, also blocks pair bond formation. [16]

An additional feature of monogamy in many animal species is the presence of intense aggression toward strangers for the defense of territory, the nest, and the mate.

In a subsequent study [17] vasopressin was found to play a role in this defensive activity and in mate preference. Further studies from this group showed that the administration of chemicals that blocked the oxytocin receptors in the brains of females, prevented pair bonding without an effect on mating behavior. [18-20] In the opposite vein, when oxytocin was infused into the brain, pair bonding was increased. The effects of oxytocin in females were not seen with the infusion of vasopressin receptor blockers or vasopressin, but these chemicals did affect pair bonding in males. *Thus oxytocin elicits pair bonding in female voles while vasopressin elicits pair bonding in male voles.*

When the oxytocin gene is removed in adult female mice, they do not lactate after giving birth. When the gene is removed in adult male mice the infants offspring are less vocal than when the gene is removed from the mother, and the adults are more aggressive in specific settings. [21] Genes can also be added. In monogamous voles the vasopressin V_1 receptor is expressed at higher levels than in the non-monogamous promiscuous voles. Transferring the vasopressin V_1 receptor gene from the monogamous vole into the ventral forebrain of promiscuous vole [22] substantially increased partner bonding. *This showed that a change in the expression of a single gene could profoundly alter social behavior.* This provides a potential molecular mechanism for the rapid evolution of complex social behavior.

In rats, the injection of oxytocin exerts potent anti-stress effects. Blood pressure and cortisol levels are decreased and the resistance to heat, the rate of wound healing and insulin levels are increased. [23]

Oxytocin and vasopressin in humans. Is oxytocin and vasopressin involved in human social behavior? A number of studies indicate the answer is yes. There is a particularly sensitive period just after the birth of a child for bonding in women. This coincides with a significant increase in a mother's oxytocin levels in the first hour after birth. [24] Breastfeeding then contributes to the continued secretion of oxytocin [23] and to continued mother-child bonding.

Oxytocin is released in response to social stimuli, [25] and this is likely to contribute to the benefits of positive social experiences. It may also provide the basis for the health-promoting effects of some alternative therapies, especially those that involve touching, talking, and group activities. The observation that oxytocin levels can become conditioned to psychological state or imagery [26] suggests it may in part mediate the benefits attributed to hypnosis and meditation. [23]

Four-year-old children who suffered emotional neglect and isolation in foreign orphanages and were then adopted into families in the United States showed significantly lower vasopressin levels than controls. [27] Following much physical contact with their adopted mothers, the neglected children also showed much less increase in oxytocin level than the control children.

Love. Love is a critical aspect of socialization and forms the basis of family ties. Both romantic and maternal love are highly rewarding experiences. Are these studies of oxytocin and vasopressin relevant to love? Orgasm releases oxytocin in both men and women [28] and contributes to the increased bonding associated with sexual relations. Brain imaging studies examining both romantic love (people in love viewing pictures of loved ones versus mere acquaintances) and maternal love (mothers viewing pictures of their own children versus children that were mere acquaintances) showed activation of regions of the brain rich in oxytocin, vasopressin, and dopamine receptors, and decreased activity in the amygdala and other regions involved in negative emotions. Thus, there was an enhancement of activity in part of the brain associated with bonding and a decrease in activity in parts of the brain involved in negative social assessments and fear. [29,30] Oxytocin and vasopressin modulate the excitatory inputs to the amygdala in opposite directions. [31] This allows for a fine-tuning of the fear response in social interactions.

Trust. Trust is indispensable in friendship, love, families, and organizations, and plays a key role in economic exchange and politics. [32] Without trust a country's institutions and political interactions would break down. Lack of trust between nations is likely to lead to wars. In a study of personal interactions that required trust, it was found that the intranasal administration of oxytocin produced a substantial increase in trust. In the setting of a trust-requiring investor game, this led to an increase in financial benefits derived from trusting social interactions. [32] In addition to oxytocin, brain imaging studies show that trust also activates the dopamine feel-good reward pathways. [33]

It is clear from these studies of voles, mice, rats, and men that oxytocin and vasopressin are important prosocial hormones and play a central role in many civilizing behaviors, including bonding, parenting, love, faithful monogamy, defending a mate and home, and engaging in trusting relationships. It is likely that unmet needs for social bonding and acceptance in early life might increase the emotional allure of groups such as gangs and religious sects, with violent and authoritarian values and leadership. [34]

The Orbitofrontal Prefrontal Cortex and the Man Who Borrowed Cars

In a one-page article in the medical journal *Lancet*, Cohen described "The Man Who Borrowed Cars." [35] He reported the case of a man whose behavior was normal until he had what seemed to be a mild stroke. He soon went back to work but began to steal cars from a local car dealer. He parked them on his lawn and over many days kept repeating this process. It did not take long for the police to determine who the culprit was. His physician suspected that the stroke may have played a key role in his sudden change in behavior. A SPECT scan was performed. The result is shown in Figure 5.

The scan showed a significant defect in blood flow within the area of the left orbitofrontal prefrontal lobe. This defect changed this man from a law-abiding citizen to one who stole cars without giving it a second thought. He displayed poor social judgment and had no feelings of guilt about his illegal activities.

Eslinger and Damasio [36] described a similar patient called "EVR," who was a successful professional, happily married, 35-year-old father of two. He led an impeccable social life and was a role model to others in his family. Unfortunately, he

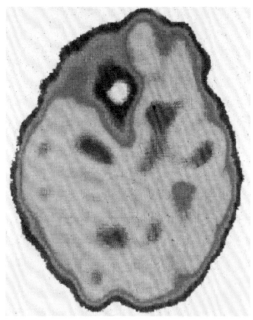

Figure 5. SPECT scan of "The Man Who Borrowed Cars."[35] *By permission from Elsevier.*

developed a brain tumor located at the site of the orbitofrontal lobes of the prefrontal cortex. After surgery, psychological testing was remarkably normal. His high IQ (129) and memory were not affected, and tests of the dorsolateral portion of the prefrontal lobes were normal. However, his social conduct was profoundly affected. He entered into disastrous business ventures, became bankrupt, and was divorced twice. His second marriage was to a prostitute and lasted only six months. He needed prompting to get started in the morning to go to work and was unable to manage his time properly. He could not hold down any paying job, was unable to learn from his mistakes, unable to support his family, and ended up living in a sheltered environment. In his book, *Descartes' Error,* Damasio[37] commented on EVR as follows:

> I never saw a tinge of emotion in my many hours of conversation with him; no sadness, no impatience, no frustration with my incessant and repetitious questioning…He could sense how topics that once had evoked a strong emotion no longer caused any reaction, positive or negative…His predicament was to know but not to feel.

Damasio and colleagues[38] performed a series of skin conductance studies on EVR and four other patients with similar surgeries. Patients with brain surgery involving other areas of the brain were used as controls. The testing consisted of showing slides to the subjects while recording their skin conductance, an electrical property of the skin that is related to the function of the sweat glands. The slides consisted of emotionally laden target objects depicting social disasters, mutilation, and nudity, along with non-target pictures of neutral scenes. There were two phases of viewing. In a passive phase, the subjects were simply asked to view the slides, while in the active phase they were asked to describe what was being shown in the slide and to give an impression about whether they liked the picture or not. In the subjects with ablation of the orbitofrontal portion of the frontal lobes, there was no skin conductance response during the passive phase but a normal skin conductance response during the active phase. The controls showed a skin conductance response during both the passive and active phases. To illustrate the importance of the body's reactions to emotion, Damasio [38] quoted from William James [39] as follows:

> What kind of emotion of fear would be left if the feeling neither of quickened heart-beats nor shallow breathing, neither of trembling lips nor of weakened limbs, neither of gooseflesh nor of visceral stirrings, were present. Can one fancy the state of rage and picture no ebullition of the chest, no flushing of the face, no dilation of the nostrils, no clenching of the teeth, no impulse to vigorous action, but in their stead limp muscles, calm breathing, and a placid face?

The implication is that emotions cannot emanate simply from a set of electrical and chemical impulses swirling around in a disconnected fashion in the brain. The color and flavor of emotional reactions, the "quickened pulse" and the "visceral stirrings" are the way the body feels things. This is what produces emotion. The classical phrase, "a gut feeling," or " I felt it in my gut," illustrates the important role that activation of the autonomic nervous system with its connection to the body plays in helping us "decide what to do" in social interactions. Anti-social personality disorder (ASPD) is associated with a disconnect between the brain and the autonomic nervous system. This can occur when the orbitofrontal lobes fail to function because of strokes or surgery. It can also occur when an individual inherits a set of genes that result in a dysfunction of the orbitofrontal area of the prefrontal lobes. This concept is shown in Figure 6.

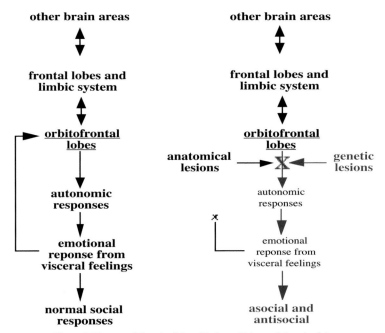

Figure 6. Diagram of the role of the orbitofrontal lobes and the role of the autonomic nervous system in feelings and emotion. See text.

The left pathway shows how the autonomic nervous system produces a visceral feeling of emotion in response to stimuli fed from the orbitofrontal lobes and other parts of the brain. The orbitofrontal lobes are connected with the autonomic nervous system via the hypothalamus. [40] The right pathway shows how this pathway can be broken by traumatic or surgical damage or by genetic damage to the orbitofrontal lobes resulting in a lack of an emotional response and feelings, lack of empathy for the feelings of others, and the development of asocial or antisocial behavior.

Neuropsychological tests specific to the function of the orbitofrontal lobes tend to be abnormal in psychopaths. [41] In addition, we have often heard the term "cold-blooded," or "he had ice in his veins" when referring to psychopathic killers. This is a reference to the hypofunction of the autonomic nervous system in psychopaths. The autonomic nervous system controls basic bodily functions such as the production of saliva, blood pressure, pulse, breathing, sweating, skin conductance, and bowel and bladder function. We can all relate to times of great emotional stress, such as taking an important test, when we had a dry mouth (shut-down of saliva production), felt short of breath, had a rapid pulse, were sweating profusely, and wanted to leave to go to the restroom. Many different studies have verified the fact that psychopaths tend to have minimal autonomic reactions to behaviors that would elicit the above responses in normal people. [38,42-45]

In addition to the cases reported by Damasio, others have confirmed that lesions of the orbitofrontal area, sometimes called the *ventromedial area,* result in aberrant social behavior. [46] In one of these studies Mah and colleagues [47] examined 31 patients with prefrontal cortex lesions of different types and compared them to 31 controls using the Interpersonal Perception Task. In this task subjects viewed videotaped social interactions and relied primarily on nonverbal cues to make interpersonal judgments, such as determining the degree of intimacy between two persons depicted in the videotaped scene. Patients whose lesions involved the orbitofrontal cortex demonstrated impaired social perception. Patients with lesions in the dorsolateral prefrontal cortex also showed deficits in using social cues to make interpersonal judgments. All patients, but especially those with lesions in the dorsolateral prefrontal cortex, showed poor insight into their deficits.

In a study of 23 patients with orbitofrontal dysfunction, 20 patients with other prefrontal lesions, and 39 controls, Berlin and coworkers [48] found that those with orbitofrontal lesions were more impulsive, experienced more subjective anger, reported less subjective happiness, and overestimated the passage of time.

The orbitofrontal cortex differs from the dorsolateral cortex in the type of encoded memories. Memorizing lists of items is a common test for episodic memory. This type of task activates the dorsolateral prefrontal cortex. This, however, is a somewhat artificial situation. In real life autobiographical memory, representing the recall of events in a person's past, is more important. This task utilizes the orbitofrontal lobes and relies on quick intuitive "feeling of rightness" to monitor the veracity and cohesiveness of retrieved memories. [49] Consistent with a strong interaction between the orbitofrontal area with the limbic system and emotions, autobiographical memories clearly have greater emotional content than dry facts.

Figure 7. The Sally-Anne task to test for the ability to mentalize. [52]

The "Theory of Mind"

The ability to infer what other people are thinking and feeling is one of the most fundamental aspects of human social interaction. [50] This is often referred to as "mentalizing," or "understanding others' intentions," or having a "Theory of Mind" (TOM). The latter especially refers to the ability to recognize when others have false beliefs. A test of this ability is illustrated in Figure 7.

Here the subject being tested is shown this illustrated scenario which can be enacted by puppets or real people. At the end the subject is asked, "Where will Sally look for her ball?" To answer the question, the subject must realize that Sally has not seen the ball being moved and therefore, Sally would falsely believe that the ball is still in the basket. [51] The ability to mentalize is an important skill of the social brain. As stated by Frith: [52]

> The capacity to understand and manipulate the mental states of other people is necessary in order to understand and alter their behavior....In everyday life, beliefs rather than reality determine what people do, and false beliefs play an important role. False beliefs can be removed by education and implanted by deception.

Mentalization developed late in evolution. It is not present in monkeys but appears in a primitive form in the great apes. In humans the ability to intuit what is in the mind of others plays an important role in daily conversation, in novels, movies, poetry and plays. The understanding that others may hold and act on false beliefs is widely held to be a cornerstone of social competence. [53]

Developmental psychologists have often addressed the question of when children first develop the ability to understand that others may have false beliefs. This has generally been assumed to begin to develop around four years of age [54] consistent with it being a cultural process tied to the development of language skills. However, one study using testing that did not depend on the presence of language skills suggested that children as young as 15 months of age may understand false beliefs. [53] This would suggest an evolutionary and innate ability for understanding false beliefs.

Many studies have shown that autistic children have significant difficulty in understanding that others can have false beliefs [55,56] They are especially poor at putting themselves in another person's place and in imaginative or pretend play. In a study of the ability of autistic children to keep an opponent from retrieving a desired object from a box, they were able to do so by physical manipulation such as locking a box containing a desired object. However, they were very poor at using deception by simply telling the opponent a lie such as "the box is locked." [57] This requires putting themselves in the mind of the other person and thus thinking they would believe such a lie.

A number of brain imaging studies using PET and fMRI have been carried out to determine which brain area is involved in mentalizing. These are quite consistent in showing involvement of the medial prefrontal cortex (MPFC, Brodmann areas 32 and 10) especially on the left. [50,52,58-63]

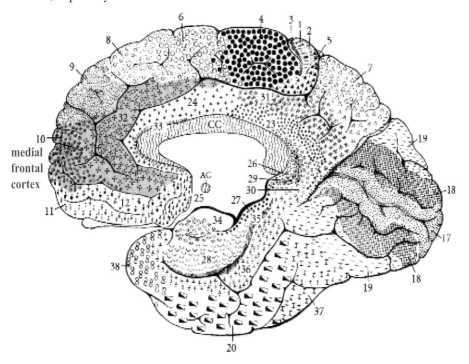

Figure 8. The medial prefrontal cortex (MPFC).

In some studies the anterior cingulate (BA 24) was also activated. [50] The amygdala may also play a role in theory of mind tasks. [64] The medial prefrontal area is activated during feelings of guilt [65] and it has been proposed as the site of self-reference or the self. [66] This is consistent with the important role of the prefrontal cortex in consciousness. Patients with destructive lesions of the right orbitofrontal prefrontal lobes show some theory of mind defects, suggesting that this social brain area also plays some role in theory of mind tasks. [67]

The Mirror System

Mirror neurons form an additional intriguing aspect of the social brain and mentalization. When Macaque monkeys perform a motor task, a specific set of neurons is activated. When they watch another monkey perform the same task, the same set of neurons is activated. This is referred to as *mirroring* and the neurons involved are called *mirror neurons*. [68] They have also been called the "monkey-see, monkey-do" cells. In monkeys they are located in area 5 and the rear part of the inferior parietal lobule. [69] Area 5 receives inputs from the prefrontal cortex (area 46) and the cingulate, thus producing a specific frontoparietal circuit for hand actions in monkeys.

The mirror neurons are activated both by the action itself and whenever there are enough visual or auditory clues to perceive the meaning of the action. Macaque monkeys are social animals that live in groups characterized by intense social interactions. It is critical to each member to recognize the actions of others and to "understand" the meaning of the observed actions in order to appropriately react to them. [70] This understanding of meaning is thought to result from the fact that an observed action activates the same neurons that are activated when that action is performed by the subject themselves. Thus, when it is observed it is recognized and implicitly understood by the observer.

A similar but somewhat more-extensive system is present in humans. [70] Mouth, hand, and foot motions involve the respective parts of the motor association area. The prefrontal cortex component includes the *pars opercularis,* which is roughly equivalent to Brodmann area 44. As in monkeys, the inferior parietal lobule is involved. These areas are shown in Figure 9.

Similar areas are involved in imitation of the movements of others. This is especially important in learning from the actions of others, learning language, decoding the intentions of others, and empathizing with their pain.

Just as autistic children have difficulty with theory of mind tasks, they also have difficulties empathizing with others, suggesting a defect in mirroring. This can be studied by analyzing EEG data for *mu* rhythm suppression. *Mu* rhythms are suppressed or blocked when the brain is engaged in performing, observing, or imagining action and correlate with the activity of the mirror neuron system. While normal subjects show *mu* rhythm suppression to both their own and to observed movements, autistic children showed *mu* rhythm suppression only to their own movements. [71]

A defect in the mirror system in autistic children has also been demonstrated using fMRI brain scanning. [72] While imitating and observing emotional expressions such as fear, anger, happiness, and sadness, autistic children showed little or no mirror brain activity in the pars opercularis. The level of mirror activity was inversely related to the severity of the social problems. Autistic children typically have difficulty with

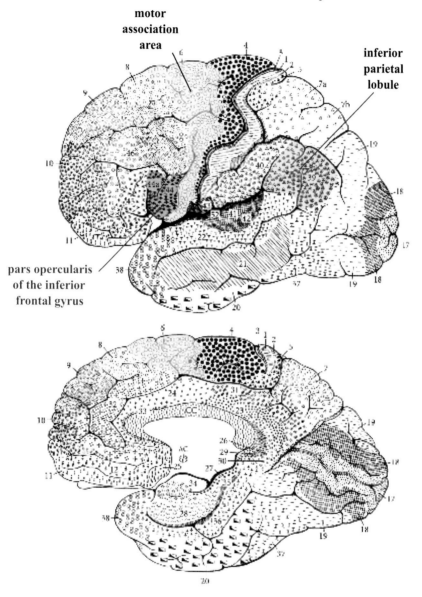

Figure 9. Brain areas involved in mirroring in humans.

metaphors, often interpreting them literally. This problem may be related to a dysfunctional mirror neuron system.

The orbitofrontal cortex and the mirror system provide two important capabilities to the social brain. The mirror system provides a fundamental mechanism for understanding the motor actions and physical intentions of others, while the orbitofrontal system provides a fundamental mechanism for understanding the emotions of others. [73]

These observations show that dysfunctions of specific parts of the social brain can lead to a range of asocial, antisocial, and amoral behaviors. The presence of neurological and genetic lesions of these areas in some individuals leads to behaviors that tend to give the rest of the human race a bad name. Most humans do not have these neurological or genetic lesions, and it is quite likely that within a societal structure providing some basic secular laws, most humans do not need threats of divine wrath to behave in a moral and caring fashion.

The social brain monitors the interactions between individuals in a society, between parents and their children, between spouses or partners, and between friends and society as a whole. Many different parts of the brain are involved, reflecting the critical role of such interactions for socialization. These parts include:

- **The limbic system that adds emotional flavoring to life.**
- **The amygdala that teaches us who and what to be afraid of.**
- **The hormones oxytocin and vasopressin that are involved in pair bonding, monogamy, love, maternal care, and trust of others.**
- **The orbitofrontal prefrontal lobes that allow us to be connected to our emotions through the limbic system and the autonomic nervous system. This system controls our emotional behavior and allows us to have empathy and understand the emotions of others. Antisocial behavior is common when this area is dysfunctional.**
- **The medial frontal cortex that is involved in "theory of mind" tasks and allows us to put ourselves into the mind of others.**
- **The inferior frontal gyrus and inferior temporal module that are involved in mirroring and allow us to understand the physical actions and intentions of others.**

References

1. Comings, D. E. *Tourette Syndrome and Human Behavior.* Hope Press, Duarte, CA, 1990.
2. Papez, J. W. A proposed mechanism of emotion. *Arch Neurol Psychiatr.* 38: 728-743, 1937.
3. MacLean, P. D. Contrasting functions of limbic and neocortical systems of the brain and their relevance to psychophysiological aspects of medicine. *Am J Medicine.* 25: 611-626, 1958.
4. Snyder, S. H. Opiate receptors and internal opiates. *Sci Amer.* 236: 44-56, 1977.
5. Sagan, C. *The Dragons of Eden.* Ballantine Books, New York, 1977.
6. Hogan, J. The forgotten era of brain chips. *Sci Am.* 293: 66-73, 2005.
7. Klüver, H. & Bucy, P. C. Preliminary analysis of functions of the temporal lobes in monkeys. *Arch Neurol Psychiatry.* 42: 979-1000, 1939.
8. Damasio, A. *The Feeling of What Happened. Body and Emotion in the Making of Consciousness.* A Harvest Book Harcourt, New York, 1999.
9. Le Doux, J. Emotion, Memory and the Brain. *Sci Am.* 270: 32-39, 1994.
10. Shumyatsky, G. P. et al. Stathmin, a Gene Enriched in the Amygdala, Controls Both Learned and Innate Fear. *Cell.* 123: 697-709, 2005.
11. Kluger, J. Secrets of the shy: why so bashful? Science finds something complex and cunning behind the curtain. *Time.* 165: 50-52, 2005.
12. Gimpl, G. & Fahrenholz, F. The oxytocin receptor system: structure, function, and regulation. *Physiol Rev.* 81: 629-683, 2001.
13. Insel, T. R. & Shapiro, L. E. Oxytocin receptor distribution reflects social organization in monogamous and polygamous voles. *Proc Natl Acad Sci USA.* 89: 5981-5985, 1992.

13a. Figure from: www.biosbcc.net/barron/physiology/endo/FG19_06.jpg

14. Young, L. J., Lim, M. M., Gingrich, B. & Insel, T. R. Cellular mechanisms of social attachment. *Horm Behav.* 40: 133-138, 2001.

15. Insel, T. R. Is social attachment an addictive disorder? *Physiol Behav.* 79: 351-357, 2003.

16. Liu, Y. & Wang, Z. X. Nucleus accumbens oxytocin and dopamine interact to regulate pair bond formation in female prairie voles. *Neuroscience.* 121: 537-544, 2003.

17. Winslow, J. T., Hastings, N., Carter, C. S., Harbaugh, C. R. & Insel, T. R. A role for central vasopressin in pair bonding in monogamous prairie voles. *Nature.* 365: 545-548, 1993.

18. Insel, T. R., Winslow, J. T., Wang, Z. X., Young, L. & Hulihan, T. J. Oxytocin and the molecular basis of monogamy. *Adv Exp Med Biol.* 395: 227-234, 1995.

19. Insel, T. R. & Hulihan, T. J. A gender-specific mechanism for pair bonding: oxytocin and partner preference formation in monogamous voles. *Behav Neurosci.* 109: 782-789, 1995.

20. Liu, Y., Curtis, J. T. & Wang, Z. Vasopressin in the lateral septum regulates pair bond formation in male prairie voles *(Microtus ochrogaster). Behav Neurosci.* 115: 910-919, 2001.

21. Winslow, J. T. et al. Infant vocalization, adult aggression, and fear behavior of an oxytocin-null mutant mouse. *Horm Behav.* 37: 145-155, 2000.

22. Lim, M. M. et al. Enhanced partner preference in a promiscious species by manipulating the expression of a single gene. *Nature.* 429: 754-757, 2004.

23. Uvnas-Moberg, K. Oxytocin may mediate the benefits of positive social interaction and emotions. *Psychoneuroendocrinology.* 23: 819-835, 1998.

24. Nissen, E., Lilja, G., Widstrom, A. M. & Uvnas-Moberg, K. Elevation of oxytocin levels early post partum in women. *Acta Obstet Gynecol Scand.* 74: 530-533, 1995.

25. Light, K. C., Grewen, K. M. & Amico, J. A. More frequent partner hugs and higher oxytocin levels are linked to lower blood pressure and heart rate in premenopausal women. *Biol Psychol.* 69: 5-21, 2005.

26. Turner, R. A., Altemus, M., Enos, T., Cooper, B. & McGuinness, T. Preliminary research on plasma oxytocin in normal cycling women: investigating emotion and interpersonal distress. *Psychiatry.* 62: 97-113, 1999.

27. Fries, A. B., Ziegler, T. E., Kurian, J. R., Jacoris, S. & Pollak, S. D. Early experience in humans is associated with changes in neuropeptides critical for regulating social behavior. *Proc Natl Acad Sci USA.* 102: 17237-17240, 2005.

28. Carmichael, M. S. et al. Plasma oxytocin increases in the human sexual response. *J Clin Endocrinol Metab.* 64: 27-31, 1987.

29. Bartels, A. & Zeki, S. The neural basis of romantic love. *Neuroreport.* 11: 3829-3834, 2000.

30. Bartels, A. & Zeki, S. The neural correlates of maternal and romantic love. *Neuroimage.* 21: 1155-1166, 2004.

31. Huber, D., Veinante, P. & Stoop, R. Vasopressin and oxytocin excite distinct neuronal populations in the central amygdala. *Science.* 308: 245-248, 2005.

32. Kosfeld, M., Heinrichs, M., Zak, P. J., Fischbacher, U. & Fehr, E. Oxytocin increases trust in humans. *Nature.* 435: 673-676, 2005.

33. Rilling, J. K., Sanfey, A. G., Aronson, J. A., Nystrom, L. E. & Cohen, J. D. Opposing BOLD responses to reciprocated and unreciprocated altruism in putative reward pathways. *Neuroreport.* 15: 2539-2543, 2004.

34. Pedersen, C. A. Biological aspects of social bonding and the roots of human violence. *Ann N Y Acad Sci.* 1036: 106-127, 2004.

35. Cohen, L., Angladette, L., Benoit, N. & Pierrot-Deseilligny, C. The Man Who Borrowed Cars. *Lancet.* 353: 334., 1999.

36. Eslinger, P. J. & Damasio, A. R. Severe disturbance of higher cognition after bilateral frontal lobe ablation. *Neurology.* 35: 1731-1741, 1985.

37. Damasio, A. R. Descartes' Error. *Emotion, Reason, and the Human Brain.* A Grosset/Putnam Book, New York, 1994.

38. Damasio, A. R., Tranel, D. & Damasio, H. Individuals with sociopathic behavior caused by frontal damage fail to respond autonomically to social stimuli. *Behav Brain Res.* 41: 81-94, 1990.

39. James, W. *The Principles of Psychology.* Henry Holt, New York, 1890.

40. MacLean, P. D. Psychosomatic disease and the visceral brain. *Psychosomatic Medicine.* 11: 338-351, 1949.

41. Lapierre, D., Braun, C. M. & Hodgins, S. Ventral frontal deficits in psychopathy: neuropsychological test findings. *Neuropsychologia.* 33: 139-151, 1995.

42. Raine, A., Venables, P. H. & Williams, M. High autonomic arousal and electrodermal orienting at age 15 years a protective factor against criminal behavior at age 29 years. *Am J Psychiatry.* 152: 1595-1600, 1995.

43. Tong, J. E. & Murphy, I. C. A review of stress reactivity research in relation to psychopathology and psychopathic behavior disorders. *J Ment Sci.* 106: 1273-1295, 1960.

44. Raine, A., Lencz, T., Bihrle, S., LaCasse, L. & Colletti, P. Reduced prefrontal gray matter volume and reduced autonomic activity in antisocial personality disorder. *Arch Gen Psychiatry.* 57: 119-127; discussion 128-129, 2000.

45. Raine, A. Autonomic nervous system factors underlying disinhibited, antisocial, and violent behavior. Biosocial

perspectives and treatment implications. *Ann N Y Acad Sci.* 794: 46-59, 1996.

46. Mah, L. W., Arnold, M. C. & Grafman, J. Deficits in social knowledge following damage to ventromedial prefrontal cortex. *J Neuropsychiatry Clin Neurosci.* 17: 66-74, 2005.

47. Mah, L., Arnold, M. C. & Grafman, J. Impairment of social perception associated with lesions of the prefrontal cortex. *Am J Psychiatry.* 161: 1247-55, 2004.

48. Berlin, H. A., Rolls, E. T. & Kischka, U. Impulsivity, time perception, emotion and reinforcement sensitivity in patients with orbitofrontal cortex lesions. *Brain.* 127: 1108-1126, 2004.

49. Gilboa, A. Autobiographical and episodic memory—one and the same? Evidence from prefrontal activation in neuroimaging studies. *Neuropsychologia.* 42: 1336-49, 2004.

50. Calarge, C., Andreasen, N. C. & O'Leary, D. S. Visualizing how one brain understands another: a PET study of theory of mind. *Am J Psychiatry.* 160: 1954-1964, 2003.

51. Baron-Cohen, S., Leslie, A. M. & Firth, U. Mechanical, behavioral and intentional understanding of picture stories in autistic children. *Br J Dev Psychology.* 4: 113, 1986.

52. Firth, C. D. & Firth, U. Interacting Minds—A biological basis. *Science.* 286: 1692-1695, 1999.

53. Onishi, K. H. & Baillargeon, R. Do 15-month-old infants understand false beliefs? *Science.* 308: 255-258, 2005.

54. Wellman, H. M., Cross, D. & Watson, J. Meta-analysis of theory-of-mind development: the truth about false belief. *Child Dev.* 72: 655-684, 2001.

55. Happe, F. G. An advanced test of theory of mind: understanding of story characters' thoughts and feelings by able autistic, mentally handicapped, and normal children and adults. *J Autism Dev Disord.* 24: 129-154, 1994.

56. Yirmiya, N., Erel, O., Shaked, M. & Solomonica-Levi, D. Meta-analyses comparing theory of mind abilities of individuals with autism, individuals with mental retardation, and normally developing individuals. *Psychol Bull.* 124: 283-307, 1998.

57. Sodian, B. & Frith, U. Deception and sabotage in autistic, retarded and normal children. *J Child Psychol Psychiatry.* 33: 591-605, 1992.

58. Goel, V., Grafman, J. & Sadato, N. Modeling other minds. *Neuroreport.* 6: 1741-1746, 1995.

59. Nieminen-von Wendt, T. et al. Changes in cerebral blood flow in Asperger syndrome during theory of mind tasks presented by the auditory route. *Eur Child Adolesc Psychiatry.* 12: 178-189, 2003.

60. Calder, A. J. et al. Reading the mind from eye gaze. *Neuropsychologia.* 40: 1129-1138, 2002.

61. Happe, F. et al. "Theory of mind" in the brain. Evidence from a PET scan study of Asperger syndrome. *Neuroreport.* 8: 197-201, 1996.

62. Walter, H. et al. Understanding intentions in social interaction: the role of the anterior paracingulate cortex. *J Cogn Neurosci.* 16: 1854-1863, 2004.

63. Stuss, D. T., Gallup, G. G., Jr. & Alexander, M. P. The frontal lobes are necessary for "theory of mind." *Brain.* 124: 279-286, 2001.

64. Fine, C., Lumsden, J. & Blair, R. J. Dissociation between "theory of mind" and executive functions in a patient with early left amygdala damage. *Brain.* 124: 287-298, 2001.

65. Takahashi, H. et al. Brain activation associated with evaluative processes of guilt and embarrassment: an fMRI study. *Neuroimage.* 23: 967-974, 2004.

66. MacRae, C. N., Heatherton, T. F. & Kelley, W. M. A Self Less Ordinary: The Medical Prefrontal Cortex. in: Gassaniga, M. S. *The Cognitive Neurosciences.* Cambridge, MA. A Bradford Book of the MIT Press. 2004.

67. Shamay-Tsoory, S. G., Tomer, R., Berger, B. D., Goldsher, D. & Aharon-Peretz, J. Impaired "affective theory of mind" is associated with right ventromedial prefrontal damage. *Cogn Behav Neurol.* 18: 55-67, 2005.

68. Gallese, V., Fadiga, L., Fogassi, L. & Rizzolatti, G. Action recognition in the premotor cortex. *Brain.* 119 (Pt 2): 593-609, 1996.

69. Gallese, V., Fadiga, L., Fogassi, L. & Rizzolatti, G. Action representation and the inferior parietal lobule. in: Prinz, W. & Hommel, B. *Common Mechanisms inPerception and Action: Attention and Performance.* Oxford, UK. Oxford University Press. 2002.

70. Rizzolatti, G. l., Fogassi, L. & Gallese, V. Cortical mechanisms subserving object graspig, action understanding, and imitation. in:. Gazzaniga, M.S. *The Cognitive Neurosciences.* p427-440 Cambridge, MA. A Bradford Book of the MIT Press. 2004.

71. Oberman, L. M. et al. EEG evidence for mirror neuron dysfunction in autism spectrum disorders. *Brain Res Cogn Brain Res.* 24: 190-198, 2005.

72. Dapretto, M. et al. Understanding emotions in others: mirror neuron dysfunction in children with autism spectrum disorders. *Nat Neurosci.* 9:28-30, 2005.

73. Gallese, V., Keysers, C. & Rizzolatti, G. A unifying view of the basis of social cognition. *Trends Cogn Sci.* 8: 396-403, 2004.

Chapter 29

The Rational Brain

Throughout this book I have referred to our spiritual brain and our thinking or rational brain. There are two views of this concept. One view is concrete and implies that these two involve separate, discrete, and localized regions of the brain. The second view is metaphorical and implies that rational thought and spiritual feelings tend to be different but they may or may not be performed by separate parts of the brain. Which of these is more correct? The following chapters will examine the evidence for the involvement of rational thoughts versus spiritual feelings in separate versus similar parts of the brain.

The concrete interpretation carries with it the implication of modularity of brain function. This has been a popular concept since there is abundant evidence that different parts of the brain subserve different functions. For example, it is clear that the occipital lobes are the primary site for processing sight, the parietal lobes process touch, the temporal lobes process hearing, and the olfactory lobes process smell. The regions of the brain with the greatest modularity are these areas for primary sensory input. The nerve tracts that communicate within these areas are referred to as intramodal or primary associations. Intermodal nerve tracts producing secondary associations provide for communication between two different modular units. For example, tracts between the visual and auditory cortex would allow the conscious brain to perceive a dog by both its appearance and its bark. The third hierarchical level of association between multiple modules occurs in the heteromodal, or tertiary, association cortex. These are the latest parts of the cortex to evolve. This is especially true of the prefrontal cortex. The three major heteromodal regions are the inferior temporal (area 20), the inferior parietal (areas 39 and 40), and prefrontal cortex. These are shown in Figure 1.

Thus, the degree of modularity of a function would depend upon whether it involved the primary, secondary, or tertiary association cortex. The heteromodal areas occupy a large percent of the brain and service many different functions, while the primary association areas service a single function. As we shall see, complex brain functions such as rational thought involve heteromodal areas.

Right Brain — Left Brain

Before launching into the studies of the neurology of rational thought, it is also necessary to examine the differing role of the right and left brain. While they have many functions in common, it is clear that speech and language are localized to the left brain and involve Broca's and Wernicke's areas while spatial orientation tends to

Heteromodal areas

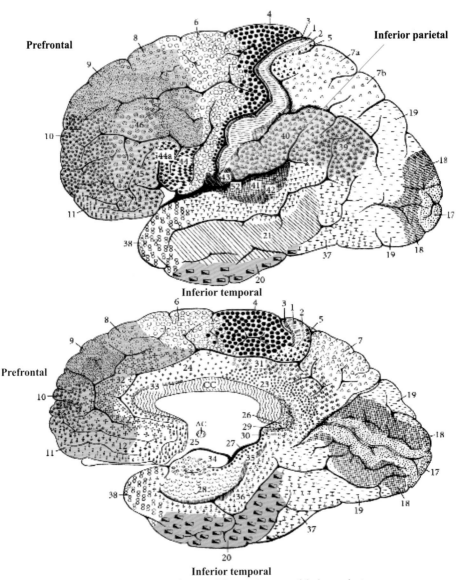

Figure 1. Tertiary or heteromodal association areas of the human brain.

be localized to the right hemisphere. This is practically illustrated by the fact that right handed individuals who have a stroke that compromises Broca's or Wernicke's area in the left hemisphere have trouble speaking, while those with strokes affecting comparable areas of the right brain have no effect on speech. Individuals with a stroke compromising the right hemisphere often have problems orienting themselves in space. In humans these specialized functions produce asymmetries in size between the right and the left brain. The fact that the same asymmetries are present in animals who don't talk and don't have language suggests some more fundamental differences may be involved. [1p42] Many books have been written in the popular science field proposing that the left brain is the rational scientific, hard, male, "just give me the facts" brain, while the right brain is the intuitive, soft, feminine, spiritual brain. If this were valid we should not have to search any further for the location of the rational and the spiritual brain. The rational brain would be on the left; the spiritual brain would be on the right. However, neuroscientists do not agree with this popular version.

Novelty Versus Routine

Elkhonon Goldberg suggested a more fundamental difference: the right brain processes novel stimuli while the left brain processes routine stimuli. [1,2] This is highly relevant to learning. At an early stage of every learning process the organism is faced with "novelty," and at the end stage of the learning process thought is "familiar" and "routine." This view provides a reinterpretation of old assumptions about the left versus the right brain. For example, it was well known that music processing and the perception of faces occurred predominantly in the right hemisphere. This, however, was mostly true for musically naïve people. Trained musicians process music mostly with the left hemisphere. [3] The perception of new faces is also processed by the right hemisphere, while the perception of familiar faces is mostly processed in the left hemisphere. [4]

These findings of the preferential processing of novel information by the right hemisphere and routine information by the left hemisphere have been supported by PET scan studies. Based on PET studies of men who viewed pictures they had never seen previously and those they had seen previously, Tulving and colleagues [5,6] proposed that the right medial temporal lobe preferentially processed novel pictures.

Martin and colleagues [7] examined the learning of several types of information — meaningful words, nonsense words, real objects, and nonsense objects. Each type of information presentation was examined twice, first as a novel task and then as a practiced task. This showed that in the right middle temporal area, activation was consistently less with the practiced task. This was not the case for the left hemisphere. The fact that the results were the same for all four types of tasks is important because it shows that the activation of the right hemisphere depends less upon the type of task and more on whether it was a novel or a routine task. While there was a trend for meaningful words to activate the left temporal lobe and for meaningless words to activate the right temporal area, the meaningless words could be considered more novel. Similar results concerning the activation of the right hemisphere by novel tasks have been found for faces and symbols, [8] and for a complex frontal lobe task involving delayed response and delayed alteration. [9] These findings weaken the classic view that the right hemisphere is specialized for certain specific functions.

The change from novelty to learned or routine also results in successively less brain work for the learned task. This was well demonstrated in a PET study of learning a popular computer puzzle called Tetris. [10] The rate of metabolism of the brain regions involved decreased with increasing practice. A seven-fold increase in skill was associated with a significant decrease in brain metabolism. This indicated that learning results in an increased efficiency of brain function. In summary, Goldberg states: [1p52]

> It appears that the cerebral orchestra is divided into two groups of players. Those sitting on the right of the aisle are quicker at basic mastery of the new repertoire, but in the long run, with due practice, those on the left of the aisle come closer to perfection.
>
> It can be argued that the whole history of human civilization has been characterized by a relative shift of the cognitive emphasis from the right hemisphere to the left hemisphere owing to the accumulation of ready-made cognitive "templates" of various kinds. These cognitive templates are stored externally through various cultural means, including language, and are internalized by individuals in the course of learning cognitive "prefabricates."

There is, however, more to the right brain/left brain issue than novelty versus routine. Further studies on roles of the left and right brain, based on split-brain and other experiments, will be discussed in more detail later.

Working Memory

The process of making decisions is carried out thousands of times per day and is aided by the *working memory*. Things such as birthdates, places, faces, and an untold number of other facts are stored in permanent memory, not in working memory. Working memory knows where this information is stored and accesses these facts, or "engrams," on a need-to-know basis. It temporarily brings these items "online," allowing the brain to place things in their proper spatial or time sequence, organize, prioritize, make decisions, and plan. It holds items online that would otherwise never meet and gives them a chance to interact. Working memory is constantly and rapidly changing its content. The dorso- lateral prefrontal cortex is the major location for working memory. [11] The efficiency of working memory is strongly correlated with IQ. [12]

Two major types of facts involve the questions "What?" and "Where?" The facts of the visual "What" system (an apple, or a cat, or a car) are stored along the occipital-temporal cortex and is referred to as the *ventral visual system*. The facts of the "Where" type (in the bathroom, the living room) and other spatial information are stored along the occipital-parietal cortex and is referred to as the *dorsal visual system* (see Figure 2.)

The inferior parietal lobule was discussed elsewhere in relation to the mirror neurons. When the relevant engrams are recalled, different parts of the prefrontal lobes are utilized. Accessing the "What" facts into working memory activates the inferior portions of the prefrontal lobes. Accessing the "Where" facts into working memory activates the superior portions of the prefrontal lobes. [13,14]

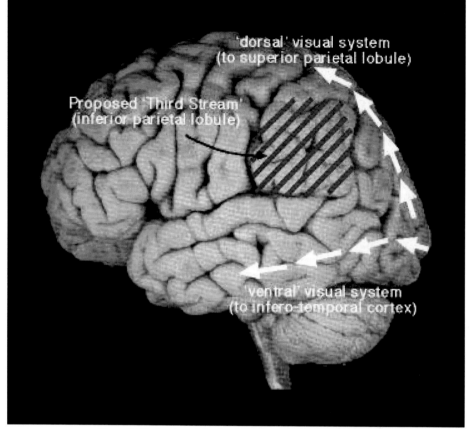

Figure 2. The location of the dorsal (Where?) and the ventral (What?) system and the inferior parietal lobule. [12a]

What is Rational Thought?

We cannot identify the brain areas involved in a rational thought unless we have a precise definition of rational thought. Decision-making is at the core of rational thought and is the skill that characterizes the rational brain. There are two types of decision-making: *veridical* and *adaptive*. Veridical is derived from the Latin verus = true + dicere = to say; thus veridical is "to say the truth." Veridical decision-making refers to making decisions about things that have a single, clearly defined value where there is only one correct answer. For example, when asked whether there are 10 or 12 months in a year, a veridical decision is involved, since the only valid decision is to say 12. By contrast, adaptive decisions refer to those where there is no absolute right answer. The answer is *ambiguous*. Some adaptive decisions have only a trivial effect on one's life, such as "Shall I order the steak or the lobster? Other adaptive decisions that a person makes can determine the future course of their life. "Shall I finish college or drop out and play basketball?" "Shall I take the high-paying job with no opportunity for advancement or the low-paying job with many opportunities for advancement?" "Shall I marry Jane or Sally?" Decisions relevant to this book would include, "Is

Darwin's theory of evolution correct, or is the account of the origin of life in Genesis correct?", "Is the Big Bang account of the origin of the universe evidence for the existence of God, or is it consistent with the laws of physics?"

The complexity of adaptive decision-making and its reliance on working memory was illustrated by Goldberg's and Podell's [15] example: "What suit shall I wear today?"

> The situation is ambiguous and it is up to the individual to make the choice. While the choice is usually made quickly and "unthinkingly," maybe half-awake, it is not random. Presumably, the individual weighs various priorities. Is it particularly important for him to be warm today? Or to look dapper? Or to look wealthy? Or to look conservative? Depending upon whether he is coming down with a cold, planning a date, trying to obtain a line of credit, or giving a job interview, he will rank the priorities differently. The priorities characterize the actor and not the contents of his closet. Once the priorities have been ranked, the situation has been disambiguated, and the remainder of the decision-making process is veridical.

Answering these questions requires working memory. If the decision about the suit requires knowing the current outside temperature, the engram containing the weather report on the morning news is accessed. If the decision about the suit relates to looking dapper, the engram containing the pictures of the styles in the latest fashion magazine is retrieved. And so on. A dance takes place between the cortex containing working memory and the adaptive decision-making cortex.

Where is Rational Thought Localized?

Since adaptive decision-making is at the core of the function of the rational brain, identifying the brain site for this process is very relevant. As referred to above, resolving the ambiguity surrounding an adaptive decision has been referred to as *disambiguating the situation*. Dealing with ambiguous situations represents the function of the frontal lobes in its finest hour. In the dementias, making adaptive decisions is one of the first skills to be lost. Making veridical decisions is more resistant to loss.

Given its importance, this aspect of cognition has been relatively ignored in cognitive neuroscience. Goldberg and Podell attempted to remedy this situation by developing a test for adaptive decision-making. [15-17] This test consists of a target which is a geometric design, followed by two additional designs. Figure 3 is an example. [15]

By presenting subjects with a number of such cards a Cognitive Bias Task (CBT) score can be calculated. This score is highest when the target and the choice are similar. For example, this would occur in the above card when the pair of blue dots was chosen. The score would be lowest when the target and the choice were different. This would occur in the above card when the red square was chosen.

Ambiguous decision. In the ambiguous decision-making, as part of the task the

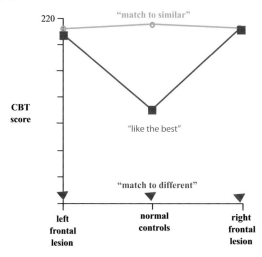

subject is simply asked to "Look at the target and select the choice you like the most." This is ambiguous because there are no wrong answers and the subject is told there are no wrong answers. The subjects actually have two options: to base their response either on the properties of the targets (in this case, shape) or on some preference unrelated to the target (in this case, color). Despite the looseness of the task the responses were quantifiable and highly repeatable. Of interest, the responses were dramatically different for subjects with frontal lobe damage compared to those without such damage, while damage to other parts of the brain had no effect.

Disambiguated decision. In the second part of the task the decision was disambiguated by asking the subjects to "Make a choice most similar to the target" and then again with the instructions to "Make a choice most different from the target." The results for females with frontal lobe lesions are shown in Figure 4.

In the "match to similar" task (green) both the normal women and women with a frontal lobe lesion had high CBT scores, and in the "match to different" task (dark blue) both had low CBT scores. In the "like the best" task, the normal controls had a CBT score between these two extremes, indicating that in the ambiguous decisions some cards were matched by shape and some by color, whichever they "liked the best" (red). However, in women with

Figure 3. A sample card from the Cognitive Bias Task. The top is the target while the bottom two present the choice. From Goldberg and Podell. Adaptive versus Veridical Decision-making and the Frontal Lobes. In Consciousness and Cognition. 8: 364-377, 1999.

Figure 4. Cognitive Bias Task for females with left or right frontal lobe lesions compared to normal controls. From Goldberg and Podell. [15]

frontal lobe lesions, the CBT scores were identical to their "match to similar" scores, indicating they had problems with the ambiguous "like the best" decisions. Goldberg stated: [1p80]

> Our experiment shows that the frontal lobes are critical to a free-choice situation, when it is up to the subject to decide how to interpret an ambiguous situation. Once the situation has been disambiguated for the subject and the task has been reduced to the computation of the only correct response possible, the input of the frontal lobes is no longer critical, even though all the other aspects of the task remain the same. Of all the aspects of the human mind none are more intriguing than intentionality, volition, and free will. But these attributes of the human mind are fully at play only in situations affording multiple choices.

Goldberg refers to ambiguous decisions as actor-centered decisions and decries the fact that both cognitive neuroscientists and educators have ignored this form of decision-making. Most educators focus on fact-laden veridical decisions, while in life the adaptive decisions are the important ones. These are also the important decisions involved in the development of civilization and in deciding one's spiritual and religious views. Adaptive decisions are uniquely human and they are performed in the prefrontal lobes.

Brain Imaging Studies

The above conclusions about the role of the prefrontal cortex in decision-making were based on studies of normal versus brain injury subjects. A number of studies using brain-imaging techniques also support the role of the prefrontal lobes in decision-making. The following are some examples:

Cognitive bias task. One study actually used the Cognitive Bias Task. [18] Twelve young adult men were studied using SPECT (Single Photon Emission Computed Tomography). This showed bilateral activation of the dorsolateral prefrontal cortices and middle temporal gyri. The middle temporal activation represented the sensory response to the images. The prefrontal activation represented the decision-making aspect of the task.

Perceptual decision-making. Heekeren and colleagues [19] from the National Institute of Mental Health presented human subjects with the perceptual decision of determining whether an image was a face or a house. Two versions were used; clear pictures referred to as *suprathreshold images,* and unclear or blurred figures referred to as *perithreshold images.* They sought to identify the brain regions that were more activated by the suprathreshold than the perithreshold images. Functional MRI showed that this region was the left superior frontal sulcus in the posterior region of the dorsolateral area (Brodmann area 8/9) shown in Figure 5.

Thus, while the images of faces versus houses are stored in separate regions of the

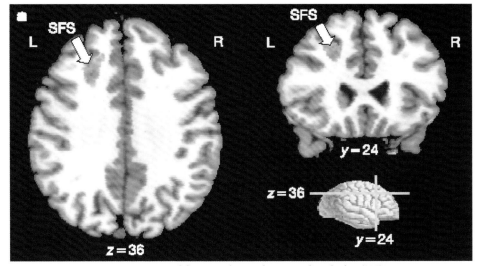

Figure 5. Perceptual decision-making in the superior frontal sulcus (SFS) of the posterior dorsolateral prefrontal cortex. From Heekeren et al.: A general mechanism for perceptual decision-making in the human brain. Reprinted by permission of Macmillan Publishing, Ltd. Nature. 431:859-862, 2004. [19]

ventral temporal cortex, the decision about which was which rested in the dorso-lateral area of the prefrontal cortex. Their study also provided insights into the role of attention in decision-making. When the targets were more ambiguous, the attentional networks were activated. When the images were clear, they were not. Other studies involving different types of decision-making [20-22] activate the same area, indicating that the *dorsolateral prefrontal region has general decision-making functions* independent of the stimulus.

Deductive and inductive reasoning. The rational brain is the brain involved in reasoning. Reasoning is a cognitive process of drawing inferences from a given set of information. Reasoned arguments involve the claim that one or more premises provide some grounds for accepting a conclusion. The arguments can be deductive or inductive. Deduction is what you do when you know the principles of something and deduce a particular case. For example, if you know the principles of arithmetic, you can deduce that 23 + 161 = 184, even if you have never seen this example before. Deductive reasoning can be judged as valid or invalid. Induction is the opposite. It is the process of reasoning in which the conclusion of an argument is very likely to be true, but this is not certain, given the premises. Inductive reason can only be judged as probable or improbable. The logic formats involved are called *syllogisms*. The following syllogisms illustrate the difference between deduction and induction. [23]

Deduction:
    All animals with 32 teeth are cats. No cats are dogs. No dogs have 32 teeth.
Induction:
    House cats have 32 teeth. Lions have 32 teeth. All felines have 32 teeth.

Goel and colleagues[23] presented 25 valid and 25 invalid deduction syllogisms and 25 probable and 25 improbable induction syllogisms to 16 subjects and asked them to judge each deduction as valid or invalid and each induction as probable or improbable. The deductive choices activated the left inferior frontal gyrus portion of the dorsolateral prefrontal cortex (Brodmann area 44 and 45). The inductive choices activated the left dorsolateral prefrontal gyrus. *Thus, as with adaptive and perceptual decision-making, both deductive and inductive reasoning also involved the dorsolateral region of the prefrontal cortex.*

Intelligence. Intelligence is assessed using intelligence or IQ tests. Statistical tests indicate that many types of IQ tests share a common factor called *g*, for general intelligence. PET studies have shown that when individuals perform tasks with high-g involvement, there is bilateral activation of the dorsolateral prefrontal cortex.[24] This is additional strong evidence of the role of this part of the brain in rational, intelligent thought.

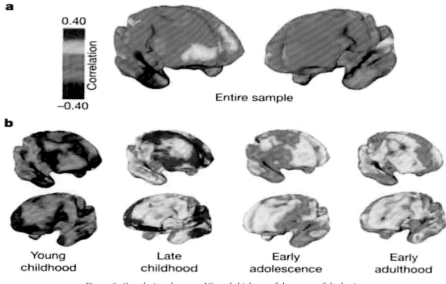

Figure 6. Correlations between IQ and thickness of the cortex of the brain. From Shaw et al: Reprinted by permission from Macmillan Publishing, Ltd. Nature. 440:676-679, 2006. By permission.

Longitudinal studies illustrate why the location of the portion of the brain that correlates with IQ testing has been difficult. Phillip Shaw and colleagues at the National Institute of Mental Health performed MRI scans on 307 children from six to 19 years of age[25]. IQ was assessed using the Wechsler Intelligence Scales. Figure 6 shows in red the areas of the brain that showed the highest correlation between IQ and the thickness of the cortex of the brain.

The striking finding was that the strongest correlations occurred during late childhood, around 10 to 12 years of age, in the prefrontal and temporal lobes on both the right and left sides of the brain. If these studies of structure rather than function had been limited to adults, this correlation would have been missed.

These findings suggest that the concept of left brain = language and rational thought while the right brain = intuitive and spiritual activities is too simplistic. The dorsolateral areas of both the right and the left prefrontal lobes represent the primary neural location of our rational brain with a contribution of the temporal lobes during development.

> **The dorsolateral prefrontal cortex is the neural site of working memory, intelligence loaded tests, abstract thought, adaptive decision-making, deductive and inductive reasoning. It is the major site of our thinking or rational brain.**

References

1. Goldberg, E. *The Executive Brain. Frontal Lobes and the Civilized Brain.* Oxford University Press, New York, 2001.
2. Goldberg, E. & Costa, L. D. Hemisphere differences in the acquisition and use of descriptive systems. *Brain Lang.* 14: 144-173, 1981.
3. Bever, T. G. & Chiarello, R. J. Cerebral dominance in musicians and nonmusicians. *Science.* 185: 537-539, 1974.
4. Marzi, C. A. & Berlucchi, G. Right visual field superiority for accuracy of recognition of famous faces in normals. *Neuropsychologia.* 15: 751-756, 1977.
5. Tulving, E., Markowitsch, H. J., Kapur, S., Habib, R. & Houle, S. Novelty encoding networks in the human brain: positron emission tomography data. *Neuroreport.* 5: 2525-2528, 1994.
6. Tulving, E., Markowitsch, H. J., Craik, F. E., Habib, R. & Houle, S. Novelty and familiarity activations in PET studies of memory encoding and retrieval. *Cereb Cortex.* 6: 71-79, 1996.
7. Martin, A., Wiggs, C. L. & Weisberg, J. Modulation of human medial temporal lobe activity by form, meaning, and experience. *Hippocampus.* 7: 587-593, 1997.
8. Henson, R., Shallice, T. & Dolan, R. Neuroimaging evidence for the dissociable forms of repetition priming. *Science.* 287: 1269-1272, 2000.
9. Gold, J. M., Berman, K. F., Randolph, C., Goldberg, T. B. & Weinberger, D. R. PET validation of a novel prefrontal task: delayed response alteration. *Neuropsychology.* 10: 3-10, 1996.
10. Haier, R. J. et al. Regional glucose metabolic changes after learning a complex visuospatial/motor task: a positron emission tomographic study. *Brain Res.* 570: 134-143, 1992.
11. Narayanan, N. S. et al. The role of the prefrontal cortex in the maintenance of verbal working memory: an event-related fMRI analysis. *Neuropsychology.* 19: 223-32, 2005.
12. Kyllonen, P. C. & Christal, R. E. Reasoning ability is (little more than) working-memory capacity? *Intelligence.* 14: 389-433, 1990.
12a. From psyche.cs.monash.edu.au/v5/psyche-5-08-turnbull1.jpg
13. Courtney, S. M., Ungerleider, L. G., Keil, K. & Haxby, J. V. Object and spatial visual working memory activate separate neural systems in human cortex. *Cereb Cortex.* 6: 39-49, 1996.
14. Funahashi, S., Bruce, C. J. & Goldman-Rakic, P. S. Mnemonic coding of visual space in the monkey's dorsolateral prefrontal cortex. *J Neurophysiol.* 61: 331-349, 1989.
15. Goldberg, E. & Podell, K. Adaptive versus veridical decision making and the frontal lobes. *Conscious Cogn.* 8: 364-377, 1999.
16. Podell, K., Lovell, M., Zimmerman, M. & Goldberg, E. The Cognitive Bias Task and lateralized frontal lobe functions in males. *J Neuropsychiatry Clin Neurosci.* 7: 491-501, 1995.
17. Goldberg, E. & Podell, K. Adaptive decision making, ecological validity, and the frontal lobes. *J Clin Exp Neuropsychol.* 22: 56-68, 2000.
18. Shimoyama, H. et al. Context-dependent reasoning in a cognitive bias task Part II. SPECT activation study. *Brain Dev.* 26: 37-42, 2004.
19. Heekeren, H. R., Marrett, S., Bandettini, P. A. & Ungerleider, L. G. A general mechanism for perceptual

decision-making in the human brain. *Nature.* 431: 859-862, 2004.

20. Koechlin, E., Ody, C. & Kouneiher, F. The architecture of cognitive control in the human prefrontal cortex. *Science.* 302: 1181-1185, 2003.

21. Petrides, M., Alivisatos, B., Evans, A. C. & Meyer, E. Dissociation of human mid-dorsolateral from posterior dorsolateral frontal cortex in memory processing. *Proc Natl Acad Sci USA.* 90: 873-877, 1993.

22. Huettel, S. A. & Misiurek, J. Modulation of prefrontal cortex activity by information toward a decision rule. *Neuroreport.* 15: 1883-1886, 2004.

23. Goel, V. & Dolan, R. J. Differential involvement of left prefrontal cortex in inductive and deductive reasoning. *Cognition.* 93: B109-121, 2004.

24. Duncan, J. et al. A neural basis for general intelligence. *Science.* 289: 457-460, 2000.

25. Shaw, P. et al. Intellectual ability and cortical development in children and adolescents. *Nature.* 440: 676-679, 2006.

I have really touched God. He came into me, myself; yes God exists, I cried, and I don't remember anything else. You all, healthy people, can't imagine the happiness which we epileptics feel during the second before our attack.

F. Dostoyevsky
The Idiot

Our deepest spiritual convictions may be nothing more than fluctuations in brain chemistry.

Albert Hoffman
Discoverer of LSD

The realization that the God Experience could be an artifact of the human brain was intellectually paralyzing.

Michael Persinger
Neuropsychological Bases of God Beliefs [1p16]

Chapter 30

The Spiritual Brain

In the previous chapters we have seen that specific brain areas are involved in consciousness, thinking and rational thought (the rational brain), pleasure (the pleasure brain), and societal interactions (the social brain). Is there also a spiritual brain, a neural location for feelings of spirituality, feelings of being connected to something larger than ourselves, feelings of immortality, feelings that we are special, and feelings that God is talking just to us? The answer is yes. This chapter reviews the evidence suggesting that the temporal lobes represent the neural location for spirituality.

Anatomy of the Temporal Lobes

Before entering this world of spiritual feelings it is important to provide a brief review of some of the important aspects of the temporal lobes. They function as the primary association area for hearing (language, music, rhythm) and smelling. They are the secondary association area for visual recognition of color and shapes including faces. They are the site for memory (hippocampus) and fear (amygdala). They link the past and present sensory and emotional experiences into a continuous self. The left temporal lobe is involved in speech. The speech circuit contains the cortex for hearing speech, for processing that speech (Wernicke's area), the nerve tracts for passing that information to Broca's area for expressive speech, and from there to the motor area for talking (Figure 1A). In response to auditory input, PET scan images of the speech circuit show activation of Wernicke's area, the auditory association cortex, and Broca's area (Figure 1B).

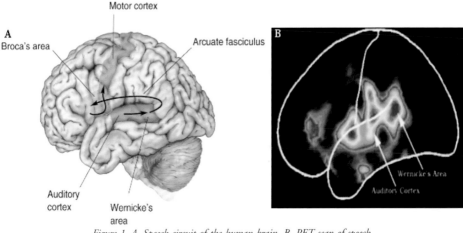

Figure 1. A. Speech circuit of the human brain. B. PET scan of speech circuit.

The association areas of the temporal lobe are shown in Figure 2.

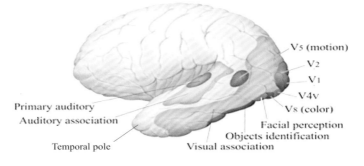

Figure 2. Visual association functions of the temporal lobes. [2]

V1 and V2 represent the visual cortex of the occipital lobe (Figure 2). The V4 area is critical for color consistency and hue discrimination. The V5 is the visual motion center. The right temporal lobes are important in spatial orientation—"where am I? How do I get home from here?" The very tips, or *poles,* of the temporal lobes are heavily connected with sensory regions and integrate sensory, emotional, and cognitive functions.

When monkeys who had both temporal poles removed were placed back in the colony, they were isolated and had very impaired social relationships. In humans, imaging studies indicate the temporal poles are involved in linking symbols to names and recalling emotional and traumatic events. The temporal pole on the dominant side is involved in recalling proper names and learning new visual patterns. Thus, individuals who have had the left temporal lobe removed have trouble recalling people's names. On the non-dominant side, the temporal pole processes words when perceiving sad faces and experiencing anger. Parts of the temporal lobe farther back from the pole participate in recalling names of objects and tools. As shown in Figure 3, the hippocampus and amygdala are located in the depths of the *mesial* or middle part of the temporal lobe.

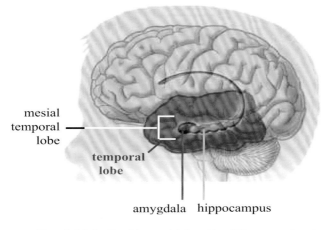

mesial
temporal
lobe

temporal
lobe

amygdala   hippocampus

Figure 3. Relationship of the amygdala (purple) and hippocampus (green) and mesial temporal lobe (red) www.BrainConnection.com, Scientific Learning Corporation, 1999. By permission. [2b]

What is the evidence that the temporal lobes are the site of the spiritual brain? Evidence comes from studies of the electrical stimulation of the brain in conscious subjects, clinical histories of individuals with temporal lobe epilepsy both during and between seizures, the effects of traumatic lesions of the temporal lobes, imaging studies, studies of near-death experiences, spontaneous and drug-induced hallucinations and studies of individuals experiencing a range of spiritual and religious feelings. Some of these conditions produce a feeling of being detached from oneself as in out-of-body experiences or a feeling of being detached from one's own emotions (depersonalization); feelings that everything is unfamiliar, strange and not real (derealization); a sense of timelessness and spacelessness; hallucinations; ecstasy; dreamy states; joy; and other experiences that foster a religious interpretation. [3] Temporal lobe epilepsy (TLE) has played a central role in deciphering the functions of the temporal lobe.

Temporal Lobe Epilepsy (TLE)—History

While any part of the brain can be the site of seizure activity, over a period of many years it became apparent that there is something uniquely spiritual about seizure activity that emanated from the temporal lobes. One of the most common causes is sclerosis of the hippocampus in the mesial temporal lobe.

Sclerosis of the hippocampus was first identified in 1885. [4] This sclerosis was reported in patients with "alienation-type" seizures. In 1899, Hughlings Jackson [5] described what are now known as psychomotor seizures. The examination of the brain tissue of individuals who had a history of psychomotor seizures [6,7] showed unique changes with fibrosis and hardening, referred to as *hippocampal sclerosis.* In 1938, Gibbs and colleagues [8] first described the EEG pattern in patients with psychomotor seizures. A few years later, in studies of the open brain, neurosurgeons [9] identified the temporal lobes as the site of psychomotor seizures.

A breakthrough in the treatment of TLE came with the recognition that EEG spikes, present in the absence of seizures, could be used to localize the exact site of the otherwise invisible lesions. [10] As a result, the brain tissue at such sites could be removed, resulting in the elimination of the seizures. In cases where the entire temporal lobe was removed, pathological examination usually showed the presence of hippocampal sclerosis. [11] The technique of placing electrodes deep into the temporal lobes during surgery allowed recordings to be made directly from the hippocampus. TLE is the most common of the drug-resistant forms of epilepsy. Of the 2.5 million people in the United States with epilepsy, 30 percent are resistant to drug treatment, and half of these, or 375,000, have temporal lobe epilepsy. [12]

A range of sensations (auras) prior to seizures are common in TLE. These can include psychic symptoms such as fear, upset stomach, and the aberrant sensation of various smells or tastes. If overt seizures occur, they are called *complex partial seizures,* consisting of freezing of motion, posturing of one arm, staring, lip-smacking, chewing, and other "automatisms." After the seizure there may be disorientation and amnesia of the event. If the seizure occurs in the left temporal lobe ,there may be a period of difficulty with speech and a verbal memory deficit. If it occurs in the right temporal lobe, there may be a visual-spatial memory deficit.

Wilder Penfield and Mapping of the Spiritual Human Brain

Just as consciousness and the "soul" are brain-based, so are spiritual and religious experiences. The evidence for this began with the studies by the famous Canadian neurosurgeon, Wilder Penfield. One advantage of animal studies in neuroscience is that it is possible to electrically stimulate different parts of the exposed brain. However, animals are not suitable for studies of spirituality since even if spiritual feelings were generated, they could not communicate those feelings to us. Since most people would object to having their brain exposed just to allow some curious scientist to probe around, such experimental studies are difficult in humans. The exception is when a brain is exposed for neurosurgical operations, as for epilepsy. A unique advantage of such surgery is that the brain has no pain receptors. It is thus possible to perform surgery on conscious, talking patients.

Taking advantage of this unique opportunity which is a part of the process in identifying the lesions causing temporal lobe epilepsy, Penfield began a systematic process of electrically stimulating different parts of the brain and recording the verbal responses in conscious subjects. He found that he was able to elicit episodes of "reliving past life" when the temporal lobe was stimulated. No other part of the brain elicited this response. He first obtained these results in 1934, when a patient related that she was reliving a past event. She "saw herself as she had been while giving birth to her baby." While Penfield immediately realized the relevance of this memory recall to the field of psychiatry, he wanted to accumulate additional careful documentation before publishing these remarkable results. Thus, it was not until he was invited to give the Mandsley lecture in 1954 that he shared two decades of his studies with his colleagues. [13-15]

Penfield classified the responses, both from seizures and from direct brain stimulation, into three types: *experiential,* having to do with the past; *interpretative,* having to do with the present; and *amnesic seizures,* with automatisms or psychomotor confusion. He noted that the electrical stimulation of the temporal lobe often brought back a period of past experience with a startling degree of vividness and detail, allowing the subject to review the sights and sounds and thinking of a previous period of time. [14] Penfield referred to these as *psychical* effects. This is not to be confused with psychotic. The word psychical was used by Hughlings Jackson to denote more complicated mental phenomena that involve the complex integration of many different neurons. Some case reports illustrate the point. The following are a few of Penfield's cases.

- A 19-year-old male had temporal lobe seizures that were sometimes precipitated by listening to music. At the beginning of each attack he experienced what he termed a flashback that was "much more distinct" than anything he could summon to his memory. During the operation, stimulation of the anterior part of the first temporal lobe convolution on the right caused him to say, "I feel as though I were in the bathroom at school." A few minutes later, when the electrode was re-applied near the same area, he said something about a "street corner." When asked where, he said, "South Bend, Indiana, corner of Jacob and Washington." A subsequent stimulation produced "music from *Guys and Dolls.*"
- A 26-year-old woman had recurring temporal lobe seizures. The attacks led her to say, "[I feel] as though I have lived through this all before." After another attack without warning she seemed to be sitting in the railroad station of a small town, which she felt was Vanceburg, Kentucky. "It was winter and the wind is blowing outside and I am waiting for a train." This was apparently an experience from her past life, but was one she had forgotten.
- A 33-year-old male had right temporal lobe epilepsy. During the operation, he was electrically stimulated at a depth of 2 cm in the right superior surface of the temporal lobe. This caused the patient to say, "That bittersweet taste on my tongue." He seemed confused and made swallowing movements. When the stimulation was turned off, the EEG showed that a 4-per-second generalized *theta* rhythm had been produced. While this was continuing the patient looked terrified and exclaimed, "Oh God! I am leaving my body." [13] These are called *out-of-body-experiences* (OBEs).
- A 30-year-old man had minor seizures apparently due to an old traumatic lesion of the left temporal lobe. During some of his minor attacks he stated that "thoughts" kept coming into his mind. When asked if they were memories he said, "No, they were more like words or combinations of words."

He tried to explain by saying that it was like having a dictionary and having different words come to mind. At another time he said it was like thinking two things at once. At such time he would look around, he said, and know what was happening and yet the thoughts kept coming. This state was followed by confusion and automatism and after the automatism was over, some slight tendency to aphasia. [13]

- A 46-year-old man from South Africa had a diagnosis of left temporal lobe epilepsy. During stimulation of the left first temporal convolution, he stated he was going back to a conversation in Johannesburg and was "spiritually" speaking to an unknown woman. [15p629]
- A 31-year-old male had a diagnosis of left temporal lobe epilepsy that was often asociated with experiential hallucinations. During stimulus of the inferior temporal lobe he said, "I am going to die." When asked if he saw anything, he said, "No, God said I am going to die." [15p636]

The different epileptic discharges from the right temporal lobe were causing him to experience a sense of *déjà vu,* a sense of fear, and reproduction of previous experiences. One of his psychical responses after brain stimulation was, "I heard voices down along a river somewhere—a man's voice and a woman's voice calling." A few minutes later after stimulation of a similar area he said, "I hear voices, it is later at night, around the carnival somewhere—some sort of traveling circus. I saw lots of big wagons that they used to haul animals in." Re-stimulation a few minutes later produced, "I seemed to hear little voices, the voices of people calling from building to building somewhere—I do not know where it is but it is very familiar to me."

As shown in Figure 4, the entire temporal lobe and parts of the parietal lobe may be involved in the *experiential* and *interpretative* psychic experiences.

Better detail concerning the precise location of the sites of stimulation eliciting experiential responses is shown in Figure. 5.

The majority of the sites are at the Sylvian fissure at the top of the temporal lobes. This map is extremely relevant to the common statement that the right but not the left temporal lobe is the spiritual brain. Clearly, both the right and left temporal lobes are involved in experiential psychical responses. This map also shows that most of the experiential responses occur in the region of the auditory association

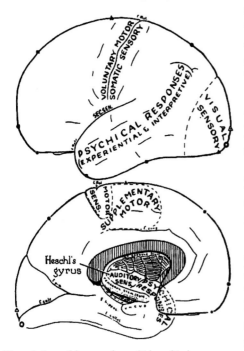

Figure 4. Areas of the cortex from which psychical responses are obtained. The upper figure shows the lateral structures; the lower figures shows medial structures. The major sensory and motor areas are also indicated. From Penfield[13] Permanent Record of the Stream of Consciousness. Acta Psychologia. *11:47–69, 1955. By permission.*

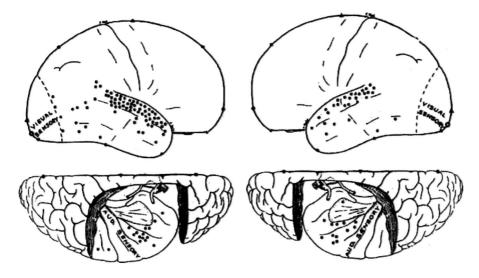

Figure 5. Summary of stimulation sites producing experiential responses. The top shows the sites from the right hemisphere (left) and left hemisphere (right). The bottom shows the comparable sites from the underside of the temporal lobes. From Penfield,[15] The Brain's Record of Auditory and Visual Experience. Brain. 84: 595–696, 1963. By permission.

cortex, as shown in Figure 2. These sites are located between the visual (occipital) and auditory (gyrus of Heschl) association areas. This is consistent with the involvement of both visual and auditory aspects of experiential responses.

It is also of note that no experiential responses were elicited from the dominant (left) speech area. The expressive or ideational speech area mapped by Penfield is shown in Figure 6.

Comparing this map with the map of the left hemispheres in Figure 5 shows the complete separation of the area of expressive speech from the areas involved in experiential responses. One additional figure from Penfield's studies allows us to see first hand the effect that the speech area has on right brain—left brain differences.

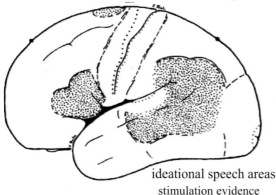

ideational speech areas
stimulation evidence

Figure 6. Map of the areas of the dominant hemisphere that are devoted to the ideational elaboration of speech. From Penfield,[15] The Brain's Record of Auditory and Visual Experience. Brain. 84: 595- 696, 1963. By permission.

The large expanse of area involved in visual experiential responses in the temporal and occipital lobe on the non-dominant side is squeezed into one small area under the region of the auditory responses on the dominant side. This again illustrates that while there is a modest predominance of experiential responses emanating from the right hemisphere, the presence

Experiential Responses

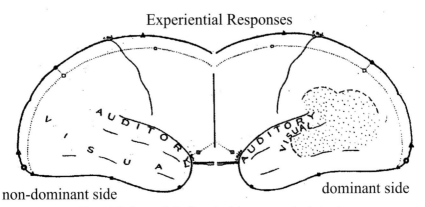

non-dominant side

dominant side

Figure 7. Auditory and visual experiential responses to stimulation shown for the lateral surfaces of both hemispheres. From Penfield,[15] The Brain's Record of Auditory and Visual Experience. Brain. *84: 595- 696, 1963. By permission.*

of the speech area has not eliminated them from the left hemisphere.

The area of the right hemisphere, corresponding to the speech area in the left hemisphere, is especially devoted to *interpretive* responses. Stimulation produces visual interpretive illusions, such as changes in the appearance of things as coming nearer or going farther away, changes in the apparent speed of things, and out-of-body experiences.

The region of the brain associated with automatisms was the amygdala; about 4 cm back from the tip of the temporal lobe and 4 cm deep into the lateral surface. [13] While in the automatic state, the patient is still conscious but in an altered state of consciousness. He may seem to be slightly or completely confused and may move about aimlessly, or may have some apparent purpose, a purpose not easily influenced by his companions. These are also called *fugue states,* and some examples will be given later. These illusions of familiarity and strangeness are almost always produced by discharge or stimulation of the non-dominant side.

There were a number of relevant characteristics and additional aspects of the psychical responses.

- Penfield felt that psychical responses were not hallucinations in the sense of psychotic or schizophrenic hallucinations because in all the cases the subject always talked to him, the "doctor," and never talked to the people in the re-play. In addition, they were not afraid. Patients having psychotic hallucinations often talk to the voices and are afraid of them.
- He also felt that the right temporal lobe was preferentially engaged in the reproduction of experiences from the past, while the left temporal lobe was preferentially involved in present experiences. This was presented as a supposition rather than fact. Whether valid or not, *psychical experiences were clearly generated from both the right and left temporal lobes.*
- Touching, music, lights and other sensory stimuli could precipitate temporal lobe

seizures. *Psychical precipitation by thoughts can also occur.*

- Hallucinations emanating from the right temporal lobe are more likely to involve non-verbal themes such as complex visual, musical, and singing themes, while hallucinations emanating from the left temporal lobe are more likely to involve verbal themes such as words and sentences. [16]

- *All subjects agreed that the psychical response was more vivid than anything they could voluntarily recall from memory.* They "never looked upon the experiential response as remembering. Instead it was a hearing — and seeing — again, a living through moments of past time."

- Penfield felt that in regard to memory, nothing was lost. The record of each man's experience was complete. He liked to describe what was happening in his psychical experiments in the following way:

> Among the millions and millions of nerve cells that clothe certain parts of the temporal lobe on each side, there runs a thread. It is the thread of time, the thread that has run through each succeeding wakeful hour of the individual's past life. Think of the thread, if you like, as a pathway through an unending sequence of nerve cells, nerve fibers and synapses. It is a pathway which can be followed again because of the continuing facilitation that has been created in the cell contacts.
>
> When, by chance, the neurosurgeon's electrode activates some portion of that thread, there is a response as though that thread were a wire recorder, or a strip of cinematographic film, on which are registered all those things of which the individual was once aware, the things he selected for his attention in that interval of time. Absent from it are impulses he ignored, the talk he did not hear.
>
> The time's strip of film runs forward, never backward, even when resurrected from the past. It seems to proceed again at time's own unchanged pace. It would seem, once one section of the strip has come alive, that a functional all-or-nothing principle steps in so as to protect the other portions of the film from activation by the electric current. As long as the electrode is held in place, the experience of a former day goes forward. There is no holding it back. When the electrode is withdrawn it stops as suddenly as it began.

In a final summary of his work [15] Penfield concluded that the interpretative temporal cortex involved in psychical experiences made possible the recall of previous perceptions, chiefly auditory and visual; the comparison of past experience with similar present experience; the subconscious elaboration of signals that interpret present experience; and the altering of previously recorded concepts such as a place, a person, a voice, or a piece of music. The religious conversions described below in individuals with TLE also indicate this revision in previously recorded concepts can involve a person's religious and spiritual orientation.

Wilder Penfield's brain mapping studies clearly placed both temporal lobes front and center as the site for many complex spiritual experiences, including the re-playing of past experiences, thought intrusions, feelings of *déjá vu,* out-of-body sensations, trances or *fugue* states, automatic behaviors, feelings of being in the presence of others, of hearing music, of hearing angelic voices, of intense meaningfulness, of being connected to some force greater than themselves, and of talking to God.

A review of the evidence accumulated since Penfield's studies also suggest the temporal lobes and its deep limbic structures, the amygdala, and hippocampus are the site of our spiritual brain.

Stimulation of the Amygdala and Hippocampus

A number of investigators have shown that deep temporal lobe stimulation in the area around the amygdala and hippocampus of the limbic system produces feelings of intense meaningfulness, of depersonalization, of a connection with God, of cosmic connectedness, of out-of-body experiences, a feeling of not being in this world, *déjá vu* (a feeling that something has been experienced before), *jamais vu* (a feeling something is happening for the first time even though it has been experienced before), fear, and hallucinations. [17-23] Figure 8 shows why "deep temporal lobe stimulation" can involve the stimulation of the amygdala or hippocampus.

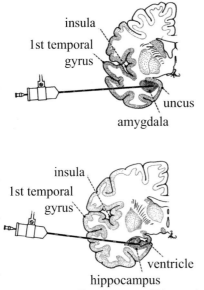

Figure 8. Demonstration of how deep temporal lobe stimulation results in the stimulation of the amygdala or hippocampus. Top: 4 cm from the temporal tip. Bottom: 6 cm from the temporal tip. From Jasper and Rasmussen. Association of Nervous and Mental Diseases. 36:316-334, 1958. [18]

Passing an electrode through the outer surface of the temporal lobes into the deeper structures passes through the white matter tracts and then, depending upon the site of insertion, enters either the amygdala or the hippocampus.

Since the amygdala has wide connections to all parts of the brain, it serves as a master association area for emotionally charged memories—the fears, the pleasures, wonderful tastes and smells, the sexual pleasures and other sweet things, the evil things, the spiritual experience, the dreams, the nightmares and all other experiences that make life meaningful. Stimulation of the amygdala and hippocampus is capable of bringing all these feelings and emotions back from the realm of the forgotten to the realm of the here and now. These features also make this area uniquely suitable for the production of visual and auditory spiritual and religious feelings.

More Out-of-Body Experiences

Blanke and colleagues[24] stimulated the right angular gyrus, also called the *inferior parietal lobule,* during surgery on a 43-year-old woman with epilepsy. This produced an OBE in which she saw her trunk and legs from above. Blanke proposed that the OBE was produced by disrupting the part of the brain responsible for feeling and knowing the position of the body. While this area is part of the parietal lobe, it is at the angle of the temporal and parietal lobe and is inside the areas reported by Penfield to produce psychical experiences.

Spiritual and Religious Experiences and Temporal Lobe Epilepsy (TLE)

The most fascinating part of TLE is the nature of the spiritual and religious feelings that may occur during the seizures and of the personality changes that often occur between the seizures. The following is a summary of some of these reports. I have gone into them in some detail because they are both fascinating and highly relevant to the subject of this book.

There have been many reports of spiritual and religious experiences associated with TLE. In one study, MRI scans were performed on 33 patients with refractory TLE.[25] All subjects also completed a religiosity scale. The volumes of the mesial temporal structures, the amygdala, and the hippocampus were compared in individuals with high and low scores on the religiosity scale. The religiosity scores were highest in those with the smallest sizes of the right hippocampus, consistent with many of these individuals having hippocampal sclerosis.

This association of religiosity with TLE is consistent with a study in Japan where 234 epileptic patients of all types were examined for seizure-related religious experiences.[26] Of these, only three were found to have had seizure-related religious experiences, but in every case the type of epilepsy was TLE. Between the seizures subjects experienced hyperreligiosity.

In a single case report, a 25-year-old female had intractable TLE. The seizures were characterized by a repetition of religious statements and a compulsive kissing behavior.[27] An MRI showed a right-sided, mesial temporal focus and hippocampal sclerosis. The auras, seizures, and religious thoughts were virtually eliminated after the removal of the right amygdala and hippocampus.

In a study of a normal population of 262 undergraduate students, MacDonald[28] had them complete an *Expressions of Spirituality Inventory* that he had designed. This assessed spirituality in five different dimensions. He also had them fill out a self-report scale related to any symptoms they may have had relevant to complex partial epileptic-like seizures. These would be similar to what Persinger (see below) would call *temporal lobe transients* (TLTs). The intriguing observation was that except for just one subscore, the presence of TLTs was strongly predicted by or correlated with each of the other four spirituality subscales. This pattern remained the same after controlling for the participants' age, sex, and reported religious involvement. Thus, *the more spiritual the students were, the more likely it was that they had some type of TLT episode.*

Ecstatic seizures. In some cases the spiritual and pleasurable content of TLE seizures is so dramatic that they have been called "ecstatic" seizures. The first case with documented EEG was published in 1980. [29] The patient had stereotyped spells of psychomotor arrest and an indescribable sense of joy associated with epileptiform discharges from the right temporal lobe. Two types of ecstatic seizures have been described. [3] The first is an emotional seizure of deep pleasure. The second is primarily *a cognitive experience of insight into the unity, harmony, joy, and divinity of all reality, usually with pleasurable effect.*

One study examined 11 patients with ecstatic seizures. [30] Of these eight had sensory hallucinations, four had erotic sensations, and five described a religious or spiritual experience. Several had symptoms that were felt to have no counterpart in human experience. EEG localization of the site of the seizures was possible in four subjects: in two the right temporal lobe was involved, while the left temporal lobe was involved in the other two. Eight patients enjoyed the experience so much they wanted to continue to have seizures. Five subjects found they could self-induce the seizures, and four simply stopped taking their medication. The authors felt that ecstatic seizures associated with TLE have had a substantial impact on our cultural and religious history (see below).

Naito and Matsui [31] described a woman with left temporal lobe epilepsy with ecstatic seizures characterized by joyous visions of God and the sun. She reported that, "My mind, my whole being was pervaded by a feeling of delight."

Fugue states. Fugue states, or dissociative episodes, would be the third type of response with temporal lobe seizures or stimulation mentioned by Penfield, i.e., the production of automatic behaviors, altered consciousness, and confusion following stimulation of the area of the amygdala. The following case report [32] illustrates the aggressive and destructive behaviors that can occur during these fugue states.

A 33-year-old engineer developed seizures at age 22 following an episode of severe gastrointestinal bleeding with shock. Attacks would typically commence with the patient complaining to his wife that some relatively minor event was not to his liking. He would proceed to brood aloud, dwell upon, and increasingly elaborate on this single theme with mounting anger, verbal abuse, and irrational accusations over a period of three to four hours, reaching a crescendo of rage which was always climaxed by an outburst of physical aggression during which he threw his children against the walls, spit or kicked at his wife, and on one occasion pinned her down while burning her bared chest with a lighted cigarette. During the latter part of these attacks, he appeared dazed and wild-eyed. As the anger spent itself in physical violence, he rather suddenly seemed to come to himself and wept violently, feeling hurt and broken. He claimed nearly total amnesia for the attack.

This example illustrates many of the features of temporal lobe fugue states. Other aggressive behaviors have included robbing, stealing, rape and murder. As discussed in the chapter on the social brain, this would clearly qualify as a socializing disorder of the brain which, if not understood, could give the rest of the human race a bad name.

Autoscopic seizures. Autoscopy is defined as a visual experience where *one sees one's double,* a hallucinatory perception of one's own body visualized in external space. Autoscopy can also include typical out of body experiences consisting of a feeling of leaving one's body and viewing it from another perspective. In one report of 43 cases of patients with seizures who had out-of-body experiences or saw their own double, the temporal lobes were involved in 86 percent of those where the focus could be identified. [33] There was no preference for the right or left hemisphere.

TLE auras and non-epileptic religious conversions. Saver and Rabin [3] call attention to the deep similarities between some features of TLE auras and the features of intense, non-epileptic religious conversions.

> Individuals undergoing sudden religious awakening or conversion often report abruptly perceiving their ordinary, unenlightened selves as hollow, empty, and unreal (depersonalization) as a prelude to finding a truer, more authentic, religiously grounded self. Similarly, a sense of suddenly seeing through a view of appearances previously taken for real (derealization) to a deeper, supernatural, genuine reality is a frequent aspect of mystical-spiritual experiences. Also, doubling of consciousness—a simultaneous perception of a higher, purer, religiously oriented self and an irreligious self, contesting for control and spirit—is a recurrent leitmotif of religious experience. Although many individuals do not associate their intellectual auras with religious experience, it seems likely that the repeated, intense, visceral experiences of the self or external world as unreal would tend to foster a belief in a supernatural ground of reality and a religious outlook.

Personality changes between seizures. One aspect of TLE are the personality changes observed between the seizures, the so-called interictal periods. Gibbs first emphasized the strong association of psychosis with TLE in 1951. [34] In a study of 275 cases of focal epilepsy, he found that the prevalence of psychosis was 17 percent for those with a temporal lobe locus, compared to two percent for those with other types of epilepsy. Others have found a frequency of psychosis in TLE of between 11 and 14 percent. [35] Most of those with psychosis have left temporal lobe involvement. [35,36] This may represent the possibility that a thought disorder is especially likely to occur when the area for language and symbolic representation is disturbed.

Dewhurst and Beard [37,38] described six patients with TLE who had religious conversion experiences. The following are some examples:

L. T. C. was a 55-year-old bus conductor with a history of left temporal lobe epilepsy. One day, in the middle of collecting fares, he had a minor seizure and was suddenly overcome with a feeling of bliss. He felt he was literally in Heaven. He collected the fares correctly, telling his passengers at the same time how pleased he was to be in Heaven. When he returned home he appeared not to recognize his wife. He later told his doctor that he felt like a bomb had burst in his head. He said that he had seen God and that his wife and family would soon join him in Heaven. He readily admitted to hearing music and voices. He remained in this state of exaltation, hearing divine and angelic voices, for two days. Two years later, following three seizures, he became elated again and stated [his] "mind had cleared." During this episode he lost his faith.

In this case, one set of temporal lobe seizures resulted in a religious conversion, while a subsequent set of seizures resulted in an anti-religious conversion. A left temporal lobectomy was performed with a cessation of seizures. He retained his belief from his second conversion and continued in an attitude of agnosticism.

D. W. H. was a 33-year-old soldier. He was raised in a strict religious home but lost his interest in religion by age 21. While serving overseas he had his first minor seizure. Two weeks later while walking alone, he suddenly felt God's reality and his own insignificance. As a result of this revelation he recovered his lost faith and was determined to live in a Christian manner. However, this conversion experience gradually lost its impact and he once again ceased concerning himself with religion. Eleven years later he had two rare grand mal attacks in one day. Within 24 hours he had another religious conversion associated with a florid religious psychosis. He had a sudden dream-like feeling, saw a flash of light, and exclaimed, "I have seen the light." He suddenly knew that God was behind the sun and that his knowledge meant power; he could have power from God if he would only ask for it. He had a series of visions in which he felt that his past life was being judged; a book appeared before him, a world atlas with a torn page; a pendulum was swinging and when it stopped the world would end. He considered that he had received a message from God to mend his ways and to help others. The fact that he had been singled out in this way meant that he was God's chosen instrument.

This patient was diagnosed with left temporal lobe epilepsy. A left temporal lobectomy was performed. This resulted in a cessation of the seizures and psychotic experiences but his religious beliefs remained.

J. P. was a 37-year-old Jewish male. He was brought up in a strictly

Jewish Orthodox faith and remained devout until age 17. Although he then ceased to attend regular worship he felt guilty about these lapses. His first religious conversion occurred in the hospital after photic stimulation. He had a vision he was in the cockpit of an airplane, flying over a mountainous region. As it brought him into a different land he felt at peace and felt that the power of God was upon him and was changing him for the better. Afterwards he became intensely interested in following the teachings of Jesus Christ and became a member of the Pentecostal church. He was diagnosed with right temporal lobe epilepsy. No surgery was done and he continued in his preoccupation with religion. He often walked the streets carrying a sign "Be prepared to meet thy God."

This case was of interest, since instead of a conversion from little interest in religion to a great interest, here there was a change from one religion to another.

J. R. was a 33-year-old male with a history of left temporal lobe epilepsy since age 18. His seizures were partially controlled on medication. At age 33 he stopped taking his medications and was soon having frequent seizures. At this point he suddenly realized that he was the Son of God; he possessed special powers of healing and could abolish cancer from the world; he had visions, and believed that he could understand other people's thoughts. Later he gave the following account of his conversion. "It was a beautiful morning and God was with me and I was thanking God. I was talking to God. I was with God. God isn't something hard looking down on us, God is trees and flowers and beauty and love. God was telling me to carry on and help the doctors."

This patient was not considered suitable for surgery and was re-started on medications. Five years later he was doing well, holding down a job, but still occasionally talking about God in an inappropriate way.

These cases and reports have been presented because of the remarkable insight they provide into the relationship between the temporal lobe events and religious and spiritual feelings, and in some cases, religious conversions. *It is clear that not all religious conversions are the result of TLE but it is equally clear that a number of individuals with TLE have experienced religious conversions.* It is also clear from these reports that *both the right and left temporal lobes can be involved.*

Cases of multiple personality and a feeling of devil or spiritual possession are rare in psychiatric practice. Despite this, Mesulam [39] reported that of 61 patients in the Behavioral Neurology Unit in Boston, 12 gave a history consistent with these syndromes. About one woman,

On repeated occasions she believed she was the Messiah and that she had a special mission to fulfill. Some of the episodes lasted for almost a year. During one she believed she was called by God to enter politics. She ran for an important public office and almost won. She explained these episodes as being "possessed by God."

In addition to being transformed by their experiences, an additional remarkable aspect of temporal lobe epilepsy is that the transformative changes in a patient's religious and spiritual outlook on life are often permanent. [40] As shown below, this is a feature they share with near-death experiences. While TLE is too rare to account for all cases of religious conversions, these results raise the question of whether certain life events might trigger sub-clinical electrical events and play a role in religious and spiritual experiences in normal individuals. This is discussed later. These observations clearly have relevance to the life-changing manner in which some people have "found God," or "discovered Jesus Christ."

In studies of three different groups of male and female college students, Persinger reported a significant correlation between signs of TLE and having paranormal experiences, such as thinking they can read another person's mind, feeling their souls have left their bodies, feeling close to a Universal Consciousness, thinking about a person they had not seen for awhile and then seeing that person a few minutes later, hearing an inner voice call their name, or hearing an inner voice telling them where to find something and subsequently finding it there. [41,42] There was also a significant correlation between the number of TLE signs and intense religious experiences. [43] Nine years later Persinger [44] studied an additional 400 men and 400 women with similar results relating to paranormal experiences.

The 4-H Syndrome. A distinct but fairly rare syndrome of TLE interictal behavior changes has been described. The symptoms include religiosity, alterations in sexual behavior, loss of a sense of humor, and a tendency toward extensive, and in some cases compulsive, writing and drawing. This was first described by Wasman and Geschwind [40] and has been referred to as the *Geschwind syndrome,* or the four H's syndrome: Hyperreligiosity, Hyposexuality, Humorlessness, and Hypergraphia. Other features include aggression, pedantic speech, a "sticky" or compulsive personality, and psychosis. [45] The personality structure included increased concern with philosophical, moral, and religious issues, and extensive writing on religious or philosophical themes, lengthy letters, diaries, and poetry. [46] Endocrine studies showing a decreased responsiveness to luteinizing hormone-releasing hormone *(LHRH)* [47,48] may explain the hyposexuality. Luteinizing hormone, which is produced by the pituitary gland, regulates the menstrual cycle and stimulates ovulation.

In one case [49] a 35-year-old man expressed the hypergraphia by painting an excessive number of buildings and houses. He also presented with hyposexuality and hyperreligiosity. An MRI showed right mesial hippocampal sclerosis.

Religious conversions have been reported in individuals with TLE of both the right and left temporal lobes. In some cases these conversions are permanent. A rare 4-H syndrome has been described

consisting of Hyperreligiosity, Hyposexuality, Humorlessness, and Hypergraphia, with increased concern with philosophical, moral and religious issues, and extensive writing on religious or philosophical themes.

Interictal behavior and the study of Bear and Fedio. An extensive study of interictal behavior in TLE was reported by Bear and Fedio. [50] They sought to answer two questions: 1) Do temporal lobe epileptics differ in behavior from controls without epilepsy, and 2) Is there a difference between right- and left-sided TLE? To test this they examined 15 patients with right temporal lobe epilepsy, 12 with left temporal lobe epilepsy, 12 normal controls, and nine patients under treatment for neuromuscular disorders unrelated to epilepsy. Each subject was given a self-report questionnaire covering 18 different types of behavior. In addition, an individual who knew the subject well (the rater) was asked to fill out the same questionnaire, with the questions changed to ask about a person other than themselves. This had both the advantage of a second opinion and of determining if a person was denying a symptom that others felt they had or exaggerating a symptom others felt they did not have. Both individuals with right and left TLE had scores for all 18 of the traits that were significantly greater than for the controls or the other group. These results suggest that a wide range of behavioral veriations occur in TLE in addition to religiosity.

Not all studies in the literature concur with the Bear and Fedio report. [52,53,57] Some have criticized it by virtue of the fact that 33 percent of the TLE cases had preexisting psychopathology and this may have driven many of the differences in the behavioral scales. [54] However, since there is general agreement that psychoses and hallucinations are significantly more common in TLE than in the general population or in other forms of epilepsy, [15,52,55,56] one could argue that directly or indirectly the differences were due to TLE.

Spiritual experiences following injury to the temporal lobe. Just as trauma to the frontal lobes provided us with insight into their function, the same is true for the role of the temporal lobes in religious experiences. In one case a 39-year-old woman had a traumatic injury to her right temporal lobe. [58] Prior to this she had no psychiatric problems. After the injury she developed an acute psychotic state similar to a schizophreniform disorder that was associated with religious delusions.

Fenwick and colleagues [59] examined the "psychic" experiences of 17 students called "sensitives," from the College of Psychic Studies and compared them to 17 church-going control subjects. The sensitives had experienced more head injuries and serious illnesses than the controls. Sixty-six percent showed evidence of right hemisphere and right temporal lobe dysfunction and of these, 35 percent had poor visual memories. There was evidence to suggest that some of their "psychic" experiences were associated with brain dysfunction. Mystical experiences showed a trend towards being related to non-dominant hemisphere dysfunction.

Hallucinations and the temporal lobe. Since ecstatic communications with God or supernatural beings are common in individuals with schizophrenia, identifying the brain location of the visual and auditory hallucinations in this disorder could provide major clues to the location of the spiritual brain. In one study, brain imaging of schizophrenic subjects with religious delusions showed increased activity of the left temporal lobe with reduced activity of the left occipital lobe. [60] In a second study from Japan, direct brain stimulation was performed on individuals with schizophrenia. Their visual hallucinations were reproduced by deep temporal lobe stimulation. [61]

The God Module. In 1997, Vilayanur Ramachandram, director of the Center for Brain and Cognition at the University of California in San Diego, presented an intriguing paper at the Society for Neuroscience meeting. They were studying subjects with temporal lobe epilepsy and found that one of the effects of the seizures was to strengthen involuntary responses to religious words as tested by changes in galvanic skin response. One subject with TLE felt a rapturous "Oneness with the Creator" that carried over into the rest of his life. When asked if he believed in God, he replied, "But what else is there?" [62p182] Other TLE patients had made statements such as, "I finally understand what it is all about. This is the moment I've been waiting for all my life. Suddenly it all makes sense." "Finally, I have insight into the true nature of the cosmos."

The scientists *suggested that the temporal lobes were naturally attuned to ideas about a supreme being.* When thinking about why such a dedicated neural machinery would have evolved they speculated it may have been to encourage tribal loyalty or reinforce kinship ties or the stability of a closely knit clan. They noted that, "These studies do not in any way negate the validity of religious experience or God, they merely provide an explanation in terms of brain regions that may be involved." This report generated a lot of attention in the press and this portion of the brain was designated *The God Module* [63] or *The God Spot.* [64] Ramachandram felt that the left temporal lobe was *The God Module.* Craig Kinsely, from the University of Richmond in Virginia, commented, "There is a quandary of whether the mind created God or God created the mind."

The Feeling of a Presence

Arzy and coworkers in Switzerland reported that the stimulation of the left temporal-parietal junction repeatedly produced a creepy feeling of the presence of another person in their extra-personal space, that sombody was close by. [63a] An epileptic focus in this area could contribute to the sensation of being close to a supernatural being.

The Role of TLE in History and Religion

These relationships between TLE and religious experiences and conversions raise the question of whether TLE was a factor in the religious leanings of major figures in history, literature and religion. The answer is yes. The following are some examples.

Ezekiel. It has been suggested [65] that the oldest-known case of TLE, dating to approximately 2,600 years ago, might be the biblical figure of Ezekiel, son of Buzi. The book of Ezekiel contains prophecies against Israel and Judah and oracles against foreign nations and about the future glory of Israel. Altschuler [65] proposed that Ezekiel possessed some of the symptoms of the 4-H syndrome, including hyperreligiosity, a compulsive personality, and repetitive hypergraphia. In addition he was aggressive, pedantic, and critical of many women, of whom he refered to as harlots. He also had other symptoms of epilepsy in general, including "fainting" spells and episodes of mutism.

Paul. The apostle Paul was raised as a religious Jew in the Pharisean sect devoted to purity of faith. Up until the time of his religious conversion, he had a notorious reputation for the thoroughness with which he hunted down and persecuted Christians. [37] During this period he was called "Saul." This was completely changed by a dramatic incident on the road to Damascus [46] in about 34 A. D. :

> As he neared Damascus in the course of his journey, suddenly a light from heaven flashed round him; he dropped to the ground and heard a voice saying to him "Saul, Saul, why do you persecute me? "Who are you?" he asked. "I am Jesus," he said "and you persecute me. Get up and go into the city; there you will be told what you are to do..."
>
> Saul got up from the ground, but though his eyes were open he could see nothing, so they took his hand and led him to Damascus. For three days he remained sightless, and neither ate nor drank.
>
> *Acts 9:3–6, 8, 9*

After three days he was visited by Ananias, a Damascus Christian, who laid his hands on him and welcomed him:

> In a moment something like scales fell off his eyes, he re-gained his sight, got up and was baptized. Then he took some food and felt strong again.
>
> *Acts 9:18, 19*

Some evidence that St. Paul had multiple seizure-like episodes comes from his letter to the church in Corinth 22 years earlier where he described multiple visions and called his illness a "thorn in the flesh" and from Satan.

> My wealth of visions might have puffed me up, so I was given a thorn in the flesh, an angel of Satan to rack me and keep me from being puffed up; three times over I prayed to the Lord to relieve me of it, but he told me, "It is enough for you to have my grace; it is a weakness that my power is fully felt."
>
> *2 Corinthians 12:1–9*

Interpretation of parts of the epistles of Paul suggests his facial motor and sensory disturbances were coming after ecstatic seizures and that his religious conversion occurred as a result of ecstatic visions associated with TLE. [37,46,66,67]

Paul was critically important in spreading the message of Christianity in the time following the death of Jesus. He was responsible for the Christian traditions such as giving up animal sacrifice and substituting the remembrance of the sacrifice of Jesus on the Cross; the substitution of wine as symbolic of the blood of Christ in place of blood from sacrificed animals; the elimination of the Jewish custom of circumcision in order to attract Gentiles; and the concept that Christ had died for their sins and that those sins would be forgiven. If it was not for these efforts and for the prolific writings of Paul, it is likely that Christianity would never have progressed beyond a tiny Roman religious sect. If the role of TLE in Paul's conversion is correct, it could be argued that without TLE Christianity would never have become the dominant religion of the Western world.

Teresa of Jesus. Garcia [68] has suggested that the vivid ecstasies of the Carmelite nun, Teresa of Jesus (Teresa de Ahumanda) were due to TLE.

Joan of Arc. For centuries romantics, historians, and scientists have debated the mystery of Joan of Arc's exceptional achievements. Foote-Smith and Bayne [69] wondered how an uneducated farmer's daughter, raised in harsh isolation in a remote village in medieval France, could have found the strength and resolution to alter the course of history. Based on her own words and the contemporary descriptions of observers, they suggested that the source of her visions and convictions was ecstatic TLE auras. In her own words from the text of her trial in Rouen in 1431, she states: [70]

> I was thirteen when I heard a Voice from God for my help and guidance. The first time that I heard this Voice, I was very much frightened; it was mid-day in the summer, in my father's garden....I heard this Voice to my right, towards the Church: rarely do I hear it without its being accompanied also by a light. This light comes from the same side as the Voice. Generally it is a great light....When I heard it for the third time, I recognized that it was the Voice of an Angel....It told me it was necessary for me to come into France...it said to me two or three times a week: "You must go into France."...It said to me "Go, raise the siege which is being made before the City of Orleans. Go!"...and I replied that I was but a poor girl, who knew nothing of riding or fighting....There was never a day when I do not hear this Voice, and I have much need of it.

These visions came upon her with increasing frequency and sustained her though the reversal of her military victories, betrayal, imprisonment, and trial. [69] A logical diagnosis would be to simply assume she had schizophrenia or a related thought disorder. However, the authors argue that her testimony was marked by caution, modesty, reasonableness in dealing with others, and clarity of thought; the episodic nature of her visions with clear sensorium interictally; the presence of a musicogenic form of epilepsy; and an ecstatic aura—all argue for TLE.

Patients with musicogenic epilepsy have seizures that are precipitated by music, especially music that has some emotional significance to the patient. [71] They may have only a brief disturbance of consciousness. In Joan of Arc's case the evidence suggests the music that induced her seizures was from church bells. She stated to the judges that she heard the voices when *Ave Maria* was played by church bells in the evening. Often when she was in the fields and heard the church bells ring, she would fall to her knees." [70] Such a type of musicogenic epilepsy has been described. [72] There is even evidence that sometimes her episodes were self-induced, since she "was accustomed to repair daily to the church at the time of Vespers, or toward evening. She had the bells rung for half an hour." [70] Joan's first reaction to her voices and apparitions was one of fright, followed by ecstasy, followed by grief and tears when the apparitions vanished. As described above, it is not unusual for patients with ecstatic seizures to attempt to precipitate more seizures. Once she had determined to accept and embark on her mission, she appeared to be in a state of chronic exhilaration. [69] Her enthusiasm was so intense that it overwhelmed the English soldiers. Joan of Arc appeared to have other aspects of the 4-H syndrome, including humorless sobriety, hypermoralism, hyposexualism, aggression, and religiosity.

Dostoevsky. Fyodor Dostoevsky, the famous Russian novelist, also appears to have had musicogenic epilepsy. [69] The following is an account of a friend relating an argument that Dostoevsky, a believer, was engaged in conversation with an atheist:

> "God exists, He exists!" Dostoevsky finally cried, beside himself with excitement. At that same moment, the bells of the neighboring church rang for Easter matins. The air was vibrant and full of sound, "And I felt," Fyodor narrates, "that heavens have come down to earth and absorbed me. I really perceived God and was imbued with him. Yes, God exists….I cried…and I do not remember any more." [69]

Joseph Smith. Joseph Smith was the founder of the Mormon Church. In the spring of 1820 he was seized with some strange power which rendered him speechless. Darkness gathered around him, and he was greatly afraid. He wrote: [73]

> Just at this moment of great alarm I saw a pillar of light exactly above my head, above the brightness of the sun, which descended gradually until I found myself delivered….When the light rested above me, I saw two personages, whose brightness and glory defy all description, standing above me in the air. One of them spake into me….When I came to myself again, I found myself lying on my back looking up at the heaven.

These circumstances are strongly suggestive of TLE. [37]

Ellen White. Ellen White, born in 1827, was the co-founder of the Seventh-Day Adventist Movement. As a nine-year-old child she was hit in the face with a rock, leaving her in a stupor for three weeks. Following this injury her friends shunned her because of her disfigured face. Her personality changed and she became an avid Bible student and an intensely religious person. She complained of impaired memory, nervousness, trouble concentrating, and fatigue and was unable to complete her formal education. When she was 12, her family became involved in the Millerite movement, members of which called themselves Adventists. A Baptist preacher, William Miller, predicted the second coming of Christ in 1844. When this did not occur it was termed the "great disappointment of 1844." With the guidance of Ellen White, Miller's disillusioned followers formed the Seventh-Day Adventist church. They also predicted the second coming of Christ but wisely did not specify exactly when this would occur.

Based on the presence of head injury, paroxysmal loss of consciousness, upward staring of the eyes, hundreds of visual hallucinations, mood and personality changes, automatisms, and hypergraphia, Hodder and Holmes[74] concluded that Ellen White had TLE. Her hypergraphia was prodigious, consisting of 5,000 periodical articles and 40 books totaling over 100,000 pages of text. Some of her writing was subsequently found to have been plagiarized from earlier religious writers.[75] Attributing White's visions, religiosity, and writing to TLE was clearly disturbing to Seventh-Day Adventists. In response to the Hodder and Holmes report, the trustees of the Ellen G. White Estate appointed a committee to examine whether she had TLE. Eight of the nine members of the committee were professors from Loma Linda University School of Medicine and Nursing, a prominent Seventh-Day Adventist school in Southern California. Not surprisingly, although not denying any of her symptoms, they concluded her writing was a divinely inspired gift of prophecy and that she did not have TLE.[76]

Other cases. In 1873, Howden published five cases of intense religiosity occurring in epileptics. He included Swedenborg, Sweden's math genius who at age 56 underwent a transformative spiritual event that was probably the result of a seizure.[77,78] He developed a messianic psychosis and subsequently spent the remaining 28 years of his life exploring the spirit world and describing his experiences in an extensive body of writings. Howden also concluded that Ann Lee, founder of the Shaker Movement, and the Islamic prophet, Mohammed, founder of Islam, had TLE.

Dewhurst and Beard[37] provided an extensive list of saints and mystics who probably had TLE. They had periodic attacks that included sensations of extreme heat and cold, trembling of the whole body, transient aphasia or paralysis, loss of consciousness, automatisms, feelings of passivity and childish regression, dissociations, hallucinations, ecstasies, and increased suggestibility. Saver and Rabin[3] have further extended the list.

> **Temporal lobe epilepsy and its spiritual manifestations may have played a major role in the religious conversions of many historical figures and in the origin of several religions.**

Near-Death Experiences

Some individuals who have come very close to dying, or who have been clinically dead for varying periods of time, report profound spiritual sensations and feelings. After they recover they often report significant changes in their attitude about God, religion, death, and personal relationships. Raymond Moody first wrote of these episodes in 1975 in his book, *Life After Life*.[79] He termed them "near-death experiences" or NDE. In those who have had NDE some of the common features include a feeling of extraordinary peace, out-of-body experiences, a sensation of being in a tunnel often ending by experiencing a brilliant white or golden light, and the "inner setting."[80] The "inner setting" refers to a feeling of being in heaven or a comparable setting such as being surrounded by flowers, trees, mountains, rivers, or streams.

Each of these symptoms is progressively less common in NDE with the extraordinary peace occurring in 60 to 75 percent, and "the inner setting," in 10 to 35 percent. Some experience a review of their past life, somewhat reminiscent of the re-playing of the tape in Penfield's studies. Grasso noted that similar NDE reports are obtained from a wide variety of subjects: "...believers and atheists, the educated and the ignorant; from old and young, saint and sinner, man and woman."[81]

NDE in pilots. This remarkable set of experiences has led many to propose that the events associated with NDE prove that heaven and God exists. A more sober and scientific account of the physiological events surrounding NDE have come from studies of the artificial induction of NDE in the laboratory. James Whinnery, an aerospace medicine physician, was asked by the navy and air force to come up with a solution to the problem of pilots blacking out during jet plane maneuvers. They were experiencing G-force-induced loss of consciousness known as *G-LOC*. To study this phenomenon a huge centrifuge was built at the Naval Warfare Center in Warminster, Pennsylvania. This centrifuge was large enough to hold a pilot and powerful enough to produce high G-forces. Extensive studies over many years identified the precise G-forces needed to produce varying durations of unconsciousness.[82] The wearing of an anti-G suit decreased length of unconsciousness and increased tolerance to higher G-forces.

Many of the pilots had an out-of-body experience while they were unconscious. Not being familiar with OBE, Whinnery referred to these as "dreamlets." In reviewing the literature he came upon the reports of NDE in patients with heart attacks and realized that this was what a number of his pilots were experiencing. The longer the period of unconsciousness and the closer they got to brain death, the greater the probability they had NDEs. The transition from grayout to unconsciousness resembled floating peacefully within a dark tunnel, which is much like some of the defining characteristics of an NDE. The pilots also reported a feeling of peace and serenity as they regained consciousness.[83] Moderate degrees of lack of oxygen (anoxia) preferentially affect the frontal lobes and it has been suggested that this is responsible for the feelings during NDEs of calm and a tranquil indifference to anything including pain.[84p192]

When G-LOC was produced gradually, it produced tunnel vision, then blindness, then blackout. This can be explained by progressive loss of blood flow to the occipital lobes producing tunnel vision, then loss of blood flow to the retina producing black-out, then anoxia for the rest of the brain, producing a total loss of consciousness. While in the centrifuge, if the pilots pressed on their eyes to increase the intraocular pressure and interfere with ocular blood flow they experienced greyout and tunnel vision.[85] The feelings of serenity and peace are likely to have been produced by the increased release of various neurotransmitters such as endorphins, serotonin, and dopamine. Thus, rather than proving that God exists, NDE proves that when the brain is deprived of oxygen for prolonged periods of time, immediately prior to brain damage a range of physiological events occur that characterize NDE. Support for the role of anoxia in the production of NDEs comes from the observation that one of the very few other things to produce NDEs is prolonged exposure to carbon dioxide. This was used to treat nervous diseases in the 1950s.[86] Since it produced severe anoxia and risked brain damage, it was discontinued. While this was long before there was an appreciation of NDEs, it was probably the resultant NDEs that produced the positive changes in behavior described below.

A person actually needs to be near death to have an NDE. Melvin Morse studied NDE in children. His interest in NDE was stimulated by an experience he had during his pediatric residency in Seattle. He performed CPR on Katie, a child that had drowned in a swimming pool and had been without a heartbeat for 19 minutes. Her pupils were fixed and dilated. Three days later Katie regained consciousness. Several weeks later he encountered her in the hospital and Katie turned to her mother and said, " That's the guy who put the tube in my nose at the swimming pool." Morse was stunned, since the child was essentially brain-dead at the time. His report[87] was the first description of NDE in a child.

Morse went on to accumulate and study many additional cases of NDE in children[88-91] and to write several books on the subject including *Closer to the Light*[92] and *Transformed by the Light.*[93] In what has been termed the Seattle study, Morse interviewed 160 children from the intensive care unit at Children's Hospital in Seattle.[91,92] He used the 16-item Greyson scale[94] to quantitate the NDEs. Of the children who had experienced near-death, 88 percent had an NDE. By contrast, none of the other children had an NDE. This was the first clear demonstration that a person actually needs to be near death to have an NDE. Morse excluded a role for any of the drugs they were given, or dreams, or hallucinations. Some of the cases were able to do what Katie did, recount aspects of the experience and of the doctors and nurses they only had contact with when they were in deep coma and apparently dead.

NDE induced permanent changes in personality. Scientific explanations of the physiology of NDE do not detract from the fact that NDEs also produce remarkable changes in personality and spirituality. Exposure to death in traumatic situations such as in combat is often associated with *post-traumatic stress disorder (PTSD).* This is a debilitating psychiatric condition characterized by flashbacks; avoidance of stimuli associated with the trauma; and symptoms of increased arousal, including insomnia, irritability, difficulty concentrating, hypervigilance, and exaggerated startle response.[95] Substance abuse is also very common.[96] In dramatic contrast to this, in individuals who have actually died, been brought back to life, and had an NDE, the experience was not associated with the dysfunctional stress reactions typical of PTSD. Instead NDE was associated with better mental health and positive coping styles.

Raymond Moody based his psychiatric practice around counseling individuals with NDEs. The personality changes he observed in individuals who had experienced an NDE included a loss of the fear of dying, a sense of the importance of love in their lives, a sense of being connected with all things, an appreciation of learning, an urgency to experience life, a new feeling of being in control, and a better-developed sense of spirituality with the abandonment of religious doctrine purely for the sake of doctrine.[97] He recounts the following story of a man who studied in the seminary before his NDE:

> My doctor told me I "died" during the surgery. But I told him that I came to life. I saw in that vision what a stuck-up ass I was with all that theory, looking down on everyone who wasn't a member of my denomination or didn't subscribe to the theological beliefs that I did.
>
> A lot of people I know are going to be surprised when they find out that the Lord isn't interested in theology. He seems to find some of it amusing, as a matter of fact, because he wasn't interested at all in anything about my denomination. He wanted to know what was in my heart, not my head.

Moody also recounts the following as an example of a significant personality change in an adult with NDE:[97p51-52]

> When I "came back" [from the NDE], no one quite knew what to make of me. When I had my heart attack, I had been a very driven and angry type A personality (aggressive, impatient and selfish). If things didn't go right for me, I was impossible to live with. That was at home as well as work. If my wife wasn't dressed on time when we had some place to go, I would blow up and make the rest of the evening miserable for her. Why she put up with it, I don't know. I guess she grew accustomed to it over the years, though, because after my near-death experience she could hardly cope with my mellowness. I didn't yell at her any more. I didn't push her to do things, or anyone else for that matter. I became the easiest person to live with and the change was almost more than she could bear. It took a lot of patience on my part—which is something I had never possessed before—to keep our marriage together. She kept saying, "You are so different since your heart attack." I think she really wanted to say, "You've gone crazy."

When Melvin Morse re-interviewed the parents of children with NDE eight years later, he found these children had become special teenagers who had excellent relationships with their families. They seemed to share a maturity and wisdom that was humbling.[92p193] There was a conspicuous absence of drug abuse and even experimentation. There was little rebellion against authority, no excessive risk-taking, and no teenage pregnancies. They all had good grades. One child described himself as more serious than his peers, but a lot happier. One girl said she saw life differently than most people. Little things that bother others did not bother her. She felt calmer and more in control. Her mother described her as "serene" and "very mature for her age." As with others in the study she did not fear death, but wanted to make sure she "lives life to the fullest." Morse felt that the right temporal lobes were the site of the positive aspects of NDEs. [92,93]

Morse met Katie again 15 years later. When asked how much she remembered of the NDE her reply encapsulates many of the personality features of individuals with NDEs: [98p17]

> "Oh, I remember everything, every little detail, and they're images that are always with me. My life is richer for it and I work every day to share that richness with my family and friends. There's so much work to do in this life. I wouldn't waste a minute of it."

In a study of adults, Morse interviewed elderly people who had an NDE as children. He noted that: [93]

> Nearly all of the people who had a NDE—no matter if it was 10 years ago or 50 — were still absolutely convinced their lives had meaning and there was a universal, unifying thread of love which provided that meaning. Matched against a control group, they scored much higher on life-attitude tests, significantly lower on fear-of-death tests, gave more money to charity, and took fewer medications. There's no other way to look at the data. These people were just transformed by the experience.

In addition, these adults had less depression, lower rates of drug and alcohol abuse, spent more time meditating, ate more fresh fruits and vegetables, did more exercise, spent more time with family members, and had increased scores relevant to good mental health and spiritual well-being. [91] Some of the adults with childhood NDEs felt they had paranormal abilities such as predicting events just before they happen. [93p84-107] Moody [97] also found that a small percent of his NDE subjects felt they had experienced some form of precognition.

There is a very high successful suicide rate among individuals who have previously attempted suicide. However, the rate of subsequent successful suicide is greatly reduced in individuals who had an NDE during their suicide attempt. [99] Of those who survived a Golden Gate bridge jump and had an NDE, none went on to commit suicide. [100] When asked whether the findings of increased mental and spiritual health among those with NDEs had any relevance to the rest of us, Morse recounted several individuals whose own lives were enriched simply by having close emotional ties to someone with NDEs.

Prim van Lommel of the Rijnstate Hospital in Arnheim, the Netherlands, reported an eight-year longitudinal study of 344 cardiac-arrest patients who were clinically dead but revived. [101] Of these, 62 reported an NDE. With the possible exception of age, the only common thread was the experience of near-death. Extensive interviews and psychological tests were administered initially and after two- and eight-year intervals. Initially, those with NDEs reported more self-awareness, social awareness, and more religious feelings than those without NDEs. At two years, those with NDEs had a far more vivid recollection of the event, an increased belief in an afterlife, and less fear of death. After eight years, the effects seen after two years were more pronounced. The NDE group was more empathetic, emotionally vulnerable, and often showed evidence of increased intuitive awareness. They still showed no fear of death and held a strong belief in the afterlife.

Out-of-body experiences (OBE). An 11-year-old boy suffered a cardiac arrest in the hospital. He was without a heartbeat for 20 minutes. Seven years later he related the following: [92]

> The next thing I knew, I was in a room, crouched in a corner of the ceiling. I could see my body below me. I could see the doctors and nurses working by me. I saw a doctor put jelly on my chest. My hair was really messed up and I wished I had washed my hair before coming to the hospital. They had cut my clothes off, but my pants were still on. I heard a doctor say, "Stand back," and he then pushed one of the buttons on the paddles. Suddenly, I was back inside my body…

Morse [92] noted that NDE subjects could recall in great detail all aspects of the resuscitation procedure, including technical things they could not have known previously. By contrast, seriously ill but non-NDE subjects had only vague and often inaccurate recollections of the emergency room setting.

Some of the reports of OBE include remarkable, almost unbelievable statements. In one case [92] the patient claimed that while she was floating around above her body she noticed that there was a shoe on the ledge of the window. The skeptical physician looked and could not find it. The patient said, "It's out there, around the corner." It was only after the physician crawled out onto the ledge and looked around the corner that she saw the shoe. These OBE stories suggest that comatose patients who seem to be in the last stages of life may actually be undergoing a profound experience that involves total awareness of what is going on around them. [92]

The light. The following account from the International Association for Near-Death Studies (IANDS) [102] about a young girl who fell in her basement illustrates an experience with the light.

> I noticed the dim light growing slowly brighter. The source of the light was not in the basement, but far behind and slightly above me. I looked over my shoulder into the most beautiful light imaginable. It seemed to be at the end of a long tunnel which was gradually getting

brighter and brighter as more and more of the light entered it. It was yellow-white and brilliant, but not painful to look at even directly. As I turned to face the Light with my full "body," I felt happier than I ever had before or have since.

Another study was also from a young girl near death from a ruptured appendix.

Then the blackness was gone and in its place was a beautiful soft pink light. All the weight was gone, and I floated back up into the room as light as a feather. I seemed to be filled with this same light, which was the most profound spirit of love that you can imagine. Nothing has ever come near it since. I opened my eyes, and the whole room was just bathed in that beautiful light. In fact, the light completely surrounded everything in the room, so there were no shadows. I felt so happy....I heard my father say, "What's she looking at?" The light lasted for a little while and it was wonderful.

The NDEs and religious history. Just as examples were given above concerning the role of TLE in religious history, Morse [92p141-144] listed a number of examples where NDEs with the light shaped individuals' life-long religious and spiritual affiliation. In one case, one of his patients experienced a light that totally engulfed him after an NDE at age 15. After that he knew he wanted to become a minister, and 30 years later was a successful mainstream Protestant minister.

Black Elk, a Native American spiritual leader, had an NDE at age nine. At the heart of his experience he was on the highest mountain of them all, and beneath him was the entire world. A bright light surrounded the earth, "wide as daylight."

The Indian guru Paramahansa Yogananda, author of *Autobiography of a Yogi*, had an NDE at age eight. He states, "There was a blinding light, enveloping my body and the entire room. My nausea and other uncontrollable symptoms disappeared; I was well." This light then stayed with him the rest of his life allowing him to illuminate others.

Jonathan Edwards, the Calvinist theologian, speaks of a divine light imparted to the soul by God. Morse wondered where Edwards learned of such a light. Some research showed that he nearly died of pleurisy as a child. This could have produced an NDE.

The inner setting. Kurt was a seven-year-old boy dying of muscular dystrophy. He had a cardiac arrest in the hospital and found himself outside his body, watching the doctors and nurses work to revive him.

Then everything became dark, until I saw angels. I was in a beautiful place with flowers and rainbows, where everything was white like it had its own light. I talked to several people while I was there, including Jesus, who wanted me to stay with him. I wanted to stay but we decided I had to come back and see my parents again. I'm not afraid to go back to that place.

This was a common theme, of feeling so peaceful that the subjects did not want to come back.

NDE and the temporal lobes. Many of the features of NDE suggest the temporal lobes are involved. This includes the findings that stimulation of the temporal lobes can produce out-of-body experiences and feelings of great meaning and being connected to a greater force, [15,18,103,33] the many spiritual aspects of TLE, and the permanent nature of the interictal personality changes. Acute and moderate-to-severe anoxia produces abnormal nervous activity in the temporal lobes [104] and especially the hippocampus. [105-107] These factors suggested to Britton and Bootzin [108] that altered temporal lobe functioning may be involved in individuals who reported having transcendental NDEs during life-threatening events. To test this they examined 43 individuals who had a significant life-threatening event, had NDE symptoms, and had a minimum score of seven on Greyson's *Near-Death Experience Scale.* [94] They also examined 20 controls who had a life-threatening experience but scored less than seven on Greyson's scale. The presence of general symptoms of epilepsy and specific symptoms of TLE was assessed by administering the *Complex Partial Epileptic Signs and the Temporal Lobe Symptoms* sub-scales of the *Personal Philosophy Inventory.* [109] The subjects were also given an EEG during sleep and monitored for the timing of onset of rapid eye movement or REM sleep.

Paroxysmal EEG activity was found in 22 percent of the NDE subjects compared to five percent of the controls. In all NDE subjects this activity emanated from the left temporal lobe, while in the controls it emanated from the right temporal lobe. As shown in Figure 9 the NDE subjects had significantly higher scores on both the *Complex Partial Epileptic Signs* and the *Temporal Lobe Symptoms* tests. The scores on both tests were significantly higher in the subjects with NDEs.

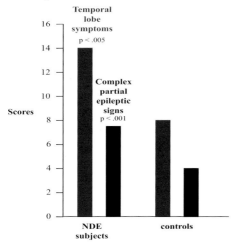

The results from the sleep studies provided some insight into why individuals with NDEs are more centered and resistant to stress. The NDE subjects had altered sleep patterns with a longer interval between the onset of sleep and rapid eye movements or REM, relative to the control group. Individuals with depression characteristically have a short sleep to REM interval averaging 60 minutes or less. A short sleep to REM interval has, in fact, proven to be an

Figure 9. Scores on the Temporal Lobe Symptoms *and* Complex Partial Epileptic Signs *scales in the subjects with NDE and controls. From Britton and Bootzin, Near-Death Experiences and the Temporal Lobe.* Psychological Science. *15: 254-258, 2004. By permission from Blackwell Publishing.*

excellent predictor of the risk of developing a major depression. The average interval is 90 minutes. In the controls without an NDE it averaged 77 minutes, while in those with NDE it averaged 109 minutes. While the cause of this increased REM latency is not known, it is likely to be related to the presence of less depression, the increased resistance to stress, and a more-spiritual outlook toward life.

> **Individuals with near-death experiences (NDE) have many features with a strong spiritual content including a feeling of great peace, depersonalization or out of body sensations, changes in visual perception interpreted as passing down a dark tunnel and coming out into a bright light, a review of one's life, and a feeling of seeing God and being in heaven. As with other forms of spiritual awakening, NDEs are often associated with a permanent decrease in an individual's susceptibility to depression and fear of death, improved overall mental health, increased tolerance of stress, and a greater appreciation for the spiritual aspects of life.**

Mechanism of NDEs. Many have claimed that NDEs prove that God, a life after death, and heaven exist. However, the above studies showing that many of the elements of NDE can be produced in pilots when gravity-induced loss of consciousness is severe or prolonged, strongly implicate oxygen deprivation (anoxia) as a major factor. This is supported by the findings of Morse[91,110] that a person actually needs to be near death to have a NDE. The studies of Britton and Bootzin[108] indicate that the temporal lobes, amygdala, and hippocampus are involved.

Studies in rats have shown that a lack of oxygen results in an increase in the concentration of glutamate and aspartate in the hippocampus.[107] These excitatory neurotransmitters are related to N-methyl-D-aspartate (NMDA) that plays a central role in memory. NMDA binds to NMDA receptors. In humans, the anesthetic ketamine induces a detached depersonalized state, positive and negative symptoms of schizophrenia, and OBEs.[111-113] It is similar to the street drug PCP (phencyclidine) and is one of the few drugs known to reproduce some of the features of NDEs. Two compounds have been isolated in animals that are produced by the brain, bind to PCP receptors and have actions similar to PCP.[114,115] These are called alpha- and beta-endopsychosin (endo = produced internally, psychosin = psychosis producing). Ketamine, PCP, alpha-, and beta-endopsychosin all act by blocking the action of the NMDA receptors by binding to the PCP domain of the receptor. The administration of these compounds reproduces several components of the NDE experience, including depersonalization, hallucinations, sensory deprivation, and elated mood. This blockage also helps to prevent the nerve damage that normally occurs when aspartic acid and glutamate are released after anoxia. Jansen[116,117] has proposed a reasonable explanation for the production of NDEs. This model suggests that in the presence of severe hypoxia, as occurs with NDEs, alpha- and beta-endopsychosins are released to attempt to prevent the hippocampal cells from dying following the release of glutamate and aspartate. This action at the NMDA receptors triggers the psychological and sensory aspects of NDEs. As discussed later, the release of DMT, or di-methyl-tryptamine, may also play a role in NDEs.

Endorphins also play a role in NDEs. The amygdala is the site of large concentrations of endorphin and enkephalin receptors. [118,119] Studies in dogs have shown that when the dogs were conscious at the time of cardiac arrest and subsequent death, there was a significant increase in brain endorphin levels. [120] This did not occur if the dogs were deeply anaesthetized at the time of death. In other animal studies, the administration of beta-endorphin into the cerebral spinal fluid produced a profound increase in neuronal activity in many parts of the limbic system at the same time that the animal became immobile. [121,122] These findings can account for the ability of this region of the brain to produce its own internal "high." Thus, instead of fear and terror there may be a state of calmness, peace, and even euphoria in the face of severe stress, pain or death. It has been suggested that, "It is this amygdala-induced opiate high that contributes to the feeling of religious rapture and the ecstasy associated with [feelings of a] life after death and the attainment of Nirvana." [16] It is likely that the release of endorphins and hypoxia of the prefrontal lobes [84p192] contribute to the pain-free bliss of NDEs. [123,124]

> **As much as some would like to use NDEs as proof that God, heaven, and a life-after-death exists, NDEs are most likely due to severe lack of oxygen to the brain. In the hippocampal portion of the temporal lobes this results in the release of two excitatory neurotransmitters, glutamate and aspartic acid, both of which cause nerve cell death. In a last ditch effort to prevent this, two endogenous psychedelic compounds are released — alpha- and beta-endopsychosin. Although they bind to and block the action of the NMDA receptors, thus preventing or delaying nerve cell death, they also produce spiritual sensations. This, in combination with the release of endorphins, produces a pain-free state of peaceful bliss. This biological explanation in no way detracts from the power of NDEs to produce life-long spiritual changes.**

REM Dreams and the Right Temporal Lobe

The four major types of human EEG waves are shown in Figure 10. They include beta waves typical of the alert waking state, alpha waves typical of a relaxed or reflecting mental state, theta waves occurring when individuals are in a drowsy state, and the slow delta waves typical of dreamless sleep. Two of the five stages of sleep are Rapid Eye Movement (REM) and non-REM sleep. EEG recordings during non-REM sleep show slow, synchronized, delta waves. By contrast REM sleep occurs during what is termed *paradoxical sleep* because electrically the brain seems active and alert, showing a beta wave pattern. [125] When individuals wake up during REM sleep they typically report that they have been dreaming. By contrast, when individuals wake up during non-REM periods they only occasionally report they have been dreaming. [126] The content of the dreams is also different. REM sleep dreams typically involve a great deal of visual imagery, emotion, and often involve implausible themes, while non-REM dreams tend to involve words and are speech-oriented with rambling monologues in the absence of visual imagery. [16,126,127]

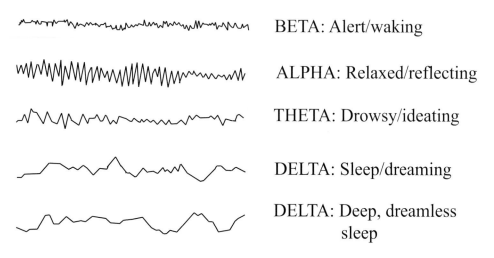

BETA: Alert/waking

ALPHA: Relaxed/reflecting

THETA: Drowsy/ideating

DELTA: Sleep/dreaming

DELTA: Deep, dreamless sleep

Figure 10. The four types of human EEG waves.

The positive effect of near-death experiences on sleep and REM latency raises the question, "What part of the brain is activated by REM versus non-REM dreams?" Given their content, it should not come as a surprise that EEG recordings show that the right hemisphere becomes highly active during REM sleep, while the left hemisphere is more active during non-REM sleep. [128,129] Brain imaging studies also support this and show greatly increased blood flow in the right temporal and parietal regions during REM sleep and in subjects who upon awakening report visual and auditory dreaming. [16,130]

Magnetic Brain Stimulation of the Temporal Lobes and Spirituality

Persinger describes an event that occurred in his laboratory. [131]

> In 1983 during a routine EEG study to monitor the effects of transcendental meditation, an experienced instructor of that technique displayed an electrical anomaly over her right temporal lobe. During an "electrical seizure," she reported she was "filled with the spirit" and felt the presence of God with her in the laboratory. The duration of the electrical transient was about 20 seconds.

To my knowledge this is the only record of a TLE-related "God Experience" that actually occurred during EEG monitoring. A portion of that EEG is shown in Figure 11. Persinger wondered if this experience could be experimentally induced. Since the brain is essentially a giant electrical machine with nerve impulses traveling across billions of axons and dendrites, the application of magnets to different parts of the skull might be expected to elicit various types of symptoms and sensations. This

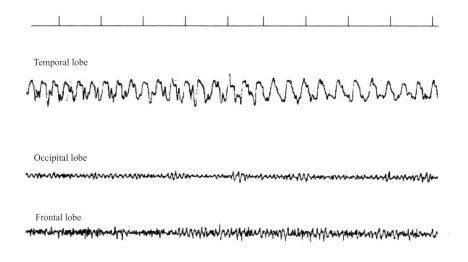

Temporal lobe

Occipital lobe

Frontal lobe

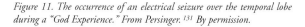

Figure 11. The occurrence of an electrical seizure over the temporal lobe during a "God Experience." From Persinger. [131] By permission.

technique is called *Transcranial Magnetic Stimulation* (TMS). It has become a popular tool for possible diagnosis and treatment of a range of conditions. When Persinger applied such a machine to his own brain, over the right temporal lobe, he found to his amazement that he experienced God for the first time. [62] Persinger [131,132] has since carried out experiments using these magnets on over 500 individuals over a period of 15 years. When the magnets were placed over the temporal lobes of normal individuals, it was reported that 80 percent had a mystical-sensed presence of a sentient or emoting being, often interpreted as the presence of God. This was referred to as the *God Machine*. These results, however, are controversial.

Granqvist and colleagues [133] in Sweden felt that since these results had not been replicated and since the magnets were very weak, a confirmatory double-blind study needed to be done. They carried out a study with 89 subjects, including a sham-treatment control group. All subjects were given a range of personality tests including the *Temporal Lobe Signs Inventory,* [134] the *Tellegen Absorption Scale* [135] to measure susceptibility to suggestion, and a *New Age Orientation Scale* [136] to assess individual differences in the adoption of a new age lifestyle orientation, with respect to broad systems of thought, as well as more specific beliefs, interests, and activities. They found no evidence for any effect of the magnets either in the entire group or in those scoring high on suggestibility. The authors suggested that the previous results were due to suggestibility and a subtle desire to please the experimenters.

A positive aspect of the study was their finding that the level of suggestibility consistently predicted the mystical and somatosensory experiences in both religious and non-religious participants. These characteristics included absorption to mind-altering experiences, the adoption of a "new age" lifestyle orientation, and signs of anomalous temporal lobe activity. This is consistent with the conclusion (see later) that *normal individuals in the population may have temporal lobe transients and that these may play a role in our spiritual experiences.*

In response to these results, Persinger [137] suggested that it was necessary to be exposed to the magnet for longer than 15 minutes to produce an effect. In reply to this, Granqvist [137] pointed out that in setting up their study, they had worked closely with Persinger; they had even used his apparatus and software. In addition, their experimental design involved a total of 30 minutes of exposure to the magnets. They also pointed out that despite claims to the contrary, none of the Persinger studies had been truly double-blinded. John Horgan, a skeptical science writer, had Persinger try the machine on him. He felt no effect. [138]

This exchange of studies and responses is in the best tradition of science. It illustrates how critical it is to carry out careful double-blind experiments when working with subjective traits such as perceiving the presence of a superior being. This study in no way negates the many results reviewed in this chapter concerning the role of the temporal lobes in spirituality. It does, however, show that caution and double-blind studies are required when claims are made that tend to induce skepticism from our rational brain.

LSD, the Temporal Lobes, and Spirituality

We have seen that hallucinations associated with the direct stimulation of the brain, with spontaneous seizures of TLE, with brain trauma, stress, and schizophrenia all emanate from the temporal lobes, especially the area of emotional memory, the amygdala and hippocampus. Psychotropic drugs such as LSD represent the remaining major cause of hallucinations. Are temporal lobe structures also involved in LSD-induced hallucinations? The intensity of the sensory experiences resulting from the ingestion of LSD is illustrated in the following account: [16]

> About half an hour after taking it I began to notice the incredible clarity and vividness of my surroundings. Colors were brighter, plants seem to sparkle…and when I stopped and touched a leaf….I could feel its energy, its life….I could taste it through my fingers…and when I got to the park I was overwhelmed with the colors, the tastes, the smells. My eyes led me to one of the mountains surrounding the valley, and oh my God, I could see right through the mountain. It was like the molecular composition of the mountain was parting into separate molecules. I could see the spaces between the molecules which were all in a frenzy of activity…it was like I had X-ray vision and I could see right through the mountain and see the sky on the other side. I raised my hand to point to this incredible sight, and instead of one hand there were these trails of hands. It was then that I realized I could see through my hand. At first I

could see the incredible cellular structure of the skin, and then the molecular structure…the pulsating molecules themselves…then my sight penetrated the skin and I could see the blood vessels, and then my eyes penetrated the blood vessels and I could see the blood platelets and the white corpuscles—and I kept thinking: how could I never have noticed this before? I had forgotten that I had taken LSD.

Another description of an LSD trip illustrates the religious experiences that psychedelics can produce. This subject was a housewife in her early thirties. [139p261.] The guide who stayed with her for her trip took her into a garden.

I felt I was there with God on the day of the Creation. Everything was so fresh and new. Every plant and tree and fern and bush has its own particular holiness. As I walked along the ground the smells of nature rose to greet me — they were sweeter and more sacred than any incense. Around me bees hummed and birds sang and crickets chirped a ravishing hymn to Creation. Between the trees I could see the sun sending down rays of warming benediction upon this Eden, this forest paradise. I continued to wander through this wood in a state of puzzled rapture, wondering how it could have been that I lived only a few steps from this place, walked in it several times a week, and yet had never really seen it before.

Later she stated that, "Since that day I had brewing in me a sense of the relevance of that forest for the other areas of my life and the life of my family. For I have come to realize that my way of seeing and hearing and smelling the forest that way was greater than any way I had ever seen and heard and smelled before."

These descriptions give us insight into how spiritually transforming the experiences produced from alterations in the function of the temporal lobes can be. The production of similar images by a spontaneous TLE seizure could understandably result in a religious conversion. What is the mechanism of such powerful imagery? The LSD molecule is structurally similar to serotonin, a major neurotransmitter implicated in a range of behavioral disorders. It and other psychedelic drugs bind to serotonin 1A, 2A and 2C receptors. [140-142] Serotonin is an inhibitory neurotransmitter that normally inhibits the neurons of the amygdala and thus filters its sensory input so that we are not constantly bombarded by all the emotionally laden sounds, visions, memories and images stored there. LSD interferes with this action of serotonin by binding to the serotonin receptors in the amygdala and hippocampus. This interaction breaks down the filters and releases all the visual, auditory and emotional imagery as illustrated by the description of the above LSD trip.

The central role of serotonin in spiritual experiences was supported by a PET scan study of a series of 15 normal males. [143] The PET scan utilized a radioactive compound that, like LSD, also binds to serotonin 1A receptors. The hippocampus and the brain stem nuclei enriched in serotonin (raphe nuclei) were examined. The subjects were administered the *Temperament and Character Inventory (TCI)*. There was an inverse association between the amount of binding to the serotonin 1A receptor and the self-transcendence scale, a measure of spirituality. It is of note that over time the self-transcendence subscale is the most stable and at the same time one of the most variable of the TCI scales. [144] None of the six other subscales showed such a relationship. Thus, *lower levels of the serotonin receptor were associated with higher spirituality scores.* The authors speculated that *the several-fold variability in serotonin 1A receptor density may explain why people vary greatly in spiritual zeal.*

A role of the temporal lobes in LSD hallucinations is indicated by studies where subjects slated for temporal lobectomy were given LSD before and after the surgery. There was a decrease in the richness of perceptual changes after the removal of the temporal lobe. [145]

Most other psychedelic drugs also interact with serotonin receptors. An exception is salvatorin A, another drug that causes hallucinations. It belongs to the mint family and has been used for its psychoactive properties in traditional spiritual practices by the Mazatecs of Oaxaca, Mexico. This drug acts primarily on kappa endorphin receptors. [146]

Psychedelic drugs are clearly potent hallucinogens. Great spiritual properties have been attributed to them, especially by the "new age" culture. In one study of 206 observed sessions of psychedelic drug use, chiefly LSD and peyote, 96 percent of the subjects experienced religious imagery of some kind, 91 percent saw religious buildings, and 58 percent encountered religious figures. [147]

The vast majority of individuals using LSD experience some type of religious imagery.

DMT and Spirituality

In 1990, Dr. Rich Strassman, a clinical psychiatrist at the University of New Mexico, obtained permission from the Drug Enforcement Agency (DEA) and other regulatory agencies to study the effects of di-methyl-tryptamine (DMT), in human volunteers. He summarized these results in his book, *DMT: The Spirit Molecule.* [148] As shown in Figure 12, DMT is closely related to serotonin.

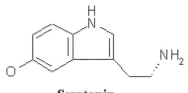

Serotonin

DMT differs from serotonin only in the presence of two methyl groups (CH3) instead of two hydrogen atoms on the N atom. Strassman was impressed with several unique characteristics of DMT. It was known to have psychedelic properties, to be normally present in the human brain, to be synthesized in the

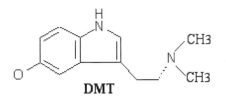

DMT

Figure 12. Serotonin and DMT.

pineal gland, and to be actively transported into the brain. Compounds do not have mechanisms to actively transport them across membranes unless they have some function in the brain. These properties indicated it was an endogenous psychedelic compound. [149] He wondered, "What was DMT doing in the human brain?" One intriguing possibility was that it was released during intense meditation or severe stress and was responsible for the feelings of spiritual transformations that can occur during meditation and with NDEs. Since it caused hallucinations, there was also a possibility that schizophrenia was due to a genetically caused excess production of DMT. DMT had been classified by the DEA as a category I drug. These are drugs that are potentially dangerous and addictive and have no known use in medical treatment.

Strassman launched a two-year effort to obtain permission from a wide range of regulatory agencies to study the clinical effects of DMT with the ultimate purpose of determining if it might be involved in schizophrenia, NDE, or meditation. He wondered if it might be the human spirituality molecule. This effort to obtain permission was eventually successful and carefully monitored, double-blind clinical studies were begun using individuals who were experienced users of psychedelic drugs such as LSD, psilocybin, and DMT. DMT is the hallucinogen in *ayahuasca,* a sacramental beverage used in some churches in South America. If drug-naïve subjects had been used, they might later sue him claiming he caused them to become dependent upon psychedelic drugs. This was avoided by using individuals who had previously used psychedelic drugs many times. This also avoided some of the "bad trip" problems of new psychedelic drug users.

In these studies DMT was given intravenously. While street users smoke DMT, this route was not used because it was difficult to determine the precise dose administered. DMT is short acting with the peak effect occurring in two minutes. The effects were usually noticed even before the injection was completed. Subjects felt they were coming down after five minutes. They could talk after 12 to 15 minutes and they felt relatively normal after 30 minutes. The following are some of the experiences related by the subjects receiving DMT. [148p146-149]

The IV dose gave a rush which some compared to a "freight train," "ground zero," or a "nuclear cannon." Almost all commented on the "vibrations," of a powerful energy pulsing through them at a very rapid rate and high frequency. There was a feeling of dissociation of body and mind, producing comments like, "I no longer have a body," "my body dissolved—I was pure awareness." Sometimes this was associated with a feeling of weightless motion: "I am falling," "lifting up," or "flying." The early effects often cause a sense of fear and anxiety lasting 15 to 30 seconds.

Visual images were the predominant sensory effects of a full dose of DMT. They ranged from kaleidoscopic, geometric patterns to "tremendously intricate tiny geometric colors, like being one inch from a color television." Some images had "Mayan," "Islamic," or "Aztec" qualities. Colors were brighter, more intense, and deeper than those of normal awareness or dreams. "It was like the blue of a desert sky, but on another planet. The colors were a hundred times deeper." The inability to tell which images were "in front" and which were "behind" led to a feeling of being in a "four-dimensional" world that was "beyond dimensionality." Specific images included "tunnels," "stairways," "ducts," "a DNA helix," and "a spinning golden disc." One group of remarkable sensations were collectively referred to as "contact," as in contact with aliens or non-human entities such as "spiders," "mantises," and "reptiles."

About half of the volunteers experienced auditory effects. Sounds were different and they heard things others did not hear. Some had an intensification of hearing, others became functionally deaf to distracting noises. They rarely heard voices or music. They heard non-word noises like "whining and whirring," "chattering," or "high-pitched noises."

Most subjects found the high-dose DMT exciting, euphoric, and extraordinarily pleasurable. For others the fear and anxiety were nearly unbearable, "menacing," and like "incredible torture." Another common effect was the loss of normal time perception. Almost all were surprised late in the session by how much time had passed.

The higher doses often caused a sense of complete loss of control. They felt utterly helpless and incapacitated. "I felt like an infant, helpless, unable to do anything." They also felt another "intelligence" or "force" directing their minds in an interactive manner. This was especially true of the contact with "beings." The following are specific statements made by some of the subjects: [148]

> "Something took my hand and yanked me. It seemed to say, 'Let's go!' Then I started flying through an intense circus-like environment. I've never been that out of my body before. We went though a maze at an incredible fast pace. I say 'we' because it seemed like I was accompanied."

> "If I could only hold onto this feeling. If everyone did this every day the world would be a much better place. Life would be a lot better. The potential for good was great. Feeling good within yourself. I guess meditation is supposed to get you to the same place."

> "There was a moment of color. The colors were words. I heard them saying 'God is in every cell of our body.'"

> "These experiences are like the height of meditation, accessing inner power and inner strength. I am in contact with something deeper and inside."

> "I felt a tremendous energy, brilliant pink light with white edges, building on my left side. I knew it was spiritual energy and love."

> "I feel very loved. It was a feeling in my chest. It was warm. My whole chest felt inflated. It was a really good feeling. I was loved by the entities or whatever they are. It was very pleasant and comforting." (In later conversations this person said it helped her by demonstrating that she

could lose control, particularly around a powerful man, and be safe and loved at the same time.)

Some of the "contact" experiences provide insight into the alien abduction reports, such as those related by the Harvard psychiatrist, John Mack in *Abduction: Human Encounters with Aliens.* [150] One of the DMT subjects stated: [148p192-197]

> They were trying to show me as much as possible. They were communicating in words. They were like clowns or jokers or jesters or imps. There were just so many of them doing their funny little thing. I settled into it. I was incredibly still and I felt like I was in an incredibly peaceful place. Then there was a message telling me that I had been given a gift, that this space was mine and I could go anytime. I should feel blessed to have form, to live. It went on forever. There were blue hands, fluttering things, then thousands of things flew out of those hands. I thought "What a show!" It was really healing.

Another related story:

> I felt like I was in an alien laboratory, in a hospital bed like this, but it was over there. A sort of landing bay, or recovery room. There were beings. They had a space for me. They weren't as surprised as I was. I was able to pay attention to every detail. There was one main creature, and he seemed to be behind it all. They activated a sexual circuit and I was flushed with an amazing orgasmic energy. A goofy chart popped up like an X-ray in a cartoon. When I was coming out I couldn't help but think "aliens."

Mack suggested that a *reconnection with spirituality* was at the heart of the abduction phenomena—sense of realness and the power of spiritual experiences. One of the most remarkable aspects of these DMT-induced contact experiences was how real they felt. The subjects knew these were drug-induced. However, if an individual had a spontaneous contact experience, triggered by personal crisis, trauma or loss, the realness of it could be overwhelming. This sense of realness was described by Strassman [148p200] as follows:

> The research subjects tenaciously resisted biological explanations because such explanations reduced the enormity, consistency, and undeniability of their encounters. How could anyone believe there were chunks of brain tissue that, when activated, flashed encounters with the beings, experimentation, and reprogramming? Neither did suggesting that it was a waking dream satisfy the volunteers' need for a model that made sense and fit their experience. One said, "This was not a dream or a hallucination. It was real. I can tell the difference. I couldn't have made it up if I wanted to." [148p314]

The same powerful sense of realness has been reported for NDEs, [151] hallucinations induced by the drugs ketamine and PCP, [116] and by hallucinations in general. The American Psychiatric Association notes that "a hallucination has the immediate sense of reality and true perception" and that "transient hallucinatory experiences are common in individuals without mental disorder." [152] These observations have clear implications for spiritual experiences in general and *provide insight into their power because they feel so real.* This relates to the issue of egocentricity discussed below, namely, "Since I experienced it, it was real." This intense sense of "feeling real" is understandable if we assume that the temporal lobes are the association areas for visual and auditory experiences. The vast majority of the time the hippocampal and amygdalar tape recorder for these experiences place into memory banks experiences that are real. In the rare cases where the experiences were internally generated, either as a spiritual experience or as a result of taking a psychedelic drug, the temporal lobes have no mechanism of distinguishing between the real and the unreal. It is as though everything coming to the temporal lobes is assumed to have really happened, to be real.

This conviction and sense of realness in the face of clear evidence of non-realness goes to the heart of the conflict between science and faith. Edmond O. Wilson claimed that you cannot tread the path of spirituality and the path of reason; you must choose between them. The DMT studies suggest this is not necessarily so since they show that even the sophisticated, science-savvy volunteers in this study felt and believed that the "contact" they experienced under DMT was not a dream, not a hallucination, but real. Thus, while the rational and the spiritual brain would always seem to be in conflict, this is not necessarily so.

It is simply necessary for the rational brain to understand that one of the characteristics of the spiritual brain is to strongly believe in something and have faith in something, even when the rational brain says it is unreasonable or that it did not and could not have happened. The rational brain needs to recognize that the spiritual brain can sometimes confuse externally generated reality with internally generated experience.

The rational brain needs to give the spiritual brain "its space," to have this faith without being derogatory and critical of its need to sometimes be irrational. It is like the marriage of an atheist to a theist—something that is perfectly possible and joyous as long as each respects the other's view of the world. These issues will be discussed again later in the part on science and religion.

The psychedelic drugs like DMT often produce a sensation of "contact," of being in the presence of and interacting with a non-human being. Highly intelligent and sophisticated test subjects who knew these feelings were drug-induced nevertheless insisted the contact had really happened. The temporal lobe-limbic system's emotional tape recorder sometimes cannot distinguish between externally generated real events and internally generated non-real experience thus providing a system in which the rational brain and

the spiritual brain are not necessarily in conflict. It is simply necessary for the rational brain to understand that one of the characteristics of the spiritual brain is to strongly believe in something, have faith in something, even when the rational brain says it is unreasonable or that it did not and could not have happened. The rational brain needs to give the spiritual brain "its space," to have this faith without being derogatory and critical of its need to sometimes be irrational.

DMT and hormone release. Strassman obtained blood samples from his subjects before and at varying times after the administration of DMT. The analyses showed that there was a sharp spike in levels of beta-endorphin, vasopressin, prolactin, growth hormone, and corticotrophin within minutes of the injection of DMT. [148p145] Corticotrophin stimulates the adrenal glands to release the stress hormone *cortisone.* It is likely that some of the psychological effects of DMT were secondary to increased release of one or more of these potent hormones.

DMT and serotonin. The consistent production of visual images, sounds, and fear indicate the primary effect of DMT is on the temporal lobes. In an effort to identify which serotonin receptors DMT was binding to, Strassman gave some of his subjects a second drug along with DMT. Two different drugs were used: pindolol, which is a serotonin 1A receptor antagonist, and cyproheptadine, a serotonin 2 receptor antagonist. While cyproheptadine had no effect, pindolol markedly enhanced the effect of DMT. This suggests that DMT was also acting as a serotonin 1A antagonist and when pindolol and DMT were given together, the psychogenic effect was enhanced. These results agree with the above PET studies showing a correlation between the spiritual transcendence score and the level of serotonin 1A receptors. Thus, DMT is likely to exert its effect by blocking the serotonin 1A receptors in the amygdala, hippocampus, and other areas of the temporal lobes.

The many similarities between DMT experiences, religious conversions, out-of-body experiences, NDEs, and alien abductions illustrate how all of these spiritual experiences can be generated by neurochemical events taking place inside the temporal lobes. It is little wonder that Strassman referred to DMT as the *Spirit Molecule.* It is also little wonder that psychedelic drugs have also been called *entheogens,* meaning *God-containing.* [138p20]

> DMT is made in the human brain and has been referred to as the *Spirit Molecule.* When given intravenously it produces a wide range of visual and auditory psychedelic and spiritual experiences that have many features in common with OBE, NDEs, alien abductions, depersonalization, derealization, "contact" with other beings, and other spiritual phenomena. Like LSD it appears to exert its effect by inhibiting serotonin receptors in the temporal lobes. The release of this endogenous psychedelic compound during periods of stress and other conditions could play a role in generating spiritual experiences.

Psilocybin and Spirituality

Psilocybin is another popular psychedelic drug. It is derived from the psilocybin mushrooms and has a duration of action of four to six hours. A double-blind study of the effects of psilocybin were carried out in 1962 by Walter Pahnke, a psychiatrist in a Harvard doctoral program on religion and society. [153] Twenty divinity students were the subjects. They received either psilocybin or a placebo. Because it was carried out in the Marsh Chapel on Good Friday it has been called the *Good Friday Experiment.* The results were dramatic. All ten subjects receiving psilocybin rated their experience much higher on mystical qualities than the placebo group. In addition, as with NDEs there were positive long-term effects with improved attitude, deeper religious faith, a more-loving attitude and empathy toward others, and a greater appreciation of life. [138,154,155] However, as with DMT, psilocybin could also produce fear, anxiety, and a terrifying sensation of dying.

In a study by Timothy Leary and colleagues of the effects of psilocybin, [156] one of the subjects wrote the following account:

> I also felt that the only reasonable way to live in the same world was to love and to realize that no one else will ever fully share or understand this basis of our actions, nor will we understand theirs. But the faith, which is completely sustained of and by itself within ourselves alone, is the basis of other's actions and provides the necessary consensus to achieve some sort of simultaneity of time and place in the universe. Love, and the faith in love, keep us from being cosmically alone.

Griffith and colleagues [156a] of Johns Hopkins University School of Medicine carried out a second double-blind study in 2006. None of the 36 volunteers had prior experience with psychogenic drugs. This had the advantage of avoiding a possible selective bias wherein individuals who had previously had a positive experience with hallucinogens might be more likely to volunteer for the study. When administered under supportive conditions, psilocybin produced experiences which were evaluated by the volunteers as having *substantial and sustained personal meaning and spiritual significance.* In a two-month follow-up, in contrast to the placebo (Ritalin), psilocybin produced significantly positive attitudes about life and themselves, positive mood changes, and altruistic and positive social effects.

As with most other psychedelic drugs, psilocybin is structurally similar to serotonin and binds to serotonin receptors. [157,158] The production of visual and auditory hallucinations, fear, and anxiety are consistent with an effect on the temporal lobes.

After Aldous Huxley took mescaline, the psychedelic compound present in some species of cactus, he was moved to write the *The Doors of Perception and Heaven and Hell.* [159] He suggested that visionary vegetables and the psychedelic drugs they contained could provide a new spiritual stimulation for the masses that was easier than going to church and safer than alcohol.

The Swiss psychiatrist Franz Vollenweidner has used PET scanning to examine the site of action of a range of psychedelic drugs. He showed that in addition to their effect on the temporal lobes and limbic system, psychedelic drugs frequently activated the frontal lobes. [160,161] These results were consistent with the important role of the frontal lobes in consciousness and the fact that the primary effect of all psychedelic drugs is to produce an altered state of consciousness.

Psychedelic drugs have also been called *psychotomimetic,* or *psychosis-mimicking.* The extensive studies of LSD in the 1960s, showing that a drug could reproduce many symptoms of schizophrenia, were the primary driving force responsible for launching the field of biological psychiatry and the de-emphasizing of Freudian psychoanalytic explanations of psychopathology. The role of abnormalities of brain chemistry in psychotic and neurotic disorders was further advanced by the discovery of drugs, such as Thorazine and Haldol, that were so effective in the treatment of schizophrenia that they literally emptied out the wards of psychiatric institutions for the chronically ill patients. Since these two drugs worked by blocking dopamine D_2 receptors, this led to one of the major chemical-based theories of schizophrenia – that of an excess of dopamine activity in some parts of the brain. This led Vollenweider to wonder if the psychedelic drugs that bind to serotonin 1A and 2 receptors might also have a secondary effect on brain dopamine levels. PET scans using radioactive agents that bind to dopamine receptors showed there was an increase in dopamine release in the basal ganglia. [162,163] Since dopamine is the pleasure neurotransmitter, it is likely that the increase in dopamine release was responsible for the elevated mood and feelings of peace, joy and pleasure that psychedelics and spiritual feelings can produce.

Right Temporal Lobe or Both Temporal Lobes?

Although many authors have emphasized the role of the right temporal lobe as the site of the spiritual brain, how strong is the evidence for this? The main differences between the left and right temporal lobes are that the left is involved in verbal skills of speech and language and in mathematics, while the right is involved in non-verbal skills and spatial orientation. Is there any more to the left-right dichotomy than this? It is clear from the studies of Penfield and of TLE that both temporal lobes are involved in psychical, spiritual, and religious feelings and experiences. On the basis of a range of studies, there are some unique attributes of the right hemispheres. Studies of individuals with lesions of the right hemispheres are especially valuable since they cut through the New Age myths to the reality of the neurological defects. For example, focal lesions of the right hemisphere impair non-word aspects of speech such as prosody. Prosody refers to aspects of speech such as intonation, pitch, rate, loudness, and rhythm. [164] An additional factor is the tendency for conversion hysteria to affect the left side of the body which is controlled by the right hemisphere. [165]

White matter in the right hemisphere. In 1980, based on blood perfusion studies, Gur [166] reported that there was more grey matter relative to white matter in the left hemisphere than in the right hemisphere, and the right hemisphere had more intermodal white matter nerve tracts. This result suggested that the left hemisphere tended to talk to itself while the right hemisphere tended to talk to the rest of the brain. This finding added to the mythology that the left-brain was the thinking and internally cognating hemisphere, while the right hemisphere was more open, communicative, intuitive, and holistically oriented. However, in 1999, Gur[167] revisited the issue using the much more sensitive and accurate MRI technique. This time the studies showed that there was in fact more grey matter in the left hemisphere, but this was mostly in men. There was slightly more white matter in the right hemisphere, but this was more so in women. Importantly, none of these differences were statistically significant. So much for the more holistic nature of the right hemisphere.

Self, spatial awareness, and the right temporal lobe. Spatial awareness has usually been attributed to the right parietal lobe. This idea has been based on the assumption that spatial neglect was typically associated with lesions of the right posterior parietal lobe. However, in monkeys, this disorder is due to lesions of the right or left superior temporal cortex. This seemed to present a puzzling species disparity. Karnath and colleagues from the Department of Cognitive Neurology in the University of Tübingen, Germany[168] carried out a careful analysis of 33 subjects with "pure spatial neglect." This showed that in humans the superior temporal gyrus (STG), not the posterior parietal cortex, was the location for spatial neglect. This STG area involved in spatial neglect is shown in Figure 13.

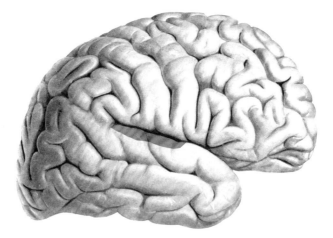

Figure 13. Superior temporal gyrus area for spatial neglect in humans. From Karnath et al.: Spatial awareness is a function of the temporal not the posterior parietal lobe. Nature. 411: 950-953, 2001.

Unlike monkeys, in humans the area of spatial neglect is localized to the right temporal lobe since the left temporal lobe is subserved for speech. The STG is located at the transition between the "what" and the "where" systems of visual processing. Since the STG receives polysensory streams from both of these areas, it is a site of multimodal sensory convergence. Karnath and colleagues concluded that in early hominids, both temporal lobes were involved in spatial awareness, but with evolution of speech spatial awareness shifted to the STG of the right temporal lobe, not to the right posterior parietal lobe.

Comparing the left portion of Figure 5, showing the areas on the right temporal lobe where Penfield elicited psychical responses, with Figure 13, indicates that Penfield's region shows a remarkable overlap with the area involved in the evaluation of the position of the "self" in space. This area is likely to play an important role in the out-of-body sensations and the depersonalization and derealization aspects of spiritual experiences.

Self, spatial awareness and limbic system. In addition to the role of the superior temporal gyrus in spatial orientation, specific parts of the limbic system also play a critical role. These are the hippocampus and a region between the hippocampus and the cortex called the *ectorhinal cortex*. The hippocampus contains "place cells" which fire when the individual is in a specific spatial location. These and other cells in the hippocampus provide a cognitive map of the layout of the environment. This map allows us to find our way back to a given site and even plan shortcuts. The ectorhinal cortex has "grid cells" which further refine knowledge of our position in space. [169] Thus, between the right superior temporal gyrus, the right and left hippocampus, and ectorhinal cortex, the temporal lobes play a major role in the of awareness of "self" in space.

Strassman eloquently defined the central role of spatial orientation in spiritual and mystical experiences. He proposed that the three pillars of a mystical experience were self, time, and space, with each undergoing a profound transfiguration.

> There is no longer any separation between the self and what is not the self. Personal identity and all of existence become one and the same. In fact, there is no "personal" identity because we understand at the most basic level the underlying unity and interdependence of all existence. Past, present, and future merge together in a timeless moment, the now of eternity. Time stops, in as much as it no longer "passes."...our self and time lose their boundaries, space becomes vast. Like time, space is no longer there but everywhere, limitless, without edges. Here and there are all the same. It is all here. [148p234]

In conclusion, the cortex of the left temporal lobe is specialized for verbal skills, including speech, reading and math, and the cortex of the right hemisphere, largely by default, is specialized for nonverbal skills, including spatial orientation and music appreciation. Other than this, there is nothing mysterious about the right hemisphere that gives it a valid reason to be exclusively reserved for spiritual and religious experiences. The left hemisphere also has an amygdala, a hippocampus, and an ectorhinal cortex and is fully capable of remembering meaningful emotional experiences, orienting the self in space and of spiritual expression.

With this background showing that the temporal lobes are often the neurological site of spiritual and religious feelings and experiences, we can now examine how three different investigators have interpreted these findings. Two of them have proposed a primary role for the right temporal lobe, as outlined above; it is clear that both temporal lobes are involved in spirituality.

Persinger, Temporal Lobe Transients, and the God Experience

Michael Persinger is a professor of psychology at the Laurentian University in Ontario, Canada. His major research interest is the clinical and experimental correlates of stimulation of the temporal lobes of mammals including man. In his book, *Neuropsychological Bases of God Beliefs*[1] he has proposed that each person's *God Belief* is composed of a combination of their *God Experiences* and their *God Concept*. The God Experiences are transient phenomena that are loaded with emotion.

> *God experiences* exist for a few seconds or minutes at any given time. Multiple experiences can occur in quick succession. During this period, the person feels that the "self," or some reference indicating "the thinking entity," becomes united or "at one" with the symbolic form of all space-time. It may be called Allah, God, Cosmic Consciousness, or even some idiosyncratic label. Slightly deviant forms include references to intellectual abstracts such as "mathematical balance," "consciousness of time," or "extraterrestrial intrusions."
>
> Usually the God Experience involves euphoria and positive emotions. The person reports a type of God-high that is characterized by a sense of profound meaningfulness, peacefulness, and cosmic serenity. Invariably the state is perfused with references to reduction of death anxiety. It is defined as the anticipated extinction of the self-concept or "the thinking entity." During the God Experience, the person suddenly feels that he or she will not die. Instead, he or she will live forever as a part or subset of the symbol of all space-time. If the symbol is a father image, then the person expects to become a child of the father. If the symbol is "imageless," the person expects to become part of a Universal Whole. [1p1-2]

Persinger has proposed that temporal lobe transients (TLTs), play a major role in peoples' most intense God Experiences and that the God Experience is a phenomenon that is associated with the construction of the temporal lobes. He does not view TLTs as the equivalent to the seizures of temporal lobe epilepsy but rather as "a normal and more organized pattern of temporal lobe activity." They may, however, represent some type of aberrant electrical activity deep within the temporal lobes suggesting that:

> *A biological capacity for God Experience was critical for the survival of the human species.* Without some experiences that could balance the terror of personal extinction, existence of the human phenomena called the "self" could not be maintained. It would have been fragmented by the

persistent, gnawing realization that death could come at any time. [1p12]

The first time that Persinger recorded a minor electrical event from the temporal lobe of a meditator and heard his reports of cosmic bliss, he was impressed with the impact of this change on the person's behavior.

> There was no convulsion of any kind, just a smile and the facial expressions of cosmic serenity. But the experience was compelling. The individual, depressed and forlorn before the episode, left with a fresh view of the world. For a few brief seconds, the person has mingled with the Great Mentality whose rudiments are found in every human culture. The person experienced a conviction shared by millions of other individuals. [1p16]

The *God Concept,* by contrast, is a learned view of one's religion or relation to God. It is a product of years spent as a child in Sunday school or a comparable form of religious instruction. It also embodies such verbal statements as, "I am a Christian," or "I am a Jew," or " I am a Muslim." Although both the God Experience and the God Concept are continuous variables, Persinger suggested that a person's God Belief system could be categorized into four major groups depending upon whether their God Experience and God Concepts were weak or strong.

Some people may have many God Experiences but primitive or poorly socialized God Concepts. They would be classified as mystics or eccentrics. Some may have never had a God Experience but have strong God Concepts as a result of frequent church, mosque, or synagogue attendance, starting at an early age and maintained by weekly attendance to maintain their God Belief.

Those with a poorly developed God Concept and no God Experiences would often be atheists, agnostics, or "spiritual but not religious" individuals. However:

> Even the professed atheist displays some form of God Belief. If the behavior of atheists rather than their verbal displays are measured, then God Beliefs are evident. There are still references to the relationship between the self and the extensions of space and time. Death may be a final termination, but this known finality can be a source of anxiety reduction for people with certain types of reward history. More often, the atheist simply substitutes the conventional God Concept for abstract forms of mysticism. The "Great Nothingness," is almost indiscriminable from the Cosmic Whole of some Asian religions. [1p3]

Finally, individuals who have both a strong God Concept and one or more God Experiences are totally convinced of the validity of their experiences and the absolute truth of the God Concept. They may kill or sacrifice themselves for its benefit, or proselytize others to believe that they have the only true belief system. They can represent the most rabid of the religious believers.

One of the most intriguing aspects of Persinger's analysis of the biological basis of religious experience are the different things that he proposed could set off the TLTs and produce spiritual feelings. They included hypoxia or lack of oxygen, low blood sugar, fever, illness, changes in cerebral blood flow, stress, a pounding beat, chanting, music, smells, and a range of drugs, especially psychedelic drugs such as LSD, peyote, mescaline, and different mushrooms. Hypoxia occurs at great heights and Persinger suggested that this might account for the fact that ancient religious figures were often known to climb to the tops of mountain. Woerlee [84] made the same point but related it to moderate hypoxia of the prefrontal lobes. At these heights, religious experiences took place. God spoke to the listener and gave special messages. For example, Moses went to the mountains to receive the ten commandments from God. While most yoga involves deep breaths, it can involve reduced breathing and Persinger felt that experienced meditators learned to control the production of TLTs.

Hypoglycemia was proposed as an especially popular method of producing the God Experience. Young initiates among American Indians were required to starve themselves until a God experience occurred and this single event influenced a person's life from then on. Wandering though the wilderness and quasi-starvation were popular Biblical techniques for obtaining the God Experience. Most communications with Jehovah occurred during protracted periods of effective starvation. As an example of a fever induced God Experience, Persinger [1p32] quotes the report of a young person with a severe case of scarlet fever:

> As I drifted in and out of consciousness, I felt I was going to die. Then suddenly I heard a voice say, "Don't worry, I am with you." I looked up and saw a soft white ray coming through the window. The voice said, "I am the Christ, through me there is salvation." I knew I had seen God. I was no longer afraid. When I awoke, my mother told me that two days had passed.

Stresses that are likely to produce God Experiences include death of the spouse or child, marriage, divorce, loss of a job or starting a new job or new responsibilities, being involved in a serious accident, leaving home for college, or a middle age crisis. Stress is likely to simulate TLTs though the release of pituitary hormones such as cortisol, vasopressin or oxytocin, or the release of neurotransmitters such as dopamine, serotonin, epinephrine, or endorphins. Most God Experiences occurring after stress, such as the death of a spouse, occur within one to four days of the death. It is common to experience the presence of the deceased person, smiling and stating, "Don't worry, I am in heaven with God." Persinger relates the following case of a woman whose husband, Fred, had died:

> I lay in bed trying to piece my life together. I lay there for hours. Suddenly, I felt Fred's presence beside me in the bed. I looked over and saw

him standing beside me. He was dressed in his old work clothes and had a big smile on his face. He said, "Don't worry, Maud, I'm in heaven now. God has let me come to you. All our friends are here too. It's all true, what we believed about God...this is only a temporary separation." I went to sleep and didn't wake for hours. The next day I felt good, the sun was shining again; there was meaning to my life. I know that God exists because I have experienced His presence.

This well illustrates the enormous degree of calming and relief of anxiety that a strong spiritual experience or God Experience can bring about. In some ways these experiences resemble NDEs with their potential to bring about long-term changes and increased resistance to stress.

Music can drive the epileptic brain into seizures and some music can probably drive the normal brain into TLTs, especially very loud music with clapping, chanting, singing, and vocalizations such as "Amens" or "Allah." These are very important elements of religious services and revivals in all religions. Sounds are probably especially powerful because of the central position of the auditory sensory cortex in the temporal lobes. Other repetitious movements such as swaying, dancing, bobbing forward and backward, bowing, or jumping are important. The repetitious genuflecting of both the Jewish and Islamic religions can stimulate the God experience. The critical feature is the monotony and rhythm of the movement.

Smell directly stimulates the olfactory lobe part of the limbic system. Perfumes, incense, and other aromatic compounds are examples. Just as the temporal lobes are the site of the auditory cortex association areas, they are also the site of the olfactory association areas.

Persinger also points out the importance of egocentrism. This does not refer to being egotistical or self-centered. This refers to the relative reliance placed on one's personal experience as proof of reality. Egocentrism is epitomized by the following:

> All of us assume that our experiences are real and true. [170] We presume our memories to be accurate representations of what has happened. We assume that if we perceive something, it must exist, or, if we have not experienced something, it does not exist.

Egocentricism has the advantage of strengthening one's faith based on one's own experiences. However, it has the downside of being used by organized religions to stoke the conviction that one's religion and one's God is the only religion and the only God. This attitude is the fodder of prejudice and the source of religious wars and religious terrorism.

A problem with the Persinger model is that it tends to pathologize spirituality and religion. Although in many cases these feelings and sensations may be the result of TLTs, everyone has the capacity for some degree of spiritual and religious experience, yet it is unlikely that everyone has some microform of temporal lobe epilepsy.

Speaking in tongues provides an example of a common learned trait that appears to stimulate the temporal lobes rather than the temporal lobes stimulating the behavior.

Speaking in Tongues (Glossolalia)

Speaking in tongues, or *glossolalia* (*glossa*—tongue, and *lalô*—speak) is one of the features of the charismatic Pentecostal churches. As outlined in the chapter on Pentecostals, the membership in these churches has rapidly expanded in the twentieth century, despite the shrinking memberships of many other denominations. This leads one to wonder why Pentecostalism is so popular? While some of the reasons are covered later, one reason may be the practice of speaking in tongues. This refers to the utterance of meaningless syllables producing what appears to be an unknown foreign or mystic language. The Pentecostals believe that speaking in tongues is a gift from God through the Holy Spirit. In fact, the term *charismatic* is derived from the Greek word *charis,* meaning a gift. This profound religious experience was believed both to come directly from the Holy Spirit and to provide proof for the existence of God.

The enormously spiritual nature of speaking in tongues raises the question of whether this might be yet another way of directly accessing the spiritual brain using a method produced by the believers themselves, rather than by the Holy Spirit. In other words, "Is glossolalia a divinely given trait or is it a self-learned skill?"

To address this question Spanos and colleagues [171] had 60 undergraduate students listen to a 60-second sample of glossolalia and then asked them to attempt to reproduce this pseudolanguage on their own. In this baseline trial 20 percent of subjects exhibited fluent glossolalia after this very brief exposure. After this, half of the subjects, termed the *trained subjects,* also received two additional training sessions including audio- and videotaped samples of glossolalia interspersed with a chance to practice glossolalia. Live modeling of glossolalia and direct instruction and encouragement were also provided. Of these trained subjects, 70 percent produced fluent glossolalia. The authors concluded that *glossolalia was a rapidly acquired, socially learned behavior, rather than a divinely inspired one.*

Since the speech center, the auditory cortex, and the emotional brain are all located in the temporal lobe, another question is, "Does glossolalia involve the temporal lobes of the brain?" One EEG study provided an answer to this question. Persinger [172] reported the occurrence of spikes within the temporal lobe of a member of the Pentecostal faith, during and only during protracted intermittent episodes of glossolalia. In the same paper he described the presence of a delta-wave dominant electrical seizure from the temporal lobe for about 10 seconds during a peak experience within a period of routine transcendental meditation by a TM teacher. He proposed that these cases were consistent with his hypothesis that transient, focal, epileptic-like electrical discharges in the temporal lobe, without convulsions, may be associated with strong spiritual and religious experiences.

Newberg and colleagues [178] performed SPECT brain imaging of five Pentecostal charismatic Christian women while they were singing or speaking in tongues there was a significant bilateral decrease in blood flow in the dorsolateral prefrontal cortices.

This was not present with simple singing. The result was interpreted as indicating less voluntary control over glossolalia than over singing. The only portions of the brain that showed increased activity for glossolalia compared to singing were the left superior parietal cortex and the amygdala of the right temporal lobe and limbic system.

Together, these studies suggest that glossolalia, like meditation, can provide a method by which normal individuals who are not mystics can activate their spiritual or emotional brain.

Speaking in tongues, as practiced by members of the charismatic Pentecostal churches, may provide an additional way for individuals to directly access their spiritual brain.

Julian Jaynes, God, and the Bicameral Mind

In 1976, the Princeton psychiatrist Julian Jaynes published a book entitled *The Origin of Consciousness in the Breakdown of the Bicameral Mind.*[173] By *bicameral mind* he meant a mind without a consciousness. Individuals without a consciousness had no sense of self and thus did not understand that their own thoughts and actions were generated from within themselves. To replace this deficit they thought that external Gods created these thoughts and actions. For example, a hungry person with a fully developed sense of self and consciousness will simply say, "I am hungry, therefore I should eat." A bicameral individual without this understanding of self would assume the gods produced the hunger.

As with many students of consciousness, Jaynes was enamored by the role of the assumed powerful role the right temporal lobe plays in feelings and spirituality. As an

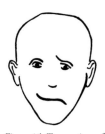

example, he presented a figure showing two identical drawings of a half smiling, half frowning face (Figure 14). They differed only in whether the smile part or the frown part is on the right or left. When asked the questions, Which is happier? Which is sadder? Most of us say the figure on the top with the smile part on the right is happier, and the figure with the frown on the right is sadder. This is the non-verbal, presumably more emotional right brain shining through.

Jayne proposed that the spiritual resources of the right temporal lobes spilled into the left hemisphere across the section of the commissures located at the level of the temporal lobes. He proposed that the Gods spoke to man from the right to the left temporal lobe. This concept is shown in Figure 15.

Jaynes proposed that consciousness did not evolve in man until quite recently, since the time of the Egyptian pharaohs. It was proposed that in the Egyptian civilization humans were

Figure 14. Two versions of a smiling-frowning face. From Jaynes.[173] *See text.* directed by the bicameral voice of their first God-king, Osiris. Jaynes' claim was that religion owed its origin to a dialogue

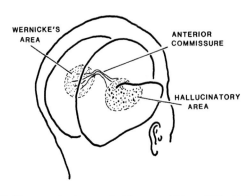

between the spiritual right temporal lobe with the rational left temporal lobe in ancient man. Prior to the development of consciousness, man was incapable of realizing that the gods were not speaking to them directly.

The concept that consciousness developed only in the last several thousand years is unlikely on many grounds. Anthropological findings dating back over 60,000 years suggest that early man was aware of his

Figure 15. The connection between the left temporal lobe and Wernicke's area and the right temporal lobe or the hallucinatory area. From Jaynes. The Origin of Consciousness in the Breakdown of the Bicameral Mind. Houghton Mifflin Co. Boston. [173p104]

own mortality, something only a well-formed consciousness and sense of self would allow. In addition, since all behavior is associated with brain activity, and ultimately with the expression of a range of genes, it is unlikely that a major, species-changing event such as consciousness could have evolved in only the last several thousand years. Jaynes realized this and claimed the change was a cultural one. However, the genetic transmission of learned behavior is unlikely. Despite the improbability of Jaynes' theory of the origin of religion, I have presented it because like other proposals, it lays spirituality at the feet of the temporal lobes.

The Temporolimbic Marker Model of Saver and Rabin

Saver and Rabin [3] proposed a temporolimbic marker model that does not rely on pathologizing spirituality. The name temporolimbic is based on the fact that while the amygdala and the hippocampus, and the emotional memories they contain, are part of the temporal lobes, they are also part of the limbic system. They play a critical role in spiritual experiences produced by brain stimulation, temporal lobe seizures, auras, NDEs, and psychedelic drugs. The term *temporolimbic system* emphasizes the important role of the limbic system.

The amygdala and hippocampus mark incoming sensory stimuli as positive or negative experiences. [174] They serve as the brain's tape recorder for emotional events. In the temporolimbic marker model, the temporal lobes and limbic system remember and mark some experiences as producing a sense of depersonalization or derealization, of spiritual importance, of being in harmony with the rest of the universe, and of ecstasy. Spiritual experiences are seen as similar to those of ordinary experiences except that they are tagged by the limbic system as of profound emotional importance, joyous and of providing a feeling of being connected to something greater than themselves. [3] A remarkable conclusion from the literature reviewed in this chapter is that a single spiritual experience has the potential of producing a permanent life-long change in an individual's spiritual or religious outlook. This is consistent with the temporolimbic marker model with its emphasis on the critical role of the hippocampus, a structure that monitors short- and long-term memory. The beauty of the marker model is that it relies on the normal functioning of the temporolimbic system, a system which is susceptible to changes in function by stress and a wide range of environmental events and as such, is applicable to everyone.

A critical advantage of incorporating the amygdala and the hippocampus, the emotional brain and the memory system into the model is the realization that the temporolimbic system is often unable to distinguish between real, external events, and non-real internally generated experiences. It records with equal fidelity whatever is presented to the tape recorder. Thus, *when internally generated spiritual and religious experiences occur they may be perceived as totally real.* While the rational brain and the spiritual brain often seem to be in conflict, this conflict is not inevitable. *It is simply necessary for the rational brain to understand that one of the characteristics of the spiritual brain is to strongly believe in something, have faith in something, even when the rational brain says it is unreasonable or that it did not and could not have happened.*

> The temporolimbic system consists of the temporal lobes and the amygdala and hippocampal portion of the limbic system. The latter two structures serve as the site of emotional memory. Different studies show that a wide range of factors that influence temporal lobe function can produce hallucinations, paranormal, spiritual, mystical, and religious experiences. These factors include the electrical stimulation of the temporal lobes; spontaneous temporal lobe epileptic auras and seizures; trauma; the severe anoxia of near death, G-forces and carbon dioxide inhalation; psychedelic drugs; speaking in tongues; and many environmental stressors.

> In addition, the superior temporal gyrus, the hippocampus, and the surrounding ectorhinal cortex have been shown to be the site of a sense of the self in space. Aberrant functioning of this area can result in the out-of-body sensations, depersonalization and derealization so common in spiritual and mystical experiences. These spiritual experiences are seen as similar to those of ordinary experiences except that they are tagged by the limbic system as of profound importance, meaningful, immensely joyous and of providing a sense of being connected to something greater than ourselves.

> The temporal lobe emotional memory system is often unable to distinguish between real, external events and non-real, internally generated non-real experiences. Thus, when these internally generated spiritual experiences occur they may be perceived as totally real. It is necessary for the rational brain to understand that one of the characteristics of the spiritual brain is to strongly believe in something and have faith in something, even when the rational brain says it is unreasonable or that it did not and could not have happened.

This is the essence of faith over reason. The temporolimbic system is our spiritual brain.

A final note. For the cover of this book I used Michelangelo's depiction of the Creation of Man from the Sistine Chapel. Michelangelo spent considerable time dissecting the human body to learn the secrets of anatomy, including removing and examining the brain. [171] It is of interest that in his fresco, God is resting on the outline of a human brain, right in the area of the temporal lobe. Whether as a part of his insightful genius or happy accident, it appears he got it right.

References

1.   Persinger, M. A. *Neurophsychological Basis of God Beliefs*. Prager, New York, 1987.

1a. From www.vnn.vn/dataimages/original/images419975_Wernicke141204.jpg

2.   Devinsky, O. The normal function of the temporal lobe. from www.medscape.com/viewarticle/468200_7. Medscape. 2004.

2b. From www.brainconnection.com/med/medart/l/hippocampus.jpg. BrainConnection.com

3.   Saver, J. L. & Rabin, J. The neural substrates of religious experience. *J Neuropsychiatry Clin Neurosci.* 9: 498-510, 1997.

4.   Bouchet, C. & Cazauvieilh, A. de l'épilepsie considérée dans ses rapports avec l'aliénation mentale. *Archives Générales de Médecine.* 9: 515-542, 10:5-50, 1825.

5.   Jackson, J. H. & Stewart, J. P. Epileptic attacks with a warning of a crude sensation of smell and with the intellectual aura (dreamy state) in a patient who had symptoms pointing to a gross organic disease of the right temporo-sphenoidal lobe. *Brain.* 22: 534-549, 1899.

6.   Sommer, W. Erkrankung des Ammonshorn als aetiologis ches Moment der Epilepsien. *Arch Psychiatr Nurs.* 10: 631-675, 1880.

7.   Bratz, E. Ammonshornbefunde bei Epileptikern. *Archives für Psychiatrie und Nervenkrankheiten.* 31: 820-825, 1899.

8.   Gibbs, F. A., Gibbs, E. L. & Lennox, W. G. Cerebral dysrhythmias of epilepsy. *Arch Neurology.* 39: 298-314, 1938.

9.   Jasper, H. H. & Kershman, J. Electroencephalographic classification of the epilepsies. *Archives of Neurology and Psychiatry.* 45: 903-943, 1941.

10. Bailey, P. & Gibbs, F. A. The surgical treatment of psychomotor epilepsy. *JAMA.* 145: 365-370, 1951.

11. Falconer, M. A. & Serafetinides, E. A. A follow-up study of surgery in temporal lobe epilepsy. *Arch Neurol Psychiatry.* 70: 40-53, 1953.

12. Engel, J. Mesial Temporal Lobe Epilepsy. From www.medscape.com/viewarticle/468200_3. 2004.

13. Penfield, W. The role of the temporal cortex in certain psychical phenomena. *The Journal of Mental Science.* 424: 1955.

14. Penfield, W. The permanent record of the stream of consciousness. *Acta Psychol (Amst).* 11: 47-69, 1955.

15. Penfield, W. & Perot. The Brain's record of auditory and visual experience. A final summary and discussion. *Brain.* 86: 595-696, 1963.

16. Joseph, R. Dreams, Spirits and the Soul. in: Joseph, R. NeuroTheology. *Brain Science, Spirituality, Religious Experience.* San Jose, CA. University Press. 2002.

17. Weingarten, S. M., Cherlow, D. G. & Holmgren, E. The relationship of hallucinations to the depth structures of the temporal lobe. *Acta Neurochir (Wien).* 199-216, 1977.

18. Jasper, H. H. & Rasmussen, T. Studies of clinical and electrical responses to deep temporal stimulation in man with some considerations of functional anatomy. *Association of Nervous and Mental Diseases.* 36: 316-334, 1958.

19. Higgins, J. W., Mahl, G. F., Delgado, M. J. & Hamlin, H. Behavioral changes during intracerebral electrical stimulation. *Archives of Neurology.* 76: 399-449, 1956.

20. Horowitz, M. D. & Adams, J. E. Hallucinations on brain stimulation: Evidence for revision of the Penfield hypothesis. in: Keup, W. *Origin and Mechanisms of Hallucinations.* Plenum Press, New York, 1970.

21. Halgren, E., Walter, R. D., Cherlow, D. G. & Crandall, P. H. Mental phenomena evoked by electrical stimulation of the human hippocampal formation and amygdala. *Brain.* 101: 83-117, 1978.

22. Gloor, P., Olivier, A., Quesney, L. F., Andermann, F. & Horowitz, S. The role of the limbic system in experiential phenomena of temporal lobe epilepsy. *Ann Neurol.* 12: 129-144, 1982.

23. Gloor, P. *The Temporal Lobe and the Limbic System.* Oxford University Press, New York, 1997.

24. Blanke, O., Ortigue, S., Landis, T. & Seeck, M. Stimulating illusory own-body perceptions. *Nature.* 419: 269-270, 2002.

25. Wuerfel, J. et al. Religiosity is associated with hippocampal but not amygdala volumes in patients with refractory epilepsy. *J Neurol Neurosurg Psychiatry.* 75: 640-642, 2004.

26. Ogata, A. & Miyakawa, T. Religious experiences in epileptic patients with a focus on ictus-related episodes. *Psychiatry Clin Neurosci.* 52: 321-325, 1998.

27. Ozkara, C. et al. Ictal kissing and religious speech in a patient with right temporal lobe epilepsy. *Epileptic Disord.* 6: 241-245, 2004.

28. MacDonald, D. A. & Holland, D. Spirituality and complex partial epileptic-like signs. *Psychol Rep.* 91: 785-792, 2002.

29. Cirignotta, F., Todesco, C. V. & Lugaresi, E. Temporal lobe epilepsy with ecstatic seizures (so called Dostoevsky's epilepsy). *Epilepsia.* 21: 705-710, 1980.

30. Asheim Hansen, B. & Brodtkorb, E. Partial epilepsy with "ecstatic" seizures. *Epilepsy Behav.* 4: 667-673, 2003.

31. Naito, H. & Matsui, N. Temporal lobe epilepsy with ictal ecstatic state and interictal behavior of hypergraphia. *J Nerv Ment Dis.* 176: 123-124, 1988.

32. Stevens, J. R., Mark, V. H., Erwin, F., P., P. & Suematsu, K. Deep temporal stimulation in man. *Archives of Neurology.* 21: 157-169, 1969.

33. Devinsky, O., Feldmann, E., Burrowes, K. & Bromfield, E. Autoscopic phenomena with seizures. *Arch Neurol.* 46: 1080-1088, 1989.

34. Gibbs, F. A. Ictal and non-ictal psychiatric disorders in temporal lobe epilepsy. *J Nervous Mental Disease.* 11: 522-528, 1951.

35. Sherwin, I. The effect of the location of an epileptogenic lesion on the occurrence of psychosis in epilepsy. *Adv Biol Psychiat* 8: 81-97, 1982.

36. Trimble, M. R. & Peres, M. M. The phenomenology of chronic psychoses of epilepsy. *Adv Biol Psychiat.* 8: 98-105, 1982.

37. Dewhurst, K. & Beard, A. W. Sudden religious conversions in temporal lobe epilepsy. *Br J Psychiatry.* 117: 497-507, 1970.

38. Dewhurst, K. & Beard, A. W. Sudden religious conversions in temporal lobe epilepsy. 1970. *Epilepsy Behav.* 4: 78-87, 2003.

39. Mesulam, M. M. Dissociative states with abnormal temporal lobe EEG. Multiple personality and the illusion of possession. *Arch Neurol.* 38: 176-81, 1981.

40. Waxman, S. G. & Geschwind, N. The interictal behavior syndrome of temporal lobe epilepsy. *Arch Gen Psychiatry.* 32: 1580-1586, 1975.

41. Persinger, M. A. Propensity to report paranormal experiences is correlated with temporal lobe signs. *Percept Mot Skills.* 59: 583-586, 1984.

42. Makarec, K. & Persinger, M. A. Temporal lobe signs: electroencephalographic validity and enhanced scores in special populations. *Percept Mot Skills.* 60: 831-842, 1985.

43. Persinger, M. A. People who report religious experiences may also display enhanced temporal-lobe signs. *Percept Mot Skills.* 58: 963-975, 1984.

44. Persinger, M. A. Paranormal and religious beliefs may be mediated differentially by subcortical and cortical phenomenological processes of the temporal (limbic) lobes. *Percept Mot Skills.* 76: 247-251, 1993.

45. Geschwind, N. Interictal behavioral changes in epilepsy. Epilepsia. 24 Suppl 1: S23-30, 1983.

46. Landsborough, D. St Paul and temporal lobe epilepsy. *J Neurol Neurosurg Psychiatry.* 50: 659-664, 1987.

47. Herzog, A. G., Russell, V., Vaitukaitis, J. L. & Geschwind, N. Neuroendocrine dysfunction in temporal lobe epilepsy. *Arch Neurol.* 39: 133-135, 1982.

48. Pritchard, P. B., Wannamaker, B. B., Sagel, J. & DeVillier, C. Endocrine dysfunction in temporal lobe epilepsy. *Arch Neurol.* 39: 786-787, 1982.

49. Trevisol-Bittencourt, P. C. & Troiano, A. R. [Interictal personality syndrome in non-dominant temporal lobe epilepsy: case report]. *Arq Neuropsiquiatr.* 58: 548-555, 2000.

50. Bear, D. M. & Fedio, P. Quantitative analysis of interictal behavior in temporal lobe epilepsy. *Arch Neurol.* 34: 454-467, 1977.

51. Bear, D. M. Temporal lobe epilepsy—a syndrome of sensory-limbic hyperconnection. *Cortex.* 15: 357-384, 1979.

52. Hermann, B. P. & Whitman, S. Behavioral and personality correlates of epilepsy: a review, methodological critique, and conceptual model. *Psychol Bull.* 95: 451-497, 1984.

53. Willmore, L. J., Heilman, K. M. & Fennell, E. Effects of chronic seizures on religiosity. *Trans of the American Neurological Associaton.* 105: 85-87, 1980.

54. Mungas, D. Interictal behavior abnormality in temporal lobe epilepsy. A specific syndrome or nonspecific psychopathology? *Arch Gen Psychiatry.* 39: 108-111, 1982.

55. Flor-Henry, P. Psychosis and temporal lobe epilepsy. A controlled investigation. *Epilepsia.* 10: 363-395, 1969.

56. Bruens, J. H. Psychoses in epilepsy. *Psychiatr Neurol Neurochir.* 74: 175-192, 1971.

57. Roberts, J. K. & Guberman, A. Religion and epilepsy. *Psychiatr J Univ Ott.* 14: 282-286, 1989.

58. Assal, G. & Bindschaedler, C. Religious delusion 13 years after brain injury. *Neurochirurgie.* 38: 381-384, 1992.

59. Fenwick, P., Galliano, S., Coate, M. A., Rippere, V. & Brown, D. 'Psychic sensitivity', mystical experience, head injury and brain pathology. *Br J Med Psychol.* 58 (Pt 1): 35-44, 1985.

60. Puri, B. K., Lekh, S. K., Nijran, K. S., Bagary, M. S. & Richardson, A. J. SPECT neuroimaging in schizophrenia with religious delusions. *Int J Psychophysiol.* 40: 143-148, 2001.

61. Ishibashi, T., Horo, H., Endo, K. & Sato, T. Hallucinations produced by electrical stimulations of temproal lobes in schizophrenic patients. *Tohuku J Exp Med.* 82: 124-139, 1964.

62. Ramachandran, V. S. & Blakeslee, S. *Phantoms in the Brain.* Quill, New York, 1998.

63. Holtz, R. E. Brai's 'God Module' may affect religious intensity. In *Los Angeles Times,* Los Angeles, October, 1997.

63a. Arzy, S. et al: Induction of an illusory shadow person. *Nature.* 443:287, 2006

64. Trull, D. The God Spot. From www.parascope.com/articles/slips/fs22_3.htm. 1997.

65. Altschuler, E. L. Did Ezekiel have temporal lobe epilepsy? *Arch Gen Psychiatry.* 59: 561-562, 2002.

66. Vercelletto, P. [Saint Paul disease. Ectasia and estatic seizures]. *Rev Neurol (Paris).* 150: 835-839, 1994.

67. Brorson, J. R. & Brewer, K. St Paul and temporal lobe epilepsy. *J Neurol Neurosurg Psychiatry.* 51: 886-887, 1988.

68. Garcia Albea, E. [The ecstatic epilepsy of Teresa of Jesus]. *Rev Neurol.* 37: 879-887, 2003.

69. Foote-Smith, E. & Bayne, L. Joan of Arc. *Epilepsia.* 32: 810-815, 1991.

70. Murray, T. D. *Jeanne D'Arc, Maid of Orleans, 1429-1431.* William Heinemann, London, 1907.

71. Critchley, M. Musicogenic epilepsy. *Brain.* 60: 13-27, 1937.

72. Poskanzer, P. C., Brown, A. E. & Miller, H. Musicogenic epilepsy caused only by a discrete frequency band of church bells. *Brain.* 85: 77-92, 1962.

73. Davenport, F. M. *Primitive Traits in Religious Revivals.* Macmillan, London, 1905.

74. Hodder, D. H. & Holmes, G. L. Ellen G. White and the Seventh-Day Adventist Church: Visions or Parial-Complex Seizures? *Neurology.* 31: 160-161, 1981.

75. Canwright, D. M. *Life of Mer. E.G. White A Seventh-Day Adventist Prophet, Her False Claims Refuted.* W. H. Olson, Washington, D.C., 1919, 1955.

76. Peterson, D. L. *Visions or Seizures: Was Ellen White the Victim of Epilepsy?* Pacific Press Publishing Association, Boise, ID, 1988.

77. Bradford, D. T. Neuropsychology of Swedenborg's visions. *Percept Mot Skills.* 88: 377-383, 1999.

78. Johnson, J. Henry Maudsley on Swedenborg's messianic psychosis. *Br J Psychiatry.* 165: 690-691, 1994.

79. Moody, R. *Life After Life.* Harper San Francisco, New York, 1975, 2001.

80. Bates, B. C. & Stanley, A. The epidemiology and differential diagnosis of near-death experience. *Am J Orthopsychiatry.* 55: 542-549, 1985.

81. Grosso, M. Toward an explanation of near-death phenomena. *J Amer Soc Psychical Res.* 75: 37-60, 1981.

82. Whinnery, J. E. & Whinnery, A. M. Acceleration-induced loss of consciousness. A review of 500 episodes. *Arch Neurol.* 47: 764-776, 1990.

83. Kotler, S. Extreme States. *Discover.* 26: 2005.

84. Woerlee, G. M. Mortal Minds. *The Biology of Near-Death Experiences.* Prometheus Books, New York, 2003, 2005.

85. Whinnery, J. E. Technique for simulating G-induced tunnel vision. *Aviat Space Environ Med.* 50: 1076, 1979.

86. Medune, L. J. *Carbon Dioxite Therap: A Neuropsychological Treatment of Nervous Disorders.* Charles C. Thomas, Springfield, IL, 1950.

87. Morse, M. A near-death experience in a 7-year-old child. *Am J Dis Child.* 137: 959-961, 1983.

88. Morse, M., Conner, D. & Tyler, D. Near-death experiences in a pediatric population. A preliminary report. *Am J Dis Child.* 139: 595-600, 1985.

89. Morse, M., Castillo, P., Venecia, D., Milstein, J. & Tyler, D. C. Childhood near-death experiences. *Am J Dis Child.* 140: 1110-1114, 1986.

90. Morse, M. L. Near-death experiences of children. *J Pediatr Oncol Nurs.* 11: 139-144; discussion 145, 1994.

91. Morse, M. L. Near death experiences and death-related visions in children: implications for the clinician. *Curr Probl Pediatr.* 24: 55-83, 1994.

92. Morse, M. *Closer to the Light. Learning from the Near-Death Experiences of Children.* Ivy Books, New York, 1990.

93. Morse, M. *Transformed by the Light: The Powerful Effect of Near-Death Experiences on People's Lives.* Villard, 1992.

94. Greyson, B. The near-death experience scale. Construction, reliability, and validity. *J Nerv Ment Dis.* 171: 369-375, 1983.

95. Frances, A., Pincus, H. A. & First, M. B. (eds.) DSM-IV-TR. *Diagnostic and Statistical Manual of Mental Disorders.* Fourth Edition. Text Revision. American Psychiatric Association, Washington, DC, 2000.

96. Hough, R. L., Jordan, B. K., Marmar, C. R. & Weiss, D. S. (eds.) *The National Vietnam Veterans Readjustment Study Brunner/Mazel,* New York, 1990.

97. Moody, R. *The Light Beyond.* Bantam, New York, 1989.

98. Morse, M. *Where God Lives. The Science of the Paranormal and How Our Brains are Linked to the Universe.* Cliff Street Books, New York, 2000.

99. Greyson, B. Near-death experiences and personal values. *Am J Psychiatry.* 140:618-620, 1983.

100. Rosen, D. H. Suicide survivors. A follow-up study of persons who survived jumping from the Golden Gate and San Francisco-Oakland Bay Bridges. *West J Med.* 122:289-294, 1975.

101. van Lommel, P., van Wees, R., Meyers, V. & Elfferich, I. Near-death experience in survivors of cardiac arrest: a prospective study in the Netherlands. *Lancet.* 358:2039-2045, 2001.

102. IANDS. Internatonal Association for Near-Death Studies. iands.org/index.php. 2005.

103. Daly, D. D. Ictal clinical manifestations of complex partial seizures. *Adv Neurol.* 11:57-83, 1975.

104. Gastaut, H. & Meyer, J. S. (eds.) *Cerebral Anoxia and the Electroencephalogram.* Charles C. Thomas, Springfield, IL, 1961.

105. Schiff, S. J. & Somjen, G. G. Hyperexcitability following moderate hypoxia in hippocampal tissue slices. *Brain Res.* 337: 337-340, 1985.

106. Aitken, P. G., Jing, J., Young, J. & Somjen, G. G. Ion channel involvement in hypoxia-induced spreading depression in hippocampal slices. *Brain Res.* 541: 7-11, 1991.

107. Benveniste, H., Brejer, J., Achouseboe, A. & Diemer, H. Elevation of the extracellular concentration of glutamate and aspartate in rat hippocampus during ischemia monitored by microdialysis. *Journal of Neurochemistry.* 43: 1369-1374, 1984.

108. Britton, W. B. & Bootzin, R. R. Near-death experiences and the temporal lobe. *Psychol Sci.* 15: 254-258, 2004.

109. Persinger, M. A. Religious and mystical experiences as artifacts of temporal lobe function: a general hypothesis. *Percept Mot Skills.* 57: 1255-1262, 1983.

110. Morse, M. *Closer to the Light.* Villard, 1990.

111. Krystal, J. H. et al. Subanesthetic effects of the noncompetitive NMDA antagonist, ketamine, in humans. Psychotomimetic, perceptual, cognitive, and neuroendocrine responses. *Arch Gen Psychiatry.* 51: 199-214, 1994.

112. Collier, B. Ketamine and the conscious mind. *Anesthesiology.* 27: 120-134, 1972.

113. Collier, B. Ketamine and the near-death experience. *Anabiosis.* 1: 87-96, 1984.

114. Contreras, P. C., DiMaggio, D. A. & O'Donohue, T. L. Evidence for an endogenous peptide ligand and antagonist for PCP receptors. *Prog Clin Biol Res.* 192:495-498, 1985.

115. DiMaggio, D. A., Contreras, P. C., Quirion, R. & O'Donohue, T. L. Isolation and identification of an endogenous ligand for the phencyclidine receptor. *NIDA Res Monogr.* 64: 24-36, 1986.

116. Jansen, K. L. Neuroscience and the near-death experience: roles for the NMSA-PCP receptor, the sigma receptor and the endopsychosins. *Med Hypotheses.* 31: 25-29, 1990.

117. Jansen, K. Neuroscience, ketamine, and the near-death experience. in: Bailey, L. W. *The Near-Death Experience*

Reader. New York. Routledge. 1996.

118. Kuhar, M. J., Pert, C. B. & Snyder, S. H. Regional distribution of opiate receptor binding in monkey and human brain. *Nature*. 245: 447-450, 1973.

119. Uhl, G. R., Kuhar, M. J. & Synder, S. H. Enkephalin-containing pathway: amygdaloid efferents in the stria *terminalis*. *Brain Res*. 149: 223-228, 1978.

120. Sotelo, J., Perez, R., Guevara, P. & Fernandez, A. Changes in brain, plasma and cerebrospinal fluid contents of beta-endorphin in dogs at the moment of death. *Neurol Res*. 17: 223-225, 1995.

121. Henriksen, S. J., Bloom, F. E., McCoy, F., Ling, N. & Guillemin, R. beta-endorphin induces nonconvulsive limbic seizures. *Proc Natl Acad Sci USA*. 75: 5221-5225, 1978.

122. Ableitner, A. & Schulz, R. Neuroanatomical sites mediating the central actions of beta-endorphin as mapped by changes in glucose utilization: involvement of *mu* opioid receptors. *J Pharmacol Exp Ther*. 262: 415-423, 1992.

123. Carr, D. Pathophysiology of stress-induced limbic lobe dysfunction: A hypothesis for NDEs. *Anabiosis*. 2: 75-90, 1982.

124. Carr, D. B. Endorphins at the approach of death. *Lancet*. 1: 390, 1981.

125. Helfand, R., Lavie, P. & Hobson, J. A. REM/NREM discrimination via ocular and limb movement monitoring: correlation with polygraphic data and development of a REM state algorithm. *Psychophysiology*. 23: 334-339, 1986.

126. Monroe, L. J., Rechtschaffen, A., Foulkes, D. & Jensen, J. Discriminability of REM And NREM Reports. *J Pers Soc Psychol*. 12: 456-460, 1965.

127. Stickgold, R., Malia, A., Fosse, R., Propper, R. & Hobson, J. A. Brain-mind states: I. Longitudinal field study of sleep/wake factors influencing mentation report length. *Sleep*. 24: 171-179, 2001.

128. Goldstein, L., Stoltzfus, N. W. & Gardocki, J. F. Changes in interhemispheric amplitude relationships in the EEG during sleep. *Physiol Behav*. 8: 811-815, 1972.

129. Hodoba, D. Paradoxic sleep facilitation by interictal epileptic activity of right temporal origin. *Biol Psychiatry*. 21: 1267-1278, 1986.

130. Meyer, J. S., Ishikawa, Y., Hata, T. & Karacan, I. Cerebral blood flow in normal and abnormal sleep and dreaming. *Brain Cogn*. 6: 266-294, 1987.

131. Persinger, M. A. Experimental simulation of the God experience. in: Joseph, R. NeuroTheology. *Brain, Science, Spirituality, Religious Experience*. University Press, San Jose, CA, 2002.

132. Hill, D. R. & Persinger, M. A. Application of transcerebral, weak (1 microT) complex magnetic fields and mystical experiences: are they generated by field-induced dimethyltryptamine release from the pineal organ? *Percept Mot Skills*. 97: 1049-1050, 2003.

133. Granqvist, P. et al. Sensed presence and mystical experiences are predicted by suggestibility, not by the application of transcranial weak complex magnetic fields. *Neurosci Lett*. 379: 1-6, 2005.

134. Makarec, M. A. & Persinger, M. A. Electroencephalographic validation of a temporal lobe signs inventory. *J Res Personality*. 24: 323-337, 1990.

135. Tellegen, A. & Atkinson, G. Openness to absorbing and self-altering experiences ("absorption"), a trait related to hypnotic susceptibility. *J Abnorm Psychol*. 83: 268-277, 1974.

136. Granqvist, P. & Hagekull, B. Seeking security in the new age: on attachment and emotional compensation. *J Soc Study Religion*. 40: 529-547, 2001.

137. Larsson, M., Larhammar, D., Fredrikson, M. & Granqvist, P. Reply to M.A. Persinger and S.A. Koren's response to Granqvist et al. "Sensed presence and mystical experiences are predicted by suggestibiity, not by application of transcranial weak magnetic fields." *Neurosci Lett*. 380: 348-350, 2005.

138. Horgan, J. *Rational Mysticism*. Houghton Mifflin Company, New York, 2003.

139. Masters, R. E. L. & Houston, J. *The Varieties of Psychedelic Experience*. A Delta Book, New York, 1966.

140. Delgado, P. L. & Moreno, F. A. Hallucinogens, serotonin and obsessive-compulsive disorder. *J Psychoactive Drugs*. 30: 359-366, 1998.

141. Riba, J., Anderer, P., Jane, F., Saletu, B. & Barbanoj, M. J. Effects of the South American psychoactive beverage ayahuasca on regional brain electrical activity in humans: a functional neuroimaging study using low-resolution electromagnetic tomography. *Neuropsychobiology*. 50: 89-101, 2004.

142. Burris, K. D., Breeding, M. & Sanders-Bush, E. (+)Lysergic acid diethylamide, but not its nonhallucinogenic congeners, is a potent serotonin 5HT1C receptor agonist. *J Pharmacol Exp Ther*. 258: 891-896, 1991.

143. Borg, J., Andree, B., Soderstrom, H. & Farde, L. The serotonin system and spiritual experiences. *Am J Psychiatry*. 160: 1965-1969, 2003.

144. Brandstrom, S. et al. Swedish normative data on personality using the Temperament and Character Inventory. *Compr Psychiatry*. 39: 122-128, 1998.

145. Serafetinides, E. A. The significance of the temporal lobes and of hemisphere dominance in the production of the LDS-25 symptomatology in man. *Neuropsychologia*. 95: 53-63, 1965.

146. Roth, B. L. et al. Salvinorin A: A potent naturally occurring nonnitrogenous kappa opioid selective agonist. *Proc*

Natl Acad Sci USA. 99: 11934-11939, 2002.

147. Masters, R. E. L. & Houston, J. *The Psychedelic Experience.* Holt, Rinehart, and Winston, New York, 1966.

148. Strassman, R., M.D. *DMT: The Spirit Molecule.* Park Street Press, Rochester, VT, 2001.

149. Barker, S. A., Monti, J. A. & Christian, S. T. N, N-dimethyltryptamine: an endogenous hallucinogen. *Int Rev Neurobiol.* 22: 83-110, 1981.

150. Mack, J. E. Abduction: *Human Encounters with Aliens.* Schribner, New York, 1994.

151. Ring, K. *Life at Death: A Scientific Investigation of the Near Death Experience.* Coward McGan, Geoghegan, NY, 1980.

152. DSM ed. *Diagnostic and Statistical Manual of Mental Disorders.* Third Edition. American Psychiatric Association, Washington D.C., 1980.

153. Pahnke, W. N. *Drugs and Mysticism: An Analysis of the Relationship between Psychedelic Drugs and the Mystical Consciousness Thesis in History and Philosophy of Religion,* Harvard, Cambridge, 1963.

154. Pahnke, W. N. Psychedelic drugs and mystical experience. Int Psychiatry Clin. 5:149-62, 1969.

155. Doblin, R. *Pahnke's Good Friday Experiment: A long term follow-up and methodological critique. J Transper Psychol.* 23: 1991.

156. Leary, T., Litwin, G. H. & Metzner, R. Reactions to Psilocybin Administered in a Supportive Environment. *J Nerv Ment Dis.* 137: 561-573, 1963.

156a. Griffiths, R. R., Richards, W. A., McCann, U. & Jesse, R. Psilocybin can occasion mystical-type experiences having substantial and sustained personal meaning and spiritual significance. *Psychopharmacology (Berl).* 187: 268-83, 2006.

157. Hasler, F., Grimberg, U., Benz, M. A., Huber, T. & Vollenweider, F. X. Acute psychological and physiological effects of psilocybin in healthy humans: a double-blind, placebo-controlled dose-effect study. *Psychopharmacology (Berl).* 172: 145-156, 2004.

158. Vollenweider, F. X., Vollenweider-Scherpenhuyzen, M. F., Babler, A., Vogel, H. & Hell, D. Psilocybin induces schizophrenia-like psychosis in humans via a serotonin-2 agonist action. *Neuroreport.* 9: 3897-3902, 1998.

159. Huxley, A. *The Doors of Perception and Heaven and Hell.* Harper & Row, New York, 1963.

160. Vollenweider, F. X. et al. Metabolic hyperfrontality and psychopathology in the ketamine model of psychosis using positron emission tomography (PET) and [18F]fluorodeoxyglucose (FDG). *Eur Neuropsychopharmacol.* 7: 9-24, 1997.

161. Vollenweider, F. X., Leenders, K. L., Oye, I., Hell, D. & Angst, J. Differential psychopathology and patterns of cerebral glucose utilisation produced by (S)- and (R)-ketamine in healthy volunteers using positron emission tomography (PET). *Eur Neuropsychopharmacol.* 7: 25-38, 1997.

162. Vollenweider, F. X., Vontobel, P., Hell, D. & Leenders, K. L. 5-HT modulation of dopamine release in basal ganglia in psilocybin-induced psychosis in man—a PET study with [11C]raclopride. *Neuropsychopharmacology.* 20: 424-433, 1999.

163. Vollenweider, F. X., Vontobel, P., Oye, I., Hell, D. & Leenders, K. L. Effects of (S)-ketamine on striatal dopamine: a [11C]raclopride PET study of a model psychosis in humans. *J Psychiatr Res.* 34: 35-43, 2000.

164. Ross, E. D. The aprosodias. Functional-anatomic organization of the affective components of language in the right hemisphere. *Arch Neurol.* 38: 561-569, 1981.

165. Merskey, H. *Analysis of Hysteria.* Bailliere Tindall, London, 1979.

166. Gur, R. C. et al. Differences in the distribution of gray and white matter in human cerebral hemispheres. *Science.* 207: 1226-1228, 1980.

167. Gur, R. C. et al. Sex differences in brain gray and white matter in healthy young adults: correlations with cognitive performance. *J Neurosci.* 19: 4065-4072, 1999.

168. Karnath, H. O., Ferber, S. & Himmelbach, M. Spatial awareness is a function of the temporal not the posterior parietal lobe. *Nature.* 411: 950-953, 2001.

169. Hafting, T., Fyhn, M., Molden, S., Moser, M. B. & Moser, E. I. Microstructure of a spatial map in the entorhinal cortex. *Nature.* 436: 801-806, 2005.

170. Browning, D. ed. *Faith and the Dynamics of Knowing.* University of Chicago Press, Chicago, IL., 1968.

171. Spanos, N. P., Cross, W. P., Lepage, M. & Coristine, M. Glossolalia as learned behavior: an experimental demonstration. *J Abnorm Psychol.* 95: 21-23, 1986.

172. Persinger, M. A. Striking EEG profiles from single episodes of glossolalia and transcendental meditation. *Percept Mot Skills.* 58: 127-233, 1984.

173. Jaynes, J. *The Origin of Consciousness in the Break-down of the Bicameral Mind.* Houghton Mifflin Company, Boston, 1976, 1990.

174. Aggleton, J. P. The contribution of the amygdala to normal and abnormal emotional states. *Trends Neurosci.* 16: 328-333, 1993.

175. Stone, Irving. *The Agony and the Ecstasy.* Doubleday & Company, New York, 1961.

176. Newberg, A. B., Wintering, N. A., Morgan, D. Waldman, M. R. The measurement of regional cerebral blood flow during glossolalia: A preliminary SPECT study. *Psychiatry Res.* 148:67-71, 2006.

Meditation is first and foremost a search for the God within.

Ken Wilbur
Grace and Grit, 1991 [1]

Chapter 31

The Meditating Brain

What is meditation? The following description [1] covers it well.

> Meditation, it is said, is a way to evoke the relaxation response. Meditation, others say, is a way to train and strengthen awareness; a method for centering and focusing the self; a way to halt constant verbal thinking and relax the body; a technique for calming the central nervous system; a way to relieve stress, bolster self-esteem, reduce anxiety, and alleviate depression. All of these things are true enough; meditation has been clinically demonstrated to do all of those things. But I would like to emphasize that meditation itself is, and always has been, a spiritual practice.

Various spiritual disciplines speak of the transformative feelings produced by different forms of meditation. These include ecstatic emotions, a sense of being lost in time and space, encounters with demonic or angelic entities, heavenly sounds and sights, a blinding white light, a feeling of having died and been re-born, contacting a powerful and loving presence underlying all reality, [2p73] pure or heightened awareness, pure consciousness, *samadhi, santori, nirvana,* [3] *ananda* (peace), [4] enlightenment, [5] inward contemplation, [6] pleasure, [7] a "eureka" moment, [3] mindfulness, and touching the Godhead. [8] These experiences cut across all denominations, faiths, and cultures. As wonderful as these descriptions sound, the vast majority of people who meditate just obtain a feeling of being very relaxed, rested, mellow, blissful and at peace with the world.

Given the intensely spiritual nature of meditation one would anticipate that the part of the brain that would be activated during meditation would be the spiritual brain — the temporal lobes. This is not necessarily the case, and for this reason I have given the meditating brain its own chapter. In the chapter on the spiritual brain, the spiritual sensations were arising spontaneously, from within, generated by electrical stimulation, epileptic auras, trauma, NDEs, psychedelic drugs, speaking in tongues, and other factors. There was no conscious effort to make the spiritual feelings happen; they just happened.

By contrast, the spiritual feelings associated with meditation are the result of a conscious effort to bring them about. This is done by evoking a highly focused attention, visualization, a range of rhythmic activities including deep breathing, chanting, vocalizing mantras or different body movements. The type of meditation and the method used will dictate which parts of the brain will be activated. The body of knowledge about meditation is vast. I will only cover the types of meditation, the physical effects of meditation, meditation and *gamma* brain waves, and which parts of the brain are involved in meditation.

The Types of Meditation

The religions of the world are commonly classified into the ecstatic religions of the West (Christianity, Judaism, Islam) and the contemplative religions of the East (Buddhism, Hinduism, Taoism, and others). Meditation had its origin in the contemplative religions of the East. It was initially introduced into the United States at the World Parliament of Religions, held in Chicago in 1893.[6] The practice of various types of meditation has seen a continuous growth ever since. It experienced a giant increase in popularity following the counter-cultural revolution of the 1960s, the widespread interest in altered states of consciousness initiated by the use of psychedelic drugs, and the influx of large number of practitioners to the United States following the Communist invasions of China, North Vietnam, North Korea, and Tibet. [6p6.]

The two major types of meditation are *those that relax* and *those that excite*. The vast majority of practitioners teach a type that relaxes. This can be attained by either *focused* or *unfocused* efforts. In focused meditation practitioners focus their attention on an object such as a peaceful place, a word such as a mantra, an action such as breathing, on muscle movement or lack of movement as in yoga, or a thought such as compassion or love of God. In unfocused meditation the emphasis is on "mindfulness," a generalized state of alertness where the mind remains unfocused but is prepared to attend to any potential stimulus. Rapid breathing is often used for the type of meditation that excites. It has been suggested that this eventually leads to a relaxation response. The following is a partial list of some of the many specific types of meditation.

Transcendental Meditation (TM). This was taught by Maharishi Mahesh Yogi, a Vedantic meditation teacher. TM began in India in 1956. It involves the quiet repetitious thinking or vocalization of a mantra. A mantra is any word or syllable. TM has been labeled by some as a cult because it offers, for money, to teach TM and to provide pupils with their own individualized mantras. In fact a student can think up their own mantra. It is simply the monotonous repetition of words or phrases that focus the mind, increase attention, and produce a restful relaxation. A common mantra in TM is Om Mani Padme Hum, or just Hum. A common position to enhance TM and other forms of meditation is to assume the physically difficult crossed-legs lotus position as shown in Figure 1. The half-lotus position with one leg crossed is much easier.

One of the purported appeals of TM is its claim to be scientifically validated. Many of these studies[9] however, were carried out at the Maharishi Mahesh International University (MIU) in Fairfield, Iowa, now called the Maharishi International School of Management. There is considerable debate about whether

Figure 1. The legs-crossed lotus position. [8a]

TM or meditation in general produces effects above and beyond those of simple eyes-closed relaxation.

Mindfulness meditation. Mindfulness is an ancient Buddhist practice of sitting quietly and emptying the mind. One practitioner said, "Just by sitting and doing nothing, we are doing a tremendous amount." The goal of Buddhist meditation is to detach oneself from desires and objects which are the cause of suffering. This is sometimes called Zen meditation. Zen considers the "blank mind" to be a higher form of consciousness because it is free of attachments. An additional goal is to have as little tension in the body as possible. The following statements about mindfulness are from Jon Kabat-Zinn's book *Wherever You Go There You Are.* [10]

> Mindfulness means paying attention in a particular way: on purpose, in the present moment, and nonjudgmentally. This kind of attention nurtures greater awareness, clarity, and acceptance of present-moment reality. It wakes us up to the fact that our lives unfold only in moments. If we are not fully present for many of those moments, we may not only miss what is most valuable in our lives but also fail to realize the richness and depth of our possibilities for growth and transformation.
>
> The funny thing about stopping is that as soon as you do it, here you are. Things get simpler. In some ways, it's as if you died and the world continued on. By "dying" now in this way, you actually become more alive now. There is nothing passive about it. Stopping actually makes the going more vivid, richer, more textured.
>
> I like to think of mindfulness simply as the art of conscious living. The most important point is to be yourself and not try to become anything that you are not already. Buddhism is fundamentally about being

in touch with your own deepest nature and letting it flow out of you unimpeded. It has to do with waking up and seeing things as they are. In fact the word "Buddha" simply means one who has awakened to his or her own true nature.

Kabat-Zinn's instructions on the art of mindfulness are:

> TRY: Stopping, sitting down, and becoming aware of your breathing once in a while throughout the day. It can be for five minutes or five seconds. Let go into full acceptance of the present moment, including how you are feeling and what you perceive to be happening. For those moments, don't try to change anything at all, just breathe and let go. In your mind and in your heart, give yourself permission to allow this moment to be exactly as it is, and allow yourself to be exactly as you are. Then, when you're ready, move in the direction your heart tells you to go, mindfully and with resolution.

Thus, instead of the clearing the mind by repeating words, mindfulness clears the mind by simply concentrating only on the present moment, not the past, not the future. Mindfulness meditation has also been called Vipassana insight meditation, in the Theravada Buddhist tradition. The fact that the word "spirit" comes from the Latin word *spirare,* meaning "to breathe," may account for the emphasis on breathing in virtually all forms of meditation.

Tantric yoga meditation. This is a form of Buddhist meditation practiced by Ananda Marga, an international society dedicated to the achievement of both social and individual spiritual goals. It involves intense concentration of attention and the subjective sense of an ongoing struggle to achieve the ultimate union with the object of concentration and total self-adsorption or *samâdhi.* The concepts of *kundalini* (spinal energy) and *chakras* (spinal energy sites) are Tantric concepts. Ananda Marga practitioners often report the subjective sense of energy discharges or "rushes" at times during meditation. Tantric tradition emphases that all the energies of the organism are potentially capable of transformation into the spiritual energy of union with the object of devotion. [11] Some researchers have suggested that practicing attention based meditation might improve the ability to concentrate in children with attention deficit disorder. [12]

The Relaxation Response. Herbert Benson, M.D. is a cardiologist at Harvard Medical School. In the late 1960s he first began to study TM practitioners, then Tibetan Buddhist meditators and people practicing other forms of relaxation. In 1975 he published *The Relaxation Response*[7] describing what he felt were the key generic elements to meditation and generation of the relaxation response. These included a quiet environment, an object to dwell upon, a passive attitude, and a comfortable position.

The object to dwell on can be a repetitive word or sound or a feeling. Some prefer to think about God. It was proposed that this helped to clear the mind so when a distracting thought occurred, returning to the repetition eliminated the thought. The passive attitude consisted of the emptying of all thoughts and distractions from one's mind. This was felt to be especially essential in eliciting the relaxation response. Sitting is essential to maintain wakefulness. If these elements were performed while lying down the subject would just fall asleep. Some keep their eyes open to further decrease the chance of falling asleep. This whole process is carried out for 20 minutes each day.

The relaxation response consists of a decrease in the heart rate, respiratory rate, blood pressure, and oxygen consumption and an increase in EEG alpha waves. It was proposed that these responses were due to a decrease in sympathetic tone and were the opposite of the fight and flight response to stress, where the pulse, respiratory rate, blood pressure and oxygen consumption all increase. It was suggested that the daily stresses of life were constantly triggering the flight or fight response, a major cause of hypertension. If meditation could reverse the flight or fight response, it might also be useful in the treatment of hypertension, and Benson's studies suggested this was the case.

The production of the relaxation response was not unique to TM meditation. Benson found that a wide range of other relaxation techniques also produced the relaxation response. These included Zen and Yoga; hypnosis; progressive relaxation, where the subject lies down and focuses on relaxing different muscles; and other similar techniques.

If the reader has not had previous experience with meditation he or she may wish to try the following simple instructions for the technique Benson gave to his subjects in his studies. [7p162]

- Sit quietly in a comfortable position.
- Close your eyes.
- Deeply relax all your muscles, beginning at the feet and progressing up to your face. Keep them relaxed.
- Breathe through your nose. Become aware of your breathing. As you breathe out, say one word, "ONE," silently to yourself. For example, breathe IN…OUT, "ONE"; IN…OUT, "ONE"; etc. Breathe easily and naturally,
- Continue for 10 to 20 minutes. You may open your eyes to check the time, but do not use an alarm. When you finish, sit quietly for several minutes, at first with your eyes closed and later with your eyes opened. Do not stand up for a few minutes.
- Do not worry about whether you are unsuccessful in achieving a deep level of relaxation. Maintain a passive attitude and permit relaxation to occur at its own pace. When distracting thoughts occur, try to ignore them by not dwelling upon them and return to repeating "ONE." With practice, the response should come with little effort. Practice the technique once or twice daily but not within two hours after any meal, since the digestive processes seem to interfere with the elicitation of the Relaxation Response.

Physical Yoga. Yoga can have many meanings. Yoga is a Sanskrit word derived from *"yuj"* which means to connect, join, or balance. In relationship to meditation the term itself means union, specifically the union between the individual's consciousness and a universal consciousness. Yoga can refer to this union, to a state of consciousness, or to the method of achieving this state of consciousness. "Yoga meditation" is often used to refer to various forms of meditation. The term "yogi" refers to an individual practitioner or teacher of meditation or yoga. Hatha yoga refers to a form of yoga that prepares the body for spiritual growth by the use of different physical positions and breathing exercises. Much of the yoga popularly practiced in the United States is some form of physical or hatha yoga. It began in the U.S. with the publication in 1966 of *Light on Yoga*[13] by B. K. S. Iyengar. In this book he explained 216 different yoga postures. This was a physically challenging form of yoga and was designed to provide treatment for a number of conditions including backache, high blood pressure, stress, depression and others. It has become enormously popular. A yoga teacher stated, "Prior to his book yoga classes were a cliché in which vegetarians gathered in dark room to meditate with burning candles and incense. Mr. Iyengar and his book literally turned the light on in the room and on the fact that yoga was not a flowery, soft, and easy practice. He showed us it could be fierce, dynamic and physical."[14] Other variations include "flow yoga" using a different set of body positions than Iyengar yoga and "hot yoga" in which yoga is practiced in a sauna-like hot room.

> **Several types of meditation and relaxation exercises have a number of features in common. These are:**
> - **a quiet environment,**
> - **an object to dwell upon, such as a repetitive word or sound, a feeling, or awareness of breathing,**
> - **a passive attitude, and**
> - **a comfortable sitting position.**
>
> **These features help to clear the mind of extraneous thoughts. The sitting position helps to maintain a wakeful level of consciousness. Some recent forms of yoga meditation incorporate various forms of physical positioning of the body to enhance the spiritual effect.**

Effects of Meditation

Many thousands of studies have been performed on the effects of meditation on a range of bodily functions. These studies have been extensively reviewed elsewhere.[5,6,15] While these studies vary widely in their scientific rigor there is a consensus that meditation results in a decrease in heart rate, respiratory rate, and blood pressure; an increase in EEG alpha and theta wave activity; an increased synchronization (coherence) of neuronal activity; a decrease in blood lactate level; decreased oxygen consumption; decreased muscle tension; increased blood phenylalanine; decreased generation of carbon dioxide by muscles; decreased use of glucose by red blood cells; decrease in stress hormones, and an increase in the secretion of vasopressin and prolactin. Many of these are only modest changes, but some are dramatic. Coherence refers to the degree of synchronization of the electrical activity of a number of neurons. Increased coherence means increased efficiency of information transfer in the brain.

While there is considerable doubt about whether meditation is any more effective in bringing about these changes than simple eyes-closed resting, [16-18] a number of studies suggest that it is. [5,19-22] It can be seen from the above description that eyes-closed rest involves three of the six steps of the meditation procedure described by Benson. The primary difference is that meditation focuses on an object, or thought, or repeating a word or phrase, and a "passive attitude" to keep the mind free of all extraneous thoughts. During simple eyes-closed rest many thoughts can still swirl about in one's brain. Emptying of the brain of random thoughts may allow for a deeper level of concentrated relaxation than simple eyes-closed rest and this may account for the greater effect of meditation. Some of the changes described above as occurring during meditation do not occur during eye-closed rest.

Most forms of meditation result in deactivation of the autonomic nervous system and a feeling of intense relaxation. In a study of expert practitioners of Tantric Yoga recruited from the Ananda Marga Training Center, Corby and colleagues [11] recorded episodes of sudden autonomic activation coinciding with reports by the practitioner of an ecstatic state of intense concentration—a true *samâdhi* episode. This type of experience indicates that some forms of meditation constitute much more than just relaxation.

The EEG is the spatial average of activity generated by the superficial nerve cells of the cortex. The tracings would sum to zero if certain groups of cells were not linked and firing together. [23] The larger the area involved in synchronized activity, the higher the frequency and amplitude of the EEG. One of the effects of meditation is to increase the degree of synchrony of nerve cells. This is called *coherence*. As described below, coherence is taken to the extreme in practitioners who have completed thousands of hours of meditation. During meditation they produce high-frequency 25–70 Hz *gamma* waves.

Claims have been made that meditation can be used to treat a dizzying number of disorders and conditions. Again there is great variation in scientific rigor in the different studies. Any improvement disappears if meditation is discontinued. The interested reader can refer to the reviews of these studies. [6,15] A potential downside of meditation is the risk of becoming addicted to it. This may result in a distancing from family, job and responsibilities and a susceptibility to being manipulated into cults that claim to have "the answer" to life. [15]

The Dalai Lama, Compassionate Meditation, and Gamma Waves

Prior to a MIT conference on meditation, the Dalai Lama spent two days visiting the University of Wisconsin laboratory of neuroscientist Richard Davidson. Davidson was interested in neuroplasticity, the concept that using the brain can physically change the brain. Hebb first proposed this in 1949. He suggested that learning, memory and other higher brain functions were accomplished by the formation of groups of nerve cells whose interactions were strengthened whenever the cells and certain pathways were activated. The research question was: As a result of neuroplasticity, are the brains of experienced Buddhist meditators different than those of non-meditators? To test this, the Dalai Lama dispatched eight of his most accomplished practitioners of Buddhist meditation to Davidson's laboratory. These practitioners had undergone mental training in the Tibetan Nyingmapa and Kagyupa traditions for 10 to 50 thousand hours over periods ranging from 10 to 40 years. The controls had no previous meditative experience but were interested in meditation and underwent training for one week prior to the experiment.

Objectless or compassionate meditation was practiced by the subjects to produce a state of "unconditional loving kindness and compassion" with an "unrestricted readiness and availability to help living beings." Unlike other forms of meditation, compassionate meditation does not require concentration on particular objects, memories, or images. Because "benevolence and compassion pervades the mind as a way of being," this state is called "pure compassion." During objectless meditation the subjects were asked to be in a non-meditative state. They were examined by power spectrum EEG during meditative and non-meditative states.

This study showed remarkable differences in high frequency 25–70 Hz *gamma* wave activity both in the neutral state and during mediation. [24] The differences in the non-meditative state were consistent with neuroplastic changes in the experienced meditators. Gamma power represents the additive effect of all the gamma waves. The gamma power results for the meditative state are shown in Figure 2.

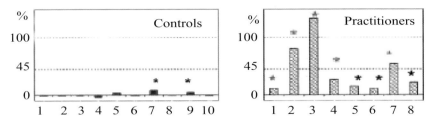

Figure 2. Relative gamma power and mental training. The numbers on the bottom represent subjects. The data on the right of each figure is the relative total gamma power as the percent ratio between the basal state and the meditative state. The blue stars represent a 2-fold increase over baseline, the red stars a 3-fold increase. The results are presented for Controls and Practitioners. From Lutz et al.: Proc Nat Acad Sci USA. 101:16369-16373. By permission of National Academy of Sciences. Copyright 2004.

There was a dramatic increase in *gamma* power during meditation for the experienced practitioners compared to the controls. Figure 3 shows *gamma* power averaged across the whole brain and illustrates the brain locations with the greatest *gamma* power.

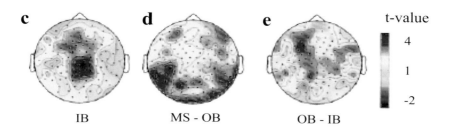

Figure 3. *Relative* gamma *power comparing controls to practitioners for different brain regions. c: initial base line (IB). d: Meditative state (MS) – ongoing baseline (OB). e: post-meditation ongoing baseline – initial baseline. From Lutz et al.: Proc Nat Acad Sci USA. 101:16369-16373. By permission National Academy of Sciences, U.S.A. Copyright 2004.*

These illustrations show the increase in *gamma* power (red areas) over the frontoparietal electrodes. The authors stated that the results demonstrated robust *gamma* wave oscillations and long-distance phase-synchrony in compassionate meditation. The movement of the *gamma* waves through the brain was far better organized and coordinated than in the controls. This indicated that massive distributed neural assemblies were synchronized with a high degree of in-phase timing for the thalamo-cortical and cortical-cortical interactions in this meditative state. The observation that these differences were more striking in the practitioners that had been training the longest is consistent with a neuroplastic effect.

What are *gamma* waves? Neural synchrony in the fast gamma band frequencies of 25 to 70 Hz has been implicated in mental processes involved in attention, working-memory, learning, information processing and conscious perception. This synchronization is thought to play a critical role in high-level cognitive functions. [25-27] There are striking similarities between these results and the proposed neural substrates for consciousness. [28]

Many in the West have assumed that meditation is just a form of relaxation. This is very likely true for the casual meditator. However, considerable evidence has been accumulated that in practitioners who have been meditating many hours a day for many years, brain blood flow, EEG, and spiritual experiences occur that are different from those obtained from simple eyes-closed relaxation.

A study of Buddhist monks with thousands of hours of mental training showed that objectless or compassionate meditation designed to produce a state of "unconditional loving kindness and compassion" was associated with high levels of EEG gamma wave activity. Gamma waves are high frequency 25–70 Hz brain waves that are indicative of a high level of synchronization of neuronal activity and are important in cognition and consciousness. The results were also consistent with the presence of neuroplastic changes in the brain of practitioners with a history of prolonged mental training.

The Effect of Meditation on Brain Function as Determined by Imaging Studies

Imaging studies are relevant to the issue of whether there is a "meditating brain." Only a small number of relevant studies have been carried out. The most well known are those by Newberg and d'Aquili, described in their book, *Why God Won't Go Away*. [29,30] They examined eight devout Buddhists who were accomplished practitioners of Tibetan "mindful" meditation. As in all meditation, the goal was to quiet the constant chatter of the conscious mind and lose themselves in the deeper, simpler reality within. Meditating practitioners were examined using a SPECT (Single Photon Emission Computed Tomography) scanner, a tool that detects emissions of a radioactive compound that is injected when the subject pulls a string to tell the investigators they are at the peak of the process. Figures 4 and 5 show the results.

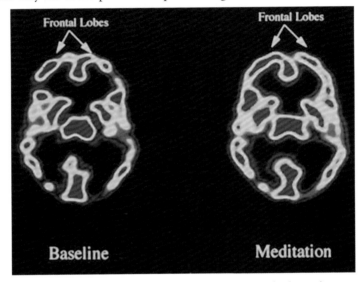

Figure 4. SPECT Scan of a Tibetan Buddhist monk at baseline and during meditation. From Newberg, University of Pennsylvania Health System. There was increased activity in the prefrontal lobes during meditation reflecting increased concentration. Reproduced with permission of the authors and publisher from: Newberg, A. Pourdenad, M. Alavi, A. & d'Aquili, E. G. Cerebral blood flow during meditative prayer: preliminary findings and methodological issues. Perceptual and Motor Skills. 97: 625-630, 2003.

These scans show a combination of activation of the inferior, orbital, and dorsolateral prefrontal cortex representing the increased concentration involved in meditation and decreased activity of the left posterior superior parietal lobe which they called the *orienting association area*. This area constantly receives and evaluates sensory input as to where one is in space and this keeps the self informed as an entity separate from the environment and from others. When input to this area is decreased by sensory isolation or by rhythmic events, such as repeating mantras or clearing the mind of thoughts. Newberg and d'Aquili suggested that the sense of self as an isolated entity was diminished and as a result, the spiritual sense of the person as part of something greater than the self was increased.

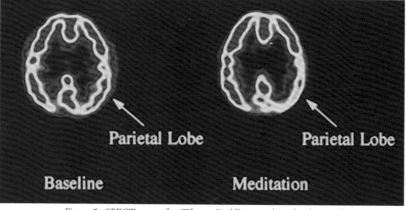

Figure 5. SPECT scan of a Tibetan Buddhist monk at baseline and during meditation. From Newberg, University of Pennsylvania Health System. There was decreased activation of the left parietal lobe (on the reader's right). Reproduced same as Figure 4.

When Franciscan nuns were examined during prayer there was a positive correlation between the blood flow in the right prefrontal cortex and the right thalamus, and a relative decrease in the right superior parietal lobe[31] (Figure 6).

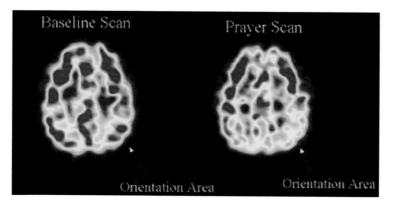

Figure 6. Franciscan nun during prayer showing decreased activation of the right parietal orientation association area. From Newberg, University of Pennsylvania Health System, by permission.

There was also activation of the speech area consistent with the silent use of words in the prayers. Newberg and colleagues believed that "the orientation association area is extremely important in the brain's sense of mystical and religious experience, which often involves altered perception of space and time, self and ego."[29p29] They make their point in more detail as follows:[29p87]

> The orientation association area — the part of the brain that helps us distinguish the self from the rest of the world and orients that self in space — requires a constant stream of sensory information to do its job well.

When that stream is interrupted, it has to work with whatever information is available. In neurological parlance, the orientation area is deafferentiated (*afferent* = neural pathway toward, *de* = unblock) — it is forced to operate on little or no neural input. The likely result of this deafferentiation is a softer, less precise definition of the boundaries of the self. This softening of the self, we believe, is responsible for the unitary experience practitioners of ritual often describe.

The same neurobiological mechanism underlying unitary experiences can also be set in motion, in a slightly different manner, by the intense, sustained practice of slow ritual activity such as chanting or contemplative prayer. These slow rhythmic behaviors stimulate the quiescent system, which, when pushed to very high level, directly activates the inhibitory effects of the hippocampus, with the eventual result of deafferentiating the orientation area and ultimately, of blurring the edges of the brain's sense of self, opening the door to the unitary states that are the primary goal of religious ritual.

In summary, it was proposed that meditation and other rituals resulted in a suppression of the area of the brain responsible for identifying the self in space. As a result, the individual merged with the oneness of the universe, with the cosmic consciousness, with God. While this is almost poetic in its inherent beauty and seems to have great heuristic value for understanding spiritual experiences, there are a couple of problems. The first is that imaging studies of meditating individuals by other investigators have given different results. The second relates to the issue of whether the posterior superior parietal area is the penultimate brain area for developing a sense of the self in space. As described in the previous chapter, the superior temporal gyrus, hippocampus, and ectorhinal cortex play the major role in spatial orientation. In addition, studies in humans after tumor resection indicate that a subcortical parietal-frontal lobe pathway is important in spatial orientation [32] and yet the frontal lobes showed no increase in activity.

Recent studies have examined the brain areas involved in the concept of self as distinct from the location of self in space. [33] It could be argued that these areas might also be deafferentiated during prayer. The areas of the brain involved in this self-network are shown in Figure 7.

These areas are the medial prefrontal cortex, [34,35] the precuneus, and the anterior insula. The medial prefrontal cortex portion, as well as the dorsolateral prefrontal cortex, were activated in the studies of meditating monks described by Newberg and d'Aquili. [30] They attributed this to focused attention. The precunus is in a similar location (Brodmann 7) as the orienting area, but in the self-network it is involved in autobiographical memories related to the identification of the self rather than a positional self.

Herzog and colleagues [36] used PET scanning to examine eight members of a yoga meditation group during a non-meditation control state and during meditative

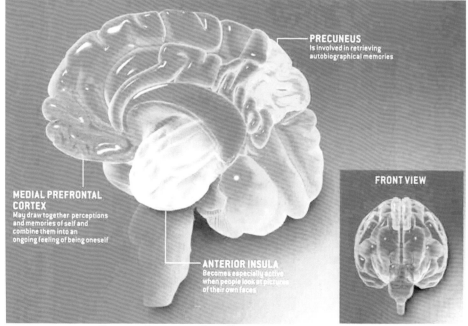

Figure 7. Components of a self-network. From Carl Zimmer, The Neurobiology of the Self. Scientific American. 293:93-101, 2005. 3FX, Inc. [33]

relaxation. They showed a slight increase in frontal lobe blood flow and a more pronounced reduction in the posterior occipital and parietal areas. They did not observe any difference in the two hemispheres. Thus, except for the lack of a primarily left-sided effect, these results tended to agree with those of Newberg and d'Aquili.

A series of studies from researchers at the University of Copenhagen have produced different results. Nine young adults who were highly experienced yoga teachers were examined by PET scanning during non-meditation and relaxation (Yoga Nidra) meditation. [37] During meditation there was activation of portions of the posterior occipital cortex involved in visual imagery. During non-meditation, there was relative activation of the prefrontal cortex and other brain areas that support focused attention. These results, showing activation of the visual imagery areas of the brain and a relative loss of executive attentional control during meditation, tended to be the opposite of the results obtained by Newberg and d'Aquili.

The Copenhagen group obtained similar results in a PET study of light sleep. [38] EEG monitoring was used to determine the stage of sleep and the subjects were interviewed after the scans to determine if they had been dreaming and, if so, what they were dreaming about. During stage-1 sleep there was an increase in blood flow to the posterior occipital cortex representing the visual secondary association areas (Figure 8). Since the eyes were closed, the primary V1 visual cortex was not activated.

There was a relative decrease in blood flow in the frontal and parietal lobes and other areas associated with goal-directed action, a function that is suppressed during sleep. They proposed that stage-1 sleep represents a dreaming state of wakefulness

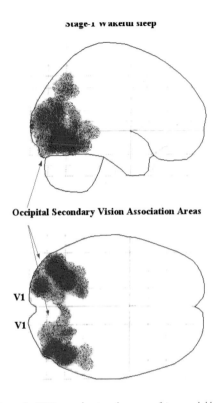

Stage-1 Wakeful sleep

Occipital Secondary Vision Association Areas

V1

V1

Figure 8. PET scan showing the areas of increased blood flow during stage-1 sleep. From Kjaer et al.: Journal of Sleep Research. 11:201-207, 2002. By permission.

associated with visual imagery, while REM sleep reflects the dreaming state of the unaware, more-soundly sleeping brain. In this regard the brain during light sleep is similar to the brain changes they found in relaxation meditation. There were also similarities to the results of PET scans during a hypnotic state. [39] Furthermore, the results also showed bilateral activation of the posterior occipital and parietal cortex and other areas especially in the left hemisphere, suggesting that the three states of altered consciousness, meditation, hypnosis, and stage-1 wakeful sleep, have much in common. [23,38]

The same group also performed PET scanning during meditation with a radio-active compound that was specific for the dopamine D_2 receptor. This showed a 65 percent increase in dopamine release in the basal ganglia during Yoga Nidra meditation and was correlated with an increase in EEG *theta* activity, a characteristic feature of meditation. Since dopamine in the basal ganglia modulates excitatory glutamate neurons, the authors suggested that one effect of meditation is to regulate glutamate pathways in the brain, and this may be the mechanism of stimulating *theta* wave activity.

In his book *Zen and the Brain*, [40] James Austin of the University of Colorado, presented a PET scan of his own brain during just "letting go" sessions of meditation. There was prominent activity over regions of the frontal lobes; in the transverse and superior temporal gyrus, hippocampus, and posterior cingulate; and in the portions of the parietal lobes closest to the occipital lobes. Austin stated he primarily presented these results in his book to illustrate to his readers the use of PET scanning and to introduce the subject of functional neuroanatomy. [15] A larger number of individuals would be needed for more definitive results.

Benson and colleagues [41] carried out a study involving five subjects with very similar results. Using functional MRI (fMRI) they examined blood flow to various parts of the brain in a number of subjects using the meditation method described by Benson to elicit the relaxation response. They observed significant increases in activity of the dorsolateral prefrontal areas, parietal cortex, hippocampus, temporal lobe, anterior cingulate and other areas. They did not observe any significant decrease in activity in the orientation area of the parietal lobes. They attributed the changes to a combination of focused attention and to the regulation of the autonomic nervous system. The activation of the posterior parietal regions is consistent with the visual imagery results of the Copenhagen group. In addition, both the Austin and Benson studies suggested some involvement of the spiritual brain since the temporal lobes, hippocampus, and cingulate were activated.

These results seem confusing. In 2003 there was a meeting involving the Dalai Lama, the exiled spiritual leader of Tibet, other Buddhists, and neuroscientists at the Massachusetts Institute of Technology. [42] The participants aired their West versus East divergent views of how the brain works. It was noted that during meditation some Buddhist practitioners specialized in attention, while others specialized in the demanding practice of visual imagery. The above confusing mix of results may be understandable in this context. The brain scan of a practitioner specializing in attention would show activation of the prefrontal lobe structures that are involved in attention and less activation in posterior cortical structures. The brain scan of a practitioner specializing in visual imagery would show activation of the posterior cortex containing the secondary association areas for vision in the occipital lobes and posterior portions of the parietal lobes. Practitioners using both techniques would show a combination of both patterns and might also activate portions of the spiritual brain, the temporal lobes and hippocampus.

The poetic and spiritual interpretations of Newberg and d'Aquili concerning their proposal that the reported decreased blood flow to the left parietal region represents the brain losing contact with itself and merging in a selfless oneness with cosmic consciousness or with God, are intriguing. Whether this interpretation is correct or not will require replication by other investigators.

Brain Imaging During Religious and Mystical Experiences

In addition to the studies of meditation, several brain imaging studies of spiritual individuals engaged in various religious activities have been described. In one study, PET imaging was used to examine the effect of a religious experience. [43] The religious subjects were members of an evangelical fundamentalist community in Germany. Religious feelings were triggered in the religious subjects by reading one of the verses from the book of *Psalms* that had a special meaning to this group. During religious recitation in the religious group there was activation of the dorsolateral prefrontal, dorsomedial frontal, and medial parietal cortex. The latter plays a role in visual memory. There are strong anatomical connections between the medial parietal cortex and the prefrontal lobes. This pathway plays a role in a variety of cognitive processes. There was no activation of the centers for emotion such as the amygdala or other areas of the limbic system. The authors interpreted their study as indicating that religious experience is a *cognitive* phenomenon. As in the Newberg and d'Aquili studies, the prefrontal cortex was activated. However, instead of inactivation of the left parietal lobe, both the right and left the parietal lobes were activated. The interpretation of the activation of the frontal and parietal lobes as cognitive process was different from the Newberg and d'Aquili interpretation of deafferentiation of the orientation association area.

Another study used fMRI imaging of 15 cloistered Carmelite nuns. [44] They were asked to relive the most intense mystical experience they ever had. They were not asked to actually achieve a state of spiritual union with God during the experiment because, as the nuns put it, "God cannot be summoned at will." As a control the nuns were asked to relive the most intense state of union with another human ever felt in their lives while in the order. The study found that reliving the mystical experiences activated more than a dozen different areas of the brain, including the right orbitofrontal cortex, right middle temporal cortex, right inferior and superior parietal lobules, left inferior parietal lobule, right and left caudate, left medial prefrontal cortex, left anterior cingulate cortex, left inferior parietal lobules, left insula and visual cortex.

The authors claimed that their research discredited the theory of a "God spot" in the brain. Many of the areas they observed overlapped with those mentioned above in studies of meditation and prayer. Since many areas of the prefrontal and parietal cortex were activated, their results tend to agree with the German study that willed religious and mystical experiences involve a *cognitive* process. These studies do not negate the concept of a spiritual brain. As mentioned at the start of this chapter the spiritual feelings associated with meditation, prayer, religious thought, reading religious verses and thinking of past mystical experiences are the result of *a conscious effort to bring about spiritual feelings*. As a result they activate many different parts of the brain especially the cognitive centers. By contrast, the spiritual sensations described in the chapter on the spiritual brain were not the result of trying to be spiritual. Instead, they were *arising spontaneously* from within, and were generated by electrical stimulation, epileptic auras, trauma, NDEs, psychedelic drugs, speaking in tongues, and other factors. They came from the temporal lobes — from the spiritual brain.

Brain imaging studies of experienced meditating practitioners have shown three general types of pattern:

- **Activation of the prefrontal lobes**
- **Activation of the occipital and posterior parietal lobes**
- **A combination of both patterns. In studies showing both, there was some activation of the temporolimbic system, suggesting some involvement of the spiritual brain.**

The activation of the frontal lobes is consistent with a meditation style involving focused attention or cognition. The activation of the occipital lobes is consistent with a meditation style involving visual imagery and closely resembles that seen in stage-1 wakeful sleep and hypnosis. For the most highly experienced practitioners meditation elicits changes in the body and brain that are different than those of simple relaxation.

Studies of Newberg and d'Aquili showed both activation of the prefrontal lobes and a reciprocal decrease in blood flow in the left superior parietal lobe, an area purported to be involved in the location of the concept of self in space and in autobiographical memory of the self. Other areas have been shown to also be involved in the sense of self in space and the concept of self. Their proposal that a decrease in activation of the superior posterior parietal lobe represents a loss of self allowing for the merging of a selfless whole with a cosmic spirit or God requires independent replication.

The spiritual experiences associated with the temporal lobes are spontaneous, internally generated and effortless, while the spiritual experiences in meditation, prayer, religious experiences, and reliving mystical experiences are due to a conscious effort to experience spirituality. The areas of the brain that are activated reflect that effort. They are largely independent of the spiritual brain.

References

1. Wilbur, K. *Grace and Grit: Spirituality and Healing in the Life and Death of Treya Killam Wilber*. Shambhala Publications, Boston, 1991.
2. Strassman, R., M. D. *DMT: The Spirit Molecule*. Park Street Press, Rochester, VT, 2001.
3. Ludwig, A. M. in *Altered States of Consciousness*. Ed. Tart, C. T.: Anchor Books, New York, 1969.
4. Isherwood, C. *Vedanta for the Western World*. The Marcel Rodd Company, New York, 1946.
5. Jevning, R., Wallace, R. K. & Beidebach, M. The physiology of meditation: a review. A wakeful hypometabolic integrated response. *Neurosci Biobehav Rev.* 16: 415-424, 1992.
6. Murphy, M. & Donovan, S. *The Physical and Psychological Effects of Meditation Institute of Noetic Sciences,* Sausalito, CA, 1997.
7. Benson, H. *The Relaxation Response*. Avon Books, New York, NY, 1975.
8. Wilber, K. *The Essential Ken Wilbur*. Shambhala Publications, Boston, MA, 1998.
8a. From www.yatan-ayur.com.au
9. Orme-Johnson, D. W. & Farrow, J. T. Eds. *Scientific Research on the Transcendental Meditation Program*. MERU Press, New York, 1977.
10. Kabat-Zinn, J. *Wherever You Go There You Are. Mindfulness Mediation in Everyday Life*. Hyperion, New York, 1994.
11. Corby, J. C., Roth, W. T., Zarcone, V. P., Jr. & Kopell, B. S. Psychophysiological correlates of the practice of Tantric Yoga meditation. *Arch Gen Psychiatry.* 35, 571-577, 1978.
12. Conis, E. in *Los Angeles Times,* F1, F7 Los Angeles, 2005.
13. Iyengar, B. K. S. *Light on Yoga*. Schocken Books, New York, 1976.
14. Stukin, S. in *Los Angeles Times,* F1, F4 Los Angeles, 2005.
15. Andresen, J. Meditation meets behavioral medicine. *Journal of Consciousness Studies.* 7, 17-73, 2000.
16. Fenwick, P. B. et al. Metabolic and EEG changes during transcendental meditation: an explanation. *Biol Psychol.* 5, 101-118, 1977.
17. Dhanaraj, V. H. & Sing, M. *Reduction of Metabolic Rate During TM*. MERU Press, Pheinweiler, Germany, 1976.
18. Holmes, D. S. Meditation and Somatic Arousal Reduction. *American Psychologist.* 39, 1-10, 1984.
19. Farrow, J. T. & Hebert, J. R. Breath suspension during the transcendental meditation technique. *Psychosom Med.* 44, 133-153, 1982.
20. Wolkove, N., Kreisman, H., Darragh, D., Cohen, C. & Frank, H. Effect of transcendental meditation on breathing and respiratory control. *J Appl Pyshcio.*: Respirat., Environ. Exercise Physiol. 56, 607-612, 1984.
21. Benson, H. & Friedman, R. A rebuttal to the conclusions of David S. Holmes article: Meditation and Somatic Arousal Reduction. *American Psychologist.* 39, 725-728, 1985.
22. Dillbeck, M. C. & Orme-Johnson, D. W. Physiological differences between transcendental meditation and rest. *American Psychologist.* 42, 879-888,1987.

23. Fenwick, P. in *The Psychology of Meditation*. Ed. West, M. W.: Clarendon Press, Oxford, 1987.

24. Lutz, A., Greischar, L. L., Rawlings, N. B., Ricard, M. & Davidson, R. J. Long-term meditators self-induce high-amplitude gamma synchrony during mental practice. *Proc Natl Acad Sci USA*. 101, 16369-16373, 2004.

25. Fries, P., Reynolds, J. H., Rorie, A. E. & Desimone, R. Modulation of oscillatory neuronal synchronization by selective visual attention. *Science*. 291, 1560-1563, 2001.

26. Miltner, W. H., Braun, C., Arnold, M., Witte, H. & Taub, E. Coherence of *gamma*-band EEG activity as a basis for associative learning. *Nature*. 397, 434-436, 1999.

27. Rodriguez, E. et al. Perception's shadow: long-distance synchronization of human brain activity. *Nature*. 397, 430-433, 1999.

28. Tononi, G. & Edelman, G. M. Consciousness and complexity. *Science*. 282, 1846-1851, 1998.

29. Newberg, A., M.D., D'Aquill, E., Ph.D. & Rause, V. *Why God Won't Go Away*. Ballantine Books, New York, 2001.

30. Newberg, A. et al. The measurement of regional cerebral blood flow during the complex cognitive task of meditation: a preliminary SPECT study. *Psychiatry Res*. 106, 113-122, 2001.

31. Newberg, A., Pourdehnad, M., Alavi, A. & d'Aquili, E. G. Cerebral blood flow during meditative prayer: preliminary findings and methodological issues. *Percept Mot Skills*. 97, 625-630, 2003.

32. Thiebaut de Schotten, M. et al. Direct evidence for a parietal-frontal pathway subserving spatial awareness in humans. *Science*. 309, 2226-2228, 2005.

33. Zimmer, C. The neurobiology of the self. *Sci Am*. 293: (November) 293-101, 2005.

34. Macrae, C. N., Moran, J. M., Heatherton, T. F., Banfield, J. F. & Kelley, W. M. Medial prefrontal activity predicts memory for self. *Cereb Cortex*. 14, 647-654, 2004.

35. Kelley, W. M. et al. Finding the self? An event-related fMRI study. *J Cogn Neurosci*. 14, 785-794, 2002.

36. Herzog, H. et al. Changed pattern of regional glucose metabolism during yoga meditative relaxation. *Neuropsychobiology*. 23, 182-187, 1990.

37. Lou, H. C. et al. A 15O-H2O PET study of meditation and the resting state of normal consciousness. *Hum Brain Mapp*. 7, 98-105, 1999.

38. Kjaer, T. W., Law, I., Wiltschiotz, G., Paulson, O. B. & Madsen, P. L. Regional cerebral blood flow during light sleep—a H(2)(15)O-PET study. *J Sleep Res*. 11, 201-207, 2002.

39. Maquet, P. et al. Functional neuroanatomy of hypnotic state. *Biol Psychiatry*. 45, 327-333, 1999.

40. Austin, J. A. *Zen and the Brain*. MIT Press, Boston, 1999.

41. Lazar, S. W. et al. Functional brain mapping of the relaxation response and meditation. *Neuroreport*. 11, 1581-1585, 2000.

42. Barinaga, M. Buddhism and neuroscience. Studying the well-trained mind. *Science*. 302, 44-46, 2003.

43. Azari, N. P. et al. Neural correlates of religious experience. *Eur J Neurosci*. 13, 1649-1652, 2001.

44. Beauregard, M., Paquette, V. Neural correlates of mystical experience in Carmelite nuns. *Neuroscience Lett*. 405:186-190, epub, 2006.

Chapter 32

The Hopeful Brain

The Hopeful Brain refers to the ability of the human brain to heal the body. This is accomplished through what is called the *placebo effect*. The placebo effect is simultaneously one of the most amazing aspects of the human brain and one of the most misunderstood. It is amazing because it shows that the brain is capable of bringing about the same level of healing for a range of disabilities as the most powerful drugs developed over the past century. It is misunderstood because many think of it as something that is "just in your mind" and has no true physiological effect on the body. This chapter shows that the placebo effect is illustrative of the ability of the mind and the brain to marshall many of the same effects that are brought about by the best that the pharmaceutical industry has to offer for healing the broken body. This is important to the theme of this book because a specific mindset, a specific belief, or a specific faith, are the critical elements to releasing the placebo effect. The placebo effect plays a major role in explaining the healing effect of prayer and of the laying on of hands by the physician, priest, witch doctor, or shaman. The placebo effect will help us to understand the healing power of spirituality.

The word *placebo* comes from Latin and means "I shall please." It is derived from the Catholic vesper service for the dead, where paid mourners participated in the funeral service. The placebo effect has had a number of definitions. One defines the placebo effect as "the bodily change due to the symbolic effect of treatment or the treatment situation and not its pharmacologic or physiologic properties." [1] The problem with this definition is that the placebo effect has its own pharmacologic and physiologic properties. A better approach is to use just the first part of this definition. Thus, as will become clear as this chapter unfolds — the placebo effect is the bodily change due to the symbolic effect of treatment or the treatment situation.

The simple act of receiving any treatment (active or not) may be effective because of the expectation of a benefit. The expectation of benefit is likely to be greater when the associated accoutrements are the most impressive. In our western society these would be a white coat, a stethoscope in the pocket or around the neck, the diplomas on the wall, and a hospital or clinic setting — the "white coat effect." In primitive societies these would be an impressive witch doctor's mask, outrageous clothing, chanting and instruments that could include rattles, snakes, fire, and smoke — the "witch doctor effect." If the treatment offered contained no effective active ingredient, then whether the ineffective treatment was a drug or a snake's tail, whether it was a "white coat effect" or a "witch doctor effect," both would be equally effective. The reason people get better is in part due to nature's innate healing ability. With the exception of a very few active drugs such as belladonna and digitalis, *until the twentieth century every non-surgical treatment used by physicians in the previous two thousand years owed any effectiveness to the placebo effect.*

So what is this amazing effect? In the following pages I present a number of studies that have shown the power of the placebo effect. Some of these studies also provide insights into how the placebo effect works.

How the Placebo Effect Complicates Drug Studies

The placebo effect is so strong that the Federal Drug Administration (FDA) determines that a drug is effective enough to be released for public use only if its effect is significantly better than placebo. The accepted standard is a random, double-blind design in which subjects who meet criteria for inclusion in a given study are randomly and blindly assigned to a treatment or a placebo group. Double-blind means that neither the patient nor the doctor knows which is which. It is critical that the doctor also be kept in the dark; if he or she knows whether the patient is on the drug or placebo, the doctor may unconsciously be biased in his or her evaluation of the response. The following example was a study of the effectiveness of a long-acting, injectable form of risperidone,

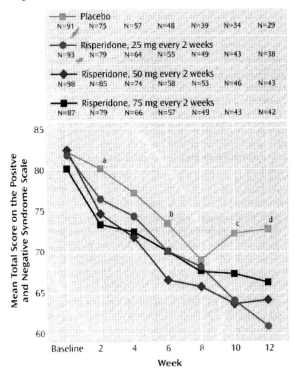

a drug used to treat schizophrenia. [2] Individuals with schizophrenia have both positive symptoms such as hallucinations and delusions and negative symptoms such as social withdrawal. A *Positive and Negative Symptom Scale* was used to evaluate the results. The injections were given every two weeks and three different doses of the drug were given: 25, 50 and 75 mg every two weeks. Figure 1 illustrates the results.

The blue line shows that the placebo was almost as effective as the active drug. By the eighth week the response to placebo was virtually indistinguishable from the effect of all three

Figure 1. Response of positive and negative symptoms of schizophrenia to risperidone and placebo. From Kane et al.: Am J Psychiatry. 160:1125-1132, 2003. By permission.

doses of risperidone. It was only after the eighth week that the effect of the placebo began to wear off, while the effect of all three doses of risperidone persisted. The same degree of effectiveness of placebo has been demonstrated for drugs used to treat a wide range of conditions. The placebo effect represents the sum of a number of effects, including the natural healing course of the disease, the subject trying to please the doctor, the simple easing of anxiety by having a diagnosis and receiving any treatment, faith in the practitioner, and expectation of improvement. [3,4] More than once a drug company has invested many millions of dollars in a new drug, only to have to abandon it when it fails to be any more effective than placebo.

Placebo and Mammary Artery Ligation. The presence of a placebo effect for drugs is impressive enough. The demonstration of a strong placebo effect for surgical procedures is even more impressive. Two of the most famous examples relate to surgical procedures to treat angina pectoris and osteoarthritis of the knee. Both of these conditions produce objective evidence of disease — a narrowing of coronary arteries or a narrowing of the cartilage plate.

In the 1950s, tying or ligating a pair of arteries called the internal mammary arteries, on the inside wall of the chest, was a popular treatment for coronary artery disease. The rationale behind the surgery was that ligating these arteries was supposed to divert more blood to the coronary arteries. It had the advantage that the heart did not have to be stopped to carry out the surgery. Seventy-five percent of patients who had the operation experienced relief of angina pain.

In 1959 Cobb and colleagues [5] reported a double-blind study of this procedure. Of 17 patients, the mammary artery ligation was performed in eight, while the other nine were given anesthesia and an incision was performed but the mammary arteries were not ligated. The study was double-blind in that neither the patient nor the physicians charged with evaluating the results knew what was behind the scar, a ligation or no ligation. *The sham operation was just as effective as the real operation.* A second independent study came to the same conclusion. [6] For both studies combined, there were a total of 21 patients who received the real ligation and 14 who had the sham operation. In both groups 71 percent showed significant improvement of their symptoms. As a result of these studies mammary artery surgery was abandoned.

Placebo and Arthroscopic Knee Surgery. Degenerative osteoarthritis of the knees is a common effect of aging. It is made worse if there had been any unusual stress on the knees, as may occur in some professional or recreational sports. It is characterized by degeneration and thinning of the cartilage plates between the tibia and femur, resulting in a narrowing of the space between these bones (Figure 2).

When medication is no longer effective, an expensive surgical procedure called "debridement" is often performed. This involves passing an arthroscope through a small incision, shaving down the cartilage, and lavage, consisting of flushing out the debris. This procedure costs about $5,000, and up to the year 2002, 650,000 were performed each year in the United States. In 2002 Moseley and colleagues [7] reported a double-blind study of this surgical procedure. A total of 180 patients were randomly assigned to the debridement and lavage, lavage only, or a sham surgery. The sham

A   B

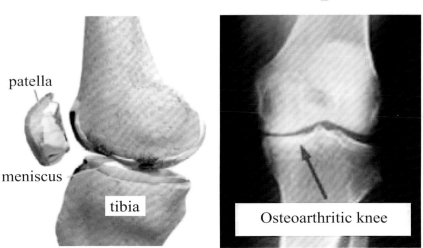

Figure 2. A. Osteoarthritis is due to the degeneration of the meniscus of cartilage between the femur and tibia. B. By X-ray this shows up as a narrowing of the space between the bones. [6a]

surgery involved all the same steps as involved in the real surgery, including surgical draping, anesthesia and splashing saline around to make the sounds of lavage. The only difference was that in the sham surgery, although an incision was made, the arthroscope was not inserted. They also spent just as much time in the recovery room as those with the real arthroscopy. The level of pain, ability to walk, and use of the knee was assessed for two years.

While the real surgery resulted in a significant decrease in pain and increase in function, *it was no greater than that in the placebo group or the lavage-only group.* Those in the placebo group who derived benefit from the procedure "believed" in effectiveness of the "surgery." In contrast to the risperidone study above, where the placebo effect only lasted eight weeks, the effect could still be measured after two years. In his book, the *Anatomy of Hope,* Groopman [8] suggested that subjects who are in chronic pain from any form of disability, become afraid of pain and allow it to become their master. As a result, movement is restricted to prevent pain, but the resultant muscle atrophy only further exacerbates their disability. Once the fear of pain is mastered, people behave as if they were cured, even if it is a "cure" based on placebo effect. Once the cycle of "worshiping the pain god" is broken, the improvement can last for years. *This provides us some insight into the role that faith and hope can play in remaining healthy.*

Pain Pathways

The physiology of pain provides some understanding of how placebos can work to alleviate pain. The ascending and descending pain pathways are shown in Figure 3.

A and C pain fibers from the body enter the dorsal horn of the spinal column. These sensations are passed to the spinothalamic tract that runs from the spinal cord,

ascending pain pathways ——————

descending pain pathways ——————

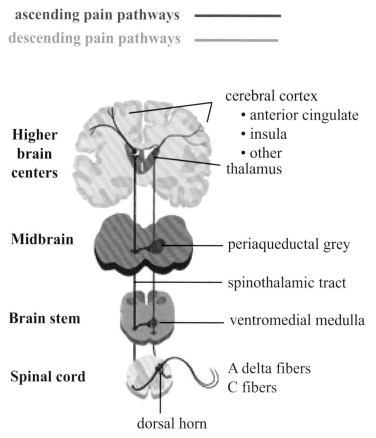

cerebral cortex
* anterior cingulate
* insula
* other

Higher brain centers

thalamus

Midbrain —— periaqueductal grey

—— spinothalamic tract

Brain stem —— ventromedial medulla

Spinal cord

A delta fibers
C fibers

dorsal horn

Figure 3. Ascending and descending pain fibers. [8a]

through the brain stem and midbrain, to the thalamus and from there to the cerebral cortex where they are interpreted as pain. Descending *inhibiting* pathways start in the anterior cingulate, insula, and other areas of the cortex, pass the thalamus, the periaqueductal grey, the ventromedial medulla, and finally back down to the spinal cord. A group of cells called "on" cells increase pain and play a role in defensive withdrawal reflexes, while another group of "off" cells turn pain off. Since the perception of pain is critical for survival, the "on" cells are usually predominant. Morphine and other drugs that relieve pain work by enhancing the effect of the "off" cells. The body has its own endogenous morphine compounds called *endorphins* (*endo* = endogenous, *orphine* = morphine) and *enkephalins* (in the head). The periaqueductal grey is especially rich in receptors for endorphins and enkephalins. In 1969 Reynolds [9] showed that the electrical stimulation of the periaqueductal grey in rats was so effective in suppressing pain that although the animals were still alert they could be operated on without feeling any pain. As soon as the current was turned off, the pain returned.

The descending pain pathways can act to either inhibit or facilitate pain. [10] Endorphins, enkephalins, serotonin and norepinephrine [11] are involved in the inhibition of pain by the descending pain pathway. Other endogenous compounds such as substance P and cholecystokinin (CCK) enhance the pain.

When drug addicts take an overdose and end up in the emergency room, they are given an injection of a drug called Naloxone. This drug binds to the opioid receptors and displaces the heroin or other narcotic drugs that are causing a potentially lethal effect. Naloxone is effective because it binds to but does not stimulate the opioid receptors. It also blocks the effects of endorphins and enkephalins.

Placebo Effect, Pain, and Endorphins

The above paragraphs illustrated the remarkable power of the placebo effect for relieving pain but did not show how it works. In 1978, a major clue was provided by Jon Levine and colleagues.[12] They examined a total of 47 patients who had an impacted third molar removed using Valium, nitrous oxide, and a local block as anesthesia. This anesthesia slowly wore off, and after two hours they were told they were going to receive a powerful anti-pain drug. Some were given morphine, while others were given a placebo. At three hours they were told they were going to receive a medication that might make the pain worse. Some were given Naloxone, while others were given placebo. They were divided into those who responded to the placebo and those who did not. The results are given in Figure 4.

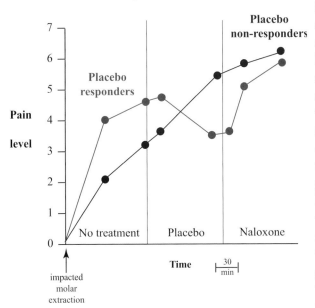

Figure 4. Effect of placebo on dental pain and effect of subsequent Naloxone in subjects who were placebo responders and those who were placebo non-responders. From Levine et al.: Lancet. 2:654-657, 1978.[12] By permission from Elsevier.

This study showed that in placebo responders, the Naloxone, which blocks opioid receptors, reversed the effect of the placebo, suggesting the placebo effect was due to the internal release of endorphins. In the placebo non-responders, the pain just continued to increase after surgery. By the end of the experiment the level of pain was the same for both groups. Numerous subsequent studies have replicated these results.

Dr. Fabrisio Benedetti of the Department of Neurosciences at the University of Turin in Italy also carried out important studies to explain how the placebo effect for pain works.[13] He and his colleagues elicited pain in volunteers by compressing a cuff around the arm. The pain was evaluated by monitoring blood pressure, pulse, sweating, and muscle contraction, and by subjective reports of the level of the pain response. In a great show of doctoral authority, the volunteer watched as a dose of morphine was injected into an intravenous line. After a few minutes the cuff was inflated again and this time there was no pain. This process was repeated several times. In subsequent tests, all aspects of the procedure were the same except that, unknown to the volunteer, saline instead of morphine was injected. Again there was no evidence of or report of pain. In later tests the placebo and naloxone were injected together. If the placebo effect was due to the endogenous release of enodorphins, the Naloxone would block the placebo effect. With this combination the pulse and blood pressure increased and the volunteers began to sweat and report pain, indicating the placebo effect had been blocked. This experiment indicated that the placebo effect elicited by the *expectation of pain relief* was produced by the release of endogenous endorphins. Additional evidence for the important role of expectation came from studies showing that when the placebo was administered out of sight of the subject, this resulted in a significant reduction in the placebo effect. [14] The administration of drugs that block the effect of cholecystokinin (CCK) enhance the placebo effect, [15] suggesting that the inhibition of CCK may contribute to the placebo effect associated with the expectation of pain relief.

In addition to pain, the placebo effect is especially effective for other subjective symptoms such as depression. While part of this effect may be mediated by changes in endogenous opiates, the neurons that contain opiate receptors are closely interlinked with a range of neurotransmitters including serotonin, dopamine, norepinephrine, and GABA (gamma-amino-butyric acid). This broader effect may play a role in the effectiveness of the placebo effect on mood and other behaviors. [16]

Placebo Effect and the Prefrontal Cortex

Despite the above studies showing that the production of endogenous endorphins play a role in the placebo effect for pain, there was still controversy about whether the effect on pain was due to inhibition of pain transmission, the emotional aspects of pain, or simply an artifact of trying to please the investigators, the so-called report bias. [4] There was also the question of how the increase in endorphins was produced. To address these issues, Tor Wagner [16a] and colleagues used fMRI to examine how the different parts of the brain were affected by the placebo effect. The parts of the brain that are activated during pain processing in humans are shown in Figure 5.

These players form the *pain matrix* and are as follows: the rostral anterior cingulate cortex, reported to track changes in pain response mediated by hypnosis; the parahippocampal complex and insula, involved in the discrimination of types of pain and the emotional context of pain; and the thalamus, the major relay station for pain fibers from the body to the brain.

The prefrontal cortex, consisting of the dorsolateral prefrontal cortex and the orbitofrontal cortex, acts to maintain and constantly update the expectations of pain, and modulates pain processing by other areas of the brain. The orbitofrontal cortex plays a role in learning based on rewards. Finally, the midbrain in the area of the pariaqueductal grey contains a high concentration of opiate neurons associated with

Human Brain Sites for Processing Pain

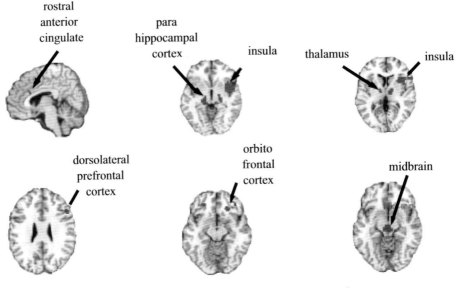

Figure 5. The parts of the human brain involved in the perception of pain. Adapted from Wagner et al., Science. 303:1162 –1167, 2004. [16a] By permission.

pain fibers coming from the body. This is the site where most of the endogenous opiates are produced, resulting in the placebo effect. Monitoring of the activity in these sites (red areas in Figure 5) allowed a number of hypotheses to be examined.

Wagner's study involved 50 subjects. Varying levels of pain were elicited by electrical or heat stimulation of the skin. Part of the study design involved the application of a cream to the skin. In some cases subjects were told the cream should help control the pain; in other cases they were told the cream contained no active ingredients and was serving as a control. An additional aspect of the study was to warn or not warn subjects that the pain was coming. This study design allowed the investigators to study the flow of blood to different parts of the brain under control versus placebo conditions and under conditions of expecting or not expecting pain. The following are some of the findings:

- The expectation of pain relief is associated with the activation of the prefrontal cortex. This activation in turn was associated with an increase in activity of the midbrain and a decrease in the activation of other parts of the pain matrix. The magnitude of the placebo response was correlated with the degree of decrease in blood flow to the regions of the brain that process pain. This supported Wagner's first hypothesis that *the placebo response was associated with a decrease in the activation of the pain matrix,* and second hypothesis that *the prefrontal cortex mediated the anticipation of pain relief.*
- The strong correlation of the activation of the dorsolateral and orbitofrontal cortex and the activation of the midbrain during anticipation of pain relief suggests that prefrontal mechanisms and cognitive control trigger the opioid

release involved in part of the placebo response.

- There is clearly more to the placebo effect than just the release of endogenous endorphins. In anticipation of pain relief, the prefrontal cortex decreases the activation of the structures of the pain matrix independent of opioid release.
- These results clearly reject the proposal that the placebo effect is due to report bias [4] or the equivalent of no treatment.
- While 72 percent of subjects showed a placebo effect, the remaining 28 percent did not. The role of genetic factors in placebo response is discussed below.

Other imaging and EEG studies have also supported a role for the prefrontal cortex in the placebo effect with expectation of pain relief [17-19] and relief of depression. [20] In the latter study, individuals whose depression improved with placebo showed a significant increase in prefrontal EEG concordance. By contrast drug responders showed a decrease in prefrontal EEG concordance.

These studies provide an important link in the ability of the mind to control the body. They indicate that the placebo effect is associated with an active cognitive brain process and is not equivalent to no treatment or biased reporting. They illustrate the importance of the mind set, in this case expectation of pain relief. This expectation factor directly relates to the "white coat" and the "witch doctor" effects noted previously.

Placebo Effect and Acupuncture

Acupuncture is a form of Traditional Chinese Medicine based on practices and theories that go back thousands of years. One of these theories is that the body's vital energy, called *chi* or *qi,* circulates through channels called meridians. Each of 12 meridians represents a major organ system. Originally there were 365 acupuncture points on these meridians but during the past 2,000 years the number has increased to about 2,000. Yin and yang are opposing forces in the body. When these get out of balance, *qi* is blocked. Inserting needles in the acupuncture points is purported to unblock the *qi.* Some practitioners place the needles near the site of the disease and some select points at different parts of the body based on the symptoms. Most do both. In electroacupuncture, an electrical current is passed through the needles to increase the effectiveness of acupuncture. [21]

The problem that Western medicine has with this theory is that there is no physical or objective evidence for the presence of these channels or meridians. However, there is no question that acupuncture can be effective. It has been used in the place of conventional anesthesia during surgery, and many have reported its effectiveness for a wide range of disorders. In a study designed to resolve this dilemma, Klaus Linde and colleagues at the University of Technology in Munich examined 302 patients suffering from migraine headaches. The study design included three groups: those who received standard acupuncture with the needles inserted into classic, meridian based acupuncture points, sham acupuncture where the needles were inserted in non-acupuncture sites, and patients on a waiting list to be treated. All subjects kept diaries on their headache symptoms. They were not told which acupuncture group they were in.

The results showed that 51 percent in the acupuncture group, 53 percent in the sham group, and 15 percent on the waiting list had a significant decrease in their headaches. The authors concluded that the effect "may be due to a non-specific physiological effect of needling, to a powerful placebo effect, or both." This study indicated that no matter how the needles were placed, acupuncture was effective. As Michael Shermer [22] suggested, this study does suggest that "*Qi* theory is full of holes."

Brain imaging by PET scan has been performed on individuals receiving acupuncture for pain due to osteoarthritis to explore the areas of the brain involved. [18] Fourteen subjects were examined in a single-blind study. Each subject received real acupuncture, sham acupuncture, and a single pin prick. The real and placebo acupuncture were associated with an expectation of pain relief, while the pin prick was not. Although none of the treatments relieved the pain, the real acupuncture and the sham acupuncture resulted in activation of the right dorsolateral prefrontal cortex, anterior cingulate and midbrain, similar to the areas involved in the study by Wagner and colleagues. This showed that the prefrontal cortex, cingulate, and midbrain were activated by the expectation of pain relief even in the absence of pain relief. While some studies of real and sham acupuncture sites suggest that only real sites activate specific brain areas, most show that both real and sham sites activate brain sites to the same degree.

Placebo, PET, and Parkinson's Disease

Parkinson's Disease (PD) is due to a degeneration of the neurons in the specific dopamine-rich areas of the brain. Since dopamine is critical for the normal initiation of movement, Parkinson's disease patients have difficulty initiating movement. This results in the typical mask like face and shuffling gait. Drugs which enhance the level of dopamine in these critical areas alleviate the symptoms. PET brain imaging can be performed with radioactive labeled compounds, such as $[^{11}C]$ raclopride (RAC), that bind to dopamine D_2 receptors. The degree to which these compounds can bind depends upon how many of the D_2 receptors are empty. The lower the level of dopamine in the synapses, the greater the binding of the radioactive compound and the greater the signal. The higher the level of dopamine in the synapses, the lower the signal. Thus PET scanning with RAC provides an objective method of determining the amount of dopamine released in the synapses of dopamine rich neurons.

An RAC study was carried out on six PD patients. [23] In one part of the study, all patients were at different times given an active drug to treat their PD symptoms or they were given a placebo. In another part of the experiment, the patients were only given the active drug. The active drug increased the release of dopamine in the synapses and decreased the binding of RAC. The placebo had the same effect and there was no significant difference between the two. Both resulted in an improvement in symptoms. As shown in the chapter on the pleasure brain, rewards release dopamine into the synapses of dopamine reward pathways. All PD patients in this study had previously received treatment and knew what to expect of their medication. The authors suggested that the unconscious expectation of reward (drug effect) resulted in the release of dopamine, whether the active drug was given or not.

Endorphins, PET, and the *COMT* Gene

Other radioactive compounds that target different neurotransmitters can also be used in PET scans. The radioactive compound [^{11}C] carfentanil binds to enkephalin receptors. Enkephalins, like endorphins, are the body's endogenous pain medications. Since placebo responses are elicited more easily in some individuals than others, genetic factors are likely to be involved. Placebo responses, especially those to pain, involve the production of endogenous endorphins and enkephalins. Thus, genes that affect the production of these endogenous pain-killing compounds could explain the difference in placebo responses. Catechol-o-methyl-transferase is one of the enzymes that break down dopamine and norepinephrine. The gene involved is called *COMT*. A common genetic variant of this gene results in the presence of either methionine (met) or valine (val) at amino acid position 158 in the *COMT* enzyme. Individuals who inherit the met allele from both parents (met/met) have lower enzyme activity than those that inherit the val allele from both parents (val/val). Met/met individuals with low *COMT* activity have higher amounts of dopamine in their synapses. Met/met homozygotes have chronically increased levels of dopamine. This in turn results in a secondary decrease in the nerve content of enkephalins and subsequently result in an increase in μ-opioid receptors. The level of μ-opioid receptors in different parts of the brain can be detected by PET scans using [^{11}C] carfentanil. These relationships are shown in Figure 6.

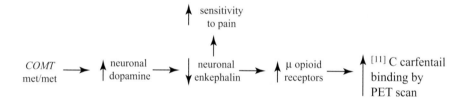

Figure 6. Method by which [^{11}C] carfentanil PET scanning can evaluate the effect of the COMT val158met polymorphism on response to pain.

Subjects with the met/met, met/val and val/val *COMT* genotypes were subjected to a painful stimulus and examined by [^{11}C] carfentanil PET scanning to determine the percent increase in enkephalin release. [24] The results are shown in Figure 7.

This showed a significant effect of *COMT* gene variants on the amount of enkephalins released in response to a painful stimulus. These changes were noted in the dorsal anterior cingulate, anterior and posterior thalamic nucleus, and amygdala, all parts of the brain involved in either the transmission or interpretation of pain. While placebo responses to pain were not examined, it is very likely that since the *COMT* gene plays a role in the regulation of the enkephalin release involved in the placebo response to pain, the *COMT gene will thus play a role in determining who will have the greatest placebo responses.* Other still-unidentified genes are also likely to produce genetic variation in the level of the placebo effect.

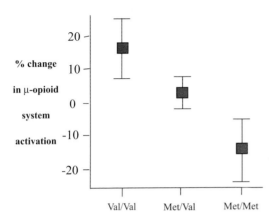

% change in μ-opioid system activation

Figure 7. *Effect of* COMT *val158met genotype on percent change in enkephalin release following a painful stimulus. From Zubleta et al. Science. 299:1240-1242, 2003.*

These results illustrate the important role that different genes play in regulating the amount of endorphins and enkephalins that can be released during the placebo effect. This suggests that *in addition to cultural differences and differences in religious indoctrination, genetic factors contribute to differences in the effectiveness of faith in maintaining good health.*

Nocebo Effect

The opposite of the placebo effect is the *nocebo* effect. Nocebo derives its meaning from the Latin term "I will harm." It refers to symptoms or bodily changes that follow the administration of an inert substance that the patient believes to be an active drug. [25] As with the placebo effect, expectation and suggestion play an important role. As an example, a placebo-controlled study of the potential effect of aspirin for the treatment of angina involved three different medical centers. At two of the centers, the consent form noted that "gastrointestinal irritation" was a possible side effect, while at the third center there was no mention of this side effect. *Patients at the first two centers reported a significantly higher incidence of GI upset than at the third center.* [26] In addition, six times as many subjects in the first two groups left the study because of these side effects than in the third center. There was no medical evidence that those complaining of GI symptoms actually had GI disease. This is the *nocebo effect — the development of adverse symptoms based on the expectation of adverse symptoms.* This has also been referred to as "negative placebo effect." [27] It might also be termed the "voodoo effect." There have been many other examples of headaches, bronchial asthma, allergic, and other symptoms in subjects taking placebos as part of randomized clinical studies that represent nocebo effects.

In some cases the nocebo effect has resulted in an epidemic of symptoms. An example was the religious sect called the "jumpers." Members of this group experienced seizure-like jerking of the head, an arm, a leg, or sometimes the entire body. One author reported seeing a person stand in one place and jerk forward and backwards with their head almost touching the floor in front and behind. Hundreds of people often jerked at one time. [27] Other examples of epidemics of psychogenic symptoms or disorders have been recorded.

The placebo effect is a powerful example of mind over body. It is especially potent when the individual has an expectation of benefit, whether a decrease in pain, a relief of depression, or other aspect of

good health. When there is relief of pain, part of the placebo effect is due to the release of endorphins and enkephalins, the body's own internal morphine-like compounds. An additional part of the placebo effect is derived from an activation of the prefrontal cognitive centers producing a decrease in activation of the pain matrix consisting of different brains areas involved in the processing of pain signals. The effectiveness of the placebo response varies in different individuals. Genetic factors play a role in this variation.

The nocebo effect is the opposite of the placebo effect. It involves the production of troublesome symptoms or side effects when given a placebo. Like the placebo effect, the expectation of a given result plays a major role.

Both the placebo and nocebo effects help us to understand the powerful role that faith and belief can play in many aspects of good health.

References

1. Brody, H. in *The Role of Complementary & Alternative Medicine*. Ed. Callahan, D. Georgetown University Press, Washington, D.C., 2002.
2. Kane, J. M. et al. Long-acting injectable risperidone: efficacy and safety of the first long-acting atypical antipsychotic. *Am J Psychiatry.* 160, 1125-1132, 2003.
3. Kaptchuk, T. J. Powerful placebo: the dark side of the randomised controlled trial. *Lancet.* 351, 1722-1725, 1998.
4. Hrobjartsson, A. & Gotzsche, P. C. Is the placebo powerless? An analysis of clinical trials comparing placebo with no treatment. *N Engl J Med.* 344, 1594-1602, 2001.
5. Cobb, L. A., Thomas, G. I., Dillard, D. H. & al, e. An evaluation of internal mammary artery ligation by double-blind technique. *N Engl J Med.* 260, 1115-1118, 1959.
6. Diamond, E. G., Kittle, F. & Crockett, J. E. Evaluation of internal mammary artery ligation and sham procedure in angina pectoris. *Circulation.* 18, 717-718, 1958.
6a. A. From www.allaboutarthritis.com B. From www.emedx.com/emedx
7. Moseley, J. B. et al. A controlled trial of arthroscopic surgery for osteoarthritis of the knee. *N Engl J Med.* 347, 81-88, 2002.
8. Groopman, J. *The Anatomy of Hope How People Prevail in the Face of Illness*. Random House, New York, 2004.
8a. From www.synapticusa.com/images/pathway_illust.jpg
9. Reynolds, D. V. Surgery in the rat during electrical analgesia induced by focal brain stimulation. *Science.* 164, 444-444, 1969.
10. Zhang, L., Zhang, Y. & Zhao, Z. Q. Anterior cingulate cortex contributes to the descending facilitatory modulation of pain via dorsal reticular nucleus. *Eur J Neurosci.* 22, 1141-1148, 2005.
11. Jones, S. L. Descending noradrenergic influences on pain. *Prog Brain Res.* 88, 381-394, 1991.
12. Levine, J. D., Gordon, N. C. & Fields, H. L. The mechanisms of placebo analgesia. *Lancet.* 2, 654-657, 1978.
13. Amanzio, M. & Benedetti, F. Neuropharmacological dissection of placebo analgesia: expectation-activated opioid systems versus conditioning-activated specific subsystems. *J Neurosci.* 19, 484-494, 1999.
14. Amanzio, M., Pollo, A., Maggi, G. & Benedetti, F. Response variability to analgesics: a role for non-specific activation of endogenous opioids. *Pain.* 90, 205-215, 2001.
15. Benedetti, F. & Amanzio, M. The neurobiology of placebo analgesia: from endogenous opioids to cholecystokinin. *Prog Neurobiol.* 52, 109-125,1997.
16. Sher, L. The placebo effect on mood and behavior: the role of the endogenous opioid system. *Med Hypotheses.* 48, 347-349, 1997.
16a. Wagner, Tor. Placebo-induced changes in fMRI in the anticipation and experience of pain. *Science.* 303:1162–1167, 2004.
17. Lieberman, M. D. et al. The neural correlates of placebo effects: a disruption account. *Neuroimage.* 22, 447-455, 2004.
18. Pariente, J., White, P., Frackowiak, R. S. & Lewith, G. Expectancy and belief modulate the neuronal substrates

of pain treated by acupuncture. *Neuroimage.* 25, 1161-1167, 2005.

19. Zubieta, J. K. et al. Placebo effects mediated by endogenous opioid activity on *mu*-opioid receptors. *J Neurosci.* 25, 7754-7762, 2005.

20. Leuchter, A. F., Cook, I. A., Witte, E. A., Morgan, M. & Abrams, M. Changes in brain function of depressed subjects during treatment with placebo. *Am J Psychiatry.* 159, 122-129, 2002.

21. Ulett, G. Beyond Yin & Yang. *How Acupuncture Really Works.* W. H. Green, New York, 1992.

22. Shermer, M. Full of Holes. The curious case of acupuncture. *Sci Am.* 30, 2005.

23. de la Fuente-Fernandez, R. et al. Expectation and dopamine release: mechanism of the placebo effect in Parkinson's disease. *Science.* 293, 1164-1166, 2001.

24. Zubieta, J. K. et al. COMT val158met genotype affects *mu*-opioid neurotransmitter responses to a pain stressor. *Science.* 299, 1240-1243, 2003.

25. Barsky, A. J., Saintfort, R., Rogers, M. P. & Borus, J. F. Nonspecific medication side effects and the nocebo phenomenon. *JAMA.* 287, 622-627, 2002.

26. Myers, M. G., Cairns, J. A. & Singer, J. The consent form as a possible cause of side effects. *Clin Pharmacol Ther.* 42, 250-253, 1987.

27. Benson, H. *Beyond the Relaxation Response.* Times Books, New York, 1984.

Success means getting what you want; happiness means wanting what you get.
Richard Bolstad [1]

A generous man will prosper; he who refreshes others will himself be refreshed.
Proverbs 11:25

Chapter 33

The Happiness Brain

Most studies of human mood have focused on pathological states such as depression. Happiness is not simply the absence of depression. It is a dimension in its own right that has only recently received research attention. People can be unhappy but not clinically depressed. It is often stated that one of the advantages of religion is that it makes people happy. Unfortunately, as discussed elsewhere it can also make people hateful, sad and miserable. This leads to the question, "What causes people to be happy?" Studies suggest humans are inherently happy and that happiness is *unrelated* to financial success or material wealth. Surveys across many countries have repeatedly shown that most members of our species are at least mildly happy. [2] Using a simple five-question happiness scale [2] on representative samples from 43 nations, Ed and Carol Diener, psychologists at the University of Illinois, found that 86 percent of people scored above neutral. In another study, 10 groups of widely different people were asked to rate the statement, "You are satisfied with your life?" on a scale of 1 (complete disagreement) to 7 (complete agreement). The results are shown in Figure 1.

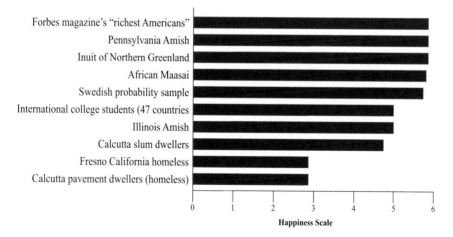

Figure 1. Results of different people being asked if they are satisfied with their lives. Based on data from Ed Diener and Martin Seligman, Beyond Money: Toward an Economy of Well Being in Psychological Science in the Public Interest, 2004, [6] and R. Biswas-Diener. [2]

Remarkably, most people were well above average regardless of their material wealth. Thus a group of the richest Americans rated no higher than the much more austere living Pennsylvania Amish, Inuit of northern Greenland, or the African Maasai. Even Calcutta slum dwellers rated themselves above average. Only the two groups of the homeless in California and Calcutta rated themselves below average.

While it is easy to understand why homeless people would be unhappy and since the slum dwellers in Calcutta who had homes were much happier, there may be some aspect of being homeless that is antithical to feeling happy. A number of studies on learned helplessness suggest that one factor is a loss of control over one's life.

The lack of correlation between wealth and happiness is further illustrated in Figure 2 showing the average rates of happiness in the U.S. did not increase over periods during which the gross national product doubled and even quintupled.

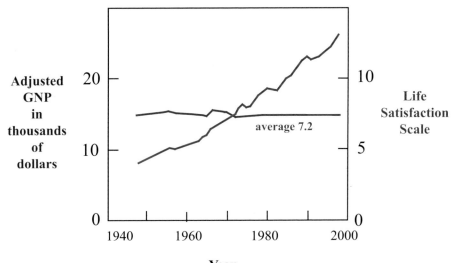

Figure 2. Lack of correlation between gross national income and level of happiness. From Easterlin Journal of Economic Behavior and Organization. *27:35-47, 1995.* [3]

A major reason for the lack of correlation between GNP and happiness is that people quickly adapt to a wide range of circumstances. Someone inheriting or winning a great deal of money may temporarily be happier, but they soon settle back to their previous innate level of happiness. The same holds for those with progressively increasing yearly incomes. After each raise, people adapt and return to a previous level of happiness, a phenomena that Allen Parducci [4] called the *hedonic treadmill.*

Just as altruism in humans is likely to be the result of its having a positive selective value in evolution, it has also been suggested that happiness is common because it also has a positive selective value. People who are in a good mood are more creative, helpful, sociable, and more energized and able to tackle the business of the day. Many studies have shown that happy people are healthier, tend to live longer, have more enduring marriages, and have better jobs. [5]

Social Relationships

To attempt to further identify what factors played the greatest role in happiness, Ed Diener and Martin Seligman examined those who scored in the top 10 percent of the happiness score and compared them to those in the bottom 10 percent. The single most important variable was the presence of social relationships. Nearly everyone in the top 10 percent were surrounded by good friends and had healthy family ties, while those in the bottom 10 percent rarely had these traits. [6]

This is consistent with studies showing that married people tend to be happier and live longer than unmarried, separated, or divorced people. [7] The relationship with health was demonstrated by a study showing that among patients who had a bone marrow transplant, those with strong social support, 54 percent survived two years compared to 20 percent for those without social support. [7] In one study, 126 randomly selected healthy Harvard graduates from the early 1950s were followed for 35 years. After that time 100 percent of those who reported low warmth and closeness from both parents had diseases such as coronary artery disease, hypertension, duodenal ulcer, and alcoholism, compared to only 47 percent with these diseases among those reporting high levels of warmth and closeness to both parents. [8]

The important role of love and caring in health [9] was also shown in a study of 10,000 Israeli men, 40 years of age and older. Those who perceived their wives to be loving and supportive had half the rate of angina of those who felt unloved and unsupported. [10]

This effect even applies to animals. In a remarkable study that was subsequently replicated two times, Nerem and colleagues [11] fed rabbits a diet high in fat and cholesterol. In one group of rabbits the assistant took them out of their cages, and petted and talked to them before feeding. The other group was just fed in the cage. The first group had 60 percent less atherosclerosis than the second group. These and other studies indicate that social relationships and a feeling of belonging and being loved and cared for play an important role in happiness and health.

Being in Control

In 1983 Laudenslager and colleagues [12] exposed some rats to electric shocks from which they could escape and others to shocks from which they could not escape. The control rats received no shocks. The rats were re-exposed to a small amount of shock 24 hours later, after which a test of their level of cellular immunity was performed. Those that were exposed to the inescapable shock showed a suppression of their immune response, while both the controls and those who could escape the shocks showed no immune suppression.

In studies in dogs [13] those that were exposed to unavoidable shocks eventually gave up on trying to prevent the shocks. When subsequently exposed to escapable shocks they did not even try to escape. This phenomenon was termed *learned helplessness*. In humans, learned helplessness resulting from a perceived loss of control over one's environment results in depression. [14] It is very likely that the low happiness scores in the homeless subjects in the study in Figure 1 were a result of learned helplessness over their situation.

The role of being "in control" in health and happiness has been shown in a number of studies. In one study done in a nursing home for the elderly, one group of subjects was given a plant and told to look after it, they were responsible for the plant's health. Another group was also given a plant but told that the staff would look after it. Over the next 18 months twice as many of those who were not "in control" of their plants died compared to those who were "in control" of their plants. [15]

It should not be surprising that the rational brain is the part of the brain involved in choosing when to be in control. In a study by Spence and Frith, [16] subjects were instructed to simply lift their right or left finger on response to a noise. Brain scans predictably showed that the auditory cortex was activated by the noise, and lifting a finger activated the region of the motor cortex for fingers. However, when the subjects were allowed to make their own free will choice about which finger to raise, the dorsolateral prefrontal cortex, one of the sites of the rational brain, was also activated. Thus, being "in control" and having free will to choose activated a different part of the brain compared to not being "in control." This area of the brain is underactive in depression.

Helping Others

As will be discussed in a later chapter, there is a strong selective value for altruism, which is defined as kind acts that put the individual at risk for the benefit of the group. There are also benefits to mental and physical health and happiness. The old phrase, "Tis better to give than receive" was scientifically validated in a study by Schwartz and colleagues. [17] They studied a random sample of 2,016 members of the Presbyterian church throughout the United States. Numerous variables were examined, including giving and receiving help, prayer activities, self-reported mental and physical health, and religious activities. Statistical analysis showed that giving help was more significantly associated with better mental health than receiving help.

One study that factored out the role of religion is important for the subject of this book. Musick and co-workers [18] tested the question of whether older volunteers benefited in terms of better health and well-being. They examined 8,832 subjects collected from 1989 to 1994. They were asked whether they had volunteered in the past year through a religious, educational, political, senior citizen, or other organization. The analysis showed the protective effect of volunteering in terms of a lowered death rate was greatest when the volunteering was for fewer than 40 hours per week and among those who lacked other social supports. Although 69 percent of the volunteer work was done through religious organizations, there was no relation between reduced mortality and degree of religious service attendance, They concluded that *volunteering, rather than its religious context, explained the beneficial effects.*

This result was supported in a study by Oman and colleagues, [19] who in 1990 examined 2,025 residents of Marin County, California, 55 years of age or older. Residents who were involved in two or more helping organizations were placed in a "high volunteerism" group. Mortality was measured from 1990 to 1995. Those in the "high volunteerism" group had a 63 percent lower likelihood of dying than the non-volunteers. After a correction for many other factors, including age, gender, exercise, general health, marital status, and religious attendance, "high volunteerism" was still associated with a 44 percent reduction in mortality. The absolute figures were a mortality rate of 30.1 percent for the non-volunteers versus 12.8 percent for the "high volunteerism" group. Remarkably, this 44 percent reduction was greater than the effect of physical mobility (39 percent), exercising four times per week (30 percent), weekly attendance at religious services (29 percent). It was only modestly lower than that associated with the granddaddy of all risk factors, not smoking (39 percent).

These are just a few of numerous studies showing that altruistic behaviors and volunteerism are associated with happiness, improved mood, enhanced self-esteem, and better mental and physical health, and that helping others per se may be a major part of the increased longevity seen in religious versus non-religious individuals. [9] It is little wonder that there has been selection for altruistic behaviors during human evolution.

Christian, Jewish, Buddhist, Islamic, and Native American spiritual traditions all emphasize the benefits that accrue from helping others. One could argue that if all of these religions are man-made, this is simply a reflection of man's inherent tendency to altruism and the happiness it brings. It was probably assumed that these "good" behaviors had to be wrapped in the authority of religious dogma to ensure they were carried out, even though they originated from man himself.

Human beings have evolved an emotional system that leads them to be generally happy, to think positively, and to quickly adjust to both positive and negative events. A strong and supportive social network of friends and family, and helping others, are among the greatest contributors to happiness. Helping others may provide a significant contribution to the positive effects of religion on longevity and health.

References

1. Bolstad, R. NLP and Happiness. www.suomennlp-yhdistys.fi/kongressi/happiness.pdf. 2006.
2. Biswas-Diener, R. The search for happiness. *Spirit & Science.* 17: 28-33, March-April, 2006.
3. Easterlin, R. A. Will raising the income of all increase the happiness of all? *Journal of Economic Behavior and Organization.* 27: 35-47, 1995.
4. Parducci, A. *Happiness, Pleasure, and Judgment: The Contextual Theory and its Application.* Lawrence Erlbaum Associates, Mahwah, New Jersey Hove, UK, 1995.
5. Fredrickson, B. L. The value of positive emotions: The emerging science of positive psychology is coming to understand why its good to feel good. *American Scientist.* 91: 330-335, 2003.
6. Diener, E. & Seligman, M. E. P. *Beyond Money.* Psychological Science in the Public Interest. 5: 1-31, 2004.
7. Myers, D. G. *The Pursuit of Happiness: Who is Happy, and Why.* Avon Books, New York, 1993.
8. Russek, L. G. & Schwartz, G. E. Perceptions of parental caring predict health status in midlife: a 35-year follow-up of the Harvard Mastery of Stress Study. *Psychosom Med.* 59: 144-9, 1997.
9. Post, S. G. Altuism, happiness, and health: it's good to be good. *Int J Behav Med.* 12: 66-77, 2005.
10. Medalie, J. H. & Goldbourt, U. Angina pectoris among 10,000 men. II. Psychosocial and other risk factors as evidenced by a multivariate analysis of a five year incidence study. *Am J Med.* 60: 910-21, 1976.
11. Nerem, R. M., Levesque, M. J. & Cornhill, J. F. Social environment as a factor in diet-induced atherosclerosis.

Science. 208: 1475-1476, 1980.

12. Laudenslager, M. L., Ryan, S. M., Drugan, R. C., Hyson, R. L. & Maier, S. F. Coping and immunosuppression: inescapable but not escapable shock suppresses lymphocyte proliferation. *Science.* 221: 568-70, 1983.

13. Maier, S. F. & Seligman, M. E. P. Learned Helplessness: Theory and Evidence. *Journal of Experimental Psychology: General.* 105: 3-46, 1976.

14. Seligman, M. E. P. *Learned Optimism.* Random House, Sydney, Australia, 1997.

15. Langer, E. J. *Mindfulness.* Addision-Wesley, Reading, MA, 1989.

16. Spence, S. A. & Frith, C. D. Towards a functional anatomy of volition. *Journal of Consciousness Studies.* 6: 11-29, 1999.

17. Schwartz, C., Meisenhelder, J. B., Ma, Y. & Reed, G. Altruistic social interest behaviors are associated with better mental health. *Psychosom Med.* 65: 778-785, 2003.

18. Musick, M. A., Herzog, A. R. & House, J. S. Volunteering and mortality among older adults: findings from a national sample. *J Gerontol B Psychol Sci Soc Sci.* 54: S173-180, 1999.

19. Oman, D., Thoresen, C. E. & McMahon, K. Volunteerism and mortality among the community-dwelling elderly. *Journal of Health Psychology.* 4: 301-316, 1999.

Chapter 34

The Biology of Faith Versus Reason

Sometimes faith is described as the belief in something in the absence of evidence. [1] By this view faith becomes the antithesis of reason. The existence of faith cuts to the core question of this book — how can reason and faith, a thinking rational brain, and a spiritual brain coexist in the same body?

Blaise Pascal (1623–1662) the famous and brilliant seventeenth century mathematician was the epitome of a person who used his rational brain. He made important contributions to the construction of mechanical calculators, the study of fluids, the concepts of pressure and vacuum, and the mathematics of projective geometry. At the tender age of 16 he contributed to the theory of probability and modern economics. He wrote powerfully in the defense of the scientific method. [2] In 1654 he came perilously close to being killed in an accident in which his horses lunged over a bridge and the carriage he was riding in almost followed. This terrifying experience left him unconscious for some time. Upon recovering 15 days later, between 10:30 p.m. and 12:30 a.m., reminiscent of near-death experiences and despite this massive and prolific use of his rational brain, Pascal had an intense religious vision and conversion. In 1657 his religious faith was further reinforced when his 10-year-old niece appeared to have been cured of a painful and infected fistula of a tear duct after she touched what was believed to have been a thorn from the crown that had tortured Christ.

How then does such an individual massively steeped in the productive use of his rational brain come to terms with endorsing the Christian faith and a believing in God? To Pascal, God was the Christian God depicted in the Bible. The Bible provided information about this Christian God but not proof for the existence of God. Pascal wormed his way out of the dilemma of how to be rational and still believe in God using what has been called Pascal's Wager, outlined in *Pensées,* the last book he wrote. The wager involved the application of decision theory to the belief in God. He argued that it was always a better "bet" to believe in God than not believe in God because the expected value of belief is greater. This rationale is summarized as follows:

You may believe in God, and if God exists, you go to heaven, your gain is infinite.

You may believe in God, and if God doesn't exist, your loss is finite and therefore negligible.

You may not believe in God, and if God doesn't exist, your gain is finite and therefore negligible.

You may not believe in God, and if God exists, you will go to hell, your loss is infinite.

In essence he felt it was better to believe in a non-existent God than to offend one that did exist. He favored the infinite gain and avoided directly addressing the question of whether God exists or not. While this may have worked for Pascal, in reality it was basically a cop-out and did not address the real question, Does God exist? It only addressed the question of whether one should believe in God.

To some authors, reason is totally excluded by faith. For example, in *De Carne Cristi,* Father Tertullian (150–225 A.D). states:

> After Jesus Christ we have no need of speculation, after the Gospel no need of research. When we come to believe, we have no desire to believe anything else; for we begin by believing that there is nothing else which we have to believe…

One could argue that Christianity itself is based on a distrust of knowledge, wisdom and reason. In Genesis, Adam and Eve were evicted from their blissful state of ignorance by eating of the tree of knowledge. Christianity views this act as the source of man's inherent sin and evil and the New Testament takes it for granted that man is sinful and evil. The view that knowledge and wisdom are evil is further confirmed in *I Corinthians* 1 verses:

> 18. I will destroy the wisdom of the wise.
>
> 20. Has not God made foolish the wisdom of this world?
>
> 21. The world through wisdom did not know God.
>
> 27. God has chosen the foolish things of the world to put to shame the wise.

The opposite extreme is authored by Clifford as quoted by William James in his 1897 book *The Will to Believe,* [3p47]

> If belief has been accepted on insufficient evidence the pleasure is a stolen one…It is sinful because it is stolen in defiance of our duty to mankind. The duty is to guard ourselves from such beliefs as from a pestilence which may shortly master our own body then spread to the rest of the town…
>
> If a man, holding a belief which he was taught in childhood or persuaded of afterward, keeps down and pushes away any doubts which arise about it in his mind, purposely avoids the reading of books and the company of men that call into question or discuss it, and regards as

impious those questions which cannot easily be asked without disturbing it — the life of that man is one of sin against mankind.

Another call for reason over faith was written by Baruch Spinoza in 1670: [4]

> ...if anything is there set down [in the Bible] which can be proved in set terms to contravene the order of nature, or not to be deductible therefrom, we must believe it to have been foisted into the sacred writings by irreligious hands; for whatsoever is contrary to nature is also contrary to reason, and whatsoever is contrary to reason is absurd, as *ipso facto,* to be rejected.

These extreme views illustrate the magnitude of the problem. As seductive as Pascal's attempt to reconcile the rational and the spiritual brain may be, it had an empty and inadequate ring. Can the neuroscience of cognition help us to better understand how the spiritual brain sometimes overwhelms the rational brain? There are several interesting aspects of this question.

One of these aspects has already been covered in the chapter, "The Spiritual Brain." For example, when certain areas of the brain were exposed to DMT, the scientists involved in the experiment absolutely believed that despite all the contrary evidence, they had been abducted by aliens. Under certain circumstances, the rational brain of rational men is totally ignored. This is likely due to the fact that the memory systems of the temporal lobe generally cannot distinguish between externally versus internally generated memories. Thus, strong spiritual experiences such as those produced by psychedelic drugs or aberrant electrical activity may seem as real, as real events. Some additional aspects are covered in Chapter 42 on the evolution of spirituality. Of several other factors, I will first examine the role of the conscious versus the unconscious mind in making simple versus complex decisions.

Complex Decisions are Made in the Unconscious; Simple Decisions in the Conscious Brain

One would think that complex questions, such as those involving faith and religion, would require a great deal of conscious thought and rumination, while simple decisions, such as whether to wear the solid red or the paisley tie, would be made automatically and unconsciously. In fact the reverse is the case. The conscious brain evaluates things held in working memory and the capacity of working memory is limited such that only simple decisions are made in the conscious brain. By contrast the unconscious brain has access to an almost unlimited number of variables based on past experience. Thus, complex decisions that involve weighing the relative merits of many different variables are best made in the unconscious brain.

This is illustrated in a study carried out in the department of psychology at the University of Amsterdam. [5] The participants all read information about four hypothetical cars. In one part of the study they were given only four characteristics (simple decision) rated positive or negative, on which to base their choice. In another part of the study they were given 12 characteristics (complex decision). The best car was characterized by 75 percent positive characteristics, the worst car by 25 percent positive characteristics, and the other two cars by 50 percent positive characteristics. Some subjects were asked to think about the cars for four minutes, then make a decision about which was best. This used the conscious brain. Other subjects were also asked to think about the four cars for four minutes but were distracted by also being asked to solve an anagram. Since the distracted subjects could not actively think about the cars, they were using their unconscious brain to make the decision. Their results, in terms of the percentage of subjects who made the correct decision about which of four cars was the most desirable, are shown in Figure 1.

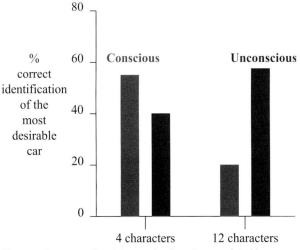

Figure 1. Percentage of participants who chose the most desirable car as a function of the complexity of the decision and conscious or unconscious mode of thought. From Dijksterhuis et al. Science. 311:1005-1007, 2006. [5]

The unconscious brain is able to juggle many different decision variables and is thus best suited for making complex decisions, while the conscious brain, capable of juggling only a few decision variables, is best at making simple decisions. The choice of whether to believe in God and to accept the many different aspects of religious belief is clearly more complex than choosing between cars. This suggests that decisions concerning complex issues such as belief in God, faith, and religion, where hundreds of different aspects of the issue are involved, are likely to bypass the conscious rational brain and utilize the unconscious brain.

The conscious, thinking, rational brain is by-passed when individuals make complex, multifaceted decisions such as those that relate to religion and faith. The rational brain is also bypassed when memory systems of the temporal lobes are internally stimulated. This may produce spiritual experiences that are indistinguishable from reality.

Man's Craving for Information and the Pleasure It Produces

One of the most pleasurable things that humans do is to acquire new information, new knowledge, or new insight into the unknown. Viewing a dramatic sunset, seascape, or snowcapped mountain; hearing a beautiful song; reading an entertaining novel; learning a new concept; or having a spiritual experience are all profoundly gratifying and bring us great pleasure. Why is this so? Irving Biederman of the department of psychology at the University of Southern California and Edward Vessel from New York University have sought to answer this question. They proposed that this enjoyment is deeply connected to an innate hunger and even craving for information. They suggest that human beings are designed to be *infovores*—seekers and devourers of new information and knowledge. "This craving begins with certain types of stimuli, then proceeds to more sophisticated levels of perception and cognition that draw on associations the brain makes with previous experience." [6] It was suggested that this craving for and acquiring of new information would have adaptive value in evolution, in that those individuals who are perceived as knowledgeable and more intelligent would have a selective advantage in mate selection. The concept of human being infovores is reminiscent of Augustine of Hippo's concept of "eros of the mind," which referred to the deep longing within the human mind to make sense of things, a passion for understanding and knowledge. It is related to Daniel Dennet's "hyperactive agent detection device" [7,8] and Karen Armstrong's [9] *logos* (word) versus *mythos* (myth) as means of making sense of the world.

Why do humans perceive the acquiring of new knowledge or understanding as pleasurable? In addition to the reward and pleasure system based on dopamine neurons described previously, opioid receptors are also involved in the subjective feeling of pleasure. Opioid receptors come in three types, *mu, kappa,* and *delta.* The *mu* receptors respond to drugs derived from the poppy plant, such as heroin and morphine. Their addictive properties are well known. These receptors did not evolve just so we could derive pleasure from and become addicted to morphine and heroin. They are present in the brain because the brain produces built-in, or endogenous, morphine-like compounds called *endorphins.* These are the compounds that play a critical role in the placebo effect for pain. Before a new drug for alleviating pain can be approved by the Federal Drug Administration (FDA) it must be shown to work better than the built-in endorphins. Endorphins are also the friend of long-distance runners, kicking in after the first few miles and providing such pleasure that running is addictive for some people. Biederman and Vessel [6] proposed that the stimulation of the *mu* opioid receptors is the mechanism by which the acquiring of new knowledge and new understanding can be very pleasurable. On what do they base this?

In addition to the presence of *mu* receptors in the pain pathways, they are also present in many other parts of the brain. For example, when we view any scene, the neurons are activated progressing along a ventral visual pathway. This pathway starts with the neurons in the V_1 to V_4 portions of the occipital lobe involved in the initial processing of vision. These areas detect color, form, contour, and texture of objects. The next part of the pathway is the primary association area for vision, consisting of the lateral occipital and ventral occipital-temporal cortex. These areas integrate the visual information to detect surfaces, objects, and places. The final portion of the pathway is the parahippocampal and rhinal cortex of the temporal lobe, where new visual information interacts with previously stored memories to determine if it is new information. While all areas of the ventral visual pathway possess opioid receptors, they are most heavily concentrated in the parahippocampal and rhinal cortexes. This is illustrated in Figure 2.

The high density of opioid receptors at the end of the visual pathway, where it intersects with the storage of memories, allows new information and new knowledge to be a pleasurable experience. Just as the pleasurable experience of taking heroin may produce a craving for more, the pleasurable experience of acquiring new information may produce a craving for more, producing an infovore. Other studies suggest that a similar increasing density of opioid receptors is present in the auditory pathway. Supporting this is the observation that the thrills experienced from listening to a stirring piece of music are eliminated by the administration of naloxone, a *mu* opioid antagonist.

New spiritual experiences, acquired either by seeing symbols of spiritual figures, by hearing a rousing sermon, or the insight produced by acquiring information leading one to believe in God, would also provide great pleasure to the recipient. It is of note that this process takes place in the temporal lobes, the spiritual brain of man. There are rich connections between these parts of the brain and the dopamine-rich striatum, suggesting the activation of the dopamine pleasure pathways may also be involved. Similar ideas of a pleasure from the stimulation of the dopamine reward system by new facts, have been proposed in learning theory. [10] It is likely that new spiritual experiences would also result in pleasure due to the stimulation of the dopamine reward system.

These mechanisms help us to understand why man is such a spiritual being and why a belief in God or other spiritual entities by most of our species is unlikely to ever go away. It is likely that the devout Jews doveting for hours before the wailing wall, the Muslims repeatedly reading and speaking the verses of the Qur'an, and the Pentecostal Christians speaking in tongues are all deriving great pleasure from their spiritual activities.

These findings can also help us to understand why faith and the spiritual brain often win out over the rational brain, and why most people in the world believe in God. While the acquiring of new scientific facts and knowledge and the creation of new music or scientific theories also bring great pleasure, because of their upbringing and early exposure to religion and culture, the majority of people in the world are more involved in spiritual activities than in rational and scientific activities. The great pleasure derived from these activities provides little incentive to change.

Man's Resistance to Changes in His Belief System

Another important aspect to the relationship between faith and reason is the fact that cognitive psychological research has repeatedly shown that people tend to seek out, recall, and interpret evidence in a manner that sustains their belief system.

The interpretation of data is often deeply shaped by the beliefs of the researcher. These implicit beliefs are often so deeply held that they affect the way in which people process information and arrive at judgments. Both religious and anti-religious belief systems are often resistant to anything that threatens to undermine, challenge, qualify, or disconfirm them. Deeply held assumptions often render these implicit theories

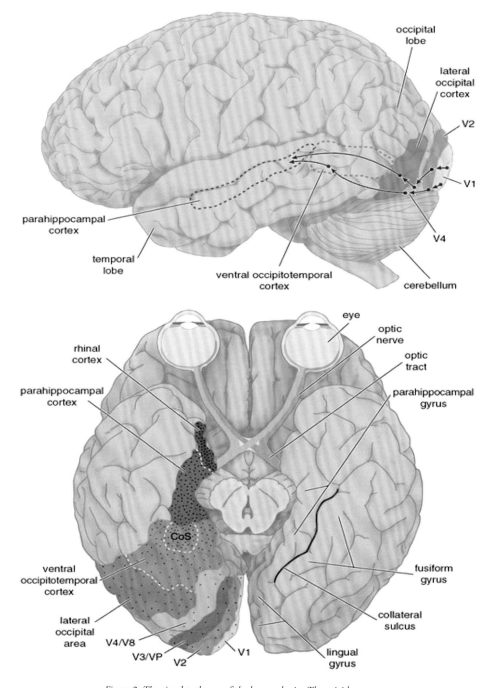

Figure 2. The visual pathways of the human brain. The opioid receptors are shown as black dots. This shows that the density of opioid receptors increases along the visual pathway and is maximal in the parahippocampal cortex and rhinal cortex. From Biederman and Vessel, Perceptual Pleasure and the Brain. American Scientist. *94:247-253, 2006. [6] By permission.*

"almost impervious to data." [1,11p83]

This is what lead my mentor in mammalogy and my friend in pre-med to violently strike out at me when I challenged their belief systems. This is what led to the phrase "Science moves funereally. Scientists don't change their minds, they just die off." [12p254] And what led Thomas Kuhn in his book, *The Structure of Scientific Revolutions* [13] to describe what he termed a *paradigm shift,* or replacement of old ideas with new ones. He described three stages. The first stage is the absolute rejection of a revolutionary new idea that threatens the old paradigm. The new ideas are, "crazy, insane, nonsense." The second stage is the beginning of a grudging, tentative acceptance of the new idea. The final stage is the rapid and full adoption of the new paradigm, often associated with claims by the original objectors that "they actually thought of it first."

Studies of how memories are stored help us to understand the neurological basis of such resistance to change. It has generally been felt that scenes and faces that come across our visual field stimulate millions of different neurons [14] and that a large number of neurons are involved in storing such scenes in memory. This is true for the average scene or the average face. But what about the memory of faces or things that we have seen thousands of times? Do these still require millions of neurons or does the process become simplified and require fewer neurons? What about only a thousand neurons? Only 10? Or even only one?

Gabriel Kreiman and colleagues [15,16,17] made recordings from single cells in the medial temporal lobes of human patients during neurosurgery. They found that for images the patients had been exposed to thousands of times, such as the face of President Clinton, only a single cell was required to store the recognition of the image. Other images did not elicit a similar response. This effect is shown in Figure 3.

The single cell responded vigorously to a line drawing, a photograph, or a group photograph of Bill Clinton. It was indifferent to images of past presidents, other unknown faces, or random images. In earlier studies these were called "grandmother cells" because studies had shown a single-cell response to pictures of subject's grandmothers but not to pictures of unrelated individuals.

These studies did not imply that only one "grandmother cell" was involved in the recognition of these repeatedly viewed objects. It is likely that several cells were involved. The important point is that very few cells were required for a rapid and efficient recall of even abstract characterizations of the objects.

The principle would be the same for individuals with a religious upbringing repeatedly exposed to pictures of Jesus Christ, or images of Christ on the Cross, or images related to other religions. The repetitive nature of childhood and adult religious instructions are likely to have produced "grandmother cells" related to religious issues. It is also relevant that these cells are closely associated with the limbic structures or the emotional brain. Thus, not only are they rapidly and easily recalled, they often have a strong emotional flavor. Since the areas involved are also part of the spiritual brain, spiritual as well as emotional flavoring may occur. Once these cells are thoroughly hardwired into the temporal lobe early in life, they may represent a form

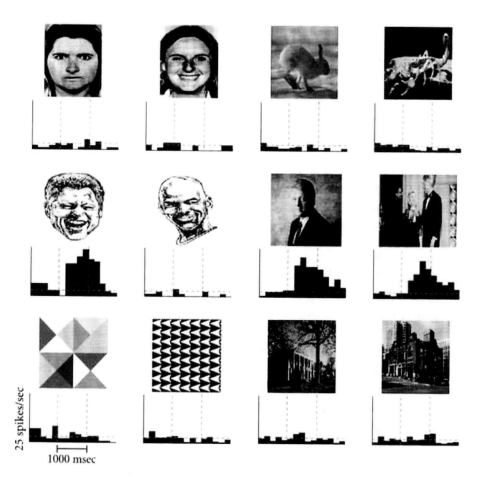

Figure 3. A cell selectively responding to different pictures of Bill Clinton. The area below the pictures show the firing pattern of a single amygdala neuron from a patient looking at drawings or photographs for one second each. Only the figures of the president elicited responses. From Koch. The Quest for Consciousness. *Roberts and Company Publishers, Englewood, CO, 2004. [18] By permission.*

of "I got here first" phenomena and thus contribute to the tendency of humans to be conservative and resistant to change.

This phenomenon is likely to be the basis of the statement of many priests, "Give me a child for five years and I will give you a Catholic for life." This may also explain the existence of scientists who have religious beliefs. This is likely due to having had a strong religious upbringing or spiritual experiences. Those belief systems, once placed into their "grandmother neurons," may be very resistant to change despite exposure to new data and often-conflicting data. It has often been stated that it is logically impossible to reconcile faith and reason. In the abstract, this is correct. It is impossible to reconcile a system based on fact with a system that makes it necessary to ignore fact. However, when reason understands the unique needs and complexities of the spiritual brain, reason and faith are less incompatible.

Many of the most complex decisions that man makes, including those relating to his spiritual nature, take place in the subconscious mind or are internally generated by the spiritual brain thus bypassing the conscious rational brain. In addition, the intake of new information, new knowledge and new insights is a pleasurable experience. This pleasure is brought about by the stimulation of opioid receptors in the higher sensory association areas located in the temporal lobes — in the spiritual brain. Through this mechanism spiritual experiences and insights may provide great pleasure. New knowledge or insights can also produce pleasure through the direct stimulation of the dopamine reward pathways. This can account for why man is such a spiritual being and derives such pleasure from participating in religious rituals.

The repeated exposure to ideas or images results in their being encoded into small number of single neurons in the temporal lobe. This process is likely to contribute to the fact that humans are resistant to any change in their belief system once they are ingrained into memory. As a result, a faith system learned in childhood is likely to persist for a lifetime.

The neurophysiology reviewed in this chapter provides us with an understanding of how the spiritual brain can sometimes overpower the fact-driven rational brain and helps us to understand how the rational and spiritual brain can peacefully coexist.

References

1. McGrath, A. Dawkins. *God Genes, Memes, and the Meaning of Life.* Blackwell Publishing, Oxford, UK, 2005.
2. Wikipedia. Blaise Pascal. en.wikipedia.org. 2006.
3. James, W. The Will to Believe. in: Burger, A. J. *The Ethics of Belief.* (1997). Roseville, CA. Dry Bones Press, Inc. 1897.
4. Spinoza, B. *A Theological-Political Treatise* (translation by R.H.M. Elwes, 1951). Dover Publications, New York, 1670.
5. Dijksterhuis, A., Bos, M. W., Nordgren, L. F. & van Baaren, R. B. On making the right choice: the deliberation-without-attention effect. *Science.* 311: 1005-1007, 2006.
6. Biederman, I. & Vessel, E. A. Perceptual pleasure and the brain. *American Scientist.* 94: 247-253, 2006.
7. Barrett, J. L. Exploring the natural foundations of religion. *Trends Cogn Sci.* 4: 29-34, 2000.
8. Dennett, D. C. *Breaking the Spell. Religion as a Natural Phenomenon.* Viking, New York, 2006.
9. Armstrong, K. *The Battle for God.* Ballantine Books, New York, 2001.
10. Waelti, P., Dickinson, A. & Schultz, W. Dopamine responses comply with basic assumptions of formal learning theory. *Nature.* 412: 43-8, 2001.
11. Nesbett, R. E. & Ross, L. D. *Human Inference: Strategies and Shortcomings of Social Judgment.* Prentice-Hall, Englewood Cliffs, NJ, 1980.
12. Comings, D. E. *The Search for the Tourette Syndrome and Human Behavior Genes.* Hope Press, Duarte, CA, 1996.
13. Kuhn, T. S. *The Structure of Scientific Revolutions.* University of Chicago Press, Chicago, 1970.
14. Levy, I., Hasson, U. & Malach, R. One picture is worth at least a million neurons. *Curr Biol.* 14: 996-1001, 2004.
15. Kreiman, G., Koch, C. & Fried, I. Imagery neurons in the human brain. *Nature.* 408: 357-61, 2000.
16. Kreiman, G., Fried, I. & Koch, C. Single-neuron correlates of subjective vision in the human medial temporal lobe. *Proc Natl Acad Sci USA.* 99: 8378-8383, 2002.
17. Kreiman, G., Koch, C. & Fried, I. Category-specific visual responses of single neurons in the human medial temporal lobe. *Nat Neurosci.* 3: 946-953, 2000.
18. Koch, C. *The Quest for Consciousness.* Roberts and Company Publishers, Englewood, CO, 2004.

Chapter 35

Neurology: Summary

To understand the power that spirituality, religion and faith can play in the lives of humans it is necessary to review some of the basic aspects of how the brain works. To conceive of how our thinking, rational brain, with its "Just give me the facts" outlook on life, can coexist with our spiritual brain with its faith-oriented "Don't confuse me with facts my mind is made up" approach, it is necessary to understand the functioning of the human brain.

None of these features can take place in the absence of consciousness. Our current knowledge of consciousness shows that its unique feature of self-awareness and 'awareness of that awareness' is the result of a high level of integration of information with inter-connection and cross-talk between many different parts of the brain. The highest level of this integration takes place in the prefrontal lobes. They serve as the master brain, the area of association of associations, the integration of integrations. The frontal lobes also serve as the executive director of the brain, with responsibility for some of our most human capabilities of compassion, empathy, long-term planning, goal-directedness, abstract reasoning, spatial memory, working memory, impulse control and paying attention. As the famous Russian neurophysiologist Luria said, the frontal lobes are "the organ of civilization."

The dopamine reward pathways are the portion of the brain most clearly related to the survival of the individual and the species. These pathways reward eating and reproduction without which we would die or become extinct. When defective, these pathways can be responsible for a wide range of addictions involving tobacco, alcohol, cocaine, crack, heroin, and other drugs, gambling and other activities. Knowledge of the pleasure brain helps us to understand that in many cases these addictive behaviors are founded in biology, in contrast to the frequently held religious view that they are the result of a pervasive moral decay.

Other parts of the brain form our social brain. They are responsible for monitoring social interactions between parents and their children, spouses or partners, friends, and society as a whole. A pair of pituitary hormones, vasopressin and oxytocin, play a major role in pair bonding, monogamy, love, maternal care, and trust of others. These admirable features of human behavior are in large part built in. This is in contrast to the conclusion of many religions that we are incapable of having these altruistic behaviors on our own and need to be forced to do them by rules, rituals, recriminations, guilt and reward of eternal happiness in heaven — if we behave.

A specific portion of the prefrontal lobes, the dorsolateral cortex, is especially involved in rational thought, reasoning, and decision-making. It is the part of the brain involved in ambiguous choices with no absolute correct answers, a characteristic of the highest form of human reasoning. This part of the brain can be viewed as our "skeptical brain." It is the portion of our brain that is in the greatest degree of conflict with the spiritual brain.

One of the most remarkable and informative aspects of the neurology of the brain is the evidence for a role of the temporolimbic system as the site of our spiritual brain. Finding God, Jesus, or religion has been widely credited with producing positive and permanent changes in human behavior. The same long-lasting positive changes associated with the sense of meaningful, profound importance, immense joy and of being connected to something greater than ourselves are produced by a range of events that affect the function of the temporolimbic system. These events include the electrical stimulation of the temporal lobes, spontaneous temporal lobe epileptic auras and seizures, trauma, near-death experiences, rituals, speaking in tongues, and psychedelic drugs. A remarkable aspect of one of these drugs, DMT, is its ability to produce the feeling of having been in contact with a non-human presence and the strong conviction that the experience was real in the face of a clear understanding that it was not. The vast majority of the time the temporolimbic tape recorder places into our memory banks experiences that were real. In rare cases where the experiences were internally generated and not real, either as a spiritual experience or the result of taking a psychedelic drug, the temporolimbic tape recorder may be unable to distinguish between what was real and what was not real. This provides us with a framework for allowing a peaceful coexistence between the rational brain and the spiritual brain. It is simply necessary for the rational brain to understand that one of the characteristics of the spiritual brain is to strongly believe in something and have faith in something, even when the rational brain says it is unreasonable or that it did not and could not have happened. That is the essence of faith over reason. It can happen. It does happen. Now we can have some insight as to why it happens.

Since various forms of meditation have been widely used to foster a sense of spirituality and connectedness to something greater than ourselves, one would anticipate that they would activate our spiritual brain. In reality, the parts of the brain that are activated or deactivated simply reflect the method of meditation used, such as highly focused attention or unfocused mindfulness. While some imaging studies have suggested that meditation may involve the dissolution of the individual "self" and merging it with a universal self, this requires independent verification.

A substantial part of spirituality, faith, and religion provide a sense of hope and healing in the face of disease or misfortune. Studies of the neurology of the placebo effect clearly show the power of the mind over the body and of the ability of a positive and believing attitude in health and healing.

The human brain is an incredible organ. It is the reason humans can call themselves human. The hardwired modules for rational thought, empathy, decision making, social interaction, pleasure, hope, mindful healing, and spirituality exist because these traits have survival value and were selected for. To be hardwired is to be genetically controlled. The following chapters examine the role of our genes in rational thought and spirituality.

Part V

The Genetics of Reason and Spirituality

Everything that our brain does is ultimately the result of an interaction between our genes and our environment. For some traits our genes play the major role, for some the environment is the primary factor, and for most it is a combination of the two. On average, depending upon the trait, the genetic contribution accounts for 40 to 90 percent of a trait.

When speaking of genetic factors, many people, including many scientists, think in terms of disorders or traits caused by a single gene. Part V is about the role of genetic factors in reason and spirituality. It is also about disorders or traits that are due to the action of multiple genes instead of single genes. The purpose of this introduction, and the next chapter, is to introduce the reader to the differences between entities due to single genes, called *Mendelian inheritance,* and entities due to multiple genes, called *polygenic inheritance.*

We all learned in high school biology that the field of genetics started with the work of Gregor Mendel, an obscure Augustinian monk who loved working with the plants in the garden of his monastery near Brünn in Austria. The prevailing paradigm of his day, based on the theory of Jean Baptiste Lamarck, was that the environment played the major role in determining different traits. In the fine tradition of experimental science, Mendel sought to demonstrate this by growing an atypical variety of a plant next to a typical variety and observing their offspring. This experiment was "designed to support Lamarck's views concerning the influence of environment upon plants." Instead, Mendel found that the plants' respective offspring retained the essential traits of the parents, and therefore were not influenced by the environment. This brilliant insight led Mendel to a series of experiments over the next seven years, examining the crosses between peas with a variety of different traits.

Mendel found there were two different ways that traits were inherited. To illustrate this I will diagram a typical family tree where females are represented as circles and males as squares. Instead of using Mendel's peas, I will simply illustrate colored genes and the colored traits they produce. All higher organisms, including plants, have two sets of genes: one from their mother and the other from their father.

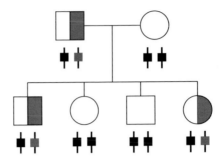

dominant trait

In this diagram the red trait is caused by the red factor, later called a *gene*. Here it is carried by the father and is passed to 50 percent of his offspring. Since only one copy of the red gene is required to cause the red trait, Mendel called this a dominant trait. The red gene is dominant over the black gene. The first set of offspring was called the F1 generation. A second set resulting from further matings was called the F2 generation. If the offspring were crossed with each other the same 50 percent ratio was observed in the F2 generation.

For some traits Mendel observed a different pattern of inheritance.

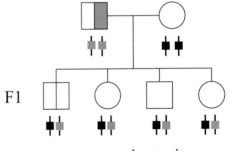

recessive trait

Here, in a cross between a father with the green trait and a mother without this trait, none of the children in the F1 generation showed the trait. However, if the offspring were crossed,

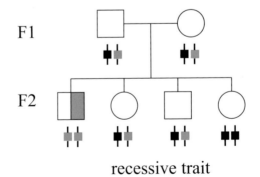

recessive trait

the trait was present in the F2 generation at Mendel's famous 1:3 ratio. One of the offspring has a double dose of the green gene and presents with the green trait. These are called *homozygotes*. Two of the offspring have a single dose and do not have the trait. These are called *heterozygotes*. The final offspring have no green gene and do not have the green trait. Since the heterozygotes with a single dose of the green gene do not have the green trait, the green gene is recessive to the black gene. Mendel called this *recessive inheritance*. Based on many different experiments Mendel formulated several laws of inheritance describing his findings concerning dominant and recessive inheritance, describing the fact that the maternal and paternal copies of a gene separate from each other in the formation of eggs and sperm and recombine at fertilization, and describing the fact that genes are inherited as independent units.

In 1865 Mendel[1] reported his findings in an article entitled *Experiments with Plant Hybrids*. It was published in an obscure journal and forgotten until it was independently rediscovered in 1900 by three different scientists. This piece of work, along with Darwin's *The Origin of Species*, are two of the most important, influential and enduring works in the history of mankind. Mendel's work represented the birth of the study of genetics, a field that in the past 100 plus years has lead to an explosive increase in knowledge, culminating with the sequencing of the entire genomes of man and many other organisms.

I have renewed the reader's knowledge of single gene inheritance for the simple purpose of illustrating what I will *not* be talking about in the following chapters. Mendelian traits represent single gene inheritance where a given trait is entirely due to one gene. The vast majority of human traits and common disorders are not inherited in this fashion. They are rather due to the combined effect of multiple different genes. This is called *polygenic inheritance*. Understanding polygenic inheritance is critical to understanding the genetics of reason and spirituality.

References
1.   Mendel, J. G. Versuche über Pflanzen-hybriden. *Verh Natur Vereins Brün.* 4: 3-57 (1865).

Chapter 36

Polygenic Inheritance

In addition to Mendel's studies of single genes, he also presented the first clear description of polygenic inheritance. [1] He made a cross between white and purple-red flowering beans. The offspring were an intermediate color. In the F2 generation, instead of the expected 1:3 ratio of white and purple-red, he observed a continuous range of colors from white to purple-red. He proposed that more than one gene was involved in determining flower color in this plant.

If the early geneticists had placed more faith in Mendel's brilliant insights, the war of words that soon ensued would not have occurred. But early geneticists such as William Bateson and Hugo DeVries [2] didn't. Contrary to Mendel, they thought these continuous variables were due to environmental factors. However, another early geneticist, Francis Galton, studied continuous variables such as height and mental ability and showed they were hereditary. For example, the children of two tall parents tend to be tall, and the children of two short parents tend to be short. Carl Pearson, the father of statistics, developed the correlation coefficient that quantitated these variations and provided a statistical test of whether the average value of a trait in one group of people was the same or different than in another group.

This led to two camps, the "Mendelians" who believed that individual genes were involved and the "biometricians" who denied the existence of discrete genes. In 1906 Yule suggested that continuous traits were due to the interaction of many individual genes each with a small effect interacting with the environment. [2] This concept was confirmed by a study of the color of wheat grains. In the F2 generation, the ratio of 1 white to 63 red grains conformed to the expectation for three genes, each of which had two variants or alleles.

Thus, early in the twentieth century all of the key elements of the inheritance of continuous traits was worked out. Polygenic inheritance was the result of the additive and interactive effect of multiple genes, each with a small effect, interacting with the environment. This is the mechanism of inheritance of height; weight; intelligence; blood pressure; coronary artery disease; autoimmune diseases such as rheumatoid arthritis and lupus erythematosis; all the mental disorders, including depression, manic depression, schizophrenia, autism, attention deficit disorder, obsessive compulsive disorder, dyslexia, learning disorders; and all of the personality traits including spirituality.

A Threshold Model

When we define a disorder, such as childhood attention deficit hyperactivity disorder (ADHD), people often get the impression that it is an all-or-none entity. In reality it is a continuous variable just like height. Our definitions just give the illusion that you either have it or you don't. This threshold effect is illustrated as follows:

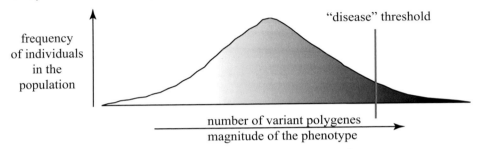

While everyone to the right of the "disease" threshold by definition has the entity and everyone to the left does not, it is clear that we are simply and arbitrarily cutting the curve into two parts (dichotomizing) a continuous trait. [3]

How Many Genes?

When we ask, "How many genes are involved?" there are two aspects of this question. We can be asking, "For a single individual, what is the minimal number of genes that can produce a given trait?" This number could be as low as two genes each, with two variants for a total of four variants. However, in reality the number of genes required to produce a given trait in a single individual is much higher than this, but the exact number is difficult to determine. Alternatively, we could be asking an easier question, "For the whole population, what is the maximum number of genes that can contribute to a given trait?" This number is easier to determine and the answer is, "many." For example, when the effect of an individual gene on a common trait is statistically examined we usually find that it accounts for only *one to two percent* of the total picture or, what we call in statistics-speak, the *variance*. If twin studies showed that environmental factors accounted for 40 percent of the variance and genes accounted for 60 percent, this would imply that on a population basis, approximately 30 different genes (60/2) would be required to produce the disorder.

Polygenes

The variant genes that play a role in polygenic disorders are often referred to as *polygenes* to distinguish them from mutant genes that cause single gene disorders. [3] Mutant genes are genes that when present in heterozygous form (dominant) or homozygous form (recessive) cause a disorder or disease all by themselves. Because they have such a deleterious effect, mutant genes are strongly selected against, and thus they are rare. The change in the nucleic acid sequence caused by the mutation usually results in a severe disruption of the function of the gene.

By contrast, the change in the nucleic acid resulting in a variant polygene usually has a minimal effect on the function of the gene. Here the function of the gene may be only modestly decreased (or increased). Because the effect is small there is little selection against individual polygenes, and as a result they may be very common in the population. Also, because the effect on gene function is modest, the cooperative effect of many different genes is required to produce a given trait. A motto for polygenic disorders is "common gene, common disorder." Table 1 [3] lists in more detail some of the differences between single gene and polygenic disorders.

Table 1. Comparison of single gene versus polygenic disorders

	Single gene disorders	*Polygenic disorders*
Number of genes involved	1	3 to dozens
Frequency of disorder	rare (<1%)	common
Gene frequency	rare (<1%)	common (5–95%)
Effect on gene function	major	minor
Method of identification	linkage analysis	association analysis
Type of subjects studied	large families	affected individuals
Variance explained per gene	100%	.5 to 5%
Specificity	disease-specific	spectrum of disorders
Type of DNA alteration	exons, splice junctions	promoters, microsatellites
	deletions, insertions	regulatory RNA genes

The method of identification refers to how the causative genes are identified. Linkage analysis requires large families of affected individuals and identifies whole regions of chromosomes that may carry the relevant variant genes. Association analysis examines the frequency of genetic variants of specific genes in affected individuals compared to controls.

Specificity refers to whether the gene defect is specific for a given disorder. For example, the mutation that causes Huntington's Disease causes Huntington's Disease and nothing else. No one without the mutant gene has Huntington's disease and everyone with the mutant gene has the disease. By contrast, individual polygenes can be associated with a wide range of related disorders and affected individuals may have a spectrum of disorders. For example, the serotonin transporter gene has been associated with ADHD, depression, anxiety, autism and other behavioral disorders, and individuals with ADHD may also suffer from the same spectrum of disorders. These are called *comorbid disorders* and tend to cluster together because they share some genes in common.

The detrimental effect of the DNA alterations involved in single gene disorders arises from altering the structure or sequence of the gene. The mild effect of the DNA alterations involved in polygenes arises from alterations in promoter regions or changes in the number of repeats in microsatellites near the promoter region. [4] or alterations in regulatory RNA genes [6].

Epistasis

Epistasis is an important aspect of polygenic inheritance. It refers to an interaction between two (or more) genes where the resulting effect is greater than the sum of the effect of each gene individually. A study by Fossella and colleagues [5] illustrates epistasis. As shown in the chapter on "The Hopeful Brain," the *COMT* gene has a valine/methionine polymorphism, and met/met individuals with two copies of the met variant have much lower levels of the catechol-o-methyltransferase enzyme than val/val subjects. Since this enzyme breaks down dopamine in the synapses, met/met subjects have higher brain dopamine levels than val/val subjects. Fossella and colleagues used a computerized assessment to test for frontal lobe executive control in 200 adult subjects. Since dopamine is an important neurotransmitter for the frontal lobes, their hypothesis was that those with higher brain dopamine levels would have better-functioning frontal lobes and thus higher scores on executive functioning. The results of the correlation between the *COMT*

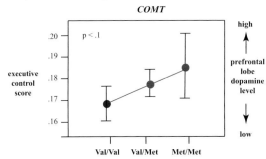

Figure 2. The correlation between a score for prefrontal lobe executive function and the COMT *gene. Fossella et al.: Assessing the molecular genetics of attention networks.* BMC Neuroscience. *3:14, 2002.* [5]

val/met genotypes and executive control scores are shown in Figure 2. As hypothesized, the executive control scores were the highest in those with the met/met genotype and progressively lower in those with the val/met and val/val genotypes. However, this trend was not significant ($p < .1$).

A second enzyme called monoamine oxidase A (MAOA) also breaks down dopamine in the synapses. The *MAOA* gene is located on the X-chromosome and has a repeat polymorphism consisting of variable number of a 30-base-pair segment of DNA in the promoter region of the gene. Individuals who only carry the 3-repeat variant have a five-fold decrease in *MAOA* enzyme levels compared to those who only carry the 4-repeat. As with the *COMT* met variant, they would also have higher brain levels of dopamine.

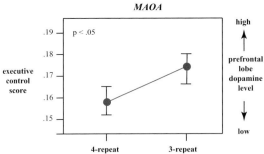

Figure 3. The correlation between a score for prefrontal lobe executive function and the MAOA *gene. Fossella et al.:* BMC Neuroscience. *3:14, 2002.* [5]

Figure 3 shows the correlation between the *MAOA* genotype and the executive control score. Again, as hypothesized, the executive control scores were the highest in those with the 3-repeat genotype and lowest in those with the 4-repeat genotypes. This trend was just barely significant ($p < .05$).

Now comes the *epistasis* part. Since both the *COMT* and *MAOA* genes regulate the breakdown of dopamine, one might anticipate that if a person carried the poorly functioning variants at both genes, the results might be more dramatic than the

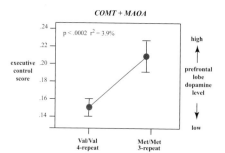

Figure 4. The correlation between a score for prefrontal lobe executive function and the COMT *and* MAOA *genes. Fossella et al.:* BMC *Neuroscience. 3:14, 2002.* [5]

simple additive effect of both genes independently. Figure 4 shows the results for individuals that carried both of the low-functioning variants (met/met and 3-repeat) versus those with both of the high-functioning variants (val/val and 4-repeat).

This shows that when individuals inherit both the *COMT* and *MAOA* low-functioning variants, the average executive function scores are much higher (21.5 %) than for either low-functioning variant alone (*COMT* 18.5 %, *MAOA* 17.5 %) and much lower (15.0 %) than for high-functioning variant alone (*COMT* 16.8 %, *MAOA* 16.0 %). In addition, the difference between the high and low values was highly significant ($p < .0002$). Together these two genes now accounted for 3.9 percent of the variance, much higher than either gene alone or the simple additive effect of both genes. Twin studies have shown that genetic factors account for 89 percent of the variance of the executive control score. If the *COMT* and *MAOA* genes account for only 3.9 % of the variance many other genes would be necessary to account for the remaining 85.1 %.

Most of the common mental and physical disorders and human behavioral traits are polygenically inherited. Polygenic inheritance is due to the additive and epistatic interaction of many different genes, each accounting for only a small percent of the total trait and interacting with the environment.

References

1. Stern, C. *Principles of Human Genetics.* W. H. Freeman, San Francisco, 1973.
2. Strickberger, M. W. *Genetics.* Macmillan, New York, 1968.
3. Comings, D. E. in: *Nature Encyclopedia of the Genome.* MacMillan, 2003.
4. Comings, D. E. Polygenic inheritance and micro/minisatellites. *Molecular Psychiatry.* 3: 21-31, 1998.
5. Fossella, J. et al. Assessing the molecular genetics of attention networks. *BMC Neurosci.* 3: 14, 2002.
6. ENCODE Consortium. Identification and analysis of functional elements in 1% of the human genome by the ENCODE pilot project. *Nature* 447:799-816, 2007.

Chapter 37

The Genetics of Bad Behavior

There are two reasons why I have included a chapter on the genetics of bad or antisocial behavior. First, many studies have been carried out on the interaction of genes and environment for this entity. These studies beautifully illustrate this important interaction. Second, one of the most frequently cited positive aspects of religion is to ensure moral behavior. But what if humans are inherently good, and amoral behavior is primarily the result of certain genes we inherit rather than the environment we are brought up in, or the amount of religious training we have revieved? This question and this possibility make an examination of the origins of amoral behavior a relevant subject.

When we speak of antisocial behavior, two different entities are involved: conduct disorder (CD) and antisocial personality disorder (ASPD). While they are essentially the same disorder, they differ primarily in that CD defines antisocial behavior in children up to the age of 20, while ASPD defines antisocial behavior in individuals 21 years of age and older and can be diagnosed only if CD was present prior to age 21. The essential feature of CD is a repetitive and persistent pattern of behavior in which the basic rights of others or major age-appropriate societal norms or rules are violated. [1] Examples include bullying and threatening others, using a weapon, cruelty to animals, arson, destroying property of others, breaking into houses, burglary, repeated running away from home, and truancy. The essential features of ASPD are the same as CD except that they refer to adulthood. These features specifically include repeated fights, assaults and arrests, conning others, a reckless disregard for the safety of others, constant irresponsibility, and lack of remorse for these behaviors.

While classically thought to be due primarily to socioeconomic and environmental factors, an increasing body of evidence indicates that genes play a major role in CD and ASPD. This conclusion is based on family, twin, and adoption studies.

Conduct disorder is a lifelong condition. One of the most highly replicated findings in the field of psychiatry is that the symptoms of childhood CD persist into adulthood and drive adult antisocial behavior. This conclusion is based on longitudinal studies where subjects are examined in childhood and then re-studied when they are adults. This approach is far more reliable than asking adults to remember their childhood behaviors. Many such longitudinal studies have been performed and they all conform to what I refer to as the 50 percent rule. On average

50 percent of children with CD have a range of antisocial behaviors as adults. This is diagrammed as follows:

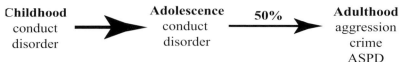

Childhood		**Adolescence**	**50%**	**Adulthood**
conduct	→	conduct	→	aggression
disorder		disorder		crime
				ASPD

The following is an example of the most famous of many of these reports. Dr. Lee Robins [2] at the Washington University School of Medicine in St. Louis carried out this early, classic study of conduct disorder and antisocial personality. In 1922, the St. Louis Psychiatric Clinic was opened in the Municipal Courts Building with the purpose of demonstrating the presumed effectiveness of psychiatric treatment of juvenile delinquents. The clinic continued to operate for 22 years, finally closing its doors in 1944. For many years the records were stored until the demands for space resulted in the proposal to burn them. Foresighted intervention got them transferred to Washington University. A sampling showed that this group included a large number of severely antisocial children, providing "a treasure trove of research materials representing the first step in the study of the natural history of the development of adult antisocial behavior." The plan was to take a population of children seen in the clinic 30 years previously, match them with a sample of normal school children, and find both groups as adults. Matching for sex, socioeconomic status, and other factors would allow the effects of these variables to be sorted out. This produced a group of 524 white children seen in the clinic for behavior problems, of which 406 were referred for antisocial behaviors. These consisted of theft, burglary, robbery, forgery, truancy, chronic tardiness at school, running away, sexual perversion, public masturbation, excess heterosexual interest or activity, vandalism, false fire alarms, carrying deadly weapons, incorrigibility, refusal to work, lying, fighting, and physical cruelty. Robins stated,

> We had expected that the deviant children referred for antisocial behavior would provide a high rate of antisocial adults, but we had not anticipated finding differences invading so many areas of their lives. Not only were antisocial children more often arrested and imprisoned as adults, as expected, but they were more mobile geographically, had more marital difficulties, poorer occupational and economic histories, impoverished social and organizational relationships, poor Armed Service records, excessive use of alcohol, and to some extent, even poorer physical health. The control subjects consistently had the most favorable outcomes. That the tendency toward deviant behavior pervades every area in which society sets norms, strongly suggests that the occurrence of deviance is a unitary phenomenon. No clear connections were found between the type of deviance in childhood and the type of deviance in adults.

Robins concluded that *antisocial behavior in childhood predicts no specific kind of deviance but rather a generalized inability to conform and perform in many areas.* The best predictor of adult antisocial behavior was the *total number of antisocial behaviors as a child, not the type of antisocial behaviors.* Although the average age of referral was 13 years, most of the children had a history of behavior problems dating back many years. *The median age of onset for boys later diagnosed with sociopathic personality was seven years.* It was also striking that *no child without serious childhood antisocial behavior became a sociopathic adult.*

These findings indicate that *adult antisocial personality disorder has its origins in early childhood,* and if a boy or girl passes through childhood without symptoms of antisocial behavior it is unlikely they will develop subsequent problems. Strong and early evidence for the role of genetic factors came from the observation that sociopathic and alcoholic fathers produced a significantly higher rate of sociopathic children (32 percent) than did fathers without this diagnosis (16 percent). *The highest risk factor for producing an adult with antisocial personality was the presence of 10 or more antisocial behaviors as a child, plus an alcoholic father.* By striking contrast, when the parents had no problems, or problems that were not of an antisocial type, there was no increased risk of the child becoming an antisocial adult.

Many sociological studies have blamed juvenile delinquency and antisocial behavior on poverty, poor housing and poor jobs. However, when Robins dissected out these variables she found that *having a sociopathic or alcoholic father was a far better predictor of a child developing an antisocial personality than was the earning power or socioeconomic status of the father.* She pointed out that

> "Families can live in slums and be on relief rolls *without* their children responding to the frustrations of poverty or to the examples of delinquency in their neighborhoods with sociopathic behavior *if* the families' poverty stems from other than antisocial behavior. It is unreasonable, then to attribute a crucial role in the production of adult antisocial behavior to the frustration consequent to low prestige and poverty in childhood."

The major finding from Robins's study was that the best predictor of adult antisocial behavior was the presence of childhood antisocial behavior, along with a family history of alcoholism or antisocial behavior. The type of behavioral problems in childhood was much less important than the number of deviant behaviors. This concept has been supported by many subsequent studies.

The following diagram shows one additional longitudinal study, this time in girls.

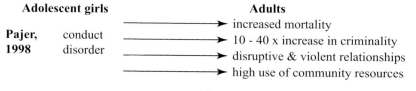

Adolescent girls		Adults
Pajer,	conduct	increased mortality
1998	disorder	10 - 40 x increase in criminality
		disruptive & violent relationships
		high use of community resources

In a paper entitled, "What Happens to 'Bad' Girls," Pajer[3] reviewed studies of the adult outcome of girls with conduct disorder as adolescents. This showed a significant increase in the frequency of both mental and physical disorders, increased mortality (often involving a violent death), a 10- to 40-fold increase in criminality, dysfunctional and often violent relationships, and high rates of using community services. In some cases the crimes committed consisted of burglary and assault rather than the usual female crimes of shoplifting, drug use, and prostitution.

Since one to 10 percent of children have CD, this disorder plays a major role in society's load of antisocial behavior. It has been repeatedly shown that most of the criminal behavior in the general population is carried out by a small number ASPD individuals who are repeat offenders.

Family studies of CD. A number of studies have shown that the fathers of children with CD commonly had CD, ASPD or criminal records themselves.[4-7] The role of genes versus the environment was examined in a study where 72 children who attended a psychiatric clinic with a diagnosis of ADHD were divided into two groups, those with at least one antisocial parent and those without an antisocial parent. In the group with an antisocial parent, the ADHD children tended to have CD, and 23.5 percent of the siblings had CD. By contrast, the ADHD children without an antisocial parent tended to have ADHD without disruptive conduct and zero siblings had CD.[8] In studies where the antisocial and aggressive behaviors were examined by a continuous scale of minimal to severe, the scores for the fathers strongly correlated with the scores for their sons.[9,10]

Simply because the fathers have CD-ASPD does not prove that CD is genetic. Their sons could have CD because of the antisocial environment provided by the father. To explore genetic factors, one study examined siblings and half-siblings. If there was a genetic component to CD, it should have been more common in boys whose fathers had antisocial behaviors than in their half-brothers whose fathers did not have antisocial behaviors. This is what was found. Twice as many sons of the fathers with antisocial behavior had CD than did half-brothers whose fathers did not have antisocial behavior.[11] While studies of half-siblings are informative, studies of twins are even more so.

Twin studies of CD. Twin studies are an important method of identifying the relative role of the genes versus the environment. Identical twins share 100 percent of their genes in common, while fraternal twins share 50 percent of their genes in common. The frequency with which a condition is present in both twins is called the *concordance rate.* For example, if a study starts by identifying a twin with CD and finds that 60 percent of the time the other twin also has CD, then the concordance rate is 60 percent. If a disorder is caused entirely by environmental factors, the concordance rate will be the same for identical and fraternal twins. If one twin comes down with a highly infectious disorder such as the flu, the other twin is likely to also get the flu, whether he or she is an identical or fraternal twin. The concordance rate would be the same for both the identical and fraternal twin. By contrast, if a condition is entirely genetic, the concordance rate would be twice as high in identical twins than in fraternal twins. For intermediate cases due to both genes and enviornmental factors, formulas allow the determination to the relative role of each.

The largest twin study of CD was reported by Slutske and coworkers [12] and utilized the Australian Twin Registry. They examined 2,682 adult twins. The remarkable finding was that genetic factors contributed to at least 71 percent of the disorder. This stands in marked contrast to the usual assumption that conduct disorder is a learned behavior and due to poor parenting, parental conflict and divorce. This very high degree of genetic loading supports the highly reproducible findings described above that CD is a life-course persistent entity as described later in this chapter.

An important aspect of the Australian study was the finding that in addition to a genetic component for the presence of three or more childhood CD symptoms there was also a significant genetic component to the presence of only one or two symptoms. This suggested a multiple threshold model in which increasing numbers of relevant genes result in a continuously increasing susceptability to the symptoms of CD.

An even larger twin study involving 7,449, seven-year-old twins examined aggression as a general trait. [13] Two types of aggression were examined, direct aggression that was essentially CD and indirect or relational aggression that involved a lot of aggressive behaviors without directly harming others. Additive genetic factors accounted for 53 to 66 percent of both types of aggression in both males and females. A number of other twin studies of CD and ASPD have also been reported. As shown in the following section, the degree of the genetic contribution in older children and adults is related to age.

Twin Studies of Juvenile Delinquency and Adult Crime

One of the most interesting findings to come out of twin studies of juvenile delinquency and criminal behavior in adults is the finding that the genetic component is minimal for juvenile delinquency but substantial for adults. This is illustrated in Figure 1.

These studies show that for juvenile delinquency the ratio of the concordance rate in fraternal versus identical twins was close to 1.0. This figure indicates there was very little genetic component to juvenile delinquency. By contrast, for adults the concordance rate for fraternal twins was less than half that for the identical twins, indicating the presence of a substantial genetic component to adult crime. The difference is due to the fact that there is a high degree of "background noise" in juvenile delinquency. In adolescents, acting out in the form of juvenile delinquency is almost a rite of passage. This is the reason why juvenile justice is more lenient than adult justice and why records of juvenile offenders can often be expunged. This result does not mean that some juvenile delinquency is not associated with genetic factors, it is just drowned out with the high level of general, non-genetic delinquency. However, most delinquent behavior fades away by adulthood. Deviant behavior tends to persist predominantly in those with a strong genetic component. As a result, crime in adults does show a genetic component.

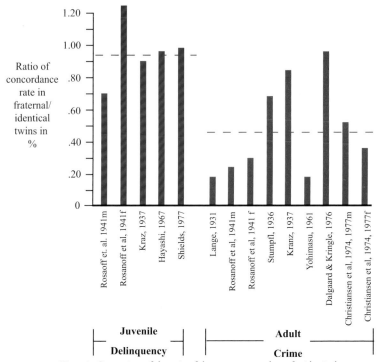

Figure 1. Comparison of the ratio of the percent concordance for identical versus fraternal twins for juvenile delinquency versus adult crime. Data from Cloninger and Gottesman, 1986 in Mednick, S. A. et al.: The Causes of Crime, Cambridge University Press.[14] Dotted lines show the means for the ratios for juvenile delinquency and adult crime.

Adoption studies of antisocial behavior. The most powerful evidence about the relative role of genes and the environment in antisocial behavior comes from adoption studies. This evidence is the result of examining four types of cross-fostering. It is possible to examine the adopted children of antisocial parents raised by either normal or antisocial parents as well as the adopted children of normal parents raised by either normal or antisocial parents. Adoption studies have shown a significantly increased rate of criminality in adoptees with criminal biological parents who were raised in non-antisocial homes.[15-21] These studies are of particular value in demonstrating that conduct disorder and antisocial behavior can occur in the absence of a negative childhood environment such as parental separation, abuse, or alcoholism.

An example of one such four-way cross-fostering study was that undertaken in Stockholm, Sweden by Cloninger and colleagues.[19-21] It included 862 men and 913 women born out of wedlock from 1930 to 1959 and adopted into families of non-relatives at an early age. There were two important aspects of this study, the relationship between alcohol abuse and crime, and the cross-fostering results. The four-way cross-fostering results are summarized for males in Figure 2.

There was only a modest increase in the frequency of criminal behavior when a child with a non-criminal parent was raised in a household with a criminal versus a non-criminal parent (7 percent vs 3 percent). However, the effect was dramatic when

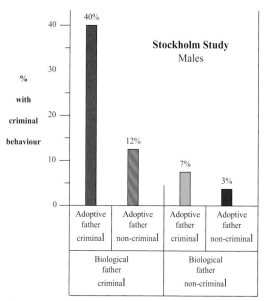

Figure 2. Summary of adoption study of Cloninger et al.: Predisposition to petty criminality. Archives of General Psychiatry. 39: 1242-1247. [19-21] Copyright 1982, American Medical Association.

the children had a criminal parent. Here 40 percent of such children raised with a criminal parent had criminal behavior, versus only 12 percent of such children raised with a non-criminal parent. Although the percentages were smaller, the ratios were even greater for females. The Stockholm studies also found no evidence for a genetic contribution to delinquency in young adolescent. This again verified the above observations that genetic factors predominantly play a role in adult criminality.

In a separate series of studies, Cadoret and colleagues [22-24] examined subjects who were adopted in the first few days of life and studied when they were 19 to 47 years of age. They examined 95 male and 102 female adopted offspring who were separated at birth from biological parents who had ASPD and/or alcoholism. An interaction between the genes and environment was demonstrated by a higher level of aggression and CD in those with both a biological parent with ASPD and an adoptive parent with one or more antisocial problems. This relationship is shown in Figure 3.

The presence of increasing problems in the adoptive parents' home had no effect on adolescent aggressive behavior in the absence of a biological parent with ASPD.

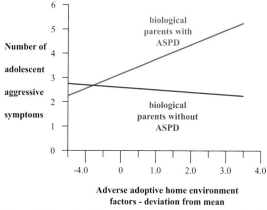

Figure 3. Interaction between genes and the environment in the prediction of adolescent aggression. From Caboret et al. [22] Archives of General Psychiatry. 52:916-924. Copyright 1995.

However, when there was a biological parent with APSD, the risk of adolescent aggression increased with more adverse factors in the adoptive home.

Adolescence limited and Life-course persistent antisocial behavior. As shown in the above twin studies, genetic factors appear to be less important for adolescent than for adult crime. This concept has been reviewed by Moffitt. [25] She addressed what she termed "two incongruous facts about antisocial behavior: A) it shows impressive continuity over age, but B) dramatically increases in frequency during adolescence. The increase during adolescence was so dramatic that to account for this she proposed there were two types of antisocial behavior, adolescence-limited and life-course persistent. This is illustrated in the Figure 4.

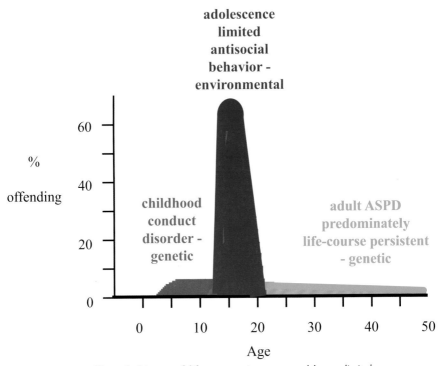

Figure 4. Diagram of life-course persistent versus adolescence-limited antisocial behavior. After Moffitt, T. E. Psychological Review. 10:674-701,1993. [25]

The majority of adult crimes were committed by the life-course persistent subjects. The life-course persistent antisocial behavior would equate to the persistent conduct disorder symptoms noted earlier and would represent the genetic form of antisocial behavior starting virtually at birth and lasting a lifetime. This is consistent with the tendency for childhood conduct disorder to persist and to be one of the best predicters of adult criminal behavior. As for the adolescence-limited antisocial behavior, Moffitt suggested that a maturity gap encourages teens to mimic antisocial behavior in ways that are normative and adjustive. The period of adolescent delinquency matches the gap between sexual maturity and the time of separation from the parents. After this they employ more socially accepted outlets such as marriage, parenthood, higher education, and employment. She proposed that the surge in adolescence-limited criminal behavior might be the result of mimicking the behavior of those with the life-course persistent antisocial behavior, thus giving this group unusual influence on the whole of adolescent delinquency. Moffitt [25] also predicted that the two groups carried out different types of crime.

Life-course-persistent offenders with poor self control, pathological interpersonal relationships, weak connections to other people, and a lifelong antisocial personality account for violence against persons as well as for crimes committed in late life. Adolescence-limited offenders account primarily for crimes which serve to meet adolescents' lust for acknowledgement and privilege: theft, vandalism, public disorder, and substance abuse.

The results of these studies have significant implications. The common view is that the environment in which children are raised plays the major role in predicting criminal behavior. These studies show that the major effect is from a combination of "bad genes" and "bad environment," not a bad environment per se. Placing a non-genetically predisposed child into a bad environment has relatively little effect on criminal outcome, suggesting that if the seed is not "bad," it will not grow. By contrast, the "bad seed" will grow in either environment but it sprouts fastest in a "bad environment."

With regard to the subject of this book, a religious upbringing is likely to have only a modest effect on preventing antisocial behavior for the majority of children, since they have a normal genetic make-up. A religious upbringing is likely to have its greatest effect for a child who has inherited genes for antisocial behavior.

The results of these studies imply that if most antisocial behavior is the result of the actions of a distinct minority of the population, the world should be perpetually blessed with peace and tranquility. Unfortunately, this is not the case. One of the reasons is that psychopaths like Hitler, Mussolini, Stalin, Sadam Hussein and others who are at ease with ruthless brutality often rise to be leaders. Once they attain power they are willing to use any means to remain in power. As a result, such individuals have a disproportionate effect on the history of mankind. As discussed in a subsequent chapter, religions themselves, with the intolerance they often foster toward other groups with different beliefs, have also contributed greatly to human conflicts and wars.

Some Specific Genes — MAO

There are two aspects to the genetics of antisocial behavior. The first, described above, relates to the use of twin and adoption studies to show that genetic factors play a major role. The second is to actually identify some of the specific genes involved. In earlier chapters the role of the two genes, *COMT* and *MAOA,* that code for the enzymes that break down dopamine were illustrated for several traits. In 1993 Brunner and colleagues [26] described a family from Holland in which numerous males had a borderline IQ and a history of aggression, including arson, attempted rape, and exhibitionism. Biochemical studies identified a C–>T mutation that resulted in inactivation of the *MAOA* gene. Since the *MAOA* gene is X-linked, only males, who carry just one X-chromosome, were affected. The extra normal X chromosome in females compensated for the defective *MAOA* gene and they are not affected. A portion of the pedigree is shown in Figure 5. This is an example of a rare single abnormal gene causing a behavioral disorder. Most behavioral disorders, including antisocial behavior, are polygenically inherited.

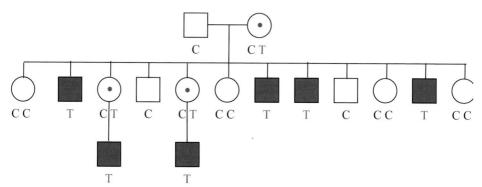

Figure 5. A part of the pedigree reported by Brunner et al. [26] Science. 262:578-580, 1993. The females with the T mutation were CT carriers and did not have symptoms. The males with only the T mutation had one or more symptom of antisocial behavior.

An excellent example of the interaction of a single gene and environmental factors also involved the *MAOA* gene. Caspi and coworkers [27] studied a large sample of children from birth to adulthood. When examined without the genetic data childhood maltreatment made little difference in antisocial behavior in the adults. However, when the interaction between the *MAOA* gene and the presence or absence of maltreatment in childhood was studied, the results, shown in Figure 6, were dramatic.

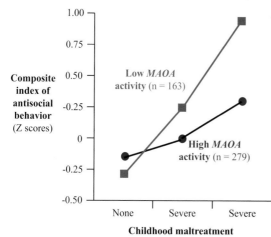

Figure 6. Interaction between the MAOA gene and the degree of maltreatment in childhood. From Caspi et al. Science. 297:851-854, 2002. By permission.

Those individuals carrying the high *MAOA* variant were less likely to show antisocial behavior regardless of whether or not they were maltreated in childhood. However, those individuals with low *MAOA* variant showed much higher levels of adult antisocial behavior if they had been maltreated as children than if they had not been maltreated.

COMT, the other gene responsible for the breakdown of dopamine, is also associated with antisocial behavior. In a study of

240 children with ADHD, the presence of comorbid CD was significantly associated with the valine allele of the val/met variant described previously. CD was also associated with low birth weight and with an interaction between the *COMT* gene and low birth weight. [28]

Genes play a significant role in adult aggressive and criminal behavior. Individuals who carry a set of genes that predispose them to antisocial behavior begin to manifest this condition by the development of conduct disorder in early childhood. In about 50 percent of cases this genetic predisposition leads to criminal and other antisocial behavior in adulthood. The likelihood of antisocial behavior is increased when an individual with such genes is exposed to maltreatment or other disruptive environmental influences.

The concept that humans are inherently predisposed to misbehave unless they are exposed to a strict religious environment is clearly incorrect. However, being raised in a supportive environment that may include a range of religious values would help to prevent antisocial behaviors in the small proportion of individuals who inherit genes for antisocial behavior.

References

1. Frances, A., Pincus, H. A. & First, M. B. (eds.) *DSM-IV-TR. Diagnostic and Statistical Manual of Mental Disorders.* Fourth Edition. Text Revision. American Psychiatric Association, Washington, D.C., 2000.

2. Robins, L. N. *Deviant Children Grown Up.* Williams & Wilkins, Baltimore, 1966.

3. Pajer, K. A. What happens to "bad" girls? A review of the adult outcomes of antisocial adolescent girls. *Am J Psychiatry.* 155: 862-870, 1998.

4. Osborn, S. G. & West, D. J. Conviction records of fathers and sons compared. *Br J Criminology.* 19: 120-133, 1979.

5. Morris, H. H., Escoll, P. J. & Wexler, R. Aggressive behavioral disorders of childhood: a follow-up study. *Am J Psychiatry.* 112: 991-997, 1956.

6. Stewart, M. A., Deblois, C. S. & Cummings, C. Psychiatric disorders in the parents of hyperactive boys and those with conduct disorder. *J Child Psychol Psychiatry.* 21: 283-292, 1980.

7. Behar, D. & Stewart, M. A. Aggressive conduct disorder of children. The clinical history and direct observations. *Acta Psychiatr Scand.* 65: 210-220, 1982.

8. August, G. J. & Stewart, M. A. Familial subtypes of childhood hyperactivity. *J Nerv Ment Dis.* 171: 362-368, 1983.

9. Stewart, M. A. & Deblois, C. S. Father-son resemblences in aggressive and antisocial behavior. *Br J Psychiatry.* 143: 319-311, 1983.

10. Vanyukov, M. M., Moss, H. B., Yu, L. M., Tarter, R. & Deka, R. Preliminary evidence for an associaton of a dinucleotide repeat polymorphism at the *MAOA* gene with early onset alcoholism/substance abuse. *Am J Med Gen (Neuropsych Genet.).* 60: 122-126, 1995.

11. Twito, T. J. & Stewart, M. A. A half-sibling study of aggressive conduct disorder. *Neuropsychobiology.* 8: 144-150, 1982.

12. Slutske, W. S. et al. Modeling genetic and environmental influences in the etiology of conduct disorder: a study of 2,682 adult twin pairs. *J Abnorm Psychol.* 106: 266-279, 1997.

13. Ligthart, L., Bartels, M., Hoekstra, R. A., Hudziak, J. J. & Boomsma, D. I. Genetic contributions to subtypes of aggression. *Twin Res Hum Genet.* 8: 483-491, 2005.

14. Cloninger, C. R. & Gottesman, I. I. Genetic and environmental factors in antisocial behavioral disorders. in: Mednick, S. A., Moffitt, T. E. & Stack, S. A. *The Causes of Crime.* New York. Cambridge Univ. Press. 1987.

15. Zur Nieden, M. The influence of constitution and environment upon development of adopted children. *J Psychol.* 31: 91-95, 1951.

16. Hutchings, B. & Mednick, S. A. Registered criminality in adoptive and biological parents of registered male criminal adoptees. in: Fieve, R. R., Rosenthal, D. & Brill, H. *Genetic Research in Psychiatry.* Baltimore. Johns Hopkins University Press, 1975.

17. Crowe, R. R. The adopted offspring of women criminal offenders: A study of their arrest records. *Arch Gen Psychiatry.* 27: 600-603, 1972.

18. Crowe, R. R. An adoption study of antisocial personality. *Arch Gen Psychiatry.* 31: 785-791, 1974.

19. Bohman, M., Cloninger, C. R., Sigvardsson, S. & AL., v. K. Predisposition to petty criminality in Swedish adoptees. I. Genetic and environmental heterogeneity. *Arch Gen Psychiatry.* 39: 1233-1241, 1982.

20. Cloninger, C. R., Sigvardsson, S., Bohman, M. & von, K. n. A. Predisposition to petty criminality in Swedish adoptees. II. Cross-fostering analysis of gene-environment interaction. *Arch Gen Psychiatry.* 39: 1242-1247, 1982.

21. Sigvardsson, S., Cloninger, C. R., Bohman, M. & von, K. n. A. Predisposition to petty criminality in Swedish adoptees. III. Sex differences and validation of the male typology. *Arch Gen Psychiatry.* 39: 1248-1253, 1982.

22. Cadoret, R. J., Yates, W. R., Troughton, E., Woodworth, G. & Stewart, M. A. Genetic-environmental interaction in the genesis of aggressivity and conduct disorders. *Arch Gen Psychiatry.* 52: 916-924, 1995.

23. Cadoret, R. J., Yates, W. R., Troughton, E., Woodworth, G. & Stewart, M. A. Adoption study demonstrating two genetic pathways to drug abuse. *Arch Gen Psychiatry.* 52: 42-52, 1995.

24. Cadoret, R. J., Yates, W. R., Troughton, E., Woodworth, G. & Stewart, M. A. An adoption study of drug abuse/depencency in females. *Compr Psychiatry.* 37: 88-94, 1996.

25. Moffitt, T. E. Adolescence-limited and life-course-persistent antisocial behavior: A developmental taxonomy. *Psychological Rev.* 10: 674-701, 1993.

26. Brunner, H. G., Nelen, M., Breakfield, X. O., Ropers, H. H. & van Oost, B. A. Abnormal behavior associated with a point mutation in the structural gene for monoamine oxidase A. *Science.* 262: 578-580, 1993.

27. Caspi, A. et al. Role of genotype in the cycle of violence in maltreated children. *Science.* 297: 851-854, 2002.

28. Thapar, A. et al. Catechol O-methyltransferase gene variant and birth weight predict early-onset antisocial behavior in children with attention-deficit/hyperactivity disorder. *Arch Gen Psychiatry.* 62: 1275-1278, 2005.

Generosity without hope of reciprocation is the rarest and most cherished of human behaviors, subtle and difficult to define, distributed in a highly selective pattern, surrounded by ritual and circumstance, and honored by medallions and emotional orations.

E. O. Wilson
On Human Nature [1]

Chapter 38

The Genetics of Good Behavior

The previous chapter pointed out that genes play a major role in the development of lifelong bad behavior as manifested by Conduct Disorder and Antisocial Personality Disorder, and that only a few percent of the population have this problem. The findings demonstrated that the majority of humans were not inherently wicked or amoral, and humans did not need to belong to a religious group to keep them from behaving in an antisocial fashion. But what about the opposite end of the spectrum? Do genes and evolution play a role in the production of individuals with good, prosocial and altruistic behavior? Are there individuals who not only do not behave badly but behave unselfishly and even place the welfare of their fellow man above that of their own? If these individuals exist, is this behavior common and is it a uniquely human trait? The evidence suggests that altruism is real, it is common, and some aspects of it are uniquely human.

Altruism

Altruism is defined as costly acts that confer benefits on other individuals, a selflessness that puts individuals at risk for the benefit of the group. From an evolutionary point of view such behavior would seem to be a counterintuitive anomaly and difficult to explain. Darwin himself recognized that altruism presented a difficulty for his theory of evolution that emphasizes self-serving survival of the more fit. [2] A number of researchers have provided important clues as to how altruism may have evolved. The following are some of the elements involved.

Kin selection. In the 1960s the evolutionary biologist William Hamilton [3] proposed a theory of kin selection. He showed that helping relatives can increase the chances that one's own genes will be passed on through them. This is a form of selective advantage for individuals who use the golden rule. [4] This is the form of altruism most likely to be seen in other primates and animals.

Direct reciprocal altruism. In the 1970s Robert Trivers [5] proposed the concept of reciprocal altruism, a "tit for tat" form of cooperation in which helping a non-relative increases one's own fitness as long as the recipient is expected to return the favor. This form of altruism, involving genetically unrelated individuals, was a signifcant expansion over kin selection where only relatives were involved. Direct reciprocal altruism would only work in situations where it is possible to keep track of who helped whom, but it allowed an extension of its effect beyond the size of the groups involved in just kin selection. This form of altruism is best described as, "You scratch my back and I'll scratch yours." [6] The degree to which humans show a division of labor and cooperate with genetically unrelated individuals is unparalleled in other animal societies. [7]

Indirect reciprocal altruism and reputation. In addition to direct reciprocal altruism, humans often help others even if the altruistic act is not likely to be returned by the recipient. [8] Different types of economic games have been used to explore different aspects of altruism in humans. Based on such studies, Martin Nowak of Harvard University and Karl Sigmund [6,9] of the University of Vienna developed the theory of indirect reciprocal altruism. It can be described as, "I help you and somebody else helps me." The term indirect comes from the fact that if other individuals observe the generous behavior they would be more likely to cooperate with the generous person. The generous person thus develops a reputation for being generous and cooperative. The authors concluded that the reputation of individuals played an important role in social interactions. As a result of reputation-building, the altruistic person will eventually benefit even if it comes from someone other than the original direct recipient.

Reputation has a powerful cooperation-enhancing effect on social interactions [10] and an individual's behavior is driven by the desire to acquire a good reputation. When a game is set up so a donor cannot acquire a good reputation, they cooperate in 37 percent of cases. When the game is set up so they can attain a good reputation, they cooperate in 74 percent of cases. [11] Clearly when someone is keeping score, individuals are more cooperative. An open display of generosity will enhance a person's reputation. As stated by Milinski [10] it helps to "Do good and talk about it." [4] The intelligence and cognitive, language, and "theory of mind" skills of humans are critical factors for the development of reputations.

Strong reciprocal altruism, altruistic rewarding, and punishing. An additional characteristic of human altruism is what has been termed *strong reciprocal altruism.* [12] This is characterized by a combination of altruistic rewarding where altruistic behavior is rewarded, and altruistic punishing where sanctions are placed on those who violate the norm and do not cooperate or help. These are called defectors, and defectors who scam the system to their advantage face reprimands and punishment. Without such punishment the defectors would quickly take over. Some have questioned whether this alone is adequate to account for why cooperation involves much larger groups in humans than in other primates. In modeling studies, Fehr and Fischbacker [7] showed that one additional factor, consisting of punishing those who were not willing to punish others was also necessary. This would be analogous to laws punishing parents who did not or could not control their own children. This effect is shown in Figure 1.

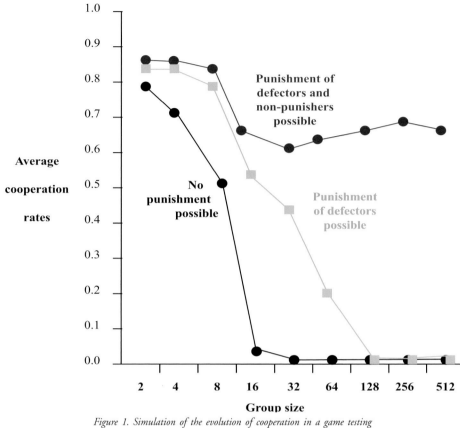

Figure 1. Simulation of the evolution of cooperation in a game testing altruism. From Fehr and Fischbacher: The Nature of Human Altruism. Reprinted by permission from Macmillan Publishing, Ltd. Nature. 425: 785-791, 2003.

After multiple generations of no punishment of any type, the average cooperation rate dropped to zero at a group size of 16. When punishment of defectors was allowed, the rate of cooperation did not drop to zero until there were 128 individuals in the group. If punishment of non-punishers was also allowed, the rate of cooperation remained very high (over 80 percent) and did not drop off in larger groups. The opportunity for reputation-building and punishment has played a major role in the evolution of human cooperation to include large groups of genetically unrelated individuals. [7]

Studies of contemporary hunter-gatherers and other evidence suggest that altruistic punishment may have been common in mobile foraging bands during the first 100,000 years of the evolution of modern man. [13] While religion may have played some role in altruism by threatening punishment by a supernatural force, [14] modeling studies show it is not a critical ingredient. Besides, *religion developed long after altruism was already well evolved.*

While humans uniquely possess altruism in extended groups, when genetic mixing between two groups occurs, rates of helping and cooperation decline

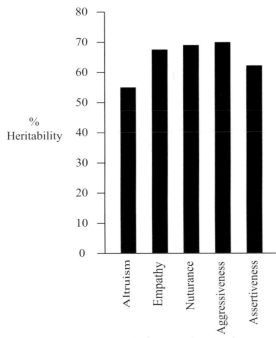

Figure 2. Heritability estimates for five traits relating to altruism and aggression. From Rushton et al.: Altruism and Aggression: The Heritability of Individual Differences. Journal of Personality and Social Psychology. 50:1192-1198, 1986. [16]

dramatically and approach zero. [15] This is indicative of one of the major problems humans have had throughout history, that of mistrusting individuals outside their own kin, social, political or religious group.

The Genetics of Altruism

Rushton and colleagues [16] from the University of London gave questionnaires that measured altruistic and aggressive tendencies to 573 twins. The heritability estimates for altruism, empathy, nurturance, aggressiveness, and assertiveness are shown in Figure 2. The majority of the variance of each scale was due to genetic factors. Specifically the heritability of altruism was 56 percent. Altruism increased with age while aggressiveness decreased. *Virtually zero percent of the variance of each trait was due to the common environment such as early religious instruction.*

Unfairness, Emotion, and Reason

The inverse of altruism is unfair behavior such as cheating and deception. Sanfey and coworkers [17] utilized fMRI studies of individuals playing the Ultimatum Game to identify the parts of the brain that were involved assessing unfair behavior. In the Ultimatum Game two players decide on how to split $10. This was a version of what children do when they are asked to share a piece of cake. To reduce conflict they often adopt the strategy of "You cut, I'll take my choice." In this study, responders played against other people or against the computer and were aware of which was which. In the Ultimatum Game the proposer offers a given cut and the responder can accept or reject the cut. An added complication is that if the responder chooses not to accept the cut, neither person gets any money. Thus, there are considerable consequences for the responders that cry foul and turn down the deal.

One might expect that the responder would accept any amount of money rather than walk away with nothing. However, studies of how people play this game in many societies show this is never the case. When the offer seems unfair, the responder often rejects the offer. The acceptance rates by offers from humans as opposed to those coming from a computer are shown in Figure 3.

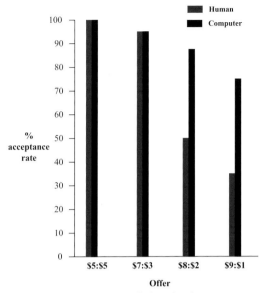

Figure 3. Acceptance rates by split offer from the Ultimatum Game played against humans or the computer. From Sanfrey et al.: Science. 300:1755-1758, 2003. [17]

The acceptance rates were much lower for unfair offers coming from humans than those coming from the computer, indicating individuals were much more likely to punish a person for unfair behavior than a computer. This suggests that unfairness engenders an emotional reaction of anger, and people are willing to sacrifice considerable financial gain to punish the unfair person.

The fMRI studies showed that unfair offers stimulated the regions of the brain involved in both emotion (the insula) and reason (dorsolateral prefrontal cortex). The activation of the insula occurs with negative emotional states. The greater the unfairness of the offer, the greater the relative activation of the insula. The activation of the insula was much greater when the unfair offer came from a person rather than from a computer, indicating the anger was directed against a fellow human and not the amount of the split.

In contrast to the emotional reaction to unfair and rejected offers, accepted offers were more likely to produce relatively more activation of the dorsolateral prefrontal cortex, even if they were unfair. This suggests that subjects used more rational thought and less emotion in deciding whether to accept an offer, and less rational thought and more emotion in deciding to reject an offer.

These studies have several important implications. The most obvious is that decision-making in humans is not purely rational—emotions play an important role and can lead to counterintuitive results. The second implication is that by producing anger and with it a desire to punish unfair activity, emotions played a critical role in the evolution of altruism.

Altruistic Behavior and Dopamine Reward Pathways

To examine the possible neural basis of altruistic behavior Rilling and colleagues performed fMRI studies on 36 women as they played the Prisoner's Dilemma Game. [18] In the game two players have a choice to cooperate, not to cooperate, or for one to cooperate while the other does not. In the latter case, cooperation incurs costs to the individual and benefits only accrue to the other player. Monetary reward is the oil that makes the game run. Repeated playing of the game results in the evolution of different strategies that different players use to maximize their gain. Mutual cooperation was associated with consistent activation in brain areas that have been linked to the reward pathways. The results suggested that the activation of reward pathways reinforced reciprocal altruism and motivated subjects to resist the temptation to selfishly accept favors without reciprocating them. There was evidence of a negative response of the dopamine system if a subject cooperated but the opponent did not.

The concept of spirituality includes being kind, doing good things, and acting for the good of one's neighbor. *Human spirituality and altruism may be linked by a common effect on reward pathways and they may have reciprocally cooperated and aided in the evolution of each other.*

Altruistic Behavior and Dopamine Genes

A study of 354 families from the general population in Israel showed a significant association of the *Selflessness Scale,* a measure of altruism, with the dopamine D_4 (*DRD4*), dopamine D_5 (*DRD5*) and insulin-like growth factor (*IGF2*) genes.[19] The *DRD4* is the same gene that we found to be associated with spirituality.[20] The association of two different dopamine genes with altruism is consistent with the fMRI studies showing that altruism stimulates the "feel good" reward pathways.

Humans show a considerably higher level of altruistic or cooperative behavior than any other species. Twin studies show a significant genetic contribution to altruistic traits and molecular genetic studies show that dopamine genes are involved. The stimulation of the dopamine reward pathways may make altruistic acts a pleasure to perform.

These factors combine to account for the presence of altruism and cooperation at levels of magnitude that are much greater for humans than for any other species. The major lesson is that man has evolved a set of biological and genetic systems that usually lead him to behave in a helpful, cooperative, and altruistic fashion toward his fellow man, independent of religion.

References

1. Wilson, E. O. *On Human Nature.* Harvard University Press, Cambridge, MA, 1978.
2. Darwin, C. *On the Origin of Species by Means of Natural Selection or the Preservation of Favored Races in the Struggle for Life.* Murray, London, 1859.
3. Hamilton, W. D. The genetical evolution of social behavior, I, II. *Journal of Theoretical Biology.* 7: 1-52, 1964.
4. Vogel, G. The evolution of the golden rule. *Science.* 303: 1128-1130, 2004.
5. Trivers, R. L. Evolution of reciprocal altruism. *Q Rev Biol.* 46: 35-57, 1971.
6. Nowak, M. A. & Sigmund, K. Evolution of indirect reciprocity. *Nature.* 437: 1291-1298, 2005.
7. Fehr, E. & Fischbacher, U. The nature of human altruism. *Nature.* 425: 785-791, 2003.
8. Alexander, R. D. *The Biology of Moral Systems.* de Gruyter, New York, 1987.
9. Nowak, M. A. & Sigmund, K. Evolution of indirect reciprocity by image scoring. *Nature.* 393: 573-577, 1998.
10. Wedekind, C. & Milinski, M. Cooperation through image scoring in humans. *Science.* 288: 850-852, 2000.
11. Engelmann, D. & Fischbacher, U. *Indirect Reciprocity and Strategic Reputation Building in an Experiment Helping Game.* Institute for Empirical Research in Economics, University of Zurich, Zurich, 2002.
12. Batson, D. C. *The Altruism Question.* Lawrence Erlbaum Associates, Hillsdale, NJ, 1991.
13. Bowles, S. & Gintis, H. Homo reciprocans. *Nature.* 415: 125-128, 2002.

14. Johnson, D. D., Stopka, P. & Knights, S. Sociology: The puzzle of human cooperation. *Nature.* 421: 911-2; discussion 912, 2003.

15. Leimar, O. & Hammerstein, P. Evolution of cooperation through indirect reciprocity. *Proc Biol Sci.* 268: 745-753, 2001.

16. Rushton, J. P., Fulker, D. W., Neale, M. C., Nias, D. K. & Eysenck, H. J. Altruism and aggression: the heritability of individual differences. *J Pers Soc Psychol.* 50: 1192-1198, 1986.

17. Sanfey, A. G., Rilling, J. K., Aronson, J. A., Nystrom, L. E. & Cohen, J. D. The neural basis of economic decision-making in the Ultimatum Game. *Science.* 300: 1755-1758, 2003.

18. Rilling, J. et al. A neural basis for social cooperation. *Neuron.* 35: 395-405, 2002.

19. Bachner-Melman, R. et al. Dopaminergic polymorphisms associated with self-report measures of human altruism: a fresh phenotype for the dopamine D_4 receptor. *Mol Psychiatry.* 10: 333-335, 2005.

20. Comings, D. E., Gonzales, N., Saucier, G., Johnson, J. P. & MacMurray, J. P. The DRD4 gene and spiritual transcendence scale of the character temperament index. *Psychiatric Genetics.* 10: 185-189, 2001.

Chapter 39

The Genetics of Reason

As described in Chapter 26, the prefrontal cortex is the neural site of abstract thought, adaptive decision-making, deductive and inductive reasoning, and represents the site of the rational brain. Adaptive decision-making, where there are no true answers, most closely represents the uniqueness of human rational thought and what I refer to when I speak of the conflict between our rational and spiritual brain. Here I ask the question, "To what extent are genetic factors involved in the ability to carry out rational thought?" To answer this in the above context would require an examination of twin studies of adaptive decision-making. Unfortunately there are no such studies, so we cannot answer this question directly. There are, however, many twin studies of intelligence and as we shall see, intelligence is related to a basic factor called g, which is correlated with the ability to carry out a wide range of cognitive or thinking behaviors including adaptive reasoning.

Intelligence Tests

As described previously Francis Galton was one of the first scientists to show that continuous traits were genetically inherited. In 1869 he published a genealogical study entitled *Hereditary Genius*. [1] He selected a representative sample of prominent men in the arts, sciences, politics, military, literature, and other areas of intellectual achievement and inquired into the status of their relatives. Figure 1 shows an example, the Gregory family.

The index person was James Gregory, "inventor of the reflecting telescope; a man of very acute and penetrating genius. He was the most important member of a very important scientific family, partly eminent as mathematicians and largely so as physicians." A brief perusal of this pedigree shows it was rife with professors, physicians, and mathematicians. While Galton understood that these individuals benefited from superior environments, he attributed most of these familiar clusters of excellence to the inheritance of innate natural ability in the form of superior intelligence. In a search for more objective measures of this innate ability, Galton set up an Anthropometric Laboratory in the Science Museum in South Kensington. For a small fee, visitors were measured for a range of traits including reaction times, visual and auditory sensitivity. Data on over 9,000 subjects was accumulated, and in studying this material Galton made many advances in the statistical methods for analyzing continuous traits.

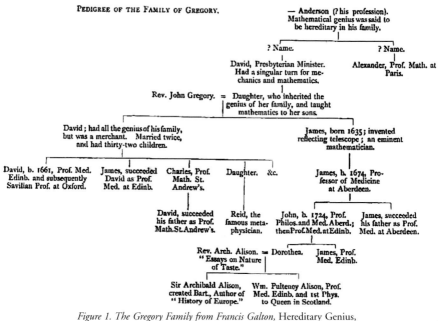

Figure 1. The Gregory Family from Francis Galton, Hereditary Genius, *1869.* [1]

One of Galton's students, James Cattell, became the first professor of psychology at the University of Pennsylvania. Like Galton, he believed that intelligence was related to reaction time. He and his students developed a range of "mental tests." [2] He became the first chairman of the American Psychological Association's Committee on Mental and Physical Tests. However, one of his own graduate students dealt a severe blow to the validity of these tests when he showed virtually no correlation between the test results and the academic performance of 300 college students. [3] Clearly a different approach to predicting academic and intellectual ability was needed.

The failure of the Cattell mental tests was due to their narrow scope, limited range of scores, and failure to measure higher mental skills. In 1895, two French psychologists, Alfred Binet and Victor Henri, published a study on individual psychological differences. They proposed that a wider variety of tests, including those that assessed higher mental functions such as imagination, comprehension, and complex memory tasks would more accurately predict academic achievement. This proved to be the case. In 1904 the French minister of public instruction asked Binet to develop a method of testing that would aid in the identification of children most likely to need assistance with special education classes. With his student, Theodore Simon, they developed what was called the *Binet-Simon Metrical Scale of Intelligence.* [4]

An important aspect of this scale was an age adjustment, which compared the performance of a given subject to others of the same age. The average score for a given age was set to 100. These came be to known as IQ tests (Intelligence Quotient). The IQ scale proved to be extremely useful in identifying mentally retarded children. Its results were consistent with independent measures, such as the evaluation of teachers and peers and the ease of trainability. In 1911, Lewis Terman, a psychology professor from Stanford, published the *Stanford Revision of the Binet-Simon* scales. This test came to be known as the Stanford-Binet and was eventually standardized on a sample of 3,000 children and adults.

In 1939 David Wechsler published his own version of an intelligence test known as the *Wechsler Adult Intelligence Scale (WAIS)*. The child version was called the *WISC-R (Wechsler Intelligence Scale for Children-Revised)*. These tests are especially valuable because of the wide range of traits they test. They are well standardized for reliability, reproducibility and validity, and are machine-scored. These characteristics made them ideal for large-scale adoption and twin studies suitable for the examination of the role of genes in intelligence.

What is Intelligence?

Intelligence tests have often been criticized because of the lack of a clear theoretical construct of what intelligence is. Intelligence is generally felt to refer to an individual's innate cognitive ability. Since innate means inherited, this upsets some who questioned the role of genes as a factor in determining intelligence. Some have factitiously stated that "intelligence is whatever intelligence tests measure." [5] Snyderman and Rothman [4] surveyed 1,023 social scientists and educators skilled in the administration of IQ tests and asked them which of 13 different descriptors they thought were most closely related to intelligence. Over 95 percent agreed that abstract thinking or reasoning, problem solving ability, and the capacity to acquire knowledge were the most relevant aspects of intelligence. Thus, contrary to the criticism that test measurers don't know what they are testing, the survey showed virtually universal agreement that the key element of intelligence is the ability to learn and to use complex mental tasks such as abstract reasoning and problem solving. By contrast, motivational and sensory abilities were not considered to be a part of innate intelligence. The Wechsler Intelligence Scales consist of six subscales to measure verbal IQ (general information, problem comprehension, arithmetic, digit span, vocabulary, and similarities) and five subscales to measure performance IQ (picture completion and arrangement, block design, object assembly and digit symbol).

An English psychologist, Charles Spearman, noted that virtually all tests of intelligence and mental ability were strongly correlated with each other. Using a statistical test he invented, called *factor analysis,* Spearman concluded that the ability to perform these tests was related to a common factor *g*, for general intelligence. [6] Further studies suggest that *g* represents a common ability underlying achievement in a wide range of cognitive skills that relate to the mental manipulation of images, symbols, words, numbers or concepts. By contrast, skills that merely call for the reproduction of highly practiced or rotely learned skills are poor measures of *g*. There was agreement among the social scientists and educators that whatever the IQ test measures, it is an important determinant of success in society.

The Genetics of Intelligence

There have been more twin studies of intelligence than any other human trait.

Bouchard and McGue[7] reviewed the world literature as of 1981. They identified 111 studies yielding 526 familial correlations based upon 113,942 twin pairings. Figure 2 presents some of the more important aspects of these results in the form of correlation coefficients between identical twins reared together, fraternal twins reared together, and siblings reared together. Correlation coefficients refer to a statistical measure that ranges from 0 for no correlation to 1.0 for a perfect correlation.

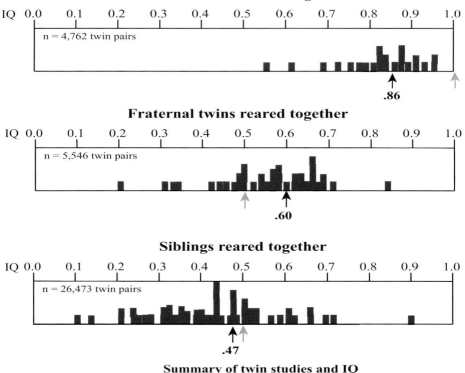

Figure 2. Diagrams of a subset of the results of twin studies of IQ reviewed by Bouchard and McGue, Science. 212:1055-1059, 1981.[7]

The blue arrows represent the correlations expected based on a simple polygenic model with no environmental or other non-gene effects. This is 1.0 for identical twins since they share 100 percent of their genes. It is 0.5 for both fraternal twins and siblings reared together since individuals in both of these groups share 50 percent of their genes in common. Correlations alone do not determine whether intelligence is due to environmental or genetic factors. For example, a disorder caused by a purely environmental factor such as a virus, could result in a correleation coefficient of 1.0. It is the relative correlation for identical twins versus fraternal twins that determines the role of genetic factors. The closer the observed results for the fraternal twins and siblings reared together come to being one half of the correlation for the identical twins, the greater the genetic component. In these studies the means are corrected for the number of pairings in different studies. Thus a study of 2,000 pairs is weighted higher than a study of 200 pairs. The weighted average correlation of IQ for the identical twins was .86. There were a small number (60) of identical twins reared apart. For them, the weighted average correlation was .76. The weighted average for the fraternal twins was .60 while the weighted average for siblings reared together was .47. When these two groups are combined, the mean weighted correlation is very close to the value of .50 expected for a polygenetic genetic model with little environmental effect.

Despite this strong evidence for the role of genes, several aspects of these results indicate that environmental factors also play a role. These are: A) the correlation coefficient for the identical twins was .86, not 1.0; B) the correlation coefficient for the identical twins reared apart was lower than for those reared together; C) the correlation for fraternal twins reared together was higher than for siblings reared together; and D) the correlation for a small number of siblings reared apart was .20, lower than for siblings reared together.

The total variance in these studies is the sum of genetic factors or heritability (G), environmental factors (E) and a gene-environment interaction factor, G-E. Several estimates of these values have been reported. On average G = .60, E = .22, and G-E = .18,[4] indicating that approximately 60 percent of intelligence is genetically determined, 22 percent is environmentally determined and 18 percent is the result of an interaction between genes and the environment.

A recent collaborative study of the genetics of cognition by scientists in three different countries, the Netherlands, Australia and Japan, involved 378 identical twins and 540 fraternal twins. The heritabilities for IQ were 87, 83, and 71 percent respectively.[8] These figures represent some of the highest genetic loading of any human trait other than single gene disorders. This is consistent with a very high degree of natural selection for intelligence. These scientists also examined the heritability of some of the basic neurological processes believed to contribute to intelligence such as reaction time, working memory[9] and spatial memory. Interestingly, the heritabilities of these were considerably lower, in the 33 to 64 percent range. However, in a study of twins 80 or more years of age,[10] the heritability of IQ was 62 percent, similar to that in the prior summary. Here the contributing basic neurological processes showed similar heritabilities of 62 percent for processing speed, 55 percent for verbal ability, and 52 percent for working memory.

Adoption studies support the results of twin studies by also indicating a significant role of genes in intelligence.[4] Some have resisted a role of genes in IQ because it implies that improvement of the environment will not increase a child's IQ. However, several studies have shown that when a child is removed from a neglectful and intellectually impoverished environment and placed into an intellectually enriched environment the children's IQs were significantly higher than for those left in a impoverished environment.[4] Thus, despite a major role for genetic factors, there is still room for improvement in IQ due to an improved environment.

Importance of IQ to Success in Society

As noted above, all of the social scientists and educators agreed that IQ was a potent predictor of success in life. Specifically significant correlations have been reported between a higher IQ and:

- a decrease in number of children
- a later age of having their first child
- a later age of first intercourse
- less poverty
- less teenage delinquency
- less tobacco smoking
- better grades
- greater college attendance
- less antisocial and criminal behavior
- fewer behavioral problems in children
- fewer problems with motor and social development
- fewer illegitimate births
- less use of welfare
- a higher socioeconomic status
- a higher income
- less drug abuse
- less alcohol use
- more years of education
- better home environments
- far less time in prison

These associations are documented elsewhere. [11,12] Some of the controversial aspects of IQ testing were not covered here since they were not relevant to the issues of this book. The interested reader is referred elsewhere. [4] It is clear that *g*, the biological factor correlated with all intelligence tests and involved in mental manipulation of images, symbols, words, numbers or concepts, plays a fundamental role in all major aspects of success in human social interactions. This suggests the presence of many different reasons for the involvement of a high level of natural selection for this important trait.

Intelligence is a measure of innate cognitive or thinking ability. The results of a wide range of tests of higher order thinking processes are strongly correlated suggesting an underlying factor, *g*, that is related to the mental manipulation of images, symbols, words and numbers. Twin studies indicate that approximately 60 percent of *g* is due to genes alone, 22 percent to the environment, and 18 percent to a gene-environment interaction. Some studies show a genetic component to IQ as high as 87 percent. IQ is positively correlated with virtually every prosocial aspect of civilized man.

References

1. Galton, F. *Hereditary Genius*. Macmillan Publishing Co., London, 1869.
2. Cattell, J. M. Mental Tests and Measurements. Mind. 15: 373ff, 1890.
3. Wissler, C. The Correlation of Mental and Physical Tests. *Psychological Review Monograph Supplement*. 3.: 1901.
4. Snyderman, M. & Rothman, S. *The IQ Controversy. The Media and Public Policy.* Transaction Books, New Brunswick, NJ, 1988.
5. Boring, E. G. *Intelligence as the Tests Test It*. New Republic. 35: 35-37, 1923.
6. Spearman, C. 'General Intelligence' objectively determined and measured. *American Journal of Psychology*. 15: 201-292, 1904.

7. Bouchard, T. J. J. & McGue, M. Familial studies of intelligence: A review. *Science.* 212: 1055-1059, 1981.

8. Wright, M. et al. Genetics of cognition: outline of a collaborative twin study. *Twin Res.* 4: 48-56, 2001.

9. Kyllonen, P. C. & Christal, R. E. Reasoning ability is (little more than) working-memory capacity? *Intelligence.* 14: 389-433, 1990.

10. McClearn, G. E. et al. Substantial genetic influence on cognitive abilities in twins 80 or more years old. *Science.* 276: 1560-1563, 1997.

11. Comings, D. E. *The Gene Bomb: Does higher education and advanced technology accelerate the selection of genes for learning disorders, ADHD, addictive, and disruptive behaviors?* Hope Press, Duarte, CA, 1996.

12. Herrnstein, R. J. & Murray, C. *The Bell Curve.* The Free Press, New York, 1994.

The predisposition to religious belief is the most complex and powerful force in the human mind and in all possibility an integral part of human nature.

E. O. Wilson
On Human Nature [1]

Chapter 40

The Genetics of Spirituality

Until very recently the field of psychology paid little attention to the possibility that genes might play a role in traits such as spirituality and religious beliefs. [2] Psychologists had simply assumed that religious attitudes and beliefs were largely shaped by the attitudes and beliefs of parents and peers.

Before entering into the subject of the genetics of spirituality, it is necessary to introduce several terms. As shown in the chapter on the genetics of antisocial behavior, twin and adoption studies are valuable methods for determining the relative role of genes versus the environment in human behavior. The three major types of variation in human behavior are: *psychiatric disorders* such as major depression, manic depressive disorder, and conduct disorder; *personality traits* such as extraversion and neuroticism; and *cultural attitudes* such as sexual, political, and religious beliefs.

Twin studies have defined the relative role of genes versus the environment and have also divided the environmental factors into two types: *shared environment* versus *unique environment*. The shared environment includes such influences as general parenting, and the economic status, political orientation, and religious upbringing of the parents and peers. Both twins would be exposed to attendance at the same church, mosque or synagogue and be exposed to the same religious and political views. These are all part of a shared environment. By contrast, many times twins are placed in separate classes, have separate teachers and friends and attend different summer camps and colleges. These represent a *unique environment*.

A final term used in twin studies is *variance*. For any continuous trait such as height, weight, or score on a given questionnaire, there will be a great deal of variation from individual to individual. This variation is called the variance. Different influences such as genes or environmental factors influence this variation. The proportion of the variance attributed to a specific factor is referred to as the percentage of the variance. Thus, for a single gene disease such as Huntington's Disease, the gene accounts for 100 percent of the variance of Huntington's Disease. In the case of the flu mentioned below, the influenza virus accounts for 100 percent of the variance of the flu.

One of the major tenets of psychology from the time of Freud was that the early shared environment was critical to later psychological development. However, twin studies of psychiatric disorders, such as conduct disorder, clearly showed that the percent of the variance contributed by the shared environment was virtually zero. Forty to 90 percent of the variance was due to genes, with the remainder being due to the unique environment. This was hard for psychologists to accept, but this could be understood if we assumed that these more severe conditions were due to a disorder of brain chemistry rather than how individuals were raised.

When twin studies of personality traits were carried out[3] the results were the same. These results really upset many psychologists and led behavioral geneticist David Rowe to state:[4]

> Given the environmental emphasis in behavior science theories, the idea that the shared environment fails to impact on personality development is radical; but it is, nevertheless, supported by an extensive literature of twin and adoption data.

Thus, twin studies of both psychiatric disorders and personality traits have shown that the shared environment plays a relatively minor role. The belief that this would not be the case for cultural attitudes was so strong that psychologists often spoke of the cultural "inheritance" of religious values without even mentioning genes.[5]

Twin Studies of Religious Belief

The view of cultural inheritance has now also changed as a result of recent twin studies which have shown that *genetic factors play as much of a role in cultural attitudes as they do in personality traits and psychiatric disorders, and that the shared environment is much less important.*

One of the first studies was reported in 1986 by Martin and colleagues.[6] They examined a sample of 825 adult twin pairs from Australia and England and reported that genetic factors accounted for 22 to 35 percent of the variance of a range of religious attitudes, including those about Bible truth, divine law, Sabbath observance, and church authority. They found little evidence for "vertical cultural inheritance." In 1990, based on the Minnesota Twin Study of twins reared together and apart, Waller and colleagues[7] reported that genes accounted for 41 to 47 percent of the variance of a range of religious variables. Again there was little or no involvement of the shared environment.

Lindon Eaves at the Virginia Commonwealth University in Richmond, Virginia, has written extensively about the genetics of religion and spirituality. This interest is derived from the fact that he was both a behavioral geneticist and an Anglican priest. Preliminary studies showed that a very large study with a broad range of different relationships would be necessary to accurately determine the role of genetic factors and shared and non-shared environment. This led to the development of a study consisting of 14,761 twins and their relatives, producing a total of 29,691 subjects. It was appropriately named the *Virginia 30,000.*[8,9] When gender was included, this study produced 80 different types of family relationships.

All the subjects completed a modified *Eysenck Personality Questionnaire* and a *Health and Lifestyles Questionnaire.* The Eysenck Questionnaire produced three major personality traits—psychoticism (pessimistic, impulsive, low self-esteem), [10] extraversion (extraverted and outgoing versus introverted and shy), and neuroticism (nervous, anxious, phobic, and panic attacks). There was also a lie scale to detect individuals who attempted to fake "looking good." The Health and Lifestyles Questionnaire produced cultural attitude scales about sex, economics, the military, politics and religious fundamentalism. Figure 1 shows the average correlation (R) between the identical versus the fraternal twins for each of these traits. [Recall that if there is no similarity or correlation, R = 0.00, while if the scores are identical with a perfect correlation, R = 1.00]

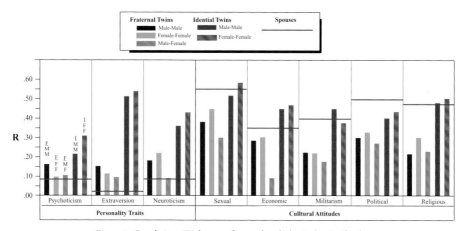

Figure 1. Correlations (R) between fraternal and identical twins for three personality variables and five cultural variables. The shades of blue bars show correlations between fraternal (F) male twins (F MM), female twins (F FF) and male-female twins (F MF). The identical twins (I) are shown in shades of red bars for males (I MM) and females (I FF). The correlations between scores for spouses are shown by the red lines. Based on data from Eaves et al. Twin Research. 2:62-80, 1999. [8]

Heritability refers to the proportion of the total variance attributable to genetic factors. It is *approximately equivalent to twice the difference between the correlation for identical versus fraternal twins.* Simple inspection of Figure 1 shows that the correlations were higher for identical twins than for fraternal twins for both the personality traits and the cultural attitudes. This indicates a significant role of genes in these variables.

The horizontal red lines show the correlations between spouses. These correlations are minimal for personality traits but quite high for cultural variables. This is understandable based on the fact that people are much more likely to marry partners with similar cultural values than with similar personality traits. This is intuitively clear for anyone who has ever been involved in computer dating. The computer profiles provide information on religious and political affiliation, type of job, income, politics and sexual attitudes, but little on personality traits—a reflection of what people judge to be important in the selection of a spouse. Figure 2 shows the estimates for the genetic contribution or heritability for males and females.

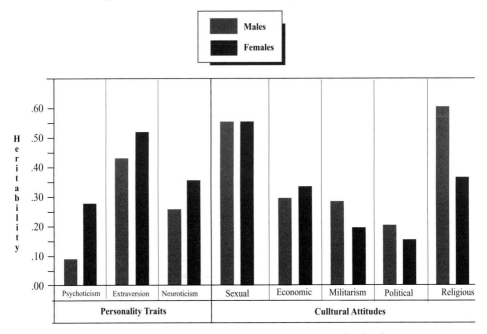

Figure 2. Heritability estimates for personality traits and cultural attitudes. Based on data from Eaves et al. Twin Research. 2:62-80, 1999. [8]

Genetic factors are most important for extraversion with heritability estimates of 42.8 percent for males and 50.4 percent for females. Several of the cultural attitude variables have remarkably high heritability estimates such as 46 percent for sexual attitudes for both males and females. The highest heritability was 64.5 percent for religion in males. It was 37 percent for females. For religious attitudes the common environment contributed to 32 percent of the variance in females but 0 percent of the variance for males. Eaves and colleagues concluded,

> The total contribution of genetic factors to differences in personality and social attitudes is significant and pervasive.

They further stated,

> The significant contribution of genetic factors to social attitudes means that virtually no measurable aspect of human behavioral variation is… far removed from the impact of events at the genetic level.

To explain this counterintuitive level of genetic involvement in cultural attitudes, the authors proposed,

Small initial genetic differences in behavior and preference are augmented over time by the incorporation into the phenotype of environmental information, correlated with the phenotype.

They were referring to the observation by Thomas Bouchard that *genes play a role in the selection of the environment.*[11] For example, an adolescent with a genetic predisposition to conduct disorder is likely to join a gang and as a result eventually become associated with an antisocial environment as a young adult. By contrast an adolescent with a high IQ and propensity to enjoy studying is likely to go to college and become associated with a much more law-abiding environment as an adult. While the eventual involvement in antisocial behavior for each of these two people would seem to be predominately due to environmental factors, genetic factors clearly played a critical and fundamental role. This is also related to what Richard Dawkins[12] referred to as the "extended genetic phenotype" and to Bouchard's[11] view of

...humans as dynamic creative organisms for whom the opportunity to learn and to experience new environments amplifies the effects of the genotype on the phenotype.

Genetic factors can make a significant contribution to cultural attitudes. This contribution is greater for religious attitudes than for economic, military, or political attitudes. The significant genetic contribution to both personality traits and cultural attitudes indicates that most aspects of human behavior are strongly influenced by our genes.

Studies of Kenneth Kendler and associates[13] indicate that the role of genes in religious attitudes can vary depending upon the nature of how those attitudes are assessed. They examined data on 1,902 twins also from the Virginia Twin Registry. Religious behavior was assessed by three scales: *personal devotion, personal conservatism,* and *institutional conservatism.*

Personal devotion was assessed by questions such as "How important are your religious beliefs in your daily life?", "When you have problems or difficulties in your family, work, or personal life, how often do you seek spiritual comfort?", and "Other than at mealtime, how often do you pray to God privately?"

Personal conservatism was assessed by questions such as, "Do you believe that God or a universal spirit observes your actions and rewards or punishes you for them?" and "Do you agree with the following statement: The Bible is the actual word of God and is to be taken literally, word for word?"

Institutional conservatism was assessed on the basis of their religious affiliation with the following being in order of decreasing conservatism: Fundamentalist Protestant (Church of God, Pentecostal Assembly of God, Jehovah's Witnesses), Baptist, Catholic, mainline Protestant, and other or unaffiliated. Figure 3 shows the results.

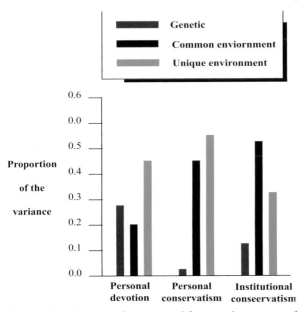

Genetic
Common enviornment
Unique environment

Proportion of the variance

0.6
0.0
0.5
0.4
0.3
0.2
0.1
0.0

Personal devotion   Personal conservatism   Institutional conseervatism

Figure 3. Role of genetic and environmental factors in three measures of religious belief. Based on data from Kendler et al. Am J Psychiatry. *154:322-329, 1997.*

There was a considerable genetic component to *personal devotion,* but only a modest genetic component to *institutional conservatism,* and no genetic component to *personal conservatism.* The latter was entirely due to environmental influences that were about equally divided between a common and unique environment. Institutional conservatism was almost entirely due to environmental factors, especially common environment. As described later, this study also examined the effect of these religious values on alcohol and tobacco use.

When religious behavior is assessed on the basis of factors that relate to religious affiliation, environmental factors play the major role.

Twins reared apart. Thomas Bouchard and colleagues[2] reported a smaller but important study of religious values. This study was important because it used the *Minnesota Study of Twins Reared Apart.* Such studies are rare since only a small proportion of twins are reared apart. They are valuable because this removes the possibility that identical twins behave the same because they are emotionally closer than fraternal twins, rather than because they share more genes in common. The authors examined genetic and environmental influences on *intrinsic religiousness* and *extrinsic religiousness.*[14,15] The *extrinsically* motivated people used their religion largely for social reasons associated with attending church, while the *intrinsically* motivated people geuninely lived their religion. There was little correlation between the two scales, indicating they tap independent dimensions. Subjects were also administered the *Multidimensional Personality Questionnaire (MPQ).* Of 14 different personality scales, the intrinsically religious scale was significantly and positively associated only with traditionalism and constraint and inversely associated with aggression. The heritability of the intrinsic religiousness scale was 43 percent; of the extrinsic religiousness scale, heritability was 39 percent, indicating that almost half of the variance of both of these variables was due to genetic factors.

Twin Studies of Spirituality

Self-transcendence refers to the capacity to reach out and find meaning in life in dimensions beyond oneself. In 1993 Dr. Robert Cloninger at Washington University in St. Louis developed a personality inventory that included four scales for temperaments and three for character. This was called the *Temperament and Character Inventory (TCI).* [16,17] One of the character dimensions was self-transcendence — a measure of spirituality. This represented the first time that a questionnaire to assess personality traits had included a scale for spirituality.

Self-transcendence consisted of three subscales: *self-forgetfulness, transpersonal identification,* and *spiritual acceptance.* The questions relating to *self-forgetfulness* included losing oneself in thought, time or space. During such states individuals may experience flashes of insight or understanding. Creativity and originality may be enhanced in this state. The questions relating to *transpersonal identification* covered issues of feeling connected to others, to nature, to the universe, and a willingness to sacrifice oneself for the good of other people to make the world a better place. Ardent environmentalists would be likely to score high on this scale.

The questions indicating a capacity for *spiritual acceptance* included believing in miracles, believing that many things cannot be scientifically explained, having a spiritual connection to others, having meaningful religious experiences, having one's life directed by a spiritual force greater than any human being, and feeling in contact with a divine and wonderful spiritual power. The other end of this scale would include people who don't believe in things that cannot be explained scientifically. Based on these questions it can be seen that the subscore for spiritual acceptance is clearly the most relevant for estimating the degree to which an individual may become involved in religious experiences and spirituality. Twin studies using the TCI provide us with information of the role of genes in spirituality. There have been several such studies.

Kirk and colleagues [18] examined the self-transcendence scale as a measure of spirituality in 1,279 Australian twins 50 years of age or older. An age of 50 or more was important since the role of family environment diminishes after individuals leave home. [19] The self-transcendence scores varied significantly by gender and across different religious affiliations. The scores were higher for females and individuals identifying themselves as evangelical and fundamentalist. They were intermediate for other religious groups and lowest for those with no religious affiliation. There were small but significant correlations with optimism, extraversion, and good general health, and for fatigue, anxiety, and depression. The results for the involvement of genetic factors, and common and unique environments for self-transcendence in male and female twins are shown in Figure 4.

In both males and females, about half of spiritual self-transcendence was the result of genetic factors and half was the result of the unique environment, with no contribution from the common environment. This was an astonishing result. It showed that spirituality was unrelated to the common environment, including religious upbringing. *This clearly indicates that spirituality is an intrinsic biological trait and is not transmitted by culture.* Most personality traits tend to share this remarkable characteristic. When all factors were considered together using a statistical tool called

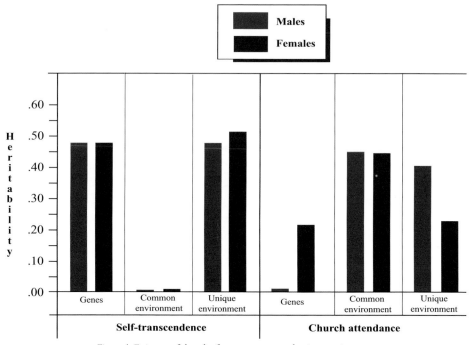

Figure 4. Estimates of the role of genes, common and unique environment for self-transcendence in 50+-year-old Australian twins. Based on data from Kirk et al. Twin Research. 2:81-87, 1999. [18]

multivariate analysis, the genetic contribution to self-transcendence averaged 40 percent for both sexes. These results were unchanged when the study size had increased to 2,517 twins. [20]

Ando and colleagues [21,22] reported twin studies for 617 pairs of adolescent and young adult twins in Japan. They examined the TCI traits and their subscales. The contribution of genes to the variance of all scales and subscales ranged from 22 to 49 percent. Specifically, genes contributed to 41 percent of the variance of self-transcendence and 39 percent of the variance of spiritual acceptance. Unique environmental factors contributed the rest. As with the Australian twins, *the shared environment, including religious upbringing, contributed nothing.* The high contribution of genes to spirituality and lack of contribution of the family environment is counterintuitive and minimizes a role of cultural perspectives or social learning in spirituality.

> **Twin studies indicate that spirituality is an intrinsic biological trait strongly controlled by genes and unique environment and is not determined by cultural influences such as religious education. *Spirituality comes from within.***

Twin Studies of *Spiritual but not Religious*

Many individuals describe themselves as *spiritual but not religious*. This raises the question of whether genetic factors play a greater role in individuals who are *spiritual and religious* or those who are *spiritual but not religious?* Dr. Ming Tsuang and colleagues from Harvard Medical School used the Vietnam Era Twin Registry to examine the role of genetic and environmental factors for these traits. [23] To do this they used a *Spiritual Well-Being Scale.* [24] This consisted of 10 questions for a "vertical dimension" that related to one's sense of well-being in relationship with God *(spiritual and religious).* An additional 10 questions related to a "horizontal dimension" for an existential sense of well-being related to perception of purpose and satisfaction in life, apart from any religious reference *(spiritual but not religious).* Genetic factors accounted for 37 percent of the spiritual and religious scale and 36 percent of the *spiritual but not religious* scale. Most of the rest was due to the non-shared environment. Thus, *genetic factors were just as important for the spiritual but not religious as the spiritual and religious scales.*

Tsuang et al. also computed an *Index of Spiritual Involvement* based on a subset of the questions from *Kass's Index of Core Spiritual Experiences.* [25] The questions sought to measure the strength of a person's religious or spiritual orientation and the time spent on religious or spiritual practices. Other assessments included the *Multidimensional Personality Questionnaire* and an assessment of any psychiatric disorders. Genetic factors accounted for 23 percent of the variance of the *Index of Spiritual Involvement.* The common environment explained 32 percent and the unique environment explained 23 percent, indicating that cultural and religious upbringing did play a role in this scale.

An additional informative aspect of this study was the correlation between the *spiritual and religious* and the *spiritual but not religious* scales and the different personality traits. The interesting result was that the religious well-being, *spiritual and religious* scale was significantly correlated only with the personality traits of traditionalism and constraint, perhaps best described as a conservative and rigid approach to life. This agreed with the results by Eaves and colleagues [8] described above.

In contrast, the *spiritual but not religious,* existential well-being scale, based on meaningful but non-religious aspects of life, was positively associated with many advantageous personality traits such as general sense of well-being, social closeness and communion as well as constraint. It was negatively correlated with disadvantageous personality traits such as a poor reaction to stress, alienation, aggression, and negative emotion, and all the negative summary traits of odd/eccentric, dramatic/erratic, and anxious/fearful. A negative correlation means that the higher the score on a well-being scale, the lower the score on the personality trait.

The results for the psychiatric disorders showed the same trend. There was a significant *negative* correlation between the *spiritual but not religious* scale and chronic depression, but not for the religious well-being scale. High scores on both of the types of scales seemed to protect against alcohol or nicotine dependence.

These results suggest that *individuals can attain a significant sense of well-being, satisfaction with life, and a sense of purpose without turning to organized religion,* and conversely, *turning to religion does not necessarily bring the same level of positive and purposeful outlook on life and satisfaction as a non-religious, existential outlook.* This "horizontal" dimension of *spiritual but not religious* is a measure of spirituality in relation to "a life purpose, satisfaction with life, and positive life experiences."[26]

> **A scale consistent with being *spiritual but not religious* was associated with positive personality traits. A scale consistent with being *spiritual and religious* was only associated with personality traits suggesting a conservative and more rigid approach to life. High scores on both traits were protective against substance abuse.**
>
> **These results suggest that being *spiritual but not religious* is asociated with better mental health than being *spiritual and religious*.**

Church Attendance

In contrast to measures of intrinsic spirituality, church attendance taps the dimension of participation in active organized religion. Many psychologists felt that certainly this trait would be influenced by the shared environment, and this proved to be the case. Studies of genetic factors in church attendance have been carried out in both the United States and Australia. In 1999 Kirk and colleagues compared the accumulated results for these two countries.[27] In the United States this involved the Virginia 30,000 study, while in Australia it involved the Australia Twin Registry.

Church attendance was more common in the United States than in Australia. For example, an average of 20 percent of subjects in the United States stated they rarely attended church while an average of 50 percent of subjects in Australia rarely attended church. In both countries attendance was greater for women than men and greater for individuals 50 years of age or greater than for younger subjects. Figure 5 compares the results for the analysis of the relative importance of genetic versus environmental factors for both countries.

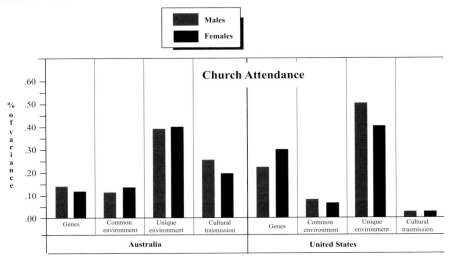

Figure 5. Twin studies of church attendance in Australia and the United States. From Kirk et al.: Twin Research. *2:99-107, 1999.*[27]

Somewhat surprisingly, the unique environment still played the greatest role in both countries. Cultural transmission, measured as parent-to-offspring environmental transmission, was more important in the Australian sample, while genetic factors were more important in the United States sample. Both genes and the environment play a significant role in church attendance in both the United States and Australia. Common environment and cultural factors are far more important than they are for spirituality. Spirituality and religiousness are separate entities and involve separate sets of genes. Spirituality comes from the inside. Religiousness comes from the outside as learned from parents, teachers, friends and church leaders.

The Role of Specific Genes

While twin and adoption studies provide evidence that genetic factors are involved in a given trait or disorder, they do not show which genes are involved. As described in Chapter 36, genetic studies using association techniques are required to identify the role of specific genes. My laboratory was the first to identify the role of a specific gene in spirituality. [28] The gene was the dopamine D₄ receptor gene *(DRD4)*. We did not initially set out to examine the genetics of spirituality. We were instead interested in determining if we could confirm studies of others that the *DRD4* gene played a role in *novelty seeking,* one of the personality traits in Cloninger's TCI questionnaire.

We tested this using a sample of university students and individuals with a history of substance abuse. Before doing the study, we reasoned that if we did not find an association between the *DRD4* gene and novelty seeking, perhaps this gene might instead be associated with one of the other of the seven dimensions in the TCI. To avoid the loss of statistical power that is associated with looking at seven different variables rather than just one, we used a statistical technique called *multivariate analysis of covariance* (MANOVA). This in essence looked at all seven traits simultaneously. This study failed to replicate the association of the *DRD4* gene with novelty seeking but did show a strong association with self-transcendence. [28] We then examined the three self-transcendence subscores of self-forgetful, transpersonal, and spiritual acceptance. There was a borderline association with the self-forgetful subscore but a strong association with spiritual-acceptance where it accounted for 6.7 percent of the variance (p < .001). Compared with most studies of single genes in complex, polygenic traits, this was a high value.

Dean Hamer, working at the National Institutes of Health was one of the scientists who first reported an association between the *DRD4* gene and novelty seeking. [29] He became interested in our results with the *DRD4* gene and spirituality and attempted to replicate them in a larger study of males and females from the general population. Instead of an association with the *DRD4* gene, he found an association with another dopamine gene, the *dopamine vesicular transporter gene —VMAT2*. Before dopamine is released from nerve terminals it is stored in small membrane-lined sacs called *vesicles*. Nothing gets through a membrane without interacting with a transporter protein specifically designed to transport it through the fatty layers. *VMAT2* is the gene for one of the two dopamine vesicular transporter proteins. Genetic heterogeneity, where different sets of genes account for the same trait in different populations of individuals, is the most likely reason for the difference between Hamer's studies and our studies.

Hamer was sufficiently impressed with his findings that he wrote a book entitled *The God Gene*[30] about the role of the *VMAT2* gene in spirituality. Since this is a polygenic trait, the book title is a stretch, since this gene accounted for only one percent of the total variance of the self-transcendence trait. He did note that the *VMAT2* gene was just one of a number of genes likely to be involved in spirituality. Hamer suggested that the involvement of dopamine genes in spirituality may be related to the fact that dopamine plays a major role in the pleasure brain, and that spiritual feelings are pleasurable. This could provide a mechanism for a significant degree of natural selection for individuals with well functioning spiritual pathways.

The fact that two different dopamine genes, *DRD4* and *VMAT2,* have now been reported to be associated with spirituality, and the fact that dopamine is the "feel good" neurotransmitter, may account for the powerful role that spirituality plays in the human condition and why the majority of people in the world derive great comfort from a belief in a God. It would also offer a partial explanation for the fact that individuals scoring high on self-transcendence are less likely to abuse alcohol. This may be because individuals whose reward pathways are activated by spirituality would have less need to artificially activate their reward pathways with alcohol or drugs.

In addition to dopamine, serotonin is another neurotransmitter that plays a major role in mood. Borg and coworkers from the Karolinska Institute in Sweden, [31] utilized PET scanning and a radioactive compound that specifically bound to serotonin 1A receptors in the brain. They found that that the binding of this compound was lowest in those with the highest scores for self-transcendence, suggesting that *such individuals had higher levels of brain serotonin.* No correlations were found for the other six dimensions of the TCI. This study implicated a role of serotonin in spiritual experiences and prompted an association study of the serotonin 1A receptor gene *(HTR1A)* for TCI variables. [32] This showed that the *HTR1A* gene was significantly associated with the self-transcendence scale and with the subscore of spiritual acceptance. This is consistent with the powerful effect of serotonin modifying psychedelic drugs that produce spiritual experiences.

Three different genes have been shown to be associated with self-transcendence and spiritual acceptance. Two are dopamine genes, suggesting a link between spiritual feelings and the pleasure pathways of the brain. Serotonin also plays a role in happiness and mood, and the other gene was a serotonin receptor gene. PET studies have shown a link between high spiritually scores and high brain serotonin levels. Since spirituality is a polygenic trait, it is likely that many other genes will eventually be shown to be associated with spirituality.

Dopamine and serotonin are the "feel good" neurotransmitters.

spirituality scores could explain the powerful effect that spirituality and religion have on the human condition.

References

1. Wilson, E. O. *On Human Nature*. Harvard University Press, Cambridge, MA, 1978.
2. Bouchard, T. J., Jr., McGue, M., Lykken, D. & Tellegen, A. Intrinsic and extrinsic religiousness: genetic and environmental influences and personality correlates. *Twin Res.* 2: 88-98, 1999.
3. Eaves, L. et al. Genes, personality, and psychopathology: A latent class analysis of liability to symptoms of attention deficit disorder in twins. in: Plomin, R. & McClearn, G. E. *Nature, Nuture, and Psychology*. American Psychological Association, Washington, D.C., 1993.
4. Rowe, D. C. Sibling interaction and self-reported delinquent behavior: Study of 265 twin pairs. *Criminology*. 23: 223-240, 1985.
5. Meyers, S. M. An interactive model of religiosity inheritance: The importance of family context. *Am Social Rev.* 61: 858-866, 1996.
6. Martin, N. G. et al. Transmission of social attitudes. *Proc Nat Acad Sci USA.* 83: 4364-4368, 1986.
7. Waller, N. G., Koketin, B. A., Bouchard, T. J. J., Lykken, D. T. & Tellegen, A. Genetic and environmental influences on religious interests, attitudes, and values: A study of twins reared apart and together. *Psychological Science*. 1: 138-142, 1990.
8. Eaves, L. et al. Comparing the biological and cultural inheritance of personality and social attitudes in the Virginia 30,000 study of twins and their relatives. *Twin Res.* 2: 62-80, 1999.
9. D'Onofrio, B. M., Eaves, L. J., Murrelle, L., Maes, H. H. & Spilka, B. Understanding biological and social influences on relgious affiliation, attitudes, and behaviors: A behavior genetic perspective. *J Personality*. 67: 953-984, 1999.
10. Howarth, E. What does Eysenck's psychoticism scale really measure? *Br J Psychol.* 77 (Pt 2): 223-227, 1986.
11. Bouchard, T. J. J. Gene, environment, and personality. *Science.* 264: 1700-1701, 1994.
12. Dawkins, R. *The Extended Phenotype: the Gene as the Unit of Selection*. Oxford University Press, Oxford, UK, 1982.
13. Kendler, K. S., Gardner, C. O. & Prescott, C. A. Religion, psychopathology, and substance use and abuse; a multimeasure, genetic-epidemiologic study. *Am J Psychiatry*. 154: 322-329, 1997.
14. Donahue, M. J. Intrisic and extrinsic religiousness: Review and meta-analysis. *J Pers Soc Psychol.* 48: 400-443, 1985.
15. Gorsuch, R. L. & Venable, G. D. Development of an "Age Universal" I-E scale. *J Sci Study Religion.* 22: 181-187, 1983.
16. Cloninger, C. R., Svrakic, D. M. & Przybeck, T. R. A psychobiological model of temperament and character. *Arch Gen Psychiatry.* 50: 975-990, 1993.
17. Svrakic, D. M., Whitehead, C., Przybeck, T. R. & Cloninger, C. R. Differential diagnosis of personality disorders by the seven-factor model of temperament and character. *Arch Gen Psychiatry.* 50: 991-999, 1993.
18. Kirk, K. M., Eaves, L. J. & Martia, N. G. Self-transcendence as a measure of spirituality in a sample of older Australian twins. *Twin Res.* 2: 81-87, 1999.
19. Eaves, L. et al. Age changes in the causes of individual differences in conservatism. *Behav Genet.* 27: 121-124, 1997.
20. Gillespie, N. A., Cloninger, C. R., Heath, A. C. & Martin, N. G. The genetic and environmental relationship between Cloninger's dimensions of temperament and character. *Personality and Individual Differences.* 35: 1931-1946, 2003.
21. Ando, J. et al. Genetic and environmental structure of Cloninger's temperament and character dimensions. *J Personal Disord.* 18: 379-393, 2004.
22. Ando, J. et al. The genetic structure of Cloninger's seven-factor model of temperament and character in a Japanese sample. *J Pers.* 70: 583-609, 2002.
23. Tsuang, M. T., Williams, W. M., Simpson, J. C. & Lyons, M. J. Pilot study of spirituality and mental health in twins. *Am J Psychiatry.* 159: 486-488, 2002.
24. Paloutzian, R. F. & Ellison, C. W. Loneliness, spiritual well-being and quality. in: Peplau, L. & Perlman, D. *Loneliness: A Sourcebook of Current Theory*. Wiley Interscience, New York, 1982.
25. Kass, J. D., Friedman, R., Leserman, J., Zuttermeister, P. C. & Benson, H. Health outcomes and a new index of spiritual experience. *J Sci Study Religion.* 30: 203-211, 1991.
26. Bolvin, M. J., Kirby, A. L., Underwood, L. K. & Silva, H. Spiritual well-being scale. in: Hill, P. C. & Hood, R. W. J. *Measures of Religosity*. Religious Education Press, Birmingham, AL, 1999.
27. Kirk, K. M. et al. Frequency of church attendance in Australia and the United States: models of family

resemblance. *Twin Res.* 2: 99-107, 1999.

28. Comings, D. E., Gonzales, N., Saucier, G., Johnson, J. P. & MacMurray, J. P. The DRD4 gene and spiritual transcendence scale of the character temperament index. *Psychiatric Genetics.* 10: 185-189, 2001.

29. Benjamin, J. et al. Population and familial association between the D_4 dopamine receptor gene and measures of novelty seeking. *Nature Genet.* 12: 81-84, 1996.

30. Hamer, D. *The God Gene. How Faith is Hardwired in our Genes.* Doubleday, New York, 2004.

31. Borg, J., Andree, B., Soderstrom, H. & Farde, L. The serotonin system and spiritual experiences. *Am J Psychiatry.* 160: 1965-1969, 2003.

32. Lorenzi, C. et al. 5-HT(1A) polymorphism and self-transcendence in mood disorders. *Am J Med Genet B Neuropsychiatr Genet.* 137: 33-35, 2005.

Part VI

Natural Selection of Reason and Spirituality

Parts IV and V showed that rational thought and spiritual experiences occur in different parts of the brain and that of these structures each is supported by a distinct set of genes. All living or fossil organisms that possess a specific structure with a specific function and a specific set of genes did not attain these things by chance. They evolved. Evolution is the result of the natural selection of a respective set of genes because those genes bring an advantage to the organism. The demonstration of a given structure, its function and the role of genetic factors is the easy part. It is easy because we can directly observe these things in living organisms. Understanding the selective forces involved is not so simple because that occurred in the past, a past that predates written historical records. We can look at fossils and at anthropological sites and try to get them to speak to us, but that speech is indirect and intuitive. Different people may hear different things. There is no absolute gold standard to prove which theory is right and which is wrong. However, there is general agreement about many aspects of this story. With these caveats in mind, the following chapters present some aspects of the evolution of intelligence and spirituality.

Chapter 41

The Evolution of Intelligence

The chapter on the genetics of intelligence presented a long list of traits and skills that were associated with a high IQ. While one could argue that the correlation with a decreased birth rate would eventually produce a race of stupid humans and a strong selection against a progressive increase in intelligence, Flynn [2,3] has shown that in the past century there has been a progressive and "massive" gain in IQ in the general population. While the reasons for this are complex they include a general improvement in test-taking skills associated with improved education and different selective factors.

The many other correlations with advantageous traits might seem to make the question, "What skills were involved in the selective process in the evolution of high intelligence?," a no-brainer. Virtually any of the long list of traits and skills associated with IQ, that were also desirable in the selection of a mate, would have a selective advantage and play a role in the evolution of IQ. However, rather than simply concluding the chapter with this statement, there are a number of interesting questions that need to be addressed: "What parts of the brain have shown the greatest evolutionary increase in size?" "What cognitive skills are unique to humans?" "What role did the multiple ice ages play in the evolution of intelligence?" "What is the time scale for the acquisition of various cultural skills associated with modern man?" and, "What is the role of social skills in the evolution of intelligence?"

What Parts of the Human Brain Have Shown the Greatest Evolutionary Increase in Size?

As described in previous chapters, the frontal lobes and especially the prefrontal lobes, are the site of creative thinking, planning of future actions, decision-making, artistic expression, working memory, abstract reasoning, spatial orientation, and other aspects of behavior critical to the development of modern civilized man. It is a widely accepted truism that the major critical feature of the evolution of humans is that the frontal lobes were proportionately larger in size than man's nearest relatives, the chimpanzee and other great apes. But is this truism true? This conclusion was based on the examination of fixed brains of humans and other primates, but fixed tissues are susceptible to shrinkage artifacts. Using 3-dimensional MRI images of living subjects eliminated these artifacts. When this was done [4] the relative size of the frontal lobes was the same for humans, chimpanzees, and orangutans (Figure 1).

When the relative areas of different sections of the frontal lobes and the relative

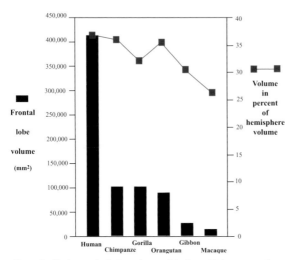

Figure 1. Absolute and relative volumes of the frontal lobes across primate species. From Semendeferi et al.: Journal of Human Evolution. *32:375-388, 1997.*[4]

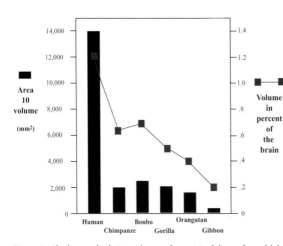

Figure 2. Absolute and relative volumes of area 10 of the prefrontal lobes across primate species. From Semendeferi et al.: American Journal of Physical Anthropology. *114:224-241, 2001.*[6]

amounts of grey versus white matter were examined the results were the same. The authors concluded: "The human frontal lobes are not larger than would be expected from a primate of our size." These results confirm what Bonin[5] stated in 1948, "Man has precisely the frontal lobes which he deserves." The assumption that a relatively greater size of the frontal lobes in humans would explain their greater intellectual capacity had to be abandoned. This similarity in the rate of evolution of the frontal lobes is not surprising given the great similarity between the human and chimpanzee genomes.

But what about the size of the prefrontal lobes or their subparts? In a subsequent study the Semenderferi group examined this question.[6] Specifically, they found a disproportionate relative increase in the size of area 10 of the frontal lobes. This is the very front-most portion of the prefrontal lobes (see Figure 2, Chapter 26). The relative size of this area in humans and other primates is shown in Figure 2.

In contrast to the results for the whole frontal lobe, area 10 of the prefrontal lobes was relatively larger for humans than for chimpanzees or other great apes. This area is involved in planning future actions, undertaking initiatives, reasoning, working memory and attention. Further studies of grey, white and total volumes showed that one of the greatest changes during the evolution of humans was an increase in prefrontal white matter.[7] Since white matter represents nerve axons, this suggests that an increase in neural interconnections played a key role in the evolution of the human brain.

Brain imaging studies of humans and the great apes show a disproportionate evolutionary increase in size and neural interconnections of area 10 of the prefrontal lobes. This area is associated with making plans for future activity, working memory, and attention. In the evolution of intelligence, an increase in connections between nerve cells is as important or even more important as an increase in size.

What Cognitive Skills are Unique to Humans?

The above studies indicate that the evolutionary increase in size and neural connections of prefrontal lobes of the great apes have almost kept pace with similar changes in humans. This suggests that we may have underestimated many of the capabilities and cognitive skills of our ape relatives. Many animal studies support this conclusion. The following is a list that summarizes the extensive literature on *human skills that have also been found to be present in chimpanzees, other great apes and other animals:*[8-10]

- a concept of self
- aggression, violence and murder
- consciousness
- cross-modal perception
- deception
- hunting
- insight
- politics
- use of language for communication

- adornment behavior
- art
- cooperation and altruism
- culture
- empathy
- incest avoidance
- mental illness
- rational thought
- use of tools

Clearly, despite the world dominance of the human species there are not many skills that we uniquely possess. The two areas that seem uniquely human are the high level of intelligence and the capacity to have awareness of our immortality, to imagine the divine, to believe in an afterlife, in heaven and in God or Gods. The potential role of selection for the latter areas is discussed in the next chapter.

The Role of the Ice Ages in the Evolution of Human Intelligence

The rapid four-fold increase in the size of the human brain began 2.5 million years ago, coincident with the onset of the ice ages. While it was often thought that each ice age was the result of gradual cooling and warming, studies of ice cores indicate that the climate changes, especially the cooling portion,[11] could be quite rapid. These abrupt changes are likely to have devastated the ecosystems on which our ancestors depended. As discussed in Chapter 16, on the finches of the Galapagos, abrupt climate changes can produce a remarkable acceleration in rates of evolution, especially when the changes persist. William Calvin [11,12,13] has suggested that the ice ages played a major role in the evolution of intelligence. Because of the rapid environmental changes, versatility and the ability to quickly adapt would provide a great advantage to our human ancestors struggling to survive. Clustering into groups would allow the combining of resources, partitioning different skills to different members of the tribe, and the sharing of food. There was a need to rapidly acquire social skills and to be able to plan ahead for the winter months. The alternative was to starve to death. The repeated cycles of the ice age changes accentuated the selective process and the progression from small groups to tribes. It is likely that we can attribute much of our high level of intelligence and social skills to the periodic presence of ice covering the Northern Hemisphere.

The Timeframe for the Evolution of Human Intelligence

Until recently it was assumed that most of the traits of modern man arouse from a cultural explosion occurring 40,000 years ago in the Upper Pleistocene. This ushered in a wide range of sophisticated behaviors, including advanced weaponry, long-distance trade networks, expression through art and music, and other characteristics of a cultural Great Leap Forward. [14] However, archeological discoveries suggest that many of the capabilities of modern humans dated to much earlier times. Figure 3 summarizes this body of data.

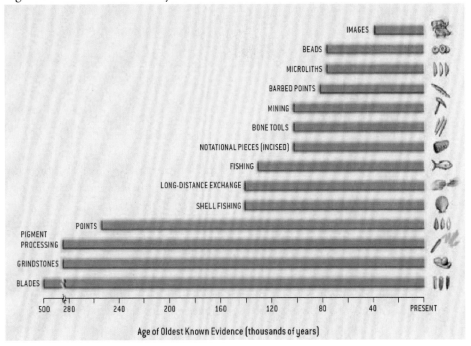

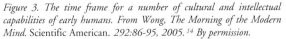

Figure 3. The time frame for a number of cultural and intellectual capabilities of early humans. From Wong, The Morning of the Modern Mind. Scientific American. 292:86-95, 2005. [14] *By permission.*

This data shows that many important aspects of intelligent behavior began as early as 280 to 500 thousand years ago. Figure 4 shows the location of some of these archeological sites.

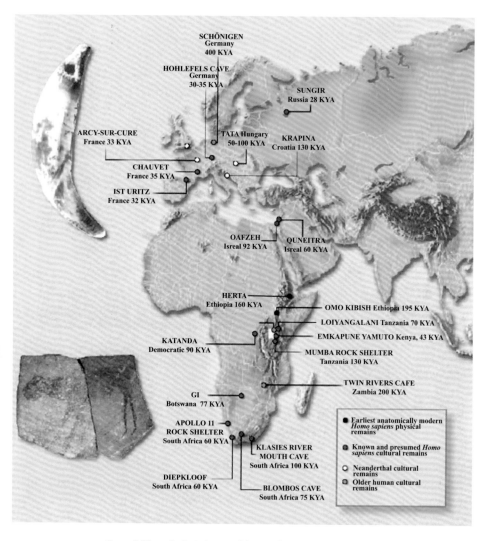

Figure 4. The archeological sites and dates in thousands of years ago (KYA) for many of the items shown in Figure 3. From Wong, The Morning of the Modern Mind. Scientific American. *292:86-95, 2005.* [14] *By permission*

Specifically, some of the older of these included a 400,000-year-old wooden throwing spear from Schöningen, Germany; a 233,000-year-old figurine from Berkekhat, Israel; and 100,000-year-old notched bone fragments from the Klasies River Mouth Cave, South Africa. [14] More recent artifacts include 77,000-year-old abstractly engraved ochres from Blombos Caves in South Africa 15 (Figure 5.)

While the meaning of these abstract images is unknown they suggest an ability to think symbolically was present over 77,000 years ago. [15]

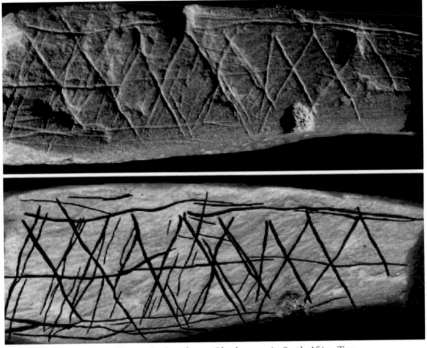

Figure 5. Engraved ochres from a Blombos cave in South Africa. Top: *oblique lighting to accentuate the surface features.* Bottom: *A tracing of the lines to emphasize the pattern. From Henshilwood et al.: Emergence of Modern Human Behavior: Middle Stone Age Engravings from South Africa.* Science. *295:1278-1280, 2002* [15] *By permission.*

The Role of Social Skills in the Evolution of Human Intelligence

Given the many ways in which humans are similar to the great apes, or vice versa, when we speak of the evolution of human intelligence we need to address those selective factors that allowed intelligence to increase to a level greater than that seen in the great apes. It is likely that the greatest degree of selection revolved around females picking a mate that was most able to succeed in life. This is still true today. These skills involve the traits that are controlled by the prefrontal lobes, the areas of the human brain that evolved most rapidly. These skills include planning future actions, initiating plans, reasoning, and paying attention. This area of the brain is also involved in working memory, a neurological function that is critical for reasoning, planning, and decision-making, and is highly correlated with IQ.

While one could speculate about the particular cognitive or social skills that are most important in the selection for intelligence, studies of intelligence tests have indicated that a wide range of tests all tap a common factor called g. In addition, a number of tests of physiological brain functions, such as working memory and reaction time, each individually correlate well with g. [16] These facts suggest that whatever trait was valued most for mate selection, including intelligence itself, it is likely to result in the continued selection of genes for improving intelligence. [16] The number of suggestions of what skills were most involved in this selection process is as varied as the number of authors writing on the subject. They include the ability to:

- be cunning and able to manipulate others [17]
- be deceptive [18]
- be predatory and able to secure food [19]
- delay impulsive behavior for a greater future gain [20p48]
- empathize [9p528]
- form into groups as defense against predators [21]
- learn social skills. [24]
- make the best tools [22]
- plan ahead [12]
- play power games in social politics [20p84]
- possess sexual attractiveness and body symmetry [23]
- socialize. [21,22]
- solve problems and learn [10p292]
- string sounds together to form meaningful sentences [12]
- tell interesting stories [20p236]
- throw spears with precision [11]
- use speech effectively [23,25]
- use symbols to represent people and concepts [20,26p191]

All of these tasks require a well-functioning brain, especially the prefrontal cortex. The greater the selection for these traits, the better the prefrontal cortex will function. The better the function of the prefrontal cortex, the greater the level of *g* and the higher the intelligence. The concept of "use it or lose it" is valid. Those who are best able to use their prefrontal lobes make the most desirous mates. The genes responsible for this improvement are selected, and intelligence and cognitive skills progressively increase. Which of the above traits were most important in this evolutionary process will never be known for certain. It is likely that they all are involved to some degree.

g is the fundamental biological factor behind a range of cognitive skills that take the measure of the mind of man. Individuals who were best able to perform a large number of those skills were most likely to win the race for sexual selection and thus pass on the responsible genes. This would result in a progressive increase in *g* and intelligence.

References

1. Piaget, J. *The Origins of Intelligence in Children.* Basic Books, New York, 1929, 1952.
2. Flynn, J. R. The mean IQ of Americans: Massive gains 1932 to 1978. *Psychological Bull.* 95: 29-51, 1984.
3. Flynn, J. R. Massive IQ gains in 14 nations: What IQ tests really measure. *Psychological Bull.* 101: 171-191, 1987.
4. Semendeferi, K., Damasio, H., Frank, R. & Van Hoesen, G. W. The evolution of the frontal lobes: a volumetric analysis based on three-dimensional reconstructions of magnetic resonance scans of human and ape brains. *J Hum Evol* 32: 375-388, 1997.
5. Bonin, G. The frontal lobes of primates: cytoarchitectural studies. *Res Publ Assoc Nerv Dis.* 27: 67-83, 1948.

6. Semendeferi, K., Armstrong, E., Schleicher, A., Zilles, K. & Van Hoesen, G. W. Prefrontal cortex in humans and apes: a comparative study of area 10. *Am J Phys Anthropol.* 114: 224-241, 2001.

7. Schoenemann, P. T., Sheehan, M. J. & Glotzer, L. D. Prefrontal white matter volume is disproportionately larger in humans than in other primates. *Nat Neurosci.* 8: 242-52, 2005.

8. Gallup, G. G. & Suarez, S. D. Overcoming our resistance to animal research: Man in comparative perspective. in: Rajecki, D. W. *Comparing Behavior: Studying Man Studying Animals.* Erbaum, Hillsdale, NJ. 1983.

9. Maser, J. D. & Gallup, G. G. J. Theism as a by-product of natural selection. *J Religion.* 70: 515-532, 1990.

10. Parker, S. T. & McKinney, M. L. *Origins of Intelligence. The Evolution of Cognitive Development in Monkeys, Apes, and Humans.* Johns Hopkins University Press, Baltimore, 1999.

11. Calvin, W. H. Pumping up intelligence: Abrupt climate jumps and the evolution of higher intellectual functions during the ice ages. in: Sternberg, R. J. & Kaufman, J. C. *The Evolution of Intelligence.* Mahwah, NJ. Lawrence Erlbaum Associates, Publishers. 2002.

12. Calvin, W. H. The Emergence of Intelligence. *Sci Am Presents.* 9: 100-107, 1998.

13. Calvin, W. H. *The Ascent of Mind. Ice Age Climates and the Evolution of Intelligence.* Bantam Books, New York, 1990.

14. Wong, K. The morning of the modern mind. *Sci Am.* 292: (June) 86-95, 2005.

15. Henshilwood, C. S. et al. Emergence of modern human behavior: Middle Stone Age engravings from South Africa. *Science.* 295: 1278-1280, 2002.

16. Mackintosh, N. J. Evolutionary psychology meets *g. Nature.* 403: 378-9, 2000.

17. Whiten, A. & Byrne, R. W. *Machiavellian intelligence. II: Extensions and evaluations.* Cambridge University Press, Cambridge, UK, 1997.

18. Flanagan, O., Hardcastle, V. G. & Nahmias, E. Is Human intelligence an adaption? Cautionary observations from the philosophy of biology. in: Sternberg, R. J. & Kaufman, J. C. *The Evolution of Intelligence.* Mahwah, NJ. Lawrence Erlbaum Associates, Publishers. 2002.

19. Brain, C. K. Do we owe our intelligence to a predatory past? *James Arthur Lect.* 70: 1-32, 2000.

20. Skoyles, J. R. & Cagan, D. *Up From Dragons. The Evolution of Human Intelligence.* McGraw Hill, New York, 2002.

21. Hart, D. & Sussman, R. W. *Man the Hunted Primates, Predators, and Human Evolution.* Westview, New York, 2005.

22. Gibson, K. R. Evolution of human intelligence: the roles of brain size and mental construction. *Brain Behav Evol.* 59: 10-20, 2002.

23. Miller, G. Sexual selection for indicators of intelligence. *Novartis Found Symp.* 233: 260-270; discussion 270-280, 2000.

24. Van Schaik, C. Why are some animals so smart? *Sci Am.* 294: 64-71, 2006.

25. Macphail, E. M. & Bolhuis, J. J. The evolution of intelligence: adaptive specializations versus general process. *Biol Rev Camb Philos Soc.* 76: 341-364, 2001.

26. Klein, R. G. & Edgar, B. *The Dawn of Human Culture.* Wiley & Sons, 2002.

The human nervous system possesses curious and profound hungers for many objects which are neither meat nor drink, neither satisfiers of oxygen need, nor of sex need, nor of material need, nor of any other more obvious visceral demand.

Gardner Murphy.
Human Potentialities [1]

Man has another mental quality which the animal lacks. He is aware of himself, of his past and of his future, which is death; of his smallness and powerlessness. Man transcends all other life because he is, for the first time, life aware of itself.

Erick Fromm [2]

All religious and philosophical systems are principally an antidote to the certainty of death.

Arthur Schopenhauer

Fear begets Gods

Lucretius, c. 99–55 BC

One of the major functions of religious belief is to reduce a person's fear of death.

Hood [3]

Chapter 42

The Evolution of Spirituality

Previous chapters have shown that the human nervous system possesses a unique capacity for spirituality. A specific part of the brain is involved; genetic factors play an important role, and a few of the specific genes involved have been identified. As with intelligence, entities that involve a specific structure and a specific set of genes do not arise by chance—they evolve. Spirituality differs from intelligence in that it is a uniquely human trait. As with intelligence, a number of theories have been proposed about how this natural selection and evolution took place, some of which are discussed in this chapter.

Is Spirituality a Spandrel?

Evolutionary psychology refers to the field of study of the role of natural selection in human behavioral traits. It had originally been termed *social biology* in deference to E.O. Wilson's 1975 book, *Sociobiology*. [4] Because of the controversial nature of sociobiology, [5] the field was renamed *evolutionary psychology*. [6] It has also been called *adaptive evolution,* where "adaptive" is used in the context of referring to traits that allow humans to flourish in a particular environment. Not every adaptive trait is the result of genes and natural selection. For example, the ability to sing well is more likely one of many uses of our vocal cords rather than a result of Darwinian natural selection for skills in singing.

While evolutionary psychology is a legitimate field of study, some have criticized it as reducing the complexity of human experience to simple genetic determinism. This is a specious argument since, as discussed in Part V, behavioral traits are due to the additive and epistatic effect of many different genes interacting with the environment. The complaint of genetic predeterminism has no validity because the effect of *the genetic component is not strong enough to produce genetic predeterminism.* The effect of genes is strong enough to alter the *probability of some behaviors* but not produce them with certainty.

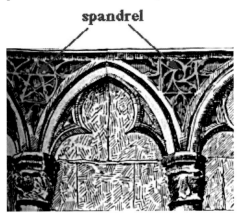

Figure 1. Spandrels formed by the intersection of two rounded arches.

Steven J. Gould and Richard Lewontin took on the whole field of evolutionary psychology in a widely cited paper entitled, "The Spandrels of San Marco and the Panglossian Paradigm: A Critique of the Adaptionist Programme."[7] Spandrels refer to the triangular spaces formed by the intersection of two rounded arches, as shown in Figure 1.

Spandrels just happen as the result of other features. The point Gould and Lewontin were making was that some behaviors might "just happen" because of certain pre-existing aspects of the structure and function of the human brain, not because there was active natural selection to produce them. An example might be the noise that a physician hears when he or she places a stethocope over the heart. These noises are the result of the flapping of the heart valves as the heart pumps blood. They are not the result of natural selection for "heart noises." The Panglossian paradigm part of the title refers to the ridicule that Voltaire heaped on Dr. Pangloss for suggesting that. "Our noses were made to carry spectacles, so we have spectacles." The spectacles were secondary to something else (poor eyesight), not due to the fact we have noses. Some have suggested that spirituality started as a spandrel that turned out to be useful and was subsequently enhanced by natural selection.[8]

Michael Shermer[9p39] proposed that magical thinking was a spandrel and was a necessary byproduct of rational thought that comes to the fore when uncertainties arise in the absence of proven scientific explanations. He gives as an example the high degree of superstition and magical thinking associated with batting in baseball, where even the best hitters connect only 30 percent of the time (uncertainty), compared to the virtual absence of magical thinking for outfielders who catch the ball over 95 percent of the time (certainty). I suspect he is correct; both causal thinking and magical thinking may be a product of a rational brain and the frontal lobes. However, I would argue that the intense feelings of spirituality and of being connected with a transcendent being is distinct from superstition and magical thinking per se and are a product of the temporal lobes.

The issue of the role of evolution in spirituality falls under the purview of *evolutionary psychology.* Does man possess spirituality as a result of natural selection because it had survival value, or is spirituality a spandrel? It is difficult to give a definitive answer, however, since spirituality has a strong genetic component, and since it is one of the most enduring and universal of human traits, and since much of spirituality appears to be associated with a specific brain structure, the temporal lobes, I propose spirituality is the result of natural selection and is not a spandrel.

Is Spirituality a Meme?

As shown in the chapter on the genetics of spirituality, cultural transmission explained some of the variance of participation in religion as measured by church attendance. In his book, *The Selfish Gene,* Richard Dawkins[10] renamed cultural transmission as *memes.* Memes refer to characteristics that are transmitted non-genetically from individual to individual and generation-to-generation. The term *memes* was meant to be analogous to genes. Dawkins referred to the work of Jenkins[11] who studied the songs of the saddleback bird on an island off New Zealand. By comparing the songs of fathers and sons, he showed the patterns were not inherited genetically. Young birds adopted the songs from their territorial neighbors by imitation. New songs arose by change in pitch. These were referred to as *cultural mutations.* As in genetic mutations there may be progressive changes in these songs. Finally, as with the punctuated equilibria of real evolution, cultural evolution may also go through long periods of stagnation followed by periods of rapid change. Dawkins referred to the centuries of cultural stagnation of the Dark Ages compared to the rapid changes of the Renaissance and Industrial Revolution as an example. Other examples of memes are tunes, ideas, catch phrases, clothes, fashions, architecture, language, poems, and a multitude of other features that define the human race.

Cultural evolution and biological evolution, or memes and genes, have much in common. They are transmitted from generation to generation, replicate, mutate, show progression and undergo periods of stagnation followed by periods of rapid change. The major distinction is that cultural or meme evolution can take place much more rapidly than biological evolution. Witness the rapidly accelerated use of the internet as a means of communication and acquisition of knowledge over a period of only a few years. This represents a cultural and behavioral change thousands of times faster than biological evolution.

The obvious question arises, "Is the development of spirituality in man the result of a meme, or of evolution by natural selection?" If spirituality was culturally transmitted, twin studies would not have shown a significant genetic component and the concordance rate would have been the same for identical versus fraternal twins. This was not the case. Twin studies of spirituality showed that genes accounted for 50 percent of the variance, the unique environment for 50 percent, and the common environment, including cultural influences, zero percent.[12] This indicated that *spirituality was an intrinsic biological trait, not a meme.* By contrast, common environment and cultural transmission accounted for a significant percent of the variance of church attendance suggesting that religion is transmitted, at least in part, as a meme. [13p480]

Spirituality Alleviates Man's Fear of His Own Death, of His Mortality

While there are many features that humans and the great apes have in common, one feature that is unique to humans is an awareness of our own mortality—an awareness that we are going to die and that death could come at any moment. In their book, *Ego in Evolution,* Ester and William Menaker [14] state:

> In the animal world from which we emerged, anxiety—or shall we say, fear—serves a survival function and appears as a warning of impending danger to be reacted to with the full panoply of automatic instinctual equipment which is available for the individual's survival. Human evolution poses a new problem, although it is motivated by the same survival need. It is obvious that the great human evolutionary acquisition, awareness [of death], must add a special dimension to fear.

Man is burdened with death awareness. Death awareness is the bitter fruit of man having risen to a high level of consciousness. Malinowski [15] stated it as follows:

> The existence of strong personal attachments and the fact of death, which *of all of human events is the most upsetting and disorganizing to man's calculations, are perhaps the main sources of religious belief. The affirmation that death is not real, that man has a soul and that this is immortal, arises out of a deep need to deny personal destruction.*

Few would argue that man is uniquely aware of his own death, but how does he cope with this knowledge? The best way to alleviate a fear of death is to maintain the belief that we actually do not die, that we possess a soul that transcends death and lives on after we die, providing us with immortality. The site where this immortality is played out is heaven. Most religions, both Western and Eastern, contain elements of this comforting concept. Such an ability to feel connected with transcendence into something beyond our own existence is at the heart of the definition of spirituality. This would alleviate the fear of death and provide a sense of peace to alleviate and balance man's unique capacity to have foreknowledge that he will die. The greater an individual's ability to feel connected with this sense of something beyond his own existence, the less his fear of death and the greater his feeling of being at peace with life. Benson [16] suggested, "In order to counter this fundamental angst, humans are 'wired' for God. "

In their article, *Theism as a By-Product of Natural Selection,* Maser and Gallup [17] suggested the role of the fear of death in spirituality as follows:

> We contend that mind is a necessary but not sufficient condition for

theistic thought. A motivational aspect to the theory is needed to explain the strong, compelling hold that theistic thought has on the lives of so many people. We maintain that the capacity to conceive of God comes with the mind, but the primary driving force is the understanding that the self is subject to annihilation.

The organism, which is aware of itself, and bearing witness to the demise of its associates, should be able to take the next logical step and conceive of a non-self, or its death. Once aware of one's own existence, one is in a position to contemplate eventual nonexistence. *The realization of the inevitability of our own demise is the unique price paid for self-awareness. In terms of our theory, death is a major motivational component forcing into use our cognitive capacity to conceive of God.*

Anthropological findings are consistent with the presence of this form of spirituality in early man. A number of Neanderthal graves have been discovered in Europe that clearly indicate the presence of "ceremonial" burials where bodies were painted with red ochre and provided with stone implements, tools, flowers, and food, presumably for use in the afterlife. [18] The red ochre is believed to have been used to create an illusion of the presence of lifegiving blood circulating through the dead body. The extensive anthropological literature indicates that a similar care of the dead was a widespread practice at the dawn of humanity. [19] One of the most beautiful and comforting poems ever written is a testament to the role of a fear of death in spirituality and religion.

Yea, though I walk through the valley of the shadow of death, I will fear no evil: For thou art with me; Thy rod and thy staff they comfort me.
Psalms 23:4

Selective value? While the development of spirituality and a belief in life after death, heaven and God is an effective way of minimizing a fear of death, how does this have survival value? The belief in an afterlife could clearly reduce the level of fear involved in dangerous tasks such as hunting animals for food and of battling competing tribes, making the individual a far braver hunter and a more fierce warrior. This is analogous to the manner in which a spiritual fervor often played a critical role in many of the victories of the First Crusaders against numerically vastly superior opposing forces. [20]

In addition to a fear of death, Alper, [21] in his paper, "The Evolutionary Origins of Spiritual Consciousness," added one more dimension created by an awareness of our death:

In light of our awareness of inevitable death, life takes on a newfound sense of existential meaninglessness. Our struggles to survive become an exercise in futility. Between death's inevitability and all of the suffering we are forced to endure, we are compelled to ask: Why go on living? What is the point? How was our species to justify its continued existence in light of such a hopeless circumstance? Why struggle today when tomorrow we won't even be here? Under such circumstances, the motivation principle of self-preservation that had sustained life for all these billions of years no longer applied to our species.

On the assumption that poorly controlled anxiety reduces fitness, Alper proposes that individuals with the greatest sense of spirituality were the most likely to survive.

> As generations of these protohumans passed, those whose cerebral constitutions most effectively dealt with the anxiety resulting from their awareness of death were selected to survive. This process continued until a cognitive function emerged that altered the way these protohumans perceived reality by adding a "spiritual" component to their perspectives....Nature selected those individuals who developed a spiritual function. That function being built is the perception that there exists an alternate and transcendental reality that supercedes the limitations of this finite physical realm which can only offer us pain, suffering and ultimately death.

Spirituality Gives Man Control over a Threatening World

An additional advantage of spirituality and religion is that they provide the individual with better sense of control over a threatening world. This is especially apparent in what we might call, with a flare of superiority, primitive religions. Edward Tylor, one of the nineteenth century pioneers in "evolutionary" cultural anthropology, stressed that primitive man saw manifestations of personified spiritual agents in living things as well as inanimate objects. This was termed *animism*. Attributing spirits to threatening objects in nature provides some sense of control since one can pray to these spirits and plead for them to behave themselves. Then it is only a modest step from praying to the spirits of inanimate objects to praying to a more sophisticated, overreaching supernatural force — a god or gods. This is an intriguing explanation for the development of a belief in God and religion that could also be transmitted from generation to generation as a meme, with no involvement of genes or natural selection. Natural selection could be involved if individuals whose level of spirituality makes them the most adept at communication with the spirits are also the most resilient to a threatening environment. This could be akin to a form of placebo effect. Those who are convinced they are protected because they prayed to the spirits may be the most resistant to the stress of a threatening environment.

Spirituality and Near-Death Experiences

The clear connection between near-death experiences and spirituality was discussed previously. Saver and Rabin [22p505] suggested that components of the near-death experience and a response to severe stress may have adaptive benefit. For example, when trapped by a predator, passive immobilization and feigning death may promote clarity of perception and insight that allows the individual to identify and carry out previously unrecognized strategies to escape desperate life-threatening circumstances.

Spirituality and Optimism

Hamer [23p10] suggested that the selection for dopaminergic spirituality genes was driven by their ability to produce an innate sense of "feel good" optimism. This would have selective value in the sense that optimism relates to the will to keep on living and procreating, despite the fact that death is ultimately inevitable. Studies have shown that optimism seems to promote better health and quicker recovery from disease, features that would have positive selective value.

Newberg and colleagues [24] suggested a different kind of association of spirituality with a "feel good" sensation. They suggested that the neurological machinery of spiritual transcendence may have arisen from the neural circuitry that evolved for mating and sexual experience. They suggested that:

> Mystics of all times and cultures have used the same expressive terms to describe their ineffable experience: bliss, rapture, ecstasy, and exaltation. They speak of losing themselves in the sublime sense of union, of melting into elation, and of the total satisfaction of desires.
>
> We believe it is no coincidence that this is also the language of sexual pleasure. Nor is it surprising, because the very neurological structures and pathways involved in transcendent experience — including the arousal, quiescent, and limbic systems — evolved primarily to link sexual pleasures to the powerful sensations of orgasm.

We saw in previous chapters that one of the most effective mechanisms of evolution was the co-option of old structures and functions into new structures and functions. It is clear that sex came before spirituality. Some of the rewarding aspects of spirituality may have co-opted the pre-existing mechanism involved in the pleasures of sex.

Spirituality, Religion, and Societal Cohesiveness

E. O. Wilson believed that any gene programming a behavior to make one small group or tribe more cohesive than another might be favored by natural selection. A band of religious hunter-gatherers might be just a little bit better at hunting and gathering than one that was less cohesive. As Wilson put it:

> When the gods are served, the Darwinian fitness of the members of the tribe is the ultimate unrecognized beneficiary. [25p184]

He also said:

Consequently religions are like other human institutions in that they evolve in directions that enhance the welfare of the practitioners. Because this demographic benefit must accrue to the group as a whole, it can be gained partly by altruism and partly by exploitation, with certain sectors profiting at the expense of others. [25p175]

Noting that religions are widespread throughout the world, however much their specific rituals and traditions vary, Wilson concluded that the religious impulse is a universal aspect of human nature. Wilson then asks what the adaptive significance of religious behavior might be.

The highest forms of religious practice, when examined more closely, can be seen to confer biological advantage. Above all they congeal identity. In the midst of the chaotic and potentially disorienting experiences each person undergoes daily, religion classifies him, provides him with unquestioned membership in a group claiming great powers, and by this means gives him a driving purpose in life compatible with his self-interest. [25p188]

In addition to congealing identity, there are many reasons why a spiritual or religious group could provide a reproductive advantage over the non-spiritual, non-religious group. Most religions include rituals related to all of the most critical aspects of reproductive life including membership in a group, rules of courtship, marriage, childbirth, and even the last rites of death. Many of these are capable of influencing reproductive fitness. An additional factor would be the ostracism and the marginalization it would produce if an individual did not join the group. This could result in a decreased likelihood of finding a mate, thus having fewer or no children.

The more spiritual an individual was, the more likely he or she would join a group of like-minded individuals, and this in turn would enhance their survivability in a hostile world. This would be analogous to the selective value of joining a tribe during the ice ages, mentioned in the previous chapter, except that the reason to join would be spirituality rather than the pervasiveness of ice. One could argue that spirituality has a self-perpetuating quality and religions are the means of ensuring that perpetuation, a theme also voiced by John Bowker.

Religion and Natural Selection

On the first page of his beautifully illustrated book, *World Religions,* John Bowker [26] speaks of religion and natural selection. He first points out that religion is derived from the word *religare,* meaning to bind things closely together. This is appropriate since religions bind people together in common practices and beliefs, and draw them together in a common goal of life. He went on to state:

Religions are the earliest protective systems we know about that enabled people to have children and to raise them to adulthood. The importance of this is obvious: natural selection and evolution means that wherever the processes of birth and bringing up children (that is passing on genes and looking after children) are best protected, their human communities survive and flourish.

Culture [from the Latin word *cultus,* meaning worship of the gods] is protective; religions, with their various patterns of belief and practice, are the earliest cultural system that we know about for the protection of gene replication and the nurture of children....religions have been the best systems that humans could devise to ensure survival.

While we might forgive Bowker for his enthusiasm for his favorite subject, these thoughts are supported by E. O. Wilson, who stated that "religions, like other human institutions, evolve so as to further the welfare of their practitioners."[4p561] This provides support for the concept that there has been selection for the genes associated with spirituality. Individuals with the greatest inherent spirituality are the ones most likely to join a religious group and thus are most likely to benefit from the protective effect of such a group.

Spirituality as a Defense Mechanism

Justin Barrett,[27] of the Institute of Cognition in Belfast, suggested that individuals who believed in a form of animism, in which any activity in the environment was assumed to have been caused by a living spiritual agent, would possess a self-protective form of hypervigilance. For example, if they assumed that a twig breaking in the forest was always the result of a living agent rather than a result of the wind, they would fare better when a breaking twig really was due to a dangerous living agent. This form of protective vigilance would provide a selective advantage for those carrying this trait.

Inborn Spirituality as a Moral Watchdog

Developmental psychologist Jesse Bering reasoned that if humans are naturally inclined to believe in God and the afterlife, then children should exhibit signs of these traits before being indoctrinated into a given religion. To test this he examined subjects in three different age groups, those in kindergarten, those in late elementary school, and adults.[28] They were all exposed to a puppet show in which a mouse is suddenly eaten by an alligator. They were then asked questions such as: Now that the mouse is dead, does it miss its mom? Is it still hungry? Did it love and hate? The total set of questions involved six different areas. They included biological questions relating brain function such as, Does the mouse need to eat?; psychological biological questions such as, Is the mouse hungry? Is the mouse thirsty? There were questions about perception such as, Can the mouse hear? Can he taste?; emotional questions such as, Does the mouse still love his mother? Is the mouse angry?; questions relating to desire such as, Does the mouse want things?; and questions about knowledge such as, Does the mouse know things? The responses to these questions are shown in Figure 2.

For every type of question the children were more likely to believe that the dead

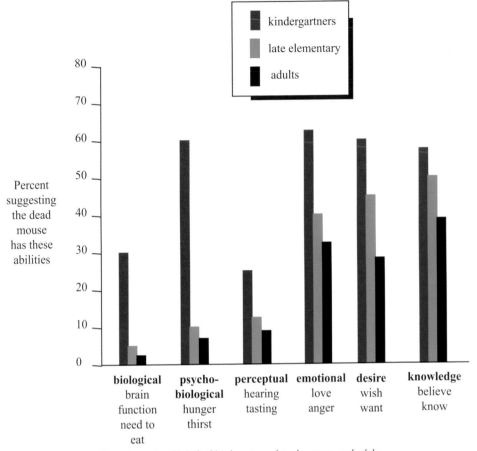

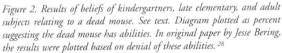

Figure 2. Results of beliefs of kindergartners, late elementary, and adult subjects relating to a dead mouse. See text. Diagram plotted as percent suggesting the dead mouse has abilities. In original paper by Jesse Bering, the results were plotted based on denial of these abilities. [28]

mouse had the different capabilities. Of interest, many of the late elementary children and adults also attributed traits relating to emotions, desires, and knowledge to the dead mouse. The drop-off with age is likely to be related to a loss of naïve ideas about death as the children better understood the biology of life. It was suggested that because no one knows what it is like to be dead, people attribute to dead agents the mental traits that they cannot imagine being without. More importantly, it suggests that a belief in supernatural agents pirates the brain's mental inference systems that are designed to reason about everyday living agents. Stated differently, *the spiritual brain often takes precedence over the rational brain.* While some psychologists have proposed that supernatural beliefs are all culturally derived, Bering suggested that afterlife beliefs are the default state, and it is in fact counterintuitive for people to deny them.

If this need to believe in the afterlife is indeed instinctual and is strong enough to countermand rational input, it is reasonable to believe that there was an evolutionary advantage for such beliefs. Bering suggested that most hunter-gatherer societies had a fear of ancestral ghosts who were constantly watching and monitoring their behavior. This would result in more pro-social as opposed to anti-social behavior, to the selective benefit of both the individual and the group.

To test this, they set up an experiment in which subjects were told they were evaluating a new test of spatial intelligence but that the program still had some glitches and would occasionally flash the correct answer on the screen. When this happened they were to immediately hit the space bar to clear the answer. The psychologist measured the time it took to hit the space bar as a measure of cheating. When some of the subjects were told that a graduate student involved in these studies had died suddenly and there had been sightings of his ghost in the room, *those students cheated less than the controls.* This suggests they consciously or unconsciously believed the ghost was monitoring their behavior. These studies suggest it might be an evolutionary advantage if humans believed that omnipotent deities would punish them if they did wrong, and as a result, they would always do right.

A Spiritual Mate

One additional selective advantage of a high level of spirituality is that such a trait would be unusually appealing to the opposite sex. Some have suggested that spiritual qualities include compassion, honesty, steadiness, and unconditional love. [29] In Cloninger's personality inventory, spiritual qualities included feeling connected to others and a willingness to sacrifice oneself for the good of others. Based on the previous paragraph, always doing the right thing could be added to this list. These traits would certainly be very attractive to a potential mate. The resulting positive sexual selection would result in the perpetuation of the relevant spirituality genes.

> **A number of factors may have been involved in the evolution of man's capacity for spirituality. These include a reduction in the fear of death, a feeling of being in better control over a hostile environment, a feeling of being monitored for moral behavior, improved social cohesiveness, and greater feelings of joy, happiness and optimism. These in turn may have had selective value by allowing spiritual individuals to more easily escape life-threatening circumstances, to make better hunters and warriors, to have greater resistance to stress and disease, to behave morally, to belong to a protective religious group, and to have greater appeal to a sexual partner.**

> **Twin and genetic studies show a significant role of genes in spirituality and no role for the common environment. This makes the idea that spirituality is a side product of other brain structures or functions (a spandrel) or a result of cultural evolution (a meme) — quite unlikely.**

> **Humans are unique in that they are aware of and fear their own mortality. A major driving force behind the invention of *The Theory of God* was to provide a way to alleviate these fears by proposing that**

humans had a soul that was imortal.

Spirituality can be defined as a feeling of a connection with something greater than oneself including any form of social order. Perhaps the greatest factor in the evolution of spirituality is that such a trait would maximize the development of man as a social animal.

References

1. Murphy, G. *Human Potentialities*. Basic Books, New York, 1958.
2. Fromm, E. Value, psychology, and human existence. in: Maslow, A. H. *New Knowledge of Human Values*. Harper Row, New York, 1959.
3. Hood, R. W. J., Spilka, B., Hunsberger, B. & Gorsuch, R. *The Psychology of Religion*. The Guilford Press, New York, 1996.
4. Wilson, E. O. *Sociobiology. The New Synthesis*. Belknap Press of Harvard University Press, Cambridge, MA, 1975, 2000.
5. Lewontin, R. C. Sociobiology as an adaptionist program. *Behavioral Science*. 24: 5-14, 1979.
6. Grossman, J. B. & Kaufman, J. C. (eds.) *Evolutionary psychology: promise and perils*, Mawrence Erlbaum Associates, Publishers, Mahwah, NJ, 2002.
7. Gould, S. J. & Lewontin, R. C. The spandrels of San Marco and the Panglossian paradigm: a critique of the adaptationist programme. *Proc R Soc Lond B Biol Sci*. 205: 581-98, 1979.
8. Boyer, P. Religion Explained. *The Evolutionary Origins of Religious Thought*. Basic Books, New York, 2001.
9. Shermer, M. How We Believe. *Science, Skepticism, and the Search for God*. Second Edition. A. W. H. Freeman Henry Holt and Company, New York, 2000.
10. Dawkins, R. *The Selfish Gene*. Oxford University Press, Oxford, 1989.
11. Jenkins, P. F. Cultural transmission of song patterns and dialect development in a free-living bird population. *Animal Behavior*. 26: 50-78, 1978.
12. Kirk, K. M., Eaves, L. J. & Martia, N. G. Self-transcendence as a measure of spirituality in a sample of older Australian twins. *Twin Res*. 2: 81-87, 1999.
13. Kirk, K. M. et al. Frequency of church attendance in Australia and the United States: models of family resemblance. *Twin Res*. 2: 99-107, 1999.
14. Menaker, E. & Menaker, W. *Ego in Evolution*. Groove Press, New York, 1965.
15. Malinowski, B. The role of magic and religion. in: Lessa, W. A. & Vogt, E. Z. *Reader in Comparative Religion*. Row Peterson, Evanston, IL, 1931.
16. Benson, H. *Timeless Healing*. Scribner, New York, 1996.
17. Maser, J. D. & Gallup, G. G. J. Theism as a by-product of natural selection. *J Religion*. 70: 515-532, 1990.
18. Hawkes, J. & Wooley, L. *Prehistory and the Beginning of Civilization. History of Mankind*. Vol 1. Harper & Row, New York, 1963.
19. Dobzhansky, T. *The Biology of Ultimate Concern*. Meridian Books, NY, 1969.
20. Asbridge, T. *The First Crusade*. Oxford University Press, New York, NY, 2004.
21. Alper, M. The "God" Part of the Brain. *A Scientific Interpretation of Human Spirituality and God*. Rogue Press, New York, 2001.
22. Saver, J. L. & Rabin, J. The neural substrates of religious experience. *J Neuropsychiatry Clin Neurosci*. 9: 498-510, 1997.
23. Hamer, D. *The God Gene: How Faith is Hardwired in our Genes*. Doubleday, New York, 2004.
24. Newberg, A., M.D., D'Aquill, E., Ph.D. & Rause, V. *Why God Won't Go Away*. Ballantine Books, New York, 2001.
25. Wilson, E. O. *On Human Nature*. Harvard University Press, Cambridge, MA, 1978.
26. Bowker, J. *World Religions*. DK Publishing, Inc., New York, 1997.
27. Barrett, J. L. Exploring the natural foundations of religion. *Trends Cogn Sci*. 4: 29-34, 2000.
28. Bering, J. M. The cognitive psychology of belief in the supernatural. *American Scientist*. 94: 142-149, 2006.
29. Janis, S. *Spirituality for Dummies*. Foster City, 2000.

Part VII

Other Aspects of Spirituality and Religion

In addition to the items already covered, there are a number of other issues and questions that are relevant to the title of this book, *Did Man Create God?* These include the issues of the origin of the world's major religions, the role of mystics, mysticism, myth, ritual, and psychedelics in the formation of the different religions.

One of the major problems with religion is the assumption by adherents that theirs is the true religion favored by God. This raises the question, Does God play favorites? Other relevant questions include, Is religion inherently evil, inherently good, or a mixture of both? In addition, one of the major problems for religion relates to what has been termed the *Problem of Evil*. How can a kind, compassionate God stand by and allow so much evil to happen to mankind?

Another question comes from the fact that major sources of religious prejudice, wars, and terrorism derive from a literal interpretation of the various sacred books. Thus, one needs to ask, Are the sacred books literally true? A final relevant question becomes — Is God Dead? An examination of Pentecostalism provides an intriguing answer.

Creating Gods is something that human beings have always done. When one religious idea ceases to work for them, it is simply replaced.

All religions change and develop. If they do not, they become obsolete.

It is far more important for a particular idea of God to work than for it to be logically or scientifically sound.

The idea of a personal God can only be a stage in our religious development.

Karen Armstrong
A History of God[1]

Chapter 43

The Origins of Religion

While the enormous diversity of man's beliefs is relevant to the question, *Did Man Create God?* anything other than a modest summary of the world's religions is beyond the scope of this book. Several excellent books on the subject are available for the reader who is interested in a more extensive review. [1-5] I will instead concentrate on a more limited objective — an examination of the origins and basic tenets of some of the world's major religions. This subject has relevance to the role that man played in placing a formal framework around his irrepressible spirituality. Developing a range of religions, each tailored to different cultures satisfied a yearning for structure. This subject also reveals how man has recognized for thousands of years that reason and religious faith were often in conflict — and how the different religions dealt with this difficult issue.

The religions of the world tend to divide into two major groups, those that look inward and those that look outward. Those that look inward seek eternal truth by the "examination of the streams and oceans of your inner nature." [3] These approaches gave rise to Hinduism, Buddhism, Jainism, and other Eastern religions. By contrast, Western religions concentrate on the outer world and relationships with other humans, but especially with a higher power recognized as God, the creator of all life, a savior, a personal companion through life who is there for the individual through the stresses of birth, marriage, life, and death, and is a provider of eternal life after death. This gave rise to Judaism, Christianity, and Islam. In a sense, many of the Eastern religions foster praying inward in the form of meditation and yoga, while Western religions foster praying outward to God. All religions make extensive use of symbolism, myths, and rituals.

Animism and the "Primitive Religions"

Animism is the oldest form of religious belief on earth and probably dates to the

Paleolithic age. It is basically a belief in the existence of spiritual beings and the belief that man shares the spiritual realm with the universe around him. Animism implies that everything has a consciousness, a spirit, and a soul. In fact, the term *animism* is derived from the Latin word *anima,* meaning breath or soul. A basic tenet of animism is that we should relate respectfully to all things.

In ancient times before the development of the monotheism of the West and the contemplative religions of the East, the rapid evolution of man's intelligence left him with the capacity to think, to wonder, to be curious, and to ask questions such as Why? and How? Why does the sun come up in the morning and set in the evening? Why the rain, thunder, and lightning? Why is there sometimes so much rain that floods are produced? Why does the rain sometimes stop, producing droughts, crop failure, and famine? Why death? Why is the world such a dangerous place? How do I control these frightening forces of nature? The objective scientific method of hypothesis formation and testing was several thousand years into the future and man's curiosity and intellect demanded immediate answers. In such a setting it is easy to see why animism, a belief in spirits, was the first manifestation of man's spirituality and was the first religion that man produced. The reasoning is straightforward. Since I have a "spirit" or a "soul" and since I am conscious and aware of my own actions, all other things must also have a "spirit"— the sky, rocks, rivers, oceans, mountains, plants, crops, animals, the whole universe. This view also implies the inverse, that all animate and inanimate objects represent the expression of the spirits.

If all objects had a spirit, the world would be a far safer and more controllable place. One can talk to the other spirits and plead with them to be less threatening. If pleading does not work, elevating them to the spiritual realm and praying to them might. Some of the things the inanimate objects do, like produce volcanic eruptions, thunder, and lightning, are so powerful and so majestic they must have come from some source that is far more powerful than man, some all-pervasive spirit, some supreme being. The spirits could also have lives of their own, giving rise to a range of man-made stories or myths. The different spirits were often represented by different symbols and could be controlled by rituals. Priests or shamans usually performed the requisite rituals. Sir Edwin Tylor first used the term animism in his 1871 book, *Primitive Cultures.* Animism is neither extinct nor necessarily restricted to primitive man. It still exists today in some form in many countries and many different cultures.

I placed "primitive religions" in quotes since one could argue that some elements of these religions could form the basis of an advanced, more rational religion of the future — closing a giant cycle and returning religion to its origins. While the assumption that inanimate objects are alive and that all objects have a soul is in contradiction to modern scientific reason, the element of feeling at one with nature and the universe, and of respecting all living and non-living things, is extremely laudable. Graham Harvey in *Animism: Respecting the Living World*[6] described these ideas as the "new animism" and referred to a second definition of animism as "a concern with knowing how to behave appropriately toward other persons, not all of whom are human." Had mankind retained some aspects of this "primitive" form of religion, millions of lives would have been spared, lives that were sacrificed in the name of "more advanced monotheistic religions" and to the prejudice that "My God is the only God, and certainly better than your god." We would also have been spared from the terrorism fostered by religious fundamentalism. In conclusion, we should be careful of whom and what we call primitive.

Polytheism

While animism and polytheism have elements in common, polytheism could be considered an evolutionary improvement in the "meme" sense in that the gods were more personalized, were formed into nuclear families, and directly interacted with human activities. This interaction involved having gods for problems with love, fertility, weather, crops, music, war, specific regions or families, and other human needs. Different gods were often adopted from earlier cultures that rose and fell in popularity. Man invented gods that most suited his needs at the time. Pantheism was popular in ancient Egypt, Greece, and Rome. It remains very popular today, playing an integral role in Hinduism, some forms of Buddhism, Confucianism, Taoism, Shintoism, and religions in Africa and the Americas. Like animism, it was nonjudgmental. People were free to worship whatever god or gods they wished.

Plato, Aristotle, and the Ancient Greeks

Given the conflict between reason and religion, it is ironic that even though Plato was passionately interested in reason and logic, many of his ideas formed the later foundations of the monotheistic religions. Plato (427–347 BCE) devoted much of his early work to defending Socrates, who fostered reason in his followers by thought-provoking questions. For his efforts, Socrates was sentenced to death in 399 BCE for the corruption of youth.

Plato is well known for his *Allegory of the Cave.* Chained prisoners in the cave can only see what is taking place behind them by observing the shadows they cast on the cave's wall. As a result they mistake the shadows for reality. Plato did not use the word "God," but he believed in the existence of the divine that was static and unchanging and could only be indirectly sensed as through the shadows. However, man was capable of regaining divine status by purification of the reasoning powers of the mind.

Aristotle (384–322 BCE) was Plato's student. He visualized the Supreme Deity as a timeless and impassable being who did not involve himself in earthly things and was remote from human needs. This was the antithesis of a personal god. The Supreme Deity was the Unmoved Mover consisting of pure thought and causing all the motion and activity in the universe. He was not composed of matter, since matter is flawed. Man was in a privileged position — his soul had the divine gift of intellect, making him kin to God and divine in nature. Aspects of these ideas of the ancient Greeks influenced all the later monotheistic religions.

Zoroastrianism

In about 1200 BCE a mystic prophet by the name of Zarathustra or Zoroaster, wrote the 17 hymns called the *Gathas*. These came to him through a series of visions from God, or *Ahura Mazda*. The Gathas stressed personal responsibility. A person's fate depended upon whether he chose to go with the good spirits called *aburas,* or the evil spirits called *daevas*. The good spirits came from the good god, *Ahura Mazda,* creator of life, while the bad or demonic spirits came from the bad god, *Angra Mainyu*. Figure 1 shows an image of Ahura Mazda.

Figure 1. The Guardian Spirit of Ahura Mazda representing the essence of god within people. From Bowker, World Religions. [3] *By permission.*

After death those who choose the good spirits went to paradise; those who choose the bad spirits went to the House of Lie, a place of torment. Since Zarathustra assumed that it was not difficult to choose the good spirits, his teachings were basically optimistic. By the seventh century BCE, Zoroastrianism had become the official state religion of the Persian Empire. A remarkable aspect of Zoroastrianism was its *tolerance of other religions based on the assumption that the ultimate judgment of a person was based on their good deeds, not on their beliefs*. Unfortunately this tolerant faith ended with the Muslim conquests in the seventh century BCE. Some elements of Zoroastrianism still persist in India today. All three of the present-day monotheistic religions borrowed concepts of good versus evil, paradise versus damnation, and heaven versus hell from Zoroastrianism.

The Eastern Religions

Hinduism. Hinduism is one of the oldest of man's religions. It had its origins among the people of the Indus valley. The Aryans, who originated from a region just north of the Tigris and Euphrates rivers, invaded northwest India in 1500 BCE. They brought with them oral teachings known as the *Vedas,* which for Hindus represent eternal truth. The Vedic religion has an elaborate plethora of gods that eventually evolved into the trinity of Brahma, Vishnu and Shiva. The Brahmins or priests dominated this religion. The society was divided into four levels with the Brahmins at the top, followed by the warriors, the traders and farmers, and the menials and servants. This may have provided the basis for the subsequent caste system in which Brahmins were at the top and the outcasts or untouchables were on the bottom. The

Hindus believed in reincarnation with the eternal soul, or *atman,* being reborn millions of times and in many forms from the heavens to the hells according to moral law, or *karma.* [3] People can be released *(moksha)* from this cycle of rebirth. There were many paths to moksha, including yoga. Hinduism is basically a method of appropriate behavior, or *dharma,* as a path to good rebirth or to release from rebirth. There are four desirable goals of life. In addition to dharma and moksha, they include *artha,* or the pursuit of legitimate worldly success, and *kama,* the pursuit of legitimate pleasure. This is certainly a long way from the sexually repressive nature of some forms of Christianity. It is believed that the essence of all reality — the earth, sun, moon, sky, birds, and animals — are one. One method of entering the power of this universe is through *mantras,* or sacred chants.

Figure 2. The four heads of Brahma. [9]

Unlike Islam, where God is unknowable and unseen, the gods of Hinduism are explicit and colorful. Brahma (Figure 2), the creator, is not worshiped like the other gods because his work was not done until the next creation of the world.

Brahma originally had five heads so he could see his lover wherever she was. Shiva destroyed one of the heads because Brahma offended him. Shiva is a bit of everything—destroyer, creator, and preserver. He is often portrayed with four hands (Figure 3), each signifying a different aspect of his power.

Figure 3. Shiva. [10]

Beginning as a minor god, Shiva gained importance and entry into the trinity after absorbing characteristics of other gods. Shivism is one of the most popular of the Hindu cults. Practitioners attempt to attain the nature of Shiva though yoga and renunciation. They mark their forehead with three horizontal marks representing the three aspects of Shiva.

Vishnu, the Supreme Being, was the *pervader* and *preserver* and represented the Universe. His was also shown with four arms representing the principal directions of space north, south, east, and west (Figure 4).

Vishnavites represent one of the largest of the Hindu groups. Vishnuism gave rise to the Hare Krishna movement once popular in the United States. The Hindu religion is rich with other gods, pilgrimages, festivals, sacrifices, and other rituals.

Buddhism. In about 538 BCE, Siddhartha Gautama was born to royalty and lived a protected life in a palace. At age 29 he saw human suffering for the first time. This led him to leave his wife and luxurious home to sit for six years at the feet of various Hindu gurus, searching for the secret of existence. He lived an ascetic life during this period known as the *Great Renunciation.* Still failing to find the answers he sought, he eventually put himself into a trance, sitting under the Bodhi tree, and attained enlightenment. Buddhism provided a new hope of liberation from suffering through the attainment of *nirvana,* the end of pain. Gautama had become the Buddha, the Enlightened One. The Hindu God Brahma convinced him to teach others, and over the next 45 years, Buddha traveled India preaching that the only stable thing in the world was *dharma,* the truth about right living. Since the gods had not helped Gautama achieve nirvana, he did not believe they were of much use to mankind, and Buddhism is not about God. He believed the ultimate reality was higher than the gods. The attainment of enlightenment is achieved though meditation and spiritual exercise and ultimately allowed practitioners to escape from constant rebirth and the suffering it entailed. The Buddha is most often depicted as rotund and in a sitting posture as shown in Figure 5.

Figure 4. Vishnu the pervader and preserver. [11]

Figure 5. Typical figure of the Buddha.

The Buddha saw Four Noble Truths during his enlightenment. The first was Existence, or *dukkha,* filled with suffering. Second, the suffering arises from a constant effort to find something permanent and stable in a transient world. Third, dukkha can cease entirely by attaining nirvana. Fourth, nirvana can be reached by following the Eightfold Path consisting of eight right steps: right understanding, thought, speech, action, livelihood, effort, mindfulness, and concentration. Right understanding includes Dependent

Organization, the concept that all things in the Universe are connected.

While Buddha believed in many of the concepts of Hinduism, he differed in one important aspect. Instead of believing in constant rebirth of the soul or atman, he felt that nothing is really permanent. One appearance simply gives rise to the next; there is no true death just a reappearance in a different form. Since even the gods were considered to be only temporary forms, he was against the Hindu practice of making animal sacrifices to the gods.

Buddhism was popular because of the appealing concept of enlightenment and moral law or karma and because individuals had control of their own fates and an opportunity for salvation. The Buddhist funeral rites dispelled fears about death, and governments appreciated it because it was seen as encouraging moral and peaceful citizens. [3]

Jainism. Jainism is named after Jain, a follower of the Jinas, the spiritual conquerors who lived in the Jain region of India in the Ganges basin. The Jains believe that 24 *tirthankaras* appear in each half-cycle of time to teach the release of the soul from its entanglement in material existence, known as karma. [3] Jainism appears to have had its origins in the ninth to the sixth century BCE. Like the Buddhists, they do not believe in a creator God.

The Jains are ascetics who take the Great Vows of nonviolence, speaking the truth, not taking what is not given, abstaining from sexual activity, a detachment from persons, places and things, and not eating after dark. The lay Jains take a less stringent set of vows that include being vegetarians and not destroying life by hunting and fishing. Being a farmer is acceptable. During the end of a Jain festival, lay people make confessions to an ascetic monk and ask him to pardon their sins. They seek to have a friendly relationship with all beings and to be unfriendly to none. The

non-violence of the Jains appeared to have deeply influenced the non-violent philosophy of Mahatma Gandhi.

Sikhism. Sikhism began in northern India in the fifteenth century with the teachings of the founder Guru Nanak. A Sikh believes in one God and the ten successive gurus of the Sikh faith. The members outwardly mark their Sikhism by keeping five K's: *Kesh,* uncut hair, showing acceptance of God's will; *Kangha,* the comb showing controlled spirituality and cleanliness; *Kirpan,* a steel dagger, showing determination to defend truth; *Kara,* a steel bangle worn on the wrists, showing unity with God and bending to the Guru; and *Kachk,* an undergarment, showing moral strength and chastity [3] (Figure 6).

Figure 6. A Sikh showing two of the K's: the uncut hair and steel dagger. [12]

Figure 7. Lao Tzu, traveling on an ox, wrote the text of the Tao Te Ching. From Bowker, World Religions. [3]

In Sikhism there is a strong emphasis on communal life, community service and the temple, the center of Sikh life where vegetarian food is often available for free to people of all religions. One of the gurus, Ram Das (1534–1581), founded Amritsar and the Golden Temple, the most sacred site for Sikhs.

Taoism. Taoism refers to the practice of seeking access to *Tao,* "the way," the supreme reality. This is done through meditation with breath control and mind-body exercises. A common theme is the harmonizing of the fundamental energies of the universe and of the cosmic currents of yin and yang to attain immortality. The two main texts of Taoism are the *Chuan Tzi* and *Tao Te Ching.* The latter has been ascribed to the sage Lao Tzu (Figure 7).

It is believed that Tao is the unchanging principle beyond the universe. *Tao Te Ching* endorses a spiritualized version of immortality arising from a natural and harmonious life, with little importance attached to material gain. It endorses a political philosophy in which rulers do not seek to impose and dominate affairs of the nation and state. There is a close connection between body, mind, and environment in Taoist thought. The human body is a vital energy system consisting of patterned flow of *ch'i.* If ch'i is solidified it forms a subtle form of sexual and emotional energy called *ching.* Further refinement results in *shen,* or spirit or consciousness. Many medical techniques in traditional Chinese medicine are based on these concepts.

> **While Gods played a role in most of the Eastern religions the primary focus was on turning inward using meditation, yoga, and other techniques to attempt to attain enlightenment or union with the absolute truth or with the oneness of the universe. As in the Western religions there was an emphasis on moral behavior and compassion for others. The great diversity of the Eastern religions shows that the human race is incredibly talented in its ability to devise structure to place around its innate spirituality.**

The Origins of Monotheism and Judaism

The temporal and theological relationship among the three major monotheistic Western Religions is Judaism –> Christianity –> Islam. Thus, if we wish to search for the origins of monotheism we need to look to the origins of Judaism and with it the origin of the concept of one God. Karen Armstrong has described this in great detail in her book, *A History of God.*[1] Figure 8 shows a map of the ancient world of the Bible.

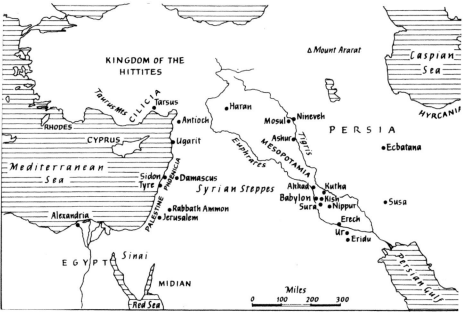

Figure 8. The ancient land of the Bible. From Karen Armstrong, A History of God. [1]

Around 4,000 BCE the Sumerians had established one of the first great cultures of the civilized world in three cities in Mesopotamia. These were located in what is now Iraq in the region of the Tigris and Euphrates rivers. The cities were Ur, Erech, and Kish. For orientation to modern Iraq, Baghdad is just north of Babylon on the Tigris river. The priests of the region recited the *Emuma Eish,* an epic poem that celebrated the victory of the gods over chaos. This story included the creation of the universe from divine stuff in the swamps of Mesopotamia. In the best tradition of polytheism, a flurry of gods emerged from this swamp including Marduk, the Sun god. He was the most perfect of the divine line and created man. Since the first man was created from the substance of gods he shared in the gods' divine nature.

A wandering chieftain left Ur and led his people to settle in Canaan, the region around Jerusalem, between the twentieth and nineteenth centuries BCE. His name was Abraham, and he is held in common by all of the three major monotheistic religions — Judaism, Christianity, and Islam. His son was Isaac and his grandson was Jacob, later renamed Israel. The Bible says that Jacob's sons became the ancestors of the twelve tribes of Israel. Abraham emigrated to Egypt during a severe famine in Canaan. He and his people were enslaved by the Egyptians but liberated by a deity called Yahweh, or God.

Although this all took place 19 centuries before the birth of Christ, it was not until the eighth century BCE that the historical account of these events was written down by two biblical authors. One was called "J" because he called God by title of

Yahweh. The other was called "E" because he preferred the more formal name for God of *Elohim.* By this time, Canaan had been divided into two parts, a northern region consisting of the Kingdom of Israel, and the southern region consisting of the Kingdom of Judah. J wrote about Judah, while E wrote about Israel. The two accounts often contain conflicting stories. It was not until the sixth century BCE that a third author, "P," wrote the chapter of Genesis and his version of creation. These historical notes are of interest since the creationists base their claims of a young universe on the belief that the Bible is the direct word of God. This history of the writing of the First Testament seems much more consistent with a small group of average human authors attempting to provide a historical and metaphorical account of events that had occurred many centuries earlier. *The story they produced is far more likely to have human than divine inspiration.*

Yahweh tells Abraham that he has a special destiny and will become the father of a mighty nation. The rest of this marvelous story is depicted in the First Testament of the Bible. The new religion of one God did not come easily to the Israelites. [1p50] Paganism was still rampant in Canaan in the fifth century BCE. Much credit for the rescue of the one God religion is given to a priest called Ezekiel. "For about five years he stayed alone in his house and did not speak to a soul. Then he had a shattering vision of Yahweh, which literally knocked him out." [1p58] He journeyed to Tel Aviv where the Second Isaiah took the cause one step further by declaring that Yahweh was the *only* God. Through their efforts "Yahweh had finally absorbed his rivals in the religious imagination of Israel. The lure of paganism had lost its attraction and the religion of Judaism had been born."

Believers in a single God benefited by having a powerful, loving, and generally merciful and just ruler. The faithful could have a personal if distant relationship with their God. However, while Paganism was an essentially tolerant faith, *Yahweh was a jealous God.* If people obeyed his laws, they would be blessed and become prosperous. If they disobeyed his laws, or worshiped other gods, the consequences could be devastating. They would be torn from the land, strewn to the ends of the earth, and terror would grip their hearts.

The Origins of Christianity

While it is known that Jesus was a charismatic faith healer from Palestine who preached charity, following the Golden Rule, and showing loving kindness toward others, the first account of his life was not penned until the Gospel of Mark was written at about 70 CE, some 40 years after his death, leaving room for a considerable degree of poetic license. Mark wrote more about what Jesus meant to his followers "than a reliable straight forward portrayal" of his life. [1p79,13,14] His followers saw Jesus as a new Moses. When he was alive, the Jews believed he was the Messiah and hailed him as the son of David, the king and spiritual leader who founded the first independent Jewish kingdom in Jerusalem. Jesus was not the only faith healer of his time, and the fact that he was crucified like a common criminal could have reasonably been such an ignominious fate that it meant the end of his influence. However, unlike many others who were crucified, there were rumors that Jesus had arisen from the dead. *Based on this miraculous event, his disciples believed that he would soon return and bring with him the Messianic Kingdom of God.* This led to the subsequent fundamentalist pre- and post-millennial apocalyptical beliefs. p564

Paul is credited with rescuing Christianity. Without his proselytizing it is quite likely the Christianity would never have survived. One of Paul's major contributions was eliminating the need for Christians to be circumcised, thus opening the faith to gentiles. Paul used the term "in Christ" in relation to his experience of Jesus. The word "Christ" was a translation of the Hebrew word *Massiach,* meaning the Anointed One.

The concept of Jesus as the Son of God also had its origins with Paul. No one in the Jewish community imagined that Yahweh actually had a son. Paul called Jesus "the Son of God" in the Jewish sense, meaning that he possessed some of God's powers. The claim that Jesus was actually the "Son of God" was one of the embellishments introduced by his later followers. The doctrine that Jesus was God in human form was not finalized until the fourth century. 1p81

Paul also introduced what was to become an additional pillar of Christianity — the concept that Jesus died for our sins. This elevated the scandalous form of his death into something he did for his followers. After several hundred years of persecution and struggle, the Roman Emperor Constantine finally legalized Christianity in 313 CE. Christians were then able to own property, worship freely, and contribute to public life.

One of the problems humans get themselves into when they write the rules of their own religions is that logical conundrums can begin to creep into the system. This was illustrated by the fierce controversy that broke out shortly after Christianity was legalized. Arius, an elder of the church, pointed out the following logical inconsistency: If there is only one true God, God the Creator, God the Almighty, how could Jesus Christ have been God in the same way as God the Father? To resolve the issue, Arius believed Jesus was not made of "God stuff" and thus was not truly divine. Another elder, Athanasius, believed Jesus was a true God. He and his followers used the term *homoousian,* meaning "made of the same stuff." One proposed solution was to instead use the term *homoiousian,* meaning of a similar but not identical nature. The ludicrous nature of this hair splitting led Gibbon to comment how absurd it was that Christian unity should have been threatened by a mere diphthong. 1p112

Eventually a trio of theologians in eastern Turkey came up with a brilliant solution that satisfied everyone. They proposed there were two aspects of the scriptures, the obvious part that consisted of the public teachings, termed *kerygma,* and an inner secret, mysterious or esoteric tradition handed down from the apostles as a "private and secret teaching." This was termed *dogma.* These elusive religious realities could only be suggested in the symbolic gestures of the liturgy, or even better, by silence. In essence, inconsistencies were handled by simply not talking about them. They were placed behind a logical shield. In a sense this dogma encompassed that which could not be seen, as in Plato's cave.

An additional understanding to emerge from this trio of theologians was the

Figure 9. The Trinity represented by King David (father), Jesus (son), and a dove (holy ghost or spirit) from a painting Virgin and Child *by Jan Provost II. 1524. National Gallery of Scotland, Edinburgh, and the Bridgemen Art Library.*

concept that God had a single essence termed *ousia,* which remained incomprehensible to humans, and three expressions, termed *hypostases,* by which He could be known. These were the Trinity of the *Father, Son,* and *Holy Spirit,* or *Holy Ghost* (Figure 9).

This interpretation was proposed to avoid confusion as to whether the Father, the Son, or the Spirit was God. If so, were there now three Gods when there was supposed to be only one? Was God being split into three parts? The answer was that none of these were God, they were only the means by which the mystery of the unknowable *ousia* of God could be glimpsed. [1p116] One of the reasons that the trio produced this formulation was to prevent God from being totally grasped by the human intellect. *This allowed the rational brain to be walled off from the spiritual brain —* an element that has persisted in all three of the monotheistic religions.

Islam

In 610 CE, Muhammad ibn Abdallah, a member of the Meccan tribe of Quraysh, was on one of his annual spiritual trips to Mount Hira during the month of Ramadan. He sat in a tiny cave praying to al-Lah (Allah) which he identified as being the same God worshipped by the Jews and Christians. However, unlike the Jews and Christians, the Arabs were feeling left out by the fact that al-Lah had never sent them a prophet or a scripture of their own analogous to Moses and Jesus and the Old and New Testament. Judaism and Christianity had made few converts in the Arab world, and at that time most worshiped a traditional form of paganism. This was due in part to the fact that the Persians and Byzantines primarily used these religions to promote their imperialistic goals.

One night during his stay in the cave, Muhammad was violently awakened by an overwhelming divine presence that commanded him to recite. He initially refused but by the third command, the words of a new scripture, the Qur'an (Koran), began to pour from his mouth. Muhammad could not read or write, so others wrote down his words. This process continued *sura* (chapter) by *sura*, *ayat* (verse) by *ayat*, over a period of 23 years. Since most Arabs of the time were also unable to read or write, the verses of the Qur'an were memorized and spoken. Armstrong. [1p140-144] makes the point that this played a major role in the rapid spread of Muhammad's new religion called *Islam.*

To a Westerner who cannot appreciate the extraordinary beauty of Arabic, the Koran seems boring and repetitive....Muslims often say that when reading the Koran in a translation, they feel that they are reading from a different book because nothing of the beauty of Arabic has been conveyed....The Koran was not meant for private perusal but for liturgical recitation. When Muslims hear a sura chanted in the mosque they are reminded of all the central tenets of their faith....In the reading Muslims claim that they experience a sense of transcendence, of an ultimate reality and power that lie behind the transient and fleeting phenomena of the mundane world....Because of the poetic beauty of the verses many were converted on the spot....It is as though Muhammad had created an entirely new literary form that some people were not ready for but which thrilled others. Without this experience of the Koran, it is extremely unlikely the Islam would have taken root.

It is thus of little wonder that Muhammad is referred to as both a poet and a prophet. As is also the case in Judaism and Christianity, there is a deep congruence between art and religion. Both are capable of touching the soul.

Poetry alone cannot be the basis of a new religion. Content is critical. What did the Koran teach? Among other things it taught that one should share their wealth with the poor. This alms-giving, or zakat, was one of the five tenets of Islam. It taught that *Muslims should make God their focus and sole priority*. Since there was only one God, and thus all religions were derived from that God, Muslims were required to recognize the validity of other religions. War was held to be abhorrent. The only war that was just was a war in self-defense. A strong sense of equality was a central tenet and the religion of al-Lah was originally very positive for women. It forbade the common practice of the day of killing female children since they were viewed as second-class citizens. It was only later after men usurped the religion that women's rights were so severely restricted.

The Kabah. The Kabah or Ka'ba is a great monolithic black cube built in the city of Mecca. Figure 10.

Figure 10. The Kabah in Mecca. From Bowker, World Religions.[3]

It is believed that the Kabah was built at God's command by Abraham and his son. It stands on a site that many consider to have been the sanctuary founded by Adam, the first man. Prior to Muhammad it was a shrine to many Arabian deities. Muhammad toppled these and re-dedicated the Kabah to the one true God. Each year millions of Muslims visit and swarm around and around the Kabah, often being spiritually overwhelmed in the process.

Sunnis and Shiites. From the very beginning there was a major division in the Islam world. Since Muhammad had no living male children, after his death a close friend, Abu Bakr was elected as the first caliph. After three elected caliphs, Ali ibn Abi Talib, Muhammad's cousin and son-in-law, was the first blood relative of Muhammad to become caliph. The Shiah called him the first *Imam,* or Leader. *The Shiah (Shiites) believed that the caliphs should all be related to Muhammad, that only members of Muhammad's family had true knowledge of God.* The Imams were believed to embody God's presence on earth. The *Sunni believed the caliphs did not need to be in Muhammad's bloodline.* These two sects have been fighting for centuries. During the time of the first crusade, the Muslim world was so splintered by internal fighting they were unable to defeat the Christian invaders. [7]

Like Judaism and Christianity before them, Islam traditionalists believed that God's essence was unfathomable by man and would always elude their understanding. God could never be wholly contained by the human mind. There was again a separation into the unknowable and the knowable, the uncreated and the created. The uncreated was the unattainable essence of God. It was like the dogma of Christianity. The created was the knowable portion meant for human consumption. The created was like the kerygma of Christianity. Thus, for some Muslims, there was once again a forced separation between reason and spirituality. Reason did not apply and could not be applied to God's essence.

The Falsafah and Reason. Unlike Christianity, which was often very threatened by science, the Koran stresses that Muslims are not to abdicate their reason but should look at the world with curiosity. This led the early Muslims to a tradition of being at peace with natural science. As part of this intellectual freedom, Islam translators made the writings of the ancient Greeks available in Arabic. In fact it was their translations that later made all of the ancient Greek writings available to the West. Muslims studied astronomy, medicine, and mathematics, and in the ninth and tenth century many scientific discoveries occurred in the Islam world. As part of this academic freedom a new type of Muslim emerged around 870 CE called the *Falsafah.* In contrast to the traditionalists, they believed it was unhealthy to relegate God to a separate intellectual category in which faith was kept isolated from other human endeavors. They had no intention of abolishing the Islam religion but wanted to purify it from its primitive and parochial elements. Instead of seeing God as a mystery, the Falsafahs believed God was reason itself. Their God was to be discovered in logical arguments. They also did not reject the Koran but felt that both the Koran and reason were valid paths to God. *They saw no fundamental contradiction between science and revelation or reason and faith.*

The Falsafah philosophers were reaching their peak by the turn of the millennium. One of the intellectual leaders held that a prophet like Muhammad was superior to any philosopher because he was not dependent upon human reason but enjoyed a direct and intuitive knowledge of God. Later another leader felt that reason could tell them that God existed but could not tell them anything about him. This led al-Ghazzali (1058–1111) to suggest, "If reason could not tell us anything about

God, what was the point of rational discussion of theological matters?"[8] He also reasoned that since the reality that we call "God" cannot be tested empirically, how could we be sure that our beliefs were not mere delusions? He eventually concluded that mystical religious experience was the only way of verifying a reality that lay beyond the reach of human intellect and thought. He proposed that some people possess "the prophetic spirit" that is higher than reason and remained convinced that it was impossible to demonstrate the existence of God by logic and rational proof. Thereafter Muslim philosophy would become inseparable from spirituality and a mystical discussion of God.

Thus, after several hundred years of attempting to bring reason into the realm of God and religion, the experiment failed and ended with the realization that God could not be rationally proven to exist. The philosophical orientation of the Falsafah appealed mostly to the intellectual elite and it remained a small sect. It did not appeal to the majority of Muslims for whom a knowledge of and *familiarity with God occurred in the realm of a religious spiritual experience, not in the realm of reason.*

The three great monotheistic religions represented a great leap forward in providing structure to the spirituality of man. All three provided a God that was the creator of man and the universe and a lifelong personal and spiritual companion. After death, as long as man followed certain well-defined moral rules, God also provided an eternal afterlife in heaven. This God was remarkably like man himself, both in appearance and personal qualities. Like man he was capable of love, hate, jealousy, anger, rage, and revenge. He judged, punished, created, and destroyed. He was especially vengeful if man chose to worship idols. This all-knowing God was the symbol of transcendence — the essence of spirituality. This transcendence was so great that the true nature of God could only be known imperfectly and indirectly. There was an overt acceptance of the fact that reason and faith occupied separate worlds. The existence or non-existence of God was not open to knowing by reason. Knowledge of and acceptance of God was a matter of faith and religious experience. Reason was not welcome.

The wide diversity of man's religions is in keeping with the statement that "Creating Gods is something that human beings have always done. When one religious idea ceases to work for them it is simply replaced."[1] The fact that the God of all three monotheistic religions so closely projected the needs, fears, desires and even appearance of man, is consistent with the probability that not only the religions, but God, the object of the religion—was created by man.

References

1. Armstrong, K. *A History of God.* Ballantine Books, New York, 1993.
2. Armstrong, K. *Buddha.* A Lipper/Viking Book, New York, 2001.
3. Bowker, J. *World Religions.* DK Publishing, Inc, New York, 1997.
4. Bowker, J. *God: A Brief History.* DK Publishing, New York, 2002.
5. Smith, H. *The World's Religions.* Harper San Francisco, New York, 1961.
6. Harvey, G. *Animism: Respecting the Living World.* 2005.
7. Asbridge, T. *The First Crusade.* Oxford University Press, NY, 2004.
8. Watt, M. *The Faith and Practice of Al Ghazzali.* One World Publications, London, 1953.
9. From www.dharmakshetra.com
10. From www.yogasite.com.br
11. From www.pitt.edu
12. From www.pilgrimage-india.com
13. Helms, R. *Gospel Fictions.* Prometheus Books, Amherst, NY, 1988.
14. Helms, R. *Who Wrote the Gospels?* Millennium Press, Altadena, CA.

Mystics are the pioneers of the spiritual world.

Evelyn Underhill
Mysticism [1]

You cannot tread the path of spirituality and the path of reason; you must choose between them.

Edward O. Wilson

Chapter 44

Mysticism

What is mysticism? The term is derived from myth and mystery, meaning to close the eyes or the mouth, to experience darkness or silence. It is the antithesis of reason. Mystical knowledge or knowing comes not from thought and thinking but from emotion and feelings unrestrained by reason. During mystical experiences there is a profound transfiguration of self, time, and space. [2] William James, in his book, *The Varieties of Religious Experience,* [3] proposed four aspects for a definition of mysticism: *ineffable,* or impossible to convey in ordinary language; *noetic,* or seeming to reveal deep, profound truth; *transient,* rarely lasting more than an hour or so; and *passive,* in which the person feels gripped by a force much greater than himself. One of the essentials of religious mysticism is a feeling of a direct union between the soul and God. [4] At a minimum there is a sense of finally understanding some aspect of absolute knowledge.

Mysticism has not been popular in the West because it is generally associated with cranks and charlatans. However, it has been very popular in various other places and times in the world. Mystics are considered to have a special direct vision of godly things, a unique spiritual talent that is shared by only a few. As an approach to God it is intuitive rather than reasoned, imaginative rather than cerebral, and ecstatic rather than placid. Mysticism is best understood as an unusual trait, not accessible to everyone, replete with visions, hallucinations, and voices often emanating from the deeper recesses of the temporal lobes, or spiritual brain, and having a life-altering effect on the individual so possessed. Mystics have attained prominence in some religious groups because their passion has allowed them to infect the less endowed with their thoughts and visions.

In true mystics we see personal religion raised to its highest power. If we accept their experience as genuine, it involves a discourse with the spiritual world, an awareness of it, which transcends the normal experience, and appears to be independent of the general religious consciousness of the community to which they belong. Mystics speak directly with God as persons and not as members of a group. They live by an immediate knowledge far more than by belief, by a knowledge achieved in those hours of direct unmediated discourse with the Transcendent when, as they say, they were "in union with God." A certitude then gained governs all of their reactions to the universe.

By the very term "mystic" we indicate a certain aloofness from the crowd suggesting that they are in possession of a secret which the community as a whole does not and cannot share, that they live at levels to which others cannot see. [4p36-37]

Much of the distrust imparted to mystics comes from this sense of aloofness and independence from the herd. One can best gain an entrée into the world of mysticism by examining the life and thought of some of the most famous mystics or mystical groups in history. Plotinus was one of the first and had a profound influence on later mystics and religious thought.

Plotinus. Drawing upon Plato's ideas, Plotinus (204–270 BCE) is considered to be the founder of the mystical and religious Neoplatonism. Considered a full-grown mystic by Underhill [4p27] he designed a system to achieve an understanding of self. Instead of seeking an explanation of the universe in science he urged his disciples to withdraw into themselves to explore their own psyche. To Plotinus, the ultimate reality was a primal unity called *the One.* In true mystic fashion he claimed the One was present everywhere but absent from those unable to perceive it. He developed a complex spiritual cosmology of three Beings consisting of Divine Reality, *the Godhead,* the absolute unconditioned One; its manifestation as nous *the Divine Mind,* or *Spirit* which inspires the "intelligible" and external world; and *the Psyche,* the life or soul of the universe. [4p16] The mystic nature of the One is illustrated by Plotinus's statement that:

> The One is nameless: If we are to think positively of the One there would be more truth in Silence. We cannot say that it exists, since as a Being itself it is not a thing but is distinct from all things. It is Everything and Nothing, it can be not of the existing things, and yet it is all. Seeking nothing, possessing nothing, lacking nothing, the One is perfect. [5p102]

There have been Jewish, Christian, and Islamic mystics and mystic sects. These include the Kabbalah for Judaism, St. Teresa of Avila for Christianity, and the Sufi for Islam.

Kabbalah. In the eleventh century in Spain, the mystic Solomon Idn Gadirol called the Jewish system of secret mysticisms the *Kabbalah,* standing for the "received' tradition of the Jews. This mystical knowledge was initially transmitted by mouth to ear. The Kabbalists were dedicated to the study of the ancient wisdom of the Talmud or Oral Torah, the book of Jewish law. They searched for mysterious connections and hidden truths. In this process they turned their attention to numbers, assigning each letter of the Hebrew alphabet a numerical value. [6] It was held that words that had the same total sum were connected in some way. In 1280 CE, Moses de Léon compiled the famous Jewish mystical work called the *Zohar (The Book of Splendor)*. While it was purported to be a treasury of ancient writings explaining God's relationship with the world in terms of *sefirot,* it is likely to have been written by de Léon himself. The

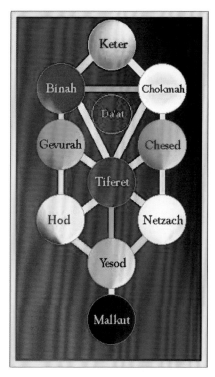

sefirot are attributions of God known as emanations though which the universe was created. [7] The Zohar emphasized that humans could affect the higher world and the pious can achieve union with God. The ten elements of the sefirot, or the *Tree of Life,* are often represented as 10 spheres as in Figure 1.

The Tree of Life originally was a Babylonian concept. It found its way into the Hebrew legend of Adam and Eve. Each circle, or *sephiroth,* represented a different aspect of God. The *Keter* was the crown, unknown and all-embracing. Others were wisdom, understanding or intelligence, kindness, power, beauty, victory and foundation. The last, Malkuth, was a funnel through which the other nine flowed and represented the Spirit of God. Each connection was identified with a letter of the Hebrew alphabet. These letters play a role in Tarot cards used by fortune-tellers.

Figure 1. The sefirot, or Tree of Life, of the Kabbalah with its 10 spheres or sephiroth. The sephiroth are arranged in a rigid hierarchy, with each lower one growing out of the one immediately above.

Different groupings by units of three sephiroth also had mystical meanings representing thought or reason, emotion, and nature that were derived from aspects of Plato, Aristotle, the Bible, and the Talmud. The common light that circulated between the sephiroth represented Knowledge, or *Da'ath,* the universal consciousness of God. The spiritual universe was termed *En Sof,* meaning infinite and standing for that which is incomprehensible, has no beginning and no end, and is inseparable from God. When all the characteristics of God are present in a region of the universe, that region is perfect. However, if God removed one of those characteristics, a point of imperfection was produced. This allowed man to have free will, something he would not have if Divine Law permeated the entire universe.

The Kabbalah reached its peak in the sixteenth and seventeenth centuries. Many believed the earth was in its final days, and Shabbetai Zevi, a self-proclaimed messiah, arrived on the scene to save the Jews. In 1666 he was captured by the Turks and given the choice of converting to Islam or being put to death. He chose conversion and was thus discredited.

The Tree of Life is emblematic of the problem with mysticism. The presence of ten different sephiroth, 22 different interconnections each of which may be positive or negative, and the many possible sub-groupings, is capable of producing a huge number of potential mystical interactions—all made up by man. The essence of mysticism is that it is based on assumptions that cannot be objectively verified and are outside the realm of reason and rationality. One of the fascinations of mysticism is that despite the total lack of objectivity, faithful followers often take the teachings as absolute truths. This ability to succumb to this self-delusion is illustrated in *The Universal Meaning of the Kabbalah,* by Leo Schaya. [8] He noted that the sephiroth were believed to have an essential and incorruptible unity because of the truths revealed by the relationships between the sephiroth, as if simply by virtue of being complex and full of mysterious interactions all of the elements of Kabbalah must be true.

Other Jewish mystics include Shimon bar Yochal, Abraham ben Samuel Abulafia, Moses ben Shem Tob de Leon, Lsaac Luria, Moshe Chaim Luzzatto, Nachman of Breslow, Abraham Isaac Kook, and Menachem Mendel Schneerson. Abraham Abulafia (1240–1291), was a highly educated man and was converted to mysticism by an intense religious experience at age 31. He evolved a Jewish form of yoga using concentration on breathing, recitation of a mantra, and the adoption of a special posture to achieve an altered form of consciousness.

Figure 2. St. Teresa of Àvila. [9]

St. Teresa of Avila. St Teresa (1515–1582) (Figure 2) was the daughter of a Spanish nobleman. She was crippled by disease as a child but was apparently cured after prayer to Saint Joseph. Against her father's will she entered a Carmelite house at age 17, and shortly thereafter again lapsed into a state of poor health. She began having ecstatic visions which were judged to have been genuine, holy, and true by the Dominicans and Jesuits. Against considerable opposition she opened her own reformed convent of Saint John of Avila.

She wrote extensively. Like other writings of medieval mystics, hers contained directions for techniques of spiritual concentration and inner contemplation. On St. Peter's Day in 1559 she believed Christ was present in her in bodily but invisible form. This vision continued for more than two years. In a separate vision, a celestial being drove a fiery golden lance into her heart, causing great spiritual pain, representative of her compassion for the suffering of Jesus.

The essence of St. Teresa's mystical writings was the ascent of the soul in four stages. These were the "heart's devotion" consisting of devout observance of Christ and penitence; the "devotion of peace," a stage of quietude in which the human will is lost in that of God's; "devotion of union," an ecstatic state with a conscious rapture in the love of God; and finally a "devotion of ecstasy," in which the consciousness of being disappears in a union with God. As shown previously there is evidence to suggest that the ecstatic mysticism of St. Teresa of Àvila was related to her having temporal lobe epilepsy.

Other Christian mystics include St. Augustine of Hippo, St. Bernard of Clairvaux, Meister Eckehart, St. Francis of Assisi, St. Hildegarde of Bingen, St. Gertrude the Great, John the Apostle, St. John of the Cross, St. Mechthild of Magdeburg, Johann Tauler, St. Jon de Ruysbroeck, St. Paul, St. Catherine of Siena, St. Catherine of Genoa, Jacob Boehme, Jacopone da Todi, George Fox, [4] and many others. St. Paul, was described previously in relation to temporal lobe epilepsy. Regarding him, Underhill [4p55] stated:

> The New Testament is thick with reports of mystical experiences. The Fourth Gospel and the Epistles of St. Paul depend for their whole character on the soaring mystical genius their writers possessed. Had St. Paul never been caught up to the third heaven [the dwelling place of God], he would have had a very different outlook on the world, and Christianity would have been a different religion in consequence.

Sufi. The Sufis were Muslims who sought a mystical approach to connecting with God. The term probably came from *suf,* the name for the woolen garment that the early Sufi wore. Like the Kabbalists who were searching for the secret meaning of the ancient Jewish writings, the Sufi were also searching for the ancient, hidden, secret, or esoteric teachings of Muhammad. These teachings were presumed to only have been given to Muhammad's immediate companions, who had the capacity to have a direct experiential knowledge of Allah, and were then passed on to their students. The early Sufis lived lives of poverty and piety and were a minor sect of Islam.

Al-Ghazali. (1058–1111) (Figure 3) Al-Ghazali was a well-educated Muslim with an appointment as professor at the Nizamiyah University of Baghdad, one of the most prestigious institutions of learning in the golden era of Muslim history. He gave up his academic appointment to become a wandering ascetic. At the end of this solitary period he became a prolific writer. He proposed that the mystical religious experience was the only way of verifying a reality that lay beyond the reach of the human intellect and reason. [5p189-191] *Reason was unable to comprehend the absolute and the infinite.*

He proposed that the only way to obtain a balance between reason and religion was to recognize that reason dealt with the finite while

Figure 3. Abu Hamid al-Ghazali, famous Muslim mystic. [11]

religion dealt with the infinite. He claimed that some people possessed a power that he called "the prophetic spirit." Those who lacked it should not deny that it exists simply because they had not experienced it.

This is consistent with the assumption that only a small subset of individuals are able to have ecstatic mystical experiences. For those who lacked this mystical ability, al-Ghazali devised a discipline to enable Muslims to cultivate a consciousness of God's reality on a daily basis. This consisted of a prescribed fasting, chanting, sleepless vigils, measured breathing, and contemplation, producing a sense of transcendental presence. To enhance concentration some used music and dancing. One order was known as the Whirling Dervishes. Their spinning dance was an aid to concentration.

Al-Ghazali was probably the greatest Islamic theologian. He eliminated the excesses of Sufism yet brought its basic tenets into the mainstream of Islamic religion. He emphasized both the obedient life through the usual laws of Islam, but added in Sufism with its mystical experience between the soul and God. [7] As a result, during the twelfth and thirteenth centuries Sufism changed from a minority mystic movement to become a dominant Islamic force, and this philosophy would become inseparable from spirituality and a mystical dimension of Allah. All Muslims became involved in a constant struggle (jihad) to find Allah in all things and to strip away everything else. While many modern Muslims may believe that Sufism is outside the sphere of Islam, it is in reality simply the name for the inner or esoteric dimensions of Islam.

Other Islamic mystics included al Hallaj, Jalal ad-Dim Rumi, Khwejeh Shams al-Din Muhammad Hafez-e Shirazi, Abdul Qadir Gilani, Abu Yazid Bistami, and others. Muhammed himself heard voices, saw visions, and sweated profusely during his mystical interludes, symptoms that are consistent with temporal lobe epilepsy.

Based on the impressive number of mystics for all three of the major monotheistic religions, it is clear that *mysticism and mystics have played a major role in helping man to flesh out the spiritual framework of his religions.* Underhill [4] expressed the following in relation to the role of mystics in the development of Christianity:

> If we ask ourselves what the history of the Church would be without the history of its mystics, then we begin to see how much its light and color emanates from them, how much of its doctrine represents their experience translated into dogmatic form.
>
> They [the mystics] are pushed out, as it were, by the visible Church like tentacles, to explore the unseen world which surrounds it, and drawn back again to its bosom that they may impart to the whole body the more abundant life which they have found. If the unfailing family of the mystics did not thus perpetually push out beyond the protective edges of the organism and bring official Christianity back into direct touch with the highest spiritual values, and so consistently reaffirm the fact — felt and experienced by them—of the intimate correspondence, the regenerating contact of God with the soul, the Church would long ago have fallen

victim to the tendency to relapse into the mechanical which dogs all organized groups.

Mysticism for the Common Man

These examples illustrate the assumption that only a select few can be linked into a direct mystical union with God. What about the common man? Is he relegated to standing on the sidelines listening to the rapturous descriptions of the chosen few? Temporal lobe epilepsy or its equivalent may have played a major role in determining who is chosen for the extreme end of these mystical abilities and who is not. In this regard the common man should not be upset by the fact that they are normal and have normal brains. We have seen that Abulafia, a Jewish mystic, St. Teresa of Àvila, a Christian mystic, and Abu Hamid al-Ghazali, a Muslim mystic have all suggested ways that the common man could, at some level, have mystical experiences. Many others, including the practitioners of the Eastern religions, have also proposed methods to allow anyone to have some mystical contact with their spiritual brain. These active methods include meditation, yoga, prayer, chanting, dancing, music, poetry, ritual, fasting, speaking in tongues, and psychedelic drugs. Passive normal or extraordinary episodes, such as life-threatening events, near death, hypoxia, grief, illness, childbirth, love-making, or natural beauty may also elicit varying levels of mystical experiences. These are all capable of producing a sense of transcendence into a realm of an altered level of consciousness and a feeling of being connected to a force greater than ourselves.

Huston Smith [10] proposed that despite the differences in the different religions, the mystical experiences of each transcend time, place, culture, and individual identity. He termed this the *perennial philosophy*. This commonality, moderated by cultural differences, is understandable, since all those involved are genetically similar members of the human race and all have similar functioning temporal lobes.

Mysticism represents a sense of knowing that emanates from the spiritual brain. During a mystical experience there is a profound transfiguration of self, time, and space and often a feeling of having a direct union between the soul and God or with the absolute truth. Knowing based on mysticism is the antithesis of reason, because it cannot be objectively verified. It is the stuff that faith is made of. Because it often emanates from the temporal lobe, hippocampus, and amygdala, it has a consuming emotional flavor and is believed to be real and true with far greater fervor and conviction than rational knowledge. It is so powerful that some have felt that without it, religions based on reason alone are likely to fail. *Without the intermittent emanations from the spiritual brain in many different individuals across the centuries and the world, it is unlikely that any of the formal religions as we know them now would exist.*

While mystic ecstasies are usually the purview of a select few, many methods have been developed, such as meditation, yoga, prayer, dance, swaying, rituals, fasting, speaking in tongues, and the taking of psychedelic drugs, to make a semblance of this mystical experience available to the common man. "Knowledge" based on mysticism is likely to be defended with far greater passion than knowledge based on reason, and therein lies its danger, since it can easily form the fodder for of despots, wars, and terrorism.

References

1. Underhill, E. *Mysticism*. E. P. Dutton & Co, Inc, New York, 1911, 1961.
2. Strassman, R., M.D. *DMT: The Spirit Molecule*. Park Street Press, Rochester, VT, 2001.
3. Arthur, J. *Mushrooms and Mankind*. The Book Tree, Escondido, CA, 2000.
4. Underhill, E. *The Essentials of Mysticism*. Oneworld, Oxford, UK, 1920.
5. Armstrong, K. *A History of God*. Ballantine Books, New York, 1993.
6. Aczel, A. D. *The Mystery of the Aleph*. Washington Square Press Pocket Books, New York, 2000.
7. Bowker, J. *World Religions*. DK Publishing, Inc., New York, 1997.
8. Schaya, L. *The Universal Meaning of the Kabbalah*. Allen & Unwin, London, 1971.
9. From www.economist.com
10. Smith, H. *The World's Religions*. Harper San Francisco, New York, 1961.
11. From www.famousmuslims.com

It seems that we will always generate Gods, powers, and other entities as first causes to explain what we observe. Indeed, we cannot do otherwise.

Human ceremonial ritual provides the "common man" access to some modified form of mystical experience.

Eugene d'Aquili and Andrew Newberg
The Mystical Mind[1]

The function of ritual is to give form to human life.

Joseph Campbell
Myths to Live By[2]

Once Gods are closely connected to salient human activities, it strenghthens the idea that gods are present and involved in our lives.

Todd Tremlin
Minds and Gods[2a]

Chapter 45

Myth and Ritual

Myth

Myths form the basis of religion. One aspect of the human mind that accompanied the evolution of a high level of intelligence was an obsession with wanting to know the answer to all possible questions. Why are we here? What is the purpose of our existence? How did we come into being? Who created us? Where do we go when we die? What causes thunder and lightning? We are like an inquisitive child. Why? Why? This desire to know was undoubtedly related to attempts by the human mind to reduce the level of anxiety associated with the threatening aspects of the unknown. In the times prior to the scientific method, if we didn't know the answer, we simply made up one.

The neurological basis of this human obsession with wanting to know and wanting to put some level of organization into the mysteries of the natural world has been labeled different things. Eugene d'Aquili and Andrew Newberg[1] referred to it as the "cognitive imperative," and suggested it was the result of a number of different cognitive operators. In the same sense that mathematics uses operators for addition (+), subtraction (-), multiplication (x) and division (/), they proposed that the human mind had seven different operators. It is these operators that force us to ask questions. The one most relevant to myth-making was the causal operator that assigns causation to events. The causal operator lies at the very heart of our scientific investigations, philosophical speculations, and religious beliefs. A binary operator was also proposed that allowed the brain to decompose continuous variables, such as a range from good to evil, into a dichotomous variable of good versus evil. Such dichotomy is prevalent in myths. A good example in modern times was presented in George Lucas's film, *Star Wars,* where the "dark side" of Darth Vader represented pure evil, and the Jedi rebels represented pure good. Unfortunately, the binary operator produces a bad precedent of reducing the shades of grey of human experience into all black or white.

It has been suggested that this obsession to know was due to a "hyperactive agent detection device," or HADD, [3,4] that not only alerts us to real dangers, such as poisonous snakes, but also generates false positive responses, such as believing that rocks and trees are imbued with spirits. The human brain is capable of perceiving reality based on observed and verifiable facts, such as the fact that the sun comes up every morning and sets every evening. However, it is also good at explaining reality based on a hyperactive causal operator that reaches a conclusion based poorly on fact, such as assuming that the sun rises and sets because it is pulled around heaven by a sun god riding a majestic chariot.

Karen Armstrong [5] referred to these two ways of acquiring knowledge as *logos* (true knowledge) and *mythos* (myth). They were both essential and complementary. Logos was rational, pragmatic, and scientific. Although based on fact, logos could leave humans with a queasy sense of unease. For thousands of years the assumed logos was that the earth was at the center of the solar system. Copernicus and Galileo showed it was not — the sun was at the center. Well at least, our solar system was at the center of our galaxy. No, this was also shown not to be true. Then at least our galaxy was the only galaxy. No, it is just one of billions in the universe. For thousands of years it was assumed that God created man and other life on earth. Then Darwin showed that life on earth evolved over millions of years by natural selection of the species that were the most fit for a given environment. In papers understandable by an elite few, Einstein showed that time slowed down at high speeds and other physicists showed that at a micro level, a particle can be in two places at once. Thus, logos, despite its claim as the ultimate form of knowledge, was not always constant. It could change. Professional skeptics called scientists drove that change. Their tool was the scientific method of hypothesis making and testing. The mark of a good scientist was that he or she did not take their theories too seriously. They needed to be ready at the drop of the next new fact or new observation to move onto a new and better theory. This shifting base, driven by an elite group whose tools, methods, and results became increasingly difficult for the non-scientist to understand, added to the sense of unease with logos. Logos was not concerned with meaning, just the facts. Logos could not explain the meaning of life. Even the discoverers of the new physics felt a sense of unease with pure logos.

By contrast, mythos was a timeless constant in human existence. It was based on faith. It could always be depended on. It provided the world with meaning, and unless humans found some meaning in their lives they tended to fall into despair. Mythos could not be verified by rational proof and was not intended to be taken literally. It was more like art, music and poetry. Mythos was associated with mysticism and intuitive insight. While science began to take over and provide answers to some of man's "Why" questions, for many, myths, taken on faith, were far more satisfying.

In the pre-modern world, unless a historical event was mythologized it could not be religious. Unlike logos that forges ahead, mythos looks backward to our sacred beginnings. It assumes that everything important has already been achieved and thought about. To assume an event was literally true was to confuse mythos with logos. [5] Making that assumption was dangerous since the next archeological dig might disprove or change logos. Not so mythos. *By not being rooted to fact, mythos could be constant and unchanging and in view of man's preference for consistency — comforting and soothing.* As science advanced it began to discount mythos and to assume only logos had validity. Although people have often tried to turn the mythos of their faith into logos, this has never really been successful. Mythos is more closely connected with our emotional and spiritual brain. *It is far more comforting than logos. Fundamentalism can best be viewed as being the result of confusing mythos with logos; of believing that the myths we have made up to explain our world are literally true;* of believing, for example, that the world is only 4,000 years old and that the mythos of the book of Genesis is logos.

Joseph Campbell [6] spent a lifetime researching mythology around the world, looking for similarities of ancient and modern societies, including Greek, Roman, Egyptian, Asian, and Nordic. Three common mythological themes emerged: First, myths involve questions about our existence, including the creation of the world, birth and death. Second, they contain conundrums raised by unresolvable contradictions relating to creation versus destruction, life versus death, gods versus humans. Third, they attempt to reconcile and make sense of these issues to resolve our fears and anxieties.

Ritual

Myth and ritual are inseparable. Joseph Campbell, the master of myth, stated that myths were the mental supports of ritual and rites and that rites were the physical enactments of myths [2] He stated that:

> By absorbing the myths of his social group and participating in its rites, the youngster is structured to accord with his social as well as natural environment, and turned from an amorphous nature product, prematurely born, into a defined and competent member of some specific, efficiently functioning social order.

This is reminiscent of the saying, "Give me a youngster for the first few years and I will give you a Catholic for life." This, of course, applies to any religion. The myths and rituals children grow up with stay with them for the rest of their lives, as well as the religions they were designed to support. D'Aquili and Newberg [1] defined ritual as having the following qualities:

- It is structured or patterned.
- It is rhythmic and repetitive.

- Within individuals it acts to synchronize various neural processes.
- Within groups it acts to synchronize the thoughts of the individual participants.

Animal studies have shown that repetitious rhythms result in the arousal of the limbic system, the emotional brain.[7,8] Studies in humans have indicated that repetitive auditory and visual stimuli can produce increased arousal and intensely pleasurable, spiritual experiences.[9] Anyone who has stood in the midst of thousands of fans in a rock concert or simply listened quietly to his or her favorite songs on an iPod implicitly understands the spiritual effects of rhythm. Prayer can be viewed as a combination of myth and ritual. Rhythmic stimuli activate a portion of the brain that produces a sense of union or oneness with the world, an important aspect of spirituality.[1]

Most animals have mating and other rituals. These are hardwired into their genetic machinery, instinctual, and critical for survival. The rituals that humans perform are not hardwired. They are culturally determined. Concerning rituals, D'Aquili and Newberg[1] commented:

> Many religious traditions indicate that states [induced by ritual] yield not only a feeling of union with a greater force or power but also an intense awareness that death is not to be feared and a sense of harmony of the individual with the universe.

> **The highly evolved intelligence of humans brought with it an intense quest for knowledge, a quest for knowing the answers to a thousand questions that start with "Why?" In the pre-modern age, with the absence of concrete knowledge, the answers were made up, producing myths (mythos). Since many myths address important spiritual issues, including the existence of a supreme being, they often form the basis of religions. Since they are not based in fact, myths can remain unchanged over the centuries, bringing a sense of stability and permanence in a changing world. By contrast, scientific facts (logos) often change with new data. Mythos is thus inherently more comforting than logos.**

> **Rituals, consisting of repetitious, rhythmic chanting, singing, or prayer, activate portions of the brain that enhance the sense of spirituality and oneness with a supreme being and represent the physical enactment of myths. Myths and rituals form an integral part of all religions.**

References

1. d'Aquili, E. & Newberg, A. B. *The Mystical Mind. Probing the Biology of Religious Experience.* Fortress Press, Minneapolis, 1999.
2. Campbell, J. *Myths to Live By.* Bantum Books, New York, 1972.
2a. Tremlin, T. *Minds and Gods.* Oxford University Press, New York, 2006

3. Barrett, J. L. Exploring the natural foundations of religion. *Trends Cogn Sci.* 4: 29-34, 2000.
4. Dennett, D. C. *Breaking the Spell. Religion as a Natural Phenomenon.* Viking, New York, 2006.
5. Armstrong, K. *The Battle for God.* Ballantine Books, New York, 2001.
6. Campbell, J. & Moyers, B. *The Power of Myth.* Anchor Books, New York, 1988.
7. Schein, M. W. & Hale, E. B. Stimuli eliciting sexual behavior. in: Beach, F. A. *Sex and Behavior.* John Wiley & Sons, New York, 1965.
8. Lorenz, K. *On Aggression.* Bantam Books, New York, 1966.
9. Walter, V. J. & Walter, W. G. The central effects of thythmic sensory stimulation. *Electroenceph Clin Neurophysiol.* 1: 57-85, 1949.

They eat the root which they call peyote, and which they venerate as though it were deity.
Aldous Huxley
The Doors of Perception, 1954

Chapter 46

Psychedelics and Religion

Mysticism played a major role in the formation of man's religions. A previous chapter emphasized this role by a select group of mystics whose unique temporal lobes poured out their intense ecstatic experiences. In many cases this was a result of epilepsy or an epilepsy equivalent. Their spirituality was the result of *intrinsic* characteristics of their own brains. As previously discussed, a second type of spirituality is produced *extrinsically* by taking a range of psychedelic drugs. These compounds provide a powerful sense of a connection with a supernatural being. As such they may have played an important role in the early spiritual development of mankind.

The four major sources of the psychedelics involved are the psilocybin-containing mushrooms; the *Ayahuasca* brews containing DMT and β-carbolines; the mescaline-containing peyote catus; and the muscimol-containing *Amanita muscaria,* or *fly-agaric* mushroom. In different cultures and locations, all four have been claimed to possess God-like qualities, and *Amanita muscaria* was even considered a god in its own right. All four played a role in the spiritual life of their users, and *Amanita muscaria* may have played a major role in the formation of at least three of the world's major religions.

The study of the role of mushrooms in religion is called *ethnomycology.* R. Gordon Wasson was father and founder of ethnomycology. Over a lifetime he wrote 10 books and over 70 articles in academic journals and magazines on the subject. His collection of over 4,000 books, pamphlets, photographs, charts, slides, and archeological artifacts currently reside in the Ethnomycological Collection in the Harvard Botanical Museum. He tells the following story of how he became so involved in mycology, the study of mushrooms. [1]

> In 1921 I fell in love with a Russian girl, Valentina Pavlovna, in London where she was studying medicine....We took our delayed honeymoon late August 1927 in Big Indian, the Catskills....On our first day, after lunch, we went for a walk, down a path....We were hand in hand and a picture of bliss. Suddenly, before I knew it, my bride threw down my hand roughly and ran up into the forest, with cries of ecstasy. She had seen toadstools growing, many kinds of toadstools. She had not seen the like since Russia, in 1917. She was in a delirium of excitement

and began gathering them right and left in her skirt. From the path I called to her, admonishing her not to gather them: they were toadstools, I said, they were poisonous.

That evening, despite his pleading, his wife cooked and ate the mushrooms. Gordon was certain he would be a widower by morning, but was not. The experience led both of them to realize that in some parts of the world, like England, the people tend to be *mycophobes,* and are deathly afraid of mushrooms and certain they are all poisonous. In other parts of the world, like Russia, the people are *mycophils,* love mushrooms, eat them, and know from long experience which are poisonous and which are not. They came to realize that something intrinsic to different cultures led to these differences. They both independently felt that religion somehow was involved. After that day, in their spare time they began a lifelong quest to understand the basis of these cultural and religious differences.

As their work progressed, Wasson and his colleagues became dissatisfied with the then current names for the effects that certain mushrooms had on the mind. They were especially not happy with the terms *hallucinogenic,* meaning "to roam or wander in one's mind," or *psychedelic,* meaning "mind-manifesting," since these tended to ignore the important spiritual effects of these compounds. A committee was formed "to devise a new word for the potions that held antiquity in awe."[1p30] They decided the best word was *entheogen,* meaning *"God generated within."* The intent of this chapter is to explore the role of entheogens in the formation of man's belief in God and the formation of man's religions.

Psilocybin Mushrooms and Mesoamerica

Mushroom stones, such as the ones shown in Figure 1, date back as far as 1,000 BCE. While they were initially misidentified, they are now understood to be effigies of a mushroom deity.[2] They have been found in the tombs of Mayan nobles, suggesting an association with the Lords of Xibalba, deity rulers of the dead.

Figure 1. Pre-Columbian Mayan mushroom stones dating to 1,000 to 500 BCE found throughout Central America but principally in the Guatemala highlands, indicating the presence of mushroom cults involving the sacramental consumption of sacred mushrooms. [2a]

The Spanish Franciscan friar, Bernardino de Sahagén, preserved extensive handwritten records of sixteenth century Mexican culture. Among other things he described how groups of people came together to eat mushrooms and how this produced visions, often of things in their future life including visions of their own death, thus bringing a compassionate acceptance of the individual's own imortality. [2]

In general the friars saw the mushroom ceremonies as devil worship and as a mockery of the consumption of the body of Christ in the Eucharistic communion rite. As a result they banned this religious practice. Back in Spain, the effects of eating the mushrooms were described in diabolical terms, such as causing uncontrollable fits and violence, [3] a practice that could easily lead to mycophobia in Spain. The suppression of the visionary mushroom cult by the Spanish clergy seemed so complete that for four centuries it disappeared from the memory of the general and scholarly public.

On September 19, 1952, Wasson received a letter from Robert Graves in Majorca, with a clipping indicating that Richard Evans Schultes, a professor of botany at Harvard and director of the Botanical Museum there, had published two papers containing the startling news that mushroom cults still existed and that Schultes had even brought back from Mexico specimens of the entheogenic mushrooms. Wasson called him the same day and learned that Schultes had visited a remote village called Huautla de Jiménez, in the State of Oaxaca, Mexico, in 1937, 1938, and 1939. He had published the two papers in 1939 and 1940. [4,5] The mushrooms were called *teonanácatl.* The Spanish interpreted this as meaning "God's flesh." This translation contributed to their claim that the mushrooms mocked the Eucharist. Wasson [6] suggested that a more-accurate translation was "wondrous or sacred mushroom," reflecting the vision-inducing qualities that provided deep spiritual insight and inspiration, traits that may have led to it being revered by the Mazatec Indians.

In 1953, Wassen visited the village during the rainy season when the mushrooms sprouted. This was the first of 10 visits he made to the region. In 1955 he asked Allan Richardson, a professional New York photographer, to join him to record the events of the journey. They met Maria Sabina, a *curandera,* or shaman, in a remote village in the state of Oaxaca. She was a *sabia,* or wise woman, a living representative of a lineage of shamanic healers reaching back to the pre-Conquest time. She was 60 years old and had been practicing her art secretly in her tiny village, known only to a very few. She was the guide for the session known as a *veladas.* Wasson described the beginning of the veladas as follows:

> We were mindful of the drama of the situation. We were attending as participants in a mushroomic supper of unique anthropological interest, which was being held pursuant to a tradition of unfathomed age, possibly going back to the time when the remote ancestors of our hosts were living in Asia, back perhaps to the dawn of man's cultural history, when he was discovering the idea of God. [7]

After they were into the session Wasson described what he saw and felt as follows:

> ...geometric patterns, angular not circular, in richest colors, such as

might adorn textiles or carpets. Then the patterns grew into architectural structures, with colonnades and architraves, patios of regal splendor, the stone-work all in brilliant colors, gold and onyx and ebony, all most harmoniously and ingeniously contrived, in richest magnificence extending beyond the reach of sight, in vistas measureless to man....They seemed to belong...to the imaginary architecture described by the visionaries of the Bible. [7]

Their experiences were described in the book that Wasson and his wife had worked on for years, called *Mushrooms, Russia and History*. [7] The book came out in a limited edition issue of only 512 copies. A separate account simultaneously appeared in an article Wasson wrote for *Life* magazine. [8] Both the book and the magazine were released on May 13, 1957. The article in *Life* caused a sensation and played an important role in launching the psychedelic revolution of the 1960s. It resulted in thousands of hippies trekking off to the mountains of Oaxaca in search of their own nirvana. This was a source of great displeasure to Wasson, who felt that the crass search for a drug high disrespected the spiritual and religious nature of the *veladas*.

To identify the nature of the entheogenic substance, Wasson sent samples of the mushrooms used in the Maria Sabina sessions to Albert Hoffman, the Sandoz chemist who discovered LSD and its mind-altering properties. He used himself and his lab assistant as the bioassay, ingesting the different analytical fractions until he had purified the active ingredient that he identified as *psilocybin*. *Psilocybin* is a very stable compound, due to the presence of an attached protective phosphorus group. After ingestion, enzymes remove the phosphorous group, producing *psilocin*. *Psilocin* is identical to DMT except that it has a hydroxyl (OH) group in the 4 position making it 4-hydroxy DMT. Wasson brought Hoffman back with him on one of his trips to revisit Maria Sabina and gave her some of this pure, synthetic *psilocybin*. She told him that the effect was the same as eating the mushrooms. There are no reports that psilocybin is addictive or causes psychological dependence or tolerance.

In 1974 Wasson wrote of his experiences among the Mazatec Indians in a book entitled *Maria Sabina and her Mazatec Mushroom Velada*. During her *veladas* Maria Sabina would sing and chant for hours with percussive clapping and slapping of her hands. To portray a fuller account of the experience, the publication also contained recordings of Maria during these sessions. [9] Of the many books that Wasson wrote, he characterized this as the one that brought him the most joy.

In addition to being spiritual guides, one of the shaman's primary duties is to heal. This healing ability was not primarily due to their own healing skills.

Figure 2. Mexican drawing of the sixteenth century showing three mushrooms, a man eating them, and a god behind him, who is speaking through the mushroom. From Gordon Wasson's 1957 article in Life *magazine.* [8]

They used the magic mushrooms to gain access to the gods, who then used the shaman as a conduit through which healing could take place. This is illustrated in Figure 2.

Following the intense interest in psilocybin, it was found that over 180 species of mushrooms and many other plants around the world contained this compound. [10-12] While *Psilocybe mexicana* is the most popular mushroom in Mexico, *Psilocybe cubensis* (Figure 3), originally called *Stroharia cubnensis,* the starborn magic mushroom, is the most widely cultivated psilocybin mushroom in the world.

Psilocybe mexicana   *Psilocybe cubensis*

Figure 3. Two common psilocybin-containing mushrooms. From Wasson, Life magazine 100: 1957. [8]

While the species of the mushroom is not known, Algerian cave paintings, dating into the Paleolithic period as far back as 9,000 BCE, show human-like figures with mushroom images all over their bodies (Figure 4). [13,10]

This is strong evidence that mushrooms were known and used in a mystic manner at the very beginning of human history. Wasson [14] suggested that the accidental ingestion of an hallucinogenic plant, probably a mushroom, constituted human beings' earliest encounter with the concept of deity, God and the supernatural. This idea was later restated in a different fashion. [6]

In the lives of us all, even those who are most earthbound, there are moments when the world stops, when the most humdrum things

Figure 4. Cave painting of Bee-Head Mushroom Goddess, from the Round-Head Culture 9,000 to 6,000 BCE, from the Tassili Plateau of Algeria. Drawing by Kathleen Harrison. From Ralph Metzner. [2]

suddenly and unaccountably clothe themselves with beauty, haunting and ravishing beauty. It now seems to me that such flashes must emerge from our unconscious well where our visions have all this time been stored, for the mushroomic visions are an endless sequence of those flashes....What an amazing thing that we should all be carrying this inventory of wonders around with us, ready to be tripped into our conscious world by mushrooms! Are Indians far wrong in calling these divine? We suspect that in its fullest sense, the creative faculty, whether in the humanities or science or industry, that most precious of man's distinctive possessions and the one most clearly partaking of the divine, is linked in some way to the area of the mind that the mushrooms unlock.

This article, written decades ago, was prophetic to the concept elaborated in this book that the temporal lobes serve as man's spiritual brain and carry within them a spirituality that can be unlocked by intrinsic and extrinsic agents. In addition, the *Life* article spoke of the theme of the independence of the rational and the spiritual brain when Wasson stated that, "the effect of the mushrooms was to bring about a fusion of the spirit with the rational side of the brain continuing to reason and to observe the sensations that the spiritual side is enjoying."

Ayahuasca and the Amazon Basin

Ayahuasca (EYE-a-wass-ca) is a hallucinogenic brew made up of two distinct Amazonian plants. The first, *Banisteriopsis caapi*, contains three different β–carbolines: harmine, harmaline, and tetrahydroharmine, all of which act as inhibitors of the enzyme monoamine oxidase (MAO). The second is *Psychotra viridis*, containing the psychedelic drug DMT, described in the chapter on the spiritual brain. When taken orally, DMT by itself has no psychedelic effects because MAO rapidly destroys it in the stomach. When taken with β–carbolines, the destructive action of the MAO is inhibited for about eight hours and the DMT can have its full psychedelic effect. Huasca means vine, and aya means soul or spirit. Thus ayahuasca is considered the "vine of the soul" or "the vine of the spirit."

Native *entheogenic* plants are widely used by shamans or priests around the world. Shamanism refers to any practice of spiritual healing and divination, or connecting to supernatural powers, that involves the induction of an altered state of consciousness, called the "shamanic journey." [15] Shamans seek spiritual and healing knowledge from the spirit world. They cultivate a direct perceptual and spiritual relationship with animals, plants, and the Earth itself. In the Northern Hemisphere they generally use music, drumming, and dance. If psychedelics are used, they tend to be derived from mushrooms or cacti. In the Southern Hemisphere ayahuasca is the most powerful and widespread of the shamanic hallucinogens. These *entheogenic* plants provide access to spiritual or transpersonal dimension of consciousness and mystical experiences that are indistinguishable from the classic religious mysticism described in a prior chapter. [15]

Not all of the ayahuasca use in South America involves tribal shamans. Three organized Christian church groups in Brazil use ayahuasca as the central sacrament. These are the *Santo Daime,* the *Barquinia,* and the *União do Vegetal (UDV).* The UDV is currently the largest, with thousands of members and some branches in North America and Europe. Gabriel de Costa, a rubber trapper, founded it in 1954. It can openly use ayahuasca in its ceremony because its leaders convinced the Brazilian government to declare the practice legal when used for religious purposes. Church members come from all walks of life, rural and urban, rich and poor, educated and uneducated. As with all religions, the social aspects involving group worship and celebration with singing and prayer strengthened community bonds and gave its members a sense of participation and belonging. In addition to their drug use, part of their appeal rests in a concern for the worldwide degradation of the ecosystem and biosphere, fostering a revival of the ancient awareness of the organic and spiritual interconnectedness of all life on the planet. In this sense it is "new Animism" plus ayahuasca.

Anthropological evidence, in the form of snuffing tubes and trays, indicates the use of hallucinogenic plants in South American dates as far back as 1,500 to 2,000 BCE. [16] As shown below, this brings the onset of the use of psychedelic substances as spiritual aids to mystic experiences to a comparable time in both the Americas and Eurasia.

Psychological effects of ayahuasca. The elements of the ayahuasca experience include a perception of the separation of the soul from the physical body associated with a sense of flying; visions of snakes and other predatory animals; a sense of contact with supernatural realms; visions of distant cities and landscapes; and a sensation of "seeing" the detailed reenactment of recent unsolved crimes. [17]

Michael Harner, an anthropologist who lived among the Jivaro Indians of the Ecuadoran Amazon, described his experience with ayahuasca as follows: [18]

> For several hours after drinking the brew, I found myself although awake, in a world literally beyond my wildest dreams. I met bird-like people, as well as a dragon-like creature who explained they were the true Gods of this world. I enlisted the services of other spirit helpers in attempting to fly through the far reaches of the Galaxy. Transported into a trance where the supernatural seemed natural, I realized that anthropologists, including myself, had profoundly underestimated the importance of the drug in affecting native ideology.

The healing aspects of ayahuasca. In addition to being a guide for the spiritual and psychedelic aspects of the use of ayahuasca, the shamans were also healers. As with the users of the psilocybin mushrooms, the shamans took the drug, sang the songs and performed the rituals to evoke the spirits which then did the healing. In the healing rituals, the spirits are referred to as "allies" and "helpers" to remove the bad or malevolent spirits. The set and setting of the ritual was as important as the ayahuasca.

Because the shamans often seemed to enjoy exceptional health and long life, in

1992 Dennis McKenna and colleagues began a study of the effect of ayahuasca use by the UDV. Fifteen long-term ayahuasca users and 15 matched control non-users were studied using a range of psychological and psychiatric tests. They found that long-term users commonly underwent experiences that changed their lives and behavior in a positive and profound way, similar to the effect of near-death experiences. Since joining the UDV they felt they had undergone a personal and spiritual transformation. On the psychological tests they appeared to be more confident, relaxed, optimistic, uninhibited, outgoing, and energetic. [17] This was not a reflection of a pre-existing personality, since prior to entry into the UDV they described themselves as impulsive, disrespectful, angry, rebellious, and aggressive. In laboratory tests there was a persistent elevation of serotonin uptake by receptors in the platelets, possibly the result of a DMT-induced elevation of serotonergic activity in the brain.

This study showed that the regular use of ayahuasca, at least within the context of the ritual and supportive environment of the UDV, appeared safe and without long-term toxicity. [19] An interesting finding was the low level of alcoholism and drug abuse among the UDV members. The authors felt that these results were not necessarily due to the ayahuasca alone, but to a partaking of ayahuasca within the ritual context of the UDV ceremonial structure. In this regard, the results, at least with alcohol and drug abuse, are similar to those obtained with the spiritually based 12-step programs to treat alcoholism and drug use, or to belonging to other more familiar religious groups that include prescriptions against alcohol or drug use.

Figure 5. Peyote cactus. [19a]

Mescaline, Peyote, and the Native American Church

Peyote, *Lophophora williamsii,* is a small, round cactus with fuzzy tufts instead of spines. The above-ground portion, containing a single white cactus flower, is the drug-containing "button" that is cut and eaten either fresh or dried (Figure 5).

The active psychedelic ingredient is mescaline. Unlike all the other entheogens, which have a structure similar to serotonin, the structure of mescaline is more closely related to dextroamphetamine. Its effects, however, resemble those of psilocybin, producing profound sensory alterations, a heightened sensitivity to sound, color, and textures, and exhilaration. Its effects last about 24 hours. Like the sacred mushrooms, peyote has a long history of use both as a medicinal and entheogen. Its first use was documented 400 years ago among the Aztecs. The Spanish invaders saw its use as a crime against God, punishable by death. Despite these attempts at suppression, the religious use of peyote is more widespread today than any of the other entheogens. It is considered divine by the Indians representing a messenger that allows them to directly communicate with God and cure all bodily and spiritual ailments.

Most peyote ceremonies consist of much drumming, singing, prayer, and story telling. Deeply meaningful and highly personalized inspirational revelation is often a very important part of the individual's experience. Mutual participation in the ceremonies often results in lifelong friendships. [20]

In the late 1800s, the great herds of animals on which the Indians depended for food had been killed off, and the Indians were defeated and decimated by starvation and disease. Those remaining were herded into reservations. During this time of impoverishment and hopelessness, the ancient peyote ceremony began to make a comeback. This was related to the ability of the peyote ceremony to provide the sensation that something is being done to and for the individuals, providing them with a feeling of power.

By the turn of the century over 50 different tribes had begun using peyote in sacramental ceremonies. One of several important leaders in this movement was James Mooney, a Smithsonian Institute archeologist. He had participated in peyote ceremonies and became convinced that it was such an important part of their culture that the Indians needed new laws to protect their right to use peyote in religious ceremonies. He helped them found and incorporate the Native American Church. This church blended ancient Indian rituals, peyote ceremonies, and Christian theology. The peyote ceremonies were not a constant component of the services but tended to be called about once a month at times of particular need such as the failing health of a member or other more joyous occasions. Laws banning peyote use were enacted in 11 southwestern states but were generally not enforced. In 1960, an Arizona Judge ruled that Native Americans were guaranteed access to the peyote sacrament under the first and fourteenth amendments of the constitution. The Native American Church currently has an estimated 250,000 members across many states and provinces in the United States and Canada.

Amanita muscaria, Soma, and Hinduism

Amanita muscaria is a beautiful and striking mushroom with a brilliant red cap covered with white specks. It has also been called the *Sacred Mushroom* (Figure 6).

In the English speaking world it was known as *fly-agaric* because it attracts flies. Maggot infestation is one of the most common reasons for making the mushroom inedible. Since it grows in association with the rootlets of certain trees, it is found in the mountains and only in areas where there are trees, especially birch, and only when there is rain. It contains several psychedelic compounds, including ibotenic acid and muscimole. The dried form is more hallucinogenic and less poisonous. When a gram or more is consumed the symptoms include relaxation, drowsiness, decreased blood pressure, increased sweating and salivation, changes in mood, euphoria, and hallucinations. In higher doses it can cause agitation as well as hallucinations. Death

Figure 6. Amanita muscaria psychedelic mushroom. From Allegro, The Sacred Mushroom and the Cross. [21]

is very rare. The deadly reputation of the *Amanita* is due to other species such as *Amanita virosa* (the Destroying Angels).

A property that is almost unique to *Amanita muscaria* relates to aspects of the metabolism of ibotenic acid. A carboxyl radical is removed, yielding muscimole. This process occurs in the liver and is very inefficient. About 80 percent of the ingested ibotenic acid passes through the body to the urine. As a result, the urine of a person who has ingested *Amanita muscaria* is itself intoxicating, and the urine of someone who drinks this urine is also intoxicating. This can be cycled several times before its potency is lost. This property would allow the priest or shaman to consume the mushrooms, suffer the unpleasant side effects and let the rest of the tribe drink his urine containing a detoxified version of the fly-agaric.

Interest in the potential role of *Amanita muscaria* in religion was initiated in 1968 with the publication of Wasson's book, *Soma, the Devine Mushroom of Immortality.* [22] He proposed that *Amanita muscaria* was used as a spiritual lubricant from the earliest beginnings of civilization, was the *Soma* of the Hindu Rig-Veda scriptures, the *Mukhomor* of the Siberian plains, and the *amrita* of Buddhist scriptures. Based on his studies, others have suggested that Soma also played a significant role in the early development of Judaism and Christianity.

Wasson reported circumstantial evidence that Soma was commonly imbibed in very ancient times, long before the advent of literacy. He proposed that it was an inebriant as far back as the period of 6,000 to 4,000 BCE, when Uralic, the precursor to over a dozen Eurasian languages, was spoken. It evoked religious adoration, and in the second millennium BCE was brought onto the Iranian plateau and to the Indus Valley. Wasson stated that fly-agaric was:

> ...a plant that could be plausibly named the Herb of Immortality responding to one of man's deepest desires in the early stages of his intellectual development. The superb fly-agaric gave him a glimpse of horizons beyond any that he knew in his hardy struggle for survival of planes of existence far removed and above his daily round of besetting cares. It contributed to the shaping of his mythological world and his religious life.

It is thus not surprising that fly-agaric was positioned to play a central role in the development of both western and eastern religions. In this regard, Wasson provides an intriguing explanation of the origin of some of the ideas that have been central to all great religions. In Siberia and other northern regions of Eurasia, where the Aryans originated, the tall Siberian birch, with its delicate dancing foliage and its dazzling white bark, was a thing of ethereal beauty. The roots of the birch tree were also the primary source of fly-agaric and of a second fungus, *Fomes fomentarius,* the source of punk, or touchwood, the primary tinder that catches the spark from a fire-drill and bursts into flames. Punk also had a mystical role in that in many primitive societies the procreation of fire was analogous to the sex act. This and a related word, *spunk,* for semen, still carry various erotic meanings. Wasson comments that:

> The birch, parent to both fly-agaric and punk, naturally held pride of place as the Tree of Life, providing punk, the key to fire for the body, and in the fly-agaric for the soul.

He further suggested,

> The peoples who emigrated from the forest belt to the southern latitudes took with them vivid memories of the herb and the imagery. The renown of the Herb of Immortality [Tree of Knowledge] and the Tree of Life spread by word of mouth far and wide, and in the South [except in the mountains] where the birch and the fly-agaric were little more than cherished tales generations and thousands of miles removed from the source of inspiration, the concepts were still stirring the imaginations of poets, story-tellers, and sages.

These poets and story-tellers very likely included those who wrote the Bible and other religious works where the concepts of a Tree of Life, the fruit of that tree, the Tree of Knowledge of Good and Evil, the Pillar of the World, the Cosmic Tree and of Immortality — all hold a central place and stem back to the birch tree and fly agaric. A prominent example is the Biblical account of Adam and Eve and the Garden of Eden. This myth states that God planted two magical trees in paradise, the Tree of Life and the Tree of Knowledge of Good and Evil, and instructed Adam not to eat the fruit of the Tree of Knowledge. This would result in enlightenment, a passing from darkness into light, knowledge of good and evil, raising them above the level of animals into God-like qualities, and signaling the sinful end of innocence. It was suggested that the forbidden fruit may have been the Sacred Mushroom which when eaten produced just such a sense of connection with divine knowledge. This concept is represented in the fresco painting in the church of Plaincourault in France, where the *Amanita muscaria* is gloriously portrayed, entwined with a serpent, while Eve stands by holding her belly (Figure 7).

Despite the fact that these figures even show the white speckles on top of a red crown, typical of the Devine Mushroom, some art historians have denied the proposal

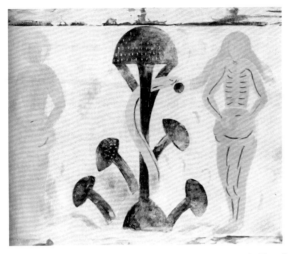

Figure 7. A Christian fresco showing the Amanita muscaria as the Tree of Knowledge of good and evil in the Garden of Eden. From Wasson, Soma, the Devine Mushroom of Immortality. [22] Copied by Mme. Bory of the Laboratoire de Crypto-gamie, Museum National d'History Naturelle, Paris.

by mycologists that this figure represents *Amanita muscaria.* Wasson suspects the mycologists were more likely have had it right. [22]

The Soma of Hinduism. When the Aryans swept into the Indus valley 3,500 years ago bringing with them the Vedas and the origins of Hinduism, they also brought magical religious ceremonies based on the cult of Soma. This cult used hallucinogenic plants, but which plants were involved remained a mystery until the publication of Wasson's book. Others investigating the source of Soma had used modern texts. This produced no clear answers. Wesson's approach was unique. He knew that the use of Soma had died out many centuries ago. Thus, to obtain clues to its nature he felt it only made sense to examine religious texts written at the time that Soma was actually used. These were the Rig Veda that dated before 4,000 BCE and represented the earliest written form of Sanskrit mantras. Of more than 1,000 holy hymns in the Rig Veda, 120 were devoted exclusively to Soma. Wasson based his conclusion that the Soma drink of the Vedic Aryans was made from the red and white *Amanita muscaria* mushroom on the following pieces of evidence taken directly from those verses.

1. The verses spoke of a plant that has neither seed nor blossom nor leaf nor root. The only plants with these characteristics were mushrooms.
2. Vedic synonyms for Soma included terms such as *aja,* meaning "one-foot," suggestive of mushrooms.
3. The Rig Veda described the soma-plant as "tawney," meaning brown. This is the color of the dried *Amanita muscaria* mushroom, its most psychoactive and least toxic form.
4. The Rig Veda constantly referred to the fact that the plant for Soma came from the mountains. This is where the birch trees, whose roots are necessary for the *Amanita muscaria* to grow, are found.
5. The verses refer to Soma as the child of thunderstorms. The fly-agaric often sprouts overnight following a rainstorm.
6. The verses referred to the two forms of Soma: a form that was taken directly, and a form that was taken in the form of the urine of any person who had ingested the mushroom. One verse spoke of the Soma from the "piss of swollen men."

These and many other clues in the ancient Rig Veda verses clearly identified *Amanita muscaria* as the source of the Soma. As Wasson stated: "The hymns of the Rig Vega fit the fly-agaric like a glove."

Soma so impressed the Indians that it became a god in its own right. Thus it was at the same time a god, a plant, and the juice of that plant. The ancient traditions recorded in the Rig Veda assert that Paranja, the god of thunder, was the father of Soma. This makes great sense because the mushroom seems to magically appear after thunderstorms. To understand these verses it is important to know there were three major gods in the Rig Veda: *Agni,* god of fire, *Soma,* moon god and personification of the soma drug, and *Indra,* who enjoyed the effects of soma and became more god-like in the process. These three gods form the basic elements of a fire-ritual in which Agni represents the sacrificial flames, Soma the sacrificial offering, and Indra the celebrant rendered divine by the soma. The following two verses illustrate some of the ways the Rig Veda refers to Soma:

Rig Veda 9.113.4 Where there are joys and pleasures, gladness and delight, where the desires of desire are fulfilled, there make me immortal. O drop of Soma, flow for Indra.

Rig Veda 9.113.7 We have drunk the Soma; we have become immortal; we have gone to the light; we have found the Gods. What can hatred and malice of mortals do to us now, O immortal one?

The Soma plant was a condensed God. Not only was Soma drinking condoned, it was the only way to guarantee entry into heaven. Patrons could pay for costly Soma sacrifices and thereby ensure their place in the everafter. Those who pressed out its intoxicating blood and drank it felt God come to life within them and were lifted up in spirit to the heavenly realms of endless light. [23] The use of Soma ended about 2,500 years ago and with it the Soma sacrifices. This was likely to have been due to an increased difficulty in obtaining it. As a result the Brahmins were forced to devise new ways to offer salvation to keep their followers. Brahminism developed as a replacement a set of complex scriptural injunctions, rituals that only Brahmin priests could administer, thus assuring their place in the spiritual life of the average Indian. It was proposed that *the widespread practice of yoga served as a Soma substitute for attaining access to the soul and that the effects of both were similar.*

The Amrita of Buddhism. *Amrita* is the Buddhist equivalent of soma. It is Sanskrit for "elixir of immortality" and literally means "deathlessness." It is similar to the Greek word *ambrosia,* which means "food of the gods" and "no death." *Amanita muscaria* was used by the practitioners of Vajrayana Buddhism during the period between 500 and 1,000 CE when Buddhism was introduced to Tibet, where it became the state religion.

The Soma of Siberia. The use of fly-agaric was widespread in northern Eurasia and has still been used in recent times in Siberia. There is a rich literature presenting different aspects of this use. In 1900 Karl von Ditmar provided the following description of fly agric use by the Koryak tribe. [22p156] *Mukhomor* is the name for Siberian Soma.

> Mukhomor eaters describe the narcosis as most beautiful and splendid. The most powerful images, such as they never see in their lives otherwise pass before their eyes and lull them into a state of most intense enjoyment. Among the numerous persons who I myself have seen intoxicated in this way, I cannot remember a single one who was raving or wild. Outwardly the effect was always thoroughly calming — I might almost say, comforting. For the most part the people sit smiling and friendly, mumbling quietly to themselves, and all their movements are slow and cautious.

In 1809 Georg Heinrich von Langsdorf had provided another view of the habits of the Koryak tribe: [22p248]

> The Koryaks have known since time immemorial that the urine of a person who has consumed fly-agaric has a stronger narcotic and intoxication power than the fly-agaric itself and this effect persists for a long time after consumption. For example, a man may be moderately drunk on fly-agaric today and by tomorrow may have completely slept off this moderate intoxication and be completely sober; but if he now drinks a cup of his own urine, he will become far more intoxicated than he was from the mushrooms the day before. It is not at all uncommon, therefore, that drunkards who have consumed the poisonous mushroom will preserve their urine as if it were a precious liqueur and will drink it as the occasion offers.

The urine can also be consumed by others, transmitting the effects of the same mushroom to many individuals. Many of the shamans, previous to their séances, eat fly-agaric in order to get into ecstatic states. Then, through their urine, this effect may be transferred to their followers who receive its benefits with fewer side effects.

While agreeing with Masson that Soma was derived from mushrooms, Terrence McKenna [24] suggested the mushroom involved was *Psilocybe (Stroharia) cubensis,* the world's most common psilocybin-containing mushroom. In India it frequently grew on cow dung.

Mushrooms and western religion. Two years after Wasson's book on Soma appeared, John Allegro published *The Sacred Mushroom and the Cross.* [21] He proposed that a secret mystic fertility sect in ancient Sumeria used *Amanita muscaria* and played a role in the spiritual beginnings of Judaism and Christianity. He suggested that certain passages were inserted into the Bible to transmit information about this secret sect to its scattered followers.

Allegro was not some crackpot new age dopehead. He was a lecturer in Old Testament and Inter-Testamental Studies at the University of Manchester. He was appointed the first British representative on an international team given the responsibility of translating and editing the Dead Sea scrolls for publication. The resulting book sold over a quarter of a million copies. He was a linguist and understood the subtle meaning of ancient Aramaic words, the language of the time of Jesus.

As pointed out in the last chapter, civilization began around 4,000 BCE in Sumeria, the region around the Tigris and Euphrates rivers. Some of the first writing consisted of wedge-shaped cuneiform letters. These were the precursors of Hebrew, Aramaic, and Arabic. The cuneiform method was well suited to the alluvial soil of the area, providing an abundance of fine clay that could be moistened and shaped into writing tablets. The early alphabetic writing was used to express only the harder consonantal sounds, while the softer vowels were left to be inserted according to the most likely intended meaning of the word. The full use of vowels was not introduced until the Christian era. This often left considerable doubt about the precise meaning of passages of the Bible. Syllables were made up of word-bricks which resisted phonetic change over time. These could be joined together to make phrases and sentences. Thus, understanding of the early Sumerian language made it possible to trace the Indo-European and Semitic verbal roots and begin to decipher the name of Gods, heroes, plants, and animals appearing in cultic mythologies. [21]

A number of these word-bricks related to concepts about fertility, which in turn were associated with God and the Word of God as the all-powerful creator of life. Because of the central role of fertility and creation, phallic designations were given to many of the Sumerian, Greek, and Semitic gods, tribal ancestors and heroes. The word Yahweh for God meant "the seed of life." The Sumerian phoneme *U,* referring to fertility and creation, was "the most important phoneme in the whole of Near Eastern Religion." The seed of God, in whatever form, was supremely holy. The terms *curse* and *sin* were derived from the idea of "seed running to waste," so sin in essence meant to "make ineffective." By contrast the term "faith" meant the opposite, to "make effective."

Allegro proposed that many of the classical and biblical stories were based on pieces of vegetation and on the sacred mushroom in particular. Its hallucinogenic properties and phallic appearance formed the basis of mystical fertility cults in the Near East that persisted for thousands of years. Allegro suggested the writers of the Bible were playing with forms of words that have subsequently become lost over the centuries, and in many cases the original words referred to the sacred mushroom. As an example of this word play he suggested that the Biblical phrase,

> *And I will give unto thee the keys of the kingdom of heaven.*
> *Matthew 16:19*

was based on the term *bolt* or *key,* referring to the sacred fungus, and the kingdom of heaven to its hallucinogenic ability to open the way to new and exciting mystical experiences. [21p47] Another example was the passage that likens the kingdom of heaven to a mustard seed.

> *Another parable put he forth unto them, saying, The kingdom of heaven is like to a grain of mustard seed, which a man took, and sowed in his field.*
>
> *Matthew 13:31*

This appears to be based on the Semitic *khardela* for "mustard," and *ardila* for "mushroom," such that the whole discussion stems from a play on the word for the secret mushroom.

Allegro suggested that the virgin birth of Jesus had its symbolic origin in the magical way in which mushrooms suddenly appeared "without seed" from God following thunderstorms and rain. The baby that resulted from this divine union was thus the "Son of God," and was more truly representative of its Heavenly Father than any other form of plant or animal life. [21p55]

In summary, based on a detailed knowledge of the subtle aspects of Aramaic, an ancient language of the time of Jesus, Allegro proposed that the plant mythology and terms that existed over the thousands of years of the ancient world provided the New Testament cryptographers with "cover" to pass on information about a secret fertility sect revolving around the hallucinogenic properties and sexual symbolism of the sacred mushroom, *Amanita muscaria*. Based on his reading of the Dead Sea Scrolls, Allegro proposed that Christianity was a derivative religion, in that a hundred years before Jesus, a "Teacher of Righteousness" was crucified for similar teachings. He proposed that this proto-Jesus was reinvented around 30 CE to appeal to Gentiles in a time of persecution by Rome and the orthodox Jewish priests. "It was the obvious device to convey to the scattered cells of the cult, reminders of their sacred doctrines and incantatory names and expressions concealed within a story of a "second Moses," another lawgiver, Joshus (Greek *Iesous,* "Jesus"). Thus was born the Gospel myth of the New Testament."

These ideas were not shared by his colleagues, and Allegro met with severe criticism for his views, considered blasphemous by many. However, elements of the story remain plausible, and all parts of this chapter illustrate the potential role of hallucinogenic mushrooms in the early spiritual stirrings of mankind. Despite the unpopularity of these proposals, Clark Heinrich expanded upon them in his 2002 book, *Magic Mushrooms in Religion and Alchemy.* [23] Wasson had eaten samples of *Amanita muscaria* without experiencing any of the spiritual experiences attributed to the mushroom. This led him to wonder if there was some secret to its preparation. Heinrich experimented extensively with ingesting a range of preparations of *Amanita muscaria*. He found that drying the mushrooms before ingestion dramatically decreased the undesirable side effects. Independent of the unpleasant side effects, he felt a tremendous vitality, as though he could conquer the world. Others felt a powerful urge to speak about the godliness and wonderful power they were experiencing, with a sense that what they said was the absolute truth and was spoken with conviction, passion, and eloquence. The elation and euphoria became amplified to the point of bliss. [23p17] The mushroom can also have an anti-hallucinogenic effect in which one sees things exactly as they are without mental overlay, mimicking the yoga-induced cessation of thought in the mind. This results in a tremendous increase in consciousness, as though one's brain has been subsumed by the mind of God.

During one period of 30 days, Heinrich and a friend ate the dried mushroom every day. For most of the time they felt immense energy, strength, spirituality, occasional sickness, and frequent euphoria, but being taken into the blissful light eluded them. Then, near the last day, following the lead of the Shamans and Indian priests, they decided to drink their own urine. Surprisingly it had a pleasant fragrance. He reported that:

> Within minutes after drinking something amazing started to happen. My body began to feel very light, as though I weighed almost nothing. It felt as if the molecules that comprised my body were separating and allowing air to pass between them, or that I could feel the space between the atoms. I became aware of tremendous energy at my feet that rose up through my body in wave after wave. "Feeling good" was rapidly changing into the most blissful feeling I had ever experienced. My mind and entire body were in the throes of a kind of meta-orgasm that wouldn't stop — not that I wanted to.

With these experiences in mind, Heinrich was particularly intrigued by how Allegro's proposal of the existence of a mystical mushroom-based sect could explain some of the most puzzling aspects of the Biblical accounts of Abraham, Moses, and Yahweh. Many of these get pretty bizarre and I leave those who are interested to read them for themselves. I will list just one — his take on circumcision.

It is not inherently apparent why God would ask Abraham to cut off not only his foreskin but the foreskin of all his descendents and anyone else who came into his household even if not related. This was ostensibly so the resultant scar would prove to everyone forever that Abraham and God had made a special holy covenant. But wouldn't a cut on the wrist, or forehead, or some type of a tattoo, been less mutilating and easier for others to see? Why circumcision? As Heinrich stated: "I don't have a foreskin today because someone almost four thousand years ago was in the throes of a paranoid delusion and everybody went along with him. I can hear the men and boys even now: 'Great idea Abraham! Let's all mutilate our penises!' "

Heinrich suggested that the idea was actually traceable to the mushroom cult. *Amanita muscaria* with its thick shaft and bulbous red head is the ultimate phallic symbol. As the sacred mushroom grows it causes the veil to separate and fall off, revealing a smaller bulb underneath, a form of mushroom self-circumcision producing a plant version of a circumcised penis. Worshipers may have wanted a way to identify other members of their secret sect and wanted their penises to look like the shaft and the concealed bulb of the sacred mushroom.

While the speculations of John Allegro and Clark Heinrich may seem singularly sacrilegious to many, there is none-the-less extensive evidence that psychedelic plants are found in virtually all parts of the world and that they played an important role in the development of religious beliefs in the Americas, Europe and Asia. Their effect on the mind of man was so powerful and so spiritual that they have been given the name *entheogenic,* meaning *God generated within.* Archeological evidence indicates they have been with mankind from its earliest beginnings and have played a major role in the development of his spiritual evolution. It is likely that without them man's belief systems and religions might be entirely different from what they are now. Wasson [25] summarized well the symbiotic relationship between sacred mushrooms and the spirituality of humans:

> As man emerged from his brutish past, thousands of years ago, there was a stage in the evolution of his awareness when the discovery of a mushroom with miraculous properties was a revelation to him, a veritable detonator to his soul, arousing in him sentiments of awe and reverence, and gentleness and love, to the highest pitch of which mankind is capable, all those sentiments and virtues that mankind has ever since regarded as the highest attributes of his kind. It made him see what his perishing mortal eye cannot see….What today is resolved into a mere drug…was for him a prodigious miracle, inspiring in him poetry and philosophy and religion.

Many different plants around the world contain a range of psychedelic drugs which are capable of strongly augmenting man's innate capacity for spirituality. They do this by providing a powerful feeling of communication with a supernatural power. It is not at all unlikely that these entheogens (god-producing substances) played a profound and critical role in facilitating man's early belief in a god or gods and in the development of his religions.

References

1. Wasson, R. G., Kramrisch, S., Ott, J. & Ruck, C. A. P. *Persephone's Quest: Entheogens and the Origins of Religion.* Yale University Press, New Haven, CT, 1986.
2. Metzner, R. Visionary mushroom of the Americas. in: Metzner, R. *Sacred Mushrooms of Visions Teonanácatl.* Park Street Press, Rochester, VT, 2004.
2a. From www.dhushara.com
3. Allen, J. W. & Arthur, J. Ethnomycology and distribution of psilocybian mushrooms. in: Metzner, R. *Sacred Mushroom of Visions:* Teonanácatl. Park Street Press,Rochester, VT, 2004.
4. Schultes, R. E. *The identification of Teonanácatl, a narcotic basidomycete of the Aztecs.* Botanical Museum Leaflets of Harvard 7: 37-54, 1939.
5. Schultes, R. E. Teonanácatl: The narcotic mushroom of the Aztecs. *American Anthropologist.* 42: 429-443, 1940.
6. Wasson, R. G. *The Wonderous Mushroom—Mycolatry in Mesoamerica.* MacGraw-Hill, New York, 1980.
7. Wasson, V. P. & Wasson, R. G. *Mushrooms, Russsia and History.* Pantheon Books, New York, 1957.
8. Wasson, R. G. Seeking the Magic Mushroom. *Life Sci.* 100: 100-102, 09-120, 1957.

9.   Wasson, R. G., Cowa, G., Cowa, F. & Rhodes, W. *Maria Sabina and her Mazatec Mushroom Velada.* Harcourt, Brace, Jovanovich, New York, 1974.

10. Gartz, J. *Magic Mushrooms Around the World—A Scientific Journey Across Cultures and Time.* Harper Collins, New York, 1996.

11. Stamets, P. *Psilocybin Mushrooms of the World—An Identification Guide.* Ten Speed Press, Berkeley, CA, 1997.

12. Schultes, R. E., Hofmann, A. & Rätsch, C. *Plants of the Gods. Their Sacred, Healing, and Hallucinogenic Powers.* Healing Arts Press, Rochester, NY, 1998.

13. Samorini, G. The oldest representations of hallucinogenic mushrooms in the world (Sahara desert. 9000-7000B.P.). *Integration: the Journal for Mind-Moving Plants and Culture.* 2: 69-78, 1992.

14. Wasson, R. G. The Divine Mushrooms: Primitive Religion and Hallucinatory Agents. *Proc Am Phil Soc.* 102: 1959.

15. Metzner, R. Introduction: Amazonian vine of visions. in: Metzner, R. *Sacred Vine of Spirits Ayahuasca.* Park Street Press, Rochester, VT, 1999, 2006.

16. Naranjo, P. Hallucinogenic plant use and related indigenous belief systems in the Ecuadorian Amazon. Journal of Enthopharmacology. 1: 121-145, 1979.

17. Metzner, R. Introduction: Amazonian vine of visions. in: Metzner, R. *Sacred Vine of Spirits Ayahuasca.* Park Street Press, Rochester, VT, 1999, 2006.

18. Harner, M. Common themes in South American Indian yage experiences. in: Tarcher, J. P. *Hallucinogens and Shaminism.* Oxford University Press, London, 1973.

19. McKenna, D. J., Grob, C. S. & Callaway, J. C. The scientific investigation of Ayahuasca: A review of past and current reserach. *Heffter Review of Psychedelic Research.* 1: 65-77, 1998.

19a. From leda.lycaeum.org. Images by permission.

20. Mercado, L. Peyote religion: Spiritual soul food. 222.csp.org/nicolas.A57html. 2005.

21. Allegro, J. M. *The Sacred Mushroom & the Cross.* Doubleday & Company, Inc, Garden City, NY, 1970.

22. Wasson, R. G. *Soma: Divine Mushroom of Immortality.* Harcourt Brace Jovnovich, 1968.

23. Heinrich, C. *Magic Mushrooms in Religion and Alchemy.* Park Street Press, Rochester, VT%, 2002.

24. McKenna, T. *Food of the Gods. The Search for the Original Tree of Knowledge.* Bantam Books, New York, 1992.

25. Wasson, R. G., Ruck, C. A. & Hofmann, A. *The Road to Eleusis: Unveiling the Secret of the Mysteries.* Harcourt Trade Publishers, San Diego, 1978.

The Lord God has chosen you to be a people for His own possession, out of all the peoples that are on the face of the earth.

Deuteronomy 7:6

The scandal of particularity is the root of all religious evil.

John Horgan
Rational Mysticism

Chapter 47

Does God Play Favorites?

The Jews claim they are the "chosen ones." The Muslims claim their Allah is "the only true God." Evangelical Christians claim that only those who are "born again" will be taken by the Rapture into heaven and the rest of the world will be lost in years of tribulation. In wars each side prays for a victory. At a more mundane level, before sports events each team prays that they will win. All of these events assume that *God plays favorites.* They assume that God has a personal investment in one religion over another, for one combatant over another, for one team over another, as though He was keeping a moral scorecard on all human activities. In *The World's Religions,* Huston Smith called this characteristic of religion the "Scandal of Particularity." [1p308]

The Chosen People. The above quote from Deuteronomy is the source of the conviction that the Jews are the "chosen people." While this would seem to be a wonderful position to be in, an alternative rabbinic view is that God offered the laws of the Torah to the world at large but only the Jews were willing to accept its rigors. [1] As a result the Jews were also elected to shoulder an enormous load of suffering that would otherwise have been shared by the rest of the world. In this sense being the chosen people had a distinct downside.

It is understandable that, since the Jews were the first people on earth to ascribe to the view of monotheism, God would be quite pleased with them, and since Abraham was willing to suffer persecution for this belief, God chose Abraham and his descendents to teach monotheism. It may be more accurate to say that the Jews chose God than to say that God chose the Jews.

Many Jews are uncomfortable with this designation because it is mindful of the Nazi concept of a supreme, superior Aryan race. Nonetheless, many are undoubtedly pleased, and some non-Jews would like to share in the distinction. For example, the Mormon Church claimed their members were descended from the Hebrews so they could share in the distinction of being among the chosen ones. Also, as illustrated in the following section on the Rapture, fundamentalist Christians have even incorporated the fact that the Jews were God's chosen ones into a portion of their plans. A skeptic might say this designation was proof that the Bible was written by men, not God. Since the men that did the writing were Jewish, they seized upon this unique opportunity to claim favored status with God.

Islam and the Infidels. The Qur'an (Koran) states,

> "O Prophet, struggle with the unbelievers and hypocrites, and be thou harsh with them."
>
> *Qur'an 9:73*

When Mohammad asked Allah for permission to fight them, permission was granted. Thus, Muslims believe that Mohammad was given a divine command to fight against people, not in self-defense but because infidels do not worship Allah. As long as they paid their taxes, Jews and Christians were exempt, but idol worshipers, including Muslims who were not believers, could be forced to embrace Islam.

> "Slay the idolaters wherever you find them."
>
> *Qur'an 9:5*

> "The unbelievers among the People of the Book [other religions] and the pagans shall burn forever in the fire of Hell. They are the vilest of all creatures."
>
> *Qur'an 98:1-8*

There are many other verses in the Qur'an that speak of religious tolerance and of granting asylum to those who ask for it. Nonetheless Islamic writings carry the clear implication that Allah favors the believers in Islam and has little tolerance for infidels. In the hands of extremist fundamentalists, this forms the basis of Islamic terrorism. Muslims are not alone in fostering the belief that one's own religion is the best religion. The Rapturists are just as adamant in their belief that God plays favorites.

The Rapture. Some fundamentalist Christians believe in the Rapture. This is the belief that at any moment a secret rapture will occur such that "born again" true believers who have accepted Jesus Christ as their savior will be swept into heaven, while all the non-believers will be subjected to seven years of a horrendous, hell-like Great Tribulation. When the seven years of hell are over, Christ will return and set up a kingdom of 1,000 years of peace on earth.

Rapturists cite the writings of St. Irenaeus as the beginning of their belief system. In 177 CE St. Irenaeus was appointed bishop of Lyons. His life's work was to combat the Gnostics. The Gnostics were supreme pessimists about the evils of life on earth, and to counter this Irenaeus taught that there would be a thousand peaceful, evil-free years immediately following the Second Coming of Christ. Since the Second Coming of Christ preceded the 1,000 years of bliss, this belief was called *premillennialism*.

An American ex-Anglican priest, John Nelson Darby expanded on this concept. Around 1830 Darby met a 15-year-old girl, Margaret McDonald, who claimed to have had a private revelation about a secret rapture that would occur shortly. By secret she meant that while the Rapture was initiated by the Second Coming of Christ, at first He did not actually set foot on earth. His return was secret and the raptured ones would "meet Him in the Clouds" and go back to heaven with him. Only a very select group of the most faithful of Christians would be included in this rapture. For the rest of the world this Rapture would usher in seven years of the Great Tribulation. This would end in the defeat of the antichrist and the judgment of Christ's followers. Then a 1,000-year reign of Christ on earth would begin for the benefit of ethnic Jews. After the millennium the enemies of Israel, Gog and Magog *(Ezekiel 38, 39; Revelation 20),* would battle Christ one final time, and the final judgment would begin. The wicked would spend an eternity without any good or God. Those who had responded to God throughout their lives, the righteous, would experience no more death and have eternal life in the presence of God forever.

The widespread dissemination of a faith in the Rapture is partially attributed to the *Scofield Reference Bible,* printed in 1909. This was the most influential study Bible in English and its notes always explained passages from the Rapturists' perspective. [2] Belief in the Rapture is surprisingly common in the United States. In 1970 Hal Lindsey's book, *The Late Great Planet Earth,* sold almost as many copies as the Bible. He predicted that the Rapture was due before the end of the 1980s. While clearly incorrect, later Rapture books such as the *Left Behind* series by Tim LaHaye and Jerry Jenkins have sold more than 50 million copies.

Throughout history Christians have believed the world would see a horrific persecution just before the second coming of Christ. This persecution is attributed to the antichrist, also called the "man of sin," the "son of perdition," and the "man of lawlessness." Much of this comes from *2 Thessalonians 2:3,* where Paul warns that people should not think that the Lord has already come, "for that day will not come, unless the rebellion comes first, and the man of lawlessness is revealed, the son of perdition."

During the Great Tribulation and before the final victory of Christ, the antichrist will take a seat in the Temple of God and proclaim himself to be God. Since this Temple is in Jerusalem, this cannot occur unless the Jews, the Chosen Ones, have retaken Jerusalem. Thus, Rapturists and Christian fundamentalists in general were delighted when the Jews recaptured Jerusalem in the wars of 1948 and 1967. They are staunch Christian-Zionists. It is also necessary that the Jewish Temple be rebuilt; otherwise how could the antichrist claim himself to be God from within that Temple? [2] There can be many antichrists, all the doing of the devil. Fundamentalist Christians often label any politician, any institution, anything they do not approve of as an antichrist. This label has variously been applied to the United Nations and many modern politicians.

Following the defeat of the antichrist, the Lord "shall stand on the Mount of Olives which lies before Jerusalem.…Then the Lord your God will come, and all the holy ones with Him *(Zechariah 14:2-5).* This accounts for why many fundamentalist Christians have moved to Israel and bought homes in view of the Mount of Olives so they can greet Him upon his return. Christ will then save the Jewish people from extinction.

Some of the implications of the Rapture are astounding. Rapturism is spiritual home for those who think the world is careening out of control. It entails a pessimistic view of the world, but one that the faithful will not have to deal with since they will be raptured into heaven. This view accounts for why many fundamentalists do not participate in the political process. They hold the view, "Why polish the brass on a sinking ship?" They do not believe this world is worth improving. Some even refuse to vote. Based on this view Currie thought that no Rapture believing fundamentalist organization would be able to remain as a long-term political force. [2] But some do get involved in politics. James Watt, the fundamentalist Reagan-era Secretary of the Interior justified the clearcutting of the nation's forests and other anti-environment "Use it or lose it" views based on the statement at his confirmation hearing of, "I do not know how many future generations we can count on before the Lord returns." [2p7]

Other implications are that born-again pilots will be raptured out of their planes leaving the unbelievers to perish in the crash. Doctors and essential civil servants will be gone. Television announcers will suddenly disappear from the screen. One of the powerful methods for recruiting new converts to this form of Christian fundamentalism comes from the statement, "Don't be left behind. Convert now before it is too late." The implied favoritism is the ultimate evangelical proselytizing tool, and it works.

The Seventh-Day Adventists propose even more severe consequences for unbelievers, in that Christ will actually destroy those who are left behind. Instead of a thousand years of Christ's rule in peace and tranquility, for a thousand years only Satan and his angels will be living on earth. A Second Coming then occurs wherein the righteous will be returned to a cleansed earth and establish a New Jerusalem. Hell does not exist as a place of eternal damnation because those who go to hell are burned up, utterly destroyed, and cease forever to exist. [3] The unrighteous who died before the Second Coming will be resurrected and consumed by fire and by God, along with Satan and his angels. The universe will then be free of sin and sinners.

The Rapture and its variants represent the ultimate in God playing favorites. Only the most faithful of the Christians will be raptured. The remaining Christians, all the Jews, Muslims, Buddhists, Hindus, Taoists, and everyone else in the world will suffer in the Great Tribulation or be destroyed outright.

It is a very human trait to want to believe we are special in some way. Many religions imply they are God's favorites and use this assumption to provide believers with an enhanced sense of self-worth and proselytizing fervor. This view is inconsistent with the existence of a fair and impartial God who loves all members of his flock equally. Wanting to be special and better than others is a human wish, not a Godly one. Its use in any context suggests that all claims of favoritism were ultimately of human authorship.

References

1.   Smith, H. *The World's Religions.* Harper San Francisco, New York, 1961.
2.   Currie, D. B. *Rapture: The End-Times Error That Leaves the Bible Behind.* Sophia Institute Press, Manchester, NH, 2003.
3.   Anonymous. Seventh-Day Adventist Church. www.religioustolerance.org/sda.htm. 2005.

With or without religion, good people can behave well and bad people can do evil but for good people to do evil — that takes religion.

Steven Weinberg,
Nobel Laureate

Religion is inherently prone to violence.

Hector Avalos
Fighting Words: The Origins of Religious Violence [1]

An only God is by nature a jealous God, who will not allow another to live.

Arthur Schopenhauer [2]

Monotheism has a violent legacy because it "abhors, reviles, rejects, and ejects whatever it defines as outside its compass."

Regina Schwartz
The Curse of Cain. The Violent Legacy of Monotheism [3]

Why do people who are obsessed with good and evil end up murdering innocents, somehow slipping into becoming more evil than the evil they aim to fight?... Purifying the world through murder.

Jessica Stern
Terror in the Name of God [4]

Religious faith represents so uncompromising a misuse of the power of our minds that it forms a kind of perverse, cultural singularity — a vanishing point beyond which rational discourse proves impossible... it is the most prolific source of violence in our history.

Sam Harris
The End of Faith [5]

Chapter 48

The Evils of Religion

If the reader incorrectly believes I am unfairly bashing religion, the chapter immediatly following this is on the Benefits of Religion. I could have placed either chapter first. In essence, both great evil and great good have been done by or in the name of religion. I will address some of the evils first. Many books have been written on the subject. [3-9] Sam Harris summarizes a common theme in *The End of Faith*: [5p13]

> Intolerance is thus intrinsic to every creed. Once a person believes — really believes — that certain ideas can lead to eternal happiness, or to its antithesis, he cannot tolerate the possibility that the people he loves might be led astray by the blandishments of unbelievers. Certainty about the next life is simply incompatible with tolerance in this one.

A few of the numerous examples of violence toward others in the name of God are discussed in this chapter.

The Old Testament

The Bible itself shows that God can be jealous, angry, wrathful, vengeful, brutal, sadistic, murderous, and violent. An example is the story of the exodus from Egypt where God led Moses and the children of Israel to freedom. To force the Pharaoh to let them go, God "slew all the males" and killed "every woman that hath known man by lying with him," killed the kings of Midian, stole all their cattle, flocks and goods, and burned their cities. God also brought on a plague of locusts and darkness *(Exodus 10)*. Further on in *Exodus,* "Thus saith the LORD God of Israel. Put every man his sword by his side, and go in and out from gate to gate throughout the camp, and slay every man his brother, and every man his companion, and every man his neighbor. And the children of Levi did according to the word of Moses: and there fell of the people that day about three thousand men" *Exodus 32:26-28.*

God's jealousness is cited in many places:

- "For you shall worship no other god, for the LORD, whose name is Jealous, is a jealous God" *Exodus 34:14.*
- "I, the LORD your God, am a jealous God" *Deuteronomy 5:9.*
- "You shall surely kill him; your hand shall be first against him to put him to death, and afterward the hand of all the people. And you shall stone him with stones until he dies, because he sought to entice you away from the LORD your God" *Deuteronomy 13:9-10.*
- "They shall be wasted with hunger, devoured by pestilence and bitter destruction; I will also send against them the teeth of beasts, with the poison of serpents of the dust" *Deuteronomy 32:24.*
- "Make no covenant with them and show them no mercy....But this is how you must deal with them: break down their altars, smash their pillars, hew down their sacred poles, and burn their idols with fire" *Deuteronomy 7.*
- Further on, *Deuteronomy 28:23-34* lists many curses for failing to obey the laws of God. They include being afflicted with madness and blindness, being oppressed and robbed, having your wife ravished, your oxen slaughtered, your donkey, sheep, sons, and daughters taken, and in general being continually abused, crushed and driven mad.
- Punishment for misdeeds is often severe. "If no proof of the girl's virginity can be found, she shall be brought to the door of her father's house and there the men of her town shall stone her to death." The penalty for adultery, fornication, and rape is equally harsh. "If a man is found sleeping with another man's wife, both the man who slept with her and the woman must die." "If a man happens to meet in a town a virgin pledged to be married and he sleeps with her, you shall take both of them to the gate of that town and stone them to death. If out in the country a man happens to meet a girl pledged to be married and rapes her, only

the man who has done this shall die" *Deuteronomy 22:20-25.*

In addition to frequent themes of violence, themes of possessing the land also abound in the Old Testament. Foreign marriages and alliances and the belief in the religion of foreigners defile the land. The land must be held in perpetuity with no pieces cultivated by foreigners. In *The Curse of Cain. The Violent Legacy of Monotheism,* Regina Schwartz[3] concluded that since the bulk of biblical narratives was composed by a dispossessed people, their myths of conquest were fantasies of victory over the oppressor. Since God has no need of land, these parts of the Bible were clearly the product of man.

Richard Dawkins summarized this God as follows:[9a]

> The God of the Old Testament is arguably the most unpleasant character in all fiction: jealous and proud of it; a petty, unjust, unforgiving control freak; a vindictive, bloodthirsty ethnic cleanser; a misogynistic, homophobic, racist, infanticidal, genocidal, filicidal, pestilential, megalomaniacal, sadomasochistic, capriciously malevolent bully.

Again, such a listing of particularly human traits supports the probability that man, not God, wrote the book.

The New Testament

It is often assumed that the God of the old, or Hebrew Bible, can be jealous, vengeful, judging and violent, while the God of the New Testament is loving and forgiving. However, in the New Testament, God still sits in judgment of all Christians, punishing them for their sins, and bringing apocalyptic ruin, destruction, and death down on non-believers. In his book, *Is Religion Killing Us?* Nelson-Pallmeyer [9p60-62] asks:

> If we believe that Jesus died for us so that we shall not be condemned, then we should ask, "Condemned by whom?" The answer is God. What remains unstated in classic Christian statements of faith is that Jesus died in order to save us from God, not from sin. More precisely, Jesus' sacrificial death saves us from a violent God who punishes sin. The idea that God sent Jesus to die for our sins makes sense only if we embrace violent and punishing images of God featured predominantly in the Hebrew scriptures.
>
> Understood in a sacrificial light, the Eucharist, or Lord's Supper, ritualizes appeasement of a bloodthirsty punishing deity. It commemorates Jesus' blood sacrifice in which Jesus stands between sinful humanity and God's violent judgment....Jesus, in order to appease a punishing deity, had to be born of a virgin in order to break the cycle by which women through childbirth passed on sin from generation to generation.

As outlined in the chapter, "Does God Play Favorites?" the apocalyptic verses in the New Testament present Jesus returning as the cosmic judge. Those who pass his test live happily everafter with Jesus in the kingdom of heaven. Those who fail the test will be subjected to years of a horrendous, hell-like Great Tribulation.

While these and hundreds of other passages hardly seem to be the actions of a kind and benevolent God, they could easily represent the behavior of a God made by man in man's image. It is little wonder that with this kind of model, mankind could behave in a murderous fashion when called upon to defend "his" God and the land of "his" God.

The Inquisitions

The word *heresy* is derived from the Greek word *hairesis* meaning to choose. In a religious sense it means to choose a belief system that differs from orthodox beliefs, with orthodox meaning "straight thinking." Heresy can work in multiple directions. To the Catholic Church, Protestantism is heretical. To Protestants, Catholicism is heretical. If the concept that "my religion is the only religion" did not exist, religious heresy would not exist.

Different inquisitions were designed to deal with different forms of heresy. Thus, there was the Medieval, or Episcopal, Inquisition established in 1184 to deal with heretical Gnostic Cathars in Europe. This was followed by the Papal Inquisition of the 1230s to deal with the failure of the Episcopal Inquisition. The Spanish Inquisition was founded in 1478 by Ferdinand and Isabella of Castile and resulted in the expulsion of many thousands of Jews and Muslims from Spain. It was followed by Portuguese, Peruvian, and Mexican Inquisitions. In addition to unspeakable tortures, an additional perverse aspect of some inquisitions was that all property belonging to a convicted heretic would be forfeited to the church. The church then shared it with local officials and the victim's accusers, as a reward for their candor. With enough candor one could become quite wealthy, as long as you were not turned in by someone else with even more candor.

Anti-Semitism was a common theme, with Jews being accused of unlikely crimes such as killing Christian infants and drinking their blood. For centuries, men and women who were guilty of little more than being ugly, old, widowed, mentally ill, or of the wrong ethnic group were convicted of impossible crimes and then murdered for God's sake. [5]

In 1542 Pope Paul III initiated the Roman Inquisition with the formation of the Congregation for the Doctrine of the Faith. This body was later responsible for the trial of Galileo Galilei in 1633 for his "grave suspicion of heresy" resulting from his support of the Copernican theory that the earth revolved around the sun. The many expulsions, burnings at the stake, tortures, and imprisonments brought about by innumerable inquisitions represent one of the most tragic faces of evil in the name of religion. Harris [5p85] blames blind, unquestioning faith itself:

The question of how the church managed to transform Jesus'

principle message of loving one's neighbor and turning the other cheek into a doctrine of murder and rapine seems to promise a harrowing mystery; but it is not mystery at all. Apart from the Bible's heterogeneity and outright self-contradiction, allowing it to justify diverse and irreconcilable aims, the culprit is clearly faith itself. Whenever a man imagines that he need only believe the truth of a proposition, without evidence — that unbelievers will go to hell, that Jews drink the blood of infants — he becomes capable of anything.

The Crusades

Pope Urban II unleashed the First Crusade when in 1095, at the French town of Clermont, he delivered an electrifying speech claiming that a race absolutely alien to God had invaded Jerusalem, the land of the Christians, and had subdued the people with sword, rapine and flame. None of this was true. In fact the Muslims of Jerusalem were living peacefully with the endogenous Christians. [10] The pope's call to the Frank knights to travel to the land of the Bible was made for political reasons.

On July 15, 1099 the Crusaders finally captured Jerusalem and unleashed incredible acts of brutality on the Muslims and other citizens. The following chilling account is from the memoirs of Raymond d'Guilers, the Bishop of Orange: [11]

> With the fall of its towers one could see marvelous works. Some of the pagans were mercifully beheaded, others pierced by arrows plunged from towers, and yet others, tortured for a long time, were then burned to death in searing flames. Piles of heads, hands and feet lay in the houses and streets, and men and knights were running to and fro over corpses…there was such a massacre that our men were wading up to their ankles in enemy blood.

The killing frenzy was so great that even non-Muslims were slaughtered:

> …they were stabbing women who had fled into palaces and dwellings; seizing infants by the soles of their feet from their mother's laps or their cradles and dashing them against the walls and breaking their necks; they were slaughtering some with weapons, or striking them down with stones; they were sparing absolutely no gentile of any place or kind. [10p317]

Even to this day, 1,000 years later, Osma bin Laden cites the Crusades as one of the reasons for his murderous rage against the non-Muslim world.

Cromwell's Slaughter of Catholics

Oliver Cromwell called himself Oliver the Protector. Others called him a cruel traitor, usurper, and hypocrite. Still others found him broad-minded, tolerant, passionately religious, and ferociously moral. Cromwell's influence as a military commander and politician during the English civil war dramatically altered the

British Isles's landscape. His suppression of Royalists in Ireland during 1649 still resonates. After its capture the massacre of nearly 3,500 people in Drogheda — comprising around 2,700 Royalist soldiers and all the men in the town carrying arms, including civilians, prisoners, and Catholic priests — fuelled Irish-English, Catholic-Protestant strife for over three centuries. [12]

The Qur'an and Islam

The Bible is not unique in it depiction of violence, retribution, and a jealous God. The heart of Islamic belief is that there is no God but God and that God is Allah.

- "God is Great" "Allah is great." "Worship none but Allah." *Qur'an 2:83*
- One's fate is determined by whether one believes this or not. For those who do not believe, "Allah has set a seal upon their hearts and upon their hearing and there is a covering of their eyes, and there is a great punishment for them." *Qur'an 2:7*
- While some passages of the Qur'an preach tolerance of other beliefs, others do not. "Of those who reject faith the patrons are the Evil Ones: from light they will lead them forth into the depths of darkness. They will be Companions of the Fire, to dwell therein." *Qur'an 2:257*
- "O you who believe! Do not take the Jews and the Christians for friends; they are friends of each other; and whoever amongst you takes them for a friend, then surely he is one of them." *Qur'an 5:51*
- "Whoever acts in opposition to Allah and His Apostle, he shall surely have the fire of hell to abide in it." *Qur'an 9:63*

These and many other passages easily provide religious fundamentalists with permission to undertake wars, violence and terrorism. Seeing the enemy as subhuman is a critical aspect of the process that allows one set of humans to kill or maim other humans. [4] Passages of both the Bible and the Qur'an can provide cover for extremists who genuinely believe those outside the faith are "infidels," "heathens," or other dehumanizing labels.

The Assassins. The Assassins operated over a period of two centuries from 1090 to 1275. As with the Islamic extremists of today they sought to spread a pure form of Islam. [4] Unlike today's terrorists who kill indiscriminately, the Assassins stabbed specific individuals, such as politicians or religious leaders. This killing in close proximity to the victim virtually assured the Assassins would be caught and often put to death themselves. In this sense they resembled the suicide bombers of today. They seriously threatened several Turkish governments.

Wahhabinism. By the 1700s the once-powerful Islamic Ottoman empire was in serious disarray. Western Europe was in its ascendancy intellectually, scientifically, commercially, and militarily, and the Islamic empire struggled unsuccessfully to keep up. In the Arabian peninsula, Muhammad ibn Abd al-Wahhab (1703–1792) broke away from Istanbul and created a state of his own. His response to the increasing secularization of the empire was to return to a more puritanical form of Islam with a strict moral code based on a literal interpretation of the Qur'an. [6] He issued a religious decree, or *fatwa,* stating that all non-Wahhabia were infidels, thus allowing the persecution of innocent people. [4] In his book, *The Crisis of Islam. Holy War and Unholy Terror,* Bernard Lewis [13p122] reports:

> Whenever they could, they enforced their beliefs with the utmost severity and ferocity, demolishing tombs, desecrating what they called false and idolatrous holy places, and slaughtering large numbers of men, women and children who failed to meet their standards of Islamic purity and authenticity. Another practice introduced by ibn Abd al-Wahhab was the condemnation and burning of books. These consisted mainly of Islamic works on theology and law deemed contrary to Wahhabi doctrine. The burning of books was often accompanied by the summary execution of those who wrote, copied, or taught them. [13p128]

Wahhabinism was only a minor Islamic sect under the Ottomans. However, it became a major global political force after oil-rich Saudi Arabia adopted its religious rigors in 1933.

> This resulted in Wahhabinism becoming the official, state-enforced doctrine of one of the most influential governments in all Islam — the custodian of the two holiest places of Islam, the host of the annual pilgrimage, which brings millions of Muslims from every part of the world to share in its rites and rituals. At the same time, the teachers and preachers of Wahhabinism had at their disposal immense financial resources, which they used to promote and spread their version of Islam.

Wahhabinism enforces a restrictive dress code, restricts the freedoms of women, cuts off the hands of thieves, and practices many other restrictive practices. In the Qur'an *jihad,* meaning "struggle," has two meanings. The meaning adopted by most Muslims refers to an internal spiritual struggle to conform to the teachings of Muhammad. A second meaning refers to a military-type struggle of Islam against infidels. The latter is the meaning adopted by Wahhabins. Wahhabinism forms the basis for the beliefs of the Taliban and Osama bin Laden. Its philosophical anti-secular, anti-modernity, anti-infidel underpinnings are largely responsible for the hatred toward Western culture seen in modern Islamic terrorism. Jessica Stern in her book, *Terror in the Name of God,* stated:

> Modernity introduces a world where the potential future paths are so varied, so unknown, and the lack of authority is so great that individuals seek assurance and comfort in the elimination of unsettling possibilities.

Too much choice, especially regarding identity, can be overwhelming and even frightening. Under these circumstances, some people crave closing off options; they crave discipline imposed from the outside. The "strictness" of militant religious groups — and the clarity they offer about self and other is part of their appeal. [4p69]

Purifying the world through holy war is addictive. Holy war intensifies the boundaries between Us and Them, satisfying the inherently human longing for a clearer identity and a definite purpose in life, creating a seductive state of bliss. [4p137]

Religion is the ideal mobilization tool for violence. [4p137] "Whatever universalist goals they may have, religions give people identity by posting a basic distinction between believers and nonbelievers, between a superior in-group and a different inferior out-group." [14]

Mixing this with the Muslim claim that "There is no correct religion besides God but Islam" [4 13398p83] makes a particularly dangerous combination. Unfortunately, "each generation of Islamic fundamentalism becomes uglier and uglier." [4p136]

Suicide bombings and Islam. Apologists for Islamic terrorism often claim Islam is a peaceful religion and that there is nothing in the Qur'an to justify suicide bombings. That is belied by the following:

> The believers who stay at home…are not the equal of those who fight for the cause of God with their goods and their persons…God has promised all a good reward; but far richer is the recompense of those who fight for Him….He that leaves his dwelling to fight for God and His apostle and is then overtaken by death, shall be rewarded by God….The unbelievers are your inveterate enemies.
>
> *Qur'an 4:95-101*

Multiple virgins are part of the promised heavenly reward. Sam Harris suggested that the Qur'an makes suicide bombing "seem like a career opportunity." [5]

Islam and the selling of nuclear secrets. Abdul Qadeer Khan was the father of Pakistan's nuclear bomb, and for decades was the highly respected head of their nuclear program. However, it later became apparent that for over a decade he masterminded a vast, clandestine, and hugely profitable enterprise of selling nuclear secrets to the rogue nations of the world — North Korea, Iran and Libya. He "did more to destabilize the planet than did many of the world's worst regimes." [15] Why did he do this? After the successful nuclear tests in 1998, bringing Pakistan into the nuclear club, Kahn became more religious, and he was doing this to bolster the standing of Muslims in the world. He has been quoted as saying, "We Muslims have to be strong and equal to any other country, and therefore I want to help some countries to be strong." The danger of placing nuclear bombs in the hands of individuals or governments who have no fear of dying and believe that dying in the name of Allah is a "career opportunity" and "Allah's will" is self-evident.

Belief in the Apocalypse

All three monotheistic traditions incorporate the concept of an apocalypse. [4p322-323] However, each believes it will be the one to prevail in the catastrophic events of the final days. This itself can lead to terrorist acts. Evangelical Christians believe that Jesus will return at the Mount of Olives overlooking the temple. Both they and Messianic Jews believe that rebuilding the Temple Mount is a prerequisite to the process of redemption. Unfortunately, the Muslim Dome of the Rock, believed to be the site where Muhammad rose to heaven, was built in 688 CE on the site of the Temple Mount. In 1984, to facilitate the rebuilding of the Temple Mount, Yoel Lerner, a radical Messianic Jew, plotted to blow up the Dome of the Rock, the third most holy site for Muslims. He believed the Messiah could not return when the sacred site was "polluted" by the Dome of the Rock? The only reason he did not carry out this task was that he could not find a Rabbi to bless the plan. In her book, *The Battle for God. A History of Fundamentalism,* Karen Armstrong notes: [6p148]

> It was a perilous moment. Not only would the bombing of the Dome of the Rock have ended the peace process, it would almost certainly have resulted in a war in which, for the first time, the whole Muslim world would have joined forces against Israel. Strategists in Washington agreed that, in the context of the Cold War, when the Soviets supported the Arabs and the United States, [supported] Israel, the destruction of the Dome of the Rock could well have sparked World War III. The specter of nuclear catastrophe did not trouble these extreme Kookists, however. They were convinced that by instigating the apocalypse here on Earth, they would activate powers in the divine world and "oblige" God to intervene on their behalf and send the Messiah to save Israel.

As with the Muslims described above, these extremists also have no fear of mass death and see it as a good thing. The horror of 9/11 and many more incidents make it quite likely that if the human race destroys itself, it will be over religious rather than political issues. Post 9/11 efforts to accelerate the apocalypse and the return of the messiah by all three Western religions may contribute to this conflict [16]. Since Evangelical Christians believe that the messiah will not return until every person on earth is converted, they are expanding their proselytizing efforts to bring this about. Christians are supportive of the Jews because they believe the messiah will return to the Temple in Jerusalem. For the Jews, the downside of this support is that the Jews who have not converted to Christianity will "be left behind." Some Jews are attempting to rebuild the ancient Temple in preparation for the appearance of their messiah. The problem with this plan has already been described.

In 2004, when Mahmoud Ahmadinejad, the president of Iran, was mayor of Tehran, he spent millions improving the city in preparation for the return of their messiah, the Mahdi. As Ahmadinejad stated in his United Nations speech, the Mahdi will emerge from a well to conquer the world and convert everyone to Islam.

Members of each religion believe that when their messiah returns the other religions will be destroyed. This clearly contains the seeds for future conflict.

Eastern Religions

While the Eastern religions are often considered to be less violent than the monotheist religions of the West, Japanese Buddhism declared all Japanese wars as holy wars. "The religious atrocities of devotees of Shinto, which inspired Japanese militarism through World War II, are too notorious to be overlooked." [17]

Sacred Texts

Given the violence portrayed in the sacred religious texts and by some people who live by these texts, the following quote from Nelson-Pallmeyer is not an unreasonable suggestion:

> The violence-of-God traditions in the Hebrew Scriptures, the Christian New Testament, and the Qur'an must be understood and challenged if we are to have any realistic hope of building a peaceful world. [9]

He also suggested that the religious violence prevalent among the followers of monotheistic faith traditions is not primarily a problem of believers distorting their "sacred" texts. It is, rather, a problem rooted in the violence-of-God traditions that lie at the heart of those "sacred" texts. The sacred texts cannot be challenged because they are perceived as being the direct word of God. [9] *A rational first step to tone down the violence done in the name of religion would be to accept that the sacred texts were not written by Yahweh, God or Allah, but by man.*

Recent Religious Wars

Sam Harris [5] has given the following listing of recent religious wars: Palestine (Jews v. Muslims), the Balkans (Orthodox Serbians v. Catholic Croatians, Bosnian and Albanian Muslims), Northern Ireland (Protestants v. Catholics), Kashmir (Muslims v. Hindus), Sudan (Muslims v. Christians and animists), Nigeria (Muslims v. Christians), Ethiopia and Eritrea (Muslims v. Christians), Sri Lanka (Sinhalese Buddhists v. Tamil Hindus), Indonesia (Muslims v. Timorese Christians), and the Caucasus (Orthodox Russians v. Chechen Muslims and Muslim Azerbaijanis v. Catholic and Orthodox Armenians). It is clear that the capacity for humans to kill each other over religious differences knows no end.

Negative Health Consequences of Religion

Religious beliefs can have a negative impact on health if beliefs based on isolated Biblical passages are taken out of context and interpreted literally. This may lead believers to the conclusion that God, rather than humans, will bring about a cure.

The negative impact of this may take the form of refusing life-saving medication or treatments, unduly delaying medical care, refusing blood transfusions, refusing childhood immunizations, refusing prenatal care and physician assisted delivery, replacing mental health care with religion, and fostering mass suicide. [18]

Some of these negative effects are amenable to objective study. For example, a religious group called Faith Assembly practices out-of-hospital, non-physician attended birthing without prenatal care. In a county in Indiana, zero percent of the Faith Assembly subjects had at least one prenatal visit compared to 99 percent for the non-Faith Assembly women. Perinatal mortality was three times greater and maternal mortality was almost 100 times greater in Faith Assembly women compared to non-Faith Assembly women. [19]

Christian Scientists who rarely consult doctors provide a second example. Age-adjusted death rates were significantly higher ($p = .003$) in Christian Science women than non-Christian Science women. [20]

Religious opposition to birth control contributes to overpopulation, and the proscription against the use of condoms and the exchange of needles, have contributed to the acceleration of the spread of AIDS in both Africa and the United States. The proscription of many religious groups against stem cell research threatens to deprive thousands of those affected with Parkinson's disease, juvenile diabetes, and other diseases of a potential cure. The proscription against abortion denies women control over their own reproduction and can be especially counterproductive when the mothers and the fathers are not ready to be responsible parents. While controversial, Steven Levitt, award-winning economist, has suggested that the recent dramatic drop in the crime rate is due, in part, to the legalization of abortion decades previously. This resulted in a decrease in the birth rate of children whose parents were unable to properly parent them. [21]

Examples of mass suicide related to religious beliefs and cults include the 800 members of the Rev. Jim Jones' People's Temple cult who died in Guyana in 1978, the 72 members of David Koresch's Branch Davidians who died in 1993, and the 39 members of Marshall Applewhite's Heaven's Gate cult who died in 1997 believing that aliens hidden behind the Hale-Bopp comet would come and take them to a better place. [18]

The literal interpretation of sacred texts. Virtually all of the evils of religion can be ascribed to the belief that the sacred texts, whether the Bible or the Qur'an or others, represent the word of God or Allah, and thus believers assume every word is literally true. Sam Harris [5p73] summarized the madness of this as follows:

Jesus Christ — who, as it turns out, was born of a virgin, cheated death, and rose bodily into the heavens — can now be eaten in the form of a cracker. A few Latin words spoken over your favorite Burgundy, and you can drink his blood as well. Is there any doubt that a lone subscriber to these beliefs would be considered mad? Rather, is there any doubt he would be mad? The danger of religious faith is that it allows otherwise normal human beings to reap the fruits of madness and consider them holy. Because each new generation of children is taught that religious propositions need not be justified in the way that all others must, civilization is still besieged by the armies of the preposterous. We are, even now, killing ourselves over ancient literature. Who would have thought something so tragically absurd could be possible?

Fundamentalism and Politics

Fundamentalists and related Christian sects tend to come in two flavors: *premillennialist* and *postmillennialist.* The premillennialist believes that the end of times will come before the return of Christ. When Christ does return he will bring with him a thousand years of peace and heaven on earth. For premillennialists, every major natural catastrophe such as earthquakes or tsunamis are believed to be the beginning of the end. Those who believe that the end of time is near tend not to become involved in politics since it would be pointless. Postmillennialists believe that righteousness and justice will gradually spread and last for a thousand years and when Christ does come again the earth will be purified for his appearance. This has important implications since if the reign of God comes gradually then it is the duty of Christians to take control of the political and secular institutions and run them according to Biblical dictates. This leads to "dominion theology" based on the first chapter of the Book of Genesis in which God, having created Adam and Eve, says to them: [22]

> Be fruitful, and multiply, and replenish the earth, and subdue it: and have dominion over the fish of the sea, and over the fowl of the air, and over every living thing that moveth upon the face of the earth.
>
> *Genesis 1:28*

Thus, according to this view, Christians are to take dominion over all major institutions and run them until Christ returns. Even premillennialists can buy into this philosophy if they make a modest adjustment in faith by believing the end of days will come before Christ appears, but this may be some time from now. The concept of Biblical law was taken to the extreme by theologian Rousas John Rushdoony. [22p393] He insisted that the Old Testament laws mandating the death penalty for adulterers, homosexuals, blasphemers, those who engage in premarital sex, astrologers, witches, and teachers of false doctrine should be enforced today. This piece of literal fundamentalist nonsense would eliminate half of the population and make the Holocaust look like child's play.

There are many examples of the inhumanity of man toward his fellow man undertaken in the name of religion. The violence-of-God traditions in the Hebrew Scriptures, the Christian New Testament, and the Qur'an must be understood and challenged if we are to have

any realistic hope of building a peaceful world. Standing in the way of this is the fact that these texts are perceived as being the direct word of God and thus are literally true.

A rational first step toward toning down the violence done in the name of religion would be to promote the understanding that the sacred texts were not written by Yahweh, God or Allah, but by man. They should be viewed as metaphorical, with the realization that one metaphor is not inherently better than another.

Without such an understanding it is more likely that mankind will self-destruct over religion than over any other issue.

References

1. Avalos, H. *Fighting Words. The Origins of Religious Violence.* Prometheus Books, Amherst, NY, 2005.
2. Schopenhauer, A. *Parga and Paralipomena: Short Philosophical Essays.* in: Payen, E. E. J. Clarendon, Oxford. 1974.
3. Schwartz, R. M. *The Curse of Cain: The Violent Legacy of Monotheism.* The University of Chicago Press, Chicago, 1997.
4. Stern, J. *Terror in the Name of God.* Harper Collins Publishers, Inc, New York, 2003.
5. Harris, S. *The End of Faith. Religion, Terror and the Future of Reason.* W. W. Norton & Company, Ltd, New York, 2005.
6. Armstrong, K. *The Battle for God. A History of Fundamentalism.* The Random House Publishing Group, New York, 2000.
7. Juergensmeyer, M. *Terror in the Mind of God.* University of Calfornia Press, Berkeley, CA, 2000.
8. Stark, R. *One True God.* Princeton University Press, Princeton, NJ, 2001.
9. Nelson-Pallmeyer, J. *Is Religion Killing Us?* Trinity Press Intenational, Harrisburg, PA, 2003.
9a. Dawkins, Richard. *The God Delusion.* Houghton Mifflin, Co., Boston, MA. 2006.
10. Asbridge, T. The First Crusade. Oxford University Press, NY, 2004.
11. Hill, J. H. & Hill, L. L. Raymond D'Aguilers: *Historia Francorum Qui Cerperunt Iherusalem.* American Philosophical Society. 1968.
12. Anonymous. Oliver Cromwell. The History Channel, 2005.
13. Lewis, B. *The Crisis of Islam.* The Modern Library, New York, 2003.
14. Huntington, S. *The Clash of Civilizations and the Remaking of World Order.* Simon and Schuster, New York, 1996.
15. Hasmaom, G. The Man Who Sold the Bomb. *Time.* 22-31, 2005.
16. Sahagun, L. Plotting the Exit Strategy. *Los Angeles Times,* Los Angeles, June 22, 2006.
17. Marty, M. E. *Is Religion the Problem?* Tikkun 2002.
18. Koenig, H. G., M.D., McCullough, M. E., Ph.D. & Larson, D. B., M.D. *Handbook of Religion and Health.* Oxford University Press, NewYork, 2001.
19. Spence, C., Danielson, T. S. & Kaunitz, A. M. The Faith Assembly: a study of perinatal and maternal mortality. *Indiana Med.* 77: 180-183, 1984.
20. Simpson, W. F. Comparative longevity in a college cohort of Christian Scientists. *The Journal of the American Medical Association.* 262: 1657-1658, 1989.
21. Levitt, S. D. & Dubner, S. J. *Freakonomics. A Rogue Economist Explores the Hidden Side of Everything.* Wiliam Morrow, New York, 2005.
22. Cox, H. *Fire from Heaven.* Da Capo Press, Cambridge, MA, 1995.

Religions are social systems whose participants avow belief in a supernatural agent or agents whose approval is to be sought.

Daniel C Dennett
Breaking the Spell[1]

By definition, a supernatural event is beyond the reach of scientific investigation.

Harold Koenig
The Healing Power of Faith[2]

Chapter 49

The Benefits of Religion

Despite the numerous evils of religion presented in the previous chapter, the positive attributes of religion far outweigh the negatives. One principle reason for this is that although the evils can negatively impact many thousands and sometimes millions of people, the positives can potentially impact most of the rest of humanity—totaling billions. Religion is mostly a matter of individual faith and has the potential to bring great comfort and peace to all who believe; as outlined previously, most members of our species believe in God. One of the premises of this book is that man is hardwired for spirituality and for belief in a supreme being. A belief in God is the ultimate outcome of the workings of the human spiritual brain, and most humans who believe in God ascribe to some formalized framework for this belief—namely religion.

A partial list of the benefits of religion includes health benefits of belief and prayer, spirituality as a life-changing event, a sense of being grounded by belonging to something larger and more important than oneself, a supportive structure for baptisms, weddings, and funerals, assurance of moral behavior, helping to provide a cohesive and stable community, a reason to help others, the comfort and support of belief, the feeling that someone is there to support you unconditionally, someone who will forgive your sins, real or imagined, and perhaps most importantly, a lessened fear of death based on a belief in a life after death. Some passages of both the Bible and Qur'an are pure poetry and provide great emotional support. An example is the Lord's Prayer given by Jesus to his disciples.

Our Father which art in heaven,
Hallowed be thy name.
Thy Kingdom come,
Thy will be done on earth,
as it is in heaven,
Give us this day our daily bread.
And forgive us our debts,

as we forgive our debtors.
And lead us not into temptation;
but deliver us from evil:
For thine is the kingdom, and the power,
and the glory, for ever, Amen.

Matthew 6:9-13 (KJV)

The comfort different versions of this prayer can provide has undoubtedly been experienced billions of times in the past two millennia. When sung by beautiful voices by a church choir even the most jaded atheist would be moved to tears. There are dozens of other equally poetic and moving passages.

The following pages review the beneficial aspects of religion and faith that are most amenable to scientific investigation. In scientific studies it is necessary to have a non-biased or epidemiologically sound study group, a control group, a hypothesis, a well-defined end point, and a valid statistical analysis of the results. As an example one might start with the hypothesis that religious faith decreases one's likelihood of being depressed. A reasonable study might choose 500 individuals who are matched by race, age, gender, geographical location, and social class. All individuals could be given a well-validated and standardized assessment of depression, and the frequency of such depression would be compared in 250 subjects who belonged to a specific religious faith versus 250 subjects who did not. If there were a statistically significant decrease in depression in the religious group, the hypothesis would appear to have been supported. Before having total confidence in the result, most scientists would wait to see if other researchers could replicate the findings.

Religion and Health

The role of religion and faith in health has been extensively studied largely because health issues provide a more objective outcome than more subjective and non-specific outcomes, such as a sense of "feeling good." The literature on this subject is very large and readers interested in a comprehensive review of hundreds of reports are referred to the *Handbook of Religion and Health*.[3] Because twin studies are often large and thus provide good statistical power, and because they also allow an examination of the role of genetic factors, I will also review some of these.

General mental health. Larson and coworkers[4] reviewed 35 reports concerning the effect of religious commitment and mental health reported in the two major American psychiatric journals between 1978 and 1989. In the majority of the reports there was a positive effect of religious commitment on mental health, especially when measured on the basis of involvement in ceremony, social support, use of prayer, and a perceived positive relationship with God.

Death anxiety. As discussed previously, awareness of one's own mortality is a unique characteristic of the human species and may have played a role in the development of religion. Support for the effectiveness of religion in assuaging such fears comes from a study of the relationship between death anxiety and religious belief in several hundred elderly people attending senior lunch programs. Of those who reported they were "very likely" to rely on religious faith and prayer when under stress, 10.3 percent experienced death anxiety, compared to 25 percent of less-religious people. [5]

Smoking. Several religions, such as the Mormons and Seventh-Day Adventists, specifically request that their members not smoke or drink. Independent of these groups, even among the more mainstream denominations, religiosity is associated with lower rates of smoking. For example, in a study of almost 4,000 older people in North Carolina, those who both attended religious services at least once a week and prayed or studied the Bible at least daily were 90 percent less likely to smoke than people not involved in these activities. [6] As outlined below, religiosity is also associated with a decrease in other types of substance abuse.

Adolescent Problem Behavior Syndrome. The relationship between the role of religion and adolescent behavior is complex. In 1977 Richard and Shirley Jessor [7] from the University of Colorado found that prevalence of alcohol abuse, drug abuse, smoking, delinquent behavior, precocious sexual intercourse and teenage pregnancies were all strongly correlated with each other. Adolescents with any one of these behaviors were more likely to have one or more of the other behaviors. This became known as the *Adolescent Problem Behavior Syndrome.* [8,9] They also found that adolescents with this syndrome were less likely to indulge in conforming behaviors such as regular attendance of school or church. Statistical analysis indicated all of these behaviors were associated with an underlying latent variable that they termed *unconventionality.* An independent study of American high school seniors by Bachman and coworkers [10] showed that while increased religious commitment was associated with a decreased use of alcohol, pot, tobacco and other drugs, a similar level of decreased use was noted for non-religious variables, such as having good grades. This is shown in Figure 1.

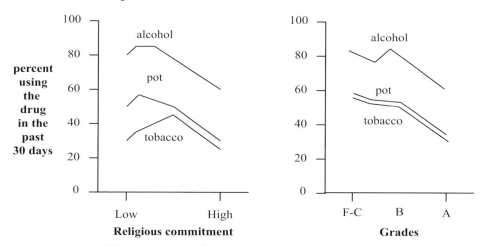

Figure 1. Association of religious commitment and good grades with decreased use of alcohol, pot, and tobacco in a group of American high school seniors. From Bachman et al., J Public Health. 71:59-69, 1981. [10] Reprinted with permission from the American Public Health Association

There was also a strong trend in those with low versus high religious commitment to increased alcohol, drug and tobacco use, high versus low truancy, radical versus conservative political views, and spending most nights out versus staying at home.

As discussed previously antisocial behavior, conduct disorder, and adolescent problem behavior syndrome have a strong genetic basis. This raises the point that studies showing a positive effect of church attendance and religious affiliation on preventing substance abuse and other antisocial behaviors may not be as straightforward as they seem on the surface. Thus, instead of the simple relationship shown in the following diagram,

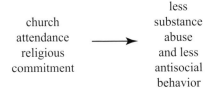

the relationship may be more complex. The following diagram is a possible example,

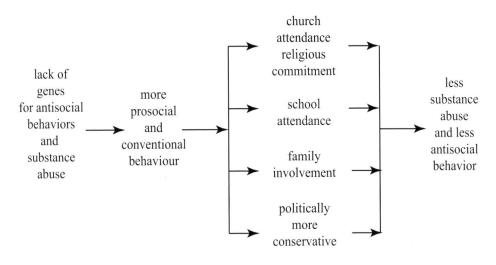

Here, part of the reason individuals with considerable religious affiliation have less antisocial or other behaviors is due to a hidden latent variable, one's genetic make-up, that primarily controls a range of problem behaviors and secondarily leads to religious commitment and other prosocial traits.

Substance abuse. A twin study by Boomsma and colleagues in the Netherlands [11] found support for the role of religious upbringing in the prevention of substance abuse and antisocial behaviors *even taking the contribution of genetics into consideration.* They examined 1,967 twins and showed that a religious upbringing *reduced the influence of genetic factors on disruptive behaviors in males.* Even more striking, a related study [12] found that in non-religious families, genetic factors accounted for 40 percent of why females started to drink. By contrast, in religious families the religious upbringing accounted for low levels of starting to drink in females, while genetic factors played no role.

In a study in Missouri of 1,687 female adolescent twins, Heath and coworkers [13] also reported a strong protective effect of religious involvement against alcohol use. This was particularly significant in African-American adolescent girls. Other studies confirm the role of religiosity in the prevention of alcohol and drug abuse in Caucasian adolescent females. [14,15]

As described previously, in the twin study by Kendler and coworkers [16] religiosity was measured by the variables of *personal devotion, personal conservatism,* and *institutional conservatism.* They found that high levels of *personal devotion* were associated with lower-than-average levels of depression but not with lower levels of anxiety or somatic complaints. There was a highly significant association of decreased alcohol use and nicotine dependence with all three measures of religiosity. [16,17] High levels of both *personal devotion* and *institutional conservatism* were associated with resistance to depression in the face of the stress of the death of a loved one or personal illness. [17]

Treatment of substance abuse. Many studies have shown the important role of religion in the treatment of substance abuse. One of the first was reported by David Desmond and J. Maddux at the University of Texas Health Science Center in San Antonio, Texas. They found that among male heroin addicts undergoing treatment at a public health service hospital, after one year into recovery those who were in a religious-based recovery program were almost eight times more likely to report abstinence than those involved in a purely secular, non-religious program. [18]

One of the major problems in treatment of drug and alcohol abuse is the presence of continual craving. There is some evidence that individuals involved in religious based programs may feel less of this intense craving than those in non-religious programs, possibly the result of a greater level of inner peace. [2p81] George Valliant, Harvard Medical School psychiatrist and pioneer in the treatment of substance abuse, suggested that to successfully recover from chronic drug and alcohol addictions, patients need "powerful new sources of self-esteem and hope" [19] and forgiveness of past sins. This may be the element that religion can supply.

Multiple studies have consistently shown that several measures of religiousness are associated with lower levels of abuse of alcohol, drugs and tobacco. Religion can also play a strong supportive role in the treatment of substance abuse.

Depression. Prevention of depression is one of the most widely replicated effects of religion. Three dimensions of religious activities are commonly recognized. These are organizational religious activities (the social aspects of religion such as church attendance), nonorganizational religious activities (private prayer and Bible reading) and subjective religiousness (importance of religion to the individual, intrinsic religiosity). So many studies have been done on the role of organizational religious activity and depression that instead of relating the individual results, it is more useful to simply state that 85 percent of these studies support a protective effect against depression. [3p124] The magnitude of this effect is illustrated by the finding that the frequency of depression was 20 to 60 percent higher in those individuals who had no involvement in organizational religious activities. The finding that non-organizational or private religious activity was less protective against depression than organizational religious activity further emphasized the role of social factors. However, statistical analysis showed that while the social aspects of organizational religious activities played an important role, they were not the entire explanation for the prevention of depression. *Intrinsic religiosity,* where religious faith was personally very important, was more protective against depression than *extrinsic religiosity,* where individuals became involved in religion for social prestige and affirmation of one's lifestyle. [3p127]

Studies also show an impressive role of intrinsic religiosity on remission of depression in depressed older adults hospitalized for medical illness. A high score for intrinsic religiosity was associated with a 70 percent increase in the rate of remission of depression. [20] A more detailed portrayal of the results is shown in Figure 2.

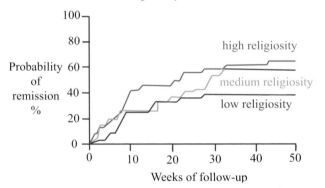

Figure 2. Survival curves for remission of depression based on level of intrinsic religiosity. From Koenig et al.: American Journal of Psychiatry. *155: 536-542, 1998. [20] By permission.*

Among the subjects whose physical illness did not improve, the rate of remission from depression doubled for each 10 percent increase in the intrinsic religiosity score.

Many studies have shown that involvement in organizational religious activity, such as church-going, and intrinsic religiosity where faith is personally important, are associated with decreased levels of depression. Rates of recovery from depression among the elderly is significantly increased with higher levels of intrinsic religiosity.

Extrinsic religiosity, where individuals are involved in religious activity simply for social prestige, is associated with increased levels of depression.

Heart disease. In a study of almost 4,000 men and women 65 years of age and older, [21] those who often attended religious service and read the Bible frequently were

40 percent less likely to have hypertension than those who attended church or read the Bible infrequently. In an even larger study of 10,059 Israeli civil servants followed over 25 years, the highly orthodox Jews experienced a lower risk of dying of coronary artery disease than less-orthodox, secular or non-religious Jews. [22] The survival curves in this study are shown in Figure 3.

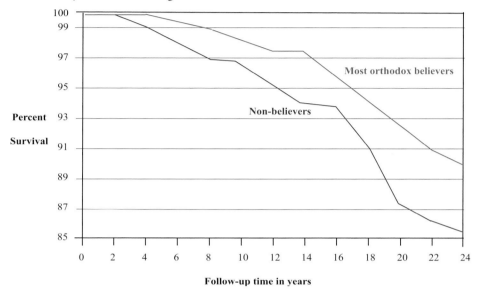

Figure 3. Survival curves showing mortality from coronary heart disease among Jewish orthodox believers and nonbelievers. From Goldbourt et al.: Cardiology. 82:100-121, 199 S. Karger AG, Basel. [22] By permission.

They were also at a lower risk of dying from all natural causes. This was not explained by health factors such as not smoking, having a lower blood pressure, or lower cholesterol level. Again, *the belief in an all-powerful God who intervenes directly in their lives was the most important factor.*

In the section below on the effectiveness of prayer, one of the endpoints was the number of complications seen following heart surgery. Oxman and coworkers [23] used this variable in a study of the role of religion in health. They selected 232 patients 55 years of age and older who were undergoing heart surgery for coronary artery disease or valve replacement. Individuals who were both socially active and derived comfort from their faith were 14 times less likely to die in the six months following surgery than those who lacked these factors. *Of the religious factors the degree of strength and comfort from religion was the most important.*

Immune function. Lymphocytes are one of the major elements of the immune system that protect us from insults including injury, bacteria and viruses. Cytokines are chemical compounds produced during the inflammatory response to these objects. High levels of one of these cytokines, interleukin-6 (IL-6), are an indicator of a weakened immune system. A study of 1,718 elderly subjects showed that those involved in a high level of attendance of religious services were 50 percent less likely to have high IL-6 levels compared to those who did not attend religious services. Religious attendance was also associated with lower levels of other immune-inflammatory markers. [24]

Life Span. It should come as no surprise that with religiosity being associated with so many health benefits that it would also be associated with a longer life span. In 1997 William Strawbridge [25] reported a large study on the role of religiosity and longevity. He followed 5,286 people between the ages of 21 and 65 living in Alameda County, California. In addition to its large size, an additional unique aspect of this study was that it continued over a long period of time—from 1965 to 1994. When complete, it showed that the hazard of dying at a given age was 36 percent less for people who attended church services frequently versus those who attended less than once per week. While close family ties and friendships were identified as one of the protective factors, when these were factored out there was still a 23 percent decrease in the rate of dying for church attendees. The association between frequent church attendance and lower mortality was greater for women than for men. The effects of a healthier lifestyle and close social ties only accounted for 30 percent of the reduction in mortality. It is likely that a sense of inner peace associated with a deep personal faith accounted for most of the effect.

These results agree with those of an earlier smaller study of 2,754 Midwestern men and women aged 35 to 69 followed for 12 years. Among women who never attended church, 17.3 percent died. By contrast, among women who attended church often, 5.4 percent died. [26] One study suggested that *deriving strength from religion was the strongest predictor of survival.* [27]

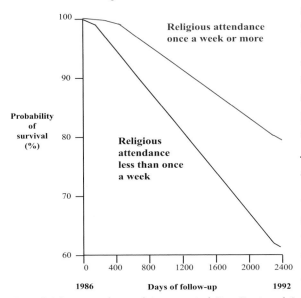

In a study designed to see if the results of the Strawbridge study could be replicated on the east coast, Koenig and colleagues [28] followed 3,968 people 65 years of age or older in the Piedomont area of North Carolina for six years. The results are shown in Figure 4.

Figure 4. Religious attendance and six-year survival. From Koenig et al.: J Gerontol A Biol Sci Med Sci. 54:M370-376, 1999. [28] By permission.

There was a significantly lower probability of dying in those with religious attendance of once a week or more. As in other studies, the effect was stronger in women than men.

The largest study of religiosity and mortality to date was by Hummer and coworkers. [29] They followed a random national sample of 21,204 adults from 1987 to

1995. Those who did not attend church lived to an average age 75.3 years. Those who attended church at least once a week lived to an average age of 81.9 years.

A number of studies suggest individuals with strong religious beliefs live longer than those without such beliefs.

Does Prayer Work?

Q: "When did you realize you were God?"
A: "While praying. I realized I was talking to myself."

Peter Medak, Director
The Ruling Class

Untold billions of inhabitants of the planet earth pray occasionally or often. Does all of this praying have any effect? The famous and outspoken atheist, Madeline Murray O'Hair, characterized praying as "Talking to yourself." If man created God then her assessment would be fundamentally correct. But, that still does not answer the question, "Does prayer work?" As shown in the chapter on placebo effect, if one strongly believes something will be effective, especially with regard to one's health, it will be effective, even when there is no active ingredient.

When attempting to scientifically evaluate the effectiveness of prayer, there are several different types of prayer. *Petitionary prayer* occurs when a person prays to God to do something such as heal an illness or protect them from death or other evil. A second form of prayer is when someone else prays for you. This is called *intercessory prayer*. It can be done either with or without the person knowing they are being prayed for. *Petitionary prayer* allows the placebo effect to play a role in effecting the outcome. Other types of prayer, such as prayer of confession, contemplative prayer, and meditative prayer do not provide the expectation of an objective result, so their effectiveness is difficult to assess. I will first examine the effectiveness of *petitionary prayer*.

Petitionary prayer. When an individual prays it is often used as a coping mechanism. A soldier who prays on the battlefield may feel he is being protected from death and thus will act more bravely. A number of studies have shown that individuals feel that praying helped them to cope with stress. The endpoint in these studies is very subjective. In a study of 100 patients filling out a *Helpfulness of Prayer Scale* immediately prior to coronary artery bypass surgery, 96 patients felt it helped them to cope. [30] Of these 70 ranked it a 15 on a scale of 0 to 15. A similar coping effect of prayer has been reported for cancer patients [31] and adult hospitalized patients. [30] Benson [32] observed objective effects of prayer in cardiac patients in the form of a decreased heart rate, blood pressure and number of episodes of angina. Similar effects have been observed with relaxation exercises and meditation. [33,34]

Affirming personal values. Part of the effectiveness of *petitionary prayer* may come about as a result of re-affirming one's personal values. In a study of 80 UCLA undergraduates, Creswell and coworkers [35] found that any *positive self-affirmation acts as a buffer against stressful events.* Prior to being exposed to a very stressful event the students in the study group were asked to reflect on values that were *especially meaningful* to them. These ranged from religious values to secular ones, including political beliefs or social values. The control group was asked to reflect on values that were *unimportant and not meaningful* to them. Blood levels of cortisol, a powerful stress hormone, were assayed after the stressful event. When stimulated continuously over time, cortisol can lead to cognitive impairments and increased risk for physical disease. There was significantly less release of cortisol in the study group who reflected on meaningful personal values before the stress than in the control group.

The authors remarked that it was "remarkable that such a brief, subtle value affirmation has the ability to mute cortisol response and serve as a buffer against stress....It's helpful to remind yourself you're a good person with talents, and remind yourself what is important to you; that can be hard to do when you're going through something that's really awful." Since religious beliefs are a very important part of the value system for many people, this study helps us to understand the powerful effect that self-affirmation in the form of prayer can have to reduce stress and increase coping. An equally important result of the study was that reflecting on non-religious value systems can also reduce stress and increase coping.

Intercessory prayer. When individuals are not aware of the praying, the power of placebo effect is removed. Evidence that intercessory prayer does not work would not prove that God does not exist since God might be ignoring those prayers. However, evidence that intercessory prayer does work would provide some presumptive evidence for the existence of God, since a supernatural force would be one of the few viable explanations for such an effect. Thus, it is not surprising that many attempts to prove or disprove the effectiveness of intercessory prayer have been undertaken.

Longevity of kings. Francis Galton, one of the fathers of statistical genetics, reasoned that since everyone in England was constantly praying for the king in the form of "Long live the king" and other prayers, if prayer was effective, kings should live longer than their subjects. Galton found that in fact, "Sovereigns were literally the shortest lived of all who have the advantage of affluence." Galton reasoned that members of the clergy should also have longer lives since they were the most "prayerful class" of all and among the most prayed for. It turned out that when Galton compared the longevity of eminent clergy with eminent doctors and lawyers, the clergy were the shortest lived of these three groups. Galton also reasoned that ships carrying missionaries should sink less often since they would be constantly praying for safe passage. There was no difference in rates of sinking of these ships compared with others.

Sex ratios. Rupert Sheldrake, a contemporary of Galton, knew that in India male children were preferred over female children, and a great deal of prayer was expended attempting to influence this outcome. However, he found that the male : female sex ratio was the same, 106:100 in both India and England.

Modern studies of intercessory prayer. Several high visibility reports that intercessory prayer is effective have been published. [36-38] However, each of these had significant problems with statistical analysis, [39] randomization of cases, [40] study design [41] or outright fraud. [41]

One of the best evaluations of intercessory prayer ever undertaken was a multi-center study led by Dr. Herbert Benson of Harvard Medical School. A total of 1,800 subjects involved in heart bypass surgery were divided into three groups of about 600 each consisting of those who were prayed for and knew they were being prayed for, those who were prayed for and only knew it was a possibility they were prayed for, and those who were not prayed for but knew it was a possibility they were prayed for. Three Christian groups were given the first name and first initial of the last name of those that they prayed for. The praying started the night before surgery and continued for two weeks. The study looked for complications within 30 days of surgery. The doctors were blind to those who were or were not prayed for. The results are shown in Figure 6.

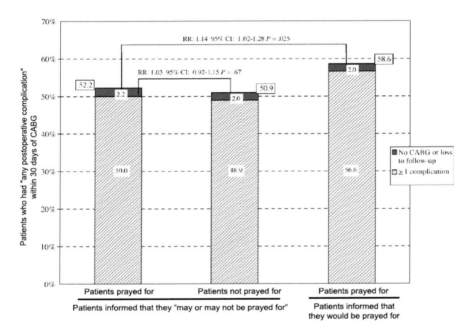

Figure 6. Results of study of Benson et al. Am Heart Journal. *151:934-942. Copyright 2006.* [42] *By permission from Elsevier.*

Fifty-nine percent of the patients who knew they were being prayed for developed a complication versus 52 percent of those who were prayed for but were told it was just a possibility and 51 percent for those who were not prayed for. Thus, those who were prayed for and knew they were prayed for actually did somewhat worse than those who were not prayed for. This difference was barely significant (p = .025). In another much smaller study, examining treatment for alcoholism, there was also a significantly worse outcome for those who were being prayed for and knew they were being prayed for than those who were not prayed for. [43] These small differences are most likely due to chance and these studies should not be taken to indicate that praying for someone can be harmful.

In petitionary prayer, where an individual prays for him- or herself, a positive outcome is often seen, especially when the outcome is better health. A belief in God and in a good outcome allows placebo effects to play a powerful role in producing a favorable outcome.

In intercessory prayer, where someone else prays for an individual who may not know he or she is being prayed for, a placebo effect is not possible, and carefully designed studies of intercessory prayer have shown it has no effect.

References

1. Dennett, D. C. *Breaking the Spell. Religion as a Natural Phenomenon.* Viking, New York, 2006.
2. Koenig, H. G. M. *The Healing Power of Faith.* Simon & Schuster, New York, 1999.
3. Koenig, H. G., M.D., McCullough, M. E., Ph.D. & Larson, D. B., M.D. *Handbook of Religion and Health.* Oxford University Press, NewYork, 2001.
4. Larson, D. B. et al. Associations between dimensions of religious commitment and mental health reported in the American Journal of Psychiatry and Archives of General Psychiatry: 1978-1989. *Am J Psychiatry.* 149: 557-559, 1992.
5. Koenig, H. G. Religious behaviour and death anxiety in later life. *The Hospice Journal.* 4: 3, 1988.
6. Koenig, H. G. et al. The relationship between religious activities and cigarette smoking in older adults. *J Gerontol A Biol Sci Med Sci.* 53: M426-434, 1998.
7. Jessor, R. & Jesson, S. *Problem Behavior and Adolescent Development.* Academic Press, New York, 1977.
8. Donovan, J. E., Jessor, R. & Jessor, L. Problem drinking in adolescence and young adulthood: A follow-up study. *J Stud Alcohol.* 44: 109-137, 1983.
9. Donovan, J. E. & Jessor, R. Structure of problem behavior in adolescence and young adulthood. *J Consult Clin Psychol.* 53: 890-904, 1985.
10. Bachman, J. G., Johnston, L. D. & O'Malley, P. M. Smoking, drinking, and drug use among American high school students: Correlates and trends, 1975-1979. *Am J Public Health.* 71: 59-69, 1981.
11. Boomsma, D. I., de Geus, E. J., van Baal, G. C. & Koopmans, J. R. A religious upbringing reduces the influence of genetic factors on disinhibition: evidence for interaction between genotype and environment on personality. *Twin Res.* 2: 115-125, 1999.
12. Koopmans, J. R., Slutske, W. S., van Baal, G. C. & Boomsma, D. I. The influence of religion on alcohol use initiation: evidence for genotype X environment interaction. *Behav Genet.* 29: 445-453, 1999.
13. Heath, A. C. et al. Resiliency factors protecting against teenage alcohol use and smoking: influences of religion, religious involvement and values, and ethnicity in the Missouri Adolescent Female Twin Study. *Twin Res.* 2: 145-155, 1999.
14. Maes, H. H., Neale, M. C., Martin, N. G., Heath, A. C. & Eaves, L. J. Religious attendance and frequency of alcohol use: same genes or same environments: a bivariate extended twin kinship model. *Twin Res.* 2: 169-179, 1999.
15. D'Onofrio, B. M. et al. Adolescent religiousness and its influence on substance use: preliminary findings from the Mid-Atlantic School Age Twin Study. *Twin Res.* 2: 156-68, 1999.
16. Kendler, K. S., Gardner, C. O. & Prescott, C. A. Religion, psychopathology, and substance use and abuse; a multimeasure, genetic-epidemiologic study. *Am J Psychiatry.* 154: 322-329, 1997.
17. Kendler, K. S., Gardner, C. O. & Prescott, C. A. Clarifying the relationship between religiosity and psychiatric illness: the impact of covariates and the specificity of buffering effects. *Twin Res.* 2: 137-144, 1999.
18. Desmond, D. P. & Maddux, J. F. Religious programs and careers of chronic heroin users. *Am J Drug Alcohol Abuse.* 8: 71-83, 1981.
19. Valliant, G. E. *The Natural History of Alcoholism: Causes, Patterns, and Paths to Recovery.* Harvard University Press, Cambridge, MA, 1983.
20. Koenig, H. G., George, L. K. & Peterson, B. L. Religiosity and remission of depression in medically ill older patients. *Am J Psychiatry.* 155: 536-542, 1998.
21. Koenig, H. G. et al. The relationship between religious activities and blood pressure in older adults. *Int J Psychiatry Med.* 28: 189-213, 1998.

22. Goldbourt, U., Yaari, S. & Medalie, J. H. Factors predictive of long-term coronary heart disease mortality among 10,059 male Israeli civil servants and municipal employees. A 23-year mortality follow-up in the Israeli Ischemic Heart Disease Study. *Cardiology.* 82: 100-21, 1993.

23. Oxman, T. E., Freeman, D. H., Jr. & Manheimer, E. D. Lack of social participation or religious strength and comfort as risk factors for death after cardiac surgery in the elderly. *Psychosom Med.* 57: 5-15, 1995.

24. Koenig, H. G. et al. Attendance at religious services, interleukin-6, and other biological parameters of immune function in older adults. *Int J Psychiatry Med.* 27: 233-250, 1997.

25. Strawbridge, W. J., Cohen, R. D., Shema, S. J. & Kaplan, G. A. Frequent attendance at religious services and mortality over 28 years. *Am J Public Health.* 87: 957-961, 1997.

26. House, J. S., Robbins, C. & Metzner, H. L. The association of social relationships and activities with mortality: prospective evidence from the Tecumseh Community Health Study. *Am J Epidemiol.* 116: 123-140, 1982.

27. Zuckerman, D. M., Kasl, S. V. & Ostfeld, A. M. Psychosocial predictors of mortality among the elderly poor. The role of religion, well-being, and social contacts. *Am J Epidemiol.* 119: 410-423, 1984.

28. Koenig, H. G. et al. Does religious attendance prolong survival? A six-year follow-up study of 3,968 older adults. *J Gerontol A Biol Sci Med Sci.* 54: M370-376, 1999.

29. Hummer, R. A., Rogers, R. G., Nam, C. B. & Ellison, C. G. Religious involvement and U.S. adult mortality. *Demography.* 36: 273-285, 1999.

30. Saudia, T. L., Kinney, M. R., Brown, K. C. & Young-Ward, L. Health locus of control and helpfulness of prayer. *Heart Lung.* 20: 60-65, 1991.

31. Sodestrom, K. E. & Martinson, I. M. Patients' spiritual coping strategies: a study of nurse and patient perspectives. *Oncol Nurs Forum.* 14: 41-46, 1987.

32. Benson, H. The faith factor. *Am Health.* 5: 50-53, 1984.

33. Hurley, J. D. Differential effects of hypnosis, biofeedback training, and trophotropic responses on anxiety, ego strength, and locus of control. *J Clin Psychol.* 36: 503-507, 1980.

34. Zaichkowsky, L. D. & Kamen, R. Biofeedback and meditation: effects on muscle tension and locus of control. *Percept Mot Skills.* 46: 955-958, 1978.

35. Creswell, J. D. et al. Affirmation of personal values buffers neuroendocrine and psychological stress responses. *Psychol Sci.* 16: 846-851, 2005.

36. Sicher, F., Targ, E., Moore, D., 2nd & Smith, H. S. A randomized double-blind study of the effect of distant healing in a population with advanced AIDS. Report of a small scale study. *West J Med.* 169: 356-363, 1998.

37. Harris, W. S. et al. A randomized, controlled trial of the effects of remote, intercessory prayer on outcomes in patients admitted to the coronary care unit. *Arch Intern Med.* 159: 2273-2278, 1999.

38. Cha, K. Y. & Wirth, D. P. Does prayer influence the success of in vitro fertilization-embryo transfer? Report of a masked, randomized trial. *J Reprod Med.* 46: 781-787, 2001.

39. Bronson, P. A prayer before dying. *Wired.* 2002.

40. Humphrey, N. The power of prayer. *Skeptical Inquirer.* 2000.

41. Flamm, B. The Columbia University 'Miracle' Study: Flawed and Fraud. *Skeptical Inquirer.* 28: 25-31, 2004.

42. Benson, H. et al. Study of the Therapeutic Effects of Intercessory Prayer (STEP) in cardiac bypass patients: a multicenter randomized trial of uncertainty and certainty of receiving intercessory prayer. *Am Heart J.* 151: 934-942, 2006.

43. Walker, S. R., Tonigan, J. S., Miller, W. R., Corner, S. & Kahlich, L. Intercessory prayer in the treatment of alcohol abuse and dependence: a pilot investigation. *Altern Ther Health Med.* 3: 79-86, 1997.

Chapter 50

The Problem of Evil

One of the most difficult conundrums that religion has had to face over the centuries is the "problem of evil." If God is a loving and compassionate being why does he let so many evil things happen? Why does he let children die of cancer and be killed in accidents? Take away a young father of five children by a heart attack? Kill hundreds of thousands in a tsunami? Allow horrendous wars? Allow genocide? The "problem of evil" has been characterized as the single greatest challenge to religious faith.

The Greek skeptic Epicurus of the fourth century BCE was the first known thinker to spell out the dilemma of the "problem of evil." He wrote, "Either God wants to abolish evil and cannot; or he can, but does not want to. If he wants to, but cannot he is impotent. If he can but does not want to, he is wicked." Either way, for God and those who believe in him, it is a lose-lose dilemma.

This chapter addresses the many different answers that priests, rabbis, clerics, imams, theologians and other keepers of the faith have proposed for one of the most problematic of the questions that religion has to deal with.

The Gnostics

This was such a difficult question that one early religious group, the Gnostics, (from *gnôsis,* meaning "knowledge"), answered it in a uniquely creative fashion. They were a group of quasi-Christian mystics who were popular in the first few centuries after the death of Christ. Instead of developing a massive set of circumlocutions based on a perfect, all-knowing, loving, and compassionate God, they simply suggested that God never had these qualities in the first place. They proposed that he was a seriously flawed, even demonic and malicious, being whom they called the *Demiurge.* This name was originally coined by Plato to represent the creator of the base world, as opposed to the world of the sublime. While most of the religious mystics of the world were optimists whose faith claimed that despite all the evil, the world was basically "all right," the Gnostic mystics were supreme pessimists and felt the world was basically "all wrong." Instead of viewing the cosmos and nature as essentially neutral, they envisioned the cosmos and nature as fundamentally hostile to human endeavor. They also believed there was a true good God called the "the True Father," who could be held blameless for the evil of the Demiurge. Part of the appeal of the Gnostics was their claim that there was a higher, less flawed world to which the soul will return, an "all right" heaven. This concept was adopted by many other religions.

The Deists

Another creative variation that was less extreme than Gnosticism was Deism. This religious philosophy affirms the existence of God the creator, but proposes that once he finished creating the early universe he retired or went off to create other universes. Deism allowed a peace treaty between Darwin's theory of evolution and creationism by providing for the existence of "old earth" creationists. God created the universe but the creation of the earth and all life on earth was the result of cosmic and biological evolution. This also got God off the hook for evil in the world. Basically he could say, as humans tend to do, "It's not my fault." God got things started, but what happened after that was due to the forces of nature he created. The trouble with the Deism solution is that the vast majority of humans are not Deists but Theists and believe in a hard-working, personal, unretired God whom they tend to hold responsible for evil.

Theodicy

Another solution is to attempt to explain away the coexistence of evil and a personal, caring God. This is called a *theodicy*. The term is derived from the Greek *theós*, meaning God, and *dikê*, meaning justice. The following are some of the common theodicy-type solutions to the "problem of evil."

The free-will solution. God gave man free will. This in itself suggests that God is very intelligent since it freed him from being responsible for the second-to-second action of every person on earth. Wise move, God! This also means that when man is responsible for evil, such as Hitler's killing of the Jews, it is not God's fault. Blame the ability of man to do what ever he wishes, to exercise his own free will. In this form evil occurs because God allowed man to have free will. The inverse form holds that God allows evil to occur so man can have free will. Both forms have the same result. This human form of evil is termed "moral evil." Of course the free will solution does not excuse "natural evil" in the form of tsunamis, hurricanes, earthquakes, and other acts of nature that God should be able to control.

Inanimate free will solution. One of the natural disasters that posed a great challenge to understanding the problem of evil occurred in Lisbon in 1755. Because it was All Saint's Day, people were attending church. An earthquake caused the stone structures to collapse killing over 100,000 people. This was a particularly onerous example of God's failure to prevent evil. To explain natural evil some have suggested the "free process solution." [1] This is based on the assumption that if humans have free will, then all of nature in general, including tectonic plates should also have free will. Thus, earthquakes and tsunamis are not God's fault; the disasters they produce are the fault of the free will of nature. This does not really explain why an all-powerful God could not have compromised just a little bit. For example, couldn't he have delayed the Lisbon earthquake by one day to Monday, when all the churches were empty?

The character-building solution. A good example of this is when a couple has a child with Down syndrome. This chromosome abnormality causes mental retardation and in previous years parents were advised to deal with this form of evil by placing the child in an institution. Over time, people stopped doing this and found that Down syndrome children are friendly, loving, and often a delight to raise, and provide true character-building for the parents. Another example is being born deaf. Some deaf people find such identity and character-building from their deafness that they refuse treatment with a cochlear implant. This solution suggests that evil helps to build man's character and to become the noble souls that God can be proud of. Of course if you are killed by the evil event, it is a bit late for character building.

The Yin and Yang solution. The Taoist religion speaks of yin and yang representing the many opposites in the universe, such as male and female and good and evil. They illustrate this concept with the following symbol of interlocking curves.

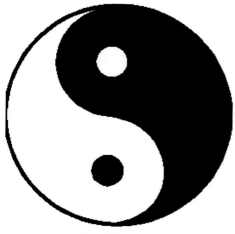

Figure 1. Yin and yang.

The yin and yang hypothesis suggests that one extreme of anything cannot exist and cannot be fully defined without the other extreme. If there was only divine perfection there would be no evil, but nothing exists in a single isolated pure state. As soon as there is some subtle variation to perfection, some dimensionality, there is automatically a window for the presence of evil. This view suggests that if there is good there must also be evil. That is just the way things are. Accept it. Don't blame God. The fifth century theologian Augustine of Hippo mounted the same solution. He couched it in terms of *privatio boni,* or a privation of good—an evil thing can only be referred to as a negative form of a good thing. In a similar vein, to the Hindu Vedantist the question of "Why does God permit evil?" is as meaningless as "Why does God permit good?" The fire burns one man and warms another, and is neither cruel nor kind. [2]

A variant of this is that in order to do good deeds, one needs individuals in need of good deeds. One cannot give alms to the poor if there are no poor, or tend to the lepers if there are no lepers, or rescue the buried victims of a powerful earthquake if there are no powerful earthquakes.

The "God's mysterious plan" solution. By far the most common explanation for God allowing evil to occur is that it was part of God's mysterious plan. God knows exactly what he is doing and in the long run the evil that happens is all part of "God's plan." We mere mortals are just too stupid to understand his long-term plans. This is the common fodder of movies where a Spencer Tracy-like priest comforts a sobbing mother after her child has died with the words, "It is all part of God's grand plan," or its variant, "He is now in a better place."

The "God is also suffering" solution. Christians believe that God has shared the suffering of humans by living a truly human life in the body of Jesus Christ on earth. This gives comfort in that God is not above our misery, but along side us in the darkness. John Polkinghorne [1] gives the example of a concentration camp in World War II. A young Jewish boy was hung and was twisting and dying in a Gestapo noose. From the crowd of his fellow Jews, forced to witness the execution, came the cry "Where is God now?" One of them tells us that he reached inside himself for the answer. "He is there, hanging in the noose." There are, of course, two ways to interpret this: either God is suffering along with us or God also just died. Polkinghorne chooses the former stating "This insight, of God as the fellow sufferer, that Christians believe was historically acted out in the cross of Jesus Christ, meets the problem of suffering at the profoundest possible level." This explanation leaves unanswered the question of why would a rational, all-powerful God want to flagellate himself?

The "We get what we deserve" solution. After the 2004 tsunami in the Indian Ocean, many religious apologists claimed that humans were being punished for a variety of ills. [3] Israel's chief Sephardic rabbi, Shlomo Amar, suggested "This is an expression of God's ire with the world. The world is being punished for wrong doing." A Hindu high priest suggested the tsunami was caused by "a huge amount of pent-up manmade evil on Earth." On MSNBC Jennifer Giroux said the tsunami was divine punishment for America's "cloning, homosexual marriages, abortion, lack of God in the schools, and taking Jesus out of Christmas." James Haught [3] suggested this was nonsense. "Why would a loving creator drown Asians in a rage over American sins?" It is also difficult to apply this solution to a young baby just diagnosed with retinoblastoma. The "We get what we deserve" solution is basically a Rorschach test for a range of upset believers and leaves a lot to be desired.

The "Man Created God" Solution

The trouble with all of these explanations is that while they are philosophically or theologically interesting, they are not inherently very satisfying or comforting. If my child is mangled and killed in a automobile accident or if massive numbers of my ancestors are killed in pogroms or other forms of genocide, none of these excuses for God allowing these things to happen are satisfactory. The very existence of the hypothesis of an all-powerful God carries with it the implication that any form of evil could have been prevented if He had simply chosen to do so. The only truly logical and satisfying answer is to take God out of the equation entirely. If he does not exist he cannot be blamed for evil. Thus, the one solution that totally eliminates the "problem of evil" is to assume that man created God.

> **The "problem of evil" is one of the greatest challenges for religion to explain. While many solutions have been proposed none adequately deals with the fact that an all powerful, personal, caring God could eliminate the worst aspects of evil if he wanted to. The one solution that is the most logically satisfying to the thinking brain is to assume that Man Created God—in which case the "problem of evil" disappears.**

References

1.   Polkinghorne, J. *Quarks, Chaos, and Christianity.* Crossroad, New York, 2000.
2.   Isherwood, C. *Vedanta for the Western World.* The Marcel Rodd Company, New York, 1946.
3.   Haught, J. A. Why would God drown children? *Free Inquiry.* 14-15, 2005.

...the idea of God as author of books is a myth, if ever there was one....The books reputed all divine are simply not filled with truth from beginning to end....They contain as many errors as books of their kind...

Alfred Loisy [1]
The Origins of the New Testament

Chapter 51

Are the Sacred Books Literally True?

Many of the most problematic aspects of religion, especially religious fundamentalism, stem from the assumption that the sacred texts such as the Bible and the Qur'an are the direct word of God and thus every word is literally true. The alternative view espoused in this book is that all the sacred books were written by human beings who sought to provide their followers with myths, rules and rituals to live by and to form the basis of their religions. Three of the ways to examine the validity of the claim that the sacred books are the direct word of God and thus inerrant are to determine a) Who really wrote them? b) Are the different parts of the texts consistent with each other? and c) Are there clear examples of where the supposed inerrant text has been recently changed by man? For English-speaking people much more on the subject of infallability has been written on the Bible than on the Qu'ran. Thus my emphasis will be on the Bible.

Who Wrote the Bible?

The New Testament, especially the Gospels of Matthew, Mark, Luke, and John, were written by unknown early Christians between 70 and 100 CE. [2,3] As pointed out by Bible scholar Randel Helms, in *Who Wrote the Gospels?,* the answer to the question of their authorship is: "Not Matthew, not Mark, not Luke, and not John." Helms further stated,

> Christians in the second century, possessing anonymous manuscripts and eager to give names to them, fastened upon four historical figures—the Apostles Matthew and John, Luke the "beloved physician" of Paul, and John Mark of Jerusalem, the "son" of Peter. It's relatively easy to show that these identifications are imaginary and based on wishful thinking. [3p1]

Each of these four canonical Gospels were largely fictional accounts concerning a historical figure, Jesus of Nazareth. As stated by Helms in *Gospel Fictions,* the Gospels are not so much about Jesus as the early Christians' own attitudes concerning Jesus. [2p16] The Gospels were intended to be a life-enhancing literature written in a fashion that would maximally enhance the acceptance of Christianity. "The Gospels are, it must be said with gratitude, works of art, the supreme fictions in our culture, narratives produced by enormously influential literary artists who put their art in the service of a theological vision." [1p11] As stated by John Meir in his biography of Jesus, "The gospels are 1st century Greco-Roman religious propaganda." [4]

Even the Old Testament was a re-written, enhanced version of the old Hebrew Bible written in Greek. "Christians, by interpretive fiat, created a new book, one that had never existed before—the "Old" Testament—turning the Hebrew Bible, especially in its Greek Septuagint translation, into a book 'really' about Jesus." [5] Some believers claimed the New Testament was true because it was predicted by the Old Testament. In reality it was a stacked deck, a tautology, since both were written, or re-written, by early Christians. As stated by Northrop Frye,

> How do we know that the Gospel story is true? Because it confirms the prophecies of the Old Testament. How do we know that the Old Testament prophecies are true? Because they are confimed by the Gospel story. Evidence, so called, is bounced back and forth between the testaments like a tennis ball; and no other evidence is given us. The two testaments form a double mirror, each reflecting the other but neither the world outside. [6p78]

Both the Old Testament and New Testament were written or re-written by largely anonomous early Christians to elevate Jesus of Nazareth to the status of a miracle worker who died for their sins, was the resurected son of God, and was a spiritual figure on which a new religion, Christianity, espousing a belief in one God, could be built. Instead of being a result of the direct word of God, the Bible is a product of early propagandists anxious to ensure the survival of a new and fragile religion.

Inconsistencies in the Bible

Christian fundamentalists, creationists, and evangelical Christians base their beliefs on the infallibility of the Bible. There is no room for metaphor. No room for allegory. No room for myth. They believe that if a single word is shown to be wrong then every word can be called into question. This belief in the inerrancy of sacred texts is not unique to Christians; Jewish and Islamic Fundamentalists also believe in the inerrancy of the Old Testament and the Qur'an.

In premodern times virtually all Christians believed in the literal truth of the Bible. For example, according to the Councilor Documents of the Catholic Church:

> The books of both the Old and New Testaments in their entirety, with all their parts, are written under the inspiration of the Holy Spirit: they have God as their author. Therefore, since everything asserted must be held to be asserted by the Holy Spirit, it follows that the books of the Scripture must be acknowledged as teaching solidly, faithfully, and

without error that truth which God wanted put into sacred writing for the sake of salvation.

Dei Verbum [11]

This view was shaken in 1860. Shortly after the publication of Darwin's *On the Origin of Species,* seven Anglican clergymen published *Essays and Reviews.* [7] This translation made a book entitled *Higher Criticisms of the Bible,* originally written in German by German Biblical scholars, available to the English-speaking public. Based on techniques of literary analysis, historical research, archeology, and comparative linguistics they argued that the first five books of the Bible, traditionally attributed to the word of God spoken to Moses, were, in fact, written much later by a number of different authors. The book of Isaiah had at least two different authors; King David did not write the *Psalms; most of the miracles should not be taken literally; many of the Biblical events were not historically true; and the Biblical tales were simply "myths.* "[8p95]

This was clearly the antithesis of the beliefs of fundamentalists. In premodern as well as modern times a significant part of believing that the Bible is literally true came from fear. For example, in referring to the rapturists, Currie [9p382] wrote:

> They must understand all passages of the Bible literally because they think that otherwise they will have left the barn door open for the horses to escape: once any passage is declared to be figurative, where do they stop, without an accepted authority as a guide? Rapturists choose to be literalistic in their interpretation of apocalyptic literature because they think that anything else is just too dangerous. Literal Scripture interpretation is their only stable spiritual authority.

One of the best places to look to when testing the inerrancy of the Bible is the Bible itself. If one passage of the Bible says one thing while another passage says the opposite, which is true? Which is divinely inspired. If God was directly responsible for the text of the Bible it should be totally free of any hint of inconsistency. *God should be the ultimate copy editor.* There are, however, over 700 inconsistencies in the Bible and the readers are invited to examine the list themselves. [10] The following are just a few examples:

- God is repeatedly portrayed as all-seeing and knowing all, as in *Proverbs 15:3* "The eyes of the LORD are in every place, Keeping watch on the evil and the good" and in *Hebrews 4:13* "And there is no creature hidden from His sight," but in *Genesis 4:9* he must ask Cain where his brother Abel was, and in *Exodus* he asks the Jews to mark their houses with blood so he will know which ones to "pass over."
- According to passages in *Exodus 20:5, Numbers 4:18,* and *Isaiah 12:21–22* children are to bear the sins of their parents, while according to *Deuteronomy 24:16* and *Ezekiel 18:20,* they are not.
- In *Leviticus 24:20* and *Deuteronomy 19:21* we are instructed to take an eye for an eye and tooth for a tooth, while in *Matthew 5:39* and *Luke 6:29* we are told to

turn the other cheek.
- The story of Noah's ark, as stated in the Bible, contains many aspects that could never have happened. The size of the ark was too great to have been built only of wood; loading it with a pair of all the animals on earth would have taken dozens of years, not a week; a worldwide flood is physically impossible; there is no evidence from DNA sequencing that all animals were derived from a single pair in recent times; and there is no geological evidence for a worldwide flood. [10] There is, however, some evidence for a catastrophic but local flood in Mesopotamia several thousand years BCE. [11] Thus, while potentially based on a kernel of truth, virtually all aspects of the Biblical accounts are metaphors.

The many examples of inconsistencies and physically or historically impossible stories in the Bible provide ample evidence that the Bible was written by man and later, to enhance its authenticity and power, claimed to have been the direct word of God. Explanations of these inconsistencies by believers in the inerrancy of the Bible are weak. These include suggesting the inconsistencies are not really inconsistent; suggesting that God put them there on purpose; or suggesting that the inerrancy of the Bible is limited to things God intended to reveal. In other words the inconsistencies are not God's word, only the consistencies are His, leaving man to sort out the difference.

Seeing the Bible not as literally true but as a metaphor for the role of God in people's lives and as source of message-laden, poetic, and spiritually lifting stories and myths allows the Bible to contain many inconsistencies and errors. Since it was written by many authors hundreds of years after the fact, it would be expected to have many inconsistencies. Since its stories were meant for their metaphorical content, it would be acceptable to contain many factual errors. These inconsistencies do not detract from the Bible as a source of rules to live by. *Holy books only become dangerous and destructive when they are assumed to be inerrant and literally true, and when the holy book of one religion is assumed to be better than the holy book of another.*

The anthropologist Andrew Wallace [12] estimated that over the course of their time on earth humans have produced 100,000 different religions. Based on his time in history, the degree to which his environment is seen as threatening, his level of knowledge of natural science, and the type of his culture—*man himself is the origin of both his religions and the Gods on which they are based.*

Man Made Changes in Sacred Texts

A problem with many religions is that their basic tenets trace back to formulations made a few thousand years ago, when the world was a different place than it is now and there was only a rudimentary amount of valid scientific knowledge. The rules and rituals made then may not always apply to modern times. Sam Harris, in his book, *The End of Faith,* [13] was particularly concerned with the irrational nature of many of the things man holds most sacred. He stated:

Because most religions offer no valid mechanism by which their core beliefs can be tested and revised, each new generation of believers is condemned to inherit the superstitions and tribal hatreds of its predecessors. [We show] a willingness to live, kill, and die on account of propositions for which we have no evidence.

Most religions have merely canonized a few products of ancient ignorance and derangement and passed them down to us as though they were primordial truths. This leaves billions of us believing what no sane person could believe on his own. If one didn't know better, one would think that man, in his fear of losing all that he loves, had created heaven, along with its gatekeeper God, in his own image.

If the rules, myths, and rituals of a given religion came directly from God they should be immutable. In reality, clear-cut man-made changes in the rules occur all the time, suggesting that the original rules were also man-made. A few of many examples are discussed here.

Limbo goes to heaven. One of the basic tenets of the Catholic church is that there is heaven and hell and two intermediate stations called purgatory and limbo. Limbo is for children who have died before they have had a chance to be baptized. They stay in limbo and do not go to heaven. However, in modern times, many of the newest recruits to Catholicism come from Africa, where the infant mortality rate is very high. This caused much distress in these new African converts because when the parents died they could not be reunited with their lost babies, since they were stuck in limbo. To solve this difficult problem and improve African conversion rates, a group of Vatican theological advisors recommended to Pope Benedict XVI that limbo be eliminated and that these babies should be allowed to go to heaven instead.

This was not the only change in the sacred realms of the afterlife. In the softer self-help world of modern times, the fire and brimstone and everlasting torture of Hell no longer brings in new believers. [14] As a result many priests have simply stopped talking about hell. To further soften *Dante's Inferno,* in 1999 Pope John Paul II redefined hell as "the state of those who freely and definitively separate themselves from God." No more fire. No more brimstone.

One of the problems with re-definitions is that once you start messing with one part, the whole landscape of the afterlife changes. It used to be that babies needed to be baptized so that when they died, either as children or adults, they could go to heaven. If babies who died now go to heaven without being baptized, is the baptismal ritual no longer necessary? Should that sacred ritual be eliminated? What happens to the untold millions of babies already in limbo, before the rules changed? Do they now march en masse into heaven? If hell is now a softer place, what happens to purgatory, the original "softer than hell" place? Is it also slated to disappear?

Mormonism, Native Americans and the Chosen People. Joseph Smith founded the Church of Jesus Christ of the the Latter-day Saints. In 1827 an angel named Moroni was supposed to have led Smith to a set of golden plates buried in a hillside near his

New York home. God gave Smith a set of special glasses and seer stones that allowed him to translate the tablets from the Reformed Egyptian language into the *Book of Mormon: Another Testament of Jesus Christ.* [This convenience alone, that ancient Egyptian texts should just happen to be buried next to his home in New York, should stretch the credulity of any rational mind.] These divine scriptures restored the Christian church to God's original version and left the rest of Christianity in a state of less-than-divine apostasy. To put this in perspective, recall that it has been suggested that Joseph Smith's visions were the result of temporal lobe epilepsy.

These sacred scriptures describe a tribe of Jews who sailed from Jerusalem to the New World in 600 BCE and split into two groups, the pure God-fearing "whites," or *Nephites,* and the idol-worshiping blacks, or *Lamanites.* By 385 CE some lighter-skinned Native American Lamanites returned to and were accepted by the church. Missionaries used this supposed ancestral link between Native Americans and Polynesians with Hebrews as a conversion tool by claiming American and Polynesian natives were also members of the "chosen race." Due in part to this enticement, millions of people from Central and South America and the South Pacific became Mormons. As stated by one Mormon attorney, "We were taught that all the blessings of the Hebrew lineage belonged to us and that we were special people. It not only made me feel special but it gave me a sense of transcendental identity, and identity with God." [15]

Unfortunately, modern science has put a major kink in Joseph Smith's vision. Analyzing mitochondrial DNA, Simon Southerton, a Mormon molecular biologists from Australia, found no trace of Middle Eastern DNA in the genetic material of today's American Indians or Pacific Islanders. [16] This produced a major problem for the Mormon leaders who cannot acknowledge any factual errors in the Book of Mormon because the prophet Joseph Smith stated it was the "most correct of any book on Earth." To admit this would result in a loss of confidence in Joseph Smith as an infallible prophet. This also produced a major problem for all those individuals who were made to feel so special because they were one of the "chosen people."

The solution was to slightly alter the original interpretation of the Book of Mormon. Instead of meaning that the Hebrews were the first and only inhabitants of the New World, the new rule is that in fact the Hebrew migration was restricted to a small region of Central America and that the DNA signature was "swallowed up" by the much larger number of pre-existing Native Americans. As Southerton pointed out, the new interpretation was counter to both a plain reading of the text and the words of Mormon leaders. It was also counter to the simple genetic fact that DNA breeds true and does not get "swallowed up." If Native Americans had some Hebrew DNA it would still be present. DNA analytical methods can pick up a few specific sequences among billions.

These DNA studies have understandably upset many. One Polynesian, who grew up believing he was a Hebrew, said, "I visualized myself among the fighting Lamanites and lived out the fantasies of the Book of Mormon as I read it. It gave me prestige to know that these were my true ancestors. Some days I am angry, and some days I feel pity for my people who have become obsessed with something that is nothing but a hoax." [15]

This is an example of the fallacy of treating mythos as logos. It is also an example where the "scandal of particularity" bites back. Trying to feel better about yourself because you think you are among the "chosen people," and then finding out you are not is perhaps more difficult than never deluding yourself in the first place.

Ayatollah Khomeini and the Shariah. The Arabic term *Shariah* means "The Path to the Watering Hole," and represents the body of sacred Islamic laws derived from the Koran. They are *immutable, divinely inspired laws* held to be the only rightly guided way of life and regulate every aspect of a Muslim's lifestyle. Khomeini, the Ayatollah of Iran, displaced the Shah and brought religious fundamentalism back to Iran. He was forced to move from theologian to secular head of state. As part of new secular duties he wanted to institute changes in certain labor laws. The problem was that the Council of Guardians was blocking these changes because they contradicted the *Shariah*. The *Shariah* were pre-industrial rules, and new rules were needed in an industrial state. In the early 1970s Khomeini proposed *Velayat-e Faqih,* or "The Mandate of the Jurist," proclaiming that *faqih,* or jurists, should head the state to ensure that society conforms to God's will as revealed in the *Shariah*. So far, no problem. However, in 1987, Khomeini made a declaration of independence in which he declared that the state was emancipated from the constraining laws of traditional religion. Then on January 12, 1988, speaker Rafsanjani, on behalf of Khomeini, gave a further new interpretation of *velayat-e faqih,* stating that *God had actually not revealed in the Koran all of the laws that Muslims needed.* He delegated to the *Majlis,* or representative assembly, the authority to make up new laws on their own initiative. Did this mean that Khomeini was embracing a Western style democracy? By no means. It was stated that this right to legislate did not come from the people but from God. Divine rulings simply passed from God to the prophet, to the Imams or religious leaders, to Imam Khomeini, and from him to the *Majlis.* [8] It was claimed that this man-made rule change produced a "democracy that was better than in the West because it was rooted in God."

This is just a small sampling of a number of man-made changes in sacred "immutable" texts.

All religions assume their sacred texts represent the direct word of God. Many thus assume they are inerrant and literally true. However, historical evidence shows that both the Old and the New Testament were written or rewritten by early Christian propagandists. In addition, there are hundreds of inconsistencies in the Bible. That is not inerrancy. Some of its stories cannot possibly be physically or historically true. That is not inerrancy. Both historically and logically Occam's razor suggests that the poetic and inspirational verses of the Bible and other holy books were instead written by poetic and inspirational humans.

An additional problem of assuming inerrancy in the sacred texts

is that after the passage of hundreds or thousands of years, customs and knowledge change and some of these "immutable" laws need to be altered. To accommodate this, man has frequently changed the sacred rules. If the texts were truly dictated by an all-knowing God who knew the future, they should have been formulated in a way that did not need changing. Again applying Occam's razor suggests that the reason the original laws are less than perfect is that they were man-made.

Over the course of their time on earth, humans have produced 100,000 different religions. God would have been better served with a "one for all, all for one religion." This clearly suggests this plethora of religions and gods were all produced by a plethora of different humans to suit their needs at the time.

With man as author of the Theory of God and writing the holy books as metaphors for rules to live by, the rationale for all fundamentalist beliefs that are based on the literal inerrancy of these texts disappears and with it all of the attendant reasons for religious wars, intolerance and terrorism.

References

1. Loisy, A. *The Origins of the New Testament* (Translation by L. P. Jacks. Reprinted in English translation in 1962). University Books, Hyde Park, NY, 1936.
2. Helms, R. *Gospel Fictions.* Prometheus Books. Amherst, NY. 1988.
3. Helms, R. *Who Wrote the Gospels?* Millennium Press. Altadena, CA, 1997.
4. Meier, J. *A Marginal Jew: Rethinking the Historical Jesus. Vol I.* Doubleday, New York. 1991.
5. Helms, R. *The Bible Against Itself. Millennium Press.* Altadena, CA, 2006.
6. Frye, N. *The Great Code: The Bible and Literature.* Harcourt Brace, NY, 1982.
7. Temple, F., Powell, B., Pattison, M., Jowett, B. & et al. *Essays and Reviews.* Longman, Green, Longman and Roberts, London, 1861.
8. Armstrong, K. *The Battle for God.* Ballantine Books, New York, 2001.
9. Currie, D. B. *Rapture: The End-Times Error That Leaves the Bible Behind.* Sophia Institute Press, Manchester, NH, 2003.
10. Morgan, D. *Biblical inconsistencies.* www.infidels.org/library/modern/donald_morgan/inconsistencies.html. 2005.
11. Anonymous. Noah's Ark: The True Story. dsc.discovery.com/tvlistings/episode. jsp?episode=0&cpi=24038&gid=0&channel=DSC. 2006.
12. Wallace, A. *Religion: An Anthropological View.* Random House, New York, 1996.
13. Harris, S. *The End of Faith. Religion, Terror and the Future of Reason.* W. W. Norton & Company, Ltd., New York, 2005.
14. Anonymous. in *L. A. Times,* Los Angeles, 2006.
15. Lobdell, W. in *L. A. Times,* Los Angeles, CA, 2006.
16. Southerton, S. G. *Losing a Lost Tribe: Native Americans, DNA, and the Mormon Church.* Signature Books, Salt Lake City, 2004.

Chapter 52

Is God Dead? Ask the Pentecostals

On October 22, 1965, *Time* magazine ran a cover story emblazoned in red block letters on a black background asking, **IS GOD DEAD?** It emphasized the fact that throughout the Western world membership in religious congregations was declining. The conclusion was that God would die of old age and exhaustion, probably within the next decade. It was just a matter of time. [1p164] The secular age was upon us. The age of religion would soon be behind us. Now, 40 years later it is clear that God is not dead.

The Russian Revolution of 1917 provided an excellent illustration of the failure of God to die. Marxism and Leninism posited that the road to socialism demanded the death of God. Karl Marx suggested that religion was simply an "opiate of the masses." However, much to the dismay of the leaders of the revolution, religion refused to become extinct, and when communism collapsed in the 1990s, religion experienced a resurgence.

At the height of Stalin's communism in 1937, the League of Militant Godless who were trying to suppress religion had to admit that as much as one-third of the urban and two-thirds of the rural population were still practicing religion in one form or another. Thus, despite over 70 years of suppression of religion by an avowed atheistic government, religion survived and thrived.

Some of the individuals who have put forth atheistic ideas, such as Feuerbach, Marx and Freud, attempted to offer explanations of why perfectly rational human beings should believe that God exists. They suggested that these ideas must lie in a malfunctioning of the mind and the subtle influences of human consciousness and unconsciousness. These individuals came to their assumptions prior to the explosion of the field of the neuroscience of cognition in the latter part of the twentieth century. [2,3]

In reality a belief in God is not due to a malfunction of the mind. It is the product of a normal mind in which spirituality plays an important role, is hardwired into neurons and genes of the brain, and is of such importance to the development of mankind that it has been perfected over thousands of years of evolution and natural selection. The Pentecostal movement is a good example of the human thirst for spiritual fulfillment.

Pentecostalism

Pentecostalism has been described as "a spiritual hurricane that has already touched half a billion people, and an alternative vision of the human future whose impact may only be at its earliest stages." [4] The half-billion estimate is probably high. More conservative estimates suggest a world membership of 115 million, [5] still a significant figure.

The term *Pentecostal* comes from the Jewish holiday called Pentecost that occurs 50 days after Passover and from the Biblical Day of Pentecost — the day that, according to *Acts 2* of the New Testament, the early Christians first experienced the phenomenon of speaking in tongues.

> *Acts 2:1. When the day of Pentecost came, they were all together in one place.*
>
> *2:2. Suddenly a sound like the blowing of a violent wind came from heaven and filled the whole house where they were sitting.*
>
> *2:3. They saw what seemed to be tongues of fire that separated and came to rest on each of them.*
>
> *2:4. All of them were filled with the Holy Spirit and began to speak in other tongues as the Spirit enabled them.*

As described previously, speaking in tongues, or *glossolalia,* refers to the utterance of meaningless syllables producing what appears to be an unknown foreign or mystic language. Despite the fact that the words produced are incomprehensible, speaking in tongues is presented as a miracle of universal translation enabling people from many parts of the world to understand each other.

Legend was that just prior to the end of history, God would pour down torrents of a "latter rain," as foreseen by the prophet Joel. This would surpass even the first Pentecost in its potency. There would be a worldwide resurgence of faith, and the healing and miracles that had been so evident in the first years of Christianity would happen again as a prelude to the second coming of Jesus Christ. [4]

Origins of Pentecostalism. While Pentecostalism is considered to be a product of the American religious ethos, it traces its origins to the primitive church in the first Christian communities of Rome and other cities, where groups of believers led lives aimed at perfection and endowed with charismatic gifts. The most prominent gift was speaking in tongues as the Apostles and disciples of Jesus did on the day of Pentecost. [6] Receiving this divine power was known as being filled with the Holy Spirit.

In the second century, an ecstatic movement was founded by Montanus and called *Montanism.* As described by historians, Montanus at times "became beside himself, and being suddenly in a sort of frenzy and ecstasy, he raved and began to babble and utter strange things." [6] By the fourth century charismatic gifts had faded from the scene.

The path to the development of charismatic faiths picked up again in America with the multiple waves of revivalism starting with the first wave from 1725–1750.

The appeal of revivalism lay more in its violent physical manifestations than in its theology.

> As long as a person had jerks, parts of his body would snap back and forth with such rapidity that the long braids of hair cracked like whips....Many western revivalists regarded the physical phenomena as heavenly visitations, while they resorted to time-tested techniques to induce them in susceptible persons....On the other hand, the better educated Presbyterian and Congregationalist ministers denounced them as vulgar animal displays. [7]

In his book, *Fire from Heaven*, Harvey Cox [4] traced the beginning of the Pentecostal movement in the United States to April 9, 1906, at 312 Azusa St., Los Angeles, when a black preacher named William Joseph Seymor began a unique type of church service. He had previously heard a woman pray aloud in a language he could not understand. Seymour was touched to the core. He could sense that the woman had somehow attained a depth of spiritual intensity he had long sought but never found. He was excited because such "speaking in tongues" was held to be a sure sign of the imminent coming of the last days and the descent of the heavenly city foreseen in *Revelation.*

The charismatic Azusa Street revivals continued day after day, month after month forming the Pacific Apostolic Faith Movement. People prayed all night and anything could happen. They spoke in tongues, leaped into the air, shouted, and fell to the floor in trances called "being slain by the Lord." The term "holy rollers" was commonly used. One man stated that when the Spirit entered him he felt as though "everything in my body was laughing with unspeakable joy." [4] Word of these uniquely spiritual services spread rapidly throughout the country. The following characteristics of Pentecostalism are what made it so popular.

Open to all. The congregation consisted of men and women, blacks and whites, rich and poor, but especially the poor and the down and out. It was felt that the dissolution of racial, gender, and economic barriers was the surest sign of the Spirit's pentecostal presence and the approaching of the New Jerusalem. One of the movement's early interpreters wrote in 1910,

> God sent this latter rain to gather up all the poor and outcast, and make us love everybody....He poured it out upon the little sons and daughters, and servants and handmaidens....God is taking the despised things, the base things, and being glorified in them.

Currently Pentecostalism has slowed considerably among white people, while its expansion among minorities and in the third world continues to accelerate.

Primal speech: Speaking in tongues. Cox [4] proposed that the appeal of Pentecostalism involved three spheres: primal speech, primal piety, and primal hope.

People had become dissatisfied with the coldness and empty formality of the standard churches and longed for something better. The so-called "text-based" churches primarily just read the Bible. This was usually done by the minister providing a dry and cerebral form of Christianity that many found unattractive and unintelligible. The Catholic church was even more structured and distant. By contrast the Pentecostal churches provided a direct, immediate, experiential connection to the Holy Spirit and God. It filled what one writer called "the ecstasy deficit." The Pentecostals had rediscovered a powerful and primal form of religious expression. There was a wonderful perceived nearness of the Spirit, as close as one's own larynx and vocal cords.

As described previously, speaking in tongues provides a powerful direct connection to the spiritual brain. The Spirit of God needs no mediators but is available to anyone in an intense and immediate way. In contrast to accessing the spiritual brain through the quiet templative meditation used by the Eastern religions, Pentecostalism utilizes a raucous, hyperactive, hypnotic and very noisy approach to the spiritual brain.

Primal piety. This refers to the resurgence in Pentecostalism of trances, visions, healings, dreams, dancing, and other archetypal religious expressions. These touch on what has been refered to as the "elementary forms" of human religiosity.

Primal hope. This points to Pentecostalism's millennial outlook and its insistence that a radically new world age is about to occur. This unmistakable expectation of a better future especially resonated with the poor and disadvantaged. Pentecostals differ from fundamentalists in that fundamentalists believe they are the only ones that will be saved at the end of time. Pentecostals "do insist they have something other believers lack, but they usually concede that they are not the only passengers on the ship of salvation."[4p275]

Faith healing. Some Pentecostal churches also utilize prayers for healing and "the laying on of hands." Rather than a substitute for modern medicine, this can be viewed as complementary to modern medicine. As described in the chapter on the placebo effect, a strong belief in the healer can trigger powerful healing responses in the human body. For those too poor to obtain modern medicine this faith healing is arguably better than nothing.

Music. While most churches utilize organ music in their service, this type of music does not get the congregation thumping their feet on the floor, clapping their hands, rocking back and forth and slapping their thighs. The music of the Pentecostal churches does this. This music provides the same primitive loud beat seen in pop concerts which serves to further tap into the spiritual brain. Cox even suggested that Pentecostalism was the religious version of jazz. Both were coming into their own at the turn of the century, both were powerfully influenced by African American culture and both manifested similar qualities of tone, style and mood.

Adaptable to any culture. Despite the incomprehensibility of speaking in tongues, this very trait allowed Pentecostalism to be adapted to any language. Nonsense syllables are pretty much the same in all languages and all cultures. The potent combination of biblical imagery and ecstatic worship unlocking existing but often repressed religious patterns enabled Pentecostalism to root itself in almost any culture. [4]

This powerful combination of factors led Cox [4] to state that

> After a mere ninety years, what began as a despised and ridiculed sect is quickly becoming both the preferred religion of the urban poor and the powerful bearer of a radically alternative vision of what the human world might one day become…At Azusa Street, a kind of primal spirituality that has been all but suffocated by centuries of western Christian moralism and rationality reemerged with explosive power. This resurfacing of archetypal modes of worship…helps explain why the movement raced across the planet with such electrifying speed.

Because of these factors Pentecostalism could become Russian in Russia, African in Africa, Chilean in Chile, Portuguese in Brazil and on and on, adapting to any culture. In fact Pentecostalism has rapidly spread to all corners of the globe.

In his book, *Is Latin America Turning Protestant?,* David Stoll [8] showed that in many Latin American countries non-Catholic Christianity is growing five to six times the rate of the general population. In Brazil, 90 percent of this increase is Pentecostal. He predicted that five or six Latin American countries will have mostly Pentecostal majorities by 2010. The Yoido Full Gospel Pentecostal Church of Korea is a further example of the rapid expansion of Pentecostalism, this time in Asia. In 1963 it had 2,000 members. This was followed by steady and rapid growth and by 1995, it had expanded to 800,000 members.

Cox [4] posited one important remaining question:

> Will the current renaissance of religions lead toward some peaceful parliament of faiths, such as the one originally envisioned by the planners of the World's Columbian Exposition in Chicago more than one hundred years ago, or will it ignite new outbursts of jihads, crusades and inquisitions?

I have chosen to use Pentecostalism as an example for the resurgence of religion in the world because of its rather dramatic character and the remarkable way that speaking in tongues provides direct access to the spiritual brain. Other proselytizing religious moments such as evangelicalism are also making significant inroads.

Alister McGrath, in his excellent book, *The Twilight of Atheism,* suggests that the resurgence of religion in the latter half of the twentieth century was due to the failure of atheism. Others have suggested that the world would be better off if we eliminated faith and religion altogether. [9,10] I would rather suggest that the resurgence of religion is not due to a failure of atheism. The resurgence is due to man's innate thirst for spirituality. A preferred form of atheism would be one that recognizes the existence of man's hardwired spiritual brain and understands that for the majority of humans, religion and a belief in God will never die. This form of atheism is totally compatible with the resurgence of religion and makes unrealistic the common belief of the 1960s that atheism would be the solution to the world's problems and that an atheistic world would have fewer wars and provide a better hope for the future. It also makes unrealistic the wish that faith and religion would disappear. In reality, atheism is a philosophy adopted by only a relatively small number individuals. The rest of the people on the planet will always believe in one faith or another. Rather than relying on atheism or the elimination of faith and religion to accomplish all these things, retaining faith and religion but eliminating the illusion that the sacred texts are literally true, is far more likely to attain the goal of an end to religious wars, intolerance and terrorism and far more likely to prevent "new outbursts of jihads, crusades, and inquisitions." [4]

In the 1960s it was commonly assumed that God was dead or dying and that the secular age was upon us. However, contrary to this perceived wisdom there has been a resurgence of interest in religion. Pentecostals represent one of the religious groups showing the most rapid rise in membership. Some of the reasons for this includes their utilization of three primal factors:

Primal speech in the form of speaking in tongues.

Primal piety in the form of trances, visions, healings, dreams, primal music, dancing, and other archetypal religious expressions which touch on what have been referred to as the elementary forms of human religiosity.

Primal hope which points to Pentecostalism's millennial outlook and its insistence that a radically new world age is about to occur.

The primal speech and piety may provide a mechanism, similar to meditation, of acquiring direct access to the spiritual brain. Man's persistent yearning for transcendent spirituality indicates that for the human species religion and a belief in God will never die.

Rather than relying on atheism or the elimination of faith to solve the problem of religious wars and terrorism, retaining faith and religion but eliminating the illusion that the sacred texts are literally true is far more likely to attain this goal and far more likely to prevent new outbursts of jihads, crusades and inquisitions.

References

1. McGrath, A. *The Twilight of Atheism. The Rise and Fall of Disbelief in the Modern World.* Galilee Doubleday, New York, 2004.
2. Gazzaniga, M. S. *The Cognitive Neurosciences II.* The MIT Press, Cambridge, MA, 2000.
3. Gazzaniga, M. S. *The Cognitive Neurosciences III.* The MIT Pres, Cambridge, MA, 2004.
4. Cox, H. *Fire from Heaven.* Da Capo Press, Cambridge, MA, 1995.
5. Wilkerson, D. *Pentecostalism.* en.wikipedia.org. 2006.

6. Damboriena, P. *Tongues As of Fire.* Corpus Books, Washington, DC, 1969.
7. Miyakawa, T. S. *Protestants and Pioneers.* Chicago University Press, Chicago, 1964.
8. Stoll, D. *Is Latin America Turning Protestant?* University of California Press, Berkeley, CA, 1991.
9. Harris, S. *The End of Faith. Religion, Terror and the Future of Reason.* W. W. Norton & Company, Ltd., New York, 2005.
10. Dawkins, R. *A Devil's Chaplain. Reflections on Hope, Lies, Science, and Love.* Houghton Mifflin Company, Boston, 2003.

What is strange, what is marvelous, is not that God really exists, the marvel is that such an idea, the idea of the necessity of God, could have entered the heart of such a savage and vicious beast as man; so holy it is, so moving, so wise, and such a great honor it does to man.

Fyodor Dostoevsky
The Brothers Karamazov

We invent God to explain the unexplainable.

Jean Paul Sartre

…[If] your God is capable of designing worlds and doing all the other godlike things…he needs an explanation in his own right.

Richard Dawkins
Climbing Mount Improbable [1p68]

If one didn't know better, one would think that man, in his fear of losing all that he loves, had created heaven, along with its gatekeeper God, in his own image.

Sam Harris
The End of Faith [2]

The Old Testament states that God created man in His own image. We would argue that just the opposite occurred. Because of our capacity to use personal experience as a means of inferring the experience of others and because of the well-studied phenomenon of generalization, humans create God(s) in their own image, rather than vice versa.

Maser and Gallup
Theism as a By-Product of Natural Selection [3p527]

I believe that gods exist to the extent that people believe in them. I believe that we created gods, not the other way around. But that doesn't make God any less "real." Indeed, it makes God all the more powerful. So, yes, I believe in, and maybe, to some extent fear, the God in your head, and all the gods in the heads of believers. They are real, omnipresent, and something approaching omnipotent.

Vince Sarich [4p11]

Part VIII

Summary: Did Man Create God?

It will never be possible to prove whether God exists or not. This has been the subject of thousands of writers over the centuries, and the conclusion is always the same — since God is a supernatural force and thus beyond the realm of natural law, the existence of God cannot be proven or disproven. Certainly, proving that something does not exist is arguably more difficult than proving it exists. If you find it, it must exist, end of story. If you don't find it, one could always argue you did not look in the right places. I start with that point as a given. As pointed out in the

Introduction, the questions "Did Man Create God?" or, "Is the Theory of God a man-made theory?" are fundamentally different from the question "Does God Exist?" It is perfectly possible that the answer to the question, "Did Man Create God?" is "Yes," and yet a God, different than the one man made, still exists.

The concept that man created God is not original to me. It has been around for a long time. While the history of this question is related to the history of atheism, I will only relate those aspects of the history of atheism that directly relate to the question, Did man create God? as distinct from the issue of whether God does or does not exist. For the interested reader, the history of the successes and failures of atheism per se, are well reviewed by Alister McGrath in his book, *The Twilight of Atheism.* [5]

One early example relating to the idea that man created God was proposed by Mary Ann Evans (1819–1880). Her pen name was George Elliot. She was a prominent advocate of atheism in Victorian England. Well versed in the German language, she translated Friedrich Strauss's book, *Life of Jesus.* Based on the growing skepticism of biblical miracles, including the resurrection, Strauss sought to explain how Christians came to believe when there was no objective historical basis for their faith. She concluded that:

> Religion is ultimately an expression of the human mind's ability to generate myths in the first place and then interpret them as truths revealed by God.

In the following sections I will use the term *Theory of God* to refer to a theory that is similar to other man-made theories such as the theory of evolution, the theory of relativity, or the theory of the atom. Theories are developed to explain the seemingly unexplainable. They may be based on a series of facts, such as the Theory of Evolution, or they may be based on thought experiments, such as the Theory of Relativity, or the Theory of God. Referring to the question of whether man was the author of the Theory of God rather than to the question "Did man create God?" might be less objectionable to some readers. However, the basic concept is the same.

Definition of God

One of the problems that arose when man formulated the Theory of God is the definition of God. The National Catholic Almanac suggests the use of the following terms to describe God: almighty, eternal, holy, immortal, immense, immutable, incomprehensible, ineffable, infinite, invisible, unknowable, just, loving, merciful, wise, omnipotent, omniscient, omnipresent, perfect, supreme, and true. [6] As pointed out by George Smith [7] most of the terms such as eternal, immortal, immense, immutable, incomprehensible, ineffable, infinite, invisible, unknowable, omnipresent, and perfect are indistinguishable from nothingness. The remaining terms such as loving, just, merciful, holy, and wise are anthropomorphic. These features suggest that when man conceived the Theory of God he created God in the image of the best parts of himself. Then to add an aura of transcendency to his creation, he added a series of impressive sounding traits that in essence were indistinguishable from nothing.

God has also been described as *omniscient,* in that he knows everything, past, present, and future. The problem with omniscience is that if God knows the future with infallible certainty, the future is predetermined and man is impotent to change it.

> Without volition, morality becomes meaningless. We cannot blame or praise a man for an action over which he has no control. Without volition the Christian scheme of salvation is a farce; men are predestined for either heaven or hell, and they have no voice in the matter…the Christian is forever plagued with the dilemma of preaching a religion of salvation to a world of men who, according to the doctrine of omniscience, are nothing more than automatons. [7p73]

All of these problems are eliminated if man is the author of the Theory of God. Man makes mistakes in logic and also produces inconsistencies in his sacred books. God does not.

The Creation Theory

Over the entire history of mankind, one of the major reasons for evoking the existence of a God or Gods was to explain what was then the unexplainable. How was the universe created? The stars? The earth? The plants and animals? Man? In the past few centuries, science has been able to produce explanations that are viable alternatives to the concept of *God The Creator.* In Parts I and II, I hope to have convinced the reader that Darwin's proposal of evolution by natural selection is perfectly adequate to explain the origin of all life on earth and there are no irreducibly complex aspects of nature that require a God to fill in the gaps. An Intelligent Designer is not required and need not apply for the job. Not only is such a designer not necessary it would only raise the question — Who created the Intelligent Designer?

In Part III, I hope to have convinced the reader that the weirdness of quantum physics includes the ability to create billions of universes out of space energy, out of virtually nothing. When the constants are just right, the random quantum fluctuations in space vacuum can result in a super rapid inflation leading to the birth of a stable universe capable of eventually supporting life. Neither the Big Bang nor the precise accuracy of specific constants as entertained in the Anthropic Principle prove the presence of an Intelligent Designer. By random chance one of the billions of embryonic quantum bubble fluctuations had the "right stuff" to make our universe. In Carl Sagan's words, [8] claiming that only a God could have managed to get the "stuff right" and the "right bubble" requires an answer to the question, "Who made the bubble maker?"

The complexity of nature, the apparent creation of the universe out of nothing, and the precision of the cosmological constants have repeatedly been proposed to have provided proof of the existence of God. The science reviewed in part III show that these arguments do not prove that God exists. However, just as they do not prove that God exists, they also do not prove that God does not exist. They do however provide strong evidence that man made up the Theory of God in an attempt to explain how the universe, the earth, and man were created. This supports the premise of this book that while the existence of God cannot be proven either way, one aspect of the question, "Did man create God?" can be answered "yes" with a reasonable degree of likelihood. Man was the originator of the portion of the Theory of God that proposed that God was the creator. Man made up this theory at a time when the level of knowledge in the natural sciences was at such a primitive level that this seemed to be the best theory available.

The Theory of the Soul

Part IV reviews the neurological location of many of the important functions of the human brain. The Theory of God has been applied to many other aspects of man's most troubling questions such as, "What happens to us when we die? Does the essence of us, our spirit and our soul live on after we die? Is there a heaven? Is there a hell? Is moral behavior rewarded by an eternal life of bliss in heaven? Are 21 virgins waiting for the Muslims who die fighting the infidels?" One of the central themes of this book is the remarkable ability of man to possess both a rational brain that critically analyzes and assesses all these important questions and a spiritual brain that does not care much about facts and just plunges ahead with its need to find the transcendent, to rise above mere mortality, and to connect with an all-encompassing spiritual presence.

As shown in the chapter on consciousness, while the exact mechanism or structures involved are still being debated, there is no debate among neuroscientists that consciousness itself is a product of the brain. Consciousness dies when the brain dies. The soul and spirit also die when the brain dies, and with it the promise of an afterlife, a heaven, a hell, eternal rewards for good behavior, and eternal damnation for bad behavior. Thus, these aspects of the Theory of God that relate to the concept of a soul, an afterlife, and eternal reward for good behavior, all die in the face of modern science.

The Prayer Theory

Other chapters in Part IV review many other components of the human brain — the areas mediating rational thought, planning for the future, experiencing pleasure, emotion, social interactions, meditation, hope and happiness. The dorsolateral frontal lobes control rational thinking. The limbic system is the emotional brain and the orbitofrontal lobes monitor social interactions and moral behavior. Pleasure, a critical aspect of basic survival, relates to eating and reproducing and is mediated by the dopaminergic reward pathways.

The brain also possesses the capacity for self-healing in the form of an enormously powerful placebo effect. The more people believe that some outside entity such as a physician, pill, herb, witch doctor or supernatural force will help them, the more likely it actually will. The more they believe that a personal God is there for them, the more effective the healing power of prayer will be. In personal prayer, the individuals pray for themselves or know they are being prayed for. This form of prayer can be effective. By contrast, in intercessory prayer, the individuals do not know someone is praying for them. This form of prayer that requires some type of supernatural power and has been shown not to work.

The Spiritual Brain

Neuroscience allows us to understand the existence of the spiritual brain, where it is and how it functions. This remarkable spiritual brain largely emanates from the temporal lobes. Within these structures lie the hippocampus, the center of regular memory, and the amygdala, the center of emotional memory. Other parts of the temporal lobes process the sensations of hearing and seeing. These come together to provide the neural substrate for powerful spiritual feelings.

A transcendent sense of spirituality may be produced when parts of the temporal lobes are stimulated by electrical probes, epileptic or partial seizures, psychedelic drugs, near-death experiences, prayer, religious services, rituals, various methods of meditation, speaking in tongues, or simply feelings of love. Some have called this the God part of the brain. It also allows us to understand that spiritual thoughts are intensely rewarding for man.

Neuroscience helps us to understand that there is a craving for a belief in something greater than ourselves, for a belief in the correctness of all aspects of the Theory of God. Understanding this also helps us to see that while the Theory of God is man-made, the feelings associated with the Theory of God are real and will never go away. This is similar to the above quote from Vince Sarich that even if man created God, it does not make God any less real or less powerful. Neuroscience helps our rational brain to understand this and to live in peace with the spiritual brain. As a result, it can be all right for an individual with a highly developed rational brain, such as a scientist, to also believe in the transcendent and, in some cases, to have a religious faith.

The last chapter of Part IV, on the biology of faith versus reason, shows how the spiritual brain can overpower the fact-driven rational brain. This is brought about by a number of factors including the fact that major decisions are made in the unconscious mind out of sight of the rational brain, and that man has evolved a built-in pleasurable craving for information and understanding that sometimes allows questions to be answered on the basis of faith in the complete absence of facts. In addition, neuroscience has shown that images, spoken words and phrases, and probably beliefs, that we have been repeatedly exposed to, can be instantly recalled from only a few neurons, and in some cases only one. This level of efficiency provides insight to why images and beliefs acquired early in childhood tend to be very resistant to change. It is understandable that an individual well steeped in the religious dogma of the family can grow up to be a scientist but still retain strong religious beliefs and irrational faiths.

An Inborn Moral Law

Part V reviewed the role of genes in controlling different aspects of our behavior. The environment, interacting with our genes, plays a role in controlling the different functions of the brain. In some cases genes play the major role, in some the environment plays the major role, while in most cases the environment and genes play about an equal role. Most functions of the brain are the result of polygenic inheritance — the interaction of many different genes, each with a small effect, and the environment. Since a given gene is usually responsible for less than one to two percent of the sum total of all forces producing a given trait, it is incorrect to speak of a "depression gene," an "alcoholism gene," or a "God gene." It is permissible to talk of depression genes, alcoholism genes, or spirituality genes.

Some have suggested that moral behavior in humans, the so-called Moral Law, could only have been divinely inspired and is thus proof of the existence of God. [9] However, based on genetic studies it is apparent that "bad behavior" or "antisocial behavior" is strongly genetic and is a relatively *rare human trait*. Good or altruistic behavior is also under significant genetic control and is as common as antisocial behavior is rare, and is exhibited by many species other than our own. Religion may help us to behave, but we can behave compassionately and well on our own. *Moral Law is an inborn behavior, not a divine one.*

Intelligence is under greater genetic control than most other human traits. Innate spirituality, independent of religion, is also under strong genetic control. Not surprisingly, religious affiliation and church-going per se are largely under environmental control, but genes also play a part. However, spirituality itself, the driving force behind a need for religion and a need for man to formulate a Theory of God, has a strong genetic component.

Spirituality: An Evolved Trait

The genes for spirituality and the functions they serve did not just happen. They evolved. Part VI shows the role of evolution and natural selection for both the high level of human intelligence and the high level of human spirituality. *Both were critical for man's survival.* A high level of intelligence provided man with the ability to make tools and function in a complex society. While the great apes also made tools and functioned in a social framework, with the added advantage of speech, humans have carried this to a much higher level. While there are many reasons why the development of spirituality had a survival value, it is likely that the most important reason was to enhance a unique level of mutually cooperative social interaction and cohesiveness.

Other Aspects of Religion and Spirituality

A number of other interesting aspects of religion and human spirituality are reviewed in Part VII. These include the origin of the world's major religions, the role of mysticism, myth, ritual, and even psychedelic drugs in the origin of religions, the question of whether God plays favorites, such that one religion is better than another, the evil and the good of religion, the problem of evil, and the question of the inerrancy of the Bible.

Multiple Religions

While there are three major religions in the West, and a somewhat greater number in the East, over the course of his time on earth, man has actually produced 100,000 different religions. Since God would have been better served with a "one for all, all for one religion," this clearly suggests that the plethora of religions and Gods were all produced by man to suit his needs at a given place and a given time.

Psychedelics and Religion

A wide range of psychedelic compounds are powerful stimulants of man's spiritual brain. The majority of these compounds are derived from plants that are common and grow throughout the world. Many studies show that these compounds have played a profound and critical role in facilitating man's early belief in God and in the development of many of his religions.

The Problem of Evil

The *Problem of Evil* refers to the question of how could a compassionate personal God allow so much evil to happen? This has always been a major problem for the Theory of God. The Problem of Evil is totally eliminated by the propositions that man was the author of the Theory of God and that man created God.

The Inerrancy of the Sacred Books

If one were asked to identify the single major factor that has allowed religion to be the source of so much evil in the world, despite its potential to do great good, that factor would be believing that the sacred books were written by God and thus are absolutely true and without error. This belief in the literal truth of sacred books, and with it the false belief that one religion is superior to another, has led to horrendous levels of religious prejudice, hatred, wars, and terrorism. If the members of the different religious faiths understood that the Theory of God and the resultant sacred books were written by man rather than by God, and that they were written using allegory and metaphor to illustrate the path to a moral and spiritual life — this evil underbelly of religion would vanish.

Is God Dead?

The final chapter of Part VII is titled "Is God Dead? Ask the Pentecostals." This chapter contains a number of important points. One is that the more directly we can stimulate the spiritual brain, the more popular the religion will be and the more compelling its faith. The second, even more important point is that not only is religion not dead, in all likelihood it will never die. Spirituality is too important to the human species to allow this to happen.

There are many other issues and questions that could not be covered because there must be some limitations on the length of this book. In the remaining part of this summary I will discuss a few remaining key points.

The Problem of Postponement

One of the methods that married couples often use when they argue about difficult issues is to say, "Can we talk about this later." This can be both an advantage and a problem. An advantage is that difficult issues can be indefinitely postponed so that the pain of resolving them never has to be endured. A disadvantage is that the pain of resolving them is never faced and they continue to fester. This could be called the "problem of postponement." In the history of man, this approach has been used repeatedly for seemingly unsolvable mysteries, such as, "Who created the universe, the earth, and man?" These difficult issues are temporarily "resolved" in the Theory of God by giving Him the role of the all-powerful creator of all things.

In the absence of scientific knowledge this was a reasonable theory. However, in modern times, many of the uncertainties that faced premodern humans have been resolved. Newton's theory of gravity explains the motion and interactions of planets, disproving the tenets of astrology; advances in statistics have led to an understanding of probabilities and a better understanding of chance events; Mendel's laws of genetics and the discovery of the structure of DNA have resolved the mystery of how traits are transmitted from generation to generation; Darwin's theory of evolution has replaced the need for a creator in the Theory of God. The total list of the successes of our rational brain is huge.

Despite this, a very large proportion of the world's population still believes that ultimately God created us and still regulates our lives. This view elicits the "problem of postponement" and leaves unresolved the questions of, "Who made the bubble-maker? Who created God? Who created the creator? Was it yet another creator? Is there a God for God? If so, is there then a God for God's God?" To avoid being drawn into this endless spiral of unanswerable questions it is easier to revert to Occam's Razor by simply saying our rational brain knows who created God — man created God and man invented the Theory of God to encompass all aspects of God. Now the "problem of postponement" is solved.

Is Religion Necessary for a Moral Life?

It is often suggested that God is necessary to provide the authority for humans to be moral. If man created God then this characteristic was instilled into the God theory by man. To do this the human authors had to be inherently moral and good. We have seen in previous chapters that in fact man is more likely to inherently behave well than behave badly. While the authors of the different sacred books were moral people they must have been concerned that other humans would not behave morally on their own. Claiming that these moral rules, such as the Ten Commandments, came from God would allow them to carry more authority and there would be a greater likelihood that they would be obeyed.

It is likely that one of the reasons Christianity is so popular is that Jesus represents the epitome of what morality is all about — a pervasive goodness, kindness, love and forgiveness—a "Do unto others as you would have them do unto you," type of person. This carries a powerful impact when combined with the spiritual nature of religion and the mythology that he was resurrected after death and died for our sins (whatever they are). The popularity of Christianity undoubtedly lies in the fact that man is inherently good and thus can relate well to the goodness of the teachings of Christ. These tenets are not unique to Christianity. With the exception of radical fundamentalist religions, virtually all other religions have the same core values consistent with the probability they were all made by man.

Is Religion Necessary for a Happy, Meaningful, or Purposeful Life?

It has often been suggested that religion brings happiness, purpose and a meaning to life. While it would seem to be reasonable that a person finding spiritual enlightenment in religion might be happy, as outlined in Chapter 33, man is an inherently happy species. A modest level of happiness has been hardwired into our brains and appears to have had some survival value. Religion is just one of many ways man can achieve both happiness and a sense of purpose. There are many other inherent purposes in life, not the least of which is to get a good education; find meaningful work; develop unique skills; get married, have children, develop loving relationships with your spouse, children, and friends; be active in the community, volunteer and give to others; create poetry, music, novels, works of art, and scientific theories; and a thousand and one other things that bring pleasure and a feeling of being happy to be alive. All of these can give a sense of purpose to one's life.

How Do We Answer the Three Questions of Pope John Paul II?

Pope John Paul II suggested there were three questions that were most important to man. These were:

Who am I?
What is there after this life?
Where have I come from and where am I going?

Who am I? Where have I come from? In previous chapters I have suggested answers to these questions. We are the product of evolution due to random mutations and natural selection. We have not evolved as a result of a purpose-driven, designed end. We have evolved as a result of a fundamentally random process and as Gould stated, if the "tape could be rewound" it is very likely that the result would have been drastically different. For example during the Cambrian explosion of the dozens of phyla produced, only one, *Pikaia,* was capable of being a chordate and thus predecessor to all of the vertebrates, including us. If this one phylum had not evolved at that critical time, it is likely that neither we nor any other intelligent beings would be here to discuss these issues.

As the Nobel Prize-winning geneticist Jacques Monod put it in his 1971 book,

Chance and Necessity, [10]

> We are utterly without purpose in the cosmos. We would like to think ourselves necessary, inevitable, ordained from all eternity. All religions, nearly all philosophies, and even a part of science testify to the unwearying, heroic effort of mankind desperately denying its own contingency [random existence].

There was no point in asking why things happened; they just did. While evolution was a great tinkerer, it had no goal.

What is there after this life? We are an intelligent, creative, complex and spiritual species and when *we die,* other than in the memories and love of those around us, we are gone forever. There is no afterlife, no hell, no heaven, no rewards for good behavior, and no hell for bad behavior. However, one could argue that a form of "heaven and hell" does exist in the memories of those who have known us. When we have behaved well our "soul" lives on in a "heaven" consisting of the pleasant memories that our friends and loved ones have of us. When we have not behaved well our "soul" lives on in a "hell" in the form of unpleasant memories that our friends and loved ones (if any) have of us. That is our eternal reward or our eternal punishment. Our soul, heaven and hell exist not in some hypothetical place above and below, but in a real place — the minds and memories of those who have known us.

Where am I going? We cannot accurately predict the future but I can state with certainty that the greatest threat to the future of mankind is not the existence of wars based on differing political philosophies but wars based on different religious philosophies. During the entire period of the cold war, the United States and Russia managed, just barely, to avoid using the atomic bomb to kill the majority of each other's citizens. However, this capacity to build nuclear bombs, or other instruments of mass destruction, is spreading to more and more nations, including those where secular rule and religion are combined and those where a fanatical religious ideology is based on the literal interpretation of sacred texts. Now, the probability that these instruments will be used for religious domination or terrorism or to bring about a prophesized end of the world is almost a certainty, especially when dying for a religious cause is viewed as a shortcut to heaven, the "will of God," [11] a great "career opportunity" [2] or a way to be sexually rewarded with 21 virgins.

Is Man Inherently Sinful and Evil?

One of the central tenets of Christianity is the concept of original sin. Ever since Eve tasted of the tree of knowledge in the Garden of Eden, man has been considered to be inherently sinful and in need of redemption and salvation. George Smith puts it as follows: [7p308]

> In exchange for obedience, Christianity promises salvation in an afterlife; but in order to elicit obedience through this promise,

Christianity must convince men that they *need* salvation, that there is something to be "saved" from. Christianity has nothing to offer a happy man living in a natural, intelligible universe. If Christianity is to gain a motivational foothold, it must declare war on earthly pleasure and happiness, and this, historically, has been its precise course of action. In the eyes of Christianity, man is sinful and helpless in the face of God, and is potential fuel for the flames of hell. Just as Christianity must destroy reason before it can introduce faith, so it must destroy happiness before it can introduce salvation.

It is not accidental that Christianity is profoundly anti-pleasure, especially in the area of sex; this bias serves a specific function. Pleasure is the fuel of life, and sexual pleasure is the most intense form of pleasure that man can experience. To deny oneself pleasure, or convince oneself that pleasure is evil, is to produce frustrations and anxiety and thereby become potential material for salvation.

While perhaps a bit extreme, it is nevertheless true that Christianity has the flavor of knocking a man down and then offering to rescue him, with the condition that he concur with the fact of his sinfulness and accept Jesus Christ as the savior from his evil nature. Man would have been better off if he had not been knocked down in the first place. Even though Christianity takes the position that man is inherently evil and sinful, and possesses "original sin" just by being born, we have seen from the prior chapters on the genetics of bad and good behavior and the biology of pleasure and happiness that humans are an inherently good and happy species. Since the natural enjoyment of sexual pleasure has been hard wired into us to ensure our survival, we might as well enjoy it without guilt.

Is Science Incompatible with Religion?

Science is dedicated to understanding reality based on the scientific method of observation and objectively testing facts and theories. By contrast, religion is dedicated to the proposition that an important segment of reality is unknowable and must be taken on faith. While hundreds of books have been written on the subject of whether science and religion are thus incompatible, the answer is simple and straightforward: Yes and No. If we are talking about religions that assume that the Bible and Qur'an are literally true, and believe the account of the creation of the universe, the earth, and man as stated in *Genesis* is true, and literally believe in miracles and other improbable features of the biblical stories, then science and religion are clearly incompatible. If we are speaking of the war that the purveyors of Intelligent Design have waged on evolution and on the scientific method itself, then science and religion are clearly incompatible. If we are speaking of the claims of the young earth creationists, then science and religion are incompatible.

However, if we are talking about religions that see the sacred texts as metaphors for a moral and spiritual life and accept the teachings of modern science, then science and this type of religion are clearly compatible. In fact the fields of neuroscience, genetics and evolution have taught us that man possesses a spiritual brain and that genetic factors play an important role in man's quest for spirituality, and that high levels of spirituality probably played an important role in natural selection and the evolution of the human species. This understanding helps make science and the latter type of religion very compatible.

Another aspect of this question is seen from the fact that many scientists are religious. This is indicated by two surveys of scientists taken in the twentieth century. [5p111] The first, in 1916, indicated that 40 percent of scientists had some form of religious belief. At the time this result was regarded as shocking or even scandalous. However, the second, taken in 1996, showed no significant reduction in this percentage. This serves as a challenge to the popular notion that as science progresses and advances it will produce a relentless erosion of religious faith.

Is the Rational Brain Incompatible With Spirituality?

To answer this requires a definition of spirituality. There are a number of dictionary definitions that refer to spirituality in relation to religious, supernatural, and sacred entities. Since a person may be spiritual without being religious and without believing in supernatural entities including God, a definition that does not include these as necessary conditions is preferable. The definition I prefer is to have a sense of awe and appreciation of entities that are greater than oneself. These entities may be God, Jesus, Buddha, or other supernatural force, but they may also be an awe and appreciation of nature, trees, the smell of flowers, the singing of birds, family, friends, the pleasure derived from a job well done, some remarkable skill, or just of love itself. The readers may easily add their own favorite transcendent items. In this sense the rational brain can become totally comfortable with spirituality.

Is the Rational Brain Incompatible with Religion and Faith?

This question is similar to the question of whether science is compatible with religion, but sufficiently different to justify its own section. A major theme of this book is not only whether man's rational brain and spiritual brain can coexist in harmony but also whether man's rational brain and religion and faith can coexist in harmony. As with the question of whether science and religion are compatible, the answer depends upon the religion and the faith. Belief systems relating to God can be divided into essentially four different levels of compatibility with the rational brain: *1. Maximally compatible, 2. Compatible with minor qualifications, 3. Compatible with major qualifications, 4. Incompatible.*

1. Maximally compatible. The following is a list of a number of examples of belief systems that are maximally compatible with the needs of the rational brain.

Atheism. A number of modern authors such as George Smith,[7] Richard Dawkins,[1,12-16] and Sam Harris,[2] have forcefully proposed that faith and religion are evil forces in society and the rational brain is only totally comfortable with atheism which is best defined as not believing in the existence of God. While this could be considered to be a belief system in its own right, it may also be considered as simply the absence of belief. [7p7]

Agnosticism. In 1869, Thomas Henry Huxley (1825–1895), the nineteenth century defender of Darwinism, proposed the term agnostic to refer to a position of uncertainty about whether God existed or not. While some individuals such as Dawkins [17p92] referred to this as a cop-out and an insult to the rational brain, Huxley had a point. If the existence of God cannot be proven one way or the other, the logical position for skeptics could be agnosticism. On the other hand if one believes that the preponderance of evidence suggests that man was the author of the Theory of God, then the rational brain would be more comfortable with atheism than agnosticism.

One could be both an agnostic and an atheist: an agnostic because one recognized that the proof of the existence or non-existence of God is impossible and an atheist because one felt that the probability that God did not exist is the more likely of the two possibilities.

Some claim that this degree of rationalism that denies the existence of God is dull and lacks the ability to produce a sense of wonder about the world. I would counter that there is almost an unlimited reservoir of aspects of nature, science, astronomy, history, poetry, literature, drama, and all of the other forms of knowledge, to provide a wonderful sense of awe and excitement about living and being alive.

One example of this can be found in Mary Robinson's *Ode inscribed to the Infant Son of S.T. Coleridge, Esq.* (1806) [5] in which she emancipates Nature from being God's creation to approaching a divinity in its own right. This type of excitement with the world of nature was also illustrated in Shelley's poem Hymn to Intellectual Beauty:

> *The awful shadow of some unseen Power*
> *Floats though unseen among us,— visiting*
> *This various world with as inconstant wing*
> *As summer winds that creep from flower to flower*

Secular humanism. Secular humanism is a philosophy that applauds reason, ethics, and justice, and specifically rejects supernatural forces. Some of the principles and beliefs of the secular humanism movement are outlined by Paul Kurtz: [18]

- the application of reason and science to the understanding of the universe and to the solving of human problems
- deplore looking to the supernatural for human salvation
- democracy is the best protection against authoritarian elites and repressive governments
- the separation of church and state
- supporting the disadvantaged and handicapped
- enjoying life here and now and developing our creative talents
- optimism rather than pessimism, hope rather than despair

- learning in the place of dogma, truth instead of ignorance
- the joy of life rather than guilt or sin
- tolerance in the place of fear
- love instead of hatred
- compassion over selfishness
- reason rather than blind faith or irrationality
- humanism as a realistic alternative to theologies of despair and of violence
- humanism as a source of personal significance and genuine satisfaction in the service of others

It is clear that *secular humanism* is a belief system that is maximally compatible with the rational brain as well as one that would end all religious and secular wars and all religious terrorism.

Buddhism. Buddha preached that the only stable thing in the world was *dharma,* the truth about right living. Since the gods had not helped Buddha to achieve nirvana he did not believe they were of much use to mankind, so Buddhism is not about God. He believed that the ultimate reality was higher than the gods. The attainment of enlightenment was achieved through spiritual exercise and meditation. Buddhism is thus a model for how humans can lead a moral and spiritual life without resorting to the Theory of God. The rational brain can be very much at peace with a spiritual brain that believes in the teachings of Buddhism.

Jainism. The rational brain can also be at peace with Jainism, a form of spirituality that also does not believe in a creator God. Jain ascetics seek to have a friendly, non-violent relationship with all living beings.

2. Compatible with minor qualifications. I would place in this category any religion that does not believe in the inerrancy of the Bible, the Qur'an or any other sacred text, either because they understand that these texts simply provide metaphors for a moral and spiritual life, or because they understand that these texts were written by man, not by God. I would also include those who believe that religion is a living entity that needs to adapt to modern life and not be frozen into rigid beliefs of 2,000 years ago, who believe in the inclusion of members even if they have doubts about some aspects of the faith (agnostics), and who believe in the inclusion of women and individuals of all sexual orientation. However, this still leaves a broad area for a range of beliefs that may have to be taken on faith. Foremost of these is a belief in God. Thus, I would also include in this group religions whose members believe in God as a transcendent being or in nature and the mysteries of the universe as a strong expression of spirituality, but do not always believe in a personal God that answers prayers, or believe in hell or a heaven that rewards one for good behavior. Such religions would qualify as being compatible with the rational brain with an understanding nod to the needs of the spiritual brain. Three examples would be the Unitarian/Universalist Church, Reform Judaism, and Taoism.

Unitarian/Universalist Church. Some of the principles and teachings of the Unitarian/Universalist church include:

- The inherent worth and dignity of every person
- Justice, equity and compassion in human relations
- Acceptance of one another and encouragement to spiritual growth in our congregations
- A free and responsible search for truth and meaning
- The goal of world community with peace, liberty, and justice for all
- Direct experience of that transcending mystery and wonder, affirmed in all cultures, which moves us to a renewal of the spirit and an openness to the forces which create and uphold life
- Words and deeds of prophetic women and men which challenge us to confront powers and structures of evil with justice, compassion, and the transforming power of love
- Wisdom from the world's religions which inspires us in our ethical and spiritual life
- Jewish and Christian teachings which call us to respond to God's love by loving our neighbors as ourselves
- Humanist teachings which counsel us to heed the guidance of reason and the results of science, and warn us against idolatries of the mind and spirit
- Spiritual teachings of earth-centered traditions which celebrate the sacred circle of life and instruct us to live in harmony with the rhythms of nature

While the section that states "Jewish and Christian teachings which call us to respond to God's love by loving our neighbors as ourselves" suggests all members believe in God, this is essentially an affirmation of the Golden Rule of treating others as we would like to be treated. Some members of the Unitarian/Universalist church believe in God, while some are atheists and some are agnostics. The church is accepting of members of all religions and faiths.

Reform Judaism. Reform Judaism began in the United States about 130 years ago under the leadership of Rabbi Isaac Mayer Wise, who brought it from Europe. It remains firmly rooted in the Jewish tradition but asserts that Judaism "frozen in time is an heirloom, not a living fountain." It "affirms belief without rejecting those who doubt." [18] While its tenets have many similarities to those of the Unitarian/Universalist Church, they may have a stronger belief in God. "We believe that all human beings are created in the image of God." They see the Torah as God-inspired, not the literal word of God. They consider children to be Jewish if they are born of a Jewish father or mother, not just if they are born of a Jewish mother. Women are accepted into all levels of the synagogue, and gays and lesbians are accorded full participation. The majority of Jews in the United States are reform Jews. In my career I have worked with many Reform Jewish scientists who were excellent scientists and still retained the rituals and myths of their religion as an integral part of their lives.

Taoism. Taoists seek to harmonize the fundamental energies of the universe consisting of the cosmic currents of *yin* and *yang* to attain immortality. They de-emphasize material gain and emphasize a close connection between the mind, body and the environment. I have placed Taoism in the category of *compatible with minor qualifications* since the rational brain has some difficulty with the concept of immortality.

3. Compatible with major qualifications. I would place most religions in this group. It includes all religions that do not insist on the inerrancy of the Bible but do believe in a personal God that responds to one's prayers. Members may or may not believe in heaven, hell, and miracles. One could reasonably ask, "How could I possibly believe that the rational brain would be comfortable with this set of beliefs?" Basically, I do not, which is why I placed it in the group of "Compatible with major qualifications." Those qualifications are that the rational brain is capable of understanding that not all people in the world are comfortable with a purely rational approach to life and that there is also a spiritual brain with its own set of needs and with its ability, as discussed previously, to bypass the rational brain and to make up its own mind about the total needs of the individual. That is the major qualification that allows the rational brain to live in some degree of peace with its more emotionally needy spiritual partner.

Scientists with a strong religious faith would belong in this category. A scientist could believe that the stories that Jesus brought dead people back to life, walked on water, or parted the seas were metaphors for his faith, without literally believing these events really happened, and without affecting his belief in Jesus' teaching of the Golden Rule and love for one's fellow man.

Spiritual but not religious is a category that is also compatible with the rational brain. This category could fit under either compatible with minor or with major qualifications depending upon the spiritual beliefs. Either way it clearly avoids the last category of being incompatible with the rational brain.

4. Incompatible. I would place all religions that believe in the inerrancy of the sacred texts in this category. This would include all fundamentalist faiths, whether Christian, Jewish, Islamic or other. I would especially include all faiths that believe in any form of the apocalypse, whether pre- or post-millennial, and that believe their religion alone is *the* true religion. While the appeal to the spiritual brain may be great, the appeal to the rational brain is zero, even when the rational brain understands the needs of the spiritual brain. In these cases the rational brain would be saying, "enough is enough." No level of qualification should allow the rational brain to be comfortable with these faiths. These are the faiths that have been responsible for most of the religious wars, intolerance, hatred, and terrorism. The elimination of the belief in the literal truth of the sacred texts and the concept that one religion is superior to another would be of enormous benefit to mankind.

Did the Rational Brain Create God as a Gift to the Spiritual Brain?

All of the evidence presented in this book suggests the rational brain created God and the *Theory of God* to explain the unknown, to assuage man's fear of death and to satisfy the urges of the spiritual brain to belong to a transcendent spirituality larger than itself.

Is Religion Doomed or is Science Doomed?

Edward O. Wilson suggested that scientific naturalism, that favorite evil word of the creationists, would spell the death knell to religion.

> We have come to the crucial stage in the history of biology when religion itself is subject to the explanation of the natural sciences. As I have tried to show, sociobiology can account for the very origin of mythology by the principle of natural selection acting on the genetically evolving material structure of the human brain. If this interpretation is correct, the final decisive edge enjoyed by scientific naturalism will come from its capacity to explain traditional religion, its chief competitor, as a wholly material phenomenon. Theology is not likely to survive as an independent intellectual discipline. [20p192]

In other words, once an evolutionary explanation for the existence of religion has been fashioned, the very idea of God is doomed. [21p183] I would argue for just the opposite. Based on many thousands of years of selective fine-tuning, the rewards of spirituality are so great that they will always be an important part of the human condition. These rewards can be achieved within or outside the bounds of a formal religion, a person can be spiritual but not religious. However, based on surveys it appears that most people will only be satisfied if they place themselves within some type of a religious setting. While some, like Richard Dawkins can be "an intellectually fulfilled atheist," [13p6] the majority of the human race will find some type of spirituality, with or without a belief in God, more satisfying.

It is even conceivable that in a thousand years, science as a discipline designed to further knowledge will have ceased, since virtually all aspects of the physical and biological world will have been discovered. "Scientists" will mostly be technicians whose job it is to keep stuff, based on discoveries made many years previously, running. I anticipate that evolution, Darwinism, and all of the other scientific discoveries of the present and the future will have been accepted and incorporated into the collective psyche of the species. We will have long since found that such knowledge is not a threat to spiritual values. Hopefully, the majority of humans will have come to understand that man was the author of the Theory of God and will have adopted one of the first three of the above options for satisfying both their rational and spiritual brain and that the ultimate — a rational spirituality — will be the glue that holds mankind together to grow in peace.

The evidence suggests that our rational brain created God to satisfy the transcendent yearnings of our spiritual brain. Instead of denying the existence and reality of the spiritual brain, we need instead to provide for an accommodation between rationality and spirituality, a way for them to live together in peaceful co-existence. Hopefully, in time, the majority of humans will recognize that man's rational brain was the author of the *Theory of God* and that man created God. As a result it will also be accepted that all religions are equally valid and that the sacred texts were written by man. Rather than being the literal word of God these works are metaphors for how we should lead moral and spiritual lives. In this context hate, terrorism, killing, and wars based on religious beliefs would become a part of mankind's past. Humans will eventually have found a way to satisfy both their rational and spiritual brain and will have attained the ultimate goal — a rational spirituality. Such a spirituality can be the glue that holds mankind together in peace.

References

1. Dawkins, R. *Climbing Mount Improbable.* W. W. Norton & Company, Inc., New York, 1996.
2. Harris, S. *The End of Faith. Religion, Terror and the Future of Reason.* W. W. Norton & Company, Ltd., New York, 2005.
3. Maser, J. D. & Gallup, G. G. J. Theism as a by-product of natural selection. *J Religion.* 70: 515-532, 1990.
4. Shermer, M. *How We Believe. Science, Skepticism, and the Search for God.* Second Edition. A. W. H.Freeman Henry Holt and Company, New York, 2000.
5. McGrath, A. *The Twilight of Atheism. The Rise and Fall of Disbelief in the Modern World.* Galilee Doubleday, New York, 2004.
6. Felician, A. & Foy, O. F. M. (eds.) *1968 National Catholic Almanac.* Patterson: St Anthony's Guild, 1968.
7. Smith, G. W. Atheism. *The Case Against God.* Prometheus Books, New York, 1979.
8. Sagan, C. *Cosmos Studios, Inc.,* Studio City, CA, 2000.
9. Collins, F. S. *The Language of God. A Scientist Presents Evidence for Belief.* Free Press, New York, 2006.
10. Monod, J. *Chance and Necessity.* 1970.
11. Krauthammer, C. Today Tehran, Tomorrow the World. *Time.* 167: 96, 2006.
12. Dawkins, R. *The Selfish Gene.* Oxford University Press, Oxford, 1989.
13. Dawkins, R. *The Blind Watchmaker. Why the Evidence of Evolution Reveals a Universe Without Design.* W. W. Norton & Company, Inc., New York N.Y., 1996.
14. Dawkins, R. A Devil's Chaplain. *Reflections on Hope, Lies, Science, and Love.* Houghton Mifflin Company, Boston, 2003.
15. Dawkins, R. *Unweaving the Rainbow: Science, Delusion and the Appetite for Wonder.* Mariner Books, 2000.
15a. Dawkins, R. *The God Delusion.* Houghton Mifflin Co, Boston, 2006.
16. Dawkins, R. *River Out of Eden.* Basic Books, New York, 1995.
17. McGrath, A. *Dawkins God Genes, Memes, and the Meaning of Life.* Blackwell Publishing, Oxford, UK, 2005.
18. Kurtz, P. The Affirmations of Humanism: Statement of Principles. www.secular humanism.org. 2006.
19. Anonymous. Reform Judaism. rj.org/index.shtml. 2006.
20. Wilson, E. O. *On Human Nature.* Harvard University Press, Cambridge, MA, 1978.
21. Miller, K. *Finding Darwin's God.* Harper Perennial, New York, 1999.

Glossary

To keep this glossary short only those abbreviations, terms and concepts that are often used or that have not been well explained in the text, are included. Thus, when inquiring about a given word the reader should first consult the Index.

apostasy renunciation of one's religion
BCE   Before common era (BC).
CE   Common era (AD).
DNA   Deoxyribonucleic acid.
KYA   Thousands of years ago.
PET   Positron emission tomography for body and brain scanning
RAC   raclopride radioactive [11C] raclopride used in PET studies
RNA   Ribonucleic acid.

Measurements:
m   milli-   one thousandth as in millimeter 10^{-3}
    micro- one millionth as in micrometer 10^{-6}
n   nano- one billionth as in nanometer 10^{-9}

Index

XII 133